AN

# APOLOGY

FOR THE

## TRUE CHRISTIAN DIVINITY

BEING AN

EXPLANATION AND VINDICATION

OF THE

PRINCIPLES AND DOCTRINES

OF THE PEOPLE CALLED

# QUAKERS.

WRITTEN IN LATIN AND ENGLISH

BY ROBERT BARCLAY.

PHILADELPHIA:
FRIENDS' BOOK-STORE,
304 ARCH STREET.

## TO

# CHARLES II.

## KING OF GREAT BRITAIN.

AND

## THE DOMINIONS THEREUNTO BELONGING:

ROBERT BARCLAY, a servant of Jesus Christ, called of God to the Dispensation of the Gospel, now again revealed, and, after a long and dark night of apostasy, commanded to be preached to all nations, wisheth health and salvation.

As the condition of kings and princes puts them in a station more obvious to the view and observation of the world, than that of other men, of whom, as Cicero observes, neither any word or action can be obscure; so are those kings, during whose appearance upon the stage of this world it pleaseth the GREAT KING of kings singularly to make known unto men the wonderful steps of his unsearchable providence, more signally observed, and their lives and actions more diligently remarked, and enquired into by posterity; especially if those things be such as not only relate to the outward transactions of this world, but also are signalized by the manifestation or revelation of the knowledge of God in matters spiritual and religious. These are the things that rendered the lives of Cyrus, Augustus Cæsar, and Constantine the Great in former times, and of Charles the Fifth, and some other modern princes in these last ages, so considerable.

But among all the transactions which it hath pleased God to permit, for the glory of his power, and the manifestation of his wisdom and providence, no age furnisheth us with things so strange and marvellous, whether with respect to matters civil or religious, as these that have fallen out within the compass of thy time; who, though thou be not yet arrived at the fiftieth year of thy age, hast yet been a witness of stranger things than many ages before produced. So that whether we respect those various troubles wherein thou foundest thyself engaged while scarce got out of thy

(3)

infancy; the many different afflictions wherewith men of thy circumstances
are often unacquainted; the strange and unparalleled fortune that befel thy
father; thy own narrow escape, and banishment following thereupon, with
the great improbability of thy ever returning, at least without very much
pains and tedious combatings; or finally, the incapacity thou wert under to
accomplish such a design; considering the strength of those that had possessed themselves of thy throne, and the terror they had inflicted upon
foreign states; and yet that, after all this, thou shouldest be restored without stroke of sword, the help or assistance of foreign states, or the contrivance and work of human policy; all these do sufficiently declare that
it is the Lord's doing; which, as it is marvellous in our eyes, so it will
be justly a matter of wonder and astonishment to generations to come;
and may sufficiently serve, if rightly observed, to confute and confound that
atheism wherewith this age doth so much abound.

As the vindication of the liberty of conscience (which thy father, by
giving way to the importunate clamours of the clergy, the answering and
fulfilling of whose unrighteous wills has often proved hurtful and pernicious
to princes, sought in some part to restrain) was a great occasion of those
troubles and revolutions; so the pretence of conscience was that which
carried it on, and brought it to that pitch it came to.  And though no doubt
some that were engaged in that work designed good things, at least in the
beginning, albeit always wrong in the manner they took to accomplish it,
viz. by carnal weapons; yet so soon as they had tasted the sweets of the
possessions of them they had turned out, they quickly began to do those
things themselves for which they had accused others.  For their hands
were found full of oppression, and " they hated the reproofs of instruction,
which are the way of life;" and they evilly intreated the messengers of the
Lord, and caused his prophets to be beaten and imprisoned, and persecuted
his people, whom he had called and gathered out from among them, whom
he had made to beat their " swords into plough-shares, and their spears
into pruning-hooks," and not to learn carnal war any more: but he
raised them up, and armed them with spiritual weapons, even with his own
Spirit and power, whereby they testified in the streets and highways, and
public markets and synagogues, against the pride, vanity, lusts, and hypocrisy of that generation, who were righteous in their own eyes; though
often cruelly intreated therefor: and they faithfully prophesied and foretold them of their judgment and downfall, which came upon them, as by
several warnings and epistles delivered to Oliver and Richard Cromwell,
the parliament, and other then powers, yet upon record, doth appear.

And after it pleased God to restore thee, what oppressions, what banishments, and evil intreatings they have met with, by men pretending thy authority, and cloaking their mischief with thy name, is known to most men in this island; especially in England, where there is scarce a prison that hath not been filled with them, nor a judge before whom they have not been haled; though they could never yet be found guilty of any thing that might deserve that usage. Therefore the sense of their innocency did no doubt greatly contribute to move thee, three years ago, to cause some hundreds of them to be set at liberty: for indeed their sufferings are singular, and obviously distinguishable from all the rest of such as live under thee in these two respects.

First: In that among all the plots contrived by others against thee since thy return into Britain, there was never any, owned of that people, found or known to be guilty, though many of them have been taken and imprisoned upon such kind of jealousies, but were always found innocent and harmless, as became the followers of Christ; not coveting after, nor contending for, the kingdoms of this world, but "subject to every ordinance of man, for conscience sake."

Secondly: In that in the hottest times of persecution, and the most violent prosecution of those laws made against meetings, being clothed with innocency, they have boldly stood to their testimony for God, without creeping into holes or corners, or once hiding themselves, as all other Dissenters have done; but daily met, according to their custom, in the public places appointed for that end; so that none of thy officers can say of them, that they have surprised them in a corner, overtaken them in a private conventicle, or catched them lurking in their secret chambers; nor needed they to send out spies to get them, whom they were sure daily to find in their open assemblies, testifying for God and his truth.

By which those who have an eye to see, may observe their Christian patience and courage, constancy and suffering joined in one, more than in any other people that differ from them, or oppose them. And yet, in the midst of those troubles, thou canst bear witness, that as on the one part, they never sought to detract from thee, or to render thee and thy government odious to the people, by nameless and scandalous pamphlets and libels; so on the other hand, they have not spared to admonish, exhort, and reprove thee; and have faithfully discharged their consciences towards thee, without flattering words, as ever the true prophets in ancient times used to do to those kings and princes, under whose power, violence and oppression was acted.

1 *

And although it is evident by experience, to be most agreeable both to divine truth and human policy, to allow every one to serve God according to their consciences, nevertheless those other sects, who for the most part durst not peep out in the times of persecution, while these innocent people stood bold and faithful, do now combine in a joint confederacy, notwithstanding all the former janglings and contentions among themselves, to render us odious; seeking unjustly to wrest our doctrine and words, as if they were inconsistent both with Christianity and civil society: so that to effectuate this their work of malice against us, they have not been ashamed to take the help, and commend the labours, of some invidious Socinians against us. So do Herod and Pontius Pilate agree to crucify Christ.

But our practice, known to thee by good experience to be more consistent with Christianity and civil society, and the peace and welfare of this island, than that of those who thus accuse us, doth sufficiently guard us against this calumny; and we may indeed appeal to the testimony of thy conscience, as a witness for us in the face of the nations.

These things moved me to present the world with a brief, but true account of this people's principles, in some short theological propositions; which, according to the will of God, proving successful beyond my expectation, to the satisfaction of several, and to the exciting in many a desire of being farther informed concerning us, as being every where evil spoken of; and likewise meeting with public opposition by some, as such will always do, so long as the devil rules in the children of disobedience; I was thereby farther engaged, in the liberty of the Lord, to present to the world this apology of the truth held by those people: which, because of thy interest in them, and theirs in thee, as having first appeared, and mostly increased, in these nations under thy rule, I make bold to present unto thee.

Thou knowest, and hast experienced their faithfulness towards their God, their patience in suffering, their peaceableness towards the king, their honesty, plainness and integrity in their faithful warnings and testimonies to thee; and if thou wilt allow thyself so much time as to read this, thou mayest find how consonant their principles are both to scripture, truth, and right reason. The simplicity of their behaviour, the generality of their condition, as being poor men and illiterate; the manner of their procedure, being without the wisdom and policy of this world; hath made many conclude them fools and madmen, and neglect them, as not being capable of reason. But though it be to them as their crown, thus to be esteemed of the wise, the great, and learned of this world, and though they rejoice to be accounted fools for Christ's sake; yet of late some, even such who in the world's account are esteemed both wise and learned, begin to judge otherwise of them, and find that they hold forth things very agreeable both o scripture, reason, and true learning.

As it is inconsistent with the truth I bear, so it is far from me to use this epistle as an engine to flatter thee, the usual design of such works; and therefore I can neither dedicate it to thee, nor crave thy patronage, as if thereby I might have more confidence to present it to the world, or be more hopeful of its success. To God alone I owe what I have, and that more immediately in matters spiritual; and therefore to him alone, and to the service of his truth, I dedicate whatever work he brings forth in me; to whom only the praise and honour appertain, whose truth needs not the patronage of worldly princes; his arm and power being that alone by which it is propagated, established, and confirmed. But I found it upon my spirit to take occasion to present this book unto thee; that as thou hast been often warned by several of that people, who are inhabitants of England; so thou may'st not want a seasonable advertisement from a member of thy ancient kingdom of Scotland; and that thou may'st know, which I hope thou wilt have no reason to be troubled at, that God is raising up and increasing that people in this nation. And the nations shall also hereby know, that the truth we profess is not a work of darkness, nor propagated by stealth; and that we are not ashamed of the " gospel of Christ," because we know it to be " the power of God unto salvation ;" and that we are no ways so inconsistent with government, nor such disturbers of the peace, as our enemies, by traducing us, have sought to make the world believe we are: for which to thee I dare appeal, as a witness of our peaceableness and Christian patience.

Generations to come shall not more admire that singular step of Divine Providence, in restoring thee to thy throne, without outward bloodshed, than they shall admire the increase and progress of this truth, without all outward help, and against so great opposition; which shall be none of the least things rendering thy memory remarkable. God hath done great things for thee; he hath sufficiently shown thee, that it is by him princes rule, and that he can pull down and set up at his pleasure. He hath often faithfully warned thee by his servants, since he restored thee to thy royal dignity, that thy heart might not wax wanton against him, to forget his mercies and providences towards thee; whereby he might permit thee to be soothed up, and lulled asleep in thy sins, by the flattering of court-parasites, who, by their fawning, are the ruin of many princes.

There is no king in the world, who can so experimentally testify of God's providence and goodness; neither is there any who rules so many free people, so many true Christians: which thing renders thy government more honourable, thyself more considerable, than the accession of many nations, filled with slavish and superstitious souls.

Thou hast tasted of prosperity and adversity; thou knowest what it is to be banished thy native country, to be over-ruled, as well as to rule, and sit upon the throne; and being oppressed, thou hast reason to know how hateful the oppressor is both to God and man: if after all these warnings and advertisements, thou dost not turn unto the Lord with all thy heart, but forget him, who remembered thee in thy distress, and give up thyself to follow lust and vanity; surely great will be thy condemnation.

Against which snare, as well as the temptation of those that may or do feed thee, and prompt thee to evil, the most excellent and prevalent remedy will be, to apply thyself to that Light of Christ, which shineth in thy conscience, which neither can, nor will flatter thee, nor suffer thee to be at ease in thy sins; but doth and will deal plainly and faithfully with thee, as those that are followers thereof have also done.

God Almighty, who hath so signally hitherto visited thee with his love, so touch and reach thy heart, ere the day of thy visitation be expired, that thou mayest effectually turn to him, so as to improve thy place and station for his name.   So wisheth, so prayeth,

Thy faithful friend and subject,

ROBERT BARCLAY.

From Ury, the place of my pilgrimage, in my native country of Scotland, the 25th of the month called November, in the year MDCLXXV.

### R. B. *Unto the Friendly Reader wisheth Salvation.*

FORASMUCH as that, which above all things I propose to myself, is to declare and defend the truth, for the service whereof I have given up and devoted myself, and all that is mine; therefore there is nothing which for its sake, by the help and assistance of God, I may not attempt. And in this confidence, I did some time ago publish certain propositions of divinity, comprehending briefly the chief principles and doctrines of truth; which appearing not unprofitable to some, and being beyond my expectation well received by many, though also opposed by some envious ones, did so far prevail, as in some part to remove that false and monstrous opinion, which lying fame, and the malice of our adversaries, had implanted in the minds of some, concerning us and our doctrines.

In this respect it seemed to me not fit to spare my pains and labour; and, therefore, being actuated by the same Divine Spirit, and the like intention of propagating the truth, by which I published the propositions themselves, I judged it meet to explain them somewhat more largely at this time, and defend them by certain arguments.

Perhaps my method of writing may seem not only different, but even contrary, to that which is commonly used by the men called divines, with which I am not concerned: inasmuch as I confess myself to be not only no imitator and admirer of the schoolmen, but an opposer and despiser of them as such, by whose labour I judge the Christian religion to be so far from being bettered, that it is rather destroyed. Neither have I sought to accommodate this my work to itching ears, who desire rather to comprehend in their heads the sublime notions of truth, than to embrace it in their hearts: for what I have written comes more from my heart than from my head; what I have heard with the ears of my soul, and seen with my inward eyes, and my hands have handled of the Word of Life, and what hath been inwardly manifested to me of the things of God, that do I declare, not so much regarding the eloquence and excellency of speech, as desiring to demonstrate the efficacy and operation of truth; and if I err sometimes in the former, it is no great matter; for I act not here the grammarian, or the orator, but the Christian; and therefore in this I have followed the certain rule of the Divine Light, and of the Holy Scriptures.

And, to make an end; what I have written, is written not to feed the wisdom and knowledge, or rather, vain pride of this world, but to starve and oppose it, as the little preface prefixed to the propositions doth show; which, with the title of them, is as followeth.

# THESES THEOLOGICÆ.

## TO

# THE CLERGY,

OF WHAT SORT SOEVER,

UNTO WHOSE HANDS THESE MAY COME;

BUT MORE PARTICULARLY

*To the Doctors, Professors, and Students of Divinity in the Universities and Schools of Great Britain, whether Prelatical, Presbyterian, or any other ;*

ROBERT BARCLAY, a Servant of the Lord God, and one of those who in derision are called Quakers, wisheth unfeigned repentance, unto the acknowledgment of the Truth.

FRIENDS,

UNTO you these following propositions are offered; in which, they being read and considered in the fear of the Lord, you may perceive that simple, naked truth, which man by his wisdom hath rendered so obscure and mysterious, that the world is even burthened with the great and voluminous tractates which are made about it, and by their vain jangling and commentaries, by which it is rendered a hundred-fold more dark and intricate than of itself it is : which great learning, so accounted of—to wit, your school divinity, which taketh up almost a man's whole life-time to learn, brings not a whit nearer to God, neither makes any man less wicked, or more righteous than he was. Therefore hath God laid aside the wise and learned, and the disputers of this world ; and hath chosen a few despicable and unlearned ii.

struments, as to letter-learning, as he did fishermen of old, to pub
lish his pure and naked truth, and to free it of those mists and fogs
wherewith the clergy hath clouded it, that the people might admire
and maintain them. And among several others, whom God hath
chosen to make known these things—seeing I also have received, in
measure, grace to be a dispenser of the same Gospel—it seemed good
unto me, according to my duty, to offer unto you these propositions;
which, though short, yet are weighty, comprehending much, and declaring what the true ground of knowledge is, even of that knowledge which leads to Life Eternal; which is here witnessed of, and
the testimony thereof left unto the Light of Christ in all your consciences.                                        Farewell,

                                                       R. B.

## THE FIRST PROPOSITION.

*Concerning the true Foundation of Knowledge.*

Seeing the height of all happiness is placed in the true knowledge of God, (" This is life eternal, to know thee John xvii. the only true God, and Jesus Christ whom thou hast sent,") [3.] the true and right understanding of this foundation and ground of knowledge, is that which is most necessary to be known and believed in the first place.

## THE SECOND PROPOSITION.

*Concerning Immediate Revelation.*

Seeing " no man knoweth the Father but the Son, and Mat. xi. 97 ne to whom the Son revealeth him ;" and seeing the reve- lation of the Son is in and by the Spirit; therefore the tes- timony of the Spirit is that alone by which the true know- ledge of God hath been, is, and can be only revealed ; who as, by the moving of his own Spirit, he converted the chaos of this world into that wonderful order wherein it was in the beginning, and created man a living soul, to rule and govern it, so by the revelation of the same Spirit he hath manifested himself all along unto the sons of men, both patriarchs, prophets, and apostles ; which revelations of God by the Spirit, whether by outward voices and ap- pearances, dreams, or inward objective manifestations in the heart, were of old the formal object of their faith, and remain yet so to be ; since the object of the saints' faith is the same in all ages, though set forth under divers admi- nistrations. Moreover, these divine inward revelations, which we make absolutely necessary for the building up of true faith, neither do nor can ever contradict the outward testimony of the scriptures, or right and sound reason. Yet from hence it will not follow, that these divine revela- tions are to be subjected to the examination, either of the outward testimony of the scriptures, or of the natural reason of man, as to a more noble or certain rule or touchstone :

2

for this divine revelation and inward illumination, is that which is evident and clear of itself, forcing, by its own evidence and clearness, the well-disposed understanding to assent, irresistibly moving the same thereunto; even as the common principles of natural truths move and incline the mind to a natural assent : as, that the whole is greater than its part; that two contradictory sayings cannot be both true, nor both false : which is also manifest, according to our adversaries' principle, who—supposing the possibility of inward divine revelations — will nevertheless confess with us, that neither scripture nor sound reason will contradict it : and yet it will not follow, according to them that the scripture, or sound reason, should be subjected to the examination of the divine revelations in the heart.

# THE THIRD PROPOSITION.

## *Concerning the Scriptures.*

From these revelations of the Spirit of God to the saints, have proceeded the scriptures of truth, which contain, 1. A faithful historical account of the actings of God's people in divers ages, with many singular and remarkable providences attending them. 2. A prophetical account of several things, whereof some are already past, and some yet to come. 3. A full and ample account of all the chief principles of the doctrine of Christ, held forth in divers precious declarations, exhortations, and sentences, which, by the moving of God's spirit, were at several times, and upon sundry occasions, spoken and written unto some churches and their pastors : nevertheless, because they are only a declaration of the fountain, and not the fountain itself, therefore they are not to be esteemed the principal ground of all truth and knowledge, nor yet the adequate primary rule of faith and manners. Nevertheless, as that which giveth a true and faithful testimony of the first foundation, they are and may be esteemed a secondary rule, subordinate to the Spirit, from which they have all their ex cellency and certainty; for as by the inward testimony of the Spirit we do alone truly know them, so they testify, that the Spirit is that guide by which the saints are led into all truth: therefore, according to the scriptures, the Spirit is the first and principal leader. And seeing we do therefore receive and believe the scriptures, because they proceeded from the Spirit; therefore also the Spirit is more originally and principally the rule, according to that received maxim in the schools, *Propter quod unumquodque est tale, illud ipsum est magis tale.* Englished thus: 'That for which a thing is such, that thing itself is more such.'

John xvi. 13. Rom. viii. 14.

## THE FOURTH PROPOSITION.

### *Concerning the Condition of Man in the Fall.*

All Adam's posterity, or mankind, both Jews and Gentiles, as to the first Adam, or earthly man, is fallen, degenerated, and dead, deprived of the sensation or feeling of this inward testimony or seed of God, and is subject unto the power, nature, and seed of the serpent, which he sows in men's hearts, while they abide in this natural and corrupted state; from whence it comes, that not their words and deeds only, but all their imaginations are evil perpetually in the sight of God, as proceeding from this depraved and wicked seed. Man, therefore, as he is in this state, can know nothing aright; yea, his thoughts and conceptions concerning God and things spiritual, until he be disjoined from this evil seed, and united to the divine light, are unprofitable both to himself and others: hence are rejected the Socinian and Pelagian errors, in exalting a natural light; as also of the Papists, and most Protestants, who affirm, That man, without the true grace of God, may be a true minister of the gospel. Nevertheless, this seed is not imputed to infants, until by transgression they actually join themselves therewith; for they are by nature the children of wrath, who walk according to the power of the prince of the air.

Rom. v. 12 15.

Eph. ii. 2

## THE FIFTH AND SIXTH PROPOSITIONS.

*Concerning the Universal Redemption by Christ, and also the Saving and Spiritual Light, wherewith every man is enlightened.*

### THE FIFTH PROPOSITION.

Ezek. xviii. 32.
Isa. xlix. 6.
John iii. 16. & i. 9.
Tit. ii. 11.
Eph. v. 13.
Heb. ii. 9.

God, out of his infinite love, who delighteth not in the death of a sinner, but that all should live and be saved, hath so loved the world, that he hath given his only Son a light, that whosoever believeth in him should be saved; who enlighteneth every man that cometh into the world, and maketh manifest all things that are reproveable, and teacheth all temperance, righteousness, and godliness: and this light enlighteneth the hearts of all in a day,* in order to salvation, if not resisted: nor is it less universal than the seed of sin, being the purchase of his death, who

1 Cor. xv. 22.

tasted death for every man; " for as in Adam all die, even so in Christ shall all be made alive."

### THE SIXTH PROPOSITION.

According to which principle (or hypothesis), all the objections against the universality of Christ's death are easily solved; neither is it needful to recur to the ministry of angels, and those other miraculous means, which, they say, God makes use of, to manifest the doctrine and history of Christ's passion unto such, who, living in those places of the world where the outward preaching of the gospel is unknown, have well improved the first and common grace; for hence it well follows, that as some of the old philosophers might have been saved, so also may now some---who by providence are cast into those remote parts of the world, where the knowledge of the history is wanting - be made partakers of the divine mystery, if they receive and resist

---

* Pro tempore: for a time.

not that grace, "a manifestation whereof is given to every 1 Cor. xii. 7. man to profit withal." This certain doctrine then being received, to wit: that there is an evangelical and saving light and grace in all, the universality of the love and mercy of God towards mankind—both in the death of his beloved Son, the Lord Jesus Christ, and in the manifestation of the light in the heart—is established and confirmed against all the objections of such as deny it. Therefore "Christ hath tasted death for every man:" not only for all Heb. ii. 9. kinds of men, as some vainly talk, but for every one, of all kinds; the benefit of whose offering is not only extended to such, who have the distinct outward knowledge of his death and sufferings, as the same is declared in the scriptures, but even unto those who are necessarily excluded from the benefit of this knowledge by some inevitable accident; which knowledge we willingly confess to be very profitable and comfortable, but not absolutely needful unto such, from whom God himself hath withheld it; yet they may be made partakers of the mystery of his death—though ignorant of the history—if they suffer his seed and light—enlightening their hearts—to take place; in which light, communion with the Father and Son is enjoyed, so as of wicked men to become holy, and lovers of that power, by whose inward and secret touches they feel themselves turned from the evil to the good, and learn to do to others as they would be done by; in which Christ himself affirms all to be included. As they then have falsely and erroneously taught, who have denied Christ to have died for all men; so neither have they sufficiently taught the truth, who affirming him to have died for all, have added the absolute necessity of the outward knowledge thereof, in order to the obtaining its saving effect; among whom the Remonstrants of Holland have been chiefly wanting, and many other asserters of Universal Redemption, in that they have not placed the extent of this salvation in that divine and evangelical principle of light and life, wherewith Christ hath enlightened every man that comes into the world, which is excellently and evidently

2 *                    c

held forth in these scriptures, Gen. vi. 3. Deut. xxx. 14.
John i. 7, 8, 9. Rom. x. 8. Tit. ii. 11.


# THE SEVENTH PROPOSITION.

## *Concerning Justification.*

As many as resist not this light, but receive the same, in
them is produced an holy, pure, and spiritual birth, bringing forth holiness, righteousness, purity, and all those other
blessed fruits which are acceptable to God; by which holy
birth, to wit, Jesus Christ, formed within us, and working
his works in us—as we are sanctified, so we are justified
in the sight of God, according to the apostle's words,
Cor. vi
11.      "But ye are washed, but ye are sanctified, but ye are justified, in the name of the Lord Jesus, and by the Spirit of
our God." Therefore it is not by our works wrought in
our will, nor yet by good works, considered as of themselves, but by Christ, who is both the gift and the giver,
and the cause producing the effects in us; who, as he hath
reconciled us while we were enemies, doth also in his
wisdom save us, and justify us after this manner, as saith
Tit. iii. 5.  the same apostle elsewhere, "According to his mercy he
saved us, by the washing of regeneration, and the renewing of the Holy Ghost."


# THE EIGHTH PROPOSITION.

## *Concerning Perfection.*

Rom. vi. 14.   In whom this holy and pure birth is fully brought forth
Id. viii. 13.
Id. vi. 2, 18.  the body of death and sin comes to be crucified and re-
1 John iii. 6.  moved, and their hearts united and subjected unto the
truth, so as not to obey any suggestion or temptation of
the evil one, but to be free from actual sinning, and transgressing of the law of God, and in that respect perfect.
Yet doth this perfection still admit of a growth; and there
remaineth a possibility of sinning, where the mind doth
not most diligently and watchfully attend unto the Lord.

# THE NINTH PROPOSITION.

*Concerning Perseverance, and the Possibility of Falling from Grace.*

Although this gift, and inward grace of God, be sufficient to work out salvation, yet in those in whom it is re
sisted it both may and doth become their condemnation.
Moreover, in whom it hath wrought in part, to purify and
sanctify them, in order to their further perfection, by disobedience such may fall from it, and turn it to wantonness,
making shipwreck of faith; and "after having tasted of 1 Tim. 1 6
the heavenly gift, and been made partakers of the Holy Heb. vi. 4, 5, 6.
Ghost, again fall away." Yet such an increase and stability in the truth may in this life be attained, from which
there cannot be a total apostasy.

# THE TENTH PROPOSITION.

*Concerning the Ministry.*

As by this gift, or light of God, all true knowledge in
things spiritual is received and revealed; so by the same,
as it is manifested and received in the heart, by the strength
and power thereof, every true minister of the gospel is ordained, prepared and supplied in the work of the ministry:
and by the leading, moving, and drawing hereof, ought
every evangelist and Christian pastor to be led and ordered
in his labour and work of the gospel, both as to the place
where, as to the persons to whom, and as to the times when
he is to minister. Moreover, those who have this authority
may and ought to preach the gospel, though without human
commission or literature; as on the other hand, those who
want the authority of this divine gift, however learned or
authorized by the commissions of men and churches, are
to be esteemed but as deceivers, and not true ministers of
the gospel. Also, who have received this holy and unspotted gift, "as they have freely received, so are they Mat. x. 8

freely to give," without hire or bargaining, far less to use it as a trade to get money by it: yet if God hath called any from their employments, or trades, by which they acquire their livelihood, it may be lawful for such, according to the liberty which they feel given them in the Lord, to receive such temporals—to wit, what may be needful to them for meat and clothing — as are freely given them by those to whom they have communicated spirituals.

## THE ELEVENTH PROPOSITION.

### Concerning Worship.

All true and acceptable worship to God is offered in the inward and immediate moving and drawing of his own Spirit, which is neither limited to places, times, or persons; for though we be to worship him always, in that we are to fear before him, yet as to the outward signification thereof in prayers, praises, or preachings, we ought not to do it where and when we will, but where and when we are moved thereunto by the secret inspirations of his Spirit in our hearts, which God heareth and accepteth of, and is never wanting to move us thereunto, when need is, of which he himself is the alone proper judge. All other worship then, both praises, prayers and preachings, which man sets about in his own will, and at his own appointment, which he can both begin and end at his pleasure, do or leave undone, as himself sees meet, whether they be a prescribed form, as a liturgy, or prayers conceived extemporarily, by the natural strength and faculty of the mind, they are all but superstitions, will-worship, and abominable idolatry in the sight of God; which are to be denied, rejected, and separated from, in this day of his spiritual arising: however it might have pleased him—who winked at the times of ignorance, with respect to the simplicity and integrity of some, and of his own innocent seed, which lay as it were buried in the hearts of men, under the mass of superstition — to blow upon the dead and dry bones,

Ezek. xiii.
Mat. x. 20.
Acts ii. 4,
xviii. 5.
John iii. 6.
and iv. 21.
Jude xix.
Acts xvii
23.

and to raise some breathings, and answer them, and that until the day should more clearly dawn and break forth.

## THE TWELFTH PROPOSITION.

### *Concerning Baptism.*

As there is one Lord and one faith, so there is " one Eph. iv. 5. baptism; which is not the putting away the filth of the 1 Pet. iii. 21. flesh, but the answer of a good conscience before God, by Rom. vi. 4. Gal. iii. 27. the resurrection of Jesus Christ." And this baptism is a Col. ii. 12. pure and spiritual thing, to wit, the baptism of the spirit John iii. 30 and fire, by which we are buried with him, that being washed and purged from our sins, we may " walk in new- 1 Cor. i. 17 ness of life;" of which the baptism of John was a figure, which was commanded for a time, and not to continue for ever. As to the baptism of infants, it is a mere human tradition, for which neither precept nor practice is to be found in all the scripture.

## THE THIRTEENTH PROPOSITION.

### *Concerning the Communion, or Participation of the Body and Blood of Christ.*

The communion of the body and blood of Christ is in- 1 Cor. x. ward and spiritual, which is the participation of his flesh John vi. 32, and blood, by which the inward man is daily nourished in 33, 35. 1 Cor. v. 8. the hearts of those in whom Christ dwells; of which things the breaking of bread by Christ with his disciples was a figure, which they even used in the church for a time, who had received the substance, for the cause of the weak; even as " abstaining from things strangled, and from Acts xv. 20 blood;" the washing one another's feet, and the anointing John xiii. 14. of the sick with oil; all which are commanded with no less James v. 14. authority and solemnity than the former; yet seeing they are but the shadows of better things, they cease in such as have obtained the substance.

## THE FOURTEENTH PROPOSITION.

*Concerning the power of the Civil Magistrate, in matters
purely religious, and pertaining to the conscience.*

Since God hath assumed to himself the power and dominion of the conscience, who alone can rightly instruct
and govern it, therefore it is not lawful for any whatsoever,
by virtue of any authority or principality they bear in the
government of this world, to force the consciences of
others ; and therefore all killing, banishing, fining, imprisoning, and other such things, which men are afflicted
with, for the alone exercise of their conscience, or difference in worship or opinion, proceedeth from the spirit of
Cain, the murderer, and is contrary to the truth ; provided
always, that no man, under the pretence of conscience,
prejudice his neighbour in his life or estate ; or do any
thing destructive to, or inconsistent with human society ;
in which case the law is for the transgressor, and justice to
be administered upon all, without respect of persons.

Luke ix.
55, 56.
Mat. vii.
12, 29.
Tit. iii. 10.

## THE FIFTEENTH PROPOSITION.

*Concerning Salutations and Recreations, &c.*

Seeing the chief end of all religion is to redeem man
from the spirit and vain conversation of this world, and to
lead into inward communion with God, before whom, if
we fear always, we are accounted happy ; therefore all the
vain customs and habits thereof, both in word and deed,
are to be rejected and forsaken by those who come to this
fear ; such as the taking off the hat to a man, the bowings
and cringings of the body, and such other salutations of
that kind, with all the foolish and superstitious formalities
attending them ; all which man has invented in his degenerate state, to feed his pride in the vain pomp and glory
of this world ; as also the unprofitable plays, frivolous

Eph. v. 11.
1 Pet. i. 14.
John v. 44.
Jer. x. 3.
Acts x. 26.
Mat. xv. 13.
Col. ii. 8.

recreations, sportings and gamings, which are invented to pass away the precious time, and divert the mind from the witness of God in the heart, and from the living sense of his fear, and from that evangelical Spirit wherewith Christians ought to be leavened, and which leads into sobriety, gravity, and godly fear; in which, as we abide, the blessing of the Lord is felt to attend us in those actions in which we are necessarily engaged, in order to the taking care for the sustenance of the outward man.

# AN
# APOLOGY

# TRUE CHRISTIAN DIVINITY.

## PROPOSITION I.

### *Concerning the true Foundation of Knowledge.*

Seeing the height of all happiness is placed in the true knowledge of God; " This is life eternal, to know thee the only true God, and Jesus Christ whom thou hast sent;" the true and right understanding of this foundation and ground of knowledge is that which is most necessary to be known and believed in the first place. *John* xvii. 3.

He that desireth to acquire any art or science, seeketh first those means by which that art or science is obtained. If we ought to do so in things natural and earthly, how much more then in spiritual? In this affair then should our enquiry be the more diligent, because he that errs in the entrance is not so easily brought back again into the right way; he that misseth his road from the beginning of his journey, and is deceived in his first marks, at his first setting forth, the greater his mistake is, the more difficult will be his entrance into the right way.

Thus when a man first proposeth to himself the knowledge of God, from a sense of his own unworthiness, and from the great weariness of his mind, occasioned by the secret checks of his conscience, and the tender, yet real *The way to the true knowledge of God.*

glances of God's light upon his heart; the earnest desires he has to be redeemed from his present trouble, and the fervent breathings he has to be eased of his disordered passions and lusts, and to find quietness and peace in the certain knowledge of God, and in the assurance of his love and good-will towards him, make his heart tender, and ready to receive any impression; and so—not having then a distinct discerning—through forwardness embraceth any thing that brings present ease. If, either through the reverence he bears to certain persons, or from the secret inclination to what doth comply with his natural disposition, he fall upon any principles or means, by which he apprehends he may come to know God, and so doth centre himself, it will be hard to remove him thence again, how wrong so ever they may be: for the first anguish being over, he becomes more hardy; and the enemy being near, creates a false peace, and a certain confidence, which is strengthened by the mind's unwillingness to enter again into new doubtfulness, or the former anxiety of a search.

This is sufficiently verified in the example of the Phari-

Jewish doctors and Pharisees resist Christ.

sees and Jewish doctors, who most of all resisted Christ, disdaining to be esteemed ignorant; for this vain opinion they had of their knowledge hindered them from the true knowledge; and the mean people, who were not so much pre-occupied with former principles, nor conceited of their own knowledge, did easily believe. Wherefore the Phari-

John vii. 48, 49.

sees upbraid them, saying, "Have any of the rulers or Pharisees believed on him? But this people, which know not the law, are accursed." This is also abundantly proved by the experience of all such, as being secretly touched with the call of God's grace unto them, do apply themselves to false teachers, where the remedy proves worse than the disease; because instead of knowing God, or the things relating to their salvation aright, they drink in wrong opinions of him; from which it is harder to be disentangled, than while the soul remains a blank, or *Tabula rasa*. For they that conceit themselves wise, are worse to deal with than they that are sensible of their ignorance. Nor hath·

it been less the device of the devil, the great enemy of mankind, to persuade men into wrong notions of God, than to keep them altogether from acknowledging him; the latter taking with few, because odious; but the other having been the constant ruin of the world: for there hath scarce been a nation found, but hath had some notions or other of religion; so that not from their denying any Deity, but from their mistakes and misapprehensions of it, hath proceeded all the idolatry and superstition of the world; yea, hence even atheism itself hath proceeded: for these many and various opinions of God and religion, being so much mixed with the guessings and uncertain judgments of men, have begotten in many the opinion, That there is no God at all. This, and much more that might be said, may show how dangerous it is to miss in this first step: "All that come not in by the door, are accounted as thieves and robbers."

Again, how needful and desirable that knowledge is, which brings life eternal, Epictetus showeth, saying excel- Epic. M 21 lently well, cap. 38, Ἴσθι ὅτι τὸ Κυριώτατον, &c. Know, that the main foundation of piety is this, To have ὀρθὰς ὑπολήψεις, right opinions and apprehensions of God.

This therefore I judged necessary, as a first principle, in the first place to affirm; and I suppose will not need much farther explanation or defence, as being generally acknowledged by all—and in these things that are without controversy I love to be brief—as that which will easily commend itself to every man's reason and conscience; and therefore I shall proceed to the next proposition; which, though it be nothing less certain, yet by the malice of Satan, and the ignorance of many, comes far more under debate.

# PROPOSITION II.

## *Of Immediate Revelation.*

**Mat. xi. 27.** Seeing " no man knoweth the Father but the Son, and he
to whom the Son revealeth him ;" and seeing the " revelation of the Son is in and by the Spirit;" therefore the
testimony of the Spirit is that alone by which the true
knowledge of God hath been, is, and can be only revealed; who as, by the moving of his own Spirit, he
disposed the chaos of this world into that wonderful
order in which it was in the beginning, and created man
a living soul, to rule and govern it, so by the revelation
of the same Spirit he hath manifested himself all along
unto the sons of men, both patriarchs, prophets, and
apostles; which revelations of God by the Spirit, whether by outward voices and appearances, dreams, or inward objective manifestations in the heart, were of old
the formal object of their faith, and remain yet so to be,
since the object of the saints' faith is the same in all
ages, though held forth under divers administrations.
Moreover, these divine inward revelations, which we
make absolutely necessary for the building up of true
faith, neither do nor can ever contradict the outward testimony of the scriptures, or right and sound reason.
Yet from hence it will not follow, that these divine revelations are to be subjected to the test, either of the
outward testimony of the scriptures, or of the natural
reason of man, as to a more noble or certain rule and
touchstone ; for this divine revelation and inward illumination, is that which is evident and clear of itself,
forcing, by its own evidence and clearness, the well-disposed understanding to assent, irresistibly moving the
same thereunto, even as the common principles of natural truths do move and incline the mind to a natural

assent: as, that the whole is greater than its part; that two contradictories can neither be both true, nor both false.

§ I. It is very probable, that many carnal and natural Christians will oppose this proposition; who being wholly unacquainted with the movings and actings of God's Spirit upon their hearts, judge the same nothing necessary; and some are apt to flout at it as ridiculous; yea, to that height are the generality of Christians apostatized and degenerated, that though there be not any thing more plainly asserted, more seriously recommended, or more certainly attested, in all the writings of the holy scriptures, yet nothing is less minded and more rejected by all sorts of Christians, than immediate and divine revelation; insomuch that once to lay claim to it is matter of reproach. Whereas of old none were ever judged Christians, but such as had the Spirit of Christ, Rom. viii. 9. But now many do boldly call themselves Christians, who make no difficulty of confessing they are without it, and laugh at such as say they have it. Of old they were accounted "the sons of God, who were led by the Spirit of God," ibid. ver. 14. But now many aver themselves sons of God, who know nothing of this leader; and he that affirms himself so led, is, by the pretended orthodox of this age, presently proclaimed an heretic. The reason hereof is very manifest, viz.: Because many in these days, under the name of Christians, do experimentally find, that they are not actuated nor led by God's Spirit; yea, many great doctors, divines, teachers, and bishops of Christianity, (commonly so called,) have wholly shut their ears from hearing and their eyes from seeing this inward guide, and so are become strangers unto it; whence they are, by their own experience, brought to this strait, either to confess tha they are as yet ignorant of God, and have only the shadow of knowledge, and not the true know edge of him, or that this knowledge is acquired without immediate revelation.

*Revelation rejected by apostate Christians.*

3 *

Knowledge
spiritual
and literal
distin-
guished.

For the better understanding then of this proposition, we do distinguish betwixt the certain knowledge of God, and the uncertain; betwixt the spiritual knowledge, and the literal; the saving heart-knowledge, and the soaring airy head knowledge. The last, we confess, may be divers ways obtained; but the first, by no other way than the inward immediate manifestation and revelation of God's Spirit, shining in and upon the heart, enlightening and opening the understanding.

§ II. Having then proposed to myself, in these propositions, to affirm those things which relate to the true and effectual knowledge which brings life eternal with it; therefore I have truly affirmed, that this knowledge is no other ways attained, and that none have any true ground to believe they have attained it, who have it not by this revelation of God's Spirit.

The certainty of which truth is such, that it hath been acknowledged by some of the most refined and famous of all sorts of professors of Christianity in all ages; who being truly upright-hearted, and earnest seekers of the Lord—however stated under the disadvantages and epidemical errors of their several sects or ages—the true seed in them hath been answered by God's love, who hath had regard to the good, and hath had of his elect ones among all; who finding a distaste and disgust in all other outward means, even in the very principles and precepts more particularly relative to their own forms and societies, have at last concluded, with one voice, that there was no true knowledge of God but that which is revealed inwardly by his own Spirit. Whereof take these following testimonies of the ancients:

Aug. ex.
Tract. Ep.
Joh. iii.

1. "It is the inward master (saith Augustine) that teacheth, it is Christ that teacheth, it is inspiration that teacheth: where this inspiration and unction is wanting, it is in vain that words from without are beaten in." And thereafter: "For he that created us, and redeemed us, and called us by faith, and dwelleth in us by his Spirit, unless he speaketh unto us inwardly, it is needless for us to cry out."

2. "There is a difference," saith Clemens Alexandrinus, "betwixt that which any one saith of the truth, and that which the truth itself, interpreting itself, saith. A conjecture of truth differeth from the truth itself; a similitude. of a thing differeth from the thing itself; it is one thing that is acquired by exercise and discipline; and another thing, which by power and faith." Lastly, the same Clemens saith, "Truth is neither hard to be arrived at, nor is it impossible to apprehend it; for it is most nigh unto us, even in our houses, as the most wise Moses hath insinuated." *Clem. Alex. l. l. Strom.* *Pædag.*

3. "How is it," saith Tertullian, "that since the devil always worketh, and stirreth up the mind to iniquity, that the work of God should either cease, or desist to act? Since for this end the Lord did send the Comforter, that because human weakness could not at once bear all things, knowledge might be by little and little directed, formed, and brought to perfection, by the holy Spirit, that vicar of the Lord. 'I have many things yet,' saith he, 'to speak unto you, but ye cannot as yet bear them; but when that Spirit of truth shall come, he shall lead you into all truth, and shall teach you these things that are to come.' But of this his work we have spoken above. What is then the administration of the Comforter, but that discipline be directed, and the scriptures revealed, &c." *Tertullianus Lib. de veland. Virginibus, cap. 1.*

4. "The law," saith Hierom, "is spiritual, and there is need of a revelation to understand it." And in his Epistle 150, to Hedibia, Quest. 11, he saith, "The whole Epistle to the Romans needs an interpretation, it being involved in so great obscurities, that for the understanding thereof we need the help of the holy Spirit, who through the apostle dictated it." *Hieron. Ep. Paulin. 103*

5. "So great things," saith Athanasius, "doth our Saviour daily: he draws unto piety, persuades unto virtue, teaches immortality, excites to the desire of heavenly things, reveals the knowledge of the Father, inspires power against death, and shows himself unto every one." *Athanasius de Incarn. Verbi Dei.*

6. Gregory the Great, upon these words [He shall teach you all things] saith, "That unless the same Spirit is pre- *Greg. Mag Hom. 30. upon the Gospel.*

sent in the heart of the hearer, in vain is the discourse of
the doctor. Let no man then ascribe unto the man that
teacheth, what he understands from the mouth of him that
speaketh ; for unless he that teacheth be within, the tongue
of the doctor, that is without, laboureth in vain."

Cyril. Alex.
in The-
sauro, lib.
xiii. c. 3.
7. Cyrillus Alexandrinus plainly affirmeth, "That men
know that Jesus is the Lord by the Holy Ghost, no otherwise, than they who taste honey know that it is sweet, even
by its proper quality."

Bernard
in Psal.
lxxxiv.
8. "Therefore," saith Bernard, "we daily exhort you,
brethren, that ye walk the ways of the heart, and that your
souls be always in your hands, that ye may hear what the
Lord saith in you." And again, upon these words of the
apostle [Let him that glorieth, glory in the Lord], "With
which threefold vice," saith he, "all sorts of religious men
are less or more dangerously affected, because they do not
so diligently attend, with the ears of the heart, to what the
Spirit of truth, which flatters none, inwardly speaks."

This was the very basis, and main foundation, upon
which the primitive reformers built.

Luther
tom. v.
p. 76.
Luther, in his book to the nobility of Germany, saith,
"This is certain, that no man can make himself a teacher
of the holy scriptures, but the holy Spirit alone." And
upon the Magnificat he saith, "No man can rightly know
God, or understand the word of God, unless he immediately receive it from the Holy Spirit ; neither can any one
receive it from the Holy Spirit, except he find it by experience in himself ; and in this experience the Holy Ghost
teacheth, as in his proper school ; out of which school nothing is taught but mere talk."

Phil. Me-
lancthon.
Philip Melancthon, in his annotations upon John vi.
"Those who hear only an outward and bodily voice, hear
the creature ; but God is a Spirit, and is neither discerned,
By the Spi-
rit alone
God is
known.
nor known, nor heard, but by the Spirit ; and therefore to
hear the voice of God, to see God, is to know and hear the
Spirit. By the Spirit alone God is known and perceived.
Which also the more serious to this day do acknowledge,
even all such who satisfy themselves not with the superfi-

cies of religion, and use it not as a cover or art. Yea, all those who apply themselves effectually to Christianity, and are not satisfied until they have found its effectual work upon their hearts, redeeming them from sin, do feel that no knowledge effectually prevails to the producing of this, but that which proceeds from the warm influence of God's Spirit upon the heart, and from the comfortable shining of his light upon their understanding."

And therefore to this purpose a modern author, viz. Dr. Smith of Cambridge, in his select discourses, saith well; "To seek our divinity merely in books and writings, is to seek the living among the dead; we do but in vain many times seek God in these, where his truth is too often not so much enshrined as entombed. *Intra te quære Deum,* Seek God within thine own soul. He is best discerned, νοερᾶ ἐπαφῆ, as Plotinus phraseth it, by an intellectual touch of him. We must see with our eyes, and hear with our ears, and our hands must handle the word of life — to express it in St. John's words. — ἔςι καὶ ψυχῆς ἄισϑησις τις, &c., the soul itself hath its sense, as well as the body. And therefore David, when he would teach us to know what the divine goodness is, calls not for speculation, but sensation: 'Taste, and see that the Lord is good.' That is not the best and truest knowledge of God which is wrought out by the labour and sweat of the brain, but that which is kindled within us, by an heavenly warmth in our hearts." And again : "There is a knowing of the truth as it is in Jesus, as it is in a Christ-like nature ; as it is in that sweet, mild, humble, and loving Spirit of Jesus, which spreads itself, like a morning sun, upon the souls of good men, full of light and life. It profits little to know Christ himself after the flesh ; but he gives his Spirit to good men, that searcheth the deep things of God." And again : "It is but a thin airy knowledge that is got by mere speculation, which is ushered in by syllogisms and demonstrations; but that which springs forth from true goodness, is ϑειότερον τι πάσης ὑποδείξεως, as Origen speaks : 'It brings

*Dr. Smith of Cambridge, concerning book-divinity.*

*Psal xxx 8.*

E

such a divine light into the soul, as is more clear and con
vincing than any demonstration.'"

§ III. That this certain and undoubted method of the
true knowledge of God hath been brought out of use, hath
been none of the least devices of the devil, to secure mankind to his kingdom.   For after the light and glory of the
Christian religion had prevailed over a good part of the
world, and dispelled the thick mists of the heathenish doc
trine of the plurality of gods, he that knew there was no
probability of deluding the world any longer that way, did
then puff man up with a false knowledge of the true God ;
setting him on work to seek God the wrong way, and persuading him to be content with such a knowledge as was
of his own acquiring, and not of God's teaching. And this
device hath proved the more successful, because accommo-
dated to the natural and corrupt spirit and temper of man,
who above all things affects to exalt himself; in which
self-exaltation, as God is greatly dishonoured, so therein the
devil hath his end ; who is not anxious how much God is
acknowledged in words, provided himself be but always
served; he matters not how great and high speculations
the natural man entertains of God, so long as he serves his
own lusts and passions, and is obedient to his evil suggestions and temptations.   Thus Christianity is become as it
were an art, acquired by human science and industry, like
any other art or science ; and men have not only assumed
the name of Christians, but even have procured themselves
to be esteemed as masters of Christianity, by certain artificial tricks, though altogether strangers to the spirit and life
of Jesus.   But if we make a right definition of a Christian,
according to the scriptures, That he is one that hath the
spirit of Christ, and is led by it, how many Christians, yea,
and of these great masters and doctors of Christianity, so
accounted, shall we justly divest of that noble title?

If those therefore who have all the other means of knowledge, and are sufficiently learned therein, whether it be
the letter of the scripture, the traditions of churches, or the
works of creation and providence, whence they are able to

*Apostasy
and a false
knowledge
introduced.*

*Christian-
ity is be-
come an
art, ac-
quired by
human
science
and indus-
try*

deduce strong and undeniable arguments—which may be true in themselves—are not yet to be esteemed Christians according to the certain and infallible definition above mentioned ; and if the inward and immediate revelation of God's Spirit in the heart, in such as have been altogether ignorant of some, and but very little skilled in others, of these means of attaining knowledge, hath brought them to salvation ; then it will necessarily and evidently follow, that inward and immediate revelation is the only sure and certain way to attain the true and saving knowledge of God.

*By revelation is the true knowledge of God.*

But the first is true : therefore the last.

Now as this argument doth very strongly conclude for this way of knowledge and against such as deny it, so in this respect it is the more to be regarded, as the propositions from which it is deduced are so clear, that our very adversaries cannot deny them. For as to the first it is acknowledged, that many learned men may be, and have been, damned. And as to the second, who will deny but many illiterate men may be, and are, saved? Nor dare any affirm, that none come to the knowledge of God and salvation by the inward revelation of the Spirit, without these other outward means, unless they be also so bold as to exclude Abel, Seth, Noah, Abraham, Job, and all the holy patriarchs from true knowledge and salvation.

*Abel, Seth Noah, &c. instanced.*

§ IV. I would however not be understood, as if hereby I excluded those other means of knowledge from any use or service to man ; it is far from me so to judge, as concerning the scriptures, in the next proposition, will more plainly appear. The question is not, what may be profitable or helpful, but what is absolutely necessary. Many things may contribute to further a work, which yet are not the main thing that makes the work go on.

The sum then of what is said amounts to this : That where the true inward knowledge of God is, through the revelation of his Spirit, there is all ; neither is there an absolute necessity of any other. But where the best, highest, and most profound knowledge is, without this there is nothing, as to the obtaining the great end of salvation.

This truth is very effectually confirmed by the first part of
the proposition itself, which in few words comprehendeth
divers unquestionable arguments, which I shall in brief
subsume.

> First, That there is no knowledge of the Father but
> by the Son.
>
> Secondly, That there is no knowledge of the Son but
> by the Spirit.
>
> Thirdly, That by the Spirit God hath always revealed
> himself to his children.
>
> Fourthly, That these revelations were the formal ob-
> ject of the saints' faith.
>
> And Lastly, That the same continueth to be the ob
> ject of the saints' faith to this day.

Of each of these I shall speak a little particularly, and
then proceed to the latter part.

Assert. i.
proved.

§ V. As to the first, viz. That there is no knowledge
of the Father but by the Son, it will easily be proved, being founded upon the plain words of scripture, and is
therefore a fit medium from whence to deduce the rest of
our assertions.

For the infinite and most wise God, who is the foundation, root and spring of all operation, hath wrought all

John i. 1,
2, 3.

things by his eternal Word and Son. "This is that Word
that was in the beginning with God, and was God, by
whom all things were made, and without whom was not
any thing made that was made." This is that "Jesus

Eph. iii 9.

Christ, by whom God created all things, by whom, and
for whom, all things were created, that are in heaven and
in earth, visible and invisible, whether they be thrones, or
dominions, or principalities, or powers," Col. i. 16. who
therefore is called, "The first-born of every creature,"
Col. i. 15. As then that infinite and incomprehensible
fountain of life and motion operateth in the creatures by
his own eternal word and power, so no creature has access
again unto him but in and by the Son, according to his
own express words, "No man knoweth the Father, but
the Son, and he to whom the Son will reveal him," Mat.

xi. 27. Luke x. 22. And again, he himself saith, "I am the way, the truth, and the life: no man cometh unto the Father but by me," John xiv. 6.

Hence he is fitly called, The mediator betwixt God and man: for having been with God from all eternity, being himself God, and also in time partaking of the nature of man, through him is the goodness and love of God conveyed to mankind, and by him again man receiveth and partaketh of these mercies.

Hence is easily deduced the proof of this first assertion, thus:

If no man knoweth the Father but the Son, and he to whom the Son will reveal him, then there is no knowledge of the Father but by the Son.

But, no man knoweth the Father but the Son:

Therefore, there is no knowledge of the Father but by the Son.

The first part of the antecedent are the plain words of scripture: the consequence thereof is undeniable; except one would say, that he hath the knowledge of the Father, while yet he knows him not; which were an absurd repugnance.

Again, If the Son be the way, the truth, and the life, and that no man cometh unto the Father, but by him; then there is no knowledge of the Father but by the Son.

But the first is true: therefore the last.

The antecedent are the very scripture words: the consequence is very evident: for how can any know a thing, who useth not the way, without which it is not knowable? But it is already proved, that there is no other way but by the Son; so that whoso uses not that way, cannot know him, neither come unto him.

§ VI. Having then laid down this first principle, I come to the second, viz.: That there is no knowledge of the Son but by the Spirit; or, That the revelation of the Son of God is by the Spirit.

Assert. u proved.

Where it is to be noted, that I always speak of the saving, certain, and necessary knowledge of God; which that it

4

cannot be acquired otherways than by the Spirit, doth also
appear from many clear scriptures. For Jesus Christ, in
and by whom the Father is revealed, doth also reveal himself to his disciples and friends in and by his Spirit. As
his manifestation was outward, when he testified and witnessed for the truth in this world, and approved himself
faithful throughout, so being now withdrawn, as to the outward man, he doth teach and instruct mankind inwardly
by his own Spirit; "He standeth at the door, and knock-
eth, and whoso heareth his voice and openeth, he comes
in" to such, Rev. iii. 20. Of this revelation of Christ in
him Paul speaketh, Gal. i. 16, in which he placeth the excellency of his ministry, and the certainty of his calling.
And the promise of Christ to his disciples, "Lo, I am
with you to the end of the world," confirmeth the same
thing; for this is an inward and spiritual presence, as all
acknowledge: but what relates hereto will again occur. I
shall deduce the proof of this proposition from two mani-

**Proof 1.** fest places of scripture: the first is, 1 Cor. ii. 11, 12.
" What man knoweth the things of a man, save the spirit

**The things** of a man which is in him? Even so the things of God
**of God are**
**known by** knoweth no man, but the Spirit of God. Now we have
**the Spirit of** received not the spirit of the world, but the Spirit which is
**God.**
of God, that we might know the things which are freely
given us of God." The apostle, in the verses before,
speaking of the wonderful things which are prepared for
the saints, after he hath declared, that "the natural man
cannot reach them," adds, that "they are revealed by the
Spirit of God," ver. 9, 10, giving this reason, "For the
Spirit searcheth all things, even the deep things of God."
And then he bringeth in the comparison, in the verses above-
mentioned, very apt, and answerable to our purpose and
doctrine, that " as the things of a man are only known by
the spirit of man, so the things of God are only known by
the Spirit of God;" that is, that as nothing below the spirit
of man (as the spirit of brutes, or any other creatures,)
can properly reach unto or comprehend the things of a
man, as being of a nobler and higher nature, so neither

can the spirit of man, or the natural man, as the apostle in the fourteenth verse subsumes, receive nor discern the things of God, or the things that are spiritual, as being also of an higher nature; which the apostle himself gives for the reason, saying, "Neither can he know them, because they are spiritually discerned." So that the apostle's words being reduced to an argument, do very well prove the matter under debate, thus:

If that which appertaineth properly to man, cannot be discerned by any lower or baser principle than the spirit of man; then cannot those things, that properly relate unto God and Christ, be known or discerned by any lower or baser thing than the Spirit of God and Christ.

But the first is true: therefore also the second.

The whole strength of the argument is contained in the apostle's words before-mentioned; which, therefore, being granted, I shall proceed to deduce a second argument, thus:

That which is spiritual can only be known and discerned by the Spirit of God.

But the revelation of Jesus Christ, and the true and saving knowledge of him, is spiritual:

Therefore the revelation of Jesus Christ, and the true and saving knowledge of him, can only be known and discerned by the Spirit of God.

The other scripture is also a saying of the same apostle, **Proof 2.** 1 Cor. xii. 3. "No man can say that Jesus is the Lord, *No man can* but by the Holy Ghost." This scripture, which is full of *call Jesus* truth, and answereth full well to the enlightened under- *Lord, &c.* standing of the spiritual and real Christian, may perhaps prove very strange to the carnal and pretended follower of Christ, by whom perhaps it hath not been so diligently re-marked. Here the apostle doth so much require the Holy Spirit in the things that relate to a Christian, that he posi-tively avers, we cannot so much as affirm Jesus to be the Lord without it; which insinuates no less, than that the *Spiritual* spiritual truths of the gospel are as lies in the mouths of *truths are* carnal and unspiritual men; for though in themselves they *lies spoken by carnal men.*

be true, yet are they not true as to them, because not known, nor uttered forth in and by that principle and spirit that ought to direct the mind and actuate it in such things : they are no better than the counterfeit representations of things in a comedy ; neither can it be more truly and properly called a real and true knowledge of God and Christ, than the actions of Alexander the Great, and Julius Cæsar, &c., if now transacted upon a stage, might be called truly and really their doings ; or the persons representing them might be said truly and really to have conquered Asia, overcome Pompey, &c.

This knowledge then of Christ, which is not by the revelation of his own Spirit in the heart, is no more properly the knowledge of Christ, than the prattling of a parrot, which has been taught a few words, may be said to be the voice of a man ; for as that, or some other bird, may be taught to sound or utter forth a rational sentence, as it hath learned it by the outward ear, and not from any living principle of reason actuating it ; so just such is that knowledge of the things of God, which the natural and carnal man hath gathered from the words or writings of spiritual men, which are not true to him, because conceived in the natural spirit, and so brought forth by the wrong organ, and not proceeding from the spiritual principle ; no more than the words of a man acquired by art, and brought forth by the mouth of a bird, not proceeding from a rational principle, are true with respect to the bird which utters them. Wherefore from this scripture I shall further add this argument:

*Like the prattling of a parrot.*

If no man can say Jesus is the Lord, but by the Holy Ghost ; then no man can know Jesus to be the Lord, but by the Holy Ghost.

But the first is true : therefore the second.

From this argument there may be another deduced, concluding in the very terms of this assertion : thus,

If no man can know Jesus to be the Lord, but by the Holy Ghost, then there can be no certain knowledge or revelation of him but by the Spirit.

But the first is true : therefore the second.

§ VII. The third thing affirmed is, That by the Spirit God always revealed himself to his children. Assert. iii. proved.

For making the truth of this assertion appear, it will be but needful to consider God's manifesting himself towards and in relation to his creatures from the beginning, which resolves itself always herein. The first step of all is ascribed hereunto by Moses, Gen. i. 2. "And the Spirit of God moved upon the face of the waters." I think it will not be denied, that God's converse with man, all along from Adam to Moses, was by the immediate manifestation of his Spirit: That reve- and afterwards, through the whole tract of the law, he lation is by spake to his children no otherways; which, as it naturally of God. followeth from the principles above proved, so it cannot be denied by such as acknowledge the scriptures of truth to have been written by the inspiration of the Holy Ghost: for these writings, from Moses to Malachi, do declare, that during all that time God revealed himself to his children by his Spirit.

But if any will object, That after the dispensation of the Object. law God's method of speaking was altered;

I answer: First, That God spake always immediately Answ. to the Jews, in that he spake always immediately to the High-Priest from betwixt the Cherubims; who, when he Sanctum entered into the Holy of Holies, returning, did relate to the Sanctorum whole people the voice and will of God, there immediately revealed. So that this immediate speaking never ceased in any age.

Secondly, From this immediate fellowship were none shut out, who earnestly sought after and waited for it; in that many, besides the High-Priest, who were not so much as of the kindred of Levi, nor of the prophets, did receive it and speak from it; as it is written, Numb. xi. 25, where the Spirit is said to have rested on the seventy elders; None shut which Spirit also reached unto two that were not in the out from tabernacle, but in the camp; whom when some would diate. fel- have forbidden, Moses would not, but rejoiced, wishing lowship. that all the Lord's people were prophets, and that he would put his Spirit upon them, ver. 29.

4 *                    F

This is also confirmed, Neh. ix., where the elders of the people, after their return from captivity, when they began to sanctify themselves by fasting and prayer, numbering up the many mercies of God towards their fathers, say, verse 20, " Thou gavest also thy good Spirit to instruct them;" and verse 30, " Yet many years didst thou forbear, and testify against them by thy Spirit in thy prophets." Many are the sayings of spiritual David to this purpose, as Psalm li. 11, 12, " Take not thy holy Spirit from me: uphold me with thy free Spirit." Psal. cxxxix. 7, " Whither shall I go from thy Spirit?" Hereunto doth the prophet Isaiah ascribe the credit of his testimony, saying, chap. xlviii. 16, " And now the Lord God and his Spirit hath sent me." And that God revealed himself to his children under the New Testament, to wit, to the apostles, evangelists, and primitive disciples, is confessed by all. How far now this yet continueth, and is to be expected, comes hereafter to be spoken to.

**Assert. iv.**    § VIII. The fourth thing affirmed is, That these revelations were the object of the saints' faith of old.

**Proved.**    This will easily appear by the definition of faith, and considering what its object is: for which we shall not dive into the curious and various notions of the school-men, but stay in the plain and positive words of the apostle Paul,

**What faith is.** who, Heb. xi. describes it two ways. " Faith," saith he, " is the substance of things hoped for, and the evidence of things not seen:" which, as the apostle illustrateth it in the same chapter by many examples, is no other but a firm and certain belief of the mind, whereby it resteth, and in a sense possesseth the substance of some things hoped for, through its confidence in the promise of God: and thus the soul hath a most firm evidence, by its faith, of things not yet seen nor come to pass. The object of this faith is the promise, word, or testimony of God, speaking in the mind. Hence it hath been generally affirmed, that the object of

**The object of faith, Deus loquens.** faith is *Deus loquens*, &c. that is, God speaking, &c. which is also manifest from all those examples deduced by the apostle throughout that whole chapter, whose faith was founded neither upon any outward testimony, nor upon the voice or writing of man, but upon the revelation of God's will, manifest unto them, and in them; as in the example of Noah, ver. 7. thus, "By faith Noah, being warned of God of things not seen as yet, moved with fear, prepared an ark to the saving of his house; by the which he condemned the world, and became heir of the righteousness which is by faith." What was here the object of Noah's faith, but God speaking unto him? He had not the writings nor prophesyings of any going before, nor yet the concurrence of any church or people to strengthen him; and yet his faith in the word, by which he contradicted the whole world, saved him and his house. Of which also Abraham is set forth as a singular example, being therefore called the Father of the faithful, who is said against hope to have believed in hope, in that he not only willingly forsook his father's country, not knowing whither he went; in that he believed concerning the coming of Isaac, though contrary to natural probability; but above all, in that he refused not to offer him up, not doubting but God was able to raise him from the dead; of whom it is said, that in Isaac shall thy seed be called. And last of all, in that he rested in the promise, that his seed should possess the land, wherein he himself was but a pilgrim, and which to them was not to be fulfilled while divers ages after. The object of Abraham's faith in all this was no other but inward and immediate revelation, or God signifying his will unto him inwardly and immediately by his Spirit.

*Noah's faith.*

*Abraham's faith.*

But because, in this part of the proposition, we made also mention of external voices, appearances, and dreams in the alternative, I think also fit to speak hereof, what in that respect may be objected; to wit,

That those who found their faith now upon immediate and objective revelation, ought to have also outward voices or visions, dreams or appearances for it.

*Object.*

It is not denied, but God made use of the ministry of angels, who, in the appearance of men, spake outwardly

*Answ.*

The minis-
try of an-
gels speak-
ing in the
appearance
of men to
the saints
of old.
to the saints of old, and that he did also reveal some things
to them in dreams and visions; none of which we will
affirm to be ceased, so as to limit the power and liberty of
God in manifesting himself towards his children. But
while we are considering the object of faith, we must
not stick to that which is but circumstantially and accidentally so, but to that which is universally and substan-
tially so.

Next again, we must distinguish betwixt that which in
itself is subject to doubt and delusion, and therefore is received for and because of another; and that which is not
subject to any doubt, but is received simply for and because
of itself, as being *prima veritas*, the very first and original
truth. Let us then consider how or how far these outward
voices, appearances, and dreams were the object of the
Revela-
tions by
dreams and
visions.
saints' faith: was it because they were simply voices, appearances, or dreams? Nay, certainly; for they were not
ignorant, that the devil might form a sound of words, convey it to the outward ear, and deceive the outward senses,
by making things to appear that are not. Yea, do we not
see by daily experience, that the jugglers and mountebanks
can do as much as all that by their legerdemain? God
forbid then that the saints' faith should be founded upon
so fallacious a foundation as man's outward and fallible
senses. What made them then give credit to these visions?
Certainly nothing else but the secret testimony of God's
Spirit in their hearts, assuring them that the voices, dreams,
and visions were of and from God. Abraham believed the
angels; but who told him that these men were angels?
We must not think his faith then was built upon his outward senses, but proceeded from the secret persuasion of
God's Spirit in his heart. This then must needs be
acknowledged to be originally and principally the object
of the saints' faith, without which there is no true and certain faith, and by which many times faith is begotten and
strengthened without any of these outward or visible
helps; as we may observe in many passages of the holy
scripture, where it is only mentioned, "And God said,"

&c. " And the word of the Lord came" unto such and such, saying, &c.

But if any one should pertinaciously affirm, That this did import an outward audible voice to the carnal ear; Object.

I would gladly know what other argument such an one could bring for this his affirmation, saving his own simple conjecture. It is said indeed, " The Spirit witnesseth with our spirit," Rom. viii. 16; but not to our outward ears. And seeing the Spirit of God is within us, and not without us only, it speaks to our spiritual, and not to our bodily ear. Therefore I see no reason, where it is so often said in scripture, The Spirit said, moved, hindered, called such or such a one, to do or forbear such or such a thing, that any have to conclude, that this was not an inward voice to the ear of the soul, rather than an outward voice to the bodily ear. If any be otherwise minded, let them, if they can, produce their arguments, and we may further consider of them. Answ. The spirit speaks to the spiritual ear not to the outward.

From all therefore which is above declared, I shall deduce an argument to conclude the proof of this assertion, thus:

That which any one firmly believes, as the ground and foundation of his hope in God, and life eternal, is the formal object of his faith.

But the inward and immediate revelation of God's Spirit, speaking in and unto the saints, was by them believed as the ground and foundation of their hope in God, and life eternal.

Therefore these inward and immediate revelations were the formal object of their faith.

§ IX. That which now cometh under debate, is what we asserted in the last place, to wit, That the same continueth to be the object of the saints' faith unto this day. Many will agree to what we have said before, who differ from us herein. Assert. proved

There is nevertheless a very firm argument, confirming the truth of this assertion, included in the proposition itself, to wit, That the object of the saints' faith is the same in all ages, though held forth under divers administrations, which I shall reduce to an argument, and prove thus:

First, Where the faith is one, the object of the faith is one.

But the faith is one: Therefore, &c.

That the faith is one, is the express words of the apostle, Eph. iv. 5. who placeth the one faith with the one God, importing no less, than that to affirm two faiths is as absurd as to affirm two gods.

Moreover, if the faith of the ancients were not one and the same with ours, *i. e.* agreeing in substance therewith, and receiving the same definition, it had been impertinent **The faith of** for the apostle, Heb. xi. to have illustrated the definition **the saints** of our faith by the examples of that of the ancients, or to **of old the** go about to move us by the example of Abraham, if Abra- **ours.** ham's faith were different in nature from ours. Nor doth any difference arise hence, because they believed in Christ with respect to his appearance outwardly as future, and we as already appeared: for neither did they then so believe in him to come, as not to feel him present with them, and witness him near; seeing the apostle saith, " They all drank of that spiritual rock which followed them, which rock was Christ;" nor do we so believe concerning his appearance past, as not also to feel and know him present with us, and to feed upon him; except Christ, saith the apostle, be in you, ye are reprobates; so that both our faith is one, terminating in one and the same thing. And as to the other part or consequence of the antecedent, to wit, That the object is one where the faith is one, the apostle also proveth it in the fore-cited chapter, where he makes all the worthies of old examples to us. Now wherein are they imitable, but because they believed in God? And what was the object of their faith, but inward and immediate revelation, as we have before proved? Their example can be no ways applicable to us, except we believe in God, as they did, that is, by the same object. The apostle clears this yet further by his own example, Gal. i. 16. where he saith, " So soon as Christ was revealed in him, he consulted not

with flesh and blood, but forthwith believed and obeyed."
The same apostle, Heb. xiii. 7, 8. where he exhorteth the
Hebrews to follow the faith of the elders, adds this reason,
" Considering the end of their conversation, Jesus Christ,
the same to-day, yesterday, and for ever:" Hereby notably
insinuating, that in the object there is no alteration.

If any now object the diversity of administration;    Object

I answer; That altereth not at all the object: for the Answ.
same apostle mentioning this diversity three times, 1 Cor.
xii. 4, 5, 6. centereth always in the same object; the same
Spirit, the same Lord, the same God.

But further ; If the object of faith were not one and the
same both to us and to them, then it would follow that we
were to know God some other way than by the Spirit.

But this were absurd: Therefore, &c.

Lastly, this is most firmly proved from a common and
received maxim of the school-men, to wit, *Omnis actus spe-
cificatur ab objecto*, ' Every act is specified from its object ;'
from which, if it be true, as they acknowledge, (though for
the sake of many I shall not recur to this argument, as
being too nice and scholastic, neither lay I much stress upon
those kind of things, as being that which commends not
the simplicity of the gospel) it would follow, that if the object were different, then the faith would be different also.

Such as deny this proposition now-a-days use here a distinction ; granting that God is to be known by his Spirit,
but again denying that it is immediate or inward, but in
and by the scriptures ; in which the mind of the Spirit (as
they say) being fully and amply expressed, we are thereby
to know God, and be led in all things.

As to the negative of this assertion, That the scriptures
are not sufficient, neither were ever appointed to be the
adequate and only rule, nor yet can guide or direct a Christian in all those things that are needful for him to know,
we shall leave that to the next proposition to be examined.
What is proper in this place to be proved is, That Christians now are to be led inwardly and immediately by the
Spirit of God, even in the same manner, though it befall

not many to be led in the same measure, as the saints **were**
of old.

§ X. I shall prove this by divers arguments, and first
from the promise of Christ in these words, John xiv. 16,
" And I will pray the Father, and he will give you another
Comforter, that he may abide with you for ever." Ver. 17.
" Even the Spirit of truth, whom the world cannot receive,
because it seeth him not, neither knoweth him ; but ye
know him, for he dwelleth with you, and shall be in you."
Again, ver. 26. " But the Comforter, which is the Holy
Ghost, whom the Father will send in my name, he shall
teach you all things, and bring all things to your remembrance." And xvi. 13. But " when he, the Spirit of truth
is come, he will guide you into all truth : for he shall
not speak of himself ; but whatsoever he shall hear he shall
speak, and he will show you things to come." We have
here first, who this is, and that is divers ways expressed,
to wit : The Comforter, the Spirit of truth, the Holy Ghost,
the Sent of the Father in the name of Christ. And hereby
is sufficiently proved the sottishness of those Socinians and
other carnal Christians, who neither know nor acknowledge
any internal Spirit or power but that which is merely natural ;
by which they sufficiently declare themselves to be of the
world, who cannot receive the Spirit, because they neither
see him nor know him. Secondly, Where this Spirit is to
be, " He dwelleth with you, and shall be in you." And
Thirdly, What his work is, " He shall teach you all things,
and bring all things to your remembrance, and guide you
into all truth," ὁδηγήσει ὑμας εἰς πᾶσαν τ᾽ ἀληθειαν.

As to the first, most do acknowledge that there is nothing
else understood than what the plain words signify ; which
is also evident by many other places of scripture that will
hereafter occur ; neither do I see how such as affirm otherways can avoid blasphemy : for, if the Comforter, the Holy
Ghost, and Spirit of truth, be all one with the scriptures,
then it will follow that the scriptures are God, seeing it is
true that the Holy Ghost is God. If these men's reasoning
might take place, wherever the Spirit is mentioned in rela-

tion to the saints, thereby might be truly and properly understood the scriptures; which, what a nonsensical monster
it would make of the Christian religion, will easily appear
to all men. As where it is said, " A manifestation of the
Spirit is given to every man to profit withal;" it might be
rendered thus: A manifestation of the scriptures is given
to every man to profit withal; what notable sense this would
make, and what a curious interpretation, let us consider by
the sequel of the same chapter, 1 Cor. xii. 9, 10, 11. " To
another the gifts of healing, by the same Spirit; to another
the working of miracles, &c. But all these worketh that
one and the self-same Spirit, dividing to every man severally as he will." What would now these great masters of
reason, the Socinians, judge, if we should place the scriptures here instead of the Spirit? Would it answer their
reason, which is the great guide of their faith? Would it
be good and sound reason in their logical schools, to affirm
that the scripture divideth severally as it will, and giveth to
some the gift of healing, to others the working of miracles?
If then this Spirit, a manifestation whereof is given to
every man to profit withal, be no other than that Spirit of
truth before-mentioned which guideth into all truth, this
Spirit of truth cannot be the scripture. I could infer an hundred more absurdities of this kind upon this sottish opinion,
but what is said may suffice. For even some of themselves,
being at times forgetful or ashamed of their own doctrine,
do acknowledge that the Spirit of God is another thing,
and distinct from the scriptures, to guide and influence the
saints.

Secondly, That this Spirit is inward, in my opinion Query 2.
needs no interpretation or commentary, " He dwelleth Where is
with you, and shall be in you." This indwelling of the his place!
Spirit in the saints, as it is a thing most needful to be
known and believed, so is it as positively asserted in the
scripture as any thing else can be. " If so be that the
Spirit of God dwell in you," saith the apostle to the Romans, chap. viii. 9. And again, " Know ye not that your
body is the temple of the Holy Ghost, 1 Cor. vi. 19. " And
5                                    G

that the Spirit of God dwelleth in you?" 1 Cor. iii. 16.
Without this the apostle reckoneth no man a Christian.
"If any man (saith he) have not the Spirit of Christ, he is
none of his." These words immediately follow those
above mentioned out of the epistle to the Romans, "But
ye are not in the flesh, but in the Spirit, if so be the Spirit
of God dwell in you." The context of which showeth,
that the apostle reckoneth it the main token of a Christian,
both positively and negatively: for in the former verses
he showeth how the carnal mind is enmity against God,
and that such as are in the flesh cannot please him. Where
subsuming, he adds concerning the Romans, that they are
not in the flesh, if the Spirit of God dwell in them. What
is this but to affirm, that they in whom the Spirit dwells
are no longer in the flesh, nor of those who please not God,
but are become Christians indeed? Again, in the same
verse he concludes negatively, that "If any man have not
the Spirit of Christ, he is none of his;" that is, he is no
Christian. He then that acknowledges himself ignorant
and a stranger to the inward in-being of the Spirit of Christ
in his heart, doth thereby acknowledge himself to be yet
in the carnal mind, which is enmity to God; to be yet in
the flesh, where God cannot be pleased; and in short,
whatever he may otherways know or believe of Christ, or
however much skilled or acquainted with the letter of the
holy scripture, not yet to be, notwithstanding all that, attained to the least degree of a Christian; yea, not once to
have embraced the Christian religion. For take but away
the Spirit, and Christianity remains no more Christianity,
than the dead carcase of a man, when the soul and spirit is
departed, remains a man; which the living can no more
abide, but do bury out of their sight, as a noisome and
useless thing, however acceptable it hath been when actuated and moved by the soul. Lastly, Whatsoever is
excellent, whatsoever is noble, whatsoever is worthy, whatsoever is desirable in the Christian faith, is ascribed to this
Spirit, without which it could no more subsist than the
outward world without the sun. Hereunto have all true

*Note in margin:* The Spirit within, the main token of a Chris-tian.

Christians, in all ages, attributed their strength and life. It is by this Spirit that they avouch themselves to have been converted to God, to have been redeemed from the world, to have been strengthened in their weakness, comforted in their afflictions, confirmed in their temptations, emboldened in their sufferings, and triumphed in the midst of all their persecutions. Yea, the writings of all true Christians are full of the great and notable things which they all affirm themselves to have done, by the power, and virtue, and efficacy of this Spirit of God working in them. "It is the Spirit that quickeneth," John vi. 63. It was the Spirit that gave them utterance, Acts ii. 4. It was the Spirit by which Stephen spake, that the Jews were not able to resist, Acts vi. 10. It is such as walk after the Spirit that receive no condemnation, Rom. viii. 1. It is the law of the Spirit that makes free, ver. 2. It is by the Spirit of God dwelling in us that we are redeemed from the flesh, and from the carnal mind, ver. 9. It is the Spirit of Christ dwelling in us that quickeneth our mortal bodies, ver. 11. It is through this Spirit that the deeds of the body are mortified, and life obtained, ver. 13. It is by this Spirit that we are adopted, and "cry ABBA Father," ver. 15. It is this "Spirit that beareth witness with our spirit that we are the children of God," ver. 16. It is this "Spirit that helpeth our infirmities, and maketh intercession for us, with groanings which cannot be uttered," ver. 26. It is by this Spirit that the glorious things which God hath laid up for us, which neither outward ear hath heard, nor outward eye hath seen, nor the heart of man conceived by all his reasonings, are revealed unto us, 1 Cor. ii. 9, 10. It is by this Spirit that both wisdom and knowledge, and faith, and miracles, and tongues, and prophecies, are obtained, 1 Cor. xii. 8, 9, 10. It is by this Spirit that we are "all baptized into one body," ver. 13. In short, what thing relating to the salvation of the soul, and to the life of a Christian, is rightly performed, or effectually obtained, without it? And what shall I say more? For the time would fail me to tell of all those things

*The great and notable acts that have been and are performed by the Spirit in all ages.*

which the holy men of old have declared, and the saints of this day do themselves enjoy, by the virtue and power of this Spirit dwelling in them. Truly my paper could not contain the many testimonies whereby this truth is confirmed; wherefore, besides what is above mentioned out of the fathers, whom all pretend to reverence, and those of Luther and Melancthon, I shall deduce yet one observable testimony out of Calvin, because not a few of the followers of his doctrine do refuse and deride (and that, as it is to be feared, because of their own non-experience thereof) this way of the Spirit's indwelling, as uncertain and dangerous; that so, if neither the testimony of the scripture, nor the sayings of others, nor right reason can move them, they may at least be reproved by the words of their own master, who saith in the third book of his institutions, cap. 2, on this wise:

Calvin, of the necessity of the Spirit's indwelling in us.

"But they allege, It is a bold presumption for any to pretend to an undoubted knowledge of God's will; which," saith he, "I should grant unto them, if we should ascribe so much to ourselves as to subject the incomprehensible counsel of God to the rashness of our understandings. But while we simply say with Paul, that 'we have received not the spirit of this world, but the Spirit which is of God,' by whose teaching we know those things that are given us of God, what can they prate against it without reproaching the Spirit of God? For if it be an horrible sacrilege to accuse any revelation coming from him, either of a lie, of uncertainty or ambiguity, in asserting its certainty wherein do we offend? But they cry out, That it is not without great temerity that we dare so boast of the Spirit of Christ. Who would believe that the sottishness of these men were so great, who would be esteemed the masters of the world, that they should so fail in the first principles of religion? Verily I could not believe it, if their own writings did not testify so much. Paul accounts those the sons of God, who are actuated by the Spirit of God; but these will have the children of God actuated by their own spirits without the Spirit of God. He will have us call God Father, the

Spirit dictating that term unto us, which only can witness to our spirits that we are the sons of God. These, though they cease not to call upon God, do nevertheless dismiss the Spirit, by whose guiding he is rightly to be called upon. He denies them to be the sons of God, or the servants of Christ, who are not led by his Spirit; but these feign a Christianity that needs not the Spirit of Christ. He takes away the hope of a blessed resurrection, unless we feel the Spirit residing in us; but these feign a hope without any such feeling; but perhaps they will answer, that they deny not but that it is necessary to have it, only of modesty and humility we ought to deny and not acknowledge it. What means he then, when he commands the Corinthians to try themselves, if they be in the faith; to examine themselves, whether they have Christ, whom who soever acknowledges not dwelling in him, is a reprobate? ' By the Spirit which he hath given us,' saith John, ' we know that he abideth in us.' And what do we then else but call in question Christ's promise, while we would be esteemed the servants of God without his Spirit, which he declared he would pour out upon all his? Seeing these things are the first grounds of piety, it is miserable blindness to accuse Christians of pride, because they dare glory of the presence of the Spirit; without which glorying, Christianity itself could not be. But by their example they declare, how truly Christ spake, saying, That his Spirit was unknown to the world, and that those only acknowledge it, with whom it remains." Thus far Calvin.

*Without the Spirit's presence, Christianity must cease.*

If therefore it be so, why should any be so foolish as to deny, or so unwise as not to seek after this Spirit, which Christ hath promised shall dwell in his children? They then that do suppose the indwelling and leading of his Spirit to be ceased, must also suppose Christianity to be ceased, which cannot subsist without it.

Thirdly, What the work of this Spirit is, is partly before shown, which Christ compriseth in two or three things, "He will guide you into all truth;" "He will teach you all things, and bring all things to your remembrance."

*Query 3. What is the work of the Spirit? John xvi. 13 and 14, 26.*

5 *

Since Christ hath provided for us so good an instructor, why need we then lean so much to those traditions and commandments of men wherewith so many Christians have burthened themselves? Why need we set up our own The Spirit the guide. carnal and corrupt reason for a guide to us in matters spiritual, as some will needs do? May it not be complained of all such, as the Lord did of old concerning Israel by the prophets, Jer. ii. 13 : " For my people have committed two evils, they have forsaken me, the fountain of living waters, and hewed them out cisterns, broken cisterns, that can hold no water?" Have not many forsaken, do not many deride and reject, this inward and immediate guide, this Spirit that leads into all truth, and cast up to themselves other ways, broken ways indeed, which have not all this while brought them out of the flesh, nor out of the world, nor from under the dominion of their own lusts and sinful affections, whereby truth, which is only rightly learned by this Spirit, is so much a stranger in the earth?

From all then that hath been mentioned concerning this promise, and these words of Christ, it will follow, that A perpetual ordinance to God's church and people. Christians are always to be led inwardly and immediately by the Spirit of God dwelling in them, and that the same is a standing and perpetual ordinance, as well to the church in general in all ages, as to every individual member in particular, as appears from this argument:

The promises of Christ to his children are Yea and Amen, and cannot fail, but must of necessity be fulfilled.

But Christ hath promised, that the Comforter, the Holy Ghost, the Spirit of truth, shall abide with his children for ever; shall dwell with them, shall be in them, shall lead them into all truth, shall teach them all things, and bring all things to their remembrance:

Therefore the Comforter, the Holy Ghost, the Spirit of truth, his abiding with his children, &c., is Yea and Amen, &c.

Again: No man is redeemed from the carnal mind, which is at enmity with God, which is not subject to the law of God, neither can be: no man is yet in the Spirit, but in the flesh, and cannot please God, except he in whom the Spirit of God dwells.

But every true Christian is in measure redeemed from the carnal mind, is gathered out of the enmity, and can be subject to the law of God; is out of the flesh, and in the Spirit, the Spirit of God dwelling in him.

Therefore every true Christian hath the Spirit of God dwelling in him.

Again: "Whosoever hath not the Spirit of Christ, is none of his;" that is, no child, no friend, no disciple of Christ.

But every true Christian is a child, a friend, a disciple of Christ:

Therefore every true Christian hath the Spirit of Christ.

Moreover: Whosoever is the temple of the Holy Ghost, in him the Spirit of God dwelleth and abideth.

But every true Christian is the temple of the Holy Ghost:

Therefore in every true Christian the Spirit of God dwelleth and abideth.

But to conclude: He in whom the Spirit of God dwelleth, it is not in him a lazy, dumb, useless thing; but it moveth, actuateth, governeth, instructeth, and teacheth him all things whatsoever are needful for him to know; yea, bringeth all things to his remembrance.

But the Spirit of God dwelleth in every true Christian:

Therefore the Spirit of God leadeth, instructeth, and teacheth every true Christian whatsoever is needful for him to know.

§ XI. But there are some that will confess, That the Spirit doth now lead and influence the saints, but that he doth it only subjectively, or in a blind manner, by enlightening their understandings, to understand and believe the truth delivered in the scriptures; but not at all by presenting those truths to the mind by way of object, and this they call, *Medium incognitum assentiendi*, as that of whose working a man is not sensible.

This opinion, though somewhat more tolerable than the

former, is nevertheless not altogether according to truth, neither doth it reach the fulness of it.

**Arg. 1.**  1. Because there be many truths, which as they are applicable to particulars and individuals, and most needful to be known by them, are in nowise to be found in the scripture, as in the following proposition shall be shown.

Besides, the arguments already adduced do prove, that the Spirit doth not only subjectively help us to discern truths elsewhere delivered, but also objectively present those truths to our minds. For that which teacheth me all things, and is given me for that end, without doubt presents those things to my mind which it teacheth me. It is not said, It shall teach you how to understand those things that are written; but, It shall teach you all things. Again, That which bringeth all things to my remembrance, must needs present them by way of object; else it were improper to say, It brought them to my remembrance; but only, that it helpeth to remember the objects brought from elsewhere.

**Arg. 2.**  My second argument shall be drawn from the nature of the new covenant; by which, and those that follow, I shall prove that we are led by the Spirit both immediately and objectively. The nature of the new covenant is expressed in divers places; and

**Proof 1.**  First, Isa. lix. 21, "As for me, this is my covenant with them, saith the Lord; My Spirit that is upon thee, and my words which I have put in thy mouth, shall not depart out of thy mouth, nor out of the mouth of thy seed, nor out of the mouth of thy seed's seed, saith the Lord, from **The leadings of the Spirit.** henceforth and for ever." By the latter part of this is sufficiently expressed the perpetuity and continuance of this promise, "It shall not depart, saith the Lord, from henceforth and for ever." In the former part is the promise itself, which is the Spirit of God being upon them, and the words of God being put into their mouths.

**1. Immediately.**  First, This was immediate, for there is no mention made of any medium; he saith not, I shall by the means of such and such writings or books, convey such and such words into your mouths; but My words, I, even I, saith the Lord, have put into your mouths.

Secondly, This must be objectively; for the words put into the mouth, are the object presented by him. He saith not, The words which ye shall see written, my Spirit shall only enlighten your understandings to assent unto; but positively, "My words, which I have put in thy mouth," &c. From whence I argue thus:

*2. Objectively.*

Upon whomsoever the Spirit remaineth always, and putteth words into his mouth, him doth the Spirit teach immediately, objectively, and continually.

But the Spirit is always upon the seed of the righteous, and putteth words into their mouths, neither departeth from them:

Therefore the Spirit teacheth the righteous immediately, objectively, and continually.

Secondly, The nature of the new covenant is yet more amply expressed, Jer. xxxi. 33, which is again repeated and re-asserted by the apostle, Heb. viii. 10, 11, in these words, "For this is the covenant that I will make with the house of Israel, after those days, saith the Lord, I will put my laws into their minds, and write them in their hearts, and I will be to them a God, and they shall be to me a people. And they shall not teach every man his neighbour, and every man his brother, saying, Know the Lord; for all shall know me, from the least to the greatest."

*Proof 2.*

The object here is God's law placed in the heart, and written in the mind; from whence they become God's people, and are brought truly to know him.

In this then is the law distinguished from the gospel; the law before was outward, written in tables of stone, but now is inward, written in the heart: of old the people depended upon their priests for the knowledge of God, but now they have all a certain and sensible knowledge of Him; concerning which Augustine speaketh well, in his book *De Litera & Spiritu;* from whom Aquinas first of all seems to have taken occasion to move this question, Whether the new law be a written law, or an implanted law? *Lex*

*The difference between the outward and inward law.*

*scripta, vel lex indita?* Which he thus resolves, affirming
that the new law, or gospel, is not properly a law written,
as the old was, but *Lex indita,* an implanted law; and that
the old law was written without, but the new law is written
within, on the table of the heart.

How much then are they deceived, who, instead of
making the gospel preferable to the law, have made the
condition of such as are under the gospel far worse? For
no doubt it is a far better and more desirable thing to converse with God immediately, than only mediately, as being
an higher and more glorious dispensation; and yet these
men acknowledge that many under the law had immediate converse with God, whereas they now cry. it is
ceased.

The gospel dispensation more glorious than that of the law.

Again: Under the law there was the holy of holies, into
which the high priest did enter, and received the word
of the Lord immediately from betwixt the cherubims, so
that the people could then certainly know the mind of the
Lord; but now, according to these men's judgment, we
are in a far worse condition, having nothing but the outward letter of the scripture to guess and divine from; concerning the sense or meaning of one verse of which, scarce
two can be found to agree. But Jesus Christ hath promised us better things, though many are so unwise as not
to believe him, even to guide us by his own unerring Spirit, and hath rent and removed the veil, whereby not only
one, and that once a year, may enter; but all of us, at all
times, have access unto him, as often as we draw near unto
him with pure hearts: he reveals his will to us by his Spirit, and writes his laws in our hearts. These things then
being thus premised, I argue,

Where the law of God is put into the mind, and written
in the heart, there the object of faith, and revelation of the
knowledge of God, is inward, immediate, and objective.

But the law of God is put into the mind, and written
in the heart of every true Christian, under the new covenant.

Therefore the object of faith, and revelation of the

knowledge of God to every true Christian, is inward, immediate, and objective.

The assumption is the express words of scripture: the proposition then must needs be true, except that which is put into the mind, and written in the heart, were either not inward, not immediate, or not objective, which is most absurd.

§ XII. The third argument is from these words of John, *Arg. 3.* 1 John ii. ver. 27, " But the anointing, which ye have re- *The anointing recommended, as* ceived of him, abideth in you, and ye need not that any man teach you: but as the same anointing teacheth you of all things, and is truth, and is no lie; and even as it hath taught you, ye shall abide in him."

First, This could not be any special, peculiar, or extra- *1.* ordinary privilege, but that which is common to all the *Common* saints, it being a general epistle, directed to all them of that age.

Secondly, The apostle proposeth this anointing in them, *2.* as a more certain touch-stone for them to discern and try *Certain.* seducers by, even than his own writings; for having in the former verse said, that he had written some things to them concerning such as seduced them, he begins the next verse, " But the anointing," &c., " and ye need not that any man teach you," &c., which infers, that having said to them what can be said, he refers them for all to the inward anointing, which teacheth all things, as the most firm, constant, and certain bulwark against all seducers.

And lastly, That it is a lasting and continuing thing; *3.* the anointing which abideth. If it had not been to abide *Lasting* in them, it could not have taught them all things, neither guarded them against all hazard. From which I argue thus,

He that hath an anointing abiding in him, which teacheth him all things, so that he needs no man to teach him, hath an inward and immediate teacher, and hath some things inwardly and immediately revealed unto him.

But the saints have such an anointing

Therefore, &c.

I could prove this doctrine from many more places of
scripture, which for brevity's sake I omit; and now come
to the second part of the proposition, where the objections
usually formed against it are answered.

OBJECT.      § XIII. The most usual is, That these revelations are
uncertain.

ANSW.        But this bespeaketh much ignorance in the opposers.
for we distinguish between the thesis and the hypothesis;
that is, between the proposition and supposition. For it is
one thing to affirm, that the true and undoubted revelation
of God's Spirit is certain and infallible; and another thing
to affirm, that this or that particular person or people is led
infallibly by this revelation in what they speak or write,
because they affirm themselves to be so led by the inward
and immediate revelation of the Spirit. The first is only
asserted by us, the latter may be called in question. The
question is not who are or are not so led? But whether
all ought not or may not be so led?

The cer-      Seeing then we have already proved that Christ hath
tainty of
the Spirit's  promised his Spirit to lead his children, and that every one
guidance      of them both ought and may be led by it, if any depart
proved.
from this certain guide in deeds, and yet in words pretend
to be led by it into things that are not good, it will not
from thence follow, that the true guidance of the Spirit is
uncertain, or ought not to be followed; no more than it
will follow that the sun showeth not light, because a blind
man, or one who wilfully shuts his eyes, falls into a ditch
at noon-day for want of light; or that no words are spoken,
because a deaf man hears them not; or that a garden full
of fragrant flowers has no sweet smell, because he that has
lost his smelling doth not smell it; the fault then is in the
organ, and not in the object.

All these mistakes therefore are to be ascribed to the
weakness or wickedness of men, and not to that Holy Spirit. Such as bend themselves most against this certain and
infallible testimony of the Spirit use commonly to allege
the example of the old Gnostics, and the late monstrous
and mischievous actings of the Anabaptists of Munster, all

which toucheth us nothing at all, neither weakens a whit our most true doctrine. Wherefore, as a most sure bulwark against such kind of assaults, was subjoined that other part of our proposition thus: Moreover these divine and inward revelations, which we establish as absolutely necessary for the founding of the true faith, as they do not so neither can they at any time contradict the Scripture's testimony, or sound reason.

Besides the intrinsic and undoubted truth of this assertion, we can boldly affirm it from our certain and blessed experience. For this Spirit never deceived us, never acted nor moved us to any thing that was amiss; but is clear and manifest in its revelations, which are evidently discerned by us, as we wait in that pure and undefiled light of God, that proper and fit organ in which they are received. Therefore if any reason after this manner, *By experience.*

That because some wicked, ungodly, devilish men have committed wicked actions, and have yet more wickedly asserted, that they were led into these things by the Spirit of God;

Therefore, No man ought to lean to the Spirit of God, or seek to be led by it,

I utterly deny the consequence of this proposition, which, were it to be received as true, then would all faith in God and hope of salvation become uncertain, and the Christian religion be turned into mere scepticism. For after the same manner I might reason thus: *The absurdity of the consequence.*

Because Eve was deceived by the lying of the serpent; Therefore she ought not to have trusted to the promise of God.

Because the old world was deluded by evil spirits; Therefore ought neither Noah, nor Abraham, nor Moses, to have trusted the Spirit of the Lord.

Because a lying spirit spake through the four hundred prophets that persuaded Ahab to go up and fight at Ramoth Gilead;

Therefore the testimony of the true Spirit in Micaiah was uncertain, and dangerous to be followed.

6

Bec: ise there were seducing spirits crept into the church of old;

Therefore it was not good, or it is uncertain, to follow the anointing, which taught all things, and is truth, and is no lie.

Who dare say that this is a necessary consequence? Moreover, not only the faith of the saints, and church cf God of old, is hereby rendered uncertain, but also the faith of all sorts of Christians now is liable to the like hazard, even of those who seek a foundation for their faith elsewhere than from the Spirit. For I shall prove by an inevitable argument, *ab incommodo*, i. e., from the inconveniency of it, that if the Spirit be not to be followed upon that account, and that men may not depend upon it as their guide, because some, while pretending thereunto, commit great evils; that then, neither tradition, nor the scriptures, nor reason, which the Papists, Protestants, and Socinians do respectively make the rule of their faith, are I. Instances any whit more certain. The Romanists reckon it an error of tradition. to celebrate Easter any other ways than that church doth. This can only be decided by tradition. And yet the Greek church, which equally layeth claim to tradition with herself, doth it otherwise. Yea, so little effectual is tradition to decide the case, that Polycarpus, the disciple of John, and Euseb. Hist. Eccles. lib. v. c. 26 Anicetus, the bishop of Rome, who immediately succeeded them, according to whose example both sides concluded the question ought to be decided, could not agree. Here of necessity one of them must err, and that following tradition. Would the Papists now judge we dealt fairly by them, if we should thence aver, that tradition is not to be regarded? Besides, in a matter of far greater importance the same difficulty will occur, to wit, in the primacy of the bishop of Rome; for many do affirm, and that by tradition, that in the first six hundred years the Roman prelates never assumed the title of Universal Shepherd, nor were acknowledged as such. And, as that which altogether overturneth this presidency, there are those that allege, and that from tradition also, that Peter never saw Rome; and that therefore the bishop of Rome cannot be his successor. Would you Romanists think this sound reasoning, to say as you do?

Many have been deceived, and erred grievously, in trusting to tradition;

Therefore we ought to reject all traditions, yea, even those by which we affirm the contrary, and, as we think, prove the truth.

Lastly, In the * council of Florence, the chief doctors of the Romish and Greek churches did debate whole sessions long concerning the interpretation of one sentence of the council of Ephesus, and of Epiphanius, and Basilius, neither could they ever agree about it.

Secondly, As to the scripture, the same difficulty occurreth: the Lutherans affirm they believe consubstantiation by the scripture; which the Calvinists deny, as that which, they say, according to the same scripture, is a gross error. The Calvinists again affirm absolute reprobation, which the Arminians deny, affirming the contrary; wherein both affirm themselves to be ruled by the scripture and reason in the matter. Should I argue thus then to the Calvinists?

Here the Lutherans and Armenians grossly err, by following the scripture;

Therefore the scripture is not a good nor certain rule; and è contrario.

Would either of them accept of this reasoning as good and sound? What shall I say of the Episcopalians, Presbyterians, Independents, and Anabaptists of Great Britain, who are continually buffeting one another with the scripture? To whom the same argument might be alleged, though they do all unanimously acknowledge it to be the rule.

And Thirdly, As to reason, I shall not need to say much; for whence come all the controversies, contentions and debates in the world, but because every man thinks he follows right reason? Hence of old came the jangles between the Stoics, Platonists, Peripatetics, Pythagoreans,

* Conc. Flor. Sess 5. decreto- quodam Conc. Eph Act. vi. Sess. 11 & 12. Conc. Flor. Sess. 18, 20. Conc. Flor. Sess. 21, p. 480 & seq.

2. Of scripture.

3 Of reason. The debates hence arising betwixt the old and late philosophers.

and Cynics, as of late betwixt the Aristotelians, Carte-
sians, and other naturalists : Can it be thence inferred, or
will the Socinians, those great reasoners, allow us to conclude, because many, and those very wise men, have
erred, by following, as they supposed, their reason, and
that with what diligence, care and industry they could, to
find out the truth, that therefore no man ought to make
use of it at all, nor be positive in what he knows certainly
to be rational? And thus far as to opinions; the same uncertainty is no less incident unto those other principles.

Anabap-
tists for
their wild
practices,
and Protes-
tants and
Papists for
their wars
and blood-
shed, each
pretending
scripture
for it.

§ XIV. But if we come to practices, though I confess I
do with my whole heart abhor and detest those wild practices which are written concerning the Anabaptists of Munster ; I am bold to say, as bad, if not worse things, have
been committed by those that lean to tradition, scripture,
and reason : wherein also they have averred themselves to
have been authorized by these rules. I need but mention
all the tumults, seditions, and horrible bloodshed, wherewith Europe hath been afflicted these divers ages; in
which Papists against Papists, Calvinists against Calvinists,
Lutherans against Lutherans, and Papists, assisted by Protestants, against other Protestants assisted by Papists, have
miserably shed one another's blood, hiring and forcing
men to kill each other, who were ignorant of the quarrel,
and strangers one to another : all, mean while, pretending
reason for so doing, and pleading the lawfulness of it from
scripture.

Tradition,
scripture
and reason,
made a co-
ver for per-
secution
and mur-
der.

For what have the Papists pretended for their many
massacres, acted as well in France as elsewhere, but tradition, scripture, and reason? Did they not say, that reason
persuaded them, tradition allowed them, and scripture
commanded them, to persecute, destroy, and burn heretics, such as denied this plain scripture, *Hoc est corpus
meum*, This is my body? And are not the Protestants as-
senting to this bloodshed, who assert the same thing, and
encourage them, by burning and banishing, while their
brethren are so treated for the same cause? Are not the
islands of Great Britain and Ireland, yea, and all the Chris-

tian world, a lively example hereof, which were divers
years together as a theatre of blood ; where many lost their
lives, and numbers of families were utterly destroyed and
ruined? For all which no other cause was principally
given, than the precepts of the scripture. If we then compare these actings with those of Munster, we shall not find
great difference ; for both affirmed and pretended they
were called, and that it was lawful to kill, burn, and destroy the wicked. We must kill all the wicked, said those
Anabaptists, that we, that are the saints, may possess the
earth. We must burn obstinate heretics, say the Papists,
that the holy church of Rome may be purged of rotten
members, and may live in peace. We must cut off seducing separatists, say the Prelatical Protestants, who trouble
the peace of the church, and refuse the divine hierarchy,
and religious ceremonies thereof. We must kill, say the
Calvinistic Presbyterians, the Profane Malignants, who
accuse the Holy Consistorial and Presbyterian government,
and seek to defend the Popish and Prelatic hierarchy ; as
also those other sectaries that trouble the peace of our
church. What difference I pray thee, impartial reader,
seest thou betwixt these?

If it be said, The Anabaptists went without, and against OBJECT.
the authority of the magistrate, so did not the other ;

I might easily refute it, by alleging the mutual testimo- ANSW.
nies of these sects against one another. The behaviour of
the Papists towards Henry the Third and Fourth of France ; Examples
their designs upon James the Sixth in the gunpowder of Popish
treason ; as also their principle of the Pope's power to
depose kings for the cause of heresy, and to absolve their
subjects from their oath, and give them to others, proves
it against them.

And as to the Protestants, how much their actions differ Protestan
from those other above-mentioned, may be seen by the violences
many conspiracies and tumults which they have been active cutions in
in, both in Scotland and England, and which they have England,
acted within these hundred years in divers towns and pro- and Hol-
vinces of the Netherlands. Have they not oftentimes sought,

6 *

not only from the Popish magistrates, but even from those that had begun to reform, or that had given them some liberty of exercising their religion, that they might only be permitted, without trouble or hindrance, to exercise their religion, promising they would not hinder or molest the Papists in the exercise of theirs? And yet did they not on the contrary, so soon as they had power, trouble and abuse those fellow-citizens, and turn them out of the city, and, which is worse, even such who together with them had forsaken the Popish religion? Did they not these things in many places against the mind of the magistrates? Have they not publicly, with contumelious speeches, assaulted their magistrates, from whom they had but just before sought and obtained the free exercise of their religion? Representing them, so soon as they opposed themselves to their hierarchy, as if they regarded neither God nor religion? Have they not by violent hands possessed themselves of the Popish churches, so called, or by force, against the magistrates' mind, taken them away? Have they not turned out of their office and authority whole councils of magistrates, under pretence that they were addicted to Popery? Which Popish magistrates nevertheless they did but a little before acknowledge to be ordained by God; affirming themselves obliged to yield them obedience and subjection, not only for fear, but for conscience' sake; to whom moreover the very preachers and overseers of the reformed church had willingly sworn fidelity; and yet afterwards have they not said, that the people are bound to force a wicked prince to the observation of God's word? There are many other instances of this kind to be found in their histories, not to mention many worse things, which we know to have been acted in our time, and which for brevity's sake I pass by.

Lutheran seditions against the reformed teachers, and assault upon the Marquis of
I might say much of the Lutherans, whose tumultuous actions against their magistrates not professing the Lutheran profession, are testified of by several historians worthy of credit. Among others, I shall propose only one example to the reader's consideration, which fell out at Berlin in

the year 1615: "Where the seditious multitude of the Lutheran citizens, being stirred up by the daily clamours of their preachers, did not only with violence break into the houses of the reformed teachers, overturn their libraries, and spoil their furniture; but also with reproachful words, yea, and with stones, assaulted the Marquis of Brandenburg, the Elector's brother, while he sought by smooth words to quiet the fury of the multitude; they killed ten of his guard, scarcely sparing himself, who at last by flight escaped out of their hands." All which sufficiently declares, that the concurrence of the magistrate doth not alter their principles, but only their method of procedure. So that for my own part, I see no difference betwixt the actings of those of Munster, and these others, whereof the one pretended to be led by the Spirit, the other by tradition, scripture, and reason, save this, that the former were rash, heady, and foolish, in their proceedings, and therefore were the sooner brought to nothing, and so into contempt and derision : but the other, being more politic and wise in their generation, held it out longer, and so have authorized their wickedness more, with the seeming authority of law and reason. But both their actings being equally evil, the difference appears to me to be only like that which is between a simple silly thief, that is easily catched, and hanged without any more ado ; and a company of resolute bold robbers, who being better guarded, though their offence be nothing less, yet by violence do, to shun the danger, force their masters to give them good terms.

From all which then it evidently follows, that they argue very ill, who despise and reject any principle because men pretending to be led by it do evil; in case it be not the natural and consequential tendency of that principle to lead unto those things that are evil.

Again : It doth follow from what is above asserted, that if the Spirit be to be rejected upon this account, all those other principles ought on the same account to be rejected. And for my part, as I have never a whit the lower esteem of the blessed testimony of the holy scriptures, nor do the

Brandenburg, &c in Germany.

Let none
reject the
certainty of
the uner-
ring Spirit
of God, be-
cause of
false pre
tenders to
it.
less respect any solid tradition, that is answerable and according to truth; neither at all despise reason, that noble
and excellent faculty of the mind, because wicked men
have abused the name of them, to cover their wickedness,
and deceive the simple; so would I not have any reject or
doubt the certainty of that unerring Spirit which God hath
given his children, as that which can alone guide them into
all truth, because some have falsely pretended to it.

§ XV. And because the Spirit of God is the fountain of
all truth and sound reason, therefore we have well said,
That it cannot contradict either the testimony of the scripture, or right reason: " Yet, as the proposition itself concludeth, to the last part of which I now come, it will not
from thence follow, that these divine revelations are to be
subjected to the examination either of the outward testimony of scripture, or of the human or natural reason of
man, as to a more noble and certain rule or touchstone;
for the divine revelation, and inward illumination, is that
which is evident by itself, forcing the well-disposed understanding, and irresistibly moving it to assent by its own
evidence and clearness, even as the common principles of
natural truths do bend the mind to a natural assent."

He that denies this part of the proposition must needs
affirm, that the Spirit of God neither can, nor ever hath
manifested itself to man without the scripture, or a distinct
discussion of reason; or that the efficacy of this supernatural principle, working upon the souls of men, is less evident than natural principles in their common operations;
both which are false.

For, First, Through all the scriptures we may observe,
that the manifestation and revelation of God by his Spirit
to the patriarchs, prophets, and apostles, was immediate
and objective, as is above proved; which they did not examine by any other principle, but their own evidence and
clearness.

The self-
evidence of
the Spirit.
Secondly, To say that the Spirit of God has less evidence upon the mind of man than natural principles have,
is to have too mean and too low thoughts of it.   How

comes David to invite us to taste and see that God is good, if this cannot be felt and tasted? This were enough to overturn the faith and assurance of all the saints, both now and of old. How came Paul to be persuaded, that nothing could separate him from the love of God, but by that evidence and clearness which the Spirit of God gave him? The apostle John, who knew well wherein the certainty of faith consisted, judged it no ways absurd, without further argument, to ascribe his knowledge and assurance, and that of all the saints, hereunto in these words; "Hereby know we that we dwell in him, and he in us, because he hath given us of his Spirit," 1 John, iv. 13. And again, chap. v. ver. 6: "It is the Spirit that beareth witness, because the Spirit is truth."

Observe the reason brought by him, "Because the Spirit is truth;" of whose certainty and infallibility I have heretofore spoken. We then trust to and confide in this Spirit, because we know, and certainly believe, that it can only lead us aright, and never mislead us; and from this certain confidence it is that we affirm, that no revelation coming from it can ever contradict the scripture's testimony nor right reason: not as making this a more certain rule to ourselves, but as condescending to such, who not discerning the revelations of the Spirit, as they proceed purely from God, will try them by these mediums. Yet those that have their spiritual senses, and can savour the things of the Spirit, as it were in prima instantia, i. e., at the first blush, can discern them without, or before they apply them either to scripture or reason; just as a good astronomer can calculate an eclipse infallibly, by which he can conclude, if the order of nature continue, and some strange and unnatural revolution intervene not, there will be an eclipse of the sun or moon such a day, and such an hour; yet can he not persuade an ignorant rustic of this, until he visibly sees it. So also a mathematician can infallibly know, by the rules of art, that the three angles of a right triangle are equal to two right angles; yea, can know them more certainly than any man by measure. And some geometrical

*[margin note:] The Spirit contradicts not scripture nor right reason.*

*[margin note:] Natural demonstrations from astronomy and geometry.*

demonstrations are by all acknowledged to be infallible,
which can be scarcely discerned or proved by the senses,
yet if a geometer be at the pains to certify some ignorant
man concerning the certainty of his art, by condescending
to measure it, and make it obvious to his senses, it will not
thence follow, that that measuring is so certain as the demonstration itself, or that the demonstration would be uncertain without it.

§ XVI. But to make an end, I shall add one argument
to prove, that this inward, immediate, objective revelation,
which we have pleaded for all along, is the only sure, certain, and unmovable foundation of all Christian faith;
which argument, when well considered, I hope will have
weight with all sorts of Christians, and it is this:

Immediate
revelation
the im-
movable
foundation
of all Chris-
tian faith.

That which all professors of Christianity, of what kind
soever, are forced ultimately to recur unto, when pressed
to the last; that for and because of which all other foundations are recommended, and accounted worthy to be believed, and without which they are granted to be of no
weight at all, must needs be the only most true, certain,
and unmovable foundation of all Christian faith.

But inward, immediate, objective revelation by the
Spirit, is that which all professors of Christianity, of what
kind soever, are forced ultimately to recur unto, &c.

Therefore, &c.

The proposition is so evident, that it will not be denied;
the assumption shall be proved by parts.

Papists'
foundation
their
church and
tradition,
why?

And first, As to the Papists, they place their foundation
in the judgment of the church and tradition. If we press
them to say, Why they believe as the church doth? Their
answer is, Because the church is always led by the infallible Spirit. So here the leading of the Spirit is the utmost
foundation. Again, if we ask them, Why we ought to trust
tradition? They answer, Because these traditions were
delivered us by the doctors and fathers of the church;
which doctors and fathers, by the revelation of the Holy
Ghost, commanded the church to observe them. Here
again all ends in the revelation of the Spirit.

And for the Protestants and Socinians, both which acknowledge the scriptures to be the foundation and rule of their faith; the one as subjectively influenced by the Spirit of God to use them, the other as managing them with and by their own reason; ask both, or either of them, Why they trust in the scriptures, and take them to be their rule? Their answer is, Because we have in them the mind of God delivered unto us by those to whom these things were inwardly, immediately, and objectively revealed by the Spirit of God; and not because this or that man wrote them, but because the Spirit of God dictated them.

*Protestants and Socinians make the scriptures their ground and foundation, why?*

It is strange then that men should render that so uncertain and dangerous to follow, upon which alone the certain ground and foundation of their own faith is built; and that they should shut themselves out from that holy fellowship with God, which only is enjoyed in the Spirit, in which we are commanded both to walk and live.

*Christians by name, and not by nature, hold revelation ceased contrary to scripture.*

If any reading these things find themselves moved, by the strength of these scripture arguments, to assent and believe such revelations necessary, and yet find themselves strangers to them, which, as I observed in the beginning, is the cause that this is so much gainsaid and contradicted, let them know, that it is not because it is ceased to become the privilege of every true Christian that they do not feel it, but rather because they are not so much Christians by nature as by name; and let such know, that the secret light which shines in the heart, and reproves unrighteousness, is the small beginning of the revelation of God's Spirit, which was first sent into the world to reprove it of sin, John xvi. 8. And as by forsaking iniquity thou comest to be acquainted with that heavenly voice in thy heart, thou shalt feel, as the old man, or the natural man, that savoureth not the things of God's kingdom, is put off, with his evil and corrupt affections and lusts; I say, thou shalt feel the new man, or the spiritual birth and babe raised, which hath its spiritual senses, and can see, feel, taste, handle, and smell the things of the Spirit; but till then the knowledge of things spiritual is but as an historical faith. But as the

description of the light of the sun, or of curious colours to
a blind man, who, though of the largest capacity, cannot
so well understand it by the most acute and lively description, as a child can by seeing them; so neither can the
natural man, of the largest capacity, by the best words,
even scripture words, so well understand the mysteries of
God's kingdom, as the least and weakest child who tasteth
them, by having them revealed inwardly and objectively by
the Spirit.

Wait then for this in the small revelation of that pure
light which first reveals things more known; and as thou
becomest fitted for it, thou shalt receive more and more,
and by a living experience easily refute their ignorance,
who ask, How dost thou know that thou art actuated by
the Spirit of God? Which will appear to thee a question
no less ridiculous, than to ask one whose eyes are open,
how he knows the sun shines at noon-day? And though
this be the surest and most certain way to answer all objections; yet by what is above written it may appear, that the
mouths of all such opposers as deny this doctrine may be
shut, by unquestionable and unanswerable reasons.

---

# PROPOSITION III.

## *Concerning the Scriptures.*

From these revelations of the Spirit of God to the saints
have proceeded the Scriptures of Truth, which contain,

I. A faithful historical account of the actings of God's people in divers ages; with many singular and remarkable
providences attending them.

II. A prophetical account of several things, whereof some
are already past, and some yet to come.

III. A full and ample account of all the chief principles of
the doctrine of Christ, held forth in divers precious de-

clarations, exhortations and sentences, which, by the moving of God's Spirit, were at several times, and upon sundry occasions, spoken and written unto some churches and their pastors.

Nevertheless, because they are only a declaration of the fountain, and not the fountain itself, therefore they are not to be esteemed the principal ground of all truth and knowledge, nor yet the adequate primary rule of faith and manners. Yet because they give a true and faithful testimony of the first foundation, they are and may be esteemed a secondary rule, subordinate to the Spirit, from which they have all their excellency and certainty: for as by the inward testimony of the Spirit we do alone truly know them, so they testify, That the Spirit is that Guide by which the saints are led into all Truth; there- John xvi 13. Rom. viii. 14. fore, according to the scriptures, the Spirit is the first and principal leader. Seeing then that we do therefore receive and believe the scriptures because they proceed-
* ed from the Spirit, for the very same reason is the Spirit more originally and principally the rule, according to the received maxim in the schools, *Propter quod unumquodque est tale, illud ipsum est magis tale:* That for which a thing is such, that thing itself is more such.

§ I. THE former part of this proposition, though it needs no apology for itself, yet it is a good apology for us, and will help to sweep away that, among many other calumnies, wherewith we are often loaded, as if we were vilifiers and deniers of the scriptures; for in that which we affirm of them, it doth appear at what high rate we value them, ac- The holy scriptures counting them, without all deceit or equivocation, the most the most excellent writings in the world; to which not only no other excellent writings are to be preferred, but even in divers respects the world. not comparable thereto. For as we freely acknowledge that their authority doth not depend upon the approbation or canons of any church or assembly; so neither can we subject them to the fallen, corrupt, and defiled reason of man · and therein as we do freely agree with the Protestants against the error of the Romanists, so on the other hand, we cannot go the length of such Protestants as make their authority to depend upon any virtue or power that is in the writings themselves; but we desire to ascribe all to that Spirit from which they proceeded.

We confess indeed there wants not a majesty in the style, a coherence in the parts, a good scope in the whole; but seeing these things are not discerned by the natural, but only by the spiritual man, it is the Spirit of God that must give us that belief of the scriptures which may satisfy our consciences; therefore some of the chief among Protestants, both in their particular writings and public confessions, are forced to acknowledge this.

*Calvin's testimony that the scripture's certainty is from the Spirit.*

Hence Calvin, though he saith he is able to prove that if there be a God in heaven, these writings have proceeded from him, yet he concludes another knowledge to be necessary. Instit. lib. 1, cap. 7, sect. 4.

" But if," saith he, " we respect the consciences, that they be not daily molested with doubts, and hesitate not at every scruple, it is requisite that this persuasion which we speak of be taken higher than human reason, judgment, or conjecture; to wit, from the secret testimony of the Spirit." And again, " To those who ask, that we prove unto them, by reason, that Moses and the prophets were inspired of God to speak, I answer, That the testimony of the Holy Spirit is more excellent than all reason." And again, " Let this remain a firm truth, that he only whom the Holy Spirit hath persuaded, can repose himself on the scripture with a true certainty." And lastly, " This then is a judgment which cannot be begotten but by an heavenly revelation," &c.

*The confession of the French churches.*

The same is also affirmed in the first public confession of the French churches, published in the year 1559, Art. 4 : " We know these books to be canonical, and the most certain rule of our faith, not so much by the common accord and consent of the church, as by the testimony and inward persuasion of the Holy Spirit."

Thus also i the fifth article of the confession of faith, Churches of Holland assert the same. of the churches of Holland, confirmed by the Synod of Dort: "We receive these books only for holy and canonical—not so much because the church receives and approves them, as because the Spirit of God doth witness in our hearts that they are of God."

And, lastly, The divines, so called, at Westminster, who Westminster confession the same. began to be afraid of, and guard against the testimony of the Spirit, because they perceived a dispensation beyond that which they were under beginning to dawn, and to eclipse them; yet could they not get by this, though they have laid it down neither so clearly, distinctly, nor honestly as they that went before. It is in these words, chap. 1. sec. 5: "Nevertheless, our full persuasion and assurance of the infallible truth thereof, is from the inward work of the Holy Spirit, bearing witness by and with the Word in our hearts."

By all which it appeareth how necessary it is to seek the certainty of the scriptures from the Spirit, and no where else. The infinite janglings and endless contests of those that seek their authority elsewhere, do witness to the truth hereof.

For the ancients themselves, even of the first centuries, Apocrypha. Conc.Laod. Can. 58, in Cod. Ec. 163. Conc.Laod. held in the year 364, excluded from the canon Eccl. the Wisdom of Solomon, Judith, Tobias, the Maccabees which the council of Carthage, held in the year 399, received. were not agreed among themselves concerning them; while some of them rejected books which we approve, and others of them approved those which some of us reject. It is not unknown to such as are in the least acquainted with antiquity, what great contests are concerning the second epistle of Peter, that of James, the second and third of John, and the Revelations, which many, even very ancient, deny to have been written by the beloved disciple and brother of James, but by another of that name. What should then become of Christians, if they had not received that Spirit, and those spiritual senses, by which they know how to discern the true from the false? It is the privilege of Christ's sheep indeed that they hear his voice, and refuse that of a stranger; which privilege being taken away, we are left a prey to all manner of wolves.

§ II. Though then we do acknowledge the scriptures to be very heavenly and divine writings, the use of them to be very comfortable and necessary to the church of Christ, and that we also admire and give praise to the Lord, for his wonderful providence in preserving these writings so pure and uncorrupted as we have them, through so long a night of apostacy, to be a testimony of his truth against the wickedness and abominations even of those whom he made instrumental in preserving them, so that they have kept them to be a witness against themselves; yet we may not call them the principal fountain of all truth and knowledge, nor yet the first adequate rule of faith and manners; because the principal fountain of truth must be the Truth itself; i. e., that whose certainty and authority depends not upon another. When we doubt of the streams of any river or flood, we recur to the fountain itself; and, having found it, there we desist, we can go no farther; because there it springs out of the bowels of the earth, which are inscrutable. Even so the writings and sayings of all men we must bring to the Word of God, I mean the Eternal Word, and if they agree hereunto, we stand there. For this Word always proceedeth, and doth eternally proceed from God, in and by which the unsearchable wisdom of God, and unsearchable counsel and will conceived in the heart of God, is revealed unto us. That then the scripture is not the principal ground of faith and knowledge, as it appears by what is above spoken, so it is proved in the latter part of the proposition, which, being reduced to an argument, runs thus:

*The Scriptures are not the principal ground of truth.*

That whereof the certainty and authority depends upon another, and which is received as truth because of its proceeding from another, is not to be accounted the principal ground and origin of all truth and knowledge:

But the scriptures' authority and certainty depend upon the Spirit by which they were dictated; and the reason why they were received as truth is, because they proceeded from the Spirit:

Therefore they are not the principal ground of truth

To confirm this argument, I added the school maxim: *Propter quod unumquodque est tale, illud ipsum magis est tale.* Which maxim, though I confess it doth not hold universally in all things, yet in this it doth and will very well hold, as by applying it, as we have above intimated, will appear.

The same argument will hold as to the other branch of the proposition, That it is not the primary adequate rule of faith and manners; thus: Neither are they the primary rule of faith and manners.

That which is not the rule of my faith in believing the scriptures themselves, is not the primary adequate rule of faith and manners:

But the scripture is not, nor can it be the rule of that faith by which I believe them, &c.

Therefore, &c.

But as to this part, we shall produce divers arguments hereafter. As to what is affirmed, that the Spirit, and not the scriptures, is the rule, it is largely handled in the former proposition; the sum whereof I shall subsume in one argument, thus: That the Spirit is the rule.

If by the Spirit we can only come to the true knowledge of God; if by the Spirit we are to be led into all truth, and so be taught of all things; then the Spirit, and not the scriptures, is the foundation and ground of all truth and knowledge, and the primary rule of faith and manners:

But the first is true, therefore also the last.

Next, the very nature of the gospel itself declareth that the scriptures cannot be the only and chief rule of Christians, else there should be no difference betwixt the law and the gospel; as from the nature of the new covenant, by divers scriptures described in the former proposition, is proved.

But besides these which are before mentioned, herein doth the law and the gospel differ, in that the law, being outwardly written, brings under condemnation, but hath not life in it to save; whereas the gospel, as it declares and makes manifest the evil, so, being an inward powerful thing, it gives power also to obey, and delivers from the Wherein the law and gospel differ.

7 *

evil. Hence it is called Εὐαγγέλιον, which is glad tidings. The law or letter, which is without us, kills; but the gospel, which is the inward spiritual law, gives life; for it consists not so much in words as in virtue. Wherefore such as come to know it, and be acquainted with it, come to feel greater power over their iniquities than all outward laws or rules can give them. Hence the apostle concludes, Rom. vi. 14, "Sin shall not have dominion over you: for ye are not under the law, but under grace." This grace then that is inward, and not an outward law, is to be the rule of Christians. Hereunto the apostle commends the elders of the church, saying, Acts xx. 32, "And now, brethren, I commend you to God, and to the word of his grace, which is able to build you up, and to give you an inheritance among all them which are sanctified." He doth not commend them here to outward laws or writings, but to the word of grace, which is inward; even the spiritual law, which makes free, as he elsewhere affirms, Rom. viii. 2, "The law of the Spirit of life in Christ Jesus, hath made me free from the law of sin and death." This spiritual law is that which the apostle declares he preached and directed people unto, which was not outward, as by Rom. x. 8, is manifest; where distinguishing it from the law, he saith, "The word is nigh thee, even in thy mouth, and in thy heart; that is the word of faith which we preach." From what is above said I argue thus:

The principal rule of Christians under the gospel is not an outward letter, nor law outwardly written and delivered, but an inward spiritual law, engraven in the heart, the law of the Spirit of life, the word that is nigh in the heart and in the mouth.

But the letter of the scripture is outward, of itself a dead thing, a mere declaration of good things, but not the things themselves:

The scrip-
ture not the
rule.

Therefore it is not, nor can be, the chief or principal rule of Christians.

§ III. Thirdly, That which is given to Christians for a rule and guide, must needs be so full, that it may clearly

and distinctly guide and order them in all things and occur-
rences that may fall out.

But in that there are numberless things, with regard to
their circumstances, which particular Christians may be concerned in, for which there can be no particular rule had in
the scriptures;

Therefore the scriptures cannot be a rule to them.

I shall give an instance in two or three particulars to
prove this proposition. It is not to be doubted but some
men are particularly called to some particular services;
their being not found in which, though the act be no general positive duty, yet in so far as it may be required of
them, is a great sin to omit; forasmuch as God is zealous
of his glory, and every act of disobedience to his will manifested, is enough not only to hinder one greatly from
that comfort and inward peace which otherwise he might
have, but also bringeth condemnation.

As for instance, some are called to the ministry of the
word: Paul saith, There was a necessity upon him to
preach the gospel; wo unto me, if I preach not.

If it be necessary that there be now ministers of the
church, as well as then, then there is the same necessity
upon some, more than upon others to occupy this place;
which necessity, as it may be incumbent upon particular
persons, the scripture neither doth nor can declare.

If it be said, That the qualifications of a minister are Object.
found in the scripture, and by applying these qualifications
to myself, I may know whether I be fit for such a place or
not;

I answer, The qualifications of a bishop, or minister, as Answ.
they are mentioned both in the epistle to Timothy and
Titus, are such as may be found in a private Christian;
yea, which ought in some measure to be in every true
Christian: so that this giveth a man no certainty. Every
capacity to an office giveth me not a sufficient call to it.

Next again, By what rule shall I judge if I be so qualified? How do I know that I am sober, meek, holy, harmless? Is it not the testimony of the Spirit in my conscience

that must assure me hereof? And suppose that I was qualified and called, yet what scripture rule shall inform me,
whether it be my duty to preach in this or that place, in
France or England, Holland or Germany? Whether I shall
take up my time in confirming the faithful, reclaiming
heretics, or converting infidels, as also in writing epistles
to this or that church?

The general rules of the scripture, viz., To be diligent
in my duty, to do all to the glory of God, and for the
good of his church, can give me no light in this thing.
Seeing two different things may both have a respect to that
way, yet may I commit a great error and offence in doing
the one, when I am called to the other. If Paul, when his
face was turned by the Lord toward Jerusalem, had gone
back to Achaia, or Macedonia, he might have supposed he
could have done God more acceptable service, in preaching and confirming the churches, than in being shut up in
prison in Judea; but would God have been pleased here-
with? Nay certainly. Obedience is better than sacrifice;
and it is not our doing that which is good simply that
pleaseth God, but that good which he willeth us to do.
Every member hath its particular place in the body, as the
Apostle showeth, 1 Cor. xii. If then, I being the foot,
should offer to exercise the office of the hand; or being the
hand, that of the tongue; my service would be troublesome, and not acceptable; and instead of helping the body,
I should make a schism in it. So that that which is good
for another to do, may be sinful to me: for as masters will
have their servants to obey them, according to their good
pleasure, and not only in blindly doing that which may
seem to them to tend to their master's profit, whereby it
may chance, the master having business both in the field
and in the house, that the servant that knows not his master's will may go to the field, when it is the mind of the
master he should stay and do the business of the house,
would not this servant then deserve a reproof, for not answering his master's mind? And what master is so sottish
and careless, as, having many servants, to leave them in

That which
is good for
one to do,
may be sin-
ful to an-
other.

such disorder as not to assign each his particular station, and not only the general terms of doing that which is profitable? which would leave them in various doubts, and no doubt end in confusion.

Shall we then dare to ascribe unto Christ, in the ordering of his church and servants, that which in man might justly be accounted disorder and confusion? The apostle showeth this distinction well, Rom. xii. 6, 7, 8, "Having then gifts differing according to the grace that is given to us; whether prophecy, let us prophesy according to the proportion of faith; or ministry, let us wait on our ministering; or he that teacheth, on teaching; or he that exhorteth, on exhortation." Now what scripture rule showeth me that I ought to exhort, rather than prophesy? or to minister, rather than teach? Surely none at all. Many more difficulties of this kind occur in the life of a Christian. *Diversities of gifts.*

Moreover, that which of all things is most needful for him to know, to wit, whether he really be in the faith, and an heir of salvation, or not, the scripture can give him no certainty in, neither can it be a rule to him. That this knowledge is exceeding desirable and comfortable all do unanimously acknowledge; besides that it is especially commanded, 2 Cor. xiii. 5, " Examine yourselves, whether ye be in the faith, prove your own selves; know ye not your own selves, how that Jesus Christ is in you, except ye be reprobates? And 2 Pet. i. 10, "Wherefore the rather, brethren, give diligence to make your calling and election sure." Now I say, What scripture rule can assure me that I have true faith? That my calling and election is sure? *Of faith and salvation can the scripture assure thee?*

If it be said, By comparing the scripture marks of true faith with mine:

I demand, Wherewith shall I make this observation? What shall ascertain me that I am not mistaken? It cannot be the scripture: that is the matter under debate.

If it be said, My own heart:

How unfit a judge is it in its own case? And how like.

to be partial, especially if it be yet unrenewed? Doth not
the scripture say, that "it is deceitful above all things?"
I find the promises, I find the threatenings, in the scripture; but who telleth me that the one belongs to me more
than the other? The scripture gives me a mere declaration
of these things, but makes no application; so that the assumption must be of my own making, thus; as for example: I find this proposition in scripture;

"He that believes, shall be saved:" thence I draw the
assumption.

But I, Robert, believe;

Therefore, I shall be saved.

The minor is of my own making, not expressed in the
scripture; and so a human conclusion, not a divine position; so that my faith and assurance here is not built upon
a scripture proposition, but upon an human principle;
which, unless I be sure of elsewhere, the scripture gives
me no certainty in the matter.

Again, If I should pursue the argument further, and
seek a new medium out of the scripture, the same difficulty
would occur: thus,

He that hath the true and certain marks of true faith,
hath true faith:

But I have those marks:

Therefore I have true faith.

For the assumption is still here of my own making, and
is not found in the scriptures; and by consequence the
conclusion can be no better, since it still followeth the
weaker proposition. This is indeed so pungent, that the
The inward
testimony
of the Spirit
the seal of
scripture
promises.
best of Protestants, who plead for this assurance, ascribe
it to the inward testimony of the Spirit; as Calvin, in that
large citation, cited in the former proposition. So that,
not to seek farther into the writings of the primitive Protestants, which are full of such expressions, even the Westminster confession of faith affirmeth, chap. xviii, sect. 12,
"This certainty is not a bare conjecture and probable persuasion, grounded upon fallible hope, but an infallible
assurance of faith, founded upon the divine truth of the

promise of salvation; the inward evidences of these graces, unto which these promises are made; the testimony of the Spirit of adoption, witnessing to our spirits that we are the children of God; which Spirit is the earnest of our inheritance whereby we are sealed to the day of redemption."

Moreover, the scripture itself, wherein we are so earnestly pressed to seek after this assurance, doth not at all affirm itself a rule sufficient to give it, but wholly ascribeth it to the Spirit, as Rom. viii. 16, " The Spirit itself beareth witness with our spirit, that we are the children of God." 1 John iv. 13, "Hereby know we that we dwell in him, and he in us, because he hath given us of his Spirit;" and chap. v. 6, " And it is the Spirit that beareth witness, because the Spirit is truth."

§ IV. Lastly, That cannot be the only, principal, nor chief rule, which doth not universally reach every individual that needeth it, to produce the necessary effect; and from the use of which, either by some innocent and sinless defect, or natural yet harmless and blameless imperfection, many who are within the compass of the visible church, and may, without absurdity, yea, with great probability, be accounted of the elect, are necessarily excluded, and that either wholly, or at least from the immediate use thereof. But it so falls out frequently concerning the scriptures, in the case of deaf people, children, and idiots, who can by no means have the benefit of the scriptures. Shall we then affirm, that they are without any rule to Godward, or that they are all damned? As such an opinion is in itself very absurd, and inconsistent both with the justice and mercy of God, so I know no sound reason can be alleged for it. Now if we may suppose any such to be under the new covenant dispensation, as I know none will deny but that we may suppose it without any absurdity, we cannot suppose them without some rule and means of knowledge; seeing it is expressly affirmed, " They shall be all taught of God," John vi. 45. " For all shall know me from the least to the greatest," Heb. viii. 11. But

*That the scriptures are not the chief rule*

*1. Deaf people, children, and idiots instanced.*

secondly, Though we were rid of this difficulty, how many illiterate and yet good men are there in the church of God, who cannot read a letter in their own mother tongue? Which imperfection, though it be inconvenient, I cannot tell whether we may safely affirm it to be sinful. These can have no immediate knowledge of the rule of their faith; so their faith must needs depend upon the credit of other men's reading or relating it unto them; where either the altering, adding, or omitting of a little word may be a foundation in the poor hearer of a very dangerous mistake, whereby he may either continue in some iniquity ignorant-

**2. Papists conceal the second commandment from the people.** ly, or believe a lie confidently. As for example, The Papists in all their catechisms, and public exercises of examinations towards the people, have boldly cut away the second command, because it seems so expressly to strike against their adoration and use of images; whereas many of these people, in whom by this omission this false opinion is fostered, are under a simple impossibility, or at least a very great difficulty, to be outwardly informed of this abuse. But further; suppose all could read the scriptures in their own language; where is there one of a thousand that hath that thorough knowledge of the original languages in which they are written, so as in that respect immediately

**3. The uncertainty of the interpreters of the scripture, and their adulterating it** to receive the benefit of them? Must not all these here depend upon the honesty and faithfulness of the interpreters? Which how uncertain it is for a man to build his faith upon, the many corrections, amendments, and various essays, which even among Protestants have been used, whereof the latter have constantly blamed and corrected the former, as guilty of defects and errors, doth sufficiently declare. And that even the last translations in the vulgar languages need to be corrected, as I could prove at large, were it proper in this place, learned men do confess.

But last of all, there is no less difficulty occurs even to those skilled in the original languages, who cannot so immediately receive the mind of the authors in these writings, as that their faith doth not at least obliquely depend upon the honesty and credit of the transcribers, since the origi-

nal copies are granted by all not to be now extant. Of
which transcribers Jerome in his time complained, saying, Hieron.
That they wrote not what they found, but what they under- Epist. 28.
stood. And Epiphanius saith, That in the good and cor- p. 247.
rect copies of Luke it was written, that Christ wept, and Epiph. in
that Irenæus doth cite it; but that the Catholics blotted it Anachor.
out, fearing lest heretics should have abused it. Other tom.3 oper.
fathers also declare, That whole verses were taken out of
Mark, because of the Manichees.

But further, the various readings of the Hebrew cha- The various
racter by reason of the points, which some plead for, as readings of
coeval with the first writings, which others, with no less character,
probability, allege to be a later invention; the disagreement &c.
of divers citations of Christ and the apostles with those
passages in the Old Testament they appeal to; the great
controversy among the fathers, whereof some highly approve
the Greek Septuagint, decrying and rendering very doubt-
ful the Hebrew copy, as in many places vitiated and altered
by the Jews; other some, and particularly Jerome, exalting
the certainty of the Hebrew, and rejecting, yea, even de-
riding the history of the Septuagint, which the primitive
church chiefly made use of; and some fathers that lived
centuries before him, affirmed to be a most certain thing:
and the many various readings in divers copies of the
Greek, and the great altercations among the fathers of the
first three centuries, who had greater opportunity to be
better informed than we can now lay claim to, concerning
the books to be admitted or rejected, as is above observed;
I say, all these and much more which might be alleged,
puts the minds even of the learned into infinite doubts,
scruples, and inextricable difficulties: whence we may very
safely conclude, that Jesus Christ, who promised to be always with his children, to lead them into all truth, to guard
them against the devices of the enemy, and to establish
their faith upon an unmovable rock, left them not to be
principally ruled by that, which was subject in itself to
many uncertainties: and therefore he gave them his Spirit,
as their principal guide, which neither moths nor time can

8

wear out, nor transcribers nor translators corrupt; which none are so young, none so illiterate, none in so remote a place, but they may come to be reached, and rightly informed by it.

Through and by the clearness which that Spirit gives us it is, that we are only best rid of those difficulties that occur to us concerning the scriptures. The real and undoubted experience whereof I myself have been a witness of, with great admiration of the love of God to his children in these latter days: for I have known some of my friends, who profess the same faith with me, faithful servants of the Most High God, and full of divine knowledge of his truth, as it was immediately and inwardly revealed to them by the Spirit, from a true and living experience, who not only were ignorant of the Greek and Hebrew, but even some of them could not read their own vulgar language, who being pressed by their adversaries with some citations out of the English translation, and finding them to disagree with the manifestation of truth in their own hearts, have boldly affirmed the Spirit of God never said so, and that it was certainly wrong; for they did not believe that any of the holy prophets or apostles had ever written so; which when I on this account seriously examined, I really found to be errors and corruptions of the translators; who, as in most translations, do not so much give us the genuine signification of the words, as strain them to express that which comes nearest to that opinion and notion they have of truth. And this seemed to me to suit very well with that saying of Augustine, Epist. 19, ad Hier. Tom ii fol. 14, after he has said, "That he gives only that honour to those books which are called canonical, as to believe that the authors thereof did in writing not err," he adds, "And if I shall meet with anything in these writings that seemeth repugnant to truth, I shall not doubt to say, that either the volume is faulty or erroneous; that the expounder hath not reached what was said; or that I have in no wise understood it." So that he supposes that in the transcription and translation there may be errors.

Wrong
translations
of scripture
discerned in
the Spirit
by the un-
learned in
letters.

§ V. If it be then asked me, Whether I think hereby to Object.
render the scriptures altogether uncertain, or useless?

I answer; Not at all. The proposition itself declares Answ. .
how much I esteem them; and provided that to the Spirit
from which they came be but granted that place the scriptures themselves give it, I do freely concede to the scriptures the second place, even whatsoever they say of themselves; which the apostle Paul chiefly mentions in two
places, Rom. xv. 4: "Whatsoever things were written
aforetime, were written for our learning, that we through
patience and comfort of the scriptures might have hope."
2 Tim. iii. 15, 16, 17: The holy scriptures are able to
make thee wise unto salvation, through faith which is in
Christ Jesus. All scripture given by inspiration of God,
is profitable—for correction, for instruction in righteousness, that the man of God may be perfect, thoroughly furnished unto all good works.

For though God doth principally and chiefly lead us by
his Spirit, yet he sometimes conveys his comfort and con-
solation to us through his children, whom he raises up and
inspires to speak or write a word in season, whereby the
saints are made instruments in the hand of the Lord to
strengthen and encourage one another, which doth also
tend to perfect and make them wise unto salvation; and
such as are led by the Spirit cannot neglect, but do natu- The saints
rally love, and are wonderfully cherished by that which mutual
comfort is
proceedeth from the same Spirit in another; because such the same
Spirit in all
mutual emanations of the heavenly life tend to quicken the
mind when at any time it is overtaken with heaviness.
Peter himself declares this to have been the end of his
writing, 2 Pet. i. 12, 13: "Wherefore I will not be neg-
ligent to put you always in remembrance of these things,
though ye know them, and be established in the present
truth; yea, I think it meet, as long as I am in this tabernacle, to stir you up, by putting you in remembrance."

God is teacher of his people himself; and there is nothing more express, than that such as are under the new
covenant, need no man to teach them: yet it was a fruit

of Christ's ascension to send teachers and pastors for perfecting of the saints. So that the same work is ascribed to the scriptures as to teachers; the one to make the man of God perfect, the other for the perfection of the saints.

As then teachers are not to go before the teaching of God himself under the new covenant, but to follow after it; neither are they to rob us of that great privilege which Christ hath purchased unto us by his blood; so neither is the scripture to go before the teaching of the Spirit, or to rob us of it.

**Answ. 2.**
**The scriptures a looking-glass.**

Secondly, God hath seen meet that herein we should, as in a looking-glass, see the conditions and experiences of the saints of old; that finding our experience answer to theirs, we might thereby be the more confirmed and comforted, and our hope of obtaining the same end strengthened; that observing the providences attending them, seeing the snares they were liable to, and beholding their deliverances, we may thereby be made wise unto salvation, and seasonably reproved and instructed in righteousness.

**The scriptures' work and service.**

This is the great work of the scriptures, and their service to us, that we may witness them fulfilled in us, and so discern the stamp of God's spirit and ways upon them, by the inward acquaintance we have with the same Spirit and work in our hearts. The prophecies of the scriptures are also very comfortable and profitable unto us, as the same Spirit enlightens us to observe them fulfilled, and to be fulfilled; for in all this it is to be observed, that it is only the spiritual man that can make a right use of them: they are able to make the man of God perfect, so it is not the natural man; and whatsoever was written aforetime, was written for our comfort, [our] that are the believers, [our] that are the saints; concerning such the apostle speaks: for as for the others, the apostle Peter plainly declares, that the unstable and unlearned wrest them to their own destruction: these were they that were unlearned in the divine and heavenly learning of the Spirit, not in human and school literature; in which we may safely presume that Peter himself, being a fisherman, had no skill; for it may with great probability, yea certainty, be affirmed, that he had no knowledge of Aristotle's logic, which both Papists and Protestants now,* degenerating from the simplicity of truth, make the hand-maid of divinity, as they call it, and a necessary introduc-tion to their carnal, natural, and human ministry. By the infinite obscure labours of which kind of men, intermixing their heathenish stuff, the scripture is rendered at this day of so little service to the simple people : whereof if Jerome complained in his time, now twelve hundred years ago, Hierom. Epist. 134, ad Cypr. Tom. 3, saying, " It is wont to befal the most part of learned men, that it is harder to understand their expositions, than the things which they go about to expound ;" what may we say then, considering those great heaps of commentaries since, in ages yet far more corrupted ?

Logic.
* 1675.

§ VI. In this respect above mentioned, then, we have shown what service and use the holy scriptures, as managed in and by the Spirit, are of to the church of God ; where-fore we do account them a secondary rule. Moreover, be-cause they are commonly acknowledged by all to have been written by the dictates of the Holy Spirit, and that the errors which may be supposed by the injury of times to have slipped in, are not such but that there is a sufficient clear testimony left to all the essentials of the Christian faith ; we do look upon them as the only fit outward judge of controversies among Christians ; and that whatsoever doctrine is contrary unto their testimony, may therefore justly be rejected as false. And for our parts, we are very willing that all our doctrines and practices be tried by them ; which we never refused, nor ever shall, in all con-troversies with our adversaries, as the judge and test. We shall also be very willing to admit it as a positive certain maxim, That whatsoever any do, pretending to the Spirit, which is contrary to the scriptures, be accounted and reckoned a delusion of the devil. For as we never lay claim to the Spirit's leadings, that we may cover ourselves in any thing that is evil ; so we know, that as every evil

The scrip tures a se condary rule.

8 *                    M

contradicts the scriptures, so it doth also the Spirit in the first place, from which the scriptures came, and whose motions can never contradict one another, though they may appear sometimes to be contradictory to the blind eye of the natural man, as Paul and James seem to contradict one another.

Thus far we have shown both what we believe, and what we believe not, concerning the holy scriptures, hoping we have given them their due place. But since they that will needs have them to be the only, certain, and principal rule, want not some show of arguments, even from the scripture itself (though it no where calls itself so) by which they labour to prove their doctrine; I shall briefly lay them down by way of objections, and answer them, before I make an end of this matter.

**OBJ 1.** § VII. Their first objection is usually drawn from Isaiah viii. 20, "To the law and to the testimony; if they speak not according to this word, it is because there is no light in them." Now this law, testimony, and word, they plead to be the scriptures.

**ANSW.** To which I answer; That that is to beg the thing in question, and remains yet unproved. Nor do I know for what reason we may not safely affirm this law and word to be inward: but suppose it was outward, it proves not the case at all for them, neither makes it against us; for it may be confessed, without any prejudice to our cause, that the outward law was more particularly to the Jews a rule, and more principally than to us; seeing their law was outward and literal, but ours, under the new covenant, as hath been already said, is expressly affirmed to be inward, and spiritual; so that this scripture is so far from making **To try all** against us, that it makes for us. For if the Jews were **things, by** directed to try all things by their law, which was without **what?** them, written in tables of stone; then if we will have this advice of the prophet to reach us, we must make it hold parallel to that dispensation of the gospel which we are under: so that we are to try all things, in the first place, by that word of faith which is preached unto us, which the apostle saith is in the heart; and by that law which God hath given us, which the apostle saith also expressly is written and placed in the mind.

Lastly, If we look to this place according to the Greek interpretation of the Septuagint, our adversaries shall have nothing from thence to carp; yea, it will favour us much; for there it is said, that "the law is given us for a help;" which very well agrees with what is above asserted.

Their second objection is from John v 39, "Search the Obj. 2. scriptures," &c.

Here, say they, we are commanded, by Christ himself, to search the scriptures.

I answer, First, That the scriptures ought to be searched, Answ. 1. we do not at all deny; but are very willing to be tried by them, as hath been above declared: but the question is, Whether they be the only and principal rule? Which this is so far from proving, that it proveth the contrary; for Christ checks them here for too high an esteem of the scriptures, and neglecting of him that was to be preferred before them, and to whom they bore witness, as the following words declare; "for in them ye think ye have Search the eternal life, and they are they which testify of me: and ye scriptures, will not come unto me, that ye might have life." This &c. shows, that while they thought they had eternal life in the scriptures, they neglected to come unto Christ to have life, of which the scriptures bore witness. This answers well to our purpose, since our adversaries now do also exalt the scriptures, and think to have life in them; which is no more than to look upon them as the only principal rule and way to life, and yet refuse to come unto the Spirit of which they testify, even the inward spiritual law, which could give them life: so that the cause of this people's ignorance and unbelief was not their want of respect to the scriptures, which though they knew, and had a high esteem of, yet Christ testifies in the former verses, that they had neither "seen the Father, nor heard his voice at any time; neither had his word abiding in them;" which had they then had, then they had believed in the Son. Moreover that place Answ. 2

may be taken in the indicative mood, Ye search the scrip‧
tures ; which interpretation the Greek word will bear, and
so Pasor translateth it : which by the reproof following
seemeth also to be the more genuine interpretation, as Cyrillus long ago hath observed.

OBJ. 3.    § VIII. Their third objection is from these words, A ts
xvii. 11, " These were more noble than those in Thessalo-
nica, in that they received the word with all readiness of
mind, and searched the scriptures daily, whether those
things were so."

Here, say they, the Bereans are commended for searching the scriptures, and making them the rule.

ANS. 1.    I answer ; That the scriptures either are the principal or
only rule, will not at all follow from this ; neither will their
searching the scriptures, or being commended for it, infer
any such thing : for we recommend and approve the use
of them in that respect as much as any ; yet will it not
follow, that we affirm them to be the principal and only
rule.

ANS. 2.    Secondly, It is to be observed that these were the Jews
The Bere-    of Berea, to whom these scriptures, which were the law
ans search-
ing the    and the prophets, were more particularly a rule ; and the
scriptures,    thing under examination was, whether the birth, life, works,
makes
them not    and sufferings of Christ, did answer to the prophecies con-
the only    cerning him ; so that it was most proper for them, being
rule to try
doctrines.    Jews, to examine the apostle's doctrine by the scriptures ;
seeing he pleaded it to be a fulfilling of them.    It is said
nevertheless, in the first place, That "they received the
word with cheerfulness ;" and in the second place, " They
searched the scriptures :" not that they searched the scriptures, and then received the word ; for then could they not
have prevailed to convert them, had they not first minded
the word abiding in them, which opened their understand
ings ; no more than the Scribes and Pharisees, who, as in
the former objection we observed, searched the scriptures
and exalted them, and yet remained in their unbelief, be‧
cause they had not the word abiding in them.

ANS. 3.    But lastly, If this commendation of the Jewish Bereans might infer that the scriptures were the only and principal rule to try the apostle's doctrine by, what should have become of the Gentiles? How should they ever have come to have received the faith of Christ, who neither knew the scriptures, nor believed them? We see in the end of the same chapter, how the apostle, preaching to the Athenians, took another method, and directed them to somewhat of God within themselves, that they might feel after him. He did not go about to proselyte them to the Jewish religion, and to the belief of the law and the prophets, and from thence to prove the coming of Christ; nay, he took a nearer way. Now certainly the principal and only rule is not different; one to the Jews, and another to the Gentiles; but is universal, reaching both: though secondary and subordinate rules and means may be various, and diversely suited, according as the people they are used to are stated and circumstantiated: even so we see that the apostle to the Athenians used a testimony of one of their own poets, which he judged would have credit with them; and no doubt such testimonies, whose authors they esteemed, had more weight with them than all the sayings of Moses, and the prophets, whom they neither knew nor would have cared for. Now because the apostle used the testimony of a poet to the Athenians, will it therefore follow he made that the principal or only rule to try his doctrine by? So neither will it follow, that though he made use of the scriptures to the Jews, as being a principle already believed by them, to try his doctrine, that from thence the scriptures may be accounted the principal or only rule.

*The Athenians instanced.*

§ IX. The last, and that which at first view seems to be the greatest objection, is this:

If the scripture be not the adequate, principal, and only rule, then it would follow that the scripture is not complete, nor the canon filled; that if men be now immediately led and ruled by the Spirit, they may add new scriptures of equal authority with the old; whereas every one that adds is cursed: yea, what assurance have we, but

*Obj. 4.*

at this rate every one may bring in a new gospel **according** to his fancy?

**Answ.** The dangerous consequences insinuated in this objection were fully answered in the latter part of the last proposition, in what was said a little before, offering freely to disclaim all pretended revelations contrary to the scriptures.

**Obj. 1.** But if it be urged, That it is not enough to deny these consequences, if they naturally follow from your doctrine of immediate revelation, and denying the scripture to be the only rule;

**Ans. 1.** I answer; We have proved both these doctrines to be true and necessary, according to the scriptures themselves; and therefore to fasten evil consequences upon them, which we make appear do not follow, is not to accuse us, but Christ and his apostles, who preached them.

**Ans. 2.** But Secondly, We have shut the door upon all such doctrine in this very position; affirming, That the scriptures give a full and ample testimony to all the principal doctrines of the Christian faith. For we do firmly believe that there is no other gospel or doctrine to be preached, but that which was delivered by the apostles; and do freely **Gal. i. 8.** subscribe to that saying, Let him that preacheth any other gospel, than that which hath been already preached by the apostles, and according to the scriptures, be accursed.

**A new revelation is not a new gospel.** So we distinguish betwixt a revelation of a new gospel, and new doctrines, and a new revelation of the good old gospel and doctrines; the last we plead for, but the first we utterly deny. For we firmly believe, That no other foundation can any man lay, than that which is laid already. But that this revelation is necessary we have already proved; and this distinction doth sufficiently guard us against the hazard insinuated in the objection.

**Books canonical.** As to the scriptures being a filled canon, I see no necessity of believing it. And if these men, that believe the scriptures to be the only rule, will be consistent with their own doctrine, they must needs be of my judgment; seeing it is simply impossible to prove the canon by the scriptures. For it cannot be found in any book of the scriptures, that these books, and just these, and no other, are canonical, as all are forced to acknowledge; how can they then evite this argument?

That which cannot be proved by scripture is no necessary article of faith.

But the canon of the scripture; to wit, that there are so many books precisely, neither more nor less, cannot be proved by scripture:

Therefore, it is no necessary article of faith.

If they should allege; That the admitting of any other **OBJ. 2.** books to be now written by the same Spirit might infer the admission of new doctrines;

I deny that consequence; for the principal or fundamental doctrines of the Christian religion are contained in the tenth part of the scripture; but it will not follow thence that the rest are impertinent or useless. If it should please God to bring to us any of those books, which by the injury of time are lost, which are mentioned in the scripture; as, The Prophecy of Enoch; the Book of Nathan, &c., or, the **Books lost.** Third Epistle of Paul to the Corinthians; I see no reason why we ought not to receive them, and place them with the rest. That which displeaseth me is, that men should first affirm that the scripture is the only and principal rule, and yet make a great article of faith of that which the scripture can give us no light in.

As for instance: How shall a Protestant prove by scripture, to such as deny the Epistle of James to be authentic, that it ought to be received?

First, If he would say, Because it contradicts not the rest; besides that there is no mention of it in any of the rest, perhaps these men think it doth contradict Paul in relation to faith and works. But, if that should be granted, it would as well follow, that every writer that contradicts not the scripture, should be put into the canon; and by this means these men fall into a greater absurdity than they fix upon us: for thus they would equal every one the writings of their own sect with the scriptures; for I suppose they judge their own confession of faith doth not contradict the scriptures : Will it therefore follow that it should be bound up with the Bible ? And yet it seems impossible, according to their principles, to bring any better argument Whether the Epistle of James be authentic, and how to know it? to prove the Epistle of James to be authentic. There is then this unavoidable necessity to say, We know it by the same Spirit from which it was written; or otherwise to step back to Rome, and say, We know by tradition that the church hath declared it to be canonical ; and the church is infallible. Let them find a mean, if they can. So that out of this objection we shall draw an unanswerable argument *ad hominem*, to our purpose.

That which cannot assure me concerning an article of faith necessary to be believed, is not the primary, adequate, only rule of faith, &c.

But the scripture cannot thus assure me ; Therefore, &c.

I prove the assumption thus :

That which cannot assure me concerning the canon of the scripture, to wit, that such books are only to be admitted, and the Apocrypha excluded, cannot assure me of this.

Therefore, &c.

**OBJ. 3.**

And lastly, As to these words, Rev. xxii. 18, That " if any man shall add unto these things, God shall add unto **Answ.** him the plagues that are written in this book ;" I desire they will show me how it relates to any thing else than to that particular prophecy. It saith not, Now the canon of the scriptures is filled up, no man is to write more from the Spirit ; yea, do not all confess that there have been prophecies and true prophets since ? The Papists deny it not. And do not the Protestants affirm, that John Hus prophesied of the reformation ? Was he therefore cursed ? Or did he therein evil ? I could give many other exam- What it means to add to the scriptures. ples, confessed by themselves. But, moreover, the same was in effect commanded long before, Prov. xxx. 6, "Add thou not unto his words, lest he reprove thee, and thou be found a liar :" Yet how many books of the prophets were written after ? And the same was said by Moses, Deut. iv. 2, " Ye shall not add unto the word which I command you; neither shall ye diminish aught from it." So that, though we should extend that of the revelation beyond the particular prophecy of that book, it cannot be understood but of a new gospel, or new doctrines, or of restraining man's spirit, that he mix not his human words with the divine; and not of a new revelation of the old, as we have said before.

---

## PROPOSITION IV.

*Concerning the Condition of Man in the Fall.*

All Adam's posterity, or mankind, both Jews and Gentiles, as to the first Adam, or earthly man, is fallen, degenerated, and dead; deprived of the sensation or feeling of this inward testimony or seed of God; and is subject Rom v. 12. unto the power, nature, and seed of the serpent, which 15. he soweth in men's hearts, while they abide in this natural and corrupted estate: from whence it comes, that not only their words and deeds, but all their imaginations, are evil perpetually in the sight of God, as proceeding from this depraved and wicked seed. Man therefore, as he is in this state, can know nothing aright; yea, his thoughts and conceptions concerning God and things spiritual, until he be disjoined from this evil seed, and united to the Divine Light, are unprofitable both to himself and others. Hence are rejected the Socinian and Pelagian errors, in exalting a natural light; as also of the Papists, and most Protestants, who affirm, That man, without the true grace of God, may be a true minister of the gospel. Nevertheless, this seed is not imputed to infants, until by transgression they actually join themselves therewith; for they are by nature "the children of wrath," who walk according to the "power Eph. ii of the prince of the air, the spirit that now worketh in the children of disobedience," having their conversation in the lusts of the flesh fulfilling the desires of the flesh and of the mind.

§ I. Hitherto we have discoursed how the true knowledge of God is attained and preserved; also of what use and service the holy scripture is to the saints.

We come now to examine the state and condition of man as he stands in the fall; what his capacity and power is; and how far he is able, as of himself, to advance in relation to the things of God. Of this we touched a little in the beginning of the second proposition; but the full, right, and thorough understanding of it is of great use and service; because from the ignorance and altercations that have been about it, there have arisen great and dangerous errors, both on the one hand and on the other. While some do so far exalt the light of nature, or the faculty of the natural man, as capable of himself, by virtue of the inward will, faculty, light, and power, that pertains to his nature, to follow that which is good, and make real progress towards heaven; and of these are the Pelagians, and Semi-Pelagians of old; and of late the Socinians, and divers others among the Papists; others again will needs run into another extreme, to whom Augustine, among the ancients, first made way in his declining age, through the heat of his zeal against Pelagius, not only confessing man incapable of himself to do good, and prone to evil; but that in his very mother's womb, and before he commits any actual transgression, he is contaminate with a real guilt, whereby he deserves eternal death: in which respect they are not afraid to affirm, That many poor infants are eternally damned, and for ever endure the torments of hell. Therefore the God of truth, having now again revealed his truth that good and even way, by his own Spirit, hath taught us to avoid both these extremes.

That then which our proposition leads to treat of is,

First, What the condition of man is in the fall; and how far incapable to meddle in the things of God.

And, secondly, That God doth not impute this evil to infants, until they actually join with it: that so, by establishing the truth, we may overturn the errors on both parts.

**Augustine's zeal against Pelagius.** [marginal note]

And as for that third thing included in the proposition itself concerning these teachers which want the Grace of God, we shall refer that to the tenth proposition, where the matter is more particularly handled.

§ II. As to the first, not to dive into the many curious **PART I.** notions which many have concerning the condition of Adam before the fall, all agree in this: That thereby he came to **Adam's fall.** a very great loss, not only in the things which related to the outward man, but in regard of that true fellowship and communion he had with God. This loss was signified unto him in the command, "For in the day thou eatest thereof, thou shalt surely die," Gen. ii. 17. This death could not be an outward death, or the dissolution of the outward man; for as to that, he did not die yet many hundred years after; so that it must needs respect his spiritual life and communion with God. The consequence of this fall, besides that which relates to the fruits of the earth, is also expressed, Gen. iii. 24, "So he drove out the man, and he placed at the east of the garden of Eden, cherubims, and a flaming sword, which turned every way, to keep the way of the tree of life." Now whatsoever literal signification this may have, we may safely ascribe to this paradise a mystical signification, and truly account it that spiritual communion and fellowship, which the saints obtain with God by Jesus Christ; to whom only these cherubims give way, and unto as many as enter by him, who calls himself the Door. So that, though we do not ascribe any whit of **Guilt not** Adam's guilt to men, until they make it theirs by the like **ascribed to Adam's** acts of disobedience; yet we cannot suppose that men, **posterity.** who are come of Adam naturally, can have any good thing in their nature, as belonging to it; which he, from whom they derive their nature, had not himself to communicate unto them.

If then we may affirm, that Adam did not retain in his nature (as belonging thereunto) any will or light capable to give him knowledge in spiritual things, then neither can his posterity; for whatsoever real good any man doth, it proceedeth not from his nature, as he is man, or the son of

Adam ; but from the seed of God in him, as a new visitation of life, in order to bring him out of this natural condition : so that, though it be in him, yet it is not of him ·
and this the Lord himself witnessed, Gen. vi. 5, where it
is said, he " saw that every imagination of the thoughts of
his heart was only evil continually :" which words, as
they are very positive, so are they very comprehensive.

Every ima-<br>gination of<br>the natural<br>man is evil. Observe the emphasis of them ; First, There is " every
imagination of the thoughts of his heart ;" so that this ad-
mits of no exception of any imagination of the thoughts
of his heart. Secondly, " Is only evil continually ;" it is
neither in some part evil continually, nor yet only evil at
some times ; but both only evil, and always and continually evil ; which certainly excludes any good, as a proper
effect of man's heart, naturally : for that which is only evil,
and that always, cannot of its own nature produce any
good thing. The Lord expressed this again a little after,
chap. viii. 21, " The imagination of man's heart is evil
from his youth." Thus inferring how natural and proper
it is unto him ; from which I thus argue :

If the thoughts of man's heart be not only evil, but always evil ; then are they, as they simply proceed from his
heart, neither good in part, nor at any time.

But the first is true ; therefore the last.

Again,

If man's thoughts be always and only evil, then are they
altogether useless and ineffectual to him in the things of
God.

But the first is true ; therefore the last.

The heart<br>of man de-<br>ceitful. Secondly, This appears clearly from that saying of the
prophet Jeremiah, chap. xvii. 9, " The heart is deceitful
above all things, and desperately wicked." For who can
with any colour of reason imagine, that that which is so
hath any power of itself, or is in any wise fit to lead a man
to righteousness, whereunto it is of its own nature directly
opposite ? This is as contrary to reason, as it is impossible in nature that a stone, of its own nature and proper
motion, shou'd fly upwards : for as a stone of its own na-

ture inclineth and is prone to move downwards towards the centre, so the heart of man is naturally prone and inclined to evil, some to one, and some to another. From this then I also thus argue:

That which is "deceitful above all things, and desperately wicked," is not fit, neither can it lead a man aright in things that are good and honest.

But the heart of man is such:

Therefore, &c.

But the apostle Paul describeth the condition of men in the fall at large, taking it out of the Psalmist. "There is none righteous, no not one: there is none that understandeth, there is none that seeketh after God. They are all gone out of the way, they are altogether become unprofitable; there is none that doth good, no not one. Their throat is an open sepulchre, with their tongues they have used deceit, the poison of asps is under their lips: whose mouths are full of cursing and bitterness. Their feet are swift to shed blood; destruction and misery are in their ways: and the way of peace have they not known. There is no fear of God before their eyes." What more positive can be spoken? He seemeth to be particularly careful to avoid that any good should be ascribed to the natural man; he shows how he is polluted in all his ways; he shows how he is void of righteousness, of understanding, of the knowledge of God; how he is out of the way, and in short unprofitable; than which nothing can be more fully said to confirm our judgment: for if this be the condition of the natural man, or of man as he stands in the fall, he is unfit to make one right step to heaven.

*Rom. iii.10. Psa. xiv. 3. and liii. 2. &c.*

*Man's estate in the fall.*

If it be said, That is not spoken of the condition of man in general; but only of some particulars, or at the least that it comprehends not all;

*Object*

The text showeth the clear contrary in the foregoing verses, where the apostle takes in himself, as he stood in his natural condition. "What then? Are we better than they? No, in no wise; for we have before proved both Jews and Gentiles, that they are all under sin, as it is

*Answ.*

9*

written:" and so he goes on; by which it is manifest that he speaks of mankind in general.

OBJECT.    If they object that which the same apostle saith in the foregoing chapter, ver 14, to wit, That the Gentiles do by nature the things contained in the law, and so consequently do by nature that which is good and acceptable in the sight of God;

ANS. 1    I answer; This nature must not, neither can be understood of man's own nature, which is corrupt and fallen; but of the spiritual nature, which proceedeth from the seed of God in man, as it receiveth a new visitation of God's love, and is quickened by it: which clearly appears by the following words, where he saith, " These having not the law," i. e., outwardly, " are a law unto themselves; which show the work of the law written in their hearts." These acts of theirs then are an effect of the law written in their hearts; but the scripture declareth, that the writing of the law in the heart is a part, yea and a great part too, of the new covenant dispensation, and so no consequence nor part of man's nature.

*By what nature the Gentiles did do the things of the law.*

ANS. 2.    Secondly, If this nature here spoken of could be understood of man's own nature, which he hath as he is a man, then would the apostle unavoidably contradict himself; since he elsewhere positively declares, That the natural man discerneth not the things of God, nor can. Now I hope the law of God is among the things of God, especially as it is written in the heart. The apostle in the viith chap. of the same epistle, saith, verse 12, that " the law is holy, just, and good;" and verse 14, the " law is spiritual, but he is carnal." Now in what respect is he carnal, but as he stands in the fall unregenerate? Now what inconsistency would here be, to say, That he is carnal, and yet not so of his own nature, seeing it is from his nature that he is so denominated? We see the apostle contra-distinguisheth the law as spiritual, from man's nature as carnal and sinful.

*The natural man discerneth not, &c.*

*Mat. vii. 16.* Wherefore, as Christ saith, There can no grapes be expected from thorns, nor figs of thistles; so neither can the fulfilling of the law, which is spiritual, holy, and just, be

expected from that nature which is corrupt, fallen, and
unregenerate. Whence we conclude, with good reason,
that the nature here spoken of, by which the Gentiles are The Gei-
said to have done the things contained in the law, is not tiles spirit-
the common nature of men; but that spiritual nature that in doing the
ariseth from the works of the righteous and spiritual law law.
that is written in the heart. I confess they of the other
extreme, when they are pressed with this testimony by the
Socinians and Pelagians, as well as by us when we use
this scripture, to show them how some of the heathen, by
the light of Christ in their heart, came to be saved, are
very far to seek; giving this answer, That there were some
relics of the heavenly image left in Adam, by which the
heathen could do some good things. Which, as it is in
itself without proof, so it contradicts their own assertions
elsewhere, and gives away their cause. For if these
relics were of force to enable them to fulfil the righteous
law of God, it takes away the necessity of Christ's coming; or at least leaves them a way to be saved without
him; unless they will say (which is worst of all) That
though they really fulfilled the righteous law of God, yet
God damned them, because of the want of that particular
knowledge, while he himself withheld all means of their
coming to him, from them; but of this hereafter.

§ III. I might also here use another argument from
these words of the apostle, 1 Cor. ii, where he so positively
excludes the natural man from an understanding in the
things of God; but because I have spoken of that scripture in the beginning of the second proposition, I will here
avoid to repeat what is there mentioned, referring there- Socinians
unto: yet because the Socinians and others, who exalt the light of the
light of the natural man, or a natural light in man, do ob- natural
ject against this scripture, I shall remove it before I pro- man.
ceed.* *Antequam
progrediar

They say, The Greek word ψυχικὸς ought to be trans- Object.
lated animal, and not natural; else, say they, it would
have been φυσικὸς. From which they seek to infer, that it
is only the animal man, and not the rational, that is ex-

cluded here from discerning the things of God. Which
shift, without disputing about the word, is easily refuted;
neither is it any wise consistent with the scope of the
place. For,

Ans. 1.
The animal
man is the
same with
natural.

First, The animal life is no other than that which man
hath in common with other living creatures; for as he is a
mere man, he differs no otherwise from beasts than by the
rational property. Now the apostle deduceth his argument
in the foregoing verses from this simile; That as the things
of a man cannot be known but by the spirit of a man, so
the things of God no man knoweth but by the Spirit of
God. But I hope these men will confess unto me, that
the things of a man are not known by the animal spirit
only, i. e. by that which he hath in common with the
beasts, but by the rational; so that it must be the rational
that is here understood. Again, the assumption shows
clearly that the apostle had no such intent as these men's
gloss would make him have, viz. : " So the things of God
knoweth no man, but the Spirit of God." According to
their judgment he should have said, The things of God
knoweth no man by his animal spirit, but by his rational
spirit: for to say, the Spirit of God, here spoken of, is no
other than the rational spirit of man, would border upon
blasphemy, since they are so often contra-distinguished.
Again, going on, he saith not that they are rationally, but
spiritually discerned.

Ans. 2.

Secondly, The apostle throughout this chapter shows
how the wisdom of man is unfit to judge of the things of
God, and ignorant of them. Now I ask these men, whether
a man be called a wise man from his animal property, or
from his rational? If from his rational, then it is not only
the animal, but also the rational, as he is yet in the natural
state, which the apostle excludes here, and whom he contra-distinguisheth from the spiritual, verse 15, But the
spiritual man judgeth all things. This cannot be said of
any man merely because rational, or as he is a man, seeing
the men of the greatest reason, if we may so esteem men,
whom the scripture calls wise, as were the Greeks of old,

The ration-
al man in
the natural
state ex-
cluded from
discerning
the things
of God.

not only may be, but often are enemies to the kingdom of God; while both the preaching of Christ is said to be foolishness with the wise men of the world, and the wisdom of the world is said to be foolishness with God. Now whether it be any ways probable that either these wise men that are said to account the gospel foolishness, are only so called with respect to their animal property, and not their rational; or that the wisdom that is foolishness with God is not meant of the rational, but only the animal property, any rational man, laying aside interest, may easily judge.

§ IV. I come now to the other part, to wit, That this evil and corrupt seed is not imputed to infants, until they actually join with it. For this there is a reason given in the end of the proposition itself, drawn from Eph. ii. For these are by nature children of wrath, who walk according to the prince of the power of the air, the spirit that now worketh in the children of disobedience. Here the apostle gives their evil walking, and not any thing that is not reduced to act, as a reason of their being "children of wrath." And this is suitable to the whole strain of the gospel, where no man is ever threatened or judged for what iniquity he hath not actually wrought: such indeed as continue in iniquity, and so do allow the sins of their fathers, God will visit the iniquity of the fathers upon the children.

Infants, no sin imputed to them.

Is it not strange then that men should entertain an opinion so absurd in itself, and so cruel and contrary to the nature as well of God's mercy as justice, concerning which the scripture is altogether silent? But it is manifest that man hath invented this opinion out of self-love, and from that bitter root from which all errors spring; for the most part of Protestants that hold this, having, as they fancy, the absolute decree of election to secure them and their children, so as they cannot miss of salvation, they make no difficulty to send all others, both old and young, to hell. For whereas self-love, which is always apt to believe that which it desires, possesseth them with a hope that their part is secure, they are not solicitous how they leave their

The absolute decree of election springs from self-love.

o

neighbours, which are the far greater part of mankind, in these inextricable difficulties. The Papists again use this opinion as an art to augment the esteem of their church, and reverence of its sacraments, seeing they pretend it is washed away by baptism; only in this they appear to be a little more merciful, in that they send not these unbaptized infants to hell, but to a certain *limbus*, concerning which the scriptures are as silent as of the other. This then is not only not authorized in the scriptures, but contrary to the express tenor of them. The apostle saith plainly, Rom. iv. 15, " Where no law is, there is no transgression." And again, ch. v. 13, " But sin is not imputed, where there is no law." Than which testimonies there is nothing more positive; since to infants there is no law, seeing as such they are utterly incapable of it; the law cannot reach any but such as have in some measure less or more the exercise of their understanding, which infants have not. So that from thence I argue thus:

*To infants there is no law, so no transgression.*

Sin is imputed to none, where there is no law.

But to infants there is no law:

Therefore sin is not imputed to them.

The proposition is the apostle's own words; the assumption is thus proved:

Those who are under a physical impossibility of either hearing, knowing, or understanding any law, where the impossibility is not brought upon them by any act of their own, but is according to the very order of nature appointed by God; to such there is no law.

But infants are under this physical impossibility:

Therefore, &c.

Secondly, What can be more positive than that of Ezek. xviii. 20, " The soul that sinneth, it shall die: the son shall not bear the iniquity of the father." For the prophet here first showeth what is the cause of man's eternal death, which he saith is his sinning; and then, as if he purposed expressly to shut out such an opinion, he assures us, " The son shall not bear the iniquity of the father." From which I thus argue:

If the son bear not the iniquity of his father, or of his Infants bear not Adam's transgression. immediate parents, far less shall he bear the iniquity of Adam.

But the son shall not bear the iniquity of his father:

Therefore, &c.

§ V. Having thus far shown how absurd this opinion is, I shall briefly examine the reasons its authors bring for it.

First, They say, Adam was a public person, and there- Obj. 1. fore all men sinned in him, as being in his loins. And for this they allege that of Rom. v. 12, "Wherefore as by one man sin entered into the world, and death by sin; and so death passed upon all men, for that all have sinned." These last words, say they, may be translated, In whom all have sinned.

To this I answer: That Adam is a public person is not Answ. denied; and that through him there is a seed of sin propagated to all men, which in its own nature is sinful, and inclines men to iniquity; yet it will not follow from thence, that infants, who join not with this seed, are guilty. As for these words in the Romans, the reason of the guilt there alleged is, "For that all have sinned." Now no man is said to sin, unless he actually sin in his own person; for the Greek words ἐφ᾿ ᾧ may very well relate to θάνατος, which is the nearest antecedent; so that they hold forth, how that Adam, by his sin, gave an entrance to sin in the world: and so death entered by sin, ἐφ᾿ ᾧ, i. e. upon which [viz. occasion] or, in which [viz. death] all others have sinned; that is, actually in their own persons; to wit, all that were capable of sinning: of which number that infants could not be, the apostle clearly shows by the following verse: "Sin is not imputed, where there is no law:" and since, as is above proved, there is no law to infants, they cannot be here included.

Their second objection is from Psalm li. 5, "Behold I Obj. 2 was shapen in iniquity, and in sin did my mother conceive me." Hence, they say, it appears that infants from their conception are guilty.

**Answ.**

**Conceived in sin answered.**

How they infer this consequence, for my part I see not. The iniquity and sin here appears to be far more ascribable to the parents than to the child. It is said indeed, " In sin did my mother conceive me ;" not my mother did conceive me a sinner. Besides, that, so interpreted, contradicts expressly the scripture before-mentioned, in making children guilty of the sins of their immediate parents, (for of Adam there is not here any mention) contrary to the plain words, " the son shall not bear the father's iniquity."

**Obj. 3.**

Thirdly, They object, " That the wages of sin is death ;" and that seeing children are subject to diseases and death, therefore they must be guilty of sin.

**Answ.**

**Death the wages of sin answered.**

I answer, That these things are a consequence of the fall, and of Adam's sin, is confessed ; but that that infers necessarily a guilt in all others that are subject to them is denied. For though the whole outward creation suffered a decay by Adam's fall, which groans under vanity; according to which it is said in Job, that the heavens are not clean in the sight of God ; yet will it not from thence follow, that the herbs, earth, and trees are sinners.

Next, death, though a consequent of the fall, incident to man's earthly nature, is not the wages of sin in the saints, but rather a sleep, by which they pass from death to life ; which is so far from being troublesome and painful to them, as all real punishments for sin are, that the apostle counts it gain: " To me," saith he, " to die is gain." Philip i. 21.

**Obj. 4.**

Some are so foolish as to make an objection farther, saying, That if Adam's sin be not imputed to those who actually have not sinned, then it would follow that all infants are saved.

**Answ.**

But we are willing that this supposed absurdity should be the consequence of our doctrine, rather than that which it seems our adversaries reckon not absurd, though the undoubted and unavoidable consequence of theirs, viz. : That many infants eternally perish, not for any sin of their own, but only for Adam's iniquity ; where we are willing

to let the controversy stop, commending both to the illuminated understanding of the Christian reader.

This error of our adversaries is both denied and refuted
by Zuinglius, that eminent founder of the Protestant
churches of Switzerland, in his book De Baptismo, for
which he is anathematized by the Council of Trent, in the
fifth session. We shall only add this information : That
we confess then that a seed of sin is transmitted to all men
from Adam, although imputed to none, until by sinning
they actually join with it ; in which seed he gave occasion
to all to sin, and it is the origin of all evil actions and
thoughts in men's hearts, ἐφ ὦ to wit, θανάτῳ, as it is in
Rom. v., i. e., in which death all have sinned. For this
seed of sin is frequently called death in the scripture, and
the body of death ; seeing indeed it is a death to the life
of righteousness and holiness : therefore its seed and its
product is called the old man, the old Adam, in which all
sin is ; for which cause we use this name to express this sin, Original sin
and not that of original sin ; of which phrase the scripture no scripture
makes no mention, and under which invented and unscrip- phrase.
tural barbarism this notion of imputed sin to infants took
place among Christians.

## PROPOSITIONS V. AND VI.

*Concerning the Universal Redemption by Christ, and also
the Saving and Spiritual Light, wherewith every Man is
enlightened.*

## PROPOSITION V.

God, out of his infinite love, who delighteth not in the Ezek xviii
death of a sinner, but that all should live and be saved, 32 & 33, 11
hath so loved the world, that he hath given his only Son
a Light, that whosoever believeth in him shall be saved,
1C

John iii. 16, who enlighteneth every man that cometh
into the world, John i. 9, and maketh manifest all
things that are reprovable, Ephes. v. 13, and teacheth
all temperance, righteousness, and godliness; and this
Light enlighteneth the hearts of all for a time, in order
to salvation; and this is it which reproves the sin of all
individuals, and would work out the salvation of all, if
not resisted. Nor is it less universal than the seed of
sin, being the purchase of his death, who tasted death
for every man: for as in Adam all die, even so in Christ
all shall be made alive, 1 Cor. xv. 22.

## PROPOSITION VI.

According to which principle or hypothesis all the objections against the universality of Christ's death are easily
solved; neither is it needful to recur to the ministry of
angels, and those other miraculous means which they
say God useth to manifest the doctrine and history of
Christ's passion unto such, who, living in parts of the
world where the outward preaching of the gospel is unknown, have well improved the first and common grace.
For as hence it well follows that some of the old philosophers might have been saved, so also may some, who
by providence are cast into those remote parts of the
world where the knowledge of the history is wanting,
be made partakers of the divine mystery, if they receive
Cor. xii. 7. and resist not that grace, a manifestation whereof is
given to every man to profit withal. This most certain
doctrine being then received, that there is an evangelical
and saving light and grace in all, the universality of the
love and mercy of God towards mankind, both in the
death of his beloved Son the Lord Jesus Christ, and in the
manifestation of the light in the heart, is established and
confirmed, against all the objections of such as deny it.
Heb ii. 9.    Therefore Christ hath tasted death for every man; not

only for all kinds of men, as some vainly talk, but for every man of all kinds; the benefit of whose offering is not only extended to such who have the distinct outward knowledge of his death and sufferings, as the same is declared in the scriptures, but even unto those who are necessarily excluded from the benefit of this knowledge by some inevitable accident; which knowledge we willingly confess to be very profitable and comfortable, but not absolutely needful unto such from whom God himself hath withheld it; yet they may be made partakers of the mystery of his death, though ignorant of the history, if they suffer his seed and light, enlightening their hearts, to take place; in which light communion with the Father and the Son is enjoyed; so as of wicked men to become holy, and lovers of that power, by whose inward and secret touches they feel themselves turned from the evil to the good, and learn to do to others as they would be done by, in which Christ himself affirms all to be included. As they have then falsely and erroneously taught, who have denied Christ to have died for all men: so neither have they sufficiently taught the truth, who, affirming him to have died for all, have added the absolute necessity of the outward knowledge thereof, in order to obtain its saving effect. Among whom the Remonstrants of Holland have been chiefly wanting, and many other asserters of universal redemption, in that they have not placed the extent of this salvation in that divine and evangelical principle of light and life wherewith Christ hath enlightened every man that cometh into the world, which is excellently and evidently held forth in these scriptures, Gen. vi. 3; Deut. xxx. 14; John i. 7, 8, 9, 16; Rom. x. 8; Titus, ii. 11.

HITHERTO we have considered man's fallen, lost, corrupted, and degenerated condition. Now it is fit to enquire how, and by what means he may come to be freed out of this miserable and depraved condition, which in these two propositions is declared and demonstrated; which

I thought meet to place together because of their affinity, the one being as it were an explanation of the other.

Absolute reproba-
tion, that
horrible and
blasphem-
ous doc-
rine, de-
cribed.
As for that doctrine which these propositions chiefly strike at, to wit, absolute reprobation, according to which some are not afraid to assert, That God, by an eternal and immutable decree, hath predestinated to eternal damnation the far greater part of mankind, not considered as made, much less as fallen, without any respect to their disobedience or sin, but only for the demonstrating of the glory of his justice ; and that for the bringing this about, he hath appointed these miserable souls necessarily to walk in their wicked ways, that so his justice may lay hold on them : and that God doth therefore not only suffer them to be liable to this misery in many parts of the world, by withholding from them the preaching of the gospel and the knowledge of Christ, but even in those places where the gospel is preached, and salvation by Christ is offered ; whom though he publicly invite them, yet he justly condemns for disobedience, albeit he hath withheld from them all grace by which they could have laid hold of the gospel, viz. : Because he hath, by a secret will unknown to all men, ordained and decreed (without any respect had to their disobedience or sin) that they shall not obey, and that the offer of the gospel shall never prove effectual for their salvation, but only serve to aggravate and occasion their greater condemnation.

I say, as to this horrible and blasphemous doctrine, our cause is common with many others, who have both wisely and learnedly, according to scripture, reason, and antiquity, refuted it. Seeing then that so much is said already and so well against this doctrine, that little can be superadded, except what hath been said already, I shall be short in this respect ; yet, because it lies so in opposition to my way, I cannot let it altogether pass.

§ I. First, We may safely call this doctrine a novelty, seeing the first four hundred years after Christ there is no mention made of it : for as it is contrary to the scripture's testimony, and to the tenor of the gospel, so all the ancient writers, teachers, and doctors of the church pass it over with a profound silence. The first foundations of it were laid in the later writings of Augustine, who, in his heat against Pelagius, let fall some expressions which some have unhappily gleaned up, to the establishing of this error; thereby contradicting the truth, and sufficiently gainsaying many others, and many more and frequent expressions of the same Augustine. Afterwards was this doctrine fomented by Dominicus a friar, and the monks of his order; and at last unhappily taken up by John Calvin, otherwise a man in divers respects to be commended, to the great staining of his reputation, and defamation both of the Protestant and Christian religion; which though it received the decrees of the synod of Dort for its confirmation, hath since lost ground, and begins to be exploded by most men of learning and piety in all Protestant churches. However, we should not oppugn it for the silence of the ancients, paucity of its asserters, or for the learnedness of its opposers, if we did observe it to have any real bottom in the writings or sayings of Christ and the apostles, and that it were not highly injurious to God himself, to Jesus Christ our Mediator and Redeemer, and to the power, virtue, nobility, and excellency of his blessed gospel, and lastly unto all mankind.

§ II. First, It is highly injurious to God, because it makes him the author of sin, which of all things is most contrary to his nature. I confess the asserters of this principle deny this consequence; but that is but a mere illusion, seeing it so naturally follows from their doctrine, and is equally ridiculous, as if a man should pertinaciously deny that one and two make three. For if God has decreed that the reprobated ones shall perish, without all respect to their evil deeds, but only of his own pleasure, and if he hath also decreed long before they were in being, or in a capacity to do good or evil, that they should walk in those wicked ways, by which, as by a secondary means, they are led to that end; who, I pray, is the first author and cause thereof but God, who so willed and decreed?

*The rise of it.*

*1. Highly injurious to God in making him the author of sin.*

10 *

This is as natural a consequence as can be: and therefore, although many of the preachers of this doctrine have sought out various, strange, strained, and intricate distinctions to defend their opinion, and avoid this horrid consequence; yet some, and that of the most eminent of them, have been so plain in the matter, as they have put it beyond all doubt. Of which I shall instance a few among many passages. *"I say, That by the ordination and will of God, Adam fell. God would have man to fall. Man is blinded by the will and commandment of God. We refer the causes of hardening us to God. The highest or remote cause of hardening is the will of God. It followeth that the hidden counsel of God is the cause of hardening." These are Calvin's expressions. †"God," saith Beza, "hath predestinated not only unto damnation, but also unto the causes of it, whomsoever he saw meet." ‡"The decree of God cannot be excluded from the causes of corruption." §"It is certain," saith Zanchius, "that God is the first cause of obduration. Reprobates are held so fast under God's almighty decree, that they cannot but sin and perish." ‖"It is the opinion," saith Paræus, "of our doctors, That God did inevitably decree the temptation and fall of man. The creature sinneth indeed necessarily, by the most just judgment of God. Our men do most rightly affirm, that the fall of man was necessary and inevitable, by accident, because of God's decree." ¶"God," saith Martyr, "doth incline and force the wills of wicked men into great sins." **"God," saith Zuinglius, "moveth the robber to kill. He killeth, God forcing him thereunto. But thou wilt say, he is forced to sin; I permit truly that he is forced." ††"Reprobate persons," saith Piscator, "are absolutely ordained to this two-fold end, to undergo everlasting punishment, and necessarily to sin; and therefore to sin, that they may be justly punished."

If these sayings do not plainly and evidently import that God is the author of sin, we must not then seek these men's opinions from their words, but some way else. It seems as if they had assumed to themselves that monstrous and

*Calvin in cap.iii.Gen. Id. 1. Inst. c. 18. s. 1. Id. lib. de Præd. Id. lib. de Provid. Id. inst. c. 23. s. 1.

† Beza lib. de Præd.

‡ Id. de Præd. ad. Art. 1.
§ Zanch. de Excæcat. q. 5. Id. lib. 5. de Nat. Dei. cap. 2. de præd.
‖ Paræus, lib. 3. de Amis. gratiæ, c. 2. Id. c. 1.

¶ Martyr in Rom.

** Zuing. lib.de Prov. c. 5.

†† Resp. ad Vorst. pa. I. p 120.

twofold will they feign of God; one by which they declare their minds openly, and another more secret and hidden, which is quite contrary to the other. Nor doth it at all help them, to say that man sins willingly, since that willingness, proclivity, and propensity to evil is, according to their judgment, so necessarily imposed upon him, that he cannot but be willing, because God hath willed and decreed him to be so. Which shift is just as if I should take a child incapable to resist me, and throw it down from a great precipice; the weight of the child's body indeed makes it go readily down, and the violence of the fall upon some rock or stone beats out its brains and kills it. Now then I pray, though the body of the child goes willingly down, for I suppose it, as to its mind, incapable of any will, and the weight of its body, and not any immediate stroke of my hand, who perhaps am at a great distance, makes it die, whether is the child or I the proper cause of its death? Let any man of reason judge, if God's part be not, with them, as great, yea, more immediate, in the sins of men, as by the testimonies above brought doth appear; whether doth not this make him not only the author of sin, but more unjust than the unjustest of men?

§ III. Secondly, This doctrine is injurious to God, because it makes him delight in the death of sinners, yea, and to will many to die in their sins, contrary to these scriptures, Ezek. xxxiii. 11; 1 Tim. ii. 4; 2 Pet. iii. 9. For if he hath created men only for this very end, that he might show forth his justice and power in them, as these men affirm, and for effecting thereof hath not only withheld from them the means of doing good, but also predestinated the evil, that they might fall into it; and that he inclines and forces them into great sins; certainly he must necessarily delight in their death, and will them to die; seeing against his own will he neither doth, nor can do any thing. *2. It makes God delight in the death of a sinner.*

§ IV. Thirdly, It is highly injurious to Christ our mediator, and to the efficacy and excellency of his gospel; for it renders his mediation ineffectual, as if he had not by *3 It renders Christ's mediation ineffectual.*

his sufferings thoroughly broken down the middle wall, nor yet removed the wrath of God, nor purchased the love of God towards all mankind, if it was afore decreed that it should be of no service to the far greater part of mankind. It is to no purpose to allege, that the death of Christ was of efficacy enough to have saved all mankind, if in effect its virtue be not so far extended as to put all mankind into a capacity of salvation.

4. It makes the gospel a mock.

Fourthly, It makes the preaching of the gospel a mere mock and illusion, if many of these, to whom it is preached, be by an irrevocable decree excluded from being benefited by it; it wholly makes useless the preaching of faith and repentance, and the whole tenor of the gospel promises and threatenings, as being all relative to a former decree and means before appointed to such; which, because they cannot fail, man needs do nothing but wait for that irresistible juncture, which will come, though it be but at the last hour of his life, if he be in the decree of election; and be his diligence and waiting what it can, he shall never attain it, if he belong to the decree of reprobation.

5. It makes the coming of Christ an act of wrath.

Fifthly, It makes the coming of Christ, and his propitiatory sacrifice, which the scripture affirms to have been the fruit of God's love to the world, and transacted for the sins and salvation of all men, to have been rather a testimony of God's wrath to the world, and one of the greatest judgments, and severest acts of God's indignation towards mankind, it being only ordained to save a very few, and for the hardening, and augmenting the condemnation of the far greater number of men, because they believe not truly in it; the cause of which unbelief again, as the divines [so called] above assert, is the hidden counsel of God: certainly the coming of Christ was never to them a testimony of God's love, but rather of his implacable wrath: and if the world may be taken for the far greater number of such as live in it, God never loved the world, according to this doctrine, but rather hated it greatly, in sending his Son to be crucified in it.

§ V. Sixthly, This doctrine is highly injurious to mankind; for it renders them in a far worse condition than the
devils in hell. For these were some time in a capacity to
have stood, and do suffer only for their own guilt; whereas many millions of men are for ever tormented, according
to them, for Adam's sin, which they neither knew of, nor
ever were accessary to. It renders them worse than the
beasts of the field, of whom the master requires no more
than they are able to perform; and if they be killed, death
to them is the end of sorrow; whereas man is for ever tormented for not doing that which he never was able to do.
It puts him into a far worse condition than Pharaoh put
the Israelites; for though he withheld straw from them,
yet by much labour and pains they could have gotten it:
but from men they make God to withhold all means of
salvation, so that they can by no means attain it; yea, they
place mankind in that condition which the poets feign of
Tantalus, who, oppressed with thirst, stands in water up to
the chin, yet can by no means reach it with his tongue;
and being tormented with hunger, hath fruits hanging at
his very lips, yet so as he can never lay hold on them with
his teeth; and these things are so near him, not to nourish
him, but to torment him. So do these men: they make
the outward creation of the works of Providence, the
smitings of conscience, sufficient to convince the heathen
of sin, and so to condemn and judge them: but not at all
to help them to salvation. They make the preaching of
the gospel, the offer of salvation by Christ, the use of the
sacraments, of prayer, and good works, sufficient to condemn those they account reprobates within the church,
serving only to inform them to beget a seeming faith and
vain hope; yet because of a secret impotency, which they
had from their infancy, all these are wholly ineffectual to
bring them the least step towards salvation; and do only
contribute to render their condemnation the greater, and
their torments the more violent and intolerable.

Having thus briefly removed this false doctrine which
stood in my way, because they that are desirous may see it

6. It ren-
ders man-
kind in a
worse con-
dition than
the de-
vils—

—Than the
Israelites
under Pha-
raoh.

Tantalus's
condition.

both learnedly and piously refuted by many others, I come
to the matter of our proposition, which is, That "God out
of his infinite love, who delighteth not in the death of a
sinner, but that all should live and be saved, hath sent his
only begotten Son into the world, that whosoever believeth
in him might be saved;" which also is again affirmed in the
sixth proposition, in these words, Christ then tasted death
for every man, of all kinds.   Such is the evidence of this
truth, delivered almost wholly in the express words of
scripture, that it will not need much probation.   Also, because our assertion herein is common with many others,
who have both earnestly and soundly, according to the
scripture, pleaded for this universal redemption, I shall be
the more brief in it, that I may come to that which may
seem more singularly and peculiarly ours.

*Christ tast-
ed death for
every man.*

§ VI.  This doctrine of universal redemption, or Christ's
dying for all men, is of itself so evident from the scripture
testimony, that there is scarce found any other article of
the Christian faith so frequently, so plainly, and so positively asserted.   It is that which maketh the preaching of
Christ to be truly termed the gospel, or an annunciation of
glad tidings to all.   Thus the angel declared the birth and
coming of Christ to the shepherds to be, Luke ii. 10, "Behold, I bring you good tidings of great joy, which shall be
to all people:" he saith not, to a few.  Now if this coming
of Christ had not brought a possibility of salvation to all,
it should rather have been accounted bad tidings of great
sorrow to most people; neither should the angel have had
reason to have sung, "Peace on earth, and good will towards men," if the greatest part of mankind had been
necessarily shut out from receiving any benefit by it.  How
should Christ have sent out his servants to "preach the
gospel to every creature," Mark xvi. 15, (a very comprehensive commission) that is, to every son and daughter of
mankind, without all exception?  He commands them to
preach salvation to all, repentance and remission of sins
to all; warning every one, and exhorting every one, as
Paul did, Col. i. 28.  Now how could they have preached

*Christ's re-
demption
universal,
contrary to
the doctrine
of absolute
reproba-
tion.*

the gospel to every man, as became the ministers of Jesus Christ, in much assurance, if salvation by that gospel had not been possible to all? What! if some of those had asked them, or should now ask any of these doctors, who deny the universality of Christ's death, and yet preach it to all promiscuously, Hath Christ died for me? How can they, with confidence, give a certain answer to this question? If they give a conditional answer, as their principle obligeth them to do, and say, If thou repent, Christ hath died for thee; doth not the same question still recur? Hath Christ died for me, so as to make repentance possible to me? To this they can answer nothing, unless they run in a circle; whereas the feet of those that bring the glad tidings of the gospel of peace are said to be beautiful, for that they preach the common salvation, repentance unto all; offering a door of mercy and hope to all, through Jesus Christ, who gave himself a ransom for all. The gospel invites all; and certainly by the gospel Christ intended not to deceive and delude the greater part of mankind, when he invites and crieth, saying; "Come unto me, all ye that labour and are heavy laden, and I will give you rest." If all then ought to seek after him, and to look for salvation by him, he must needs have made salvation possible to all; for who is bound to seek after that which is impossible? Certainly it were a mocking of men to bid them do so. And such as deny, that by the death of Christ salvation is made possible to all men, do most blasphemously make God mock the world, in giving his servants a commission to preach the gospel of salvation unto all, while he hath before decreed that it shall not be possible for them to receive it. Would not this make the Lord to send forth his servants with a lie in their mouth, (which were blasphemous to think) commanding them to bid all and every one believe that Christ died for them, and had purchased life and salvation? whereas it is no such thing, according to the forementioned doctrine. But seeing Christ, after he arose and perfected the work of our redemption, gave a commission to preach repentance, remis-

The gospel is preached to every man.

The absurdity of that doctrine of absolute reprobation.

sion of sins, and salvation to all, it is manifest that he died
for all. For, He that hath commissionated his servants thus
to preach, is a God of truth, and no mocker of poor mankind; neither doth he require of any man that which is
simply impossible for him to do: for that no man is bound
to do that which is impossible, is a principle of truth engraven in every man's mind. And seeing he is both a most
righteous and merciful God, it cannot at all stand, either
with his justice or mercy, to bid such men repent or believe, to whom it is impossible.

§ VII. Moreover, if we regard the testimony of the scripture in this matter, where there is not one scripture, that I
know of, which affirmeth Christ not to die for all, there are
divers that positively and expressly assert, He did; as 1

*To pray for all; for Christ died for all—* Tim. ii. 1, 3, 4, 6: "I exhort therefore, that first of all,
supplications, prayers, intercessions, and giving of thanks,
be made for all men," &c. "For this is good and acceptable in the sight of God our Saviour, who will have all
men to be saved, and to come to the knowledge of the
truth; who gave himself a ransom for all, to be testified in
due time." Except we will have the apostle here to assert
quite another thing than he intended, there can be nothing
more plain to confirm what we have asserted. And this
scripture doth well answer to that manner of arguing which
we have hitherto used: for, first, the apostle here recom-
mends them to pray for all men; and to obviate such an
objection, as if he had said with our adversaries, Christ
prayed not for the world, neither willeth he us to pray for
all; because he willeth not that all should be saved, but
hath ordained many to be damned, that he might show forth
his justice in them; he obviates, I say, such an objection,

*— And will have all men to be saved.* telling them, that "it is good and acceptable in the sight
of God, who will have all men to be saved." I desire to
know what can be more expressly affirmed? or can any two
propositions be stated in terms more contradictory than
these two? God willeth not some to be saved; and, God
willeth all men to be saved, or, God will have no man perish. If we believe the last, as the apostle hath affirmed,

the first must be destroyed; seeing of contradictory propositions, the one being admitted, the other is destroyed.
Whence, to conclude, he gives us a reason of his willingness that all men should be saved, in these words, " Who
gave himself a ransom for all ;" as if he would have said,
Since Christ died for all, since he gave himself a ransom
for all, therefore he will have all men to be saved. This
Christ himself gives as a reason of God's love to the world,
in these words, John iii. 16 : " God so loved the world,
that he gave his only begotten Son, that whosoever believeth in him should not perish, but have everlasting life ;"
compared with 1 John iv. 9. This [whosoever] is an in-
definite term, from which no man is excluded. From all
which then I thus argue :

For whomsoever it is lawful to pray, to them salvation **Arg. 1.**
is possible :

But it is lawful to pray for every individual man in the
whole world :

Therefore salvation is possible unto them.

I prove the major proposition thus ;

No man is bound to pray for that which is impossible to **Arg. 2.**
be attained :

But every man is bound and commanded to pray for all
men :

Therefore it is not impossible to be obtained.

I prove also this proposition further, thus ;

No man is bound to pray, but in faith :
                                                 **Arg. 3**

But he that prayeth for that, which he judges simply impossible to be obtained, cannot pray in faith :

Therefore, &c.

Again,

That which God willeth is not impossible :
                                                 **Arg. 4**

But God willeth all men to be saved :

Therefore it is not impossible.

And lastly ;

Those for whom our Saviour gave himself a ransom, to **Arg. 5**
such salvation is possible :

But our Saviour gave himself a ransom for all :

11                                       Q

Therefore salvation is possible unto them.

**Proof 1.**      § VIII.. This is very positively affirmed, Heb. ii. 9, in these words, " But we see Jesus, who was made a little lower than the angels, for the suffering of death crowned with glory and honour, that he by the grace of God should taste death for every man." He that will but open his eyes, may see this truth here asserted : if he " tasted death for every man," then certainly there is no man for whom he did not taste death ; then there is no man who may not be made a sharer of the benefit of it ; for he came not " to condemn the world, but that the world through him might be saved," John iii. 17. " He came not to judge the world, but to save the world," John xii. 47. Whereas, according to the doctrine of our adversaries, he rather came to condemn the world, and judge it ; and not that it might be saved by him, or to save it. For if he never came to bring salvation to the greater part of mankind, but that his coming, though it could never do them good, yet shall augment their condemnation ; from thence it necessarily follows, that he came not of intention to save, but to judge and condemn the greater part of the world, contrary to his own express testimony ; and as the apostle Paul, in the words above cited, doth assert affirmatively, That God willeth the salvation of all, so doth the apostle Peter assert negatively, That he willeth not the perishing of any, 2 Pet. iii. 9. " The Lord is not slack concerning his promise, as some men count slackness ; but is long suffering to us-ward, not willing that any should perish, but that all should come to repentance." And this is correspondent to that of the prophet Ezekiel, xxxiii. 11 : " As I live, saith the Lord, I have no pleasure in the death of the wicked ; but that the wicked turn from his way and live." If it be safe to believe God, and trust in him, we must not think that he intends to cheat us by all these expressions through his servants, but that he was in good earnest. And that this will and desire of his hath not taken effect, the blame is on our parts, as shall be after spoken of ; which could not be, if we never were in any capacity of salva-

*Our adver- saries' false doctrine of a great part of mankind being pre- ordained for damnation. refuted.*

**Proof 2.**

tion, or that Christ had never died for us, but left us under an impossibility of salvation. What mean all those earnest invitations, all those serious expostulations, all those regretting contemplations, wherewith the holy scriptures are full? As, Why will ye die, O house of Israel! Why will ye not come unto me, that ye might have life? I have waited to be gracious unto you: I have sought to gather you: I have knocked at the door of your hearts: Is not your destruction of yourselves? I have called all the day long. If men who are so invited be under no capacity of being saved, if salvation be impossible unto them, shall we suppose God in this to be no other but like the author of a romance, or master of a comedy, who amuses and raises the various affections and passions of his spectators by divers and strange accidents; sometimes leading them into hope, and sometimes into despair; all those actions, in effect, being but a mere illusion, while he hath appointed what the conclusion of all shall be?

Thirdly, This doctrine is abundantly confirmed by that of the apostle, 1 John ii. 1, 2: "And if any man sin, we have an advocate with the Father, Jesus Christ the righteous. And he is the propitiation for our sins; and not for ours only, but also for the sins of the whole world." The way which our adversaries take to evite this testimony, is most foolish and ridiculous: the world here, say they, is the world of believers: for this commentary we have nothing but their own assertion, and so while it manifestly destroys the text, may be justly rejected. For, first, let them show me, if they can, in all the scripture, where the whole world is taken for believers only; I shall show them where it is many times taken for the quite contrary; as, The world knows me not: The world receives me not: I am not of this world: besides all these scriptures, Psalm xvii. 14; Isai. xiii. 11; Mat. xviii. 7; John vii. 7, and viii. 26, and xii. 19, and xiv. 17, and xv. 18, 19, and xvii. 14, and xviii. 20; 1 Cor. i. 21, and ii. 12, and vi. 2; Gal. vi. 14; James i. 27; 2 Pet. ii. 20; 1 John ii. 15, and iii. 1, and iv. 4, 5, and many more. Secondly,

*Proof 3.*

*Adversaries' comment on the words, "the whole world."*

The apostle in this very place contra-distinguisheth ne
world from the saints thus; "And not for ours only, but
for the sins of the whole world :" What means the apostle
by ours here? Is not that the sins of believers? Was
not he one of those believers? And was not this an universal epistle, written to all the saints that then were? So
that according to these men's comment, there should be a
very unnecessary and foolish redundancy in the apostle's
words; as if he had said, He is a propitiation not only for
the sins of all believers, but for the sins of all believers:
Is not this to make the apostle's words void of good sense?
Let them show us wherever there is such a manner of speaking in all the scripture, where any of the penmen first name
the believers *in concreto* with themselves, and then contradis-
tinguish them from some other whole world of believers?
That whole world if it be of believers, must not be the
world we live in. But we need no better interpreter for
the apostle than himself, who uses the very same expression
and phrase in the same epistle, ch. v. 19, saying, "We
know that we are of God, and the whole world lieth in
wickedness." There cannot be found in all the scripture
two places which run more parallel; seeing in both, the
same apostle, in the same epistle to the same persons, con-
tradistinguisheth himself, and the saints to whom he writes,
from the whole world; which, according to these men's
commentary, ought to be understood of believers: as if
John had said, We know particular believers are of God;
but the whole world of believers lieth in wickedness. What
absurd wresting of scripture were this? And yet it may
be as well pleaded for as the other; for they differ not at
all. Seeing then that the apostle John tells us plainly, That
Christ not only died for him, and for the saints and members of the church of God, to whom he wrote, but for the
whole world, let us then hold it for a certain and undoubted
truth, notwithstanding the cavils of such as oppose.

This might also be proved from many more scripture
testimonies, if it were at this season needful. All the
fathers, so called, and doctors of the church, for the first

four centuries, preached this doctrine; according to which
they boldly held forth the gospel of Christ, and efficacy of
his death; inviting and entreating the heathen to come
and be partakers of the benefits of it, showing them how
there was a door opened for them all to be saved through
Jesus Christ; not telling them that God had predestinated
any of them to damnation, or had made salvation impossible to them, by withholding power and grace, necessary to
believe, from them. But of many of their sayings, which
might be alleged, I shall only instance a few.

*The hea-
then in-
vited to sal-
vation;
none pre-
destinated
to damna-
tion.*

Augustine on the xcvth Psalm saith, "The blood of
Christ is of so great worth, that it is of no less value than
the whole world."

*Proof 4.
The testi-
monies of
the doctors
and fathers
of the first
church, that
Christ died
for all*

Prosper ad Gall. c. 9: "The redeemer of the world
gave his blood for the world, and the world would not be
redeemed, because the darkness did not receive the light.
He that saith, the Saviour was not crucified for the redemption of the whole world, looks not to the virtue of
the sacrament, but to the part of infidels; since the blood
of our Lord Jesus Christ is the price of the whole world;
from which redemption they are strangers, who either de-
lighting in their captivity would not be redeemed, or after
they were redeemed returned to the same servitude."

The same Prosper, in his answer to Vincentius's first
objection: "Seeing therefore because of one common nature and cause in truth, undertaken by our Lord, all are
rightly said to be redeemed, and nevertheless all are not
brought out of captivity; the property of redemption without doubt belongeth to those from whom the prince of this
world is shut out, and now are not vessels of the devil, but
members of Christ; whose death was so bestowed upon
mankind, that it belonged to the redemption of such who
were not to be regenerated. But so, that that which was
done by the example of one for all, might, by a singular
mystery, be celebrated in every one. For the cup of immortality, which is made up of our infirmity and the divine
power, hath indeed that in it which may profit all; b it if
it be not drunk, it doth not heal."

11 *

The author *de vocat. gentium*, lib. 11. cap. 6 : " There is no cause to doubt but that our Lord Jesus Christ died for sinners and wicked men. And if there can be any found, who may be said not to be of this number, Christ hath not died for all; he made himself a redeemer for the whole world."

Chrysostom on John i. : " If he enlightens every man coming into the world, how comes it that so many men remain without light? For all do not so much as acknowledge Christ. How then doth he enlighten every man? He illuminates indeed so far as in him is; but if any of their own accord, closing the eyes of their mind, will not

The cause they remain in darkness.

direct their eyes unto the beams of this light, the cause that they remain in darkness is not from the nature of the light, but through their own malignity, who willingly have rendered themselves unworthy of so great a gift. But why believed they not? Because they would not: Christ did his part."

The Arelatensian synod, held about the year 490, " Pronounced him accursed,. who should say that Christ hath not died for all, or that he would not have all men to be saved."

Ambrose on Psalm cxviii. Serm. 8 : " The mystical Sun of Righteousness is arisen to all; he came to all; he suffered for all; and rose again for all: and therefore he suffered, that he might take away the sin of the world. But if any one believe not in Christ, he robs himself of this general benefit, even as if one by closing the windows should

The sunbeams shut out, heat not.

hold out the sun-beams. The sun is not therefore not arisen to all, because such a one hath so robbed himself of its heat: but the sun keeps its prerogative; it is such a one's imprudence that he shuts himself out from the common benefit of the light."

The same, in his 11th book of Cain and Abel, cap. 13, saith : " Therefore he brought unto all the means of health, that whosoever should perish, may ascribe to himself the causes of his death, who would not be cured when he had the remedy by which he might have escaped."

§ IX. Seeing then that this doctrine of the universality of Christ's death is so certain and agreeable to the scripture testimony, and to the sense of the purest antiquity, it may be wondered how so many, some whereof have been esteemed not only learned, but also pious, have been capable to fall into so gross and strange an error. But the cause of this doth evidently appear, in that the way and method by which the virtue and efficacy of his death is communicated to all men, hath not been rightly understood, or indeed hath been erroneously taught. The Pelagians, ascribing all to man's will and nature, denied man to have any seed of sin conveyed to him from Adam. And the Semi-Pelagians, making grace as a gift following upon man's merit, or right improving of his nature, according to their known principle, *Facienti quod in se est, Deus non denegat gratiam.* *Pelagian errors.*

This gave Augustine, Prosper, and some others occasion, labouring, in opposition to these opinions, to magnify the grace of God, and paint out the corruption of man's nature, as the proverb is of those that seek to make straight a crooked stick, to incline to the other extreme. So also the reformers, Luther and others, finding among other errors the strange expressions used by some of the Popish scholastics concerning free will, and how much the tendency of their principles is to exalt man's nature and lessen God's grace, having all those sayings of Augustine and others for a pattern, through the like mistake ran upon the same extreme: though afterwards the Lutherans, seeing how far Calvin and his followers drove this matter, who, as a man of subtle and profound judgment, foreseeing where it would land, resolved above board to assert that God had decreed the means as well as the end, and therefore had ordained men to sin, and excites them thereto, which he labours earnestly to defend, and that there was no avoiding the making of God the author of sin, thereby received occasion to discern the falsity of this doctrine, and disclaimed it, as appears by the later writings of Melancthon, and the Mompelgartensian conference, where *Extremes fallen into by some, making God the author of sin*

Lucas Osiander, one of the collocutors, terms it impious, calls it a making God the author of sin, and an horrid and horrible blasphemy. Yet because none of those who have asserted this universal redemption since the reformation have given a clear, distinct, and satisfactory testimony how it is communicated to all, and so have fallen short of fully declaring the perfection of the gospel dispensation, others have been thereby the more strengthened in their errors; which I shall illustrate by one singular example.

The Arminians, and other assertors of universal grace, use this as a chief argument:

That which every man is bound to believe, is true:

But every man is bound to believe that Christ died for him:

Therefore, &c.

Of this argument the other party deny the assumption, saying: That they who never heard of Christ, are not obliged to believe in him; and seeing the Remonstrants (as they are commonly called) do generally themselves acknowledge, that without the outward knowledge of Christ there is no salvation, that gives the other party yet a stronger argument for their precise decree of reprobation. For, say they, seeing we all see really, and in effect, that God hath withheld from many generations, and yet from many nations, that knowledge which is absolutely needful to salvation, and so hath rendered it simply impossible unto them; why may he not as well withhold the grace necessary to make a saving application of that knowledge, where it is preached? For there is no ground to say, That this were injustice in God, or partiality, more than his leaving those others in utter ignorance; the one being but a withholding grace to apprehend the object of faith, the other a withdrawing the object itself. For answer to this, they are forced to draw a conclusion from their former hypothesis of Christ's dying for all, and God's mercy and justice, saying, That if these heathen, who live in these remote places, where the outward knowledge of Christ is not, did improve that common knowledge they have, to whom the outward creation is for an object of faith, by which they may gather that there is a God, then the Lord would, by some providence, either send an angel to tell them of Christ, or convey the scriptures to them, or bring them some way to an opportunity to meet with such as might inform them. Which, as it gives always too much to the power and strength of man's will and nature, and savours a little of Socinianism and Pelagianism, or at least of Semi-Pelagianism, so, since it is only built upon probable conjectures, neither hath it evidence enough to convince any strongly tainted with the other doctrine; nor yet doth it make the equity and wonderful harmony of God's mercy and justice towards all so manifest to the understanding. So that I have often observed, that these assertors of universal grace did far more pithily and strongly overturn the false doctrine of their adversaries, than they did establish and confirm the truth and certainty of their own. And though they have proof sufficient from the holy scriptures to confirm the universality of Christ's death, and that none are precisely, by any irrevocable decree, excluded from salvation, yet I find when they are pressed in the respects above mentioned, to show how God hath so far equally extended the capacity to partake of the benefit of Christ's death unto all, as to communicate unto them a sufficient way of so doing, they are somewhat in a strait, and are put more to give us their conjectures from the certainty of the former presupposed truth; to wit, that because Christ hath certainly died for all, and God hath not rendered salvation impossible to any, therefore there must be some way or other by which they may be saved; which must be by improving some common grace, or by gathering from the works of creation and providence; than by really demonstrating, by convincing and spiritual arguments, what that way is.

§ X. It falls out then, that as darkness, and the great apostasy, came not upon the Christian world all at once, but by several degrees, one thing making way for another; until that thick and gross vail came to be overspread, where-

*None, by an irrevocable decree excluded from salvation.*

with the nations were so blindly covered, from the seventh
and eighth, until the sixteenth century; even as the darkness of the night comes not upon the outward creation at
once, but by degrees, according as the sun declines in
each horizon; so neither did that full and clear light and
knowledge of the glorious dispensation of the gospel of
Christ appear all at once; the work of the first witnesses
being more to testify against and discover the abuses of
the apostasy, than to establish the truth in purity. He that
comes to build a new city, must first remove the old rubbish, before he can see to lay a new foundation; and he
that comes to an house greatly polluted and full of dirt,
will first sweep away and remove the filth, before he put up
his own good and new furniture. The dawning of the day
dispels the darkness, and makes us see the things that are
most conspicuous: but the distinct discovering and discerning of things, so as to make a certain and perfect observation, is reserved for the arising of the sun, and its
shining in full brightness. And we can, from a certain
experience, boldly affirm, that the not waiting for this, but
building among, yea, and with, the old Popish rubbish, and
setting up before a full purgation, hath been to most Protestants the foundation of many a mistake, and an occasion

The more full discovery of the gospel reserved to this our age.

of unspeakable hurt. Therefore the Lord God, who as he
seeth meet doth communicate and make known to man the
more full, evident, and perfect knowledge of his everlasting
truth, hath been pleased to reserve the more full discovery
of this glorious and evangelical dispensation to this our
age; albeit divers testimonies have thereunto been borne
by some noted men in several ages, as shall hereafter appear. And for the greater augmentation of the glory of
his grace, that no man might have whereof to boast, he
hath raised up a few despicable and illiterate men, and for
the most part mechanics, to be the dispensers of it; by
which gospel all the scruples, doubts, hesitations and objections above mentioned are easily and evidently answered,
and the justice as well as mercy of God, according to their
divine and heavenly harmony, are exhibited, established,

and confirmed. According to which certain light and gospel, as the knowledge thereof has been manifested to us by the revelation of Jesus Christ in us, fortified by our own sensible experience, and sealed by the testimony of the Spirit in our hearts, we can confidently affirm, and clearly evince, according to the testimony of the holy scriptures, the following points :

§ XI. First, That God, who out of his infinite love sent **Prop. I** his Son, the Lord Jesus Christ, into the world, who tasted death for every man, hath given to every man, whether **A day of** Jew or Gentile, Turk or Scythian, Indian or Barbarian, of **visitation to all.** whatsoever nation, country, or place, a certain day or time of visitation ; during which day or time it is possible for them to be saved, and to partake of the fruit of Christ's death.

Secondly, That for this end God hath communicated **Prop. II.** and given unto every man a measure of the light of his **A measure** own Son, a measure of grace, or a measure of the Spirit, **of light in all.** which the scripture expresses by several names, as sometimes of the seed of the kingdom, Mat. xiii. 18, 19 ; the Light that makes all things manifest, Eph. v. 13 ; the Word of God, Rom. x. 17 ; or manifestation of the Spirit given to profit withal, 1 Cor. xii. 7 ; a talent, Mat. xxv. 15 ; a little leaven, Mat. xiii. 33 ; the gospel preached in every creature, Col. i. 23.

Thirdly, That God, in and by this Light and Seed, in- **Prop. III.** vites, calls, exhorts, and strives with every man, in order to save him ; which, as it is received and not resisted, **God's sal-** works the salvation of all, even of those who are ignorant **vation wrought by** of the death and sufferings of Christ, and of Adam's fall, **the light in all.** both by bringing them to a sense of their own misery, and to be sharers in the sufferings of Christ inwardly, and by making them partakers of his resurrection, in becoming holy, pure, and righteous, and recovered out of their sins. By which also are saved they that have the knowledge of Christ outwardly, in that it opens their understanding rightly to use and apply the things delivered in the scriptures, and to receive the saving use of them : but that this may be resisted and rejected in both, in which then God is said to be resisted and pressed down, and Christ to be again crucified, and put to open shame in and among men. And to those who thus resist and refuse him, he becomes their condemnation.

**Conseq. 1.** First, then, According to this doctrine the mercy of God is excellently well exhibited, in that none are necessarily shut out from salvation; and his justice is demonstrated, in that he condemns none but such to whom he really made offer of salvation, affording them the means sufficient thereunto.

**Conseq. 2.** Secondly, This doctrine, if well weighed, will be found to be the foundation of Christianity, salvation, and assurance.

**Conseq. 3.** Thirdly, It agrees and answers with the whole tenor of the gospel promises and threats, and with the nature of the ministry of Christ; according to which, the gospel, salvation, and repentance are commanded to be preached to every creature, without respect of nations, kindred, families, or tongues.

**Conseq. 4.** Fourthly, It magnifies and commends the merits and death of Christ, in that it not only accounts them sufficient to save all, but declares them to be brought so nigh unto all, as thereby to be put into the nearest capacity of salvation.

**Conseq. 5.** Fifthly, It exalts above all the grace of God, to which it attributeth all good, even the least and smallest actions that are so; ascribing thereunto not only the first beginnings and motions of good, but also the whole conversion and salvation of the soul.

**Conseq. 6.** Sixthly, It contradicts, overturns, and enervates, the false doctrine of the Pelagians, Semi-Pelagians, Socinians, and others, who exalt the light of nature, the liberty of man's will, in that it wholly excludes the natural man from having any place or portion in his own salvation, by any acting, moving, or working of his own, until he be first quickened, raised up, and actuated by God's Spirit.

**Conseq 7.** Seventhly, As it makes the whole salvation of man solely and alone to depend upon God, so it makes his condemnation wholly and in every respect to be of himself, in that he refused and resisted somewhat that from God wrestled and strove in his heart, and forces him to acknowledge God's just judgment in rejecting and forsaking of him.

Eighthly, It takes away all ground of despair, in that it gives every one cause of hope and certain assurance that they may be saved; neither doth feed any in security, in that none are certain how soon their day may expire: and therefore it is a constant incitement and provocation, and lively encouragement to every man, to forsake evil, and close with that which is good. Conseq 8.

Ninthly, It wonderfully commends as well the certainty of the Christian religion among infidels, as it manifests its own verity to all, in that it is confirmed and established by the experience of all men; seeing there was never yet a man found in any place of the earth, however barbarous and wild, but hath acknowledged, that at some time or other, less or more, he hath found somewhat in his heart reproving him for some things evil which he hath done, threatening a certain horror if he continued in them, as also promising and communicating a certain peace and sweetness, as he has given way to it, and not resisted it. Conseq. 9

Tenthly, It wonderfully showeth the excellent wisdom of God, by which he hath made the means of salvation so universal and comprehensive, that it is not needful to recur to those miraculous and strange ways; seeing, according to this most true doctrine, the gospel reacheth all, of whatsoever condition, age, or nation. Conseq. 10

Eleventhly, It is really and effectively, though not in so many words, yet by deeds, established and confirmed by all the preachers, promulgators, and doctors of the Christian religion that ever were, or now are, even by those that otherways in their judgment oppose this doctrine, in that they all, wherever they have been or are, or whatsoever people, place, or country they come to, do preach to the people, and to every individual among them, that they may be saved; entreating and desiring them to believe in Christ, Conseq 11

who hath died for them. So that what they deny in the
general, they acknowledge of every particular; there being
no man to whom they do not preach in order to salvation,
telling him Jesus Christ calls and wills him to believe and
be saved; and that if he refuse, he shall therefore be condemned, and that his condemnation is of himself. Such
is the evidence and virtue of Truth, that it constrains its
adversaries even against their wills to plead for it.

**Conseq. 12.**  Lastly, According to this doctrine, the former argument
used by the Arminians, and evited by the Calvinists, concerning every man's being bound to believe that Christ
died for him, is, by altering the assumption, rendered invincible; thus,

That which every man is bound to believe, is true:

But every man is bound to believe that God is merciful
unto him:

Therefore, &c.

This assumption no man can deny, seeing his mercies
are said to be over all his works. And herein the scripture
every where declares the mercy of God to be, in that he invites and calls sinners to repentance, and hath opened a
way of salvation for them: so that though those men be
not bound to believe the history of Christ's death and passion who never came to know of it, yet they are bound to
believe that God will be merciful to them, if they follow
his ways; and that he is merciful unto them, in that he
reproves them for evil, and encourages them to good.

**Our adver-**
**saries' un-**
**merciful as-**
**sertion of**
**God.**
Neither ought any man to believe that God is unmerciful
to him, or that he hath from the beginning ordained him
to come into the world that he might be left to his own evil
inclinations, and so do wickedly as a means appointed by
God to bring him to eternal damnation; which, were it
true, as our adversaries affirm it to be of many thousands,
I see no reason why a man might not believe; for certainly
a man may believe the truth.

As it manifestly appears from the thing itself, that these
good and excellent consequences follow from the belief of
this doctrine, so from the proof of them it will yet more

evidently appear; to which before I come, it is requisite to speak somewhat concerning the state of the controversy, which will bring great light to the matter : for from the not right understanding of a matter under debate, sometimes both arguments on the one hand, and objections on the other, are brought, which do no way hit the case; and hereby also our sense and judgment therein will be more fully understood and opened.

§ XII. First, then, By this day and time of visitation, which we say God gives unto all, during which they may be saved, we do not understand the whole time of every man's life; though to some it may be extended even to the very hour of death, as we see in the example of the thief converted upon the cross; but such a season at least as sufficiently exonerateth God of every man's condemnation, which to some may be sooner, and to others later, according as the Lord in his wisdom sees meet. So that many men may outlive this day, after which there may be no possibility of salvation to them, and God justly suffers them to be hardened, as a just punishment of their unbelief, and even raises them up as instruments of wrath, and makes them a scourge one against another. Whence to men in this condition may be fitly applied those scriptures which are abused to prove that God incites men necessarily to sin. This is notably expressed by the apostle, Rom. i, from verse 17 to the end, but especially verse 28, "And even as they did not like to retain God in their knowledge, God gave them over to a reprobate mind, to do those things which are not convenient." That many may outlive this day of God's gracious visitation unto them, is shown by the example of Esau, Heb. xii. 16, 17, who sold his birthright; so he had it once, and was capable to have kept it; but afterwards, when he would have inherited the blessing, he was rejected. This appears also by Christ's weeping over Jerusalem, Luke xix. 42, saying, "If thou hadst known in this thy day the things that belong unto thy peace; but now they are hid from thine eyes." Which plainly imports a time when they might have known them,

QUES. 1. The stating of the question.

That many may outlive the day of God's visitation.

which now was removed from them, though they were yet
alive : but of this more shall be said hereafter.

Ques. 2.

§ XIII. Secondly, By this seed, grace, and word of
God, and light wherewith we say every one is enlightened,
and hath a measure of it, which strives with him in order
to save him, and which may, by the stubbornness and
wickedness of man's will, be quenched, bruised, wounded,
pressed down, slain and crucified, we understand not the
proper essence and nature of God precisely taken, which
is not divisible into parts and measures, as being a most
pure, simple being, void of all composition or division, and
therefore can neither be resisted, hurt, wounded, crucified,

The light,
what it is,
and its pro-
perties de-
scribed.

or slain by all the efforts and strength of men ; but we
understand a spiritual, heavenly, and invisible principle, in
which God, as Father, Son and Spirit, dwells ; a measure
of which divine and glorious life is in all men as a seed,
which of its own nature, draws, invites, and inclines to
God ; and this some call *vehiculum Dei*, or the spiritual
body of Christ, the flesh and blood of Christ, which came
down from heaven, of which all the saints do feed, and are
thereby nourished unto eternal life. And as every unrighteous action is witnessed against and reproved by this
light and seed, so by such actions it is hurt, wounded, and
slain, and flees from them even as the flesh of man flees
from that which is of a contrary nature to it. Now because
it is never separated from God nor Christ, but wherever it

1 Tim.
16

is, God and Christ are as wrapped up therein, therefore
and in that respect as it is resisted, God is said to be resisted ; and where it is borne down, God is said to be
pressed as a cart under sheaves, and Christ is said to be
slain and crucified. And on the contrary, as this seed is
received in the heart, and suffered to bring forth its natural
and proper effect, Christ comes to be formed and raised,
of which the scripture makes so much mention, calling it
the new man ; Christ within, the hope of glory. This
is that Christ within, which we are heard so much to speak
and declare of ; every where preaching him up, and exhorting people to believe in the light, and obey it, that

:hey may come to know Christ in them, to deliver them from all sin.

But by this, as we do not at all intend to equal ourselves to that holy man the Lord Jesus Christ, who was born of the virgin Mary, in whom all the fulness of the Godhead dwelt bodily, so neither do we destroy the reality of his present existence, as some have falsely calumniated us. For though we affirm that Christ dwells in us, yet not immediately, but mediately, as he is in that seed, which is in us; whereas he, to wit, the Eternal Word, which was with God, and was God, dwelt immediately in that holy man. He then is as the head, and we as the members; he the vine, and we the branches. Now as the soul of man dwells otherwise and in a far more immediate manner in the head and in the heart, than in the hands or legs; and as the sap, virtue, and life of the vine lodgeth far otherwise in the stock and root than in the branches, so God dwelleth otherwise in the man Jesus than in us. We also freely reject the heresy of Apollinarius, who denied him to have any soul, but said the body was only actuated by the Godhead. As also the error of Eutyches, who made the manhood to be wholly swallowed up of the Godhead. Wherefore, as we believe he was a true and real man, so we also believe that he continues so to be glorified in the heavens in soul and body, by whom God shall judge the world, in the great and general day of judgment.

*That the fulness of the Godhead dwells in Christ bodily, &c.*

§ XIV. Thirdly, We understand not this seed, light, or grace to be an accident, as most men ignorantly do, but a real spiritual substance, which the soul of man is capable to feel and apprehend; from which that real, spiritual, inward birth in believers arises called the new creature, the new man in the heart. This seems strange to carnal-minded men, because they are not acquainted with it; but we know it, and are sensible of it, by a true and certain experience. Though it be hard for man in his natural wisdom to comprehend it, until he come to feel it in himself; and if he should, holding it in the mere notion, it would avail him little; yet we are able to make it appear

*Ques. 3. That the light is a spiritual substance, which may be felt in the soul and apprehended.*

to be true, and that our faith concerning it is not withou:
a solic ground: for it is in and by this inward and substantial seed in our hearts as it comes to receive nourish
ment, and to have a birth or geniture in us, that we come
to have those spiritual senses r ised by which we are made
capable of tasting, smelling, seeing, and handling the
things of God: for a man cannot reach unto those things
by his natural spirit and senses, as is above declared.

Next, We know it to be a substance, because it subsists
:n the hearts of wicked men, even while they are in then
wickedness, as shall be hereafter proved more at large.
Now no accident can be in a subject without it give the
subject its own denomination; as where whiteness is in a

*The ae-
grees of its
operation in
the soul of
man.*

subject, there the subject is called white. So we distinguish betwixt holiness, as it is an accident, which deno-
minates man so, as the seed receives a place in him, and
betwixt this holy substantial seed, which many times lies in
man's heart as a naked grain in the stony ground. So also
as we may distinguish betwixt health and medicine; health
cannot be in a body without the body be called healthful,
because health is an accident; but medicine may be in a
body that is most unhealthful, for that it is a substance.
And as when a medicine begins to work, the body may in
some respect be called healthful, and in some respect unhealthful, so we acknowledge as this divine medicine
receives place in man's heart, it may denominate him in
some part holy and good, though there remain yet a corrupted unmortified part, or some part of the evil humours
unpurged out; for where two contrary accidents are in one
subject, as health and sickness in a body, the subject receives its denomination from the accident which prevails
most. So many men are called saints, good and holy men,
and that truly, when this holy seed hath wrought in them
in a good measure, and hath somewhat leavened them into
its nature, though they may be yet liable to many infirmities
and weaknesses, yea and to some iniquities: for as the
seed of sin and ground of corruption, yea and the capacity
of yielding thereunto, and sometimes actually falling, doth

not denominate a good and holy man impious; so neither doth the seed of righteousness in evil men, and the possibility of their becoming one with it, denominate them good or holy.

§ XV. Fourthly, We do not hereby intend any ways to Qves. 4. lessen or derogate from the atonement and sacrifice of Jesus Christ; but on the contrary do magnify and exalt it. For as we believe all those things to have been certainly transacted which are recorded in the holy scriptures concerning the birth, life, miracles, sufferings, resurrection and ascension of Christ; so we do also believe that it is the duty of every one to believe it to whom it pleases God to reveal the same, and to bring to them the knowledge of it; yea we believe it were damnable unbelief not to believe it, when so declared; but to resist that holy seed, which as minded would lead and incline every one to believe it as it is offered unto them, though it revealeth not in every one the outward and explicit knowledge of it, nevertheless it always assenteth to it, *ubi declaratur*, where it is declared. Nevertheless as we firmly believe it was necessary that Christ should come, that by his death and sufferings he might offer up himself a sacrifice to God for our sins, who his own self " bare our sins in his own body on the tree;" so we believe that the remission of sins which any partake *That re-* of, is only in and by virtue of that most satisfactory sacri- *mission of* fice, and no otherwise. For it is by the obedience of that *and alone* one that the free gift is come upon all to justification. For *by Christ.* we affirm, that as all men partake of the fruit of Adam's fall, in that by reason of that evil seed, which through him is communicated unto them, they are prone and inclined unto evil, though thousands of thousands be ignorant of Adam's fall, neither ever knew of the eating of the forbidden fruit; so also many may come to feel the influence of this holy and divine seed and light, and be turned from evil to good by it, though they knew nothing of Christ's coming in the flesh, through whose obedience and sufferings it is purchased unto them. And as we affirm it is absolutely needful that those do believe the history of Christ's outward appearance, whom it pleased God to bring to the knowledge of it ; so we do freely confess, that even that outward know ledge is very comfortable to such as are subject to and led by the inward seed and light. For not only doth the sense of Christ's love and sufferings tend to humble them, but they are thereby also strengthened in their faith, and encouraged to follow that excellent pattern which he hatl left us, " who suffered for us," as saith the apostle Peter, 1 Pet. ii. 21, " leaving us an example that we should follow his steps :" and many times we are greatly edified and refreshed with the gracious sayings which proceed out of his mouth. The history then is profitable and comfortable with the mystery, and never without it ; but the mystery is and may be profitable without the explicit and outward knowledge of the history.

*The history is profitable with the mystery.*

*Ques. 5. How Christ is ir. all men.*

But Fifthly, This brings us to another question, to wit, Whether Christ be in all men or no ? Which sometimes hath been asked us, and arguments brought against it ; because indeed it is to be found in some of our writings that Christ is in all men ; and we often are heard, in our public meetings and declarations, to desire every man to know and be acquainted with Christ in them, telling them that Christ is in them ; it is fit therefore, for removing of all mistakes, to say something in this place concerning this matter. We have said before how that a divine, spiritual, and supernatural light is in all men ; how that that divine supernatural light or seed is *vehiculum Dei ;* how that God and Christ dwelleth in it, and is never separated from it ; also how that, as it is received and closed with in the heart, Christ comes to be formed and brought forth : but we are far from ever having said, that Christ is thus formed in all men, or in the wicked : for that is a great attainment, which the apostle travailed that it might be brought forth in the Galatians. Neither is Christ in all men by way of union, or indeed, to speak strictly, by way of inhabitation ; because this inhabitation, as it is generally taken, imports union, or the manner of Christ's being in the saints : as it is written " 1 will dwell in them, and walk in them," 2 Cor. vi. 16

But in regard Christ is in all men as in a seed, yea, and that he never is nor can be separate from that holy pure seed and light which is in all men; therefore may it be said in a larger sense, that he is in all, even as we observed before. The scripture saith, Amos ii. 13, God is pressed down as a cart under sheaves; and Heb. vi. 6, Christ is crucified in the ungodly; though to speak properly and strictly, neither can God be pressed down, nor Christ, as God, be crucified. In this respect then, as he is in the seed which is in all men, we have said Christ is in all men, and have preached and directed all men to Christ in them, who lies crucified in them by their sins and iniquities, that they may look upon him whom they have pierced, and repent: whereby he that now lies as it were slain and buried in them, may come to be raised, and have dominion in their hearts over all. And thus also the apostle Paul preached to the Corinthians and Galatians, Christ crucified in them, ἐν ὑμῖν as the Greek hath it, 1 Cor. ii. 2; Gal. iii. 1. This Jesus Christ was that which the apostle desired to know in them, and make known unto them, that they might come to be sensible how they had thus been crucifying Christ, that so they might repent and be saved. And forasmuch as Christ is called that light that enlightens every man, the light of the world, therefore the light is taken for Christ, who truly is the fountain of light, and hath his habitation in it for ever. Thus the light of Christ is sometimes called Christ, *i. e.* that in which Christ is, and from which he is never separated.

*Christ crucified in man by iniquities.*

§ XVI. Sixthly, It will manifestly appear by what is above said, that we understand not this divine principle to be any part of man's nature, nor yet to be any relics of any good which Adam lost by his fall, in that we make it a distinct separate thing from man's soul, and all the faculties of it: yet such is the malice of our adversaries, that they cease not sometimes to calumniate us, as if we preached up a natural light, or the light of man's natural conscience. Next, there are that lean to the doctrine of Socinus and Pelagius, who persuade themselves through mistake, and out of no ill design to injure us, as if this which we preach up were some natural power and faculty of the soul, and that we only differ in the wording of it, and not in the thing itself; whereas there can be no greater difference than is betwixt us in that matter: for we certainly know that this light of which we speak is not only distinct, but of a different nature from the soul of man, and its faculties.

The faculties of man's reason. Indeed that man, as he is a rational creature, hath reason as a natural faculty of his soul, by which he can discern things that are rational, we deny not; for this is a property natural and essential to him, by which he can know and learn many arts and sciences, beyond what any other animal can do by the mere animal principle. Neither do we deny but by this rational principle man may apprehend in his brain, and in the notion, a knowledge of God and spiritual things; yet that not being the right organ, as in the second proposition hath more at length been signified, it cannot profit him towards salvation, but rather hindereth; and indeed the great cause of the apostasy hath been, that man hath sought to fathom the things of God in and by this natural and rational principle, and to build up a religion in it, neglecting and overlooking this principle and seed of God in the heart; so that herein, in the most universal and catholic sense, hath Anti-Christ in every man set up himself, and sitteth in the temple of God as God, and above every thing that is called God. For men being the temple of the Holy Ghost, as saith the apostle, 1 Cor. iii. 16, when the rational principle sets up itself there above the seed of God, to reign and rule as a prince in spiritual things, while the holy seed is wounded and bruised, there is Anti-Christ in every man, or somewhat exalted above and against Christ. Nevertheless we do not hereby affirm as if man had received his reason to no purpose, or to be of no service unto him, in no wise; we look upon reason as fit to order and rule man in things natural. For as God gave two great lights to rule the outward world, the sun and moon, the greater light to rule the day, and the lesser light to rule the night; so hath he given man the light of

Anti Christ in the temple of God.

The divine light and natural reason distinguished.

his Son, a spiritual divine light, to rule him in things spiritual, and the light of reason to rule him in things natural. And even as the moon borrows her light from the sun, so ought men, if they would be rightly and comfortably ordered in natural things, to have their reason enlightened by this divine and pure light. Which enlightened reason, in those that obey and follow this true light, we confess may be useful to man even in spiritual things, as it is still subservient and subject to the other; even as the animal life in man, regulated and ordered by his reason, helps him in going about things that are rational. We do further rightly distinguish this from man's natural conscience; for conscience being that in man which ariseth from the natural faculties of man's soul, may be defiled and corrupted. It is said expressly of the impure, Tit. i. 15, "That even their mind and conscience is defiled;" but this light can never be corrupted nor defiled; neither did it ever consent to evil or wickedness in any: for it is said expressly, that it makes all things manifest that are reprovable, Eph. v. 13, and so is a faithful witness for God against every unrighteousness in man. Now conscience, to define it truly, comes from *conscire*, and is that knowledge which ariseth in man's heart from what agreeth, contradicteth, or is contrary to any thing believed by him. whereby he becomes conscious to himself that he transgresseth by doing that which he is persuaded he ought not to do. So that the mind being once blinded or defiled with a wrong belief, there ariseth a conscience from that belief, which troubles him when he goes against it. As for example: A Turk who hath possessed himself with a false belief that it is unlawful for him to drink wine, if he do it, his conscience smites him for it; but though he keep many concubines, his conscience troubles him not, because his judgment is already defiled with a false opinion that it is lawful for him to do the one, and unlawful to do the other. Whereas if the light of Christ in him were minded, it would reprove him, not only for committing fornication, but also, as he became obedient thereunto, inform him that

*The light distinguished from man's natural conscience.*

*Conscience defined.*

*Example o a Turk.*

Mahomet was an impostor; as well as Socrates was informed by it, in his day, of the falsity of the heathen's gods.

*Example of a Papist.* So if a Papist eat flesh in Lent, or be not diligent enough in adoration of saints and images, or if he should contemn images, his conscience would smite him for it, because his judgment is already blinded with a false belief concerning these things: whereas the light of Christ never consented to any of those abominations. Thus then man's natural conscience is sufficiently distinguished from it; for conscience followeth the judgment, doth not inform it; but this light, as it is received, removes the blindness of the judgment, opens the understanding, and rectifies both the judgment and conscience. So we confess also, that conscience is an excellent thing, where it is rightly informed and enlightened; wherefore some of us have fitly compared it to the lanthorn, and the light of Christ to a candle: a lanthorn is useful, when a clear candle burns and shines in it; but otherwise of no use. To the light of Christ then in the conscience, and not to man's natural conscience, it is that we continually commend men; this, not that, is it which we preach up, and direct people to, as to a most certain guide unto life eternal.

*The natural conscience compared to a lanthorn, and the light of Christ to a candle.*

Lastly, This light, seed, &c., appears to be no power or natural faculty of man's mind; because a man that is in his health can, when he pleases, stir up, move, and exercise the faculties of his soul; he is absolute master of them; and except there be some natural cause or impediment in the way, he can use them at his pleasure: but this light and seed of God in man he cannot move and stir up when he pleaseth; but it moves, blows, and strives with man, as the Lord seeth meet. For though there be a possibility of salvation to every man during the day of his visitation, yet cannot a man, at any time when he pleaseth, or hath some sense of his misery, stir up that light and grace, so as to procure to himself tenderness of heart; but he must wait for it: which comes upon all at certain times and seasons, wherein it works powerfully upon the soul,

*The waiting upon the movings of the light and grace.*

mightily tenders it, and breaks it; at which time, if man resist it not, but closes with it, he comes to know salvation by it. Even as the lake of Bethesda did not cure all those that washed in it, but such only as washed first after the angel had moved upon the waters; so God moves in love to mankind, in this seed in his heart, at some singular times, setting his sins in order before him, and seriously inviting him to repentance, offering to him remission of sins and salvation; which if man accept of, he may be saved. Now there is no man alive, and I am confident there shall be none to whom this paper shall come, who, if they will deal faithfully and honestly with their own hearts, will not be forced to acknowledge that they have been sensible of this in some measure, less or more; which is a thing that man cannot bring upon himself with all his pains and industry. This then, oh man and woman! is the day of God's gracious visitation to thy soul, which if thou resist not, thou shalt be happy for ever. This is the day of the Lord, which, as Christ saith, is like the lightning, which shineth from the east unto the west; and the wind or spirit, which blows upon the heart, and no man knows whither it goes, nor whence it comes. *Mat. xxiv. 27. John iii. 8.*

§ XVII. And lastly, This leads me to speak concerning *Ques. 7.* the manner of this seed or light's operation in the hearts of all men, which will show yet more manifestly, how widely we differ from all those that exalt a natural power or light in man; and how our principle leads above all others to attribute our whole salvation to the mere power, spirit, and grace of God.

To them then that ask us after this manner, How do ye differ from the Pelagians and Arminians? For if two men have equal sufficient light and grace, and the one be saved by it, and the other not; is it not because the one improves it, the other not? Is not then the will of man the cause of the one's salvation beyond the other? I say, to such we thus answer: That as the grace and light in all is suffi- *The light's* cient to save all, and of its own nature would save all; so *operations* it strives and wrestles with all in order to save them; ne *salvation.*

that resists its striving, is the cause of l.s own condemnation; he that resists it not, it becomes his salvation : so that in him that is saved, the working is of the grace, and not of the man ; and it is a passiveness rather than an act ; though afterwards, as man is wrought upon, there is a will raised in him, by which he comes to be a co-worker with the grace : for according to that of Augustine, "He that made us without us, will not save us without us." So that the first step is not by man's working, but by his not contrary working. And we believe, that at these singular seasons of every man's visitation above mentioned, as man is wholly unable of himself to work with the grace, neither can he move one step out of the natural condition, until the grace lay hold upon him ; so it is possible for him to be passive, and not to resist it, as it is possible for him to resist it. So we say, the grace of God works in and upon man's nature ; which, though of itself wholly corrupted and defiled, and prone to evil, yet is capable to be wrought upon by the grace of God ; even as iron, though a hard and cold metal of itself, may be warmed and softened by the heat of the fire, and wax melted by the sun. And as iron or wax, when removed from the fire or sun, returneth to its former condition of coldness and hardness ; so man's heart, as it resists or retires from the grace of God, returns to its former condition again. I have often had the manner of God's working, in order to salvation towards all men, illustrated to my mind by one or two clear examples, which I shall here add for the information of others.

The example of a diseased man and the physician.

The first is, Of a man heavily diseased ; to whom I compare man in his fallen and natural condition. I suppose God, who is the great physician, not only to give this man physic, after he hath used all the industry he can for his own health, by any skill or knowledge of his own ; as those that say, If a man improve his reason or natural faculties, God will superadd grace ; or, as others say, that he cometh and maketh offer of a remedy to this man outwardly, leaving it to the liberty of man's will either to receive it or reject it. But He, even the Lord, his great physician, cometh and poureth the remedy into his mouth, and as it were layeth him in his bed; so that if the sick man be but passive, it will necessarily work the effect: but if he be stubborn and untoward, and will needs rise up and go forth into the cold, or eat such fruits as are hurtful to him, while the medicine should operate; then, though of its nature it tendeth to cure him, yet it will prove destructive to him, because of those obstructions which it meeteth with. Now as the man that should thus undo himself would certainly be the cause of his own death; so who will say, that, if cured, he owes not his health wholly to the physician, and not to any deed of his own; seeing his part was not any action, but a passiveness?

The second example is, Of divers men lying in a dark pit together, where all their senses are so stupified, that they are scarce sensible of their own misery. To this I compare man in his natural, corrupt, fallen condition. I suppose not that any of these men, wrestling to deliver themselves, do thereby stir up or engage one able to deliver them to give them his help, saying within himself, I see one of these men willing to be delivered, and doing what in him lies, therefore he deserves to be assisted; as say the Socinians, Pelagians, and Semi-Pelagians. Neither do I suppose that this deliverer comes to the top of the pit, and puts down a ladder, desiring them that will to come up; and so puts them upon using their own strength and will to come up; as do the Jesuits and Arminians: yet, as they say, such are not delivered without the grace; seeing the grace is that ladder by which they were delivered. But I suppose that the deliverer comes at certain times, and fully discovers and informs them of the great misery and hazard they are in, if they continue in that noisome and pestiferous place; yea, forces them to a certain sense of their misery, (for the wickedest men at times are made sensible of their misery by God's visitation,) and not only so, but lays hold upon them, and gives them a pull, in order to lift them out of their misery; which if they resist not will save them; only they may resist it. This being applied as the former.

*The example of men lying stupified in a dark pit, and their deliverer.*

doth the same way illustrate the matter. Neither is the grace of God frustrated, though the effect of it be diverse, according to its object, being the ministration of mercy and love in those that reject it not, but receive it, John i. 12, but the ministration of wrath and condemnation in those

**A similie of the sun's melting and hardening power.**

that do reject it, John iii. 19, even as the sun, by one act or operation, melteth and softeneth the wax, and hardeneth the clay. The nature of the sun is to cherish the creation, and therefore the living are refreshed by it, and the flowers send forth a good savour, as it shines upon them, and the fruits of the trees are ripened; yet cast forth a dead carcass, a thing without life, and the same reflection of the sun will cause it to stink, and putrefy it; yet is not the sun said thereby to be frustrated of its proper effect. So every man during the day of his visitation is shined upon by the sun of righteousness, and capable of being influenced by it, so as to send forth good fruit, and a good savour, and to be melted by it; but when he hath sinned out his day, then the same sun hardeneth him, as it doth the clay, and makes his wickedness more to appear and putrefy, and send forth an evil savour.

**All have grace sufficient for salvation given them of God.**

§ XVIII. Lastly, As we truly affirm that God willeth no man to perish, and therefore hath given to all grace sufficient for salvation; so we do not deny, but that in a special manner he worketh in some, in whom grace so prevaileth, that they necessarily obtain salvation; neither doth God suffer them to resist. For it were absurd to say, that God had not far otherwise extended himself towards the virgin Mary and the apostle Paul, than towards many others: neither can we affirm that God equally loved the beloved disciple John and Judas the traitor; yet so far, nevertheless, as none wanted such a measure of grace by which they might have been saved, all are justly inexcusable. And also God working in those to whom this prevalency of grace is given, doth so hide himself, to shut out all security and presumption, that such may be humbled, and the free grace of God magnified, and all reputed to be of the free gift; and nothing from the strength of self.

Those also who perish, when they remember those times of God's visitation towards them, wherein he wrestled with them by his Light and Spirit, are forced to confess, that there was a time wherein the door of mercy was open unto them, and that they are justly condemned, because they rejected their own salvation.

Thus both the mercy and justice of God are established, and the will and strength of man are brought down and rejected; his condemnation is made to be of himself, and his salvation only to depend upon God. Also by these positions two great objections, which often are brought against this doctrine, are well solved.

The first is deduced from those places of scripture, Object. wherein God seems precisely to have decreed and predestinated some to salvation; and for that end, to have ordained certain means, which fall not out to others; as in the calling of Abraham, David, and others, and in the conversion of Paul; for these being numbered among such to whom this prevalency is given, the objection is easily loosed.

The second is drawn from those places, wherein God Predestina seems to have ordained some wicked persons to destruc- tion to salvation, and
tion; and therefore to have obdured their hearts to force pre-ordina-
tion to de-
them unto great sins, and to have raised them up, that he struction,
might show in them his power, who, if they be numbered answered
amongst those men whose day of visitation is passed over, that objection is also solved; as will more evidently appear to any one that will make a particular application of those things, which I at this time, for brevity's sake, thought meet to pass over.

§ XIX. Having thus clearly and evidently stated the question, and opened our mind and judgment in this matter, as divers objections are hereby prevented, so will it make our proof both the easier and the shorter.

The first thing to be proved is, That God hath given to Prof. I.
every man a day or time of visitation, wherein it is possible Proved
for him to be saved. If we can prove that there is a day and time given, in which those might have been saved that

13*

Proof 1.

Those that perish had a day of mercy offered them.

Instances
1. Cain.

2. The old world.

God is long suffering, and long waiting to be gracious unto all—

actually perish, the matter is done: for none deny but those that are saved have a day of visitation. This then appears by the regrets and complaints which the Spirit of God throughout the whole scriptures makes, even to those that did perish; sharply reproving them, for that they did not accept of, nor close with God's visitation and offer of mercy to them. Thus the Lord expresses himself then first of all to Cain, Gen. iv. 6, 7, "And the Lord said unto Cain, Why art thou wroth? and why is thy countenance fallen? If thou dost well, shalt thou not be accepted? If thou dost not well, sin lieth at the door." This was said to Cain before he slew his brother Abel, when the evil seed began to tempt him, and work in his heart; we see how God gave warning to Cain in season, and in the day of his visitation towards him, acceptance and remission if he did well: for this interrogation, "Shalt thou not be accepted?" imports an affirmative, "Thou shalt be accepted, if thou dost well." So that if we may trust God Almighty, the fountain of all truth and equity, it was possible in a day, even for Cain to be accepted. Neither could God have proposed the doing of good as a condition, if he had not given Cain sufficient strength, whereby he was capable to do good. This the Lord himself also shows, even that he gave a day of visitation to the old world, Gen. vi. 3, "And the Lord said, My Spirit shall not always strive in man;" for so it ought to be translated. This manifestly implies, that his Spirit did strive with man, and doth strive with him for a season; which season expiring, God ceaseth to strive with him, in order to save him: for the Spirit of God cannot be said to strive with man after the day of his visitation is expired; seeing it naturally, and without any resistance, works its effect then, to wit, continually to judge and condemn him. From this day of visitation, that God hath given to every one, is it that he is said to "wait to be gracious," Isa. xxx. 18, and to be "long suffering," Exod. xxxiv. 6; Numb. xiv. 18; Psal. lxxxvi. 15; Jer. xv. 15. Here the prophet Jeremy, in his prayer, lays hold upon the "long suffering of God;" and in his expostulating

with God, he shuts out the objection of our adversaries in
the 18th verse: " Why is my pain perpetual, and my
wound incurable, which refuseth to be healed? Wilt thou
altogether be unto me as a liar, and as waters that fail?"
Whereas according to our adversaries' opinion, the pain
of the most part of men is perpetual, and their wound altogether incurable; yea, the offer of the gospel, and of salvation unto them, is as a lie, and as waters that fail, being
never intended to be of any effect unto them. The apostle
Peter says expressly, that this long suffering of God waited
in the days of Noah for those of the old world, 1 Pet. iii.
20, which, being compared with that of Gen. vi. 3, before
mentioned, doth sufficiently hold forth our proposition.
And that none may object that this long suffering or striving of the Lord was not in order to save them, the same —In order
apostle saith expressly, 2 Pet. iii. 15, That the long suf- to save
fering of God is to be accounted salvation; and with them.
this " long suffering," a little before in the 9th verse, he
couples, " That God is not willing that any should perish."
Where, taking him to be his own interpreter, as he is most
fit, he holdeth forth, That those to whom the Lord is long
suffering, which he declareth he was to the wicked of the
old world, and is now to all, " not willing that any should
perish," they are to account this long suffering of God to
them salvation.    Now how or in what respect can they
account it salvation, if there be not so much as a possibility
of salvation conveyed to them therein? For it were not
salvation to them, if they could not be saved by it. In
this matter Peter further refers to the writings of Paul,
holding forth this to have been the universal doctrine.
Where it is observable what he adds upon this occasion,
how there are some things in Paul's epistles hard to be    Some
understood, which the unstable and unlearned wrest to    things in
their own destruction; insinuating plainly this of those    tles hard to
expressions in Paul's epistles, as Rom. ix., &c., which    be under-
some, unlearned in spiritual things, did make to contradict    stood.
the truth of God's long suffering towards all, in which he
willeth not any of them should perish, and in which they

all may be saved. Would to God many had taken more
heed than they have done to this advertisement! That
place of the apostle Paul, which Peter seems here most
particularly to hint at, doth much contribute also to clear
the matter, Rom. ii. 4, " Despisest thou the riches of his
goodness, and forbearance, and long suffering, not knowing that the goodness of God leadeth thee to repentance?"
Paul speaketh here to the unregenerate, and to the wicked,
who, in the following verse he saith, " Treasure up wrath
unto the day of wrath;" and to such he commends the
riches of the forbearance and long suffering of God; showing that the tendency of God's goodness leadeth to repentance. How could it necessarily tend to lead them to
repentance, how could it be called riches or goodness to
them, if there were not a time wherein they might repent
by it, and come to be sharers of the riches exhibited in it?
From all which I thus argue:

ARG.
God's Spi-
rit strives
in the wick-
ed.

If God plead with the wicked, from the possibility of
their being accepted; if God's Spirit strive in them for a
season, in order to save them, who afterwards perish; if
he wait to be gracious unto them; if he be long suffering
towards them; and if this long suffering be salvation to
them while it endureth, during which time God willeth
them not to perish, but exhibiteth to them the riches of his
goodness and forbearance to lead them to repentance;
then there is a day of visitation wherein such might have
been, or some such now may be saved, who have perished,
and may perish, if they repent not:

But the first is true; therefore also the last.

R. II.

§ XX. Secondly, This appeareth from the prophet
Isaiah, v. 4, " What could I have done more to my vineyard?" For in verse 2, he saith: He had fenced it, and
gathered out the stones thereof, and planted it with the
choicest vine; and yet, saith he, " when I looked it
should have brought forth grapes, it brought forth wild
grapes." Wherefore he calleth the inhabitants of Jerusalem, and men of Judah, to judge betwixt him and his
vineyard, saying; " What could I have done more to my

The vine-
yard plant-
ed brought
forth wild
grapes.

vineyard, than I have done in it? and yet," as is said, "it brought forth wild grapes:" which was applied to many in Israel who refused God's mercy. The same example is used by Christ, Mat. xxi. 33; Mark xii. 1; Luke xx. 9, where Jesus shows, how to some a vineyard was planted, and all things given necessary for them, to get them fruit to pay or restore to their master; and how the master many times waited to be merciful to them, in sending servants after servants, and passing by many offences, before he determined to destroy and cast them out. First then, this cannot be understood of the saints, or of such as repent and are saved; for it is said expressly, "He will destroy them." Neither would the parable any ways have answered the end for which it is alleged, if these men had not been in a capacity to have done good; yea, such was their capacity, that Christ saith in the prophet, "What could I have done more?" So that it is more than manifest, that by this parable, repeated in three sundry evangelists, Christ holds forth his long suffering towards men, and their wickedness, to whom means of salvation being afforded, do nevertheless resist, to their own condemnation. To these also are parallel these scriptures, Pro. i. 24, 25, 26; Jer. xviii. 9, 10; Mat. xviii. 32, 33, 34; Acts xiii. 46.

Lastly, That there is a day of visitation given to the **Pr. III.** wicked, wherein they might have been saved, and which being expired, they are shut out from salvation, appears evidently by Christ's lamentation over Jerusalem, expressed **Christ's la**- in three sundry places, Matth. xxiii. 37; Luke xiii. 34; **mentation** and xix. 41, 42; "And when he was come near, he be- **salem** held the city, and wept over it, saying: If thou hadst known, even thou, at least in this thy day, the things which belong unto thy peace; but now they are hid from thine eyes!" Than which nothing can be said more evident to prove our doctrine. For, First, he insinuates that there was a day wherein the inhabitants of Jerusalem might have known those things that belonged to their peace. Secondly, That during that day he was willing to have gathered them, even as an "hen gathereth her chickens."

A familiar example, yet very significative in this case
which shows that the offer of salvation made unto them
was not in vain on his part, but as really, and with as great
cheerfulness and willingness, as a "hen gathereth her
chickens." Such as is the love and care of the hen toward
her brood, such is the care of Christ to gather lost men and
women, to redeem them out of their corrupt and degenerate state. Thirdly, That because they refused, the things
belonging to their peace were hid from their eyes. Why
were they hid? Because ye would not suffer me to gather
you; ye would not see those things that were good for
you, in the season of God's love towards you; and therefore now, that day being expired, ye cannot see them:
and, for a farther judgment, God suffers you to be hardened in unbelief.

**When men's hearts are hardened.**

So it is, after real offers of mercy and salvation rejected,
that men's hearts are hardened, and not before. Thus that
saying is verified, "To him that hath, shall be given; and
from him that hath not, shall be taken away even that which
he hath." This may seem a riddle, yet it is according to
this doctrine easily solved. He hath not, because he hath
lost the season of using it, and so to him it is now as nothing; for Christ uses this expression, Matth. xxv. 26, upon

**The one talent was sufficient.**

the occasion of the taking the one talent from the slothful
servant, and giving it to him that was diligent; which
talent was no ways insufficient of itself, but of the same
nature with those given to the others; and therefore the
Lord had reason to exact the profit of it proportionably, as
well as from the rest: so I say, it is after the rejecting of
the day of visitation, that the judgment of obduration is
inflicted upon men and women, as Christ pronounceth t
upon the Jews out of Isa. vi. 9, which all the four evangelists make mention of, Matth. xiii. 14; Mark iv. 12; Luke
viii. 10; John xii. 40; and last of all the apostle Paul,
after he had made offer of the gospel of salvation to the
Jews at Rome, pronounceth the same, Acts xxviii. 26,
after that some believed not; "Well spake the Holy Ghost,
by Isaiah the prophet, unto our fathers, saying, Go unto

this people, and say, Hearing ye shall hear, and shall not understand; and seeing ye shall see, and shall not perceive. For the heart of this people is waxed gross, and their ears are dull of hearing, and their eyes have they closed; lest they should see with their eyes, and hear with their ears, and understand with their hearts, and should be converted, and I should heal them." So it appears, that God would have them to see, but they closed their eyes; and therefore they are justly hardened. Of this matter Cyrillus Alexandrinus upon John, lib. 6, cap. 21, speaks well, answering to this objection. "But some may say, if Christ be come into the world, that those that see may be blinded, their blindness is not imputed unto them; but it rather seems that Christ is the cause of their blindness, who saith, 'He is come into the world, that those that see may be blinded.' But," saith he, "they speak not rationally, who object these things unto God, and are not afraid to call him the author of evil. For, as the sensible sun is carried upon our horizon, that it may communicate the gift of its clearness unto all, and make its light shine upon all; yet if any one close his eyelids, or willingly turn himself from the sun, refusing the benefit of its light, he wants its illumination, and remains in darkness, not through the defect of the sun, but through his own fault. So that the true Sun, who came to enlighten those that sat in darkness, and in the region of the shadow of death, visited the earth for this cause, that he might communicate unto all the gift of knowledge and grace, and illuminate the inward eyes of all by a spiritual splendour: but many reject the gift of this heavenly light freely given to them, and have closed the eyes of their minds, lest so excellent an illumination or irradiation of the eternal light should shine unto them. It is not then through defect of the true Sun that they are blinded, but only through their own iniquity and hardness; 'for,' as the wise man saith, Wisdom ii., 'their wickedness hath blinded them.'"

From all which I thus argue:

If there was a day wherein the obstinate Jews might have

Cyril. Alex

The cause of man's remaining in darkness, the closing his eyes.

The obstinate Jews had a day.

known the things that belonged to their peace, which, because they rejected it, was hid from their eyes; if there was a time wherein Christ would have gathered them, who, because they refused, could not be gathered; then such as might have been saved do actually perish, that slighted the day of God's visitation towards them, wherein they might have been converted and saved.

But the first is true; therefore also the last.

PROP. II. Proved.

§ XXI. Secondly, That which comes in the second place to be proved is, That whereby God offers to work this salvation during the day of every man's visitation; and that is, That he hath given to every man a measure of saving, sufficient, and supernatural light and grace. This I shall do, by God's assistance, by some plain and clear testimonies of the scripture.

PROOF I.

The light enlightening every man, &c.

First, From that of John i. 9: " That was the true light, which lighteth every man that cometh into the world." This place doth so clearly favour us, that by some it is called the Quaker's text; for it doth evidently demonstrate our assertion; so that it scarce needs either consequence or deduction, seeing itself is a consequence of two propositions asserted in the former verses, from which it followeth as a conclusion in the very terms of our faith. The first of these propositions is, " The life that is in him is the light of men:" the second, " The light shineth in the darkness:" and from these two he infers, and " He is the true light, which lighteth every man that cometh into the world."

OBS. 1.

From whence I do in short observe, That this divine apostle calls Christ the light of men, and giveth us this as one of the chief properties, at least considerably and especially to be observed by us; seeing hereby, as he is the light, and as we walk with him in that light which he communicates to us, we come to have fellowship and communion with him; as the same apostle saith elsewhere, 1 John i.

—Not to a certain number of men, but every man.

7. Secondly, That this light shineth in darkness, though the darkness comprehend it not. Thirdly, That this true light enlighteneth every man that cometh into the world. Where the apostle, being directed by God's Spirit, hath

carefully avoided their captiousness, that would have restricted this to any certain number: where every one is,
there is none excluded.  Next, should they be so obstinate,
as sometimes they are, as to say that this [every man] is
only every one of the elect; these words following, "every
man that cometh into the world," would obviate that objection.  So that it is plain there comes no man into the world,
whom Christ hath not enlightened in some measure, and
in whose dark heart this light doth not shine; though the
" darkness comprehend it not," yet it shineth there; and
the nature thereof is to dispel the darkness, where men
shut not their eyes upon it.  Now for what end this light The light
is given, is expressed in verse 7, where John is said to dispelling<br>darkness
come for a " witness, to bear witness to the light, that all begets
men through it might believe;" to wit, through the light, faith.
δι αυτε, which doth very well agree with φωτος, as being the
nearest antecedent, though most translators have (to make
it suit with their own doctrine) made it relate to John, as
if all men were to believe through John.  For which, as
there is nothing directly in the text, so it is contrary to the
very strain of the context. For, seeing Christ hath lighted
every man with this light, Is it not that they may come to
believe through it ?  All could not believe through John,
because all men could not know of John's testimony;
whereas every man being lighted by this may come there-
through to believe.  John shined not in darkness; but this
light shineth in the darkness, that having dispelled the darkness, it may produce and beget faith.  And lastly, We
must believe through that, and become believers through
that, by walking in which, fellowship with God is known
and enjoyed ; but, as hath been above observed, it is by
walking in this light that we have this communion and fellowship; not by walking in John, which were nonsense.
So that this relative δι αυτε, must needs be referred to the
light, whereof John bears witness, that through that light,
wherewith Christ hath lighted every man, all men might
come to believe.  Seeing then this light is the light of Jesus
Christ, and the light through which men come to believe,

14

The light is supernatural, saving, and sufficient. I think it needs not to be doubted, but that it is a super natural, saving, and sufficient light. If it were not supernatural, it could not be properly called the light of Jesus; for though all things be his, and of him, and from him; yet those things which are common and peculiar to our nature, as being a part of it, we are not said in so special a manner to have from Christ. Moreover, the evangelist is holding out to us here the office of Christ as mediator, and the benefits which from him as such, do redound unto us.

OBS. 2.      Secondly, It cannot be any of the natural gifts or faculties of our soul, whereby we are said here to be enlightened, because this light is said to " shine in the darkness," The darkness is man's natural state and condition. and cannot be comprehended by it. Now this darkness is no other but man's natural condition and state; in which natural state he can easily comprehend, and doth comprehend, those things that are peculiar and common to him as such. That man in his natural condition is called darkness, see Eph. v. 8: " For ye were sometimes darkness, but now are ye light in the Lord." And in other places, as Acts xxvi. 18, Col. i. 13, 1 Thess. v. 5, where the condition of man in his natural state is termed darkness: therefore I say this light cannot be any natural property or faculty of man's soul, but a supernatural gift and grace of Christ.

OBS. 3.      Thirdly, It is sufficient and saving.

ARG. 1.      That which is given " that all men through it may believe," must needs be saving and sufficient: that, by walking in which, fellowship with the saints and the blood of Christ, " which cleanseth from all sin," is possessed, must be sufficient:

But such is the LIGHT, 1 John, i. 7.

Therefore, &c.

Moreover;

ARG. 2.      That which we are commanded to believe in " that we may become the children of the light," must be a supernatural, sufficient, and saving principle:

But we are commanded to believe in this light:

Therefore, &c.

The proposition cannot be denied.   The assumption is Christ's own words, John xii. 36 : " While ye have the light, believe in the light, that ye may be the children of the light."

To this they object, That by light here is understood OBJECT. Christ's outward person, in whom he would have them believe.

That they ought to have believed in Christ, that is, that ANSW. he was the MESSIAH that was to come, is not denied; but how they evince that Christ intended that here, I see not : Whether nay the place itself shows the contrary, by these words, Christ's outward " While ye have the light ;" and by the verse going before, person was the light. " Walk while ye have the light, lest darkness come upon you :" which words import, that when that light in which they were to believe was removed, then they should lose the capacity or season of believing.   Now this could not be understood of Christ's person, else the Jews might have believed in him ; and many did savingly believe in him, as all Christians do at this day, when the person, to wit, his bodily presence, or outward man, is far removed from them.   So that this light in which they were commanded The light to believe must be that inward spiritual light that shines in of Christ is not Christ's their hearts for a season, even during the day of man's outward man or per visitation ; which while it continueth to call, invite and ex- son. hort, men are said to have it, and may believe in it ; but when men refuse to believe in it, and reject it, then it ceaseth to be a light to show them the way ; but leaves the sense of their unfaithfulness as a sting in their conscience ; which is a terror and darkness unto them, and upon them, in which they cannot know where to go, neither can work any ways profitably in order to their salvation.   And therefore to such rebellious ones the day of the Lord is said to be darkness, and not light, Amos v. 18.

From whence it appears, that though many receive not the light, as many comprehend it not, nevertheless this saving light shines in all, that it may save them.   Concerning which also Cyrillus Alexandrinus saith well, and

Cyrillus
Alexandrinus upon
John, lib. i.
chap. 11.

defends our principle: " With great diligence and watchfulness," saith he, " doth the apostle John endeavour to anticipate and prevent the vain thoughts of men: for there is here a wonderful method of sublime things, and overturning of objections. He had just now called the Son the true light, by whom he affirmed that every man coming into the world was enlightened; yea, that he was in the world, and the world was made by him. One may then object, If the word of God be the light, and if this light enlighten the hearts of men, and suggest unto men piety and the understanding of things; if he was always in the world, and was the creator or builder of the world, why was he so long unknown unto the world? It seems rather to follow because he was unknown to the world, therefore the world was not enlightened by him, nor he totally light. Lest any should so object, he divinely infers, and the world knew him not. Let not the world," saith he, " accuse the word of God, and his eternal light, but its own weakness; for the son enlightens, but the creature rejects the grace that is given unto it, and abuseth the sharpness of understanding granted it, by which it might have naturally known God; and, as a prodigal, hath turned its sight to the creatures, neglecting to go forward, and through laziness and negligence buried the illumination, and despised this grace. Which that the disciple of Paul might not do, he was commanded to watch; therefore it is to be imputed to their wickedness, who are illuminated, and not unto the light. For as albeit the sun riseth upon all, yet he that is blind receiveth no benefit thereby; none thence can justly accuse the brightness of the sun, but will ascribe the cause of not seeing to the blindness; so I judge it is to be understood of the only begotten Son of God: for he is the true light, and sendeth forth his brightness upon all; but the god of this world, as Paul saith, hath blinded the minds of those that believe not, 2 Cor. iv. 4, that the light of the gospel shine not unto them. We say then that darkness is come upon men, not because they are altogether deprived of light, for nature retaineth still the strength of understand-

The son
enlightens,
but man
through
negligence
buries illumination.

ing divinely given it, but because man is dulled by an evil habit, and become worse, and hath made the measure of grace in some respect to languish. When therefore the like befalls man, the Psalmist justly prays, crying, 'Open mine eyes, that I may behold the wonderful things of thy law.' For the law was given that this light might be kindled in us, the blearedness of the eyes of our minds being wiped away, and the blindness being removed which detained us in our former ignorance. By these words then the world is accused as ungrateful and insensible, not knowing its author, nor bringing forth the good fruit of the illumination; that it may now seem to be said truly of all, which was of old said by the prophet of the Jews, I expected that it should have brought forth grapes, but it brought forth wild grapes. For the good fruit of the illumination was the knowledge of the only Begotten, as a cluster hanging from a fruitful branch," &c.

From which it appears Cyrillus believed that a saving illumination was given unto all. For as to what he speaks of nature, he understands it not of the common nature of man by itself, but of that nature which hath the strength of understanding divinely given it: for he understands this universal illumination to be of the same kind with that grace of which Paul makes mention to Timothy, saying, "Neglect not the grace that is in thee." Now it is not to be believed that Cyrillus was so ignorant as to judge that grace to have been some natural gift. *Grace no natural gift*

§ XXII. That this saving light and seed, or a measure of it, is given to all, Christ tells us expressly in the parable of the sower, Mat. xiii. from ver. 18; Mark iv., and Luke viii. 11, he saith, That this seed sown in those several sorts of grounds is the word of the kingdom, which the apostle calls the word of faith, Rom. x. 8, James i. 21, οʽ Λόγος ἔμφυλος, the "implanted ingrafted word, which is able to save the soul;" the words themselves declare that it is that which is saving in the nature of it, for in the good ground it fructified abundantly. *Proof II. The seed of the kingdom is sown in several sorts of grounds without distinction.*

Let us then observe, that this seed of the kingdom, this

14* v

saving, supernatural, and sufficient word, was really sown
in the stony thorny ground, and by the wayside, where it
did not profit, but became useless as to these grounds: it
was, I say, the same seed that was sown in the good ground.
It is then the fear of persecution and deceitfulness of
riches, as Christ himself interpreteth the parable, which
hindereth this seed to grow in the hearts of many: not
but that in its own nature it is sufficient, being the
same with that which groweth up and prospereth in the
hearts of those who receive it. So that though all are not
saved by it, yet there is a seed of salvation planted and
sown in the hearts of all by God, which would grow up
and redeem the soul, if it were not choked and hindered.
Concerning this parable Victor Antiochenus on Mark iv.,
as he is cited by Vossius, in his Pelagian History, book vii.,
saith, " That our Lord Christ hath liberally sown the divine
seed of the word, and proposed it to all, without respect
of persons; and as he that soweth distinguisheth not betwixt ground and ground, but simply casteth in the seed
without distinction, so our Saviour hath offered the food
of the divine word so far as was his part, although he was
not ignorant what would become of many. Lastly, He so
behaved himself, as he might justly say, What should I
have done that I have not done?" And to this answered
the parable of the talents, Mat. xxv., he that had two talents was accepted, as well as he that had five, because he
used them to his master's profit: and he that had one
might have done so; his talent was of the same nature of
the rest; it was as capable to have proportionably brought
forth its interest as the rest. And so though there be not
a like proportion of grace given to all, to some five-talents,
to some two talents, and to some but one talent; yet there
is given to all that which is sufficient, and no more is required than according to that which is given: " For unto
whomsoever much is given, from him shall much be required," Luke xii. 48. He that had the two talents was
accepted for giving four, nothing less than he that gave the
ten: so should he also that gave the one, if he had given

two; and no doubt one was capable to have produced two, as well as five to have produced ten, or two four.

§ XXIII. Thirdly, This saving spiritual light is the gospel, which the apostle saith expressly is preached " in every creature under heaven;" even that very " gospel whereof Paul was made a minister," Col. i. 23. For the gospel is not a mere declaration of good things, being the " power of God unto salvation to all those that believe," Rom. i. 16. Though the outward declaration of the gospel be taken sometimes for the gospel; yet it is but figuratively, and by a metonymy. For to speak properly, the gospel is this inward power and life which preacheth glad tidings in the hearts of all men, offering salvation unto them, and seeking to redeem them from their iniquities, and therefore it is said to be preached " in every creature under heaven:" whereas there are many thousands of men and women to whom the outward gospel was never preached. Therefore the apostle Paul, Romans i., where he saith " the gospel is the power of God unto salvation," adds, that " therein is revealed the righteousness of God from faith to faith;" and also the " wrath of God against such as hold the truth of God in unrighteousness:" for this reason, saith he, " because that which may be known of God is manifest in them; for God hath showed it unto them." Now that which may be known of God, is known by the gospel, which was manifest in them. For those of whom the apostle speaks had no outward gospel preached unto them; so that it was by the inward manifestation of the knowledge of God in them, which is indeed the gospel preached in man, " that the righteousness of God is revealed from faith to faith;" that is, it reveals to the soul that which is just, good, and righteous; and that as the soul receiveth it and believes, righteousness comes more and more to be revealed from one degree of faith to another. For though, as the following verse saith, the outward creation declares the power of God; yet that which may be known of him is manifest within : by which inward manifestation we are made capable to see and discern the Eternal Power and Godhead in

PROOF III.

The light is the gospel, the power of God preached in every creature under heaven.

the outward creation ; so were it not for this inward prin
ciple, we could no more understand the invisible things of
God by the outward visible creation, than a blind man can
see and discern the variety of shapes and colours, or judge
of the beauty of the outward creation. Therefore he saith,
first, " That which may be known of God is manifest in
them," and in and by that they may read and understand
the power and Godhead in those things that are outward
and visible. And though any might pretend that the outward creation doth of itself, without any supernatural or
saving principle in the heart, even declare to the natural
man that there is a God ; yet what would such a knowledge
avail, if it did not also communicate to me what the will
of God is, and how I shall do that which is acceptable to

The out-
ward crea-
tion may
beget a per-
suasion in
man of an
eternal
power or
virtue

him ? For the outward creation, though it may beget a
persuasion that there is some eternal power or virtue by
which the world hath had its beginning ; yet it doth not
tell me, nor doth it inform me of that which is just, holy,
and righteous ; how I shall be delivered from my temptations and evil affections, and come unto righteousness ,
that must be from some inward manifestation in my heart.
Whereas those Gentiles of whom the apostle speaks knew
by that inward law and manifestation of the knowledge of
God in them to distinguish betwixt good and evil, as in
the next chapter appears, of which we shall speak hereafter.
The prophet Micah, speaking of man indefinitely, or in
general, declares this, Mic. vi. 8, " He hath showed thee,
O man, what is good. And what doth the Lord require
of thee, but to do justly, and to love mercy, and to walk
humbly with God ?" He doth not say God requires, till
he hath first assured that he hath showed unto them. Now
because this is showed unto all men, and manifest in them,
therefore, saith the apostle, is the " wrath of God revealed
against them, for that they hold the truth in unrighteousness ;" that is, the measure of truth, the light, the seed, the
grace in them : for that they hide the talent in the earth ,
that is, in the earthly and unrighteous part in their hearts,
and suffer it not to bring forth fruit, but to be choked with

the sensual cares of this life, the fear of reproach, and the deceitfulness of riches, as by the parables above mentioned doth appear. But the apostle Paul opens and illustrates this matter yet more, Rom. x., where he declares, "That the word which he preached" (now the word which he preached, and the gospel which he preached, and whereof he was a minister, is one and the same) "is not far off, but nigh in the heart and in the mouth;" which done, he frameth as it were the objection of our adversaries in the 14th and 15th verses, "How shall they believe in him of whom they have not heard? And how shall they hear without a preacher?" This he answers in the 18th verse, saying, "But, I say, have they not heard? Yes, verily, their sound went into all the earth, and their words unto the ends of the world;" insinuating that this divine preacher hath sounded in the ears and hearts of all men: for of the outward apostles that saying was not true, neither then, nor many hundred years after; yea, for aught we know, there may be yet great and spacious nations and kingdoms that never have heard of Christ nor his apostles as outwardly. This inward and powerful word of God is yet more fully described in the epistle to the Hebrews, chap. iv. 12, 13: "For the word of God is quick and powerful, and sharper than any two-edged sword, piercing even to the dividing asunder of soul and spirit, and of the joints and marrow, and is a discerner of the thoughts and intents of the heart." The virtues of this spiritual word are here enumerated: it is quick, because it searches and tries the hearts of all; no man's heart is exempt from it: for the apostle gives this reason of its being so in the following verse: "But all things are naked and opened unto the eyes of him with whom we have to do: and there is not any creature that is not manifest in his sight." Though this ultimately and mediately be referred to God, yet nearly and immediately it relates to the word or light, which, as hath been before proved, is in the hearts of all, else it had been improper to have brought it in here. The apostle shows how "every intent and thought of the heart is discerned by the word of

*The divine preacher, the word nigh, hath sounded in the ears and hearts of all men.*

*Before whom all things are manifest.*

Any every thought and intent of the heart.

God," because all things are naked before God; which imports nothing else but it is in and by this word whereby God sees and discerns man's thoughts; and so it must needs be in all men, because the apostle saith, "there is no creature that is not manifest in his sight." This then is

The faithful witness.

that faithful witness and messenger of God that bears witness for God, and for his righteousness in the hearts of all men: for he hath not left man without a witness, Acts xiv. 17, and he is said to be "given for a witness to the people," Isa. lv. 4.    And as this word beareth witness for God, so it is not placed in men only to condemn them: for as he is given for a "witness," so saith the prophet,

A leader and commander.

he is given for a leader and commander.    The light is given, that all through it may believe, John i. 7, "for faith cometh by hearing, and hearing by the word of God," which is placed in man's heart, both to be a witness for God, and to be a means to bring man to God through faith and repentance: it is therefore powerful, that it may divide

A two-edged sword.

betwixt the soul and the spirit: it is like a two-edged sword, that it may cut off iniquity from him, and separate betwixt the precious and the vile; and because man's heart is cold and hard like iron naturally, therefore hath God

A fire and a hammer.

placed this word in him, which is said to be like a fire, and like a hammer, Jer. xxiii. 29, that like as by the heat of the fire the iron, of its own nature cold, is warmed, and softened, and by the strength of the hammer is framed according to the mind of the worker; so the cold and hard heart of man is by the virtue and powerfulness of this word of God near and in the heart, as it resists not, warmed and softened, and receiveth a heavenly and celestial impression and image.    The most part of the fathers have spoken at large touching this word, seed, light, and saving voice calling all unto salvation, and able to save.

Clem. Alex.

Clemens Alexandrinus saith, lib. 2, Stromat., "The divine word hath cried, calling all, knowing well those that will not obey; and yet, because it is in our power either to obey or not to obey, that none may have a pretext of ignorance, it hath made a righteous call, and requireth but

.hat which is according to the ability and strength of every one." The selfsame, in his warning to the Gentiles: "For cs," saith he, "that heavenly ambassador of the Lord, 'the grace of God, that brings salvation, hath appeared unto all,' &c. This is the new song, coming and manifestation of the word, which now shows itself in us, which was in the beginning, and was first of all." And again, "Hear, therefore, ye that are afar off; hear, ye who are near; the word is hid from none, the light is common to all, and shineth to all. There is no darkness in the word; let us hasten to salvation, to the new birth, that we being many, may be gathered into the one alone love." *Ibid.* he saith, "That there is infused into all, but principally into those that are trained up in doctrine, a certain divine influence, τῆς ἀπόῤῥοια θεία." And again he speaks concerning the innate witness, "worthy of belief, which of itself doth plainly choose that which is most honest." And again he saith, "That it is not impossible to come unto the truth, and lay hold of it, seeing it is most near to us, in our own houses, as the most wise Moses declareth, living in three parts of us, viz. in our hands, in our mouth, and in our heart. This," saith he, "is a most true badge of the truth, which is also fulfilled in three things, namely, in counsel, in action, in speaking." And again he saith also unto the unbelieving nations, "Receive Christ, receive light, receive sight, to the end thou mayest rightly know both God and man. The word that hath enlightened us is more pleasant than gold, and the stone of great value." And again he saith, "Let us receive the light, that we may receive God; let us receive the light, that we may be the scholars of the Lord." And again he saith to those infidel nations, "The heavenly Spirit helpeth thee; resist and flee pleasure." Again, lib. 5, Strom., he saith, "God forbid that man be not a partaker of divine acquaintance, θείας ἐννοίας, who in Genesis is said to be a partaker of inspiration." And Pæd. lib. 1, cap. 3, "There is," saith he, "some lovely and some desirable thing in man, which is called the in-breathing of God, ἐμφύσημα Θεῦ." The same

*The gathering unto the one and alone love.*

*The enlightening word.*

man, lib. 10, Strom., directeth men unto the light and
water in themselves, who have the eye of the soul darkened
or dimmed through evil education and learning : let them
enter in unto their own domestic light, or unto the light
which is in their own house, πρὸς τὸ οἰκεῖον φῶς βαδιζέτω, unto
the truth, which manifests accurately and clearly these
things that have been written.

**J. Martyr.**  Justin Martyr, in his first Apology, saith, "That the
word which was and is, is in all; even that very same
word which, through the prophets, foretold things to
come."

**Auth. de**  The writer of the Calling of the Gentiles, saith, lib. 1,
**Voc. Gent.**  cap. 2, "We believe according to the same, viz. scripture,
and most religiously confess, that God was never wanting
in care to the generality of men ; who although he did lead
by particular lessons a people gathered to himself unto
godliness, yet he withdrew from no nation of men the
gifts of his own goodness, that they might be convinced
that they had received the words of the prophets, and legal
commands in services and testimonies of the first principles." Cap. 7, he saith, "That he believes that the
help of grace hath been wholly withdrawn from no man."
Lib. 2, cap. 1, "Because, albeit salvation is far from sinners, yet there is nothing void of the presence and virtue
of his salvation." Cap. 2, "But seeing none of that people
over whom was set both the doctrines, were justified but
through grace by the spirit of faith, who can question but
that they, who of whatsoever nation, in whatsoever times,
could please God, were ordered by the Spirit of the grace
of God, which although in fore-time it was more sparing
and hid, yet denied itself to no ages, being in virtue one,
in quantity different, in counsel unchangeable, in operation
multifarious."

**PROP III.**  § XXIV. The third proposition which ought to be
**Proved.**  proved is, That it is by this light, seed, or grace that God
**God's sal-**  works the salvation of all men, and many come to partake
**vation**
**wrought by**  of the benefit of Christ's death, and salvation purchased by
**the light in**
**all.**  him. By the inward and effectual operations of which, as

many heathen have come to be partakers of the promises who were not of the seed of Abraham after the flesh. so may some now, to whom God hath rendered the knowledge of the history impossible, come to be saved by Christ. Having already proved that Christ hath died for all, that there is a day of visitation given to all, during which salvation is possible to them, and that God hath actually given a measure of saving grace and light unto all, preached the gospel to and in them, and placed the word of faith in their hearts, the matter of this proposition may seem to be proved. Yet shall I a little, for the farther satisfaction of all who desire to know the truth, and hold it as it is in Jesus, prove this from two or three clear scripture testimonies, and remove the most common as well as the more strong objections usually brought against it.

Our theme then hath two parts; First, That those that 1 Part. have the gospel and Christ outwardly preached unto them, are not saved but by the working of the grace and light in their hearts.

Secondly, That by the working and operation of this, 2 Part. many have been, and some may be saved, to whom the gospel hath never been outwardly preached, and who are utterly ignorant of the outward history of Christ.

As to the first, though it be granted by most, yet because 1 Part it is more in words than deeds, the more full discussing of proved. which will occur in the next proposition concerning justification, I shall prove it in few words. And first from the words of Christ to Nicodemus, John iii. 3, " Verily, verily I say unto thee, except a man be born again, he cannot see the kingdom of God." Now this birth cometh not by The new the outward preaching of the gospel, or knowledge of birth or re generation Christ, or historical faith in him; seeing many have that, cometh not and firmly believe it, who are never thus renewed. The by the out-ward know apostle Paul also goes so far, while he commends the ne- ledge of cessity and excellency of this new creation, as in a certain Christ; respect to lay aside the outward knowledge of Christ, or the knowledge of him after the flesh, in these words, 2 Cor. v. 16, 17, " Wherefore henceforth know we no man after the flesh; yea, though we have known Christ after the flesh, yet now henceforth know we him no more. Therefore if any man be in Christ, he is a new creature; old things are passed away, behold all things are become new." Whence it manifestly appears, that he makes the knowledge of Christ after the flesh but as it were the rudiments which young children learn, which after they are become better scholars, are of less use to them, because they have and possess the very substance of those first precepts in their minds. As all comparisons halt in some part, so shall I not affirm this to hold in every respect; yet so far will this hold, that as those that go no farther than the rudiments are never to be accounted learned, and as they grow beyond these things, so they have less use of them, even so such as go no farther than the outward knowledge of Christ shall never inherit the kingdom of heaven. But such as come to know this new birth, to be in Christ indeed, to be a new creature, to have " old things passed away, and all things become new," may safely say with the apostle, " Though we have known Christ after the *but by the* flesh, yet now henceforth know we him no more." Now *work of* this new creature proceeds from the work of this light and *light and* *grace in the* grace in the heart: it is that word which we speak of, that *heart.* is sharp and piercing, that implanted word, able to save the soul, by which this birth is begotten; and therefore Christ has purchased unto us this holy seed, that thereby this birth might be brought forth in us, which is therefore also called " the manifestation of the Spirit, given to every one to profit withal;" for it is written, that " by one Spirit we are all baptized into one body." And the apostle Peter also ascribeth this birth to the seed and word of God, which we have so much declared of, saying, 1 Pet. i. 23, " Being born again, not of corruptible seed, but of incorruptible, by the word of God, which liveth and abideth for ever." Though then this seed be small in its appearance, so that Christ compares it to a " grain of mustard-seed, which is the least of all seeds," Matth. xiii. 31, 32, and that it be hid in the earthly part of man's heart; yet therein is life and salvation towards the sons of men wrapped up, which comes to be revealed as they give way to it. And in this seed in the hearts of all men is the kingdom of God, as in a capacity to be produced, or rather exhibited, according as it receives depth, is nourished, and not choked: hence Christ saith, that the kingdom of God was in the very Pharisees, Luke xvii. 20, 21, who did oppose and resist him, and were justly accounted as serpents, and a generation of vipers. Now the kingdom of God could be no otherways in them than in a seed, even as the thirty-fold and the hundred-fold is wrapt up in a small seed, lying in a barren ground, which springs not forth because it wants nourishment: and as the whole body of a great tree is wrapped up potentially in the seed of the tree, and so is brought forth in due season; and as the capacity of a man or woman is not only in a child, but even in the very embryo, even so the kingdom of Jesus Christ, yea Jesus Christ himself, Christ within, who is the hope of glory, and becometh wisdom, righteousness, sanctification and redemption, is in every man's and woman's heart, in that little incorruptible seed, ready to be brought forth, as it is cherished and received in the love of it. For there can be no men worse than those rebellious and unbelieving Pharisees were; and yet this kingdom was thus within them, and they were directed to look for it there: so it is neither lo here, nor lo there, in this or the other observation, that this is known, but as this seed of God in the heart is minded and entertained. And certainly hence it is, even because this light, seed, and grace that appears in the heart of man is so little regarded, and so much overlooked, that so few know Christ brought forth in them. The one sort, to wit, the Calvinists, they look upon grace as an irresistible power, and therefore neglect and despise this eternal seed of the kingdom in their hearts, as a low, insufficient, useless thing as to their salvation. On the other hand, the Papists, Arminians, and Socinians, they go about to set up their natural power and will with one consent, denying that this little seed, this small appearance of the light, is

*The kingdom of God is in the seed in the hearts of all men.*

*Calvinists, Papists, Arminians and Socinians' errors denying the light to be saving.*

that supernatural saving grace of God given to every man to save him. And so upon them is verified that saying of the Lord Jesus Christ, " This is the condemnation of the world, that light is come into the world, but men love darkness rather than light;" the reason is added, " because their deeds are evil." All confess they feel this; but they will not have it to be of that virtue. Some will have it to be reason; some a natural conscience; some, certain relics of God's image that remained in Adam. So that Christ, as he met with opposition from all kinds of professors in his outward appearance, doth now also in his inward. It was the meanness of his outward man that made many despise him, saying, " Is not this the son of the carpenter? Are not his brethren and sisters among us? Is not this a Galilean? And came there ever a prophet out of Galilee?" And such like reasonings. For they expected an outward deliverer, who as a prince, should deliver them with great ease from their enemies, and not such a MESSIAH as should be crucified shamefully, and as it were lead them into many sorrows, troubles, and afflictions. So the meanness of this appearance makes the crafty Jesuits, the pretended rational Socinians, and the learned Arminians overlook it; desiring rather something that they might exercise their subtilty, reason, and learning about, and use the liberty of their own wills. And the secure Calvinists, they would have a Christ to save them without any trouble; to destroy all their enemies for them without them, and nothing or little within, and in the mean while to be at ease to live in their sins secure. Whence, when all is well examined, the cause is plain; it is " because their deeds are evil," that with one consent they reject this light: for it checks the wisest of them all, and the learnedest of them all in secret, it reproves them; neither can all their logic silence it, nor can the securest among them stop its voice from crying, and reproving them within, for all their confidence in the outward knowledge of Christ, or of what he hath suffered outwardly for them. For, as hath been often said, " in a day it strives with all, wrestles with all;" and it is the un-

*The meanness of Christ's appearance in the flesh.*

*The nature of the light.*

mortified nature, the first nature, the old Adam, yet alive
in the wisest, in the learnedest, in the most zealous for the
outward knowledge of Christ, that denies this, that despises
it, that shuts it out, to their own condemnation. They
come all under this description, "Every one that doth evil,
hateth the light, neither cometh to the light, lest his deeds
should be reproved," John iii. 20. So that it may be said
now, and we can say from a true and certain experience,
as it was of old, Psalm cxviii. 22; Mat. xxi. 42; Mark
xii. 10; Luke xx. 17; Acts iv. 11, The stone which
the builders of all kinds have rejected, the same is become
unto us the head of the corner. Glory to God for ever'
who hath chosen us as first fruits to himself in this day,
wherein he is arisen to plead with the nations; and therefore hath sent us forth to preach this everlasting gospel unto
all, Christ nigh to all, the light in all, the seed sown in the
hearts of all, that men may come and apply their minds to
it. And we rejoice that we have been made to lay down
our wisdom and learning, such of us as have had some of
it, and our carnal reasoning, to learn of Jesus; and sit
down at the feet of Jesus in our hearts, and hear him, who
there makes all things manifest, and reproves all things by
his light, Eph. v. 13. For many are wise and learned in
the notion, in the letter of the scripture, as the Pharisees
were, and can speak much of Christ, and plead strongly
against Infidels, Turks, and Jews, and it may be also
against some heresies, who, in the mean time, are crucifying Christ in the small appearance of his seed in their
hearts. Oh! better were it to be stripped and naked of
all, to account it as dross and dung, and become a fool
for Christ's sake, thus knowing him to teach thee in thy
heart, so as thou mayest witness him raised there, feel the
virtue of his cross there, and say with the apostle, "I glory
in nothing, save in the cross of Christ, whereby I am crucified to the world, and the world unto me." This is better than to write thousands of commentaries, and to preach
many sermons. And it is thus to preach Christ, and direct
people to his pure light in the heart, that God hath raised

The wise
and learned
in the no-
tion, cruci-
fiers of
Christ.

15 *

us up, and for which the wise men of this world account us fools; because by the operation of this cross of Christ in our hearts, we have denied our own wisdom and wills in many things, and have forsaken the vain worships, fashions, and customs of this world. For these divers centuries the world hath been full of a dry, fruitless, and barren knowledge of Christ, feeding upon the husk, and neglecting the kernel; following after the shadow, out strangers to the substance. Hence the devil matters not how much of that knowledge abounds, provided he can but possess the heart, and rule in the will, crucify the appearance of Christ there, and so keep the seed of the king-

dom from taking root. For he has led them abroad, lo here, and lo there, and has made them wrestle in a false zeal so much one against another, contending for this outward observation, and for the other outward observation, seeking Christ in this and the other external thing, as in bread and wine; contending one with another how he is there, while some will have him to be present therein this way, and some the other way; and some in scriptures, in books, in societies, and pilgrimages, and merits. But some, confiding in an external barren faith, think all is well, if they do but firmly believe that he died for their sins past, present, and to come; while in the mean time Christ lies crucified and slain, and is daily resisted and

gainsayed in his appearance in their hearts. Thus, from a sense of this blindness and ignorance that is come over Christendom, it is that we are led and moved of the Lord so constantly and frequently to call all, invite all, request all, to turn to the light in them, to mind the light in them, to believe in Christ, as he is in them: and that in the name, power, and authority of the Lord, not in school-arguments and distinctions, for which many of the wise men of this world account us fools and mad men, we do charge and command them to lay aside their wisdom, to come down out of that proud, airy, brain-knowledge, and to stop that mouth, how eloquent soever to the worldly ear it may appear, and to be silent, and sit down as in the

dust, and to mind the light of Christ in their own consciences; which, if minded, they would find as a sharp
two-edged sword in their hearts, and as a fire and a hammer,
that would knock against and burn up all that carnal,
gathered, natural stuff, and make the stoutest of them all
tremble, and become Quakers indeed; which those that
come not to feel now, and kiss not the Son while the day
lasteth, but harden their hearts, will feel to be a certain
truth when it is too late. To conclude, as saith the apostle,
All ought to examine themselves, whether they be in the
faith indeed; and try their ownselves: for except Jesus
Christ be in them, they are certainly reprobates. 2 Cor.
xiii. 5.

§ XXV. Secondly, That which remains now to be proved
is, That by the operation of this light and seed some have
been and may yet be saved, to whom the gospel is not outwardly preached, nor the history of Christ outwardly known.
To make this the easier, we have already shown how that
Christ hath died for all men; and consequently these are
enlightened by Christ, and have a measure of saving light
and grace; yea, that the gospel, though not in any outward dispensation, is preached to them, and in them: so
that thereby they are stated in a possibility of salvation.
From which I may thus argue: *2 Par. prove 1. That many by the light may be saved, that have not the outward knowledge of Christ.*

To whom the gospel, the power of God unto salvation, *Axo.*
is manifest, they may be saved, whatever outward knowledge they want:

But this gospel is preached in every creature; in which
is certainly comprehended many that have not the outward
knowledge:

Therefore of those many may be saved.

But to those arguments, by which it hath been proved,
That all men have a measure of saving grace, I shall add
one, and that very observable, not yet mentioned, viz., that
excellent saying of the apostle Paul to Titus, chap. ii., ver.
11, "The grace of God, that brings salvation, hath appeared to all men; teaching us, that denying ungodliness and
worldly lusts, we should live soberly, righteously, and

godly, in this present world :" than which there can be nothing more clear, it comprehending both the parts of the
controversy. First, It testifies that it is no natural principle
or light, but saith plainly, It brings salvation. Secondly,
It says not, that it hath appeared to a few, but unto all
men. The fruit of it declares also how efficacious it is,
seeing it comprehends the whole duty of man: it both
teacheth us, first, to forsake evil, to deny ungodliness and
worldly lusts; and then it teacheth us our whole duty.
First, to live soberly; that comprehends temperance, chas-
tity, meekness, and those things that relate unto a man's
self. Secondly, righteously; that comprehends equity,
justice, and honesty, and those things which relate to our
neighbours. And lastly, godly; which comprehends piety,
faithfulness, and devotion, which are the duties relating to
God. So then there is nothing required of man, or is needful to man, which this grace teacheth not. Yet I have heard
a public preacher (one of those that are accounted zealous
men) to evite the strength of this text, deny this grace to
be saving, and say, It was only intended of common favours
and graces, such as is the heat of the fire, and outward light
of the sun. Such is the darkness and ignorance of those
that oppose the truth; whereas the text saith expressly, that
it is saving. Others, that cannot deny but it is saving, allege,
This *all* comprehends not every individual, but only all
kinds: but is a bare negation sufficient to overturn the
strength of a positive assertion? If the scriptures may be
so abused, what so absurd, as may not be pleaded for from
them? or what so manifest, as may not be denied? But
we have no reason to be staggered by their denying, so
long as our faith is found in express terms of the scripture;
they may as well seek to persuade us, that we do not intend
that which we affirm, though we know the contrary, as
make us believe, that when the apostle speaks forth our
doctrine in plain words, yet he intends theirs, which is
quite the contrary. And indeed, can there be any thing
more absurd, than to say, where the word is plainly *all*,
*few* is only intended? For they will not have *all* taken

The saving
grace of
God teach-
eth the
whole duty
of man.

The absur-
dity of our
adversa-
ries' com-
ment upon
the word
*all*, denying
grace to be
saving,
Tit. ii. 2, 11.

here for the greater number. Indeed, as the case may be sometimes, by a figure *all* may be taken, of two numbers, for the greater number; but let them show us, if they can, either in scripture, or profane or ecclesiastical writings, that any man that wrote sense did ever use the word *all* to express, of two numbers, the lesser. Whereas they affirm, that the far lesser number have received saving grace; and yet will they have the apostle, by *all*, to have signified so. Though this might suffice, yet, to put it further beyond all question, I shall instance another saying of the same apostle, that we may use him as his own commentator, Rom. v. 18: "Therefore as by the offence of one, judgment came upon all men to condemnation, even so by the righteousness of one, the free gift came upon all men unto justification of life." Here no man of reason, except he will be obstinately ignorant, will deny, but this similitive particle *as* makes the *all* which goes before, and comes after, to be of one and the same extent; or else let them show one example, either in scripture or elsewhere, among men that speak proper language, where it is otherwise. We must then either affirm that this loss, which leads to condemnation, hath not come upon all; or say, that this free gift is come upon all by Christ. Whence I thus argue:

If all men have received a loss from Adam, which leads Arg. to condemnation; then all men have received a gift from Christ, which leads to justification:

But the first is true; therefore also the last.

From all which it naturally follows, that all men, even Even the the heathen, may be saved: for Christ was given as a may be "light to enlighten the Gentiles," Isai. xlix. 6. Now, to say the light. that though they might have been saved, yet none were, is to judge too uncharitably. I see not what reason can be alleged for it; yea, though it were granted, which never can be, that none of the heathen were saved; it will not from thence follow, that they could not have been saved: or that none now in their condition can be saved. For, *A non esse ad non posse non datur sequela*, i. e., That consequence is false, that concludes a thing cannot be, because it is not.

**OBJECT**

But if it be objected, which is the great objection, That there is no name under heaven, by which salvation is known, but by the name JESUS:

Therefore they (not knowing this) cannot be saved:

**ANSW.**

I answer; Though they know it not outwardly, yet if they know it inwardly, by feeling the virtue and power of

*The literal knowledge of Christ is not saving, but the real experimental.*

it, the name JESUS indeed, which signifies a Saviour, to free them from sin and iniquity in their hearts, they are saved by it: I confess there is no other name to be saved by: but salvation lieth not in the literal, but in the experimental knowledge; albeit, those that have the literal knowledge are not saved by it, without this real experimental knowledge: yet those that have the real knowledge may be saved without the external; as by the arguments hereafter brought will more appear. For if the outward distinct knowledge of him, by whose means I receive benefit, were necessary for me before I could reap any fruit of it; then, by the rule of contraries, it would follow, that I could receive no hurt, without I had also the distinct knowledge of him that occasioned it; whereas experience proves the contrary. How many are injured by Adam's fall, that know nothing of there ever being such a man in the world, or of his eating the forbidden fruit? Why may they not then be saved by the gift and grace of Christ in them, making them righteous and holy, though they know not distinctly how that was purchased unto them by the death and sufferings of Jesus that was crucified at Jerusalem; especially seeing God hath made that knowledge simply impossible to them? As many men are killed by poison infused into their meat, though they neither know what the poison was, nor who infused it; so also on the other hand, how many are cured of their diseases by good remedies, who know not how the medicine is prepared, what the ingredients are, nor oftentimes who made it? The like may also hold in spiritual things, as we shall hereafter prove.

§ XXVI. First, If there were such an absolute necessity for this outward knowledge, that it were even of the essentials of salvation, then none could be saved without it; whereas our adversaries deny not, but readily confess, that many infants and deaf persons are saved without it: so that here they break that general rule, and make salvation possible without it. Neither can they allege, that it is because such are free from sin; seeing they also affirm, that all infants, because of Adam's sin, deserve eternal condemnation, as being really guilty in the sight of God; and of deaf people, it is not to be doubted, and experience shows us, that they are subject to many common iniquities, as well as other men. *The outward knowledge not essential to salvation: instance in infants and deaf persons.*

If it be said, That these children are the children of believing parents: *Obj. 1.*

What then? They will not say that they transmit grace to their children. Do they not affirm, that the children of believing parents are guilty of original sin, and deserve death as well as others? How prove they that that makes up the loss of all explicit knowledge? *Answ.*

If they say, Deaf people may be made sensible of the gospel by signs: *Obj. 2.*

All the signs cannot give them any explicit knowledge of the history of the death, sufferings, and resurrection of Christ. For what signs can inform a deaf man, That the Son of God took on him man's nature, was born of a virgin, and suffered under Pontius Pilate? *Answ.*

And if they should further allege, That they are within the bosom of the visible church, and partakers of the sacraments: *Obj. 3*

All that gives no certainty of salvation; for, as the Protestants confess, they confer not grace *ex opere operato.* And will they not acknowledge, that many are in the bosom of the church, who are visibly no members of it? But if this charity be extended towards such who are where the gospel is preached, so that they may be judged capable of salvation, because they are under a simple impossibility of distinctly knowing the means of salvation; what reason *Answ* can be alleged why the like charity may not be had to such, as though they can hear, yet are under a simple impossibility of hearing, because it is not spoken unto them? Is not

A Chinese or Indian excusable for not knowing the history of the death of Christ, &c.

a man in China, or in India, as much to be excused for not knowing a thing which he never heard of, as a deaf man here, who cannot hear? For as the deaf man is not to be blamed, because God hath been pleased to suffer him to lie under this infirmity; so is the Chinese or the Indian as excusable, because God hath withheld from him the opportunity of hearing. He that cannot hear a thing, as being necessarily absent, and he that cannot hear it, as being naturally deaf, are to be placed in the same category.

Ans. 2.

Secondly, This manifestly appears by that saying of Peter, Acts x. 34: "Of a truth I perceive that God is no respecter of persons; but in every nation, he that feareth him, and worketh righteousness, is accepted of him." Peter was before liable to that mistake that the rest of the Jews were in; judging that all were unclean, except themselves, and that no man could be saved, except they were proselyted to their religion and circumcised. But God showed Peter otherways in a vision, and taught him to call nothing

God regarded the prayers of Cornelius, stranger to the law.

common or unclean; and therefore, seeing that God regarded the prayers of Cornelius, who was a stranger to the law and to Jesus Christ as to the outward, yet Peter saw that God had accepted him; and he is said to fear God before he had this outward knowledge: therefore Peter concludes that every one in every nation, without respect of persons, that feareth God and worketh righteousness, is accepted of him. So he makes the fear of God and the working of righteousness, and not an outward historical knowledge, the qualification: they then that have this, wherever they be, they are saved. Now we have already proved, that to every man that grace is given, whereby he may live godly and righteously; and we see, that by this grace Cornelius did so and was accepted, and his prayers came up for a memorial before God, before he had this outward knowledge. Also, Was not Job a perfect and upright man, that feared God, and eschewed evil? Who

taught Job this? How knew Job Adam's fall? And from
what scripture learned he that excellent knowledge he had, From what
and that faith, by which he knew his Redeemer lived? scripture
did Job
For many make him as old as Moses. Was not this by learn his
an inward grace in the heart? Was it not that inward knowledge?
grace that taught Job to eschew evil, and to fear God?
And was it not by the workings thereof that he became a
just and upright man? How doth he reprove the wickedness of men, chap. xxiv.? And after he hath numbered
up their wickedness, doth he not condemn them, verse 13,
for rebelling against this light, for not knowing the way
thereof, nor abiding in the paths thereof? It appears then
Job believed that men had a light, and that because they
rebelled against it, therefore they knew not its ways, and
abode not in its paths; even as the Pharisees, who had the
scriptures, are said to err, not knowing the scriptures. And
also Job's friends, though in some things wrong; yet who Job's
taught them all those excellent sayings and knowledge friends,
their excel
which they had? Did not God give it them, in order to lent say-
save them? or was it merely to condemn them? Who ings.
taught Elihu, That "the inspiration of the Almighty giveth
understanding; that the Spirit of God made him, and the
breath of the Almighty gave him life?" And did not the
Lord accept a sacrifice for them? And who dare say that
they are damned? But further, the apostle puts this controversy out of doubt; for, if we may believe his plain
assertions, he tells us, Rom. ii., "That the heathen did
the things contained in the law." From whence I thus
argue:

In every nation, he that feareth God, and worketh right- Arg.
eousness, is accepted:

But many of the heathen feared God, and wrought
righteousness:

Therefore they were accepted.

The minor is proved from the example of Cornelius; but
I shall further prove it thus;

He that doth the things contained in the law, feareth
God, and worketh righteousness·

But the heathen did the things contained in the law:

Therefore they feared God, and wrought righteousness.

Can there be any thing more clear? For if to do the things contained in the law, be not to fear God, and work righteousness, then what can be said to do so, seeing the apostle calls the law spiritual, holy, just, and good? But this appears manifestly by another medium, taken out of the same chapter, verse 13; so that nothing can be more clear: the words are, "The doers of the law shall be justified." From which I thus argue, without adding any word of my own;

**ARG.**

The doers of the law shall be justified:

But the Gentiles do the things contained in the law:

The Gentiles justified doing the law

All, that know but a conclusion, do easily see what follows from these express words of the apostle. And indeed, he through that whole chapter labours, as if he were contending now with our adversaries, to confirm this doctrine, verses 9, 10, 11, "Tribulation and anguish upon every soul of man that doth evil, to the Jew first, and also to the Gentile: for there is no respect of persons with God." Where the apostle clearly homologates, or confesses to the sentence of Peter before mentioned; and shows that Jew and Gentile, or as he himself explains in the following verses, both they that have an outward law and they that have none, when they do good shall be justified. And to put us out of all doubt, in the very following verses he tells, That "the doers of the law are justified;" and that the "Gentiles did the law." So that except we think he spake not what he intended, we may safely conclude, that such Gentiles were justified, and did partake of that honour, glory, and peace, which comes upon every one that doth good; even the Gentiles, that are without the law, when they work good; seeing with God there is no respect of persons. So as we see, that it is not the having the outward knowledge that doth save, without the inward; so neither doth the want of it, to such to whom God hath made it impossible, who have the inward, bring condemnation. And many that have wanted the outward, have nad a knowledge of this inwardly, by virtue of that inward grace and light given to every man, working in them, by which they forsook iniquity, and became just and holy, as is above proved; who, though they knew not the history of Adam's fall, yet were sensible in themselves of the loss that came by it, feeling their inclinations to sin, and the body of sin in them: and though they knew not the coming of Christ, yet were sensible of that inward power and salvation which came by him, even before as well as since his appearance in the flesh. For I question whether these men can prove, that all the patriarchs and fathers before Moses had a distinct knowledge either of the one or the other, or that they knew the history of the tree of knowledge of good and evil, and of Adam's eating the forbidden fruit; far less that Christ should be born of a virgin, should be crucified, and treated in the manner he was. For it is justly to be believed, that what Moses wrote of Adam, and of the first times, was not by tradition, but by revelation; yea, we see that not only after the writing of Moses, but even of David and all the prophets, who prophesied so much of Christ, how little the Jews, that were expecting and wishing for the Messiah, could thereby discern him when he came, that they crucified him as a blasphemer, not as a Messiah, by mistaking the prophecies concerning him; for Peter saith expressly, Acts iii. 17, to the Jews, That both they and their rulers did it through ignorance. And Paul saith, 1 Cor. ii. 8, "That had they known it, they would not have crucified the Lord of Glory." Yea, Mary herself, to whom the angel had spoken, and who had laid up all the miraculous things accompanying his birth in her heart, she did not understand how, when he disputed with the doctors in the temple, that he was about his father's business. And the apostles that had believed him, conversed daily with him, and saw his miracles, could not understand, neither believe those things which related to his death, sufferings, and resurrection, but were in a certain respect stumbled at them.

§ XXVII. So we see how that it is the inward **work,**

Many wanting the history, were sensible of the loss by Adam, and salvation come by Christ in themselves.

How little the Jews knew Christ, mistaking the prophets.

and not the outward history and scripture, that gives the true knowledge; and by this inward light many of the heathen philosophers were sensible of the loss received by Adam, though they knew not the outward history: hence Plato asserted, That "man's soul was fallen into a dark cave, where it only conversed with shadows." Pythagoras saith, "Man wandereth in this world as a stranger, banished from the presence of God." And Plotinus compareth "man's soul, fallen from God, to a cinder, or dead coal, out of which the fire is extinguished." Some of them said, That "the wings of the soul were clipped or fallen off, so that they could not flee unto God." All which, and many more such expressions, that might be gathered out of their writings, show, that they were not without a sense of this loss. Also they had a knowledge and discovery of Jesus Christ inwardly, as a remedy in them, to deliver them from that evil seed, and the evil inclinations of their own hearts, though not under that particular denomination.

*The heathen were sensible of the loss received by Adam.*

*Heathen philosophers' divine knowledge. Plato. Pythag. Plotin.*

Some called him a Holy Spirit, as Seneca, Epist. 41, who said, " There is a Holy Spirit in us, that treateth us as we treat him." Cicero calleth it an " innate light," in his book *De Republica*, cited by Lactantius, 6 Inst., where he calls this " right reason, given unto all, constant and eternal, calling unto duty by commanding, and deterring from deceit by forbidding." Adding, " That it cannot be abrogated, neither can any be freed from it, neither by senate nor people; that it is one eternal, and the same always to all nations; so that there is not one at Rome, and another at Athens: Whoso obeys it not, must flee from himself, and in this is greatly tormented, although he should escape all other punishments." Plotinus also calls him light, saying, That " as the sun cannot be known but by its own light, so God cannot be known but with his own light: and as the eye cannot see the sun but by receiving its image, so man cannot know God but by receiving his image; and that it behoveth man to come to purity of heart before he could know God;" calling him also Wisdom, a name frequently given him in scripture; see Prov

*Cicero calls it an innate light. Lactan. in Sect.*

>. 20, to the end; and Prov. viii. 9, 34, where Wisdom is
said to cry, entreat, and invite all to come unto her, and
learn of her: and what is this Wisdom but Christ? Hence
such as came among the heathen, to forsake evil, and
cleave to righteousness, were called philosophers, that is, Philoso-
lovers of wisdom. They knew this wisdom was nigh unto phers,
whence so
them, and that "the best knowledge of God, and divine called?
mysteries, was by the inspiration of the wisdom of God."
Phocylides affirmed, that "the word of the wisdom of Phocylides.
God was best." His words in the Greek are, Τῆς δὲ
Θεοπνεύςης σοφίας λόγος ἐς ἰν ἄριςος.

And much more of this kind might be instanced, by
which it appears they knew Christ; and by his working in
them were brought from unrighteousness to righteousness,
and to love that power by which they felt themselves redeemed; so that, as saith the apostle, "They show the
work of the law written in their hearts, and did the things
contained in the law;" and therefore, as all doers of the
law are, were no doubt justified, and saved thus by the
power of Christ in them. And as this was the judgment
of the apostle, so was it of the primitive Christians. Hence
Justin Martyr stuck not to call Socrates a Christian, saying, Socrates a
that "all such as lived according to the divine word in &c.
Christian,
them, which was in all men, were Christians, such as Socrates and Heraclitus, and others among the Greeks," &c.
"That such as live with the word, are Christians without
fear or anxiety."

Clemens Alexandrinus saith, Apol. ii., Strom. lib. i., Clem. Alex
That "this wisdom or philosophy was necessary to the
Gentiles, and was their schoolmaster to lead them unto
Christ, by which of old the Greeks were justified."

"Nor do I think," saith Augustine, in his book of the Augustin.
City of God, lib. xviii., cap. 47, "that the Jews dare affirm de Civ. Dei
that none belonged unto God but the Israelites." Upon
which place Ludovicus Vives saith, That "thus the Gen- Lud. Vives
tiles, not having a law, were a law unto themselves; and
the light of so living is the gift of God, and proceeds from

16 *                              Y

the Son ; of whom it is written, that he ' enlighteneth every man that cometh into the world.' "

The Plato-<br>nists saw<br>the word in<br>the begin-<br>ning; which<br>was light. Augustine also testifies in his confessions, lib. i., cap. 9, That " he had read in the writings of the Platonists, though not in the very same words, yet that which by many and multiplied reasons did persuade, that ' in the beginning was the word, and the word was with God ; this was in the beginning with God, by which all things were made, and without which nothing was made that was made : in him was life, and the life was the light of men : and the light shined in the darkness, and the darkness did not comprehend it.' And, albeit the soul gives testimony concerning the light, yet it is not the light, but the word of God; for ' God is the true Light, which enlighteneth every man that cometh into the world ;' " and so repeats to verse 14, of John i., adding, " These things have I there read."

Hai Eben<br>Yokdan. Yea, there is a book translated out of the Arabic, which gives an account of one Hai Eben Yokdan ; who living in an island alone, without converse of man, attained to such a profound knowledge of God, as to have immediate converse with him, and to affirm, " That the best and most certain knowledge of God is not that which is attained by The su-<br>preme in-<br>tellect en-<br>joyed by the<br>mind of<br>man. premises premised, and conclusions deduced ; but that which is enjoyed by conjunction of the mind of man with the supreme intellect, after the mind is purified from its corruptions, and is separated from all bodily images, and is gathered into a profound stillness."

§ XXVIII. Seeing then it is by this inward gift, grace, and light, that both those that have the gospel preached unto them, come to have Jesus brought forth in them, and to have the saving and sanctified use of all outward helps and advantages ; and also by this same light, that all may come to be saved ; and that God calls, invites, and strives with all, in a day, and saveth many, to whom he hath not The day of<br>the Lord<br>proclaimed. seen meet to convey this outward knowledge ; therefore we, having the experience of the inward and powerful work of this light in our hearts, even Jesus revealed in us, cannot cease to proclaim the day of the Lord that is arisen in it, crying out with the woman of Samaria; "Come and see one that hath told me all that ever I have done: Is not this the Christ?" That others may come and feel the same in themselves, and may know, that that little small thing that reproves them in their hearts, however they have despised and neglected it, is nothing less than the gospel preached in them; Christ, the wisdom and power of God, being in and by that seed seeking to save their souls.

Of this light therefore Augustine speaks in his confessions, lib. xi., cap. 9: "In this beginning, O God! thou madest the heavens and the earth, in thy word, in thy Son, in thy virtue, in thy wisdom, wonderfully saying, and wonderfully doing. Who shall comprehend it? Who shall declare it? What is that which shineth in unto me, and smites my heart without hurt, at which I both tremble, and am inflamed? I tremble, in so far as I am unlike unto it; and I am inflamed in so far as I am like unto it: it is wisdom, wisdom which shineth in unto me, and dispelleth my cloud, which had again covered me, after I was departed from it, with darkness and the heap of my punishments." And again he saith, lib. x., cap. 27, "It is too late that I have loved thee, O thou beautifulness, so ancient and so new! late have I loved thee, and behold thou wast within, and I was without, and there was seeking thee! thou didst call, thou didst cry, thou didst break my deafness, thou glancedst, thou didst shine, thou chasedst away my darkness." *Augustine trembled at the in-shinings of the light unto him, and why?*

Of this also our countryman George Buchanan speaketh thus in his book, *De Jure regni apud Scotos:* "Truly I understand no other thing at present than that light which is divinely infused into our souls: for when God formed man, he not only gave him eyes to his body, by which he might shun those things that are hurtful to him, and follow those things that are profitable; but also hath set before his mind as it were a certain light, by which he may discern things that are vile from things that are honest. Some call this power 'nature,' others the 'law of nature;' I truly judge it to be divine, and am persuaded that nature *Buchanan testifying to the light.*

and wisdom never say different things. Moreover, God hath given us a compend of the law, which in few words comprehends the whole; to wit, that we should love him from our hearts, and our neighbours as ourselves. And of this law all the books of the holy scriptures, which pertain to the forming of manners, contain no other but an explication."

Jew and Gentile, Scythian and Barbarian partakers of the salvation of Christ.This is that universal evangelical principle, in and by which this salvation of Christ is exhibited to all men, both Jew and Gentile, Scythian and Barbarian, of whatsoever country or kindred he be: and therefore God hath raised up unto himself, in this our age, faithful witnesses and evangelists to preach again his everlasting gospel, and to direct all, as well the high professors, who boast of the law and the scriptures, and the outward knowledge of Christ, as the infidels and heathen that know not him that way, that they may all come to mind the light in them, and know Christ in them, "the just one, *τὸν Δίκαιον*, whom they have so long killed, and made merry over, and he hath not resisted," James v. 6, and give up their sins, iniquities, false faith, professions, and outside righteousness, to be crucified by the power of his cross in them, so as they may know Christ within to be the hope of glory, and may come to walk in his light and be saved, who is that "true light that enlighteneth every man that cometh into the world."

---

# PROPOSITION VII.

## *Concerning Justification.*

As many as resist not this light, but receive the same, it becomes in them a holy, pure, and spiritual birth, bringing forth holiness, righteousness, purity, and all those other blessed fruits which are acceptable to God by which holy birth, to wit, Jesus Christ formed within us, and working his works in us, as we are sanctified, so are we justified in the sight of God, according to the apostle's words; "But ye are washed, but ye are sanctified, but ye are justified in the name of the Lord Jesus, and by the Spirit of our God," 1 Cor. vi. 11. There-fore it is not by our works wrought in our will, nor yet by good works considered as of themselves; but by Christ, who is both the gift and the giver, and the cause producing the effects in us; who, as he hath reconciled us while we were enemies, doth also in his wisdom save us and justify us after this manner, as saith the same apostle elsewhere; "According to his mercy he saved us, by the washing of regeneration, and the renewing of the Holy Ghost," Tit. iii. 5.

§ I. The doctrine of justification comes well in order after the discussing of the extent of Christ's death, and of the grace thereby communicated, some of the sharpest con-tests concerning this having from thence their rise. Many are the disputes among those called Christians concerning this point; and indeed, if all were truly minding that which justifieth, there would be less noise about the no-tions of justification. I shall briefly review this controversy as it stands among others, and as I have often seriously observed it; then in short state the controversy as to us, and open our sense and judgment of it; and lastly prove it, if the Lord will, by some scripture testimonies, and the certain experience of all that ever were truly justified.

§ II. That this doctrine of justification, hath been and is greatly vitiated in the church of Rome, is not by us questioned; though our adversaries, who for want of better arguments do often make lies their refuge, have not spared in this respect to stigmatize us with popery, but how un-truly will hereafter appear. For to speak little of their *meritum ex condigno*, which was no doubt a very common doctrine of the Romish church, especially before Luther, though most of their modern writers, especially in their controversies with Protestants, do partly deny it, partly qualify it, and seem to state the matter only as if they were propagators and pleaders for good works by the others denied; yet if we look to the effects of this doctrine among

Observat. The me-thod of jus-tification taken by the church of Rome.

them, as they appear in the generality of their church members, not in things disapproved, but highly approved and

commended by their father the pope and all his clients,
as the most beneficial casualty of all his revenue, we shall
find that Luther did not without great ground oppose himself to them in this matter : and if he had not run himself
into another extreme, of which hereafter, his work would
have stood the better. For in this, as in most other things,
he is more to be commended for what he pulled down of
Babylon, than for what he built of his own. Whatever
then the Papists may pretend, or even some good men
among them may have thought, experience showeth, and
it is more than manifest by the universal and approved
practice of their people, that they place not their justification so much in works that are truly and morally good,
and in the being truly renewed and sanctified in the mind,
as in such things as are either nor good nor evil, or may
truly be called evil, and can no otherways be reckoned

good than because the pope pleases to call them so. So
that if the matter be well sifted, it will be found, that the
greatest part of their justification depends upon the authority
of his bulls, and not upon the power, virtue, and grace of
Christ revealed in the heart, and renewing of it, as will ap-

pear, First, From their principle concerning their sacraments, which they say confer grace *ex opere operato*. So
that if a man partake but of them, he thereby obtains
remission of sin, though he remains as he was; the virtue
of the sacraments making up the want that is in the man.
So that this act of submission and faith to the laws of the
church, and not any real inward change, is that which
justifieth him. As for example ; if a man make use of the

sacrament, as they call it, of penance, so as to tell over
his sins to a priest, though he have not true contrition,
which the Lord hath made absolutely necessary for penitent sinners, but only attrition, a figment of their own, that
is, if he be sorry he hath sinned, not out of any love to
God, or his law which he hath transgressed, but for fear
of punishment, yet doth the virtue of the sacrament, as

they affirm, procure to him remission of sins; so that being absolved by the priest, he stands accepted and justified in the sight of God. This man's justification then proceedeth not from his being truly penitent, and in any measure inwardly changed and renewed by the working of God's grace in his heart, but merely from the virtue of the sacrament, and authority of the priest, who hath pronounced him absolved; so that his justification is from somewhat without him, and not within him.

Secondly, This will yet more appear in the matter of indulgences, where remission of all sins, not only past but for years to come, is annexed to the visiting such and such churches and relics, saying such and such prayers; so that the person that so doth is presently cleared from the guilt of his sin, and justified and accepted in the sight of God. As for example: he that in the great jubilee will go to Rome, and present himself before the gate of Peter and Paul, and there receive the pope's blessing; or he that will go a pilgrimage to James's sepulchre in Spain, or to Mary of Loretto, is upon the performance of those things promised forgiveness of sins. Now if we ask them the reason how such things as are not morally good in themselves come to have virtue, they have no other answer but "because of the church and pope's authority," who being the great treasurer of the magazine of Christ's merits, lets them out upon such and such conditions. Thus also the invention of saying mass is made a chief instrument of justification; for in it they pretend to offer Christ daily to the Father a propitiatory sacrifice for the sins of the living and dead: so that a man for money can procure Christ thus to be offered for him when he pleases; by which offering he is said to obtain remission of sins, and to stand justified in the sight of God. From all which, and much more of this nature which might be mentioned, it doth appear, that the Papists place their justification, not so much in any work of holiness really brought forth in them, and real forsaking of iniquity, as in the mere performance of some ceremonies, and a blind belief which their teachers

*[margin: Proof II. Papist indulgences]*

*[margin: Papist mass; what it is.]*

have begotten in them, that the church and the pope
having the absolute dispensation of the merits of Christ,
have power to make these merits effectual for the remission
of sins, and justification of such as will perform these ceremonies. This is the true and real method of justification
taken by the generality of the church of Rome, and highly
commended by their public preachers, especially the monks,
in their sermons to the people, of which I myself have been
an ear and an eye-witness; however some of their modern
writers have laboured to qualify it in their controversies.

Luther and the Pro-testants op-posing the pope's doc-trine of works, fell into the other ex-treme of no good works necessary to justifica-tion. This doctrine Luther and the Protestants then had good
reason to deny and oppose; though many of them ran into
another extreme, so as to deny good works to be necessary
to justification, and to preach up not only remission of
sins, but justification by faith alone, without all works,
however good. So that men do not obtain their justification according as they are inwardly sanctified and renewed,
but are justified merely by believing that Christ died for
them; and so some may be perfectly justified, though they
be lying in gross wickedness; as appears by the example
of David, who they say was fully and perfectly justified
while he was lying in the gross sins of murder and adultery. As then the Protestants have sufficient ground to
quarrel and confute the Papists concerning those many
abuses in the matter of justification, showing how the doctrine of Christ is thereby vitiated and overturned, and the
word of God made void by many and useless traditions,
the law of God neglected, while foolish and needless ceremonies are prized and followed, through a false opinion of
being justified by the performance of them; and the merits
and sufferings of Christ, which is the only sacrifice appointed of God for remission of sins, derogated from, by
Papists' de-vice to get money. the setting up of a daily sacrifice never appointed by God,
and chiefly devised out of covetousness to get money by;
so the Protestants on the other hand, by not rightly establishing and holding forth the doctrine of justification according as it is delivered in the holy scriptures, have opened
a door for the Papists to accuse them, as if they were

neglecters of good works, enemies to mortification and holiness, such as esteem themselves justified while lying in great sins: by which kind of accusations, for which too great ground hath been given out of the writings of some rigid Protestants, the reformation hath been greatly defamed and hindered, and the souls of many ensnared. Whereas, whoever will narrowly look into the matter, may observe these debates to be more *in specie* than *in genere*, seeing both do upon the matter land in one; and like two men in a circle, who though they go sundry ways, yet meet at last in the same centre.

For the Papists say, "They obtain remission of sins, and are justified by the merits of Christ, as the same are applied unto them in the use of the sacraments of the church, and are dispensed in the performance of such and such ceremonies, pilgrimages, prayers, and performances, though there be not any inward renewing of the mind, nor knowing of Christ inwardly formed; yet they are remitted and made righteous *ex opere operato*, because of the power and authority accompanying the sacraments and the dispensers of them." *Papists' belief of justification meets in the same centre with the—*

The Protestants say, "That they obtain remission of sins, and stand justified in the sight of God by virtue of the merits and sufferings of Christ, not by infusing righteousness into them, but by pardoning their sins, and by accounting and accepting their persons as righteous, they resting on him and his righteousness by faith; which faith, the act of believing, is not imputed unto them for righteousness." *—Protestants' belief. So saith the Westminster Confession of Faith, chap. xi. sect. 1.*

So the justification of neither here is placed in any inward renewing of the mind, or by virtue of any spiritual birth, or formation of Christ in them; but only by a bare application of the death and sufferings of Christ outwardly performed for them: whereof the one lays hold on a faith resting upon them, and hoping to be justified by them alone; the other by the saying of some outward prayers and ceremonies, which they judge makes the death of Christ effectual unto them. I except here, being unwill-

ing to wrong any, what things have been said as o the necessity of inward holiness, either by some moder a Papists,
or some modern Protestants, who in so far as they have
laboured after a midst betwixt these two extremes have
come near to the truth, as by some citations out of them
hereafter to be mentioned will appear: though this doctrine
hath not since the apostasy, so far as ever I could observe,
been so distinctly and evidently held forth according to
the scripture's testimony, as it hath pleased God to reveal
it and preach it forth in this day, by the witnesses of his
truth whom he hath raised to that end; which doctrine,
though it be briefly held forth and comprehended in the
*State of the controversy.* thesis itself, yet I shall a little more fully explain, and show
the state of the controversy as it stands betwixt us and those
that now oppose us.

*Expl. 1.*     § III. First then, as by the explanation of the former
thesis appears, we renounce all natural power and ability
in ourselves, in order to bring us out of our lost and fallen
condition and first nature; and confess, that as of ourselves we are able to do nothing that is good, so neither
can we procure remission of sins or justification by any
act of our own, so as to merit it, or draw it as a debt from
*Justifica-tion springs of and from the love of God.* God due unto us; but we acknowledge all to be of and
from his love, which is the original and fundamental cause
of our acceptance.

*Expl. 2.*     Secondly, God manifested this love towards us, in the
sending of his beloved Son, the Lord Jesus Christ, into the
*Christ giv-ing himself a sacrifice for us.* world, who gave himself for us an offering and a sacrifice
to God, for a "sweet-smelling savour;" and having made
peace through the blood of his cross, that he might reconcile us unto himself, and by the Eternal Spirit offered himself without spot unto God, and suffered for our sins, the
just for the unjust, that he might bring us unto God.

*Expl. 3.*     Thirdly then, Forasmuch as all men who have come to
man's estate (the man Jesus only excepted) have sinned,
therefore all have need of this Saviour, to remove the wrath
of God from them due to their offences; in this respect he
is truly said to have borne the iniquities of us all in his

body on the tree, and therefore is the only Mediator, having qualified the wrath of God towards us; so that our former sins stand not in our way, being by virtue of his most satisfactory sacrifice removed and pardoned. Neither do we think that remission of sins is to be expected, sought, or obtained any other way, or by any works or sacrifice whatsoever; though, as has been said formerly, they may come to partake of this remission that are ignorant of the history. So then Christ by his death and sufferings hath reconciled us to God, even while we are enemies; that is, he offers reconciliation unto us; we are put into a capacity of being reconciled; God is willing to forgive us our iniquities, and to accept us, as is well expressed by the apostle, 2 Cor. v. 19: "God was in Christ, reconciling the world unto himself, not imputing their trespasses unto them, and hath put in us the word of reconciliation." And therefore the apostle, in the next verses, entreats them in "Christ's stead to be reconciled to God;" intimating that the wrath of God being removed by the obedience of Christ Jesus, he is willing to be reconciled unto them, and ready to remit the sins that are past, if they repent.

*To remission of sins*

*The only mediator betwixt God and man.*

We consider then our redemption in a two-fold respect or state, both which in their own nature are perfect, though in their application to us the one is not, nor cannot be, without respect to the other.

*A two-fold redemption.*

The first is the redemption performed and accomplished by Christ for us in his crucified body without us: the other is the redemption wrought by Christ in us, which no less properly is called and accounted a redemption than the former. The first then is that whereby man, as he stands in the fall, is put into a capacity of salvation, and hath conveyed unto him a measure of that power, virtue, spirit, life, and grace that was in Christ Jesus, which, as the free gift of God, is able to counterbalance, overcome, and root out the evil seed, wherewith we are naturally, as in the fall, leavened.

*I. The redemption of Christ without us*

The second is that whereby we witness and know this pure and perfect redemption in ourselves, purifying, cleans-

II.

The redemption wrought by Christ in us.

ing, and redeeming us from the power of corruption, and bringing us into unity, favour, and friendship with God. By the first of these two, we that were lost in Adam, plunged into the bitter and corrupt seed, unable of ourselves to do any good thing, but naturally joined and united to evil, forward and propense to all iniquity, servants and slaves to the power and spirit of darkness, are, notwithstanding all this, so far reconciled to God by the death of his Son, while enemies, that we are put into a capacity of salvation, having the glad tidings of the gospel of peace offered unto us, and God is reconciled unto us in Christ, calls and invites us to himself, in which respect we understand these scriptures; * He slew the enmity in himself. He loved us first; seeing us in our blood, he said unto us, Live; he who did not sin his own self, bare our sins in his own body on the tree; and he died for our sins, the just for the unjust.

*Eph. ii. 15.
1 John iv.
10. Ezek.
xvi. 6.  1
Pet. ii. 22,
24, &. iii.
18.

By the second, we witness this capacity brought into act, whereby receiving and not resisting the purchase of his death, to wit, the light, spirit, and grace of Christ revealed in us, we witness and possess a real, true, and inward redemption from the power and prevalency of sin, and so come to be truly and really redeemed, justified, and made righteous, and to a sensible union and friendship with God. Thus he died "for us, that he might redeem us from all iniquity;" and thus "we know him and the power of his resurrection, and the fellowship of his sufferings, being made conformable to his death." This last follows the first in order, and is a consequence of it, proceeding from it, as an effect from its cause: so as none could have enjoyed the last, without the first had been, such being the will of God; so also can none now partake of the first, but as he witnesseth the last. Wherefore as to us, they are both causes of our justification; the first the procuring efficient, the other the formal cause.

Tit. ii. 14.
Phil. iii. 10.

EXPL. 4.

Fourthly, We understand not by this justification by Christ, barely the good works even wrought by the Spirit of Christ; for they, as Protestants truly affirm, are rather

an effect of justification than the cause of it; but we understand the formation of Christ in us, Christ born and
brought forth in us, from which good works as naturally
proceed as fruit from a fruitful tree. It is this inward
birth in us, bringing forth righteousness and holiness in us,
.hat doth justify us; which having removed and done
away the contrary nature and spirit that did bear rule and
bring condemnation, now is in dominion over all in our
hearts. Those then that come to know Christ thus formed
in them, do enjoy him wholly and undivided, who is " the
LORD our RIGHTEOUSNESS," Jer. xxiii. 6. This is
to be clothed with Christ, and to have put him on, whom
God therefore truly accounteth righteous and just. This
is so far from being the doctrine of Papists, that as the generality of them do not understand it, so the learned among
them oppose it, and dispute against it, and particularly
Bellarmine. Thus then, as I may say, the formal cause of
justification is not the works, to speak properly, they being
but an effect of it; but this inward birth, this Jesus brought
forth in the heart, who is the well-beloved, whom the
Father cannot but accept, and all those who thus are
sprinkled with the blood of Jesus, and washed with it. By
this also comes that communication of the goods of Christ
unto us, " by which we come to be made partakers of the
divine nature," as saith Peter, 2 Pet. i. 4, and are made
one with him, as the branches with the vine, and have a
title and right to what he hath done and suffered for us; so
that his obedience becomes ours, his righteousness ours,
his death and sufferings ours. And by this nearness we
come to have a sense of his sufferings, and to suffer with
his seed, that yet lies pressed and crucified in the hearts of
the ungodly, and so travail with it, and for its redemption,
and for the repentance of those souls that in it are crucifying as yet the " Lord of Glory." Even as the apostle
Paul, who by his sufferings is said to " fill up that which
is behind of the afflictions of Christ for his body, which is
the church." Though this be a mystery sealed up from
all the wise men that are yet ignorant of this seed in them-

*The forma-
tion of
Christ in us
begets good
works.*

*Christ's
obedience,
righteous-
ness, death
and suffer-
ings are
ours.*

17 *

selves, and oppose it, nevertheless some Protestants speak
of this justification by Christ inwardly put on, as shall hereafter be recited in its place.

**Expl. 5.**    Lastly, Though we place remission of sins in the righteousness and obedience of Christ performed by him in the
flesh, as to what pertains to the remote procuring cause,
and that we hold ourselves formally justified by Christ
Jesus formed and brought forth in us, yet can we not, as
**Good**          some Protestants have unwarily done, exclude works from
**works are**     justification. For though properly we be not justified for
**not exclud-**   them, yet are we justified in them ; and they are necessary,
**ed justifica-** even as *causa sine quâ non,* i. e., the cause, without which
**tion.**         none are justified. For the denying of this, as it is contrary to the scripture's testimony, so it hath brought a great
scandal to the Protestant religion, opened the mouths of
Papists, and made many too secure, while they have
believed to be justified without good works. Moreover,
though it be not so safe to say they are meritorious, yet
seeing they are rewarded, many of those called the Fathers
have not spared to use the word *merit*, which some of us
have perhaps also done in a qualified sense, but no ways
to infer the Popish abuses above mentioned. And lastly,
if we had that notion of good works which most Protestants have, we could freely agree to make them not only
not necessary, but reject them as hurtful, viz. : That the
best works even of the saints are defiled and polluted.
For though we judge so of the best works performed by
man, endeavouring a conformity to the outward law by
his own strength, and in his own will, yet we believe that
such works as naturally proceed from this spiritual birth
and formation of Christ in us are pure and holy, even as
the root from which they come ; and therefore God accepts
them, justifies us in them, and rewards us for them of his
own free grace. The state of the controversy being thus
laid down, these following positions do from hence arise in
the next place to be proved.

**Posit. I.**    § IV. First, That the obedience, sufferings, and death
of Christ is that by which the soul obtains remission of

sins, and is the procuring cause of that grace, by whose inward workings Christ comes to be formed inwardly, and the soul to be made conformable unto him, and so just and justified. And that therefore, in respect of this capacity and offer of grace, God is said to be reconciled; not as if he were actually reconciled, or did actually justify, or account any just, so long as they remain in their sins really impure and unjust.

Secondly, That it is by this inward birth of Christ in Posit. II. man that man is made just, and therefore so accounted by God: wherefore, to be plain, we are thereby, and not till that be brought forth in us formally, if we must use that word, *justified* in the sight of God; because *justification* is both more properly and frequently in scripture taken in its proper signification for making one just, and not reputing one merely such, and is all one with *sanctification*.

Thirdly, That since good works as naturally follow from Posit. III. this birth as heat from fire, therefore are they of absolute necessity to justification, as *causa sine quâ non*, i. e. though Good not as the cause for which, yet as that in which we are, works are causa sine and without which we cannot be justified. And though *quâ non—* they be not meritorious, and draw no debt upon God, yet of justifica-tion. he cannot but accept and reward them: for it is contrary to his nature to deny his own, since they may be perfect in their kind, as proceeding from a pure holy birth and root. Wherefore their judgment is false and against the truth that say; that the holiest works of the saints are defiled and sinful in the sight of God: for these good works are not the works of the law, excluded by the apostle from justification.

§ V. As to the first, I prove it from Rom. iii. 25: Posit. I. "Whom God hath set forth to be a propitiation through Proof I. faith in his blood, to declare his righteousness for the The effi-remission of sins that are past, through the forbearance of cacy of Christ's God." Here the apostle holds forth the extent and efficacy death to re of Christ's death, showing that thereby, and by faith deem man out of evil therein, remission of sins that are past is obtained, as being that wherein the forbearance of God is exercised towards mankind. So that though men for the sins they daily commit deserve eternal death, and that the wrath of God should lay hold upon them ; yet, by virtue of that most satisfactory sacrifice of Christ Jesus, the grace and seed of God moves in love towards them, during the day of their visitation ; yet not so as not to strike against the evil, for that must be burnt up and destroyed, but to redeem man out of the evil.

PROOF II.     Secondly, If God were perfectly reconciled with men, and did esteem them just while they are actually unjust, and do continue in their sins, then should God have no controversy with them ;* how comes he then so often to complain, and to expostulate so much throughout the whole scripture with such as our adversaries confess to be justified, telling them " that their sins separate betwixt him and them ?" Isai. lix. 2. For where there is a perfect and full reconciliation, there is no separation. Yea, from this doctrine it necessarily follows, either that such for whom Christ died, and whom he hath thus reconciled, never sin, or that when they do so, they are still reconciled, and their sins make not the least separation from God ; yea, that they are justified in their sins. From whence also would follow this abominable consequence, that the good works and greatest sins of such are alike in the sight of God, seeing neither the one serves to justify them, nor the other to break their reconciliation, which occasions great security, and opens a door to every lewd practice.

PROOF III.     Thirdly, This would make void the whole practical doc-trine of the gospel, and make faith itself needless. For if faith and repentance, and the other conditions called for throughout the gospel, be a qualification upon our part necessary to be performed, then, before this be performed

---

* I do not only speak concerning men before conversion, who after-wards are converted, whom yet some of our antagonists, called Anti-nomians, do aver were justified from the beginning; but also touching those who, according to the common opinion of Protestants, have been converted ; whom albeit they confess they persist always in some misdeeds, and sometimes in heinous sins, as is manifest in David's adultery and murder, yet they assert to be perfectly and wholly justi-fied.

by us, we are either fully reconciled to God, or but in a capacity of being reconciled to God, he being ready to reconcile and justify us as these conditions are performed; which latter, if granted, is according to the truth we profess. And if we are already perfectly reconciled and justified before these conditions are performed, (which conditions are of that nature that they cannot be performed at one time, but are to be done all one's lifetime,) then can they not be said to be absolutely needful; which is contrary to the very express testimony of scripture, which is acknowledged by all Christians: "For without faith it is impossible to please God." "They that believe not are condemned already, because they believe not in the only begotten Son of God." Except ye repent, ye cannot be saved: "for if ye live after the flesh, ye shall die." And of those that were converted; I will remove your candlestick from you, unless ye repent. Should I mention all the scriptures that positively and evidently prove this, I might transcribe much of all the doctrinal part of the Bible. For since Christ said, "It is finished," and did finish his work sixteen hundred years ago and upwards; if he so fully perfected redemption then, and did actually reconcile every one that is to be saved, not simply opening a door of mercy for them, offering the sacrifice of his body, by which they may obtain remission of their sins when they repent, and communicating unto them a measure of his grace, by which they may see their sins, and be able to repent; but really making them to be reputed as just, either before they believe, as say the Antinomians, or after they have assented to the truth of the history of Christ, or are sprinkled with the baptism of water, while nevertheless they are actually unjust, so that no part of their redemption is to be wrought by him now, as to their reconciliation and justification; then the whole doctrinal part of the bible is useless, and of no profit: in vain were the apostles sent forth to preach repentance and remission of sins; and in vain do all the preachers bestow their labour, spend their breath, and give forth writings; yea, much more in vain

*Margin notes:*
Heb. xi. 6.
John iii. 18.
Luke xiii. 3.
Rom. viii. 13.

Apoc. ii. 5.

A door of mercy opened by Christ upon repentance

The Antinomians' opinion of reconciliation and justification.

do the people spend their money which they give them for preaching; seeing it is all but *actum agere*, but a vain and ineffectual essay, to do that which is already perfectly done without them.

**PROOF IV.**   But lastly, To pass by their human labours, as not worth the disputing whether they be needful or not, since, as we shall hereafter show, themselves conress the best of them is sinful; this also makes void the present intercession of Christ for men.   What will become of that great article of faith, by which we affirm, " That he sits at the right hand of God, daily making intercession for us; and for which end the Spirit itself maketh intercession for us with groanings which cannot be uttered?"   For Christ maketh not intercession for those that are not in a possibility of salvation; that is absurd.   Our adversaries will not admit that he prayed for the world at all; and to pray for those that are already reconciled, and perfectly justified, is to no purpose: to pray for remission of sins is yet more needless, if all be remitted, past, present, and to come.   Indeed there is not any solid solving of this, but by acknowledging according to the truth, That Christ by his death removed the wrath of God, so far as to obtain remission of sins for as many as receive that grace and light that he communicates unto them, and hath purchased for them by his blood; which, as they believe in, they come to know remission of sins past, and power to save them from sin, and to wipe it away, so often as they may fall into it by unwatchfulness or weakness, if, applying themselves to this grace, they truly repent; for " to as many as receive him, he gives power to become the sons of God:" so none are sons, none are justified, none reconciled, until they thus receive him in that little seed in their hearts : And life eternal is offered to those, who by patient continuance in well-doing, seek for glory, honour, and immortality: for if the righteous man depart from his righteousness, his righteousness shall be remembered no more.   And therefore on the other part, none are longer sons of God, and justified, than they patiently continue in righteousness and

*Christ's daily making intercession for us.*

well-doing. And therefore Christ lives always making intercession, during the day of every man's visitation, that they may be converted: and when men are in some measure converted, he makes intercession that they may continue and go on, and not faint, nor go back again. Much more might be said to confirm this truth; but I go on to take notice of the common objections against it, which are the arguments made use of to propagate the errors contrary to it.

§ VI. The first and chief is drawn from that saying of the apostle before mentioned, 2 Cor. v. 18, 19, "God hath reconciled us to himself by Jesus Christ: God was in Christ reconciling the world unto himself, not imputing their trespasses unto them."

From hence they seek to infer, That Christ fully per- Cbj. 1. fected the work of reconciliation, while he was on earth.

I answer; If by *reconciliation* be understood the re- Answ. moving of wrath, and the purchase of that grace by which we may come to be reconciled, we agree to it; but that that place speaks no more, appears from the place itself: for when the apostle speaks in the perfect time, saying, "He hath reconciled us," he speaks of himself and the saints; who having received the grace of God purchased The diffe-by Christ, were through faith in him actually reconciled. ence be-But as to the world, he saith *reconciling* not *reconciled*; *conciled to* which *reconciling*, though it denotes a time somewhat past, *reconciling*. yet it is by the imperfect time, denoting that the thing begun was not perfected. For this work Christ began towards all in the days of his flesh, yea, and long before; for He was the mediator from the beginning, and the lamb slain from the foundation of the world: but in his flesh, after he had perfectly fulfilled the law, and the righteousness thereof, had rent the veil, and made way for the more clear and universal revelation of the gospel to all, both Jew and Gentile; he gave up himself a most satisfactory sacrifice for sin; which becomes effectual to as many as receive him in his inward appearance, in his light in the heart. Again, this very place showeth that no other reconciliation is intended, but the opening of a door of mercy upon God's part, and a removing of wrath for sins that are past; so as men, notwithstanding their sins, are stated in a capacity of salvation: for the apostle, in the following verse, saith, "Now then we are ambassadors for Christ, as though God did beseech you by us; we pray you in Christ's stead be ye reconciled to God." For if their reconciliation had already been perfectly accomplished, what need any entreating then to be reconciled? Ambassadors are not sent after a peace already perfected, and reconciliation made, to entreat for a reconciliation; for that implies a manifest contradiction.

**Obj. 2.**

Secondly, They object, verse 21st of the same chapter, "For he hath made him to be sin for us, who knew no sin, that we might be made the righteousness of God in him." From whence they argue, That as our sin is imputed to Christ, who had no sin; so Christ's righteousness is imputed to us, without our being righteous.

**Answ.**

But this interpretation is easily rejected; for though "Christ bare our sins," and "suffered for us," and was among men "accounted a sinner," and "numbered among transgressors;" yet that God reputed him a sinner, is nowhere proved. For it is said, He was found before him holy, harmless, and undefiled, neither was there found any guile in his mouth. That we deserved these things, and much more for our sins, which he endured in obedience to the Father, and according to his counsel, is true; but that ever God reputed him a sinner, is denied: neither did he ever die that we should be reputed righteous, though no more really such than he was a sinner, as hereafter appears. For indeed, if this argument hold, it might be stretched to that length, as to become very pleasing to wicked men that love to abide in their sins: for if we be made righteous, as Christ was made a sinner, merely by imputation; then as there was no sin, not in the least in Christ, so it would follow, that there needed no more righteousness, no more holiness, no more inward sanctification in us, than there was sin in him. So then, by his "being made sin for us"

**Heb. vii. 26.**
**1 Pet. ii. 22.**

**Men's imputed righteousness solidly refuted.**

must be understood his suffering for our sins, that we might be made partakers of the grace purchased by him; by the workings whereof we are made the righteousness of God in him. For that the apostle understood here a being made really righteous, and not merely a being reputed such, appears by what follows, seeing in vers. 14, 15, 16, of the following chapter, he argues largely against any supposed agreement of light and darkness, righteousness and unrighteousness; which must needs be admitted, if men are to be reckoned engrafted in Christ, and real members of him, merely by an imputative righteousness, wholly without them, while they themselves are actually unrighteous. And indeed it may be thought strange, how some men have made this so fundamental an article of their faith, which is so contrary to the whole strain of the gospel: a thing which Christ in none of all his sermons and gracious speeches ever willed any to rely upon; always recommending to us works, as instrumental in our justification. And the more it is to be admired at, because that sentence or term, so frequently in their mouths, and so often pressed by them, as the very basis of their hope and confidence, to wit, The imputed righteousness of Christ, is not to be found in all the bible, at least as to my observation. Thus have I passed through the first part, and that the more briefly, because many, who assert this justification by bare imputation, do nevertheless confess, that even the elect are not justified until they be converted; that is, not until this imputative justification be applied to them by the Spirit. *Christ's imputed righteousness not found in all the bible.*

§ VII. I come then to the second thing proposed by me, which is; That it is by this inward birth, or Christ formed within, that we are, so to speak, formally justified in the sight of God. I suppose I have said enough already to demonstrate how much we ascribe to the death and sufferings of Christ, as that whereby satisfaction is made to the justice of God, remission of sins obtained, and this grace and seed purchased, by and from which this birth proceeds. The thing now to be proved is, That by Christ *Posit. II. By Christ formed within we are justified.*

18

Jesus formed in us, we are justified, or made just. Let it be marked, I use *justification* in this sense upon this occasion.

**PROOF 1.**

First then, I prove this by that of the apostle Paul, 1 Cor. vi. 11, "And such were some of you; but ye are washed, but ye are sanctified, but ye are justified in the name of the Lord Jesus, and by the Spirit of our God." First, This *justified* here understood, must needs be a being really made just, and not a being merely imputed such; else *sanctified* and *washed* might be reputed a being esteemed so, and not a being really so; and then it quite overturns the whole intent of the context. For the apostle showing them in the preceding verses, how the "unrighteous cannot inherit the kingdom of God," and descending to the several species of wickedness, subsumes, That they were sometimes such, but now are not any more such. Wherefore, as they are now washed and sanctified, so are they justified: for if this justification were not real, then it might be alleged that the Corinthians had not forsaken these evils; but, though they still continued in them, were notwithstanding justified: which as in itself it is most absurd, so it very clearly overturneth the very import and intent of the place; as if the Corinthians turning Christians had not wrought any real change in them, but had only been a belief of some barren notions, which had wrought no alteration in their affections, will, or manner of life. For my own part, I neither see any thing, nor could ever yet hear or read any thing, that with any colour of reason did evince *justified* in this place to be understood any other ways than in its own proper and genuine interpretation of being made just. And for the more clear understanding hereof, let it be considered, that this word *justify* is derived either from the substantive *justice*, or the adjective *just*: both which words import the substantive, that true and real virtue in the soul, as it is in itself; to wit, it signifies *really*, and not *suppositively*, that excellent quality expressed and understood among men by the word *justice*; and the adjective *just* as applied signi-

*Justified, i. e. being made just really, not by imputation.*

*The derivation of the word justified considered, &c.*

fies a man or woman who is just, that is, in whom this quality of justice is stated: for it would not only be great impropriety, but also manifest falsity, to call a man just, merely by supposition; especially if he were really unjust. Now this word *justify* formed from *justice*, or *just*, doth beyond all question signify a making just; it being nothing else but a composition of the verb *facio*, and the adjective *justus*, which is nothing else than thus, *justifico*, i. e., *justum facio*, I make just; and *justified* of *justus* and *fio*, as *justus fio*, I become just, and *justificatus*, i. e. *justus factus*, I am made just. Thus also is it with verbs of this kind, as *sanctifico*, from *sanctus*, holy, and *facio; honorifico*, from *honor* and *facio; sacrifico*, from *sacer* and *facio:* all which are still understood of the subject really and truly endued with that virtue and quality from which the verb is derived. Therefore, as none are said to be sanctified that are really unholy, while they are such; so neither can any be truly said to be justified, while they actually remain unjust. Only this verb *justify* hath, in a metaphorical and figurative sense, been otherwise taken, to wit, in a law sense; as when a man really guilty of a crime is freed from the punishment of his sin, he is said to be justified; that is, put in the place as if he were just. For this use of the word hath proceeded from that true supposition, That none ought to be acquitted, but the innocent. Hence also that manner of speaking, I will justify such a man, or I will justify this or that, is used from the supposition that the person and thing is really justifiable: and where there is an error and abuse in the matter, so far there is also in the expression.

*Justified none are, while they actually remain unjust.*

This is so manifest and apparent, that Paræus, a chief Protestant, and a Calvinist also in his opinion, acknowledges this; "We never at any time said," saith he, "nor thought, that the righteousness of Christ was imputed to us, that by him we should be named formally just, and not be so, as we have divers times already showed; for that would no less soundly fight with right reason, than if a guilty man absolved in judgment should say, that he him-

*Paræus de Just. cont. Bell. l. ii. c. vii. p.469*

self was formally just by the clemency of the judge granting him his life." Now is it not strange, that men should be so facile in a matter of so great concernment, as to build the stress of their acceptance with God upon a mere borrowed and metaphorical signification, to the excluding, Holiness required, therefore good works are. or at least esteeming that not necessary, without which the scripture saith expressly, " No man shall ever see God?" For if holiness be requisite and necessary, of which this is said, then must good works also; unless our adversaries can show us a holy man without good works. But, moreover, *justified* in this figurative sense is used for *approved ;* and indeed for the most part, if not always in scripture, when the word *justify* is used, it is taken in the worst part; that is, that as the use of the word that way is a usurpation, so it is spoken of such as usurp the thing to themselves, while it properly doth not belong unto them; as will appear to those that will be at the pains to examine these places: Exod. xxiii. 7; Job. ix. 20, and xxvii. 5; Prov. xvii. 15; Isai. v. 23; Jer. iii. 11; Ezek. xvi. 51, 52; Luke x. 29, and xvi. 15, which are all spoken of men "justifying the wicked," or of " wicked men justifying themselves;" that is, approving themselves in their wickedness. If it be at any time in this signification taken in good part, it is very seldom, and that so obvious and plain by the context, as leaves no scruple. But the question is not so much of the use of the word, where it is passingly or occasionally used, as where the very doctrine of justification is handled. Where indeed to mistake it, viz. in its proper place, so as to content ourselves with an imaginary justification, while God requires a real, is of most dangerous consequence. For the disquisition of which, let it be considered, that in all these places to the Romans, Corinthians, Galatians, and elsewhere, where the apostle handles this theme, the word may be taken in its own proper signification without any absurdity. As, where it is often asserted in the above-mentioned epistles to the Romans and Galatians, That " a man cannot be justified by the law of Moses, nor by the works of the law;" there is no absurdity nor danger in understanding it according to its own proper signification, to wit, that a man cannot be made just by the law of Moses; seeing this so well agrees with that saying of the same apostle, That "the law makes nothing perfect." And also where it is said, "We are justified by faith," it may be very well understood of being made just; seeing it is also said, That "faith purifies the heart;" and no doubt the pure in heart are just; and "the just live by faith." Again, where it is said, We are justified by grace, we are justified by Christ, we are justified by the Spirit; it is no ways absurd to understand it of being made just, seeing by his Spirit and grace he doth make men just. But to understand it universally the other way, merely for acceptance and imputation, would infer great absurdities, as may be proved at large; but because I judged it would be acknowledged, I forbear at present for brevity's sake. But further, in the most weighty places where this word *justify* is used in scripture, with an immediate relation to the doctrine of justification, our adversaries must needs acknowledge it to be understood of making just, and not barely in the legal acceptation: as first, in that of 1 Cor. vi. 11, "But ye are washed, but ye are sanctified, but ye are justified," as I before have proved; which also many protestants are forced to acknowledge. "Neither diffide we," saith Thysius, "because of the most great and strict connexion, that justification doth sometimes seem also to comprehend sanctification as a consequence, as in Rom. viii. 30; Tit. iii. 7; 1 Cor. vi. 11, 'And such sometimes were ye, but ye are washed,'" &c. Zanchius, having spoken concerning this sense of justification, adds, saying: "There is another signification of the word, viz: for a man from unjust to be made just, even as *sanctified* signifies from unholy to be made holy: in which signification the apostle said, in the place above cited, 'And such were some of you,' &c., that is, of unclean ye are made holy, and of unjust ye are made just by the Holy Spirit, for Christ's sake, in whom ye have believed. Of this signification is that, Rev. xxii. 11, 'Let

*Justified,* in its proper signification.

Justification signifies a making just.

Thysius Disp. de Just. Thes. 3.

Zanchius in cap. 2. ad Eph. v. 4. loc. de Just.

him that is just, be just still ;' that is, really from just be‧
come more just, even as from unjust he became just. And
according to this signification the Fathers, and especially
Augustine, have interpreted this word." Thus far he.

**H. Bulli‧g.**  H. Bullinger, on the same place, 1 Cor. vi., speaketh thus,
" By divers words," saith he, " the apostle signifies the
same thing, when he saith, ' Ye are washed, ye are sancti‧
fied, ye are justified.' "

**Proof II.**  Secondly, In that excellent saying of the apostle, so
much observed, Rom. viii. 30, " Whom he called, them
he also justified, and whom he justified, them he also glori‧
fied :" this is commonly called the golden chain, as being
acknowledged to comprehend the method and order of
salvation.  And therefore, if *justified* were not understood
here in its proper signification of being made just, sancti‧
fication would be excluded out of this chain.  And truly
it is very worthy of observation, that the apostle, in this
succinct and compendious account, makes the word *justi‧
fied* to comprehend all betwixt calling and glorifying;
Righteous-  thereby clearly insinuating, that the being really righteous
ness the
only me-  is that only medium by which from our calling we pass to
dium by
which from  glorification.  Almost all do acknowledge the word to be
our calling  so taken in this place ; and not only so, but most of those
we pass to
glorifica-  who oppose are forced to acknowledge, that as this is the
tion.  most proper, so the most common signification of it : thus
divers famous Protestants acknowledge.  " We are not,"
D. Cham.  saith D. Chamierus, " such impertinent esteemers of words,
Tom. iii. de
Sanct l. x.  as to be ignorant, nor yet such importunate sophists, as to
▸. 1.  deny that the words *justification* and *sanctification* do infer
one another ; yea, we know that the saints are chiefly for
this reason so called, because that in Christ they have re‧
ceived remission of sins : and we read in the revelations,
' Let him that is just, be just still ;' which cannot be under‧
stood, except of the fruit of inherent righteousness.  Nor
do we deny, but perhaps in other places they may be pro‧
miscuously taken, especially by the Fathers."  " I take,"
Beza in c.  saith Beza, " the name of justification largely, so as it com‧
ᵴ. aᴅ Tit.  prehends whatsoever we acquire from Christ, as well by
ver. 7.

imputation, as by the efficacy of the Spirit in sanctifying us. So likewise is the word *justification* taken, Rom. viii. 30." Melancthon saith, "That to be justified by faith, signifies in scripture not only to be pronounced just, but also of unrighteous to be made righteous." Also some chief Protestants, though not so clearly, yet in part, hinted at our doctrine, whereby we ascribe unto the death of Christ remission of sins, and the work of justification unto the grace of the Spirit acquired by his death. Martinus Boræus, explaining that place of the apostle, Rom. iv. 25: "Who was given for our sins, and rose again for our justification," saith: "There are two things beheld in Christ, which are necessary to our justification; the one is his death, the other is his arising from the dead. By his death, the sins of this world behoved to be expiated: by his rising from the dead, it pleased the same goodness of God to give the Holy Spirit, whereby both the gospel is believed, and the righteousness, lost by the fault of the first Adam, is restored." And afterwards he saith: "The apostle expresseth both parts in these words, 'Who was given for our sins,' &c. In his death is beheld the satisfaction for sin; in his resurrection, the gift of the Holy Spirit, by which our justification is perfected." And again, the same man saith elsewhere: "Both these kinds of righteousness are therefore contained in justification, neither can the one be separate from the other. So that in the definition of *justification*, the merit of the blood of Christ is included, both with the remission of sins, and with the gift of the Holy Spirit of justification and regeneration." Martinus Bucerus saith: "Seeing by one sin of Adam the world was lost, the grace of Christ hath not only abolished that one sin, and death which came by it; but hath together taken away those infinite sins, and also led into full justification as many as are of Christ; so that God now not only remits unto them Adam's sin, and their own, but also gives them therewith the Spirit of a solid and perfect righteousness, which renders us conform unto the image of the firstbegotten." And upon these words, *by Jesus Christ*, he

Melanct. in Apol. Conf. Aug.

Boræus, in Gen. c. xv. Credidit Abraham Deo, p. 161.

Idem, lib. iii. Reg. cap. ix. v. 4, p. 681.

Bucerus, in Rom. iv. ad ver. 16.

Righteousness a conformity to the image of the first begotten.

saith : "We always judge that the whole benefit of Christ tends to this, that we might be strong through the gift of righteousness, being rightly and orderly adorned with all virtue, that is, restored to the image of God."    And lastly,

W. Forbes
in Consider.
Modest. de
Just., lib. ii.
sect. 8.
William Forbes, our countryman, bishop of Edinburgh, saith : "Whensoever the scripture makes mention of the justification before God, as speaketh Paul, and from him (besides others) Augustine, it appears that the word *justify* necessarily signifies not only to pronounce just in a law sense, but also really and inherently to make just; because that God doth justify a wicked man otherwise than earthly

How God
ustifies the
wicked.
judges.    For he, when he justifies a wicked or unjust man, doth indeed pronounce him as these also do ; but by pronouncing him just, because his judgment is according to truth, he also makes him really of unjust to become just." And again, the same man, upon the same occasion, answering the more rigid Protestants, who say, That God first justifies, and then makes just; he adds : "But let them have a care, lest by too great and empty subtilty, unknown both to the scriptures and the fathers, they lessen and diminish the weight and dignity of so great and divine a benefit, so much celebrated in the scripture, to wit, justification of the wicked.    For if to the formal reason of justification of the ungodly doth not at all belong his justification (so to speak), *i. e.*, his being made righteous, then in the justification of a sinner, although he be justified, yet the stain of sin is not taken away, but remains the same in his soul as before justification ; and so, notwithstanding the benefit of justification, he remains as before, unjust and a sinner ; and nothing is taken away, but the guilt and obligation to pain, and the offence and enmity of God through non-imputation.    But both the scriptures and fathers do affirm, that in the justification of a sinner, their sins are not only remitted, forgiven, covered, not imputed, but also taken away, blotted out, cleansed, washed, purged, and very far removed from us, as appears from many places of the holy scriptures."    The same Forbes shows us at length, in the following chapter, That this was the con-

fessed judgment of the fathers, out of the writings of those who hold the contrary opinion; some whereof, out of him, I shall note. As, first, Calvin saith : "That the judgment of Augustine, or at least his manner of speaking, is not throughout to be received; who although he took from man all praise of righteousness, and ascribed all to the grace of God, yet he refers grace to sanctification, by which we are regenerate through the Spirit unto newness of life." Calv. Inst. l. iii., c. **xi.** sect. 15.

Chemnitius saith : That they "do not deny, but that the fathers take the word *justify* for *renewing*, by which works of righteousness are wrought in us by the Spirit." And p. 130 : "I am not ignorant, that the fathers indeed often use the word *justify* in this signification, to wit, of making just." Chemnit. in Exam. Conc. Trid. de Just., p 129.

Zanchius saith : "That the fathers, and chiefly Augustine, interpret the word *justify* according to this signification, to wit, of making just ; so that, according to them, to be justified was no other than of unjust to be made just, through the grace of God for Christ." He mentioneth more, but this may suffice to our purpose. Zanchius in c. ii. ad Ep. ver. 4. loc. de Just. Thes. xiii.

§ VIII. Having thus sufficiently proved, that by justification is to be understood a really being made righteous, I do boldly affirm, and that not only from a notional knowledge, but from a real, inward experimental feeling of the thing, That the immediate, nearest, or formal cause (if we must in condescendence to some use this word) of a man's justification in the sight of God, is, the revelation of Jesus Christ in the soul, changing, altering, and renewing the mind, by whom (even the author of this inward work) thus formed and revealed, we are truly justified and accepted in the sight of God. For it is as we are thus covered and clothed with him, in whom the Father is always well pleased, that we may draw near to God, and stand with confidence before his throne, being purged by the blood of Jesus inwardly poured into our souls, and clothed with his life and righteousness therein revealed. And this is that order and method of salvation held forth by the apostle in that divine saying, Rom. v. 10 : "For if when we were enemies, we were reconciled to God by the death of his Asser. I. Christ revealed and formed in the soul of a man, is the formal cause of man's justification. Proof I.

Son; much more, being reconciled, we shall be saved by his life." For the apostle first holding forth the reconciliation wrought by the death of Christ, wherein God is near to receive and redeem man, holds forth his salvation and justification to be by the life of Jesus. Now, that this life is an inward, spiritual thing revealed in the soul whereby it is renewed and brought forth out of death, where it naturally has been by the fall, and so quickened and made alive unto God, the same apostle shows, Eph. ii. 5: " Even when we were dead in sins, he hath quickened us together with Christ (by whose grace ye are saved) and hath raised us up together." Now this none will deny to be the inward work of renovation, and therefore the apostle gives that reason of their being saved by g  ·; which is the inward virtue and power of Christ in the soul: but of this place more hereafter. Of the revelation of this inward life the apostle also speaketh, 2 Cor. iv. 10: " That the life also of Jesus might be made manifest in our body;" and ver. 11: " That the life also of Jesus might be made manifest in our mortal flesh." Now this inward life of Jesus is that whereby, as is before observed, he said, " we are saved."

**PROOF II.**     Secondly, That it is by this revelation of Jesus Christ, and the new creation in us, that we are justified, doth evidently appear from that excellent saying of the apostle included in the proposition itself, Tit. iii. 5: " According to his mercy he hath saved us, by the washing of regeneration, and renewing of the Holy Ghost," &c. Now that whereby we are saved, that we are also no doubt justified by; which words are in this respect synonymous. Here *The immediate cause of justification is the inward work of regeneration.* the apostle clearly ascribes the immediate cause of justification to this inward work of regeneration, which is Jesus Christ revealed in the soul, as being that which formally states us in a capacity of being reconciled with God; the washing of regeneration being that inward power and virtue, whereby the soul is cleansed, and clothed with the righteousness of Christ, so as to be made fit to appear before God.

Thirdly, This doctrine is manifest from 2 Cor. xiii. 5 : PR. III.
" Examine your ownselves, whether ye be in the faith;
prove your ownselves: know ye not your ownselves, how
that Jesus Christ is in you, except ye be reprobates?"
First, It appears here how earnest the apostle was that they
should know Christ in them ; so that he presses this exhortation upon them, and inculcates it three times.    Secondly, The cause
He makes the cause of reprobation, or not-justification, the of reproba
                                                             tion is
want of Christ thus revealed and known in the soul: Christ not
                                                             known by
whereby it necessarily follows, by the rule of contraries, inward re-
where the parity is alike (as in this case it is evident), that velation.
where Christ is inwardly known, there the persons subjected to him are approved and justified.    For there can
be nothing more plain than this, That if we must know
Christ in us, except we be reprobates, or unjustified persons ; if we know him in us, we are not reprobates, and
consequently justified ones.    Like unto this is that other
saying of the same apostle, Gal. iv. 19 : " My little children, of whom I travail in birth again, until Christ be formed
in you ;" and therefore the apostle terms this, " Christ
within, the hope of glory," Col. i. 27, 28.    Now that
which is the hope of glory, can be no other than that which
we immediately and most nearly rely upon for our justification, and that whereby we are really and truly made just.
And as we do not hereby deny, but the original and fundamental cause of our justification is the love of God manifested in the appearance of Jesus Christ in the flesh, who Christ by
                                                             his death
by his life, death, sufferings, and obedience, made a way and suffer
for our reconciliation, and became a sacrifice for the remis- ings has
                                                             opened a
sion of sins that are past, and purchased unto us this seed way for ou
and grace, from which this birth arises, and in which Jesus reconcilia-
                                                             tion.
Christ is inwardly received, formed, and brought forth in
us, in his own pure and holy image of righteousness, by
which our souls live unto God, and are clothed with him,
and have put him on, even as the scripture speaks, Eph.
iv. 23, 24 ; Gal. iii. 27, we stand justified and saved in
and by him, and by his Spirit and grace ; Rom. iii. 24 ; 1
Cor. vi. 11 ; Tit. iii. 7.    So again, reciprocally, we are

hereby made partakers of the fulness of his merits, and his
cleansing blood is near, to wash away every sin and infirmity, and to heal all our backslidings, as often as we turn
towards him by unfeigned repentance, and become renewed
by his Spirit.  Those then that find him thus raised, and
ruling in them, have a true ground of hope to believe that
they are justified by his blood.  But let not any deceive
themselves, so as to foster themselves in a vain hope and
confidence, that by the death and sufferings of Christ they
are justified, so long as "sin lies at their door," Gen. iv.
7, iniquity prevails, and they remain yet unrenewed and
unregenerate; lest it be said unto them, "I know you not."
Let that saying of Christ be remembered, "Not every one
that saith Lord, Lord, shall enter, but he that doth the will
of my father," Matt. vii. 21.  To which let these excellent
sayings of the beloved disciple be added; "Little children, let no man deceive you; he that doth righteousness
is righteous, even as he is righteous.  He that committeth
sin is of the devil; for if our heart condemn us, God is
greater than our heart and knoweth all things," 1 John iii.
7 and 20.

Many famous Protestants bear witness to this inward
justification by Christ inwardly revealed and formed in
man.  As M. Boræus: "In the imputation," saith he,
"wherein Christ is ascribed and imputed to believers for
righteousness, the merit of his blood, and the Holy Ghost
given unto us by virtue of his merits, are equally included.
And so it shall be confessed, 'that Christ is our righteousness,' as well from his merit, satisfaction, and remission of
sins obtained by him, as from the gifts of the Spirit of
righteousness.  And if we do this, we shall consider the
whole Christ proposed to us for our salvation, and not any
single part of him."  The same man, p. 169, "In our
justification then Christ is considered, who breathes and
lives in us, to wit, by his Spirit put on by us; concerning
which putting on the apostle saith, 'Ye have put on Christ.'"
And again, p. 171, "We endeavour to treat in justification,
not of part of Christ, but him wholly, in so far as he is our

*Marginal notes:*
Boræus in
Gen. p. 161.

The testi-
monies of
famous
Protestants
of inward
justifica-
tion.

righteousness every way." And a little after: "As tnen blessed Paul, in our justification, when he saith, 'Whom he justified, them he glorified,' comprehends all things which pertain to our being reconciled to God the Father, and our renewing, which fits us for attaining unto glory, such as faith, righteousness, Christ, and the gift of righteousness exhibited by him, whereby we are regenerated, to the fulfilling of the justification which the law requires; so we also will have all things comprehended in this cause, which are contained in the recovery of righteousness and innocency" And p. 181: "The form," saith he, "of our justification is the divine righteousness itself, by which we are formed just and good. This is Jesus Christ, who is esteemed our righteousness, partly from the forgiveness of sins, and partly from the renewing and the restoring of that integrity, which was lost by the fault of the first Adam: so that this new and heavenly Adam being put on by us, of which the apostle saith, 'Ye have put on Christ,' ye have put him on, I say, as the form, so the righteousness, wisdom, and life of God." So also affirmeth Claudius Alberius Inuncunanus, see his *Orat. Apodict. Lausaniæ* Inuncunan. *Excus.*, 1587. *Orat.* ii., p. 86, 87. Zuinglius also, in Zuinglius his epistle to the princes of Germany, as cited by Himelius, c. vii., p. 60, saith, "That the sanctification of the Spirit is true justification, which alone suffices to justify." Estius, Estius. upon 1 Cor. vi. 11, saith, "Lest Christian righteousness should be thought to consist in the washing alone, that is, in the remission of sins, he addeth the other degree or part, 'but ye are sanctified;' that is, ye have attained to purity, so that ye are now truly holy before God. Lastly, expressing the sum of the benefit received in one word, which includes both the parts, 'But ye are justified,' the apostle adds, 'in the name of the Lord Jesus Christ,' that is, by his merits, and in the Spirit of our God, that is, the Holy Spirit, proceeding from God, and communicated to us by Christ." And lastly, Richard Baxter, a famous R. Baxter. English preacher, in his book called Aphorisms of Justification, p. 80. saith "That some ignorant wretches gnash their teeth at this doctrine, as if it were fl t Popery not understanding the nature of the righteousness of the new covenant; which is all out ' Christ in ourselves, though wrought by the power of the Spirit of Christ in us."

**Pos. III.** § IX. The third thing proposed to be considered is, concerning the necessity of good works to justification. I suppose there is enough said before to clear us from any imputation of being popish in this matter.

**Object.** But if it be queried, Whether we have not said, or will not affirm, that a man is justified by works?

**Answ.** I answer; I hope none need, neither ought to take offence, if in this matter we use the plain language of the holy scripture, which saith expressly in answer hereunto, *That works are necessary to justification.* James ii. 24, "Ye see then how that by works a man is justified, and not by faith only." I shall not offer to prove the truth of this saying, since what is said in this chapter by the apostle is sufficient to convince any man that will read and believe it; I shall only from this derive this one argument:

**Arg** If no man can be justified without faith, and no faith be living, nor yet available to justification without works, then works are necessary to justification.

But the first is true; therefore the last.

For this truth is so apparent and evident in the scriptures, that for the proof of it we might transcribe most of the precepts of the gospel. I shall instance a few, which of themselves do so clearly assert the thing in question, that they need no commentary, nor farther demonstration And then I shall answer the objections made against this which indeed are the arguments used for the contrary opinion, Heb. xii. 14, "Without holiness no man shall see God." *Not the sayers, but the doers are blessed.* Mat. vii. 21, "Not every one that saith unto me. Lord, Lord, shall enter into the kingdom of heaven, but he that doth the will of my Father which is in heaven." John xiii. 17, "If ye know these things, happy are ye if ye do them." 1 Cor. vii. 19, "Circumcision is nothing, and uncircumcision is nothing, but the keeping of the commandments of God." Rev. xxii. 14, "Blessed are they that do his commandments, that they may have right to the tree of life, and may enter in through the gates into the city:" and many more that might be instanced. From all which I thus argue:

If those only can enter into the kingdom that do the Arg. will of the Father; if those be accounted only the wise builders and happy that do the sayings of Christ; if no observation avail, but only the keeping of the commandments; and if they be blessed that do the commandments, and thereby have right to the tree of life, and entrance through the gates into the city; then works are absolutely necessary to salvation and justification:

But the first is true; and therefore also the last.

The consequence of the antecedent is so clear and evident, that I think no man of sound reason will call for a proof of it.

§ X. But they object, That works are not necessary to Obj. 1. justification: First, because of that saying of Christ, Luke xvii. 10, "When ye shall have done all these things Unprofit that are commanded you, say, we are unprofitable ser- able ser- vants," &c. vants.

Answer; As to God we are indeed unprofitable, for he Answ. needeth nothing, neither can we add any thing unto him: God need eth nothing but as to ourselves, we are not unprofitable; else it might be said, that it is not profitable for a man to keep God's commandments; which is most absurd, and would contradict Christ's doctrine throughout. Doth not Christ, Mat. v., through all those beatitudes, pronounce men blessed for their purity, for their meekness, for their peaceableness, &c.? And is not then that for which Christ pronounceth men blessed, profitable unto them? More- Those that over, Mat. xxv. 21, 23, Doth not Christ pronounce the had im- proved men "good and faithful servants" that improved their ta- their ta- lents? Was not their doing of that then profitable unto lents, were called good them? And ver. 30, it is said of him that hid his talent, and faithful and did not improve it, "Cast ye the unprofitable servant servants. into utter darkness." If then not improving of the talent made the man unprofitable, and he was therefore cast into

utter darkness, it will follow by the rule of contraries, so
far at least that the improving made the other profitable;
seeing, if our adversaries will allow us to believe Christ's
words, this is made a reason, and so at least a cause instrumental of their acceptance; " Well done, good and
faithful servant, thou hast been faithful over a few things,
I will make thee ruler over many things; enter thou into
the joy of thy Lord."

OBJ. 2.   Secondly, They object those sayings of the apostle,
where he excludes the deeds of the law from justification;
as first, Rom. iii. 20, " Therefore by the deeds of the law
there shall no flesh be justified in his sight." And verse
28, " Therefore we conclude, that a man is justified by
faith, without the deeds of the law."

Aws. 1.   Answer: We have shown already what place we give to
works, even to the best of works, in justification; and how
we ascribe its immediate and formal cause to the worker
brought forth in us, but not to the works.   But in answer
to this objection, I say, there is a great difference betwixt
The works  the works of the law, and those of grace, or of the gospel.
of the gos-  The first are excluded, the second not, but are necessary.
pel or grace
distinguish-  The first are those which are performed in man's own will,
ed from     and by his strength, in a conformity to the outward law
those of the
law.        and letter; and therefore are man's own imperfect works,
or works of the law, which makes nothing perfect: and to
this belong all the ceremonies, purifications, washings, and
traditions of the Jews.   The second are the works of the
Spirit of grace in the heart, wrought in conformity to the
inward and spiritual law; which works are not wrought in
man's will, nor by his power and ability, but in and by the
power and Spirit of Christ in us, and therefore are pure
and perfect in their kind, as shall hereafter be proved, and
may be called Christ's works, for that he is the immediate
author and worker of them: such works we affirm absolutely necessary to justification, so that a man cannot be
justified without them; and all faith without them is dead
and useless, as the apostle James saith.   Now, that such
a distinction is to be admitted, and that the works excluded

by the apostle in the matter of justification are of the first kind, will appear, if we consider the occasion of the apostle's mentioning this, as well here, as throughout his epistle to the Galatians, where he speaks of this matter and to this purpose at large: which was this, That whereas many of the Gentiles, that were not of the race or seed of Abraham, as concerning the flesh, were come to be converted to the Christian faith, and to believe in him, some of those, that were of the Jewish proselytes, thought to subject the faithful and believing Gentiles to the legal ceremonies and observations, as necessary to their justification: this gave the apostle Paul occasion at length, in his epistle to the Romans, Galatians, and elsewhere, to show the use and tendency of the law, and of its works, and to contra-distinguish them from the faith of Christ, and the righteousness thereof; showing how the former was ceased and become ineffectual, the other remaining, and yet necessary. And that the works excluded by the apostle are of this kind of works of the law, appears by the whole strain of his epistle to the Galatians, chap. i., ii., iii., and iv. For after, in chap. iv., he upbraideth them for their returning unto the observation of days and times, and that, in the beginning of chap. v., he showeth them their folly, and the evil consequence of adhering to the ceremonies of circumcision, then he adds, ver. 6, "For in Christ Jesus neither circumcision nor uncircumcision availeth, but faith, which worketh by love;" and thus he concludes again, chap. vi. ver. 15, "For in Christ Jesus neither circumcision availeth, nor uncircumcision, but a new creature." From which places appeareth that distinction of works before mentioned, whereof the one is excluded, the other necessary to justification. For the apostle showeth here, that circumcision, which word is often used to comprehend the whole ceremonies and legal performances of the Jews, is not necessary, nor doth avail. Here then are the works which are excluded, by which no man is justified; but faith, which worketh by love, but the new creature, this is that which availeth, which is absolutely necessary:

*The occasion of the apostle's speaking of the works of the law which are excluded.*

19 *

for faith, that worketh by love, cannot be without works,
for, as it is said in the same 5th chapter, ver. 22, love
is a work of the Spirit; also the new creature, if it avail
and be necessary, cannot be without works; seeing it is
natural for it to bring forth works of righteousness. Again,
that the apostle no ways intends to exclude such good
works appears, in that in the same epistle he exhorts the

**The useful-** Galatians to them, and holds forth the usefulness and ne-
**ness and** cessity of them, and that very plainly, chap. vi. ver. 7, 8,
**necessity** 9: "Be not deceived," saith he, "God is not mocked;
**of good** for whatsoever a man soweth, that shall he also reap: for
**works.**
he that soweth to the flesh, shall of the flesh reap corruption; but he that soweth to the Spirit, shall of the Spirit
reap life everlasting. And let us not be weary in well-
doing, for in due season we shall reap, if we faint not."
Doth it not hereby appear, how necessary the apostle would
have the Galatians know that he esteemed good works to
be? To wit, not the outward ceremonies and traditions
of the law, but the fruits of the Spirit, mentioned a little
before; by which Spirit he would have them to be led, and
walk in those good works: as also, how much he ascribed
to these good works, by which he affirms life everlasting is
reaped. Now, that cannot be useless to man's justification, which capacitates him to reap so rich a harvest.

**Ans. 2.**        But lastly; For a full answer to this objection, and for
the establishing of this doctrine of good works, I shall
instance another saying of the same apostle Paul, which
our adversaries also in the blindness of their minds make
use of against us; to wit, Tit. iii. 5: "Not by works of

**Justified** righteousness which we have done, but according to his
**not by our** mercy he saved us, by the washing of regeneration, and
**legal per-** renewing of the Holy Ghost." It is generally granted by
**formances,** all, that *saved* is here all one as if it had been said *justi-*
**but the**
**fruit of the** *fied.* Now there are two kinds of works here mentioned:
**Spirit.** one by which we are not saved, that is, not justified; and
another by which we are saved, or justified. The first, the
works of righteousness which we have wrought, that is,
which we in our first fallen nature, by our own strength,

have wrought, our own legal performances, and therefore may truly and properly be called ours, whatever specious appearances they may have. And that it must needs and ought to be so understood, doth appear from the other part: "By the washing of regeneration, and renewing of the Holy Ghost;" seeing regeneration is a work, comprehensive of many good works, even of all those which are called the fruits of the Spirit.

Now in case it should be objected, That these may also OBJECT. be called ours, because wrought in us, and also by us many times as instruments;

I answer; It is far otherwise than the former: for in the ANSW. first we are yet alive in our own natural state, unrenewed, working of ourselves, seeking to save ourselves, by imitating and endeavouring a conformity to the outward letter of the law; and so wrestling and striving in the carnal mind, that is enmity to God, and in the cursed will not yet subdued. But in this second we are "crucified with Christ," we are become "dead with him," have "partaken of the fellowship of his sufferings," are made "conformable to his death;" and our first man, our "old man with all his deeds," as well the openly wicked as the seemingly righteous, our legal endeavours and foolish wrestlings, are all buried and nailed to the cross of Christ; and so it is no more we, but Christ alive in us, the worker in Not we, but us. So that though it be we in a sense, yet it is accord- is the work-ing to that of the apostle to the same Galatians, ch. ii., ver. er of right eousness. 20: "I am crucified with Christ, nevertheless I live, yet not I, but Christ liveth in me;" not I, but the grace of Christ in me. These works are especially to be ascribed to the Spirit of Christ, and the grace of God in us, as being immediately thereby acted and led in them, and enabled to perform them. And this manner of speech is not strained, but familiar to the apostles, as appears, Gal. ii. 8: "For he that wrought effectually in Peter to the apostleship of the circumcision, the same was mighty in me," &c. Phil. ii. 13: "For it is God which worketh in you, both to will and to do," &c. So that it appears by this place, that since the washing of regeneration is necessary to justification, and that regeneration comprehends works, works are necessary; and that these works of the law that are excluded, are different from these that are necessary and admitted.

§ XI. Thirdly, They object that no works, yea, not the works of Christ in us, can have place in justification, because nothing that is impure can be useful in it; and all the works wrought in us are impure. For this they allege that saying of the prophet Isaiah, lxiv. 6: "All our righteousnesses are as filthy rags;" adding this reason, "That seeing we are impure, so must our works be; which though good in themselves, yet as performed by us, they receive a tincture of impurity, even as clean water passing through an unclean pipe is defiled."

That no impure works are useful to justification is confessed; but that all the works wrought in the saints are such is denied. And for answer to this, the former distinction will serve. We confess, that the first sort of works above mentioned are impure; but not the second: because the first are wrought in the unrenewed state, but not the other. And as for that of Isaiah, it must relate to the first kind; for though he saith, "All our righteousnesses are as filthy rags," yet that will not comprehend the righteousness of Christ in us, but only that which we work of and by ourselves. For should we so conclude, then it would follow, that we should throw away all holiness and righteousness; since that which is as filthy rags, and as a menstruous garment, ought to be thrown away; yea, it would follow, that all the fruits of the Spirit, mentioned Gal. v., were as filthy rags: whereas, on the contrary, some of the works of the saints are said to have a " sweet savour in the nostrils of the Lord;" are said to be an " ornament of great price in the sight of God;" are said to " prevail with him," and to be " acceptable to him;" which filthy rags and a menstruous garment cannot be. Yea, many famous Protestants have acknowledged, that this place is not therefore so to be understood. Calvin upon this place saith,

"That it is used to be cited by some, that they may prove Calvin and others, their sense concerning Isa. lxiv. 6, of our righteousness. there is so little merit in our works, that they are before God filthy and defiled; but this seems to me to be different from the prophet's mind," saith he, "seeing he speaks not here of all mankind." Musculus upon this place saith, Musculus "That it was usual for this people to presume much of their legal righteousness, as if thereby they were made clean; nevertheless, they had no more cleanness than the unclean garment of a man. Others expound this place concerning all the righteousness of our flesh; that opinion indeed is true; yet I think that the prophet did rather accommodate these sayings to the impurity of that people in legal terms." The author (commonly supposed Bertius), Bertius, Epistolæ præfixæ dissert. ann. speaking concerning the true sense of the 7th chapter of the epistle to the Romans, hath a digression touching this of Isaiah, saying; "This place is commonly corrupted by a pernicious wresting: for it is still alleged, as if the meaning thereof inferred the most excellent works of the best Christians," &c. James Coret, a French minister in Jas. Coret Apol. Impress., Paris, ann. 1597, p. 78 the church of Basil, in his Apology concerning Justification against Alescales, saith: "Nevertheless, according to the counsel of certain good men, I must admonish the reader, that it never came into our minds to abuse that saying of Isaiah, lxiv. 6, against good works, in which it is said, that 'all our righteousnesses are as filthy rags,' as if we would have that which is good in our good works, and proceedeth from the Holy Spirit, to be esteemed as a filthy and unclean thing."

§ XII. As to the other part, That seeing the best of men are still impure and imperfect, therefore their works must be so; it is to beg the question, and depends upon a proposition denied; and which is to be discussed at farther length in the next proposition. But though we should suppose a man not thoroughly perfect in all respects, yet will not that hinder, but good and perfect works in their kind may be brought forth in him by the Spirit of Christ: neither doth the example of water going through an unclean pipe hit the matter; because though water may

be capable to be tinctured with uncleanness, yet the Spirit
of God cannot, whom we assert to be the immediate author
of those works that avail in justification: and therefore
Jesus Christ's works in his children are pure and perfect,
and he worketh in and through that pure thing of his own
forming and creating in them.  Moreover, if this did hold,
according to our adversaries' supposition, That no man ever
was or can be perfect, it would follow, that the very mira-

Were the miracles and works of the apostles, wrought by the power of Christ in them, impure and imperfect?

cles and works of the apostles, which Christ wrought in
them, and they wrought in and by the power, Spirit and
grace of Christ, were also impure and imperfect; such as
their converting of the nations to the Christian faith; their
gathering of the churches, their writing of the holy scriptures; yea, and their offering up and sacrificing of their
lives for the testimony of Jesus.  What may our adversaries think of this argument, whereby it will follow, that
the holy scriptures, whose perfection and excellency they
seem so much to magnify, are proved to be impure and
imperfect, because they came through impure and imperfect vessels?  It appears by the confessions of Protestants,
that the Fathers did frequently attribute unto works of this
kind that instrumental work, which we have spoken of in
justification, albeit some ignorant persons cry out it is
Popery, and also divers, and that famous Protestants, do

A. Polan.

of themselves confess it.  Amandus Polanus, in his *Sym
phonia Catholica*, cap. 27, *de Remissione Peccatorum*, p.

Our doctrine of justification and works is not Popery.

651, places this thesis as the common opinion of Protestants, most agreeable to the doctrine of the Fathers: " We
obtain the remission of sins by repentance, confession,
prayers, and tears, proceeding from faith, but do not merit,
to speak properly; and therefore we obtain remission of
sins, not by the merit of our repentance and prayers, but

Gentiletus ex Impress. Gen. 1516.

by the mercy and goodness of God."  Innocentius Gentiletus, a lawyer of great fame among Protestants, in his
Examen of the Council of Trent, p. 66, 67, of justification, having before spoken of faith and works, adds these
words: " But seeing the one cannot be without the other,
we call them both conjunctly instrumental causes."  Zan

chius, in his fifth book, *De Naturâ Dei*, saith ; "We do Zanchius.
not simply deny, that good works are the cause of salvation, to wit, the instrumental, rather than the efficient cause,
which they call *sine quâ non*." And afterwards, "Good
works are the instrumental cause of the possession of life
eternal: for by these, as by a means and a lawful way,
God leads unto the possession of life eternal." G. Ame- G. Ames.
sius saith, "That our obedience, albeit it be not the prin- in Medulla
S. Theolo-
cipal and meritorious cause of life eternal, is nevertheless giæ, l. ii.
c. 1 Thes.
a cause in some respect, administering, helping, and advan- xxx.
cing towards the possession of the life." Also Richard R. Baxter.
Baxter, in his book above cited, p. 155, saith, "That we
are justified by works in the same kind of causality as by
faith, to wit, as being both causes *sine quâ non*, or conditions of the new covenant on our part requisite to justification." And p. 195, he saith, "It is needless to teach
any scholar, who hath read the writings of Papists, how
this doctrine differs from them."

But lastly, Because it is fit here to say something of the Of the merit and re-
merit and reward of works, I shall add something in this ward of
place of our sense and belief concerning that matter. We works.
are far from thinking or believing, that man merits any thing
by his works from God, all being of free grace ; and therefore do we, and always have denied that Popish notion of
*meritum ex condigno*. Nevertheless we cannot deny, but
that God, out of his infinite goodness wherewith he hath
loved mankind, after he communicates to him his holy
Grace and Spirit, doth, according to his own will, recom- God rewards the
pense and reward the good works of his children ; and good works
therefore this merit of congruity or reward, in so far as the of his children.
scripture is plain and positive for it, we may not deny ;
neither wholly reject the word, in so far as the scripture
makes use of it. For the same Greek ἄξιον, which signifies
*merit*, is also in those places where the translators express
it *worth*, or *worthy*, as Mat. iii. 8; 1 Thess. ii. 12 ; 2 Thess.
i. 5, 11. Concerning which R. Baxter saith, in the book
above cited, p. 8, "But in a larger sense, as promise is an
obligation, and the thing promised is said to be debt, so

the performers of the conditions are called *worthy*, and that which they perform *merit;* although properly all be of grace, and not of debt." Also those, who are called the Fathers of the church, frequently used this word of *merit,* whose sayings concerning this matter I think not needful to insert, because it is not doubted, but evident, that many Protestants are not averse from this word, in the sense that we use it. The apology for the Augustan confession, art. 20, hath these words; " We agree that works are truly meritorious, not of remission of sins, or justification ; but they are meritorious of other rewards corporal and spiritual, which are indeed as well in this life, as after this life." And further, " Seeing works are a certain fulfilling of the law, they are rightly said to be meritorious ; it is rightly said, that a reward is due to them."

Conference of Oldenburgh. In the acts of the conference of Oldenburgh, the electoral divines, p. 110 and 265, say, " In this sense our churches also are not averse from the word *merit* used by the Fathers ; neither therefore do they defend the Popish doctrine of merit."

G. Vossius, of the word *merit.* G. Vossius, in his theological thesis concerning the merits of good works, saith ; " We have not adventured to condemn the word *merit* wholly, as being that which both many of the ancients use, and also the reformed churches have used in their confessions. Now that God judgeth and accepteth men according to their works, is beyond doubt to those that seriously will read and consider these scriptures," Mat. xvi. 27; Rom. ii. 6, 7, 10; 2 Cor. v. 10; James i. 25; Heb. x. 35; 1 Pet. i. 17; Rev. xxii. 12. .

§ XIII. And to conclude this proposition, let none be so bold as to mock God, supposing themselves justified and accepted in the sight of God, by virtue of Christ's death and sufferings, while they remain unsanctified and Job. viii 13 unjustified in their own hearts, and polluted in their sins, lest their hope prove that of the hypocrite, which perisheth. Neither let any foolishly imagine, that they can by their own works, or by the performance of any ceremonies or traditions, or by the giving of gold or money, or by afflicting their bodies in will-worship and voluntary numility, or foolishly striving to conform their way to the outward letter of the law, flatter themselves that they merit before God, or draw a debt upon him, or that any man or men have power to make such kind of things effectual to their justification, lest they be found foolish boasters and strangers to Christ and his righteousness indeed.   But blessed for ever are they, that having truly had a sense of their own unworthiness and sinfulness, and having seen all their own endeavours and performances fruitless and vain, and beheld their own emptiness, and the vanity of their vain hopes, faith, and confidence, while they remained inwardly pricked, pursued, and condemned by God's holy witness in their hearts, and so having applied themselves thereto, and suffered his grace to work in them, are become changed and renewed in the spirit of their minds, passed from death to life, and know Jesus arisen in them, working both the will and the deed ; and so having "put on the Lord Jesus Christ," in effect are clothed with him, and partake of his righteousness and nature ; such can draw near to the Lord with boldness, and know their acceptance in and by him ; in whom, and in as many as are found in him, the Father is well pleased.

---

# PROPOSITION VIII.

## *Concerning Perfection.*

In whom this pure and holy birth is fully brought forth, the body of death and sin comes to be crucified and removed, and their hearts united and subjected to the truth ; so as not to obey any suggestions or temptations of the evil one, but to be free from actual sinning and transgressing of the law of God, and in that respect perfect : yet doth this perfection still admit of a growth ; and there remaineth always in some part a possibility of sinning, where the mind doth not most diligently and watchfully attend unto the Lord.

20

§ I. Since we have placed justification in the revelation of Jesus Christ formed and brought forth in the heart, there working his works of righteousness, and bringing forth the fruits of the Spirit, the question is, How far he may prevail in us while we are in this life, or we over our souls, enemies, in and by his strength? Those that plead for justification wholly without them, merely by imputative righteousness, denying the necessity of being clothed with real and inward righteousness, do consequently affirm,

*These are the words of the Westminster larger catechism.* "That it is impossible for a man, even the best of men, to be free of sin in this life, which, they say, no man ever was; but on the contrary, that none can, neither of himself, nor by any grace received in this life, [O wicked saying against the power of God's grace,] keep the commandments of God perfectly; but that every man doth break the commandments in thought, word and deed;" whence

*Whether it is possible to keep the commandments of God?* they also affirm, as was a little before observed, "That the very best actions of the saints, their prayers, their worships are impure and polluted." We on the contrary, though we freely acknowledge this of the natural fallen man, in his first state, whatever his profession or pretence may be, so long as he is unconverted and unregenerate, yet we do believe, that to those in whom Christ comes to

*Part I.* be formed, and the new man brought forth, and born of the incorruptible seed, as that birth, and man in union therewith, naturally doth the will of God, it is possible so far to keep to it, as not to be found daily transgressors of

*Controversy stated.* the law of God. And for the more clear stating of the controversy, let it be considered:

*Notional knowledge.* § II. First, That we place not this possibility in man's own will and capacity, as he is a man, the son of fallen Adam, or as he is in his natural state, however wise or knowing, or however much endued with a notional and literal knowledge of Christ, thereby endeavouring a conformity to the letter of the law, as it is outward.

*The new birth.* Secondly, That we attribute it wholly to man, as he is born again, renewed in his mind, raised by Christ, knowing Christ alive, reigning and ruling in him, and guiding and leading him by his Spirit, and revealing in him the law of the Spirit of life; which not only manifests and reproves sin, but also gives power to come out of it.

Thirdly, That by this we understand not such a perfection as may not daily admit of a growth, and consequently mean not as if we were to be as pure, holy, and perfect as God in his divine attributes of wisdom, knowledge, and purity; but only a perfection proportionable and answerable to man's measure, whereby we are kept from transgressing the law of God, and enabled to answer what he requires of us; even as he that improved his two talents so as to make four of them, perfected his work, and was so accepted of his Lord as to be called a " good and faithful servant," nothing less than he that made his five ten. Even as a little gold is perfect gold in its kind, as well as a great mass, and a child hath a perfect body as well as a man, though it daily grow more and more. Thus Christ is said, Luke ii. 52, to have " increased in wisdom and stature, and in favour with God and man;" though before that time he had never sinned, and was no doubt perfect, in a true and proper sense.

*Growth in perfection*

*He that improved his two talents was nothing less accept able than he with the five.*

Fourthly, Though a man may witness this for a season, and therefore all ought to press after it; yet we do not affirm but those that have attained it in a measure may, by the wiles and temptations of the enemy, fall into iniquity, and lose it sometimes, if they be not watchful, and do not diligently attend to that of God in the heart. And we doubt not but many good and holy men, who have arrived to everlasting life, have had divers ebbings and flowings of this kind; for though every sin weakens a man in his spiritual condition, yet it doth not so as to destroy him altogether, or render him incapable of rising again.

*Wiles of the enemy*

*Every sin weakens a man in his spiritual condition, but doth not destroy him altogether.*

Lastly, Though I affirm, that after a man hath arrived at such a state, in which he may be able not to sin, yet he may sin: nevertheless, I will not affirm that a state is not attainable in this life, in which to do righteousness may be so natural to the regenerate soul, that in the stability of that condition he cannot sin. Others may speak more

*Righteousness become natural.*

certainly of this state, if they have arrived at it. With respect to myself, I speak modestly, because I ingenuously confess that I have not yet attained it; but I cannot deny that there is such a state, as it seems to be so clearly asserted by the apostle, 1 John iii. 9, "Whosoever is born of God doth not commit sin; for his seed remaineth in him: and he cannot sin, because he is born of God."

PART II.
SECT. 1.

The controversy being thus stated, which will serve to obviate objections, I shall proceed, First, to show the absurdity of that doctrine that pleads for sin for term of life, even in the saints.

SECT. 2.

Secondly, To prove this doctrine of perfection from many pregnant testimonies of the holy scripture.

SECT. 3.

And, Lastly, To answer the arguments and objections of our opposers.

SECT. I.
PROOF 1.
The doctrine of pleading for sin for term of life absurd.
* Hab. i. 13.

§ III. First then, This doctrine, viz.: That the saints nor can nor ever will be free of sinning in this life, is inconsistent with the wisdom of God, and with his glorious power and majesty, "who is of purer eyes than to behold iniquity;"* who having purposed in himself to gather to him that should worship him, and be witnesses for him on earth, a chosen people, doth also no doubt sanctify and purify them. For God hath no delight in iniquity, but abhors transgression; and though he regard man in transgression so far as to pity him, and afford him means to come out of it; yet he loves him not, neither delights in him, as he is joined thereunto. Wherefore if man must be always joined to sin, then God would always be at a distance with him; as it is written, Isa. lix. 2, "Your iniquities have separated between you and your God, and your sins have hid his face from you;" whereas on the contrary, the saints are said to partake, even while here, "of the divine nature," 2 Pet. i. 4, and to be one spirit with the Lord, 1 Cor. vi. 17. Now no unclean thing can be so. It is expressly written, that there is no communion betwixt light and darkness, 2 Cor. vi. 14; but God is light, and every sin is darkness in a measure. What greater stain then can there be than this upon God's wisdom, as if he had been wanting to prepare a means whereby his children might perfectly serve and worship him, or had not provided a way whereby they might serve nim in any thing, but that they must withal still serve the devil no less, yea more than himself? For "he that sinneth is the servant of sin," Rom. vi. 16, and every sin is an act of service and obedience to the devil. So then if the saints sin daily in thought, word, and deed, yea, if the very service they offer to God be sin, surely they serve the devil more than they do God: for besides that they give the devil many entire services, without mixture of the least grain to God, they give God not the least service in which the devil hath not a large share; and if their prayers and all their spiritual performances be sinful, the devil is as much served by them in these as God, and in most of them much more, since they confess that many of them are performed without the leadings and influence of God's Spirit. Now who would not account him a foolish master among men, who being able to do it, and also desirous it might be so, yet would not provide a way whereby his children and servants might serve him more entirely than his avowed enemy; or would not guard against their serving of him, but be so imprudent and unadvised in his contrivance, that whatever way his servants and children served him, they should no less, yea, often much more, serve his enemy? What may we then think of that doctrine that would infer this folly upon the Omnipotent and Only Wise God?

§ IV. Secondly, It is inconsistent with the justice of God. For since he requires purity from his children, and commands them to abstain from every iniquity, so frequently and precisely as shall hereafter appear, and since his wrath is revealed against all ungodliness and unrighteousness of men, it must needs follow, that he hath capacitated man to answer his will, or else that he requires more than he has given power to perform; which is to declare him openly unjust, and with the slothful servant to be a hard master. We have elsewhere spoken of the injustice these men ascribe to God, in making him to damn the

Hath God's wisdom been wanting to prepare a means to serve and worship him perfectly?

Proof II Its inconsistency with the justice of God.

20*  2 E

wicked, to whom they allege he never afforded any means of being good; but this is yet an aggravation more irrational and inconsistent, to say that God will not afford to those, whom he hath chosen to be his own, whom they confess he loveth, the means to please him. What can follow then from so strange a doctrine?

This imperfection in the saints either proceeds from God or from themselves: If it proceeds from them, it must be because they are short in improving or making use of the power given them, whereby they are capable to obey; and so it is a thing possible to them, as indeed it is by the help of that power: but this our adversaries deny: they are then not to be blamed for their imperfection and continuing in sin, since it is not possible for them to do otherwise. If it be not of themselves, it must be of God, who hath not seen meet to allow them grace in that degree to produce that effect: and what is this but to attribute to God the height of injustice, to make him require his children to forsake sin, and yet not to afford them sufficient means for so doing? Surely this makes God more unrighteous than wicked men, who if, as Christ saith, their children require bread of them, will not give them a stone; or instead of a fish a serpent. But these men confess we ought to seek of God power to redeem us from sin, and yet believe they are never to receive such a power; such prayers then cannot be in faith, but are all vain. Is not this to make God as unjust to his children as Pharoah was to the Israelites, in requiring brick and not giving them straw? But blessed be God, he deals not so with those that truly trust in him, and wait upon him, as these men vainly imagine; for such faithful ones find of a truth that his grace is sufficient for them, and know how by his power and spirit to overcome the evil one.

*Who shall give their children a stone instead of bread?*

PROOF III. § V. Thirdly, This evil doctrine is highly injurious to Jesus Christ, and greatly derogates from the power and virtue of his sacrifice, and renders his coming and ministry, as to the great end of it, ineffectual. For Christ, as for other ends, so principally he appeared for the removing of sin, for the gathering a righteous generation, that might serve the Lord in purity of mind, and walk before him in fear, and to bring in everlasting righteousness, and that evangelical perfection which the law could not do. Hence he is said, Tit. ii. 14, " to have given himself for us, that he might redeem us from all iniquity, and purify unto himself a peculiar people, zealous of good works." This is certainly spoken of the saints while upon earth ; but, contrary thereunto, these men affirm, that we never are redeemed from all iniquity, and so make Christ's giving of himself for us void and ineffectual, and give the apostle Paul the lie plainly, by denying that " Christ purifieth to himself a peculiar people, zealous of good works." How are they zealous of good works, who are ever committing evil ones? How are they a purified people, that are still in impurity, as they are that daily sin, unless sin be accounted no impurity? Moreover, it is said expressly, 1 John iii. 5, 8, That " for this purpose the Son of God was manifested, that he might destroy the works of the devil ; and ye know that he was manifested to take away our sins." But these men make this purpose of none effect ; for they will not have the Son of God to destroy the works of the devil in his children in this world, neither will they at all believe that he was manifest to take away our sins, seeing they plead a necessity of always living in them. And lest any should wrest this place of the apostle, as if it were spoken only of taking away the guilt of sin, as if it related not to this life, the apostle, as if of purpose to obviate such an objection, adds in the following verses, " Whosoever abideth in him sinneth not," &c. I hope then they sin not daily in thought, word, and deed. " Let no man deceive you ; he that doth righteousness is righteous ; even as he is righteous ; he that committeth sin is of the devil ;"* but he that sinneth daily in thought, word, and deed, committeth sin ; how comes such a one then to be the child of God? And if Christ was manifest to take away sin, how strangely do they overturn the doctrine of Christ that deny that it is ever taken away here ?

*Marginal note (right side):* The great and principal end of Christ's coming and appearance was for the removing of sin, and to redeem us from all iniquity.

*Footnote:* * 1 John iii. 6, 7.

And how injurious are they to the efficacy and power of
Christ's appearance? Came not Christ to gather a people
out of sin into righteousness; from the kingdom of Satan
into the kingdom of the dear Son of God? And are not
they that are thus gathered by him his servants, his children, his brethren, his friends? who as he was, so are they
to be in this world, holy, pure, and undefiled. And doth
not Christ still watch over them, stand by them, pray for
them, and preserve them by his power and Spirit, walk in

The devil
dwells
among the
reprobates

them, and dwell among them; even as the devil on the
other hand doth among the reprobate ones? How comes
it then that the servants of Christ are less his servants than
the devil's are his? Or is Christ unwilling to have his servants thoroughly pure? Which were gross blasphemy to
assert, contrary to many scriptures. Or is he not able by
his power to preserve and enable his children to serve him?
Which were no less blasphemous to affirm of him, concerning whom the scriptures declare, That he has overcome sin, death, hell, and the grave, and triumphed over
them openly, and that all power in heaven and earth is
given to him. But certainly if the saints sin daily in
thought, word and deed, as these men assert, they serve
the devil daily, and are subject to his power; and so he
prevails more than Christ doth, and holds the servants of
Christ in bondage, whether Christ will or not. But how
greatly then doth it contradict the end of Christ's coming?
as it is expressed by the apostle, Eph. v. 25, 26, 27,
" Even as Christ also loved the church, and gave himself
for it, that he might sanctify and cleanse it with the wash
ing of water by the word: that he might present it to himself a glorious church, not having spot or wrinkle, or any
such thing, but that it should be holy, and without blemish." Now if Christ hath really thus answered the thing
he came for, then the members of his church are not always sinning in thought, word, and deed, or there is no
difference betwixt being sanctified and unsanctified, clean
and unclean, holy and unholy, being daily blemished with
sin, and being without blemish.

§ VI. Fourthly, This doctrine renders the work of the ministry, the preaching of the word, the writing of the scripture, and the prayers of holy men altogether useless and ineffectual. As to the first, Eph. iv. 11, 12, 13, Pastors and teachers are said to be " given for the perfection of the saints," &c., " until we all come in the unity of the faith, and of the knowledge of the Son of God, unto a perfect man, unto the measure of the stature of the fulness of Christ." Now if there be a necessity of sinning daily, and in all things, then there can be no perfection; for such as do so cannot be esteemed perfect. And if for effectuating this perfection in the saints the ministry be appointed and disposed of God, do not such as deny the possibility hereof render the ministry useless, and of no profit? Seeing there can be no other true use assigned, but to lead people out of sin into righteousness. If so be these ministers assure us that we need never expect to be delivered from it, do not they render their own work needless? What needs preaching against sin, for the reproving of which all preaching is, if it can never be forsaken? Our adversaries are exalters of the scriptures in words, much crying up their usefulness and perfection : now the apostle tells us, 2 Tim. iii. 17, That the " scriptures are for making the man of God perfect ;" and if this be denied to be attainable in this life, then the scriptures are of no profit ; for in the other life we shall not have use for them. It renders the prayers of the saints altogether useless, seeing themselves do confess they ought to pray daily that God would deliver them from evil, and free them from sin, by the help of his Spirit and grace, while in this world. But though we might suppose this absurdity to follow, that their prayers are without faith, yet were not that so much, if it did not infer the like upon the holy apostles, who prayed earnestly for this end, and therefore no doubt believed it attainable, Col. iv. 12, " Labouring fervently for you in prayers, that ye may stand perfect," &c., 1 Thess. iii. 13 ; and v. 23, &c.

§ VII. But Fifthly, This doctrine is contrary to common

Proof IV.

Pastors, teachers, and scriptures are given for perfecting of the saints.

Proof V

Darkness
and .ight,
sin and
righteous-
ness incon
sistent to-
gether.

Prov. xvii.
45.

reason and sense. For the two opposite principles,
whereof the one rules in the children of darkness, the other
in the children of light, are sin and righteousness; and as
they are respectively leavened and actuated by them, so
they are accounted either as reprobated or justified, seeing
it is abomination in the sight of God, either to justify
the wicked, or condemn the just. Now to say that men
cannot be so leavened by the one as to be delivered from
the other, is in plain words to affirm, that sin and righteousness are consistent; and that a man may be truly
termed righteous, though he be daily sinning in every thing
he doth; and then what difference betwixt good and evil?
Is not this to fall into that great abomination of putting
light for darkness, and calling good evil, and evil good?
Since they say the very best actions of God's children are
defiled and polluted, and that those that sin daily in
thought, word, and deed are good men and women, the
saints and holy servants of the holy pure God. Can there
be any thing more repugnant than this to common reason?
Since the subject is still denominated from that accident
that doth most influence it; as a wall is called white when
there is much whiteness, and black when there is much
blackness, and such like; but when there is more unrighteousness in a man than righteousness, that man ought
rather to be denominated unrighteous than righteous.

It all daily
sin, where
is the
righteous
man then
spoken of
in scrip-
ture ?

Then surely if every man sin daily in thought, word, and
deed, and that in his sins there is no righteousness at all,
and that all his righteous actions are polluted and mixed
with sin, then there is in every man more unrighteousness
than righteousness; and so no man ought to be called
righteous, no man can be said to be sanctified or washed.
Where are then the children of God? Where are the
purified ones? Where are they who were sometimes unholy, but now holy; that sometimes were darkness, but
now are light in the Lord? There can none such be found
then at this rate, except that unrighteousness be esteemed
so: and is not this to fall into that abomination above
mentioned of justifying the ungodly? This certainly

lands in that horrid blasphemy of the Ranters, that affirm there is no difference betwixt good and evil, and that all is one in the sight of God. I could show many more gross absurdities, evil consequences, and manifest contradictions implied in this sinful doctrine; but this may suffice at present, by which also in a good measure the proof of the truth we affirm is advanced. Yet nevertheless, for the further evidencing of it, I shall proceed to the second thing proposed by me, to wit, to prove this from several testimonies of the holy scriptures. *The blasphemy of the Ranters or Liber tines.*

§ VIII. And first, I prove it from the peremptory positive command of Christ and his apostles, seeing this is a maxim engraven in every man's heart naturally, that no man is bound to do that which is impossible: since then Christ and his apostles have commanded us to keep all the commandments, and to be perfect in this respect, it is possible for us so to do. Now that this is thus commanded without any commentary or consequence, is evidently apparent from these plain testimonies, Matt. v. 48, and vii. 21; John xiii. 17; 1 Cor. vii. 19; 2 Cor. xiii. 11; 1 John ii. 3, 4, 5, 6, and iii. 2, 3, 4, 5, 6, 7, 8, 9, 10. These scriptures intimate a positive command for it; they declare the absolute necessity of it; and therefore, as if they had purposely been written to answer the objections of our opposers, they show the folly of those that will esteem themselves children or friends of God, while they do otherwise. *Sect. II. Proof I.* *Be ye perfect, &c. Keep my command ments.*

Secondly, It is possible, because we receive the gospel and law thereof for that effect; and it is expressly promised to us, as we are under grace, as appears by these scriptures, Rom. vi. 14: "Sin shall not have dominion over you; for ye are not under the law, but under grace:" and Rom. viii. 3: "For what the law could not do, in that it was weak through the flesh, God sending his own Son," &c., "that the righteousness of the law might be fulfilled in us," &c. For if this were not a condition both requisite, necessary, and attainable under the gospel, there were no difference betwixt the bringing in of a better hope, *Proof II. The possi bility of it.* *The differ ence of the law and gospel.*

and the law which made nothing perfect; neither betwixt those which are under the gospel, or who under the law enjoyed and walked in the life of the gospel and mere legalists. Whereas the apostle, throughout the whole sixth to the Romans, argues not only the possibility but the necessity of being free from sin, from their being under the gospel, and under grace, and not under the law; and therefore states himself and those to whom he wrote in that condition in these verses, 2, 3, 4, 5, 6, 7; and therefore in the 11, 12, 13, 16, 17, 18 verses he argues both the possibility and necessity of this freedom from sin almost in the same manner we did a little before; and in the 22d he declares them in measure to have attained this condition in these words, "But now being made free from sin, and become servants to God, ye have your fruit unto holiness, and the end everlasting life." And as this perfection or freedom from sin is attained and made possible where the gospel and inward law of the Spirit is received and known, so the ignorance hereof has been and is an occasion of opposing this truth. For man, not minding the light or law within his heart, which not only discovers sin but leads out of it, and so being a stranger to the new life and birth that is born of God, which naturally does his will, and cannot of its own nature transgress the commandments of God, doth, I say, in his natural state look at the commandments as they are without him in the letter; and finding himself reproved and convicted, is by the letter killed, but not made alive. So man, finding himself wounded, and not applying himself inwardly to that which can heal, labours in his own will after a conformity to the law as it is without him, which he can never obtain, but finds the more he wrestles, the more he falleth short. So this is the Jew still in effect, with his carnal commandment, with the law without, in the first covenant state, which "makes not the comers thereunto perfect, as pertaining to the conscience," Heb. ix. 9: though they may have here a notion of Christianity, and an external faith in Christ. This hath made them strain and wrest the scriptures for an imputative

*Perfection and freedom from sin attained and made possible by the gospel.*

*The letter kills, and maketh not alive.*

righteousness wholly without them, to cover their impurities; and this hath made them imagine an acceptance with God possible, though they suppose it impossible ever to obey Christ's commands. But alas! O deceived souls! that will not avail in the day wherein God will judge every man according to his work, whether good or bad. It will not save thee to say, it was necessary for thee to sin daily in thought, word and deed; for such as do so have certainly obeyed unrighteousness; and what is provided for such but tribulation and anguish, indignation and wrath; even as glory, honour, and peace, immortality and eternal life, to such as have done good, and patiently continued in well-doing. So then, if thou desirest to know this perfection and freedom from sin possible for thee, turn thy mind to the light and spiritual law of Christ in the heart, and suffer the reproofs thereof; bear the judgment and indignation of God upon the unrighteous part in thee as therein it is revealed, which Christ hath made tolerable for thee, and so suffer judgment in thee to be brought forth into victory, *How we partake of Christ's sufferings, and are made conformable unto his death.* and thus come to partake of the fellowship of Christ's sufferings, and be made conformable unto his death, that thou mayest feel thyself crucified with him to the world by the power of his cross in thee; so that that life that sometimes was alive in thee to this world, and the love and lusts thereof, may die, and a new life be raised, by which thou mayest live henceforward to God, and not to or for thyself; and with the apostle thou mayest say, Gal. ii. 20: It is no more I, "but Christ liveth in me;" and then thou wilt be a Christian indeed, and not in name only, as too many are; then thou wilt know what it is to have "put off the old man with his deeds," who indeed sins daily in thought, word, and deed; and to have put on the new man, that is renewed in holiness, after the image of him that hath created him, Eph. iv. 24: and thou wilt witness thyself to be God's workmanship, created in Christ Jesus unto good works, and so not to sin always. And to this new man "Christ's yoke is easy, and his burden is light;" *Matt. xi. 30 1 John v. 3.* though it be heavy to the old Adam; yea, the command-

ments of God are not unto this man grievous; for it is his
meat and drink to be found fulfilling the will of God.

**PROOF 3.**
**Many have**
**attained**
**perfection.**

Lastly, This perfection or freedom from sin is possible,
because many have attained it, according to the express
testimony of the scripture; some before the law, and some
under the law, through witnessing and partaking of the
benefit and effect of the gospel, and much more many under the gospel. As first, it is written of Enoch, Gen. v. 22,
24, that he walked with God, which no man while sinning
can; nor doth the scripture record any failing of his. It
is said of Noah, Gen. vi. 9, and of Job. i. 8, and of Zacharias and Elizabeth, Luke i. 6, that they were perfect; but
under the gospel, besides that of the Romans above mentioned, see what the apostle saith of many saints in general, Eph. ii. 4, 5, 6, " But God, who is rich in mercy, for
his great love wherewith he hath loved us, even when we
were dead in sins, hath quickened us together with Christ,
by grace ye are saved; and hath raised us up together,
and made us sit together in heavenly places in Christ
Jesus," &c. I judge while they were sitting in these
heavenly places, they could not be daily sinning in thought,
word and deed; neither were all their works which they
did there as filthy rags, or as a menstruous garment. See
what is further said to the Hebrews, xii. 22, 23, " Spirits
of just men made perfect." And to conclude, let that of
the Revelations, xiv. 1, 2, 3, 4, 5, be considered, where
though their being found without fault be spoken in the
present time, yet it is not without respect to their innocency
while upon earth; and their being " redeemed from among
men, and no guile found in their mouth," is expressly
mentioned in the time past. But I shall proceed now, in
the third place, to answer the objections, which indeed are
the arguments of our opposers.

**Enoch**
**walked**
**with God,**
**and was**
**perfect.**

**SEC. III.**

**OBJ. 1.**

§ IX. I shall begin with their chief and great argument,
which is the words of the apostle, 1 John i. 8, " If we say
that we have no sin, we deceive ourselves, and the truth
is not in us." This they think invincible.

**ANS. 1.**

But is it not strange to see men so blinded with partial

ity? How many scriptures tenfold more plain do they reject, and yet stick so tenaciously to this, that can receive so many answers? As first, "If we say we have no sin," &c., will not import the apostle himself to be included. Sometimes the scripture useth this manner of expression when the person speaking cannot be included; which manner of speech the grammarians call *metaschematismus.* Thus James iii. 9, 10, speaking of the tongue, saith, "Therewith bless we God, and therewith curse we men;" adding, "These things ought not so to be." Who from this will conclude that the apostle was one of those cursers? But Secondly, This objection hitteth not the matter; he saith not, We sin daily in thought, word, and deed; far less that the very good works which God works in us by his Spirit are sin: yea the very next verse clearly shows, that upon confession and repentance we are not only forgiven, but also cleansed; "He is faithful to forgive us our sins, and to cleanse us from all unrighteousness."* Here is both a forgiveness and removing of the guilt, and a cleansing or removing of the filth; for to make forgiveness and cleansing to belong both to the removing of the guilt, as there is no reason for it from the text, so it were a most violent forcing of the words, and would imply a needless tautology. The apostle having shown how that not the guilt only, but even the filth also of sin is removed, subsumes his words in the time past in the 10th verse, "If we say we have not sinned, we make him a liar." Thirdly, As Augustine well observed, in his exposition upon the epistle to the Galatians, It is one thing not to sin, and another thing not to have sin. The apostle's words are not If we say we sin not, or commit not sin daily, but "if we say we have no sin:" and betwixt these two there is a manifest difference; for in respect all have sinned, as we freely acknowledge, all may be said in a sense to have sin. Again, sin may be taken for the seed of sin, which may be in those that are redeemed from actual sinning; but as to the temptations and provocations proceeding from it being resisted by the servants of God, and not yielded to, they

*Marginal notes:* If we say we have no sin, &c. objected. Ans. 2. *1 John i 9. Ans. 3. It is one thing not to sin, and another thing not to have sin.

are the devil's sin that tempteth, not the man's that is pre-
**Ans. 4.** served. Fourthly, This being considered, as also how
positive and plain once and again the same apostle is in
that very epistle, as in divers places above cited, is it equal
or rational to strain this one place, presently after so qualified and subsumed in the time past, to contradict not only
other positive expressions of his, but the whole tendency
of his epistle, and of the rest of the holy commands and
precepts of the scripture?

**Obj. 2.** Secondly, Their second objection is from two places of
scripture, much of one signification: the one is, 1 Kings
viii. 46, "For there is no man that sinneth not." The
other is, Eccles. vii. 20, "For there is not a just man
upon earth, that doth good, and sinneth not."

**Answ.** I answer, First, These affirm nothing of a daily and continual sinning, so as never to be redeemed from it; but
only that all have sinned, or that there is none that doth
not sin, though not always, so as never to cease to sin;
and in this lies the question. Yea, in that place of the
Kings he speaks within two verses of the returning of such
"with all their souls and hearts;" which implies a possi-
Diversity bility of leaving off sin. Secondly, There is a respect to
of seasons be had to the seasons and dispensations; for if it should be
and dispen-
sations re- granted that in Solomon's time there was none that sinned
spected. not, it will not follow that there are none such now, or
that it is a thing not now attainable by the grace of God
under the gospel: For *a non esse ad non posse non valet
sequela*. And lastly, This whole objection hangs upon a
false interpretation; for the Hebrew word וחטא may be
read in the potential mood, thus, There is no man who
may not sin, as well as in the indicative: so both the old
Latin, Junius and Tremellius, and Vatablus have it; and
the same word is so used, Psalm cxix. 11, "I have hid
thy word in my heart," : למען לא אתטא לך that is to say, That
I may not sin against thee, in the potential mood, and not
in the indicative; which being more answerable to the
universal scope of the scriptures, the testimony of the truth
and the sense almost of all interpreters, doubtless ought to

be so understood, and the other interpretation rejected as spurious.

Thirdly, They object some expressions of the apostle Obj 3. Paul, Rom. vii. 19, "For the good that I would, I do not; but the evil which I would not, that I do." And verse 24, "O wretched man that I am! who shall deliver me from the body of this death?"

I answer, This place infers nothing, unless it were ap- Answ. parent that the apostle here were speaking of his own condition, and not rather in the person of others, or what he himself had sometimes borne; which is frequent in scripture, as in the case of cursing, in James before mentioned. But there is nothing in the text that doth clearly signify the apostle to be speaking of himself, or of a condition he was then under, or was always to be under; yea, on the contrary, in the former chapter, as afore is at large shown, he declares, they were dead to sin; demanding how such should yet live any longer therein? Secondly, It appears Paul personates the wretched man to show them the Redeemer. that the apostle personated one not yet come to a spiritual condition, in that he saith, verse 14, "But I am carnal, sold under sin." Now is it to be imagined that the apostle Paul, as to his own proper condition, when he wrote that epistle, was a carnal man, who in chap. i. testifies of himself, That he was separated to be an apostle, capable to impart to the Romans spiritual gifts; and chap. viii. 2, That "the law of the Spirit of Life in Christ Jesus" had "made him free from the law of sin and death?" So then he was not carnal. And seeing there are spiritual men in this life, as our adversaries will not deny, and is intimated through the whole 8th chapter to the Romans, it will not be denied but the apostle was one of them: so then as his calling himself carnal in chap. vii. cannot be understood of his own proper state, neither can the rest of what he speaks there of that kind be so understood: yea, after, verse 24, where he makes that exclamation, he adds in the next verse, "I thank God, through Jesus Christ our Lord;" signifying that by him he witnessed deliverance; and so goeth on, showing how he had obtained it in the next

21 *

chapter, viz. viii. ver. 35, "Who shall separate us from the love of Christ?" And ver. 37, "But in all these things we are more than conquerors:" and in the last verse, "Nothing shall be able to separate us," &c. But wherever there is a continuing in sin, there is a separation in some degree, seeing every sin is contrary to God, and ἀνομία, i. e. "a transgression of the law," 1 John iii. 4, and whoever committeth the least sin, is overcome of it, and so in that respect is not a conqueror, but conquered. This condition then, which the apostle plainly testified he with some others had obtained, could not consist with continual remaining and abiding in sin.

**Whom sin has conquered, he is no conqueror.**

**Obj. 4.** Fourthly, They object the faults and sins of several eminent saints, as Noah, David, &c.

**Answ.** I answer, That doth not at all prove the case: for the question is not whether good men may not fall into sin, which is not denied; but whether it be not possible for them not to sin? It will not follow because these men sinned, that therefore they were never free of sin, but always sinned: for at this rate of arguing, it might be urged, according to this rule, *Contrariorum par ratio*, i. e., The reason of contraries is alike, that if, because a good man hath sinned once or twice, he can never be free from sin, but must always be daily and continually a sinner all his life long; then by the rule of contraries, if a wicked man have done good once or twice, he can never be free from righteousness, but must always be a righteous man all his life-time: which as it is most absurd in itself, so it is contrary to the plain testimony of the scripture, Ezek. xxxiii. 12 to 18.

**Can they that sin be never freed from sin?**

**Object.** Lastly, They object, That if perfection or freedom from sin be attainable, this will render mortification of sin useless, and make the blood of Christ of no service to us, neither need we any more pray for forgiveness of sins.

**Answ.** I answer, I had almost omitted this objection, because of the manifest absurdity of it: for can mortification of sin be useless, where the end of it is obtained? seeing there is no attaining of this perfection but by mortification. Doth

the hope and belief of overcoming render the fight unne- Who fights
cessary? Let rational men judge which hath most sense in hopes to
it, to say as our adversaries do, It is necessary that we overcome
fight and wrestle, out we must never think of overcoming, his foe?
we must resolve still to be overcome; or to say, Let us
fight, because we may overcome? Whether do such as
believe they may be cleansed by it, or those that believe
they can never be cleansed by it, render the blood of
Christ most effectual? If two men were both grievously
diseased, and applied themselves to a physician for remedy,
which of those do most commend the physician and his
cure, he that believeth he may be cured by him, and as he
feels himself cured, confesseth that he is so, and so can say
this is a skilful physician, this is a good medicine, behold
I am made whole by it, or he that never is cured, nor ever
believes that he can so long as he lives? As for praying
for forgiveness, we deny it not; for that all have sinned, Praying for
and therefore all need to pray that their sins past may be of sin.
blotted out, and that they may be daily preserved from
sinning. And if hoping or believing to be made free from
sin hinders praying for forgiveness of sin, it would follow
by the same inference that men ought not to forsake murder, adultery, or any of these gross evils, seeing the more
men are sinful, the more plentiful occasion there would be
of asking forgiveness of sin, and the more work for
mortification. But the apostle hath sufficiently refuted
such sin-pleasing cavils in these words, Rom. vi. 1, 2,
"Shall we continue in sin that grace may abound? God
forbid."

But lastly, It may be easily answered, by a retortion to
those that press this from the words of the Lord's Prayer,
"forgive us our debts," that this militates no less against
perfect justification than against perfect sanctification: for
if all the saints, the least as well as the greatest, be perfectly justified in that very hour wherein they are converted, as our adversaries will have it, then they have
remission of sins long before they die. May it not then
be said to them, What need have ye to pray for remission

of sin, who are already justified, whose sins are long ago forgiven, both past and to come?

Testimonies of the fathers concerning perfection or freedom from sin.

§ X. But this may suffice : concerning this possibility Jerome speaks clearly enough, lib. iii., *adver. Pelagium*, " This we also say, that a man may not sin, if he will, for a time and place, according to his bodily weakness, so long as his mind is intent, so long as the cords of the Cithara relax not by any vice ;" and again in the same book, " Which is that that I said, that it is put in our power, to wit, being helped by the grace of God, either to sin or not to sin." For this was the error of Pelagius, which we indeed reject and abhor, and which the Fathers deservedly withstood, " That man by his natural strength, without the help of God's grace, could attain to that state so as not to sin." And Augustine himself, a great opposer of the Pelagian heresy, did not deny this possibility as attainable by the help of God's grace, as in his book *de Spiritu & literâ*, cap. ii., and his book *de Naturâ & Gratiâ* against Pelagius, cap. xlii., l., lx., and lxiii., *de Gestis Concilii Palæstini*, cap. vii., and ii., and *de Peccato Originali*, lib. ii., cap. ii. Gelasius also, in his disputation against Pelagius, saith, " But if any affirm that this may be given to some saints in this life, not by the power of man's strength, but by the grace of God, he doth well to think so confidently, and hope it faithfully ; for by this gift of God all things are possible." That this was the common opinion of the Fathers, appears from the words of the Aszansic Council, canon the last, " We believe also this according to the Catholic faith, that all who are baptized, through grace by baptism received, and Christ helping them, and co-working, may and ought to do whatsoever belongs to salvation, if they will faithfully labour."

Jerome.

Augustine.

Gelasius.

That by the gift of God all things are possible.

Conclusion.

§ XI. Blessed then are they that believe in him, who is both able and willing to deliver as many as come to him through true repentance from all sin, and do not resolve, as these men do, to be the devil's servants all their lifetime, but daily go on forsaking unrighteousness, and forgetting those things that are behind, " press forward toward the mark, for the prize of the high calling of God in Christ Jesus;" such shall not find their faith and confidence to be in vain, but in due time shall be made conquerors through him in whom they have believed; and so over-coming, shall be established as pillars in the house of God, so as they shall go no more out, Rev. iii. 12.

Phil. iii. 14. Press for-ward to the mark, for the prize and over-coming.

---

## PROPOSITION IX.

*Concerning Perseverance, and the Possibility of Falling from Grace.*

Although this gift and inward grace of God be sufficient to work out salvation, yet in those in whom it is resisted it both may and doth become their condemnation. Moreover they in whose hearts it hath wrought in part to purify and sanctify them in order to their further per-fection, may, by disobedience, fall from it, turn it to wantonness, Jude 4, make shipwreck of faith, 1 Tim. i. 19, and after having tasted the heavenly gift, and been made partakers of the Holy Ghost, again fall away, Heb. vi. 4, 5, 6, yet such an increase and stability in the truth may in this life be attained, from which there can be no total apostasy.

§ I. The first sentence of this proposition hath already been treated of in the fifth and sixth propositions, where it hath been shown that that light which is given for life and salvation, becomes the condemnation of those that refuse it, and therefore is already proved in those places, where I did demonstrate the possibility of man's resisting the grace and Spirit of God; and indeed it is so apparent in the scriptures, that it cannot be denied by such as will but seriously consider these testimonies, Prov. i. 24, 25, 26; John iii. 18, 19; 2 Thess. ii. 11, 12; Acts vii. 51, and xiii. 46; Rom. i. 18. As for the other part of it, that they in whom this grace may have wrought in a good

2 G

measure in order to purify and sanctify them, tending to their further perfection, may afterwards, through disobedience, fall away, &c., the testimonies of the scripture included in the proposition itself are sufficient to prove it to men of unbiassed judgment; but because as to this part our cause is common with many other Protestants, I shall be the more brief in it: for it is not my design to do that which is done already, neither do I covet to appear knowing by writing much; but simply purpose to present to the world a faithful account of our principles, and briefly to let them understand what we have to say for ourselves.

**I.**
**A falling from grace by disobedience evinced.**
**ARG. 1.**

§ II. From these scriptures then included in the proposition, not to mention many more which might be urged, I argue thus:

If men may turn the grace of God into wantonness, then they must once have had it:

But the first is true, therefore also the second.

**ARG. 2.**

If men may make shipwreck of faith, they must once have had it; neither could they ever have had true faith without the grace of God:

But the first is true, therefore also the last.

**ARG. 3.**

If men may have tasted of the heavenly gift, and been made partakers of the Holy Spirit, and afterwards fall away, they must needs have known in measure the operation of God's saving grace and Spirit, without which no man could taste the heavenly gift, nor yet partake of the Holy Spirit:

But the first is true, therefore also the last.

**II.**
**The doctrine of election and reprobation is inconsistent with preaching and daily exhortation.**

Secondly, Seeing the contrary doctrine is built upon this false hypothesis, That grace is not given for salvation to any, but to a certain elect number, which cannot lose it, and that all the rest of mankind, by an absolute decree, are debarred from grace and salvation; that being destroyed, this falls to the ground. Now as that doctrine of theirs is wholly inconsistent with the daily practice of those that preach it, in that they exhort people to believe and be saved while in the mean time, if they belong to the decree of reprobation, it is simply impossible for them so to do; and if to the decree of election, it is needless, seeing it is as impossible to them to miss of it, as hath been before demonstrated. So also in this matter of perseverance, their practice and principle are no less inconsistent and contradictory. For while they daily exhort people to be faithful to the end, showing them if they continue not they shall be cut off, and fall short of the reward ; which is very true, but no less inconsistent with that doctrine that affirms there is no hazard, because no possibility of departing from the least measure of true grace ; which if true, it is to no purpose to beseech them to stand, to whom God hath made it impossible to fall. I shall not longer insist upon the probation of this, seeing what is said may suffice to answer my design ; and that the thing is also abundantly proved by many of the same judgment. That this was the doctrine of the primitive Protestants thence appears, that the Augustine Confession condemns it as an error of the Anabaptists to say, That they who once are justified, cannot lose the Holy Spirit. Many such like sayings are to be found in the common places of Philip Melancthon. Vossius, in his Pelagian History, lib. vi. testifies, that this was The opinion of the common opinion of the Fathers. In the confirmation fathers of the twelfth thesis, page 587, he hath these words: concerning " That this which we have said was the common sentiment falling of antiquity, those at present can only deny, who otherways perhaps are men not unlearned, but nevertheless, in antiquity altogether strangers," &c. These things thus observed, I come to the objections of our opposers.

§ III. First, They allege, That those places mentioned Obj 1. of making shipwreck of faith, are only to be understood of seeming faith, and not of a real true faith.

This objection is very weak, and apparently contrary to Answ. the text, 1 Tim. i. 19, where the apostle addeth to faith a good conscience, by way of complaint; whereas if their A good and faith had been only seeming and hypocritical, the men had evil conscience. been better without it than with it; neither had they been worthy of blame for losing that which in itself was evil. But the apostle expressly adds " and of a good conscience," which shows it was real; neither can it be supposed that men could truly attain a good conscience without the operation of God's saving grace; far less that a good conscience doth consist with a seeming false and hypocritical faith. Again, these places of the apostle being spoken by way of regret, clearly import that these attainments they had fallen from were good and real, not false and deceitful, else he would not have regretted their falling from them; and so he saith positively, "They tasted of the heavenly gift, and were made partakers of the Holy Ghost," &c., not that they seemed to be so, which showeth this objection is very frivolous.

**Obj. 2.** Secondly, They allege, Phil. i. 6, "Being confident of this very thing, that he which hath begun a good work in you will perform it until the day of Jesus Christ," &c., and 1 Pet. i. 5: "Who are kept by the power of God through faith unto salvation."

**Answ.** These scriptures, as they do not affirm any thing positively contrary to us, so they cannot be understood otherwise than as the condition is performed upon our part, *Salvation is proposed upon certain conditions to be performed by us.* seeing salvation is no otherways proposed there but upon certain necessary conditions to be performed by us, as hath been above proved, and as our adversaries also acknowledge, as Rom. viii. 13: "For if ye live after the flesh, ye shall die; but if ye through the spirit do mortify the deeds of the body, ye shall live." And Heb. iii. 14: "We are made partakers of Christ, if we hold the beginning of our confidence steadfast unto the end." For if these places of the scripture upon which they build their objection were to be admitted without these conditions, it would manifestly overturn the whole tenor of their exhortations throughout all their writings. Some other objections there are of the same nature, which are solved by the same answers, which also, because largely treated of by others, I omit, to come to that testimony of the truth which is more especially ours in this matter, and is contained in the latter part of the proposition in these words: Yet such an increase ınd **stability** in the truth may in this life be attained, from which there cannot be a total apostasy.

§ IV. As in the explanation of the fifth and sixth propositions I observed, that some that had denied the errors cʳ others concerning reprobation, and affirmed the universality of Christ's death, did notwithstanding fall short ır sufficiently holding forth the truth, and so gave the contrary party occasion by their defects to be strengthened in their errors, so it may be said in this case. As upon the one hand they err who affirm that the least degree of true and saving grace cannot be fallen from, so do they err upon the other hand that deny any such stability to be attained from which there cannot be a total and final apostasy. And betwixt these two extremes lieth the truth apparent in the scriptures, which God hath revealed unto us by the testimony of his Spirit, and which also we are made sensible of by our own experience. And even as in the former controversy was observed, so also in this, the defence of truth will readily appear to such as seriously weigh the matter ; for the arguments upon both hands, rightly applied, will as to this hold good ; and the objections, which are strong as they are respectively urged against the two opposite false opinions, are here easily solved, by the establishing of this truth. For all the arguments which these allege that affirm there can be no falling away, may well be received upon the one part, as of those who have attained to this stability and establishment, and their objections solved by this confession ; so upon the other hand, the arguments alleged from scripture testimonies by those that affirm the possibility of falling away, may well be received of such as are not come to this establishment, though having attained a measure of true grace. Thus then the contrary batterings of our adversaries, who miss the truth, do concur the more strongly to establish it, while they are destroying each other. But lest this may not seem to suffice to satisfy such as judge it always possible for the best of men before they die to fall

*The two extremes some run into by asserting a final falling or not falling from grace im- possible.*

away, I shall add, for the proof of it, some brief con siderations from some few testimonies of the scripture.

I.
Watchful-
ness and
diligence is
of indispen-
sable ne-
cessity to
all.

§ V. And first, I freely acknowledge that it is good for all to be humble, and in this respect not over confident, so as to lean to this, to foster themselves in iniquity, or lie down in security, as if they had attained this condition, seeing watchfulness and diligence is of indispensable necessity to all mortal men, so long as they breathe in this world; for God will have this to be the constant practice of a Christian, that thereby he may be the more fit to serve him, and better armed against all the temptations of the enemy. For since the wages of sin is death, there is no man, while he sinneth, and is subject thereunto, but may lawfully suppose himself capable of perishing. Hence the apostle Paul himself saith, 1 Cor. ix. 27: "But I keep under my body, and bring it into subjection, lest that by any means, when I have preached to others, I myself should be a cast-away." Here the apostle supposes it possible for him to be a cast-away, and yet it may be judged he was far more advanced in the inward work of regeneration, when he wrote that epistle, than many who now-a-days too presumptuously suppose they cannot fall away, because they feel themselves to have attained some small degree of true grace. But the apostle makes use of this supposition or possibility of his being a cast-away, as I before observed, as an inducement to him to be watchful; "I keep under my body, lest," &c. Nevertheless the same apostle, at another time, in the sense and feeling of God's holy power, and in the dominion thereof, finding himself a conqueror there-through over sin and his soul's enemies, maketh no difficulty to affirm, Rom. viii. 38: "For I am persuaded that neither death nor life," &c., which clearly showeth that he had attained a condition from which he knew he could not fall away.

But secondly, It appears such a condition is attainable, because we are exhorted to it; and, as hath been proved before, the scripture never proposeth to us things impossible. Such an exhortation we have from the apostle

2 Pet. i. 10 : "Wherefore the rather, brethren, give dili- A condition
gence to make your calling and election sure, for if ye do attainable
these things ye shall never fall." And though there be a from which
condition here proposed, yet since we have already proved falling
that it is possible to fulfil this condition, then also the pro- away.
mise annexed thereunto may be attained. And since,
where assurance is wanting, there is still a place left for
doubtings and despairs, if we should affirm it never attainable, then should there never be a place known by the
saints in this world, wherein they might be free of doubting and despair ; which as it is most absurd in itself, so it
is contrary to the manifest experience of thousands.

Thirdly, God hath given to many of his saints and chil-            III.
dren, and is ready to give unto all a full and certain  A certain
assurance that they are his, and that no power shall be able  and estab-
to pluck them out of his hand.  But this assurance would  given of
be no assurance, if those who are so assured were not  God to
established and confirmed beyond all doubt and hesita-  saints and
tion : if so, then surely there is no possibility for such to  children.
miss of that which God hath assured them of.  And that
there is such assurance attainable in this life, the scripture
abundantly declareth, both in general and as to particular
persons.  As first, Rev. iii. 12 : "Him that overcometh
will I make a pillar in the temple of my God, and he shall
go no more out," &c., which containeth a general promise
unto all.  Hence the apostle speaks of some that are sealed,
2 Cor. i. 22 : "Who hath also sealed us, and given the
earnest of the Spirit in our hearts :" wherefore the Spirit
so sealing is called the earnest or "pledge of our inheritance," Eph. i. 13, "In whom ye were sealed with
that Holy Spirit of promise."  And therefore the apostle
Paul, not only in that of the Romans above noted, declareth himself to have attained that condition, but 2 Tim.
iv. 7, he affirmeth in these words, "I have fought a good
fight," &c., which also many good men have and do witness.  And therefore, as there can be nothing more evident
than that which the manifest experience of this time showeth and therein is found agreeable to the experience of

former times, so we see there have been both of old and
of late that have turned the grace of God into wantonness,
and have fallen from their faith and integrity; thence we
may safely conclude such a falling away possible. We
also see that some of old and of late have attained a certain assurance, some time before they departed, that they
should inherit eternal life, and have accordingly died in
that good hope, of and concerning whom the Spirit of God
testified that they are saved. Wherefore we also see such a
state is attainable in this life, from which there is not a falling away: for seeing the Spirit of God did so testify, it
was not possible that they should perish, concerning whom
he who cannot lie thus bare witness.

---

## PROPOSITION X.

### *Concerning the Ministry.*

As by the light or gift of God all true knowledge in things
spiritual is received and revealed, so by the same, as it
is manifested and received in the heart, by the strength
and power thereof, every true minister of the gospel is
ordained, prepared, and supplied in the work of the
ministry; and by the leading, moving, and drawing
hereof, ought every evangelist and Christian pastor to be
led and ordered in his labour and work of the gospel,
both as to the place where, as to the persons to whom,
and as to the time wherein he is to minister. Moreover,
they who have this authority may and ought to preach
the gospel, though without human commission or literature; as on the other hand, they who want the authority
of this divine gift, however learned, or authorized by the
commission of men and churches, are to be esteemed but
as deceivers, and not true ministers of the gospel. Also
they who have received this holy and unspotted gift, as
they have freely received it, so are they freely to give it,
without hire or bargaining, far less to use it as a trade to

The gospel
to be
preached
freely.
Mat. x. 8.

get money by: yet if God hath called any one from their employment or trades, by which they acquire their live-lihood, it may be lawful for such, according to the liberty which they feel given them in the Lord, to receive such temporals (to wit, what may be needful for them for meat and clothing) as are given them freely and cordially by those, to whom they have communicated spirituals.

§ I. HITHERTO I have treated of those things which relate to the Christian faith and Christians, as they stand each in his private and particular condition, and how and by what means every man may be a Christian indeed, and so abide. Now I come in order to speak of those things that relate to Christians, as they are stated in a joint fellowship and communion, and come under a visible and outward society, which society is called the church of God, and in scripture compared to a body, and therefore named the body of Christ. As then in the natural body there be divers members, all concurring to the common end of preserving and confirming the whole body, so in this spiritual and mystical body there are also divers members, according to the different measures of grace and of the Spirit diversely administered unto each member; and from this diversity ariseth that distinction of persons in the visible society of Christians, as of apostles, pastors, evangelists, ministers, &c. That which in this proposition is proposed, is, What makes or constitutes any a minister of the church, what his qualifications ought to be, and how he ought to behave himself. But because it may seem somewhat preposterous to speak of the distinct offices of the church, until something be said of the church in general, though nothing positively be said of it in the proposition; yet, as here implied, I shall briefly premise something thereof, and then proceed to the particular members of it.

*The church of God is the spiritual body of Christ.*

§ II. It is not in the least my design, to meddle with those tedious and many controversies, wherewith the Papists and Protestants do tear one another concerning this thing; but only according to the truth manifested to me, and I revealed in me by the testimony of the Spirit, according to that proportion of wisdom given me, briefly to hold forth as a necessary introduction both to this matter of the ministry and of worship which followeth, those things which I, together with my brethren, do believe concerning the church.

The church then, according to the grammatical signification of the word, as it is used in the holy scripture, signifies an assembly or gathering of many into one place; for the substantive ἐκκλησία comes from the word ἐκκαλέω, I call out of, and originally from καλέω, I call; and indeed, as this is the grammatical sense of the word, so also it is the real and proper signification of the thing, the church being no other thing but the society, gathering, or company of such as God hath called out of the world, and worldly spirit, to walk in his Light and Life. The church then so defined is to be considered, as it comprehends all that are thus called and gathered truly by God, both such as are yet in this inferior world, and such as having already laid down the earthly tabernacle, are passed into their heavenly mansions, which together do make up the one catholic church, concerning which there is so much controversy. Out of which church we freely acknowledge there can be no salvation; because under this church and its denomination are comprehended all, and as many, of whatsoever nation, kindred, tongue, or people they be, though outwardly strangers, and remote from those who profess Christ and Christianity in words, and have the benefit of the scriptures, as become obedient to the holy light and testimony of God in their hearts, so as to become sanctified by it, and cleansed from the evils of their ways. For this is the universal or catholic spirit, by which many are called from all the four corners of the earth, and shall sit down with Abraham, Isaac, and Jacob: by this the secret life and virtue of Jesus is conveyed into many that are afar off, even as by the blood that runs into the veins and arteries of the natural body, the life is conveyed from the head and heart unto the extreme parts. There may be members

*The etymology of the word ἐκκλησία the church, and signification of it.*

*No salvation without the church.*

*What the church is.*

therefore of this catholic church both among heathen, Turks, Jews, and all the several sorts of Christians, men and women of integrity and simplicity of heart, who though blinded in some things in their understanding, and perhaps burdened with the superstitions and formality of the several sects in which they are engrossed, yet being upright in their hearts before the Lord, chiefly aiming and labouring to be delivered from iniquity, and loving to follow righteousness, are by the secret touches of this holy light in their souls enlivened and quickened, thereby secretly united to God, and there-through become true members of this catholic church. Now the church in this respect hath been in being in all generations; for God never wanted some such witnesses for him, though many times slighted, and not much observed by this world; and therefore this church, though still in being, hath been oftentimes as it were invisible, in that it hath not come under the observation of the men of this world, being, as saith the scripture, Jer. iii. 14, "one of a city, and two of a family." And yet though the church thus considered may be as it were hid from wicked men, as not then gathered into a visible fellowship, yea and not observed even by some that are members of it, yet may there notwithstanding many belong to it; as when Elias complained he was left alone, 1 Kings xix. 18, God answered unto him, "I have reserved to myself seven thousand men, who have not bowed their knees to the image of Baal;" whence the apostle argues, Rom. xi., the being of a remnant in his day.

§ III. Secondly, The church is to be considered as it signifies a certain number of persons gathered by God's Spirit, and by the testimony of some of his servants raised up for that end, unto the belief of the true principles and doctrines of the Christian faith, who through their hearts being united by the same love, and their understandings informed in the same truths, gather, meet, and assemble together to wait upon God, to worship him, and to bear a joint testimony for the truth against error, suffering for the same, and so becoming through this fellowship as one

*[marginal note:]* Turks and Jews may become members of this church.

*[marginal note:]* II. The definition of the church of God, as gathered into a visible fellowship

family and household in certain respects, do each of them
watch over, teach, instruct, and care for one another, ac
cording to their several measures and attainments: such
were the churches of the primitive times gathered by the
apostles; whereof we have divers mentioned in the holy
scriptures. And as to the visibility of the church in this
respect, there hath been a great interruption since the
apostles' days, by reason of the apostasy, as will hereafter
appear.

**How to become a member of that church.** § IV. To be a member then of the Catholic church,
there is need of the inward calling of God by his light in
the heart, and a being leavened into the nature and spirit
of it, so as to forsake unrighteousness, and be turned to
righteousness, and in the inwardness of the mind, to be
cut out of the wild olive tree of our own first fallen
nature, and ingrafted into Christ by his Word and Spirit
in the heart. And this may be done in those who are
strangers to the history, God not having pleased to make
them partakers thereof, as in the fifth and sixth propositions
hath already been proved.

**The outward profession of the members of the true church.** To be a member of a particular church of Christ, as this
inward work is indispensably necessary, so is also the out-
ward profession of, and belief in Jesus Christ, and those
holy truths delivered by his Spirit in the scriptures; seeing
the testimony of the Spirit recorded in the scriptures, doth
answer the testimony of the same Spirit in the heart, even
as face answereth face in a glass. Hence it follows, that
the inward work of holiness, and forsaking iniquity, is
necessary in every respect to the being a member in the
church of Christ; and that the outward profession is necessary to be a member of a particular gathered church, but
not to the being a member of the Catholic church; yet it
is absolutely necessary, where God affords the opportunity
of knowing it: and the outward testimony is to be believed,
where it is presented and revealed; the sum whereof hath
upon other occasions been already proved.

§ V. But contrary hereunto, the devil, that worketh and
hath wrought in the mystery of iniquity, hath taught his

followers to affirm, That no man, however holy, is a member of the church of Christ without the outward profession; and unless he be initiated thereinto by some outward ceremonies. And again, That men who have this outward profession, though inwardly unholy, may be members of the true church of Christ, yea, and ought to be so esteemed. This is plainly to put light for darkness, and darkness for light; as if God had a greater regard to words than actions, and were more pleased with vain professions than with real holiness; but these things I have sufficiently refuted heretofore. Only from hence let it be observed, that upon this false and rotten foundation Antichrist hath built his Babylonish structure, and the Antichristian church in the apostasy hath hereby reared herself up to that height and grandeur she hath attained; so as to exalt herself above all that is called God, and sit in the temple of God as God.

*The members of the Antichristian church in the apostasy, their empty profession.*

For the particular churches of Christ, gathered in the apostles' days, soon after beginning to decay as to the inward life, came to be overgrown with several errors, and the hearts of the professors of Christianity to be leavened with the old spirit and conversation of the world. Yet it pleased God for some centuries to preserve that life in many, whom he emboldened with zeal to stand and suffer for his name through the ten persecutions: but these being over, the meekness, gentleness, love, long-suffering, goodness, and temperance of Christianity began to be lost. For after that the princes of the earth came to take upon them that profession, and that it ceased to be a reproach to be a Christian, but rather became a means to preferment; men became such by birth and education, and not by conversion and renovation of spirit: then there was none so vile, none so wicked, none so profane, who became not a member of the church. And the teachers and pastors thereof becoming the companions of princes, and so being enriched by their benevolence, and getting vast treasures and estates, became puffed up, and as it were drunken with the vain pomp and glory of this world: and so marshalled

*The decay of the church.*

*When men became Christians by birth, and not by conversion, Christianity came to be lost.*

themselves in manifold orders and degrees; not without innumerable contests and altercations who should have the precedency.* So the virtue, life, substance, and kernel of the Christian religion came to be lost, and nothing remained but a shadow and image; which dead image, or carcase of Christianity, to make it take the better with the superstitious multitude of heathen that were engrossed in it, not by any inward conversion of their hearts, or by becoming less wicked or superstitious, but by a little change in the object of their superstition, not having the inward ornament and life of the Spirit, became decked with many outward and visible orders, and beautified with the gold, silver, precious stones, and the other splendid ornaments of this perishing world; so that this was no more to be accounted the Christian religion, and Christian church, notwithstanding the outward profession, than the dead body of a man is to be accounted a living man; which, however cunningly embalmed, and adorned with ever so much gold or silver, or most precious stones, or sweet ointments, is but a dead body still, without sense, life, or motion. For that apostate church of Rome has introduced

In the church of Rome are no less superstitions and ceremonies introduced, than were either among Jews or heathen.

no fewer ceremonies and superstitions into the Christian profession, than were either among Jews or heathen; and that there is and hath been as much, yea, and more pride, covetousness, uncleanness, luxury, fornication, profaneness and atheism among her teachers and chief bishops, than ever was among any sort of people, none need doubt, that have read their own authors, to wit, Platina and others.

Whether, and what difference there is betwixt the Protestants and Papists in superstitions?

Now, though Protestants have reformed from her in some of the most gross points and absurd doctrines relating to the church and ministry, yet, which is to be regretted, they have only lopped the branches, but retain and plead earnestly for the same root, from which these abuses have sprung. So that even among them, though all that mass of superstition, ceremonies, and orders be not again estab-

---

* As was betwixt the bishop of Rome, and the bishop of Constantinople

lished, yet the same pride, covetousness and sensuality is found to have overspread and leavened their churches and ministry, and the life, power and virtue of true religion is lost among them; and the very same death, barrenness, dryness and emptiness, is found in their ministry. So that in effect they differ from Papists, but in form and some ceremonies; being with them apostatised from the life and power the true primitive church and her pastors were in: so that of both it may be said truly, without breach of charity, that having only a form of godliness, and many of them not so much as that, they are deniers of, yea, enemies to, the power of it. And this proceeds not simply from their not walking answerably to their own principles, and so degenerating that way, which also is true; but, which is worse, their laying down to themselves, and adhering to certain principles, which naturally, as a cursed root, bring forth these bitter fruits: these therefore shall afterwards be examined and refuted, as the contrary positions of truth in the proposition are explained and proved.

For as to the nature and constitution of a church,* abstract from their disputes concerning its constant visibility, infallibility, and the primacy of the church of Rome, the Protestants, as in practice, so in principles, differ not from Papists; for they engross within the compass of their church, whole nations, making their infants members of it, by sprinkling a little water upon them; so that there is none so wicked or profane who is not a fellow-member; no evidence of holiness being required to constitute a member of the church. Nay, look through the Protestant nations, and there will no difference appear in the lives of the generality of the one, more than of the other; he, who ruleth in the children of disobedience, reigning in both: so that the reformation, through this defect, is only in holding some less gross errors in the notion, but not in having the heart reformed and renewed, in which mainly the life of Christianity consisteth.

*i. e. national. The Protestant church, how they become members thereof.

Christianity chiefly consisteth in the renewing of the heart.

§ VI. But the Popish errors concerning the ministry, which they have retained, are most of all to be regretted,

by which chiefly the life and power of Christianity is bar
red out among them, and they kept in death, barrenness
and dryness: there being nothing more hurtful than an
error in this respect.  For where a false and corrupt
ministry entereth, all manner of other evils follow upon it,

according to that scripture adage, "Like people, like
priest:" for by their influence, instead of ministering life
and righteousness, they minister death and iniquity.  The
whole backslidings of the Jewish congregation of old are
hereto ascribed: " The leaders of my people have caused
them to err."  The whole writings of the prophets are full
of such complaints; and for this cause, under the New
Testament, we are so often warned and guarded to " beware of false prophets, and false teachers," &c.  What
may be thought then, where all, as to this, is out of order;
where both the foundation, call, qualifications, maintenance,
and whole discipline are different from and opposite to the
ministry of the primitive church; yea, and necessarily tend
to the shutting out of a spiritual ministry, and the bringing in and establishing of a carnal?  This shall appear by
parts.

§ VII. That then which comes first to be questioned in
this matter, is concerning the call of a minister; to wit,
What maketh, or how cometh a man to be, a minister,
pastor, or teacher in the church of Christ?

We answer; By the inward power and virtue of the
Spirit of God.  For, as saith our proposition, Having received the true knowledge of things spiritual by the Spirit
of God, without which they cannot be known, and being
by the same in measure purified and sanctified, he comes
thereby to be called and moved to minister to others; being able to speak, from a living experience, of what he
himself is a witness; and therefore knowing the terror of
the Lord, he is fit to persuade men,  &c., 2 Cor. v. 11,
and his words and ministry, proceeding from the inward
power and virtue, reach to the heart of his hearers, and
make them approve of him, and be subject unto him.  Our
adversaries are forced to confess, that this were indeed

desirable and best; but this they will not have to be absolutely necessary. I shall first prove the necessity of it, and then show how much they err in that which they make more necessary than this divine and heavenly call.

First; That which is necessary to make a man a Christian, so as without it he cannot be truly one, must be much more necessary to make a man a minister of Christianity; seeing the one is a degree above the other, and has it included in it; nothing less than he that supposeth a master, supposeth him first to have attained the knowledge and capacity of a scholar. They that are not Christians, cannot be teachers and ministers among Christians.

*Arg. 1. The necessity of an inward call to make a man a Christian.*

But this inward call, power and virtue of the Spirit of God, is necessary to make a man a Christian; as we have abundantly proved before in the second proposition, according to these scriptures, "He that hath not the Spirit of Christ, is none of his." "As many as are led by the Spirit of God, are the Sons of God:"

Therefore this call, moving and drawing of the Spirit, must be much more necessary to make a minister.

Secondly; All ministers of the New Testament ought to be ministers of the Spirit, and not of the letter, according to that of 2 Cor. iii. 6, and as the old Latin hath it, "Not by the letter, but by the Spirit." But how can a man be a minister of the Spirit, who is not inwardly called by it, and who looks not upon the operation and testimony of the Spirit as essential to his call? As he could not be a minister of the letter who had thence no ground for his call, yea, who was altogether a stranger to and unacquainted with it, so neither can he be a minister of the Spirit who is a stranger to it, and unacquainted with the motions thereof, and knows it not to draw, act, and move him, and go before him in the work of the ministry. I would willingly know, how those that take upon them to be ministers, as they suppose, of the gospel, merely from an outward vocation, without so much as being any ways sensible of the work of the Spirit, or any inward call therefrom, can either satisfy themselves or others that they are

*2. The ministry of the Spirit requires the operation and testimony of the Spirit.*

23                    2 I

ministers of the Spirit, or wherein they differ from the
ministers of the letter? For,

**3. Under the law the people needed not to doubt, who should be priests and ministers.**

Thirdly; If this inward call, or testimony of the Spirit,
were not essential and necessary to a minister, then the
ministry of the New Testament would not only be no ways
preferable to, but in divers respects far worse than that of
the law. For under the law there was a certain tribe
allotted for the ministry, and of that tribe certain families
set apart for the priesthood and other offices, by the immediate command of God to Moses; so that the people
needed not be in any doubt who should be priests and
ministers of the holy things: yea, and besides this, God
called forth, by the immediate testimony of his Spirit,
several at divers times to teach, instruct, and reprove his
people, as Samuel, Nathan, Elias, Elisha, Jeremiah, Amos,
and many more of the prophets: but now under the new
covenant, where the ministry ought to be more spiritual,
the way more certain, and the access more easy unto the
Lord, our adversaries, by denying the necessity of this inward and spiritual vocation, make it quite otherways. For
there being now no certain family or tribe to which the
ministry is limited, we are left in uncertainty, to choose
and have pastors at a venture, without any certain assent
of the will of God; having neither an outward rule nor
certainty in this affair to walk by: for that the scripture
cannot give any certain rule in this matter, hath in the
third proposition concerning it been already shown.

**4. Christ the door.**

**John x. 1.**

Fourthly; Christ proclaims them all thieves and robbers, that enter not by him the door into the sheepfold,
but climb up some other way; whom the sheep ought not
to hear: but such as come in without the call, movings,
and leadings of the Spirit of Christ, wherewith he leads
his children into all truth, come in certainly not by Christ,
who is the door, but some other way, and therefore are not
true shepherds.

§ VIII. To all this they object the succession of the
church; alleging, That since Christ gave a call to his
apostles and disciples, they have conveyed that call to

their successors, having power to ordain pastors and teachers; by which power the authority of ordaining and making ministers and pastors is successively conveyed to us; so that such, who are ordained and called by the pastors of the church, are therefore true and lawful ministers; and others, who are not so called, are to be accounted but intruders. Hereunto also some Protestants add a necessity, though they make it not a thing essential; That besides this calling of the church, every one, being called, ought to have the inward call of the Spirit, inclining him so chosen to his work: but this they say is subjective, and not objective; of which before.

*Succession pleaded by the false church from Christ and his apostles.*

As to what is subjoined of the inward call of the Spirit, in that they make it not essential to a true call, but a supererogation as it were, it showeth how little they set by it: since those they admit to the ministry are not so much as questioned in their trials, whether they have this or not. Yet, in that it hath been often mentioned, especially by the primitive Protestants in their treatises on this subject, it showeth how much they were secretly convinced in their minds, that this inward call of the Spirit was most excellent, and preferable to any other; and therefore in the most noble and heroic acts of the reformation, they laid claim unto it; so that many of the primitive Protestants did not scruple both to despise and disown this outward* call, when urged by the Papists against them. But now Protestants, having gone from the testimony of the Spirit, plead for the same succession; and being pressed (by those whom God now raiseth up by his Spirit to reform those abuses that are among them) with the example of their forefathers' practice against Rome, they are not at all ashamed utterly to deny that their fathers were called to their work by the inward and immediate vocation of the Spirit; clothing themselves with that call, which they say their forefathers had, as pastors of the Roman church. For thus (not to go further) affirmeth Nicolaus Arnoldus,† in a pamphlet written

*Answ.*

*The call of the Spirit preferred to any other by primitive Protestants.*

* Succession.
Modern Protestants denying the call of the Spirit.

---

† Who gives himself out Doctor and Professor of Sacred Theology at Franequer.

against the same propositions, called, A Theological Exercitation, sect. xl., averring, That they pretended not to an immediate act of the Holy Spirit; but reformed by the virtue of the ordinary vocation which they had in the church, as it then was, to wit, that of Rome, &c.

§ IX. Many absurdities do Protestants fall into, by deriving their ministry thus through the church of Rome. As, first, They must acknowledge her to be a true church of Christ, though only erroneous in some things; which contradicts their forefathers so frequently, and yet truly, calling her Antichrist. Secondly, They must needs acknowledge, that the priests and bishops of the Romish church are true ministers and pastors of the church of Christ, as to the essential part; else they could not be fit subjects for that power and authority to have resided in; neither could they have been vessels capable to receive that power, and again transmit it to their successors. Thirdly, It would follow from this, that the priests and bishops of the Romish church are yet really true pastors and teachers: for if Protestant ministers have no authority but what they received from them, and since the church of Rome is the same she was at that time of the reformation in doctrine and manners, and she has the same power now she had then, and if the power lie in the succession, then these priests of the Romish church now, which derive their ordination from those bishops that ordained the first reformers, have the same authority which the successors of the reformed have, and consequently are no less ministers of the church than they are. But how will this agree with that opinion which the primitive Protestants had of the Romish priests and clergy, to whom Luther did not only deny any power or authority, but contrary-wise affirmed, That it was wickedly done of them, to assume to themselves only this authority to teach, and be priests and ministers, &c. For he himself affirmed, That every good Christian (not only men, but even women also) is a preacher.

§ X. But against this vain succession, as asserted either

Absurdities Protestants fall into, by deriving their ministry through the church of Rome.

Luther affirmed, that a woman might be a preacher.

by the Papists or Protestants as a necessary thing to the call of a minister, I answer; That such as plead for it, as a sufficient or necessary thing to the call of a minister, do thereby sufficiently declare their ignorance of the nature of Christianity, and how much they are strangers to the life and power of a Christian ministry, which is not entailed to succession, as an outward inheritance; and herein, as hath been often before observed, they not only make the gospel not better than the law, but even far short of it. For Jesus Christ, as he regardeth not any distinct particular family or nation in the gathering of his children; but only such as are joined to and leavened with his own pure and righteous seed, so neither regards he a bare outward succession, where his pure, immaculate, and righteous life is wanting; for that were all one. He took not the nations into the new covenant, that he might suffer them to fall into the old errors of the Jews, or to approve them in their errors, but that he might gather unto himself a pure people out of the earth. Now this was the great error of the Jews, to think they were the church and people of God, because they could derive their outward succession from Abraham; whereby they reckoned themselves the children of God, as being the offspring of Abraham, who was the Father of the Faithful. But how severely doth the scripture rebuke this vain and frivolous pretence! Telling them, That God is able of the stones to raise children unto Abraham; and that not the outward seed, but those that were found in the faith of Abraham, are the true children of faithful Abraham. Far less then can this pretence hold among Christians, seeing Christ rejects all outward affinity of that kind: These, saith he, are my mother, brethren and sisters, who do the will of my Father which is in heaven: And again; he looked round about him, and said, Who shall do the will of God, these, saith he, are my brethren. So then, such as do not the commands of Christ, as are not found clothed with his righteousness, are not his disciples; and that which a man hath not, he cannot give to another: and it is clear, that no man nor church, though truly called of

*The pretended succession of Papists and Protestants explained.*

*The Jews' error of Abraham's outward succession.*

*Mat.xii. 48, &c.*
*Mark iii. 33, &c.*

23*

God, and as such having the authority of a church and minister, can any longer retain that authority, than they retain the power, life, and righteousness of Christianity

**The form of godliness is entailed to the power and substance, and not the substance to the form.** for the form is entailed to the power and substance, and not the substance to the form. So that when a man ceaseth inwardly in his heart to be a Christian (where his Christianity must lie) by turning to Satan, and becoming a reprobate, he is no more a Christian, though he retain the name and form, than a dead man is a man, though he hath the image and representation of one, or than the picture or statue of a man is a man: and though a dead man may serve to a painter to retain some imperfect representation of the man, that once was alive, and so one picture may serve to make another by, yet none of those can serve to make a true living man again, neither can they convey the life and spirit of the man; it must be God, that made the man at first, that alone can revive him. As death then

**Succession interrupted.** makes such interruption of an outward natural succession, that no art nor outward form can uphold, and as a dead man, after he is dead, can have no issue, neither can dead images of men make living men: so that it is the living that are only capable to succeed one another; and such as die, so soon as they die cease to succeed, or to transmit succession. So it is in spiritual things; it is the life of Christianity, taking place in the heart, that makes a Chris-

**The living members make the church: life lost, the church is ceased.** tian: and so it is a number of such, being alive, joined together in the life of Christianity, that make a church of Christ; and it is all those that are thus alive and quickened, considered together, that make the Catholic church of Christ: therefore when this life ceaseth in one, then that one ceaseth to be a Christian; and all power, virtue, and authority, which he had as a Christian, ceaseth with it; so that if he hath been a minister or teacher, he ceaseth to be so any more: and though he retain the form, and hold to the authority in words, yet that signifies no more, nor is it of any more real virtue and authority, than the mere image of a dead man. And as this is most agreeable to reason, so it is to the scripture's testimony; for it is said of Judas,

Acts. i. 25, That Judas fell from his ministry and apostle-ship by transgression; so his transgression caused him to cease to be an apostle any more: whereas, had the apostle-ship been entailed to his person, so that transgression could not cause him to lose it, until he had been formally degraded by the church (which Judas never was so long as he lived) Judas had been as really an apostle, after he betrayed Christ, as before. And as it is of one, so of many, yea, of a whole church: for seeing nothing makes a man truly a Christian, but the life of Christianity inwardly ruling in his heart; so nothing makes a church, but the gathering of several true Christians into one body. Now where all these members lose this life, there the church ceaseth to be, though they still uphold the form, and retain the name: for when that which made them a church, and for which they were a church, ceaseth, then they cease also to be a church: and therefore the Spirit, speaking to the church of Laodicea, because of her lukewarmness, Rev. iii. 16, threateneth to spue her out of his mouth. Now, suppose the church of Laodicea had continued in that lukewarmness, and had come under that condemnation and judgment, though she had retained the name and form of a church, and had had her pastors and ministers, as no doubt she had at that time, yet surely she had been no true church of Christ, nor had the authority of her pastors and teachers been to be regarded, because of an outward succession, though perhaps some of them had it immediately from the apostles. From all which I infer, That since the authority of the Christian church and her pastors is always united, and never separated from the inward power, virtue, and righteous life of Christianity; where this ceaseth, that ceaseth also. But our adversaries acknowledge, That many, if not most of those, by and through whom they derive this authority, were altogether destitute of this life and virtue of Christianity: therefore they could neither receive, have, nor transmit any Christian authority.

But if it be objected, That though the generality of the bishops and priests of the church of Rome, during the

*Judas fell from his ministry by transgression.*

*The luke warmness of the church of Laodicea.*

*Object*

apostasy, were such wicked men; yet Protestants affirm, and thou thyself seemest to acknowledge, that there were some good men among them, whom the Lord regarded, and who were true members of the Catholic church of Christ; might not they then have transmitted this authority?

**ANSW.**

I answer; This saith nothing, in respect Protestants do not at all lay claim to their ministry as transmitted to them by a direct line of good men; which they can never show, nor yet pretend to; but generally place this succession as inherent in the whole pastors of the apostate church. Neither do they plead their call to be good and valid, because they can derive it through a line of good men, separate and observably distinguishable from the rest of the bishops and clergy of the Romish church; but they derive it as an authority residing in the whole: for they think it heresy, to judge that the quality or condition of the administrator doth any ways invalidate or prejudice his work.

The Protestants plead for a succession inherent.

This vain and pretended succession not only militates against, and fights with the very manifest purpose and intent of Christ in the gathering and calling of his church, but makes him (so to speak) more blind and less prudent than natural men are in conveying and establishing their outward inheritances. For where an estate is entailed to a certain name and family, when that family weareth out, and there is no lawful successor found of it, that can make a just title appear, as being really of blood and affinity to the family: it is not lawful for any one of another race or blood, because he assumes the name or arms of that family, to possess the estate, and claim the superiorities and privileges of the family; but by the law of nations the inheritance devolves into the prince, as being *Ultimus Hæres*; and so he giveth it again immediately to whom he sees meet, and makes them bear the name and arms of the family, who then are entitled to the privileges and revenues thereof. So in like manner, the true name and title of a Christian, by which he hath right to the heavenly in-

An estate void of heirship devolves to the prince, none claims it, but he to whom he sees meet o give it: so the heirship of life is enjoyed from Christ the true heir.

heritance, and is a member of Jesus Christ, is inward
righteousness and holiness, and the mind redeemed from
the vanities, lusts, and iniquities of this world; and a
gathering or company, made up of such members, makes
a church. Where this is lost, the title is lost; and so the
true seed, to which the promise is, and to which the inheritance is due, becomes extinguished in them, and they
become dead as to it; and so it retires, and devolves itself
again into Christ, who is the righteous heir of life; and he
gives the title and true right again immediately to whom it
pleaseth him, even to as many as being turned to his pure
light in their consciences, come again to walk in his righteous and innocent life, and so become true members of his
body, which is the church. So the authority, power and
heirship are not annexed to persons, as they bear the mere
names, or retain a form, holding the mere shell or shadow
of Christianity; but the promise is to Christ, and to the
seed, in whom the authority is inherent, and in as many as
are one with him, and united unto him by purity and holiness, and by the inward renovation and regeneration of
their minds.

Moreover, this pretended succession is contrary to scripture definitions, and the nature of the church of Christ,
and of the true members. For, first, The church is the
house of God, the pillar and ground of truth, 1 Tim. iii.
15. But according to this doctrine, the house of God is
a polluted nest of all sort of wickedness and abominations,
made up of the most ugly, defiled, and perverse stones
that are in the earth; where the devil rules in all manner
of unrighteousness. For so our adversaries confess, and
history informs, the church of Rome to have been, as some
of their historians acknowledge; and if that be truly the
house of God, what may we call the house of Satan? Or
may we call it therefore the house of God, notwithstanding
all this impiety, because they had a bare form, and that
vitiated many ways also; and because they pretended to
the name of Christianity, though they were antichristian,
devilish, and atheistical in their whole practice and spirit,

I.
The house
of God is
no polluted
nest; no
atheist nor
pretender
can rest
there.

and also in many of their principles? Would not this infer yet a greater absurdity, as if they had been something to be accounted of, because of their hypocrisy and deceit, and false pretences? Whereas the scripture looks upon that as an aggravation of guilt, and calls it blasphemy, Rev. ii. 9. Of two wicked men, he is most to be abhorred, who covereth his wickedness with a vain pretence of God and righteousness; even so these abominable beasts, and fearful monsters, who looked upon themselves to be bishops in the apostate church, were never a whit the better, that they falsely pretended to be the successors of the holy apostles; unless to lie be commendable, and that hypocrisy be the way to heaven. Yea, were not this to fall into that evil condemned among the Jews, Jer. vii. 4: "Trust ye not in lying words, saying, The temple of the Lord, the temple of the Lord, the temple of the Lord are these; thoroughly amend your ways," &c., as if such outward names and things were the thing the Lord regarded, and not inward holiness? Or can that then be the pillar and ground of truth, which is the very sink and pit of wickedness, from which so much error, superstition, idolatry, and all abomination spring? Can there be any thing more contrary both to scripture and reason?

II.

**Christ is the head, his body undefiled.**

Secondly, The church is defined to be the kingdom of the dear Son of God, into which the saints are translated, being delivered from the power of darkness. It is called the body of Christ, which from him by joints and bands having nourishment ministered and knit together, increaseth with the increase of God, Col. ii. 19. But can such members, such a gathering as we have demonstrated that church and members to be, among whom they allege their pretended authority to have been preserved, and through which they derive their call; can such, I say, be the body of Christ, or members thereof? Or is Christ the head of such a corrupt, dead, dark, abominable stinking

**What fellowship hath Christ with Belial?**

carcase? If so, then might we not as well affirm against the apostle, 2 Cor. vi. 14: "That righteousness hath fellowship with unrighteousness, that light hath communion with darkness, that Christ hath concord with Belial, that a believer hath part with an infidel, and that the temple of God hath agreement with idols?" Moreover no man is called the temple of God, nor of the Holy Ghost, but as his vessel is purified, and so he fitted and prepared for God to dwell in; and many thus fitted by Christ become his body, in and among whom he dwells and walks, according as it is written, "I will dwell in them, and walk in them, and I will be their God, and they shall be my people." It is therefore that we may become the temple of Christ, and people of God, that the apostle in the following verse exhorts, saying out of the prophet, "Wherefore come out from among them, and be ye separate, saith the Lord, and touch not the unclean thing, and I will receive you; and I will be a father unto you, and ye shall be my sons and daughters, saith the Lord Almighty." But to what purpose is all this exhortation? And why should we separate from the unclean, if a mere outward profession and name be enough to make the true church; and if the unclean and polluted were both the church and lawful successors of the apostles, inheriting their authority, and transmitting it to others? Yea, how can the church be the kingdom of the Son of God, as contra-distinguished from the kingdom and power of darkness? And what need, yea, what possibility, of being translated out of the one into the other, if those that make up the kingdom and power of darkness be real members of the true church of Christ, and not simply members only, but the very pastors and teachers of it? But how do they increase in the increase of God, and receive spiritual nourishment from Christ the head, that are enemies of him in their hearts by wicked works, and openly go into perdition? Verily as no metaphysical and nice distinctions, that though they were practically as to their own private states enemies to God and Christ, and so servants of Satan; yet they were, by virtue of their office, members and ministers of the church, and so able to transmit the succession; I say, as such invented and frivolous distinctions will not please the

*2 Cor. vi. 17, 18.*

*Priests' frivolous distinction of enemies to God by practice and members of his church by office.*

Lord God, neither will he be deluded by such, nor make up the glorious body of his church with such mere outside hypocritical shows, nor be beholden to such painted se pulchres to be members of his body, which is sound, pure and undefiled, and therefore he needs not such false and corrupt members to make up the defects of it; so neither will such distinctions satisfy truly tender and Christian consciences; especially considering the apostle is so far from desiring us to regard this, that we are expressly commanded to turn away from such as have a form of godliness, but deny the power of it. For we may well object against these, as the poor man did against the proud prelate, that went about to cover his vain and unchristian-like sumptuousness, by distinguishing that it was not as bishop but as prince he had all that splendor. To which the poor rustic wisely is said to have answered, When the prince goeth to hell, what shall become of the prelate? And indeed this were to suppose the body of Christ to be defective, and that to fill up these defective places, he puts counterfeit and dead stuff instead of real living members; like such as lose their eyes, arms, or legs, who make counterfeit ones of wood or glass instead of them. But we cannot think so of Christ, neither can we believe, for the reasons above adduced, that either we are to account, or that Christ doth account, any man or men a whit the more members of his body, because though they be really wicked, they hypocritically and deceitfully clothe themselves with his name, and pretend to it; for this is contrary to his own doctrine, where he saith expressly, John xv. 1, 2, 3, 4, 5, 6, &c., That he is the vine, and his disciples are the branches; that except they abide in him, they cannot bear fruit; and if they be unfruitful, they shall be cast forth as a branch, and wither. Now I suppose these cut and withered branches are no more true branches nor members of the vine; they can no more draw sap nor nourishment from it, after that they are cut off, and so have no more virtue, sap, nor life: What have they then to boast or glory of any authority, seeing they want that

*The answer of a poor rustic to a proud prelate.*

*A withered branch can draw no nourishment, so hath no life nor virtue.*

life, virtue, and nourishment from which all authority comes? So such members of Christ as are become dead to him through unrighteousness, and so derive no more virtue nor life from him, are cut off by their sins, and wither, and have no longer any true or real authority, and their boasting of any is but an aggravation of their iniquity by hypocrisy and deceit. But further, would not this make Christ's body a mere shadow and phantasm? Yea, would it not make him the head of a lifeless, rotten, stinking carcase, having only some little outward false show, while inwardly full of rottenness and dirt? And what a monster would these men make of Christ's body by assigning it a real, pure, living, quick head, full of virtue and life, and yet tied to such a dead lifeless body as we have already described these members to be, which they allege to have been the church of Christ? Again, the members of the church of Christ are specified by this definition, to wit, as being the sanctified in Christ Jesus, 1 Cor. i. 2. But this notion of succession supposeth not only some unsanctified members to be of the church of Christ, but even the whole to consist of unsanctified members; yea, that such as were professed necromancers and open servants of Satan were the true successors of the apostles, and in whom the apostolic authority resided, these being the vessels through whom this succession is transmitted; though many of them, as all Protestants and also some Papists confess, attained these offices in the, so called, church not only by such means as Simon Magus sought it, but by much worse, even by witchcraft, traditions, money, treachery, and murder, which Platina himself confesseth* of divers bishops of Rome.

*A living head upon a lifeless body, what a monster would that be?*

§ XI. But such as object not this succession of the church, which yet most Protestants begin now to do, distinguish in this matter, affirming, that in a great apostasy, such as was that of the church of Rome, God may raise up

---

* In the Life of Benedict IV., of John XVI., of Sylvester III., of Boniface VIII., of Steph. VI., of Joan VIII. Also Onuphrius's Annotations upon this Papess, or Popess, towards the end.

some singularly by his Spirit, who from the testimony of
the scriptures perceiving the errors into which such as bear
the name of Christians are fallen, may instruct and teach
them, and then become authorized by the people's joining
with and accepting of their ministry only. Most of them
also will affirm, That the Spirit herein is subjective, and
not objective.

**OBJECT.** But they say, That where a church is reformed, such as
they pretend the Protestant churches are, there an ordinary
orderly call is necessary ; and that of the Spirit, as extraordinary, is not to be sought after : alleging, that *res aliter
se habet in ecclesiâ constituendâ, quàm in ecclesiâ constitutâ ;*
that is, There is a difference in the constituting of a church,
and after it is constituted.

**ANSW.** I answer, This objection as to us saith nothing, seeing
we accuse, and are ready from the scriptures to prove the
A differ-   Protestants guilty of gross errors, and needing reformation,
ence object-  as well as they did and do the Papists ; and therefore we
ed between
constituting  may justly lay claim, if we would, to the same extraordi-
a church
and one as  nary call, having the same reason for it, and as good
constituted  evidence to prove ours as they had for theirs. As for that
maxim, viz. : That the case is different in constituting a
church, and a church constituted, I do not deny it ; and
therefore there may be a greater measure of power required
to the one than to the other, and God in his wisdom dis-
tributes the same as he sees meet ; but that the same
immediate assistance of the Spirit is not necessary for
ministers in a gathered church as well as in gathering one,
I see no solid reason alleged for it : for surely Christ's
promise was to be with his children to the end of the
world, and they need him no less to preserve and guide
his church and children than to gather and beget them.
Nature taught the Gentiles this maxim, *Non minor est vir-
tus, quam quærere, parta tueri,* ' To defend what we attain,
requires no less strength than what is necessary to acquire
it.' For it is by this inward and immediate operation of
the Spirit, which Christ hath promised to lead his children
with into all truth, and to teach them all things, that

Christians are to be led in all steps, all well last as first, which relate to God's glory and their own salvation, as we have heretofore sufficiently proved, and therefore need not now repeat it. And truly this device of Satan, whereby he has got people to put the immediate guidings and leadings of God's Spirit as an extraordinary thing afar off, which their forefathers had, but which they now are neither to wait for nor expect, is a great cause of the growing apostasy upon the many gathered churches, and is one great reason why a dry, dead, barren, lifeless, spiritless ministry, which leavens the people into the same death, doth so much abound, and is so much overspreading even the Protestant nations, that their preaching and worships, as well as their whole conversation, is not to be discerned from Popish by any fresh living zeal, or lively power of the Spirit accompanying it, but merely by the difference of some notions and opinions.

*It is a device of Satan for men to put the Spirit's leadings far off to former times.*

§ XII. Some unwise and unwary Protestants do sometimes object to us, That if we have such an immediate call as we lay claim to, we ought to confirm it by miracles.

*Object.*

But this being an objection once and again urged against the primitive Protestants by the Papists, we need but in short return the answer to it that they did to the Papists, to wit, That we need not miracles, because we preach no new gospel, but that which is already confirmed by all the miracles of Christ and his apostles; and that we offer nothing but that which we are ready and able to confirm by the testimony of the scriptures, which both already acknowledge to be true: and that John the Baptist and divers of the prophets did none that we hear of, and yet were both immediately and extraordinarily sent. This is the common Protestant answer, therefore may suffice in this place; though, if need were, I could say more to this purpose, but that I study brevity.

*Answ.*

*Whether miracles be now necessary to confirm the gospel?*

*John Baptist and divers prophets did none.*

§ XIII. There is also another sort of Protestants, to wit, the English Independents, who differing from the Calvinistical Presbyterians, and denying the necessity of this suc-

The consti-
tution of
the inde-
pendent
church.

cession, or the authority of any national church, take another
way; affirming, That such as have the benefit of the scriptures, any company of people agreeing in the principles of
truth as they find them there declared, may constitute among
themselves a church, without the authority of any other,
and may choose to themselves a pastor, who by the church
thus constituted and consenting, is authorized, requiring
only the assistance and concurrence of the pastors of the
neighbouring churches, if any such there be; not so much
as absolutely necessary to authorize, as decent for order's
sake. Also they go so far as to affirm, That in a church so

Gifted bre-
thren.

constituted, any gifted brother, as they call them, if he find
himself qualified thereto, may instruct, exhort, and preach
in the church; though, as not having the pastoral office,
he cannot administer those which they call their sacraments.

To this I answer, That this was a good step out of the
Babylonish darkness, and no doubt did proceed from a
real discovery of the truth, and from the sense of a great
abuse of the promiscuous national gatherings. Also this
preaching of the gifted brethren, as they called them, did
proceed at first from certain lively touches and movings

Their loss
and decay.

of the Spirit of God upon many; but alas! because they
went not forward, that is much decayed among them; and
the motions of God's Spirit begin to be denied and rejected among them now, as much as by others.

The scrip-
tures give
no call to
persons in-
dividual.

But as to their pretended call from the scripture, I answer, The scripture gives a mere declaration of true things,
but no call to particular persons; so that though I believe
the things there written to be true, and deny the errors
which I find there testified against, yet as to those things
which may be my particular duty, I am still to seek; and
therefore I can never be resolved in the scripture whether
I (such a one by name) ought to be a minister? And for
the resolving this doubt I must needs recur to the inward
and immediate testimony of the Spirit, as in the proposition
concerning the scriptures is shown more at large.

§ XIV. From all this then we do firmly conclude, that

not only in a general apostasy it is needful men be extraordinarily called, and raised up by the Spirit of God, but that even when several assemblies or churches are gathered by the power of God, not only into the belief of the principles of truth, so as to deny errors and heresies, but also into the life, spirit, and power of Christianity, so as to be the body and house of Christ indeed, and a fit spouse for him, that he who gathers them doth also, for the preserving them in a lively, fresh, and powerful condition, raise up *True ministers' qualifications, call, and title.* and move among them by the inward immediate operation of his own Spirit, ministers and teachers, to instruct and teach, and watch over them, who being thus called, are manifest in the hearts of their brethren, and their call is thus verified in them, who by the feeling of that life and power that passeth through them, being inwardly builded up by them daily in the most holy faith, become the seals of their apostleship. And this is answerable to another saying of the same apostle Paul, 2 Cor. xiii. 3 : "Since ye seek a proof of Christ's speaking in me, which to youwards is not weak, but is mighty in you." So this is that *Their laying on of hands a mock to God and man; a keeping the shadow whilst the substance is wanting.* which gives a true substantial call and title to a minister, whereby he is a real successor of the virtue, life, and power that was in the apostles, and not of the bare name : and to such ministers we think the outward ceremony of ordination or laying on of hands not necessary, neither can we see the use of it, seeing our adversaries who use it acknowledge that the virtue and power of communicating the Holy Ghost by it is ceased among them. And is it not then foolish and ridiculous for them, by an apish imitation, to keep up the shadow, where the substance is wanting? And may not they by the same rule, where they see blind and lame men, in imitation of Christ and his apostles, bid them see and walk? Yea, is it not in them a mocking of God and men, to put on their hands, and bid men receive the Holy Ghost, while they believe the thing impossible, and confess that that ceremony hath no real effect? Having thus far spoken of the call, I shall proceed next to treat of the qualifications and work of a true minister.

Ques. 2.
The quali-
fication of
a minister.

§ XV. As I have placed the true call of a minister in the motion of this Holy Spirit, so is the power, life, and virtue thereof, and the pure grace of God that comes therefrom, the chief and most necessary qualification, without which he can no ways perform his duty, neither acceptably to God nor beneficially to men. Our adversaries in this case affirm, that three things go to the making up of a minister, viz. 1. Natural parts, that he be not a fool. 2. Acquired parts, that he be learned in the languages, in philosophy and school divinity. 3. The grace of God.

Philoso-
phy and
school divi-
nity will
never make
a gospel
minister.

The two first they reckon necessary to the being of a minister, so as a man cannot be one without them; the third they say goeth to the well-being of one, but not to the being; so that a man may truly be a lawful minister without it, and ought to be heard and received as such. But we, supposing a natural capacity, that one be not an idiot, judge the grace of God indispensably necessary to the very being of a minister, as that without which any can neither be a true, nor lawful, nor good minister. As for letter-learning, we judge it not so much necessary to the well-being of one, though accidentally sometimes in certain respects it may concur, but more frequently it is hurtful than helpful, as appeared in the example of Taulerus, who being a learned man, and who could make an eloquent preaching, needed nevertheless to be instructed in the way of the Lord by a poor laic. I shall first speak of the necessity of grace, and then proceed to say something of that literature which they judge so needful.

A poor
laic in-
structed
the learned
Taulerus.

Proof I.

First then, as we said in the call, so may we much more here, if the grace of God be a necessary qualification to make one a true Christian, it must be a qualification much more necessary to constitute a true minister of Christianity. That grace is necessary to make one a true Christian I think will not be questioned, since it is "by grace we are saved," Eph. ii. 8. It is the grace of God that teacheth us to deny ungodliness, and the lusts of this world, and to live godly and righteously, Tit. ii. 11. Yea, Christ saith expressly, That without him we can do nothing, John

God's
grace alone
doth consti-
tute a true
and lawful
teacher.

xv. 5 ; and the way whereby Christ helpeth, assisteth, and worketh with us is by his grace : hence he saith to Paul, "My grace is sufficient for thee." A Christian without grace is indeed no Christian, but an hypocrite, and a false pretender. Then I say, If grace be necessary to a private Christian, far more to a teacher among Christians, who must be as a father and instructor of others, seeing this dignity is bestowed upon such as have attained a greater measure than their brethren. Even nature itself may teach us that there is more required in a teacher than in those that are taught, and that the master must be above and before the scholar in that art or science which he teacheth others. Since then Christianity cannot be truly enjoyed, neither any man denominated a Christian without the true grace of God, therefore neither can any man be a true and lawful teacher of Christianity without it.

Secondly, No man can be a minister of the church of Christ, which is his body, unless he be a member of the body, and receive of the virtue and life of the head.

But he that hath not true grace, can neither be a member of the body, neither receive of that life and nourishment which comes from the head :

Therefore far less can he be a minister to edify the body.

That he cannot be a minister who is not a member is evident; because he who is not a member is shut out and cut off, and hath no place in the body ; whereas, the ministers are counted among the most eminent members of the body. But no man can be a member unless he receive of the virtue, life, and nourishment of the head ; for the members that receive not this life and nourishment decay and wither, and then are cut off. And that every true member doth thus receive nourishment and life from the head, the apostle expressly affirmeth, Eph. iv. 16: "From whom the whole body being fitly joined together, and compacted by that which every joint supplieth, according to the effectual working in the measure of every part, maketh increase of the body unto the edifying of itself in love." Now this

*PROOF II. ARG.*
*Who first must be a member of the body, and then life is received, and virtue from the head.*

that. thus is communicated, and which thus uniteth. the whole, is no other than the grace of God; and therefore the apostle in the same chapter, ver. 7, saith, "But unto every one of us is given grace according to the measure of the gift of Christ;" and ver. 11, he showeth how that by this grace and gift both apostles, prophets, evangelists, pastors, and teachers are given for the work of the ministry, and edifying of the body of Christ.    And certainly then no man destitute of grace is fit for this work, seeing that all that Christ gives are so qualified; and these that are not so qualified, are not given nor sent of Christ, are not to be heard, nor received, nor acknowledged as ministers of the gospel, because his sheep neither ought nor will hear the voice of a stranger.    This is also clear from 1 Cor. xii. throughout; for the apostle in that chapter, treating of the diversity of gifts and members of the body, showeth how by the workings of the same Spirit in different manifestations or measures in the several members of the body the whole body is edified, saying, ver. 13, That "we are all baptized by the one Spirit into one body;" and then, ver. 28, he numbers up the several dispensations thereof, which by God are set in the church through the various workings of his Spirit for the edification of the whole.    Then if there be no true member of the body which is not thus baptized by the Spirit, neither any thing that worketh to the edifying of it, but according to a measure of grace received from the Spirit, surely without grace none ought to be admitted to work or labour in the body, because their labour and work, without this grace and Spirit, would be but ineffectual.

*The sheep of Christ neither ought nor will hear the stranger's voice.*

PROOF II.    § XVI. Thirdly, That this grace and gift is a necessary qualification to a minister, is clear from that of the apostle Peter, 1 Pet. iv. 10, 11, "As every man hath received the gift, even so minister the same one to another, as good stewards of the manifold grace of God. If any man speak let him speak as the oracles of God: if any man minister, let him do it as of the ability which God giveth; that God in all things may be glorified through Jesus Christ; to whom be praise and dominion for ever, Amen." From which it appears, that those that minister must minister according to the gift and grace received; but they that have not such a gift, cannot minister according thereunto. Secondly, As good stewards of the manifold grace of God: but how can a man be a good steward of that which he hath not? Can ungodly men, that are not gracious themselves, be good stewards of the manifold grace of God? And therefore in the following verses he makes an exclusive limitation of such that are not thus furnished, saying, "If any man speak, let him speak as the oracles of God; and if any man minister, let him do it as of the ability that God giveth:" which is as much as if he had said, they that cannot thus speak, and thus minister, ought not to do it: for this *if* denotes a necessary condition. Now what this ability is, is manifest by the former words, to wit, the gift received, and the grace whereof they are stewards, as by the immediate context and dependency of the words doth appear. Neither can it be understood of a mere natural ability, because man in this condition is said "not to know the things of God," and so he cannot minister them to others. And the following words show this also, in that he immediately subjoineth, "that God in all things may be glorified;" but surely God is not glorified, but greatly dishonoured, when natural men, from their mere natural ability, meddle in spiritual things, which they neither know nor understand.

*The ministering must be by the gift and grace received.*

*Good stewardship of what? Of God's abounding grace, which is the ability and stewardship received.*

Fourthly, That grace is a most necessary qualification for a minister, appears by those qualifications which the apostle expressly requires, 1 Tim. iii. 2; Tit. i., &c., where he saith, "A bishop must be blameless, vigilant, sober, of good behaviour, apt to teach, patient, a lover of good men, just, holy, temperate, as the steward of God, holding fast the faithful word as he hath been taught." Upon the other hand, He must neither be given to wine, nor a striker, nor covetous, nor proud, nor self-willed, nor soon angry. Now I ask if it be not impossible that a man can have all these above-named virtues, and be free of all

*PROP IV.*

How can a
bishop have
these vir-
tues with-
out the
grace of
God?
these evils, without the grace of God? If then these virtues, for the producing of which in a man grace is absolutely necessary, be necessary to make a true minister of
the church of Christ according to the apostle's judgment,
surely grace must be necessary also.

Concerning this thing a learned man, and well skilled
in antiquity, about the time of the reformation, writeth
thus: " Whatsoever is done in the church, either for ornament or edification of religion, whether in choosing magistrates or instituting ministers of the church, except it be
done by the ministry of God's Spirit, which is as it were the
soul of the church, it is vain and wicked. For whoever
hath not been called by the Spirit of God to the great
office of God and dignity of apostleship, as Aaron was,
and hath not entered in by the door, which is Christ, but
hath otherways risen in the church by the window, by the
favours of men, &c., truly such a one is not the vicar of
Christ and his apostles, but a thief and robber, and the
vicar of Judas Iscariot and Simon the Samaritan. Hence
it was so strictly appointed concerning the election of prelates, which holy Dionysius calls the sacrament of nomi-
nation, that the bishops and apostles who should oversee
the service of the church should be men of most entire
manners and life, powerful in sound doctrine, to give a
reason for all things." So also another,* about the same
time, writeth thus: " Therefore it can never be, that by
the tongues or learning any can give a sound judgment
concerning the holy scriptures, and the truth of God.
Lastly," saith he, "the sheep of Christ seeks nothing but
the voice of Christ, which he knoweth by the Holy Spirit,
wherewith he is filled: he regards not learning, tongues,
or any outward thing, so as therefore to believe this or that
to be the voice of Christ, his true shepherd; he knoweth
that there is need of no other thing but the testimony of the
Spirit of God."

Whatso-
ever is done
in the
church
without the
ministry of
God's
Spirit
is vain and
wicked.

Who is Ju-
das Iscari-
ot's vicar?

* Franciscus Lambertus Avenionensis, in his book concerning Prophecy, Learning, Tongues, and the Spirit of Prophecy. Argent. *excus.*
*anno* 1516, *de prov.* cap. xxiv.

§ XVII. Against this absolute necessity of grace they Obj. 1.
object, That if all ministers had the saving grace of God,
then all ministers should be saved, seeing none can fall
away from or lose saving grace.

But this objection is built upon a false hypothesis, Answ.
purely denied by us; and we have in the former proposition concerning perseverance already refuted it.

Secondly, It may be objected to us, That since we affirm Obj. 2.
that every man hath a measure of true and saving grace,
there needs no singular qualification either to a Christian or
minister; for seeing every man hath this grace, then no man
needs forbear to be a minister for want of grace.

I answer, We have above shown that there is necessary Answ.
to the making a minister a special and particular call from
the Spirit of God, which is something besides the universal
dispensation of grace to all, according to that of the apostle,
"No man taketh this honour unto himself, but he that is Heb. v. 4
called of God, as was Aaron." Moreover, we understand All have
by grace as a qualification to a minister, not the mere mea- God's grac,
which call
sure of light, as it is given to reprove and call him to right- to righteousness; but we understand grace as it hath converted eousness,
but all are
the soul, and operateth powerfully in it, as hereafter, con- not so
cerning the work of ministers, will further appear. So we into its na-
understand not men simply as having grace in them as a ture as to
seed, which we indeed affirm all have in a measure; but fruits of a
blameless
we understand men that are gracious, leavened by it into holy life
the nature thereof, so as thereby to bring forth those good
fruits of a blameless conversation, and of justice, holiness,
patience, and temperance, which the apostle requires as
necessary in a true Christian bishop and minister.

Thirdly, They* object the example of the false prophets, Obj. 3.
of the Pharisees, and of Judas.

But First, As to the false prophets, there can nothing be Answ.
more foolish and ridiculous; as if because there were
false prophets, really false, without the grace of God, therefore grace is not necessary to a true Christian minister.

---

* So Nic. Arnoldus, sect. xxxii. upon Thesis iv.

The false not the true prophets want the grace of God.

Indeed if they had proved that true prophets wanted this grace, they had said something; but what have false prophets common with true ministers, but that they pretend falsely that which they have not? And because false prophets want true grace, will it therefore follow, that true prophets ought not to have it, that they may be true and not false? The example of the Pharisees and priests under the law will not answer to the gospel times, because

The service under the law was not purely spiritual, but figurative, for the performance of which, as they behoved to be purified from their outward pollutions, so the ministers of the gospel must be inwardly without blemish.

God set apart a particular tribe for that service, and particular families, to whom it belonged by a lineal succession; and also their service and work was not purely spiritual, but only the performance of some outward and carnal observations and ceremonies, which were but a shadow of the substance that was to come; and therefore their work made not the comers thereunto perfect, as appertaining to the conscience, seeing they were appointed only according to the law of a carnal commandment, and not according to the power of an endless life. Notwithstanding as in the figure they were to be without blemish as to their outward man, and in the performance of their work they were to be washed and purified from their outward pollutions so now, under the gospel times, the ministers in the antitype must be inwardly without blemish in their souls and spirits, being, as the apostle requires, blameless, and in their work and service must be pure and undefiled from their inward pollutions, and so clean and holy, that they may "offer up spiritual sacrifices acceptable to God by Jesus Christ," 1 Pet. ii. 5.

The ministry of the disciples of Christ before the work was finished was more legal than evangelical.

As to Judas, the season of his ministry was not wholly evangelical, as being before the work was finished, and while Christ himself and his disciples were yet subject to the Jewish observances and constitutions, and therefore his commission, as well as that which the rest received with him at that time, was "only to the house of Israel," Mat. x. 5, 6; by virtue of that commission the rest of the apostles were not empowered to go forth and preach after the resurrection until they had waited at Jerusalem for the pouring forth of the Spirit: so that it appears Judas's ministry was more legal than evanᵍelical. Secondly, Judas's case, as all will acknowledge, was singular and extraordinary, he being immediately called by Christ himself, and accordingly furnished and empowered by him to preach, and do miracles; which immediate commission our adversaries do not so much as pretend to, and so fall short of Judas, who trusted in Christ's words, and therefore went forth and preached, will out gold or silver, or scrip for his journey; giving freely as he had freely received; which our adversaries will not do, as hereafter shall be observed: also that Judas at that time had not the least measure of God's grace, I have not as yet heard proved. But is it not sad, that even Protestants should lay aside the eleven good and faithful apostles, and all the rest of the holy disciples and ministers of Christ, and betake them to that one, of whom it was testified that he was a devil, for a pattern and example to their ministry? Alas! it is to be regretted, that too many of them resemble this pattern over much.

*Judas was immediately called of Christ, and preached freely, which our adversaries will not do; although they make him a pattern of their graceless ministry, saying, he had not the least measure of God's grace at that time.*

Another objection is usually made against the necessity of grace,* That in case it were necessary, then such as wanted it could not truly administer the sacraments; and consequently the people would be left in doubts and infinite scruples, as not knowing certainly whether they had truly received them, because not knowing infallibly whether the administrators were truly gracious men.

*Object. * Ibid. Nic Arnoldus.*

But this objection hitteth not us at all, because the nature of that Spiritual and Christian worship, which we according to the truth plead for, is such as is not necessarily attended with these carnal and outward institutions, from the administering of which the objection ariseth; and so hath not any such absurdity following upon it, as will afterwards more clearly appear.

*Answ.*

§ XVIII. Though then we make not human learning necessary, yet we are far from excluding true learning; to wit, that learning which proceedeth from the inward teachings and instructions of the Spirit, whereby the soul learneth the secret ways of the Lord, becomes acquainted with many inward travails and exercises of the mind; and

*What true learning is.*

learneth by a living experience how to overcome evil, and the temptations of it, by following the Lord, and walking in his light, and waiting daily for wisdom and knowledge immediately from the revelation thereof; and so layeth up these heavenly and divine lessons in the good treasure of the heart, as honest Mary did the sayings which she heard, and things which she observed: and also out of this treasure of the soul, as the good scribe, brings forth things new and old, according as the same Spirit moves, and gives true liberty, and as the glory of God requires, for whose glory the soul, which is the temple of God, learneth to do all things. This is that good learning which we think necessary to a true minister; by and through which learning a man can well instruct, teach, and admonish in due season, and testify for God from a certain experience; as did David, Solomon, and the holy prophets of old, and the blessed apostles of our Lord Jesus Christ, Who testified of what they had seen, heard, felt, and handled of the word of life, 1 John i. 1, Ministering the gift according as they had received the same, as good stewards of the manifold grace of God ; and preached not the uncertain rumors of men by hearsay, which they had gathered merely in the comprehension, while they were strangers to the thing in their own experience in themselves: as to teach people how to believe, while themselves were unbelieving ; or how to overcome sin, while themselves are slaves to it, as all ungracious men are; or to believe and hope for an eternal reward, which themselves have not as yet arrived at, &c.

The good learning which is necessary to a true minister.

§ XIX. But let us examine this literature, which they make so necessary to the being of a minister; as in the first place, the knowledge of the tongues, at least the Latin, Greek, and Hebrew. The reason of this is, That they may read the scripture, which is their only rule, in the original languages, and thereby be the more capable to comment upon it, and interpret it, &c. That also which made this knowledge be the more prized by the primitive Protestants, was indeed the dark barbarity that was over the world in

Literature is first the knowledge of Latin, Greek, and Hebrew.

the centuries immediately preceding the reformation; the knowledge of the tongues being about that time, until it was even then restored by Erasmus and some others, almost lost and extinct. And this barbarity was so much the more abominable, that the whole worship and prayers of the people were in the Latin tongue; and among that vast number of priests, monks and friars, scarce one of a thousand understood his breviary, or that mass which he daily read and repeated: the scripture being, not only to the people, but to the greater part of the clergy, even as to the literal knowledge of it, as a sealed book. I shall not at all discommend the zeal that the first reformers had against this Babylonish darkness, nor their pious endeavours to translate the holy scriptures: I do truly believe, according to their knowledge, that they did it candidly: and therefore to answer the just desires of those that desire to read them, and for other very good reasons, as maintaining a commerce and understanding among divers nations by these common languages, and others of that kind, we judge it necessary and commendable that there be public schools for the teaching and instructing such youth, as are inclinable thereunto, in the languages. And although that papal ignorance deserved justly to be abhorred and abominated, we see nevertheless, that the true reformation consists not in that knowledge; because although since that time the Papists, stirred up through emulation of the Protestants, have more applied themselves to literature, and it now more flourisheth in their universities and cloisters, than before, especially in the Ignatian or Jesuitic sect, they are as far now as ever from a true reformation, and more hardened in their pernicious doctrines. But all this will not make it a necessary qualification to a minister, far less a more necessary qualification than the grace of God and his Spirit; because the Spirit and grace of God can make up this want in the most rustic and ignorant; but this knowledge can no ways make up the want of the Spirit in the most learned and eloquent. For all that which man by his own industry, learning and knowledge in the languages,

*Before the reformation the prayers of the people were in the Latin tongue.*

*The zeal and endeavours of the first reformers commended.*

*The knowledge of languages commendable, and schools necessary.*

*The Papists literature and knowledge, especially the Jesuits.*

The Spirit is the truest interpreter of the scriptures, whether from the original languages, or without them.

cai interpret of the scriptures, or find out, is nothing without the Spirit; he cannot be certain, but may still miss of the sense of it: whereas a poor man, that knoweth not a letter, when he heareth the scriptures read, by the same Spirit he can say, This is true; and by the same Spirit he can understand, open, and interpret it, if need be: yea, finding his condition to answer the condition and experience of the saints of old, he knoweth and possesseth the truths there delivered, because they are sealed and witnessed in his own heart by the same Spirit. And this we have plentiful experience of in many of those illiterate men, whom God hath raised up to be ministers in his church in this day; so that some such, by his Spirit, have corrected some of the errors of the translators, as in the third proposition concerning the scriptures I before observed. Yea,

A poor shoemaker, that could not read, refutes a professor of divinity's false assertions from scripture.

I know myself a poor shoemaker, that cannot read a word, who being assaulted with a false citation of scripture, from a public professor of divinity, before the magistrate of a city, when he had been taken up for preaching to some few that came to hear him; I say, I know such a one, and he is yet alive, who though the professor, who also is esteemed a learned man, constantly asserted his saying to be a scripture sentence, yet affirmed, not through any certain letter-knowledge he had of it, but from the most certain evidence of the Spirit in himself, that the professor was mistaken; and that the Spirit of God never said any such thing as the other affirmed: and the bible being brought, it was found as the poor shoemaker had said.

2. Logic and philosophy not needful to a preacher.

§ XX. The second part of their literature is logic and philosophy, an art so little needful to a true minister, that if one that comes to be a true minister hath had it, it is safest for him to forget and lose it; for it is the root and ground of all contention and debate, and the way to make a thing a great deal darker, than clearer. For under the pretence of regulating man's reason into a certain order and rules, that he may find out, as they pretend, the truth, it leads into such a labyrinth of contention, as is far more fit to make a sceptic than a Christian, far less a minister of Christ: yea, it often hinders man from a clear understanding of things that his own reason would give him; and therefore through its manifold rules and divers inventions, it often gives occasion for a man, that hath little reason, foolishly to speak much to no purpose; seeing a man, that is not very wise, may notwithstanding be a perfect logician. And then, if ye would make a man a fool to purpose that is not very wise, do but teach him logic and philosophy; and whereas before he might have been fit for something, he shall then be good for nothing, but to speak nonsense; for these notions will so swim in his head, that they will make him extremely busy about nothing. The use that wise and solid men make of it, is, to see the emptiness thereof; therefore saith one, It is an art of contention and darkness, by which all other sciences are rendered more obscure, and harder to be understood.

The use of logic is to see its emptiness.

If it be urged, That thereby the truth may be maintained and confirmed, and heretics confuted;

I answer, The truth, in men truly rational, needeth not the help thereof; and such as are obstinate, this will not convince; for by this they may learn twenty tricks and distinctions, how to shut out the truth: and the truth proceeding from an honest heart, and spoken forth from the virtue and Spirit of God, will have more influence, and take sooner and more effectually, than by a thousand demonstrations of logic; as that heathen philosopher* acknowledged, who, disputing with the Christian bishops in the council of Nice, was so subtile, that he could not be overcome by them; but yet by a few words spoken by a simple old rustic, was presently convinced by him, and converted to the Christian faith; and being enquired how he came to yield to that ignorant old man, and not to the bishops; he said, That they contended with him in his own way, and he could still give words for words; but there came from the old man that virtue, which he was not able to resist. This secret virtue and power ought to be the logic and

Answ.

A heathen philosopher disputing with the bishops in the council of Nice, was converted to the Christian faith by an ignorant old man, when they could not.

---

* <i>Lucæ Osiandri Epit. Hist. Eccles.</i>, lib. ii., cap. 5., cent. 4.

25 *

philosophy wherewith a true Christian minister should be furnished; and for which they need not be beholden to

Natural lo-
gic useful.

Aristotle. As to natural logic, by which rational men, without that art and rules, or sophistical learning, deduce a certain conclusion out of true propositions, which scarce any man of reason wants, we deny not the use of it; and I have sometimes used it in this treatise; which also may

3. Ethics,
or the man-
ner-rules to
Christians
not needful.

serve without that dialectic art. As for the other part of philosophy, which is called moral, or ethics, it is not so necessary to Christians, who have the rules of the holy scriptures, and the gift of the Holy Spirit, by which they

4. Physics
and the me-
taphysics,
make no
preachers
of the truth.

can be much better instructed. The physical and meta-physical part may be reduced to the arts of medicine and the mathematics, which have nothing to do with the essence of a Christian minister. And therefore the apostle Paul, who well understood what was good for Christian minis-ters, and what hurtful, thus exhorted the Colossians, Col. ii. 8, "Beware lest any man spoil you through philosophy and vain deceit." And to his beloved disciple Timothy he writes also thus, 1 Tim. vi. 20, "O Timothy, keep that which is committed to thy trust, avoiding profane and vain babblings, and oppositions of science, falsely so called."

III. The
learned
school-di-
vinity ob-
noxious; a
monster;
a letter-
knowledge
heathen-
ized.

§ XXI. The third and main part of their literature is school-divinity, a monster, made up of some scriptural no-tions of truth, and the heathenish terms and maxims; being, as it were, the heathenish philosophy christianized, or rather, the literal external knowledge of Christ heathen-ized. It is man in his first, fallen, natural state, with his devilish wisdom, pleasing himself with some notions of truth, and adorning them with his own sensual and carnal wisdom, because he thinks the simplicity of the truth too low and mean a thing for him; and so despiseth that simplicity, wheresoever it is found, that he may set up and exalt him-self, puffed up with this his monstrous birth. It is the devil, darkening, obscuring, and veiling the knowledge of God, with his serpentine and worldly wisdom; that so he may the more securely deceive the hearts of the simple, and make the truth, as it is in itself, despicable and hard to be known and understood, by multiplying a thousand difficult and needless questions, and endless contentions and debates. All which, he who perfectly knoweth, is not a whit less the servant of sin than he was; but ten times more s), in that he is exalted, and proud of iniquity, and so much the farther from receiving, understanding, or learning the truth, as it is in its own naked simplicity; because he is full, learned, rich, and wise in his own conceit: and so those that are most skilled in it, wear out their day, and spend their precious time about the infinite and innumerable questions they have feigned and invented concerning it. A certain learned man called it, A twofold discipline, like the race of the Centaurs, partly proceeding from divine sayings, partly from philosophical reasons. A thousand of their questions they confess themselves to be no-ways necessary to salvation; and yet many more of them they could never agree upon, but are, and still will be, in endless janglings about them. The volumes that have been written about it, a man in his whole age could scarce read, though he lived to be very old; and when he has read them all, he has but wrought himself a great deal more vexation and trouble of spirit than he had before. These certainly are the words multiplied without knowledge; by which counsel hath been darkened, Job xxxviii. 2. They make the scripture the text of all this mass; and it is concerning the sense of it that their voluminous debates arise. But a man of a good upright heart may learn more in half an hour, and be more certain of it, by waiting upon God, and his Spirit in the heart, than by reading a thousand of their volumes; which by filling his head with many needless imaginations, may well stagger his faith, but never confirm it: and indeed those that give themselves most to it, are most capable to fall into error, as appeareth by the example of Origen, who, by his learning, was one of the first, that falling into this way of interpreting the scriptures, wrote so many volumes, and in them so many errors, as very much troubled the church. Also Arius, led by this curiosity and human scrutiny, despising the simplicity of

*Its needless questions and endless janglings.*

the gospel, fell into his error, which was the cause of that horrible heresy which so much troubled the church. Methinks the simplicity, plainness, and brevity of the scriptures themselves, should be a sufficient reproof for such a science; and the apostles, being honest, plain, illiterate men, may be better understood by such kind of men now, than with all that mass of scholastic stuff, which neither Peter, nor Paul, nor John, ever thought of.

§ XXII. But this invention of Satan, wherewith he began the apostasy, hath been of dangerous consequence; for thereby he at first spoiled the simplicity of truth, by keeping up the heathenish learning, which occasioned such
Many of
the Fathers
do not only
contradict
each other,
but themselves also,
and why.
uncertainty, even among those called Fathers, and such debate, that there are few of them to be found, who, by reason of this mixture, do not only frequently contradict one another, but themselves also. And therefore when the apostasy grew greater, he, as it were, buried the truth with this veil of darkness, wholly shutting out people from true knowledge, and making the learned (so accounted) busy themselves with idle and needless questions; while the weighty truths of God were neglected, and went, as it were, into disuse.

Now, though the grossest of these abuses be swept away by Protestants; yet the evil root still remains, and is nourished and upheld; and the science kept up, as being deemed necessary for a minister: for, while the pure learning of the Spirit of truth is despised and neglected, and made ineffectual, man's fallen earthly wisdom is upheld; and so in that he labours and works with the scriptures, being out of the Life and Spirit which those that wrote them were in, by which only they are rightly understood, and made use of. And so he that is to be a minister, must
learn this art or trade of merchandizing with the scriptures, and be that which the apostle would not be, to wit, a trader with them, 2 Cor. ii. 17. That he may acquire a knack from a verse of scripture, by adding his own barren notions and conceptions to it, and his uncertain conjectures, and what he hath stolen out of books; for which end he must

have of necessity a good many by him, and may each Sabbath-day, as they call it, or oftener, make a discourse for an hour long; and this is called the preaching of the word: whereas the gift, grace, and Spirit of God, to teach, open, and instruct, and to preach a word in season, is neglected; and so man's arts and parts, and knowledge, and wisdom, which is from below, are set up and established in the temple of God, yea, and above the little seed; which in effect is Antichrist, working in the mystery. And so the devil may be as good and able a minister as the best of them; for he has better skill in languages, and more logic, philosophy and school-divinity, than any of them; and knows the truth in the notion better than they all, and can talk more eloquently than all those preachers. But what availeth all this? Is it not all but as death, as a painted sepulchre, and dead carcase, without the power, life and spirit of Christianity, which is the marrow and substance of a Christian ministry? And he that hath this, and can speak from it, though he be a poor shepherd, or a fisherman, and ignorant of all that learning, and of all those questions and notions; yet speaking from the Spirit, his ministry will have more influence towards the converting of a sinner unto God, than all of them who are learned after the flesh; as in that example of the old man at the council of Nice did appear.

§ XXIII. And if in any age, since the apostles' days, God hath purposed to show his power by weak instruments, for the battering down of that carnal and heathenish wisdom, and restoring again the ancient simplicity of truth, this is it. For in our day, God hath raised up witnesses for himself, as he did fishermen of old; many, yea, most of whom, are labouring and mechanic men, who, altogether without that learning, have, by the power and Spirit of God, struck at the very root and ground of Babylon; and in the strength and might of this power, have gathered thousands, by reaching their consciences, into the same power and life, who, as to the outward part, have been far more knowing than they, yet not able to resist the virtue

*Side notes:*

And this they call the preaching of the word.

Thus Antichrist is established above the seed of the kingdom.

How the devil may be a minister of the priests' gospel.

The power of God by weak instruments restoring the simplicity of truth.

2 N

that proceeded from them. Of which I myself am a true witness; and can declare from certain experience, because my heart hath been often greatly broken and tendered by that virtuous life that proceeded from the powerful ministry of those illiterate men : so that by their very countenance, as well as words, I have felt the evil in me often chained down, and the good reached to and raised. What shall I then say to you, who are lovers of learning, and admirers of knowledge ? Was not I also a lover and admirer of it, who also sought after it, according to my age and capacity ? But it pleased God, in his unutterable love, early to withstand my vain endeavours, while I was yet but eighteen years of age; and made me seriously to consider (which I wish also may befal others) That without holiness and regeneration, no man can see God ; and that the fear of the Lord is the beginning of wisdom, and to depart from iniquity, a good understanding; and how much knowledge puffeth up, and leadeth away from that inward quietness, stillness, and humility of mind, where the Lord appears, and his heavenly wisdom is revealed. If ye consider these things, then will ye say with me, that all this learning, wisdom and knowledge, gathered in this fallen nature, is but as dross and dung, in comparison of the cross of Christ ; especially being destitute of that power, life and virtue, which I perceived these excellent (though despised, because illiterate) witnesses of God to be filled with : and therefore seeing, that in and among them, I, with many others, have found the heavenly food that gives contentment, let my soul seek after this learning, and wait for 't for ever.

§ XXIV. Having thus spoken of the call and qualifications of a gospel-minister, that which comes next to be considered, is, What his proper work is, how, and by what rule, he is to be ordered ? Our adversaries do all along go upon externals, and therefore have certain prescribed rules and methods, contrived according to their human and earthly wisdom : we, on the contrary, walk still upon the same foundation, and lean always upon the immediate as-

*[Margin notes:]*

*The powerful ministry of illiterate men.*

*The time of the author's first convincement. Job xxviii. 24.*

*Ques. 3.*

*The work of a minister.*

sistance and influence of that Holy Spirit, which God hath The Holy Spirit, a Spirit of order and not of confusion. given his children, to teach them all things, and lead them in all things: which Spirit, being the Spirit of order, and not of confusion, leads us, and as many as follow it, into such a comely and decent order as becometh the church of God. But our adversaries, having shut themselves out from this immediate counsel and influence of the Spirit, have run themselves into many confusions and disorders, seeking to establish an order in this matter. For some will Popish orders and offices, &c have first a chief bishop, or pope, to rule and be a prince over all; and under him, by degrees, cardinals, patriarchs, archbishops, priests, deacons, sub-deacons; and besides these, Acoluthi, Tonsorati, Ostiarii, &c. And in their theology (as they call it) professors, bachelors, doctors, &c. And others would have every nation independent of another, having its own metropolitan or patriarch; and the rest in order subject to him, as before. Others again are against all precedency among pastors, and constitute their subordination not of persons, but of powers: as first the consistory, or session; then the class, or presbytery; then the provincial; and then the national synod or assembly. Thus they tear one another, and contend among themselves concerning the ordering, distinguishing, and making their several orders and offices; concerning which there hath been no less contest, not only by way of verbal dispute, but even by fighting, tumults, wars, devastations, and Wars and bloodshed about church government. bloodshed, than about the conquering, overturning, and establishing of kingdoms. And the histories of late times are as full of the various tragedies, acted on account of this spiritual and ecclesiastical monarchy and commonwealth, as the histories of old times are of the wars and contests that fell out both in the Assyrian, Persian, Greek and Roman empires: these last upon this account, though among those that are called Christians, have been no less bloody and cruel than the former among heathen, concerning their outward empires and governments. Now all this, The ground and cause thereof. both among Papists and Protestants, proceedeth, in that they seek in imitation to uphold a form and shadow of things, though they want the power, virtue and substance, while for many of their orders and forms they have not so much as the name in the scripture. But in opposition to all this mass of formality, and heap of orders, rules and governments, we say, the substance is chiefly to be sought after, and the power, virtue and spirit, is to be known and waited for, which is one in all the different names and offices the scripture makes use of; as appears by 1 Cor. xii. 4, (often before mentioned) "There are diversities of gifts, but the same Spirit." And after the apostle, throughout the whole chapter, hath shown how one and the selfsame Spirit worketh in and quickeneth each member; then in verse 28, he showeth how thereby God hath set in the church, first apostles, secondly prophets, teachers, &c. And likewise to the same purpose, Eph. iv. 11, he showeth, how by these gifts "he hath given some apostles, some prophets, some evangelists, some pastors, some teachers," &c. Now it never was Christ's purpose, nor the apostles', that Christians should, without this Spirit and heavenly gift, set up a shadow and form of these orders, and so make several ranks and degrees, to establish a carnal ministry of men's making, without the life, power and Spirit of Christ: this

The work of Antichrist and mystery of iniquity.

is that work of Antichrist, and mystery of iniquity, that hath got up in the dark night of apostasy. But in a true church of Christ, gathered together by God, not only into the belief of the principles of truth, but also into the power, life and Spirit of Christ, the Spirit of God is the orderer, ruler and governor; as in each particular, so in the general. And when they assemble together to wait upon God, and

Such as the Spirit sets apart, to the ministry, their brethren hear them.

to worship and adore him; then such as the Spirit sets apart for the ministry, by its divine power and influence opening their mouths, and giving them to exhort, reprove, and instruct with virtue and power; these are thus ordained of God and admitted into the ministry, and their brethren cannot but hear them, receive them, and also honour them for their work's sake. And so this is not monopolized by

The clergy and laics.

a certain kind of men, as the clergy (who are to that purpose educated and brought up as other carnal artists) and

the rest to be despised as laics; but it is left to the free
gift of God to choose any whom he seeth meet thereunto,
whether rich or poor, servant or master, young or old, yea,
male or female. And such as have this call, verify the *Women*
gospel, by preaching not in speech only, but also in *may*
power, and in the Holy Ghost, and in much fulness, 1 *preach.*
Thess. i. 5, and cannot but be received and heard by the
sheep of Christ.

§ XXV. But if it be objected here, That I seem hereby *OBJECT.*
to make no distinction at all betwixt ministers and others;
which is contrary to the apostle's saying, 1 Cor. xii. 29,
"Are all apostles? Are all prophets? Are all teachers?"
&c. From thence they insinuate, That I also contradict
his comparison in that chapter, of the church of Christ with
a human body; as where he saith, verse 17, " If the whole
body were an eye, where were the hearing? If the whole
were hearing, where were the smelling?" &c. Also the
apostle not only distinguisheth the ministers of the church
in general from the rest of the members, but also from themselves; as naming them distinctly and separately, apostles,
prophets, evangelists, pastors, teachers, &c.

As to the last part of this objection, to which I shall first *ANS. 1.*
answer; it is apparent, that this diversity of names is not *Diversity*
to distinguish separate offices, but to denote the different *of names*
*makes no*
and various operations of the Spirit; a manner of speech *distinct*
frequent with the apostle Paul, wherein he sometimes *offices; but*
*which may*
expatiates to the illustrating of the glory and praise of *coincide. or*
*be together*
God's grace : as in particular, Rom. xii. 6 : " Having then *in one per-*
*son.*
gifts differing according to the grace that is given us,
whether prophecy, let us prophesy according to the proportion of faith ; or ministry, let us wait on our ministering ; or he that teacheth, on teaching; or he that exhor
teth, on exhortation." Now none will say from all this,
that these are distinct offices, or do not or may not coincide in one person, as may all those other things mentioned
by him in the subsequent verses, viz., Of loving, being
kindly affectioned, fervency of spirit, hospitality, diligence,
blessing, rejoicing, &c., which he yet numbers forth as dif-

26

ferent gifts of the Spirit, and according to this objection
might be placed as distinct and separate offices, which
were most absurd.

Secondly, In these very places mentioned it is clear
that it is no real distinction of separate offices; because
all acknowledge, that pastors and teachers, which the
apostle there no less separateth and distinguisheth, than
pastors and prophets, or apostles, are one and the same,
and coincide in the same office and person ; and therefore
may be said so of the rest. For prophecy as it signifies
the foretelling of things to come, is indeed a distinct gift,
but no distinct office ; and therefore our adversaries do
not place it among their several orders: neither will they
deny, but that it both may be and hath been given of God
to some, that not only have been pastors and teachers, and
that there it hath coincided in one person with these other
offices, but also to some of the laics : and so it hath been
found, according to their own confession, without the
limits of their clergy.  Prophecy in the other sense, to wit,
as it signifies a speaking from the Spirit of truth, is not
only peculiar to pastors and teachers, who ought so to
prophesy ; but even a common privilege to the saints.
For though to instruct, teach and exhort, be proper to such
as are more particularly called to the work of the ministry ;
yet it is not so proper to them, as not to be, when the
saints are met together, as any of them are moved by the
Spirit, common to others: for some acts belong to all in
such a relation ; but not only to those within that relation :
*Competunt omni, sed non soli.*  Thus to see and hear are
proper acts of a man ; seeing it may be properly predi-
cated of him, that he heareth and seeth: yet are they
common to other creatures also.  So to prophesy in this
sense, is indeed proper to ministers and teachers ; yet not
so, but that it is common and lawful to other saints, when
moved thereunto, though it be not proper to them by way
of relation: because, notwithstanding that motion, they
are not particularly called to the work of the ministry, as
appears by 1 Cor. xiv., where the apostle at large declar-

*(marginal notes)*

Prophecy
and prophe-
sying, its
twofold sig-
nification.

To prophe-
sy, a privi-
lege of
teachers,
and of all
the saints.

ing the order and ordinary method of the church, saith, ver. 30, 31; " But if any thing be revealed to another that sitteth by, let the first hold his peace; for ye may all prophesy one by one, that all may learn, and all be comforted:" which showeth that none here is excluded. But yet that there is a subordination, according to the various measures of the gift received, the next verse showeth: " And the spirits of the prophets are subject to the prophets: for God is not the author of confusion, but of peace." Now that prophesying, in this sense, may be common to all saints, appears by verse 39, of the same chapter, where speaking to *all* in general, he saith, " Wherefore, brethren, covet to prophesy;" and verse 1, he exhorts them, saying, " Desire spiritual gifts, but rather that ye may prophesy."

Secondly, As to evangelists the same may be said; for whoever preacheth the gospel is really an evangelist, and so consequently every true minister of the gospel is one; else what proper office can they assign to it, unless they should be so foolish as to affirm that none were evangelists but Matthew, Mark, Luke, and John, who wrote the account of Christ's life and sufferings? and then it were neither a particular office, seeing John and Matthew were apostles, Mark and Luke pastors and teachers, so that there they coincided in one. And indeed it is absurd to think, that upon that particular account the apostle used the word *evangelist*. Calvin acknowledgeth, that such as preach the gospel in purity, after some time of apostasy, may be truly called evangelists, and therefore saith, that there were apostles in his time; and hence the Protestants at their first coming forth, termed themselves *evangelici*, or evangelics.

*Who are evangelists; and whether any may term themselves so now-a-day.*

Lastly, an *apostle*, if we look to the etymology of the word, signifies *one that is sent;* and in respect every true minister is sent of God, in so far he is an apostle; though the twelve, because of their being specially sent of Christ, were therefore called apostles κατ᾿ ἐξοχὴν, or *per eminentiam*, i. e., by way of excellency. And yet that there was no limi-

*Who is an apostle*

They were
not limited
to such a
number.

tation to such a number, as some foolishly imagine,
appears, because after that number was filled up, the
apostle Paul was afterwards so called; therefore we judge
that these are no distinct separate offices, but only names
used upon occasion to express the more eminent arising
and shining forth of God's grace. As if any minister of
Christ should now proselyte and turn a whole nation to the

Whether
any man be
called an
apostle at
this day.

Christian faith, though he had no distinct office, yet I doubt
not but both Papists and Protestants would judge it tolerable to call such an one an apostle, or an evangelist; for
on this account the Jesuits call some of their sect apostles
of India and of Japan; and Calvin testifies that there
were apostles and evangelists in his time, in respect to the

Upon what
account
John Knox
was called
the apostle
of Scotland.

reformation; upon which account also we have known
John Knox often called the apostle of Scotland. So that
we conclude that ministers, pastors, or teachers do comprehend all, and that the office is but one, and therefore in
that respect we judge there ought to be no precedency
among them: to prove which I shall not here insist, seeing
it is shown largely, and treated of by such as have denied
the Diocesan Episcopacy, as they call it.

Ans. 1

§ XXVI. As to the first part of the objection, viz., That
I seem to make no distinction betwixt the minister and

Liberty to
prophesy
all have by
the Spirit.

people, I answer, If it be understood of a liberty to speak
or prophesy by the Spirit, I say all may do that, when
moved thereunto, as above is shown; but we do believe
and affirm that some are more particularly called to the
work of the ministry, and therefore are fitted of the Lord
for that purpose; whose work is more constantly and particularly to instruct, exhort, admonish, oversee, and watch
over their brethren; and that as there is something more
incumbent upon them in that respect than upon every
common believer, so also, as in that relation, there is due
to them from the flock such obedience and subjection as is
mentioned in these testimonies of the scripture, Heb. xiii.
17; 1 Thess. v. 12, 13; 1 Tim. v. 17; 1 Pet. v. 5. Also
besides these who are thus particularly called to the ministry, and constant labour in the word and doctrine, there

are also the elders, who though they be not moved to a **The elders take care for the wi dows, the poor, and fatherless** frequent testimony by way of declaration in words, yet as such are grown up in the experience of the blessed work of truth in their hearts, they watch over and privately admonish the young, take care for the widows, the poor, and fatherless, and look that nothing be wanting, but that peace, love, unity, concord, and soundness be preserved in the church of Christ; and this answers to the deacons mentioned Acts vi.

That which we oppose, is the distinction of laity and **The distinction of clergy and laity not to be found in scripture.** clergy, which in the scripture is not to be found, whereby none are admitted unto the work of the ministry but such as are educated at schools on purpose, and instructed in logic and philosophy, &c., and so are at their apprenticeship to learn the art and trade of preaching, even as a man learns any other art, whereby all other honest mechanic men, who have not got this heathenish art, are excluded from having this privilege. And so he that is a scholar thus bred up must not have any honest trade whereby to get him a livelihood, if he once intend for the ministry, but he must see to get him a place, and then he hath his set hire for a livelihood to him. He must also be distinguished **Their garb** from the rest by the colour of his clothes; for he must only wear black, and must be a master of arts: but more of this hereafter.

§ XXVII. As this manner of separating men for the ministry is nothing like the church in the apostles' days, so great evils have and do follow upon it. For first, Parents seeing both the honour and profit that attends the clergy, do allot their children sometimes from their infancy to it, and so breed them up on purpose. And others, come to age, upon the same account betake them to the same trade, and having these natural and acquired parts that are judged the necessary qualifications of a minister, are thereby admitted, and so are bred up in idleness and pleasure, thinking it a disgrace for them to work with their hands; and so just study a little out of their books, to make a discourse once or twice a week during the running of an hour-glass

The clergy's study out of books, the gift of God neglected.

whereas the gift, grace, and Spirit of God, to call and qualify for the ministry, is neglected and overlooked. And many covetous, corrupt, earthly, carnal men, having a mere show and form, but strangers to, and utterly ignorant of, the inward work of grace upon their hearts, are brought in and intrude themselves, and so through them death, barrenness, and darkness, and by consequence, superstition, error, and idolatry have entered and leavened the church. And they that will narrowly observe, shall find that it was thus the apostasy came to take place; of the truth of which I could give many examples, which for brevity's sake I omit. Thus the office, reverence, and respect due to it were annexed to the mere name, so that when once a man was ordained a bishop or a priest, he was heard and believed, though he had nothing of the Spirit, power, and life that the true apostles and ministers were in. And thus in a short time the succession came to be of the name and title, and the office was thereto annexed; and not of the nature, virtue, and life; which in effect made them to cease to be the ministry and ministers of Christ, but only a shadow and vain image of it; which also decaying, was in some ages so metamorphosed, that not only the substance was lost, but the very form wholly

The marred church compared to Theseus's pieced boat.

vitiated, altered, and marred; so that it may be far better said of the pretended Christian church, as was disputed of Theseus's boat, which by the piecing of many new pieces of timber was wholly altered, whether indeed it were the same or another? But in case that the first had been of oak, and the pieces last put in but of rotten fir, and that also the form had been so far changed as to be nothing like the first, I think it would have suffered no dispute, but might have easily been concluded to be quite another, retaining nothing but the name, and that also unjustly.

The abuse following the distinction of laity and clergy.

Secondly, From this distinction of laity and clergy this abuse also follows, that good, honest, mechanic men, and others who have not learned the art and trade of preaching, and so are not licentiated according to these rules they prescribe unto themselves; such, I say, being possessed with a false opinion that it is not lawful for them to meddle with the ministry, nor that they are any ways fit for it, because of the defect of that literature, do thereby neglect the gift in themselves, and quench many times the pure breathings of the Spirit of God in their hearts; which, if given way to, might prove much more for the edification of the church than many of the conned sermons of the learned. And so by this means the apostle's command and advice is slighted, who exhorteth, 1 Thess. v. 19, 20, "not to quench the Spirit, nor despise prophesyings." And all this is done by men pretending to be Christians, who glory that the first preachers and propagators of their religion were such kind of plain mechanic men, and illiterate. And even Protestants do no less than Papists exclude such kind of men from being ministers among them, and thus limit the Spirit and gift of God; though their Fathers, in opposition to Papists, asserted the contrary; and also their own histories declare how that kind of illiterate men did, without learning, by the Spirit of God, greatly contribute in divers places to the Reformation. *Both Protestants and Papists exclude mechanic men from preaching, who greatly contributed to the reformation.*

By this it may appear, that as in calling and qualifying so in preaching and praying, and the other particular steps of the ministry, every true minister is to know the Spirit of God by its virtue and life to accompany and assist him; but because this relates to worship, I shall speak of it more largely in the next proposition, which is concerning worship.

The last thing to be considered and inquired into is, concerning the maintenance of a gospel minister; but before I proceed, I judge it fit to speak something in short concerning the preaching of women, and to declare what we hold in that matter.

Seeing male and female are one in Christ Jesus, and that he gives his Spirit no less to one than to the other, when God moveth by his Spirit in a woman, we judge it no ways unlawful for her to preach in the assemblies of God's people. Neither think we that of Paul, 1 Cor. xiv. 34, to reprove the inconsiderate and talkative women among the *Women's public preaching and praying asserted.*

Corinthians, who troubled the church of Christ with their unprofitable questions, or that, 1 Tim. ii. 11, 12, that "women ought to learn in silence, not usurping authority over the man," any ways repugnant to this doctrine; because it is clear that women have prophesied and preached in the church, else had that saying of Joel been ill applied by Peter, Acts ii. 17. And seeing Paul himself, in the same epistle to the Corinthians, giveth rules how women should behave themselves in their public preaching and praying, it would be a manifest contradiction, if that other place were taken in a larger sense. And the same Paul speaks of a woman that laboured with him in the work of the gospel: and it is written that Philip had four daughters that prophesied. And lastly, It hath been observed, that God hath effectually in this day converted many souls by the ministry of women; and by them also frequently comforted the souls of his children; which manifest experience puts the thing beyond all controversy. But now I shall proceed to speak of the maintenance of ministers.

§ XXVIII. We freely acknowledge, as the proposition holds forth, that there is an obligation upon such to whom God sends, or among whom he raiseth up a minister, that, if need be, they minister to his necessities. Secondly, That it is lawful for him to receive what is necessary and convenient. To prove this I need not insist, for our adversaries will readily grant it to us; for the thing we affirm is, that this is all that these scripture testimonies relating to this thing do grant, Gal. vi. 6; 1 Cor. ix. 11, 12, 13, 14; 1 Tim. v. 18. That which we then oppose in this matter is, First, That it should be constrained and limited. Secondly, That it should be superfluous, chargeable, and sumptuous. And Thirdly, The manifest abuse thereof, of which I shall also briefly treat.

As to the First, our adversaries are forced to recur to the example of the law; a refuge they use in defending most of their errors and superstitions, which are contrary to the nature and purity of the gospel.

They say, God appointed the Levites the tithes, there-

*Margin notes:*
Acts xxi. 9.

Ques. 4. Ministers' maintenance.

The ministers' food and their maintenance stated.

1. Against constrained main'e- nance.

fore they belong also to such as minister in holy things OBJECT.
under the gospel.

I answer, All that can be gathered from this is, that as ANS.
the priests had a maintenance allowed them under the law,
so also the ministers and preachers under the gospel, which Tithes
is not denied; but the comparison will not hold that they were appointed for
should have the very same; since, First, There is no ex- the Levites, not
press gospel command for it, neither by Christ nor his for gospel
apostles. Secondly, The parity doth no ways hold betwixt preachers.
the Levites under the law, and the preachers under the
gospel; because the Levites were one of the tribes of
Israel, and so had a right to a part of the inheritance of the
land as well as the rest of their brethren; and having none,
had this allotted to them in lieu of it. Next, The tenth of
the tithes was only allowed to the priests that served at the
altar, the rest being for the Levites, and also to be put up
in store-houses, for entertaining of widows and strangers.
But these preachers, notwithstanding they inherit what they
have by their parents, as well as other men, yet claim the
whole tithes, allowing nothing either to widow or stranger.
But as to the tithes I shall not insist, because divers others
have clearly and learnedly treated of them apart, and also
divers Protestants do confess them not to be *jure divino;*
and the parity as to the quota doth not hold, but only in
general as to the obligation of a maintenance; which maintenance, though the hearers be obliged to give, and fail of
their duty if they do not, yet that it ought neither to be
stinted, nor yet forced, I prove; because Christ, when he REASON 1.
sent forth his apostles, said, "Freely ye have received, The gospel
freely to be
freely give," Mat. x. 8, and yet they had liberty to receive preached
meat and drink from such as offered them, to supply their without so
much a
need. Which shows that they were not to seek or require year.
anything by force, or to stint, or make a bargain beforehand, as the preachers as well among Papists as Protestants
do in these days, who will not preach to any until they be
first sure of so much a year; but on the contrary, these
were to do their duty, and freely to communicate, as the

Lord should order them, what they had received, without
seeking or expecting a reward.

Nic. Ar-
noldus's
answer to
' Freely ye
have re-
ceived,'
&c.
The answer given to this by Nicolaus Arnoldus, Exercit.
Theolog. Sect. 42, 43, is not to be forgotten, but indeed
to be kept upon record for a perpetual remembrance of him
and his brethren; for he frankly answers after this manner,
We have not freely received, and therefore are not bound
to give freely. The answer I confess is ingenuous and
good; for if those that receive freely are to give freely, it
would seem to follow by the rule of contraries, that those
that receive not freely ought not to give freely, and I shall
grant it; only they must grant me, that they preach not by
and according to the gift and grace of God received, nor
can they be good stewards of the manifold grace of God,
as every true minister ought to be ; or else they have gotten
this gift or grace by money, as Simon Magus would have
been compassing it, since they think themselves not bound
to give it without money again. But to be plain, I believe
he intended not that it was from the gift or grace of God
they were to preach, but from their acquired arts and stu-
dies, which have cost them much labour and also some
money at the university; and therefore, as he that puts his
stock into the public bank expects interest again, so these
scholars, having spent some money in learning the art of
preaching, think they may boldly say they have it not
freely ; for it hath cost them both money and pains, and
therefore they expect both money and ease again. And
therefore, as Arnoldus gets money for teaching his young
students the art and trade of preaching, so he intends they
should be repaid before they give it again to others. It
All things
are set to
sale at
Rome, to
Franequer
applied.
was of old said, *Omnia venalia Romæ*, i. e., ' All things
are set to sale at Rome ;' but now the same proverb may
be applied to Franequer. And therefore Arnoldus's students, when they go about to preach, may safely seek and
require hereby, telling their hearers their master's maxim,
*Nos gratis non accepimus, ergo neque gratis dare tenemur.*
But then they may answer again, That they find them and
their master to be none of his ministers, who when he sent

forth his disciples, gave them this command, "Freely ye have received, freely give," and therefore we will have none of your teaching, because we perceive you to be of the number of those "that look for their gain from their quarter." *Isai. lvi. 11*

§ XXIX. Secondly, The scripture testimonies that urge this are in the same nature of those that press charity and liberality towards the poor, and command hospitality, &c., but these are not nor can be stinted to a certain quantity, because they are deeds merely voluntary, where the obedience to the command lieth in the good will of the giver, and not in the matter of the thing given, as Christ showeth in the example of the widow's mite. So that though there be an obligation upon Christians to minister of outward things to their ministers, yet there can be no definition of the quantity but by the giver's own consent, and a little from one may more truly fulfil the obligation than a great deal from another. And therefore as acts of charity and hospitality can neither be limited nor forced, so neither can this. *Reason II. Mere voluntary deeds no man can stint them.*

If it be objected, That ministers may and ought to exhort, persuade, yea and earnestly press Christians, if they find them defective therein, to acts of charity and hospitality, and so may they do also to the giving of maintenance ; *Object.*

I answer, All this saith nothing for a stinted and forced maintenance, for which there cannot so much as the show of one solid argument be brought from scripture. I confess ministers may use exhortation in this as much as in any other case, even as the apostle did to the Corinthians, showing them their duty ; but it were fit for ministers that so do (that their testimony might have the more weight, and be the freer of all suspicion of covetousness and self-interest) that they might be able to say truly in the sight of God that which the same apostle subjoins upon the same occasion, 1 Cor. ix. 15, 16, 17, 18 : "But I have used none of these things ; neither have I written these things, that it should be so done unto me : for it were better for *Answ. Paul's labour was that the gospel might be without charge.*

me to die, than that any man should make my glorying
void. For though I preach the gospel, I have nothing to
glory of; for necessity is laid upon me, yea woe is unto
me if I preach not the gospel. For if I do this thing willingly, I have a reward; but if against my will, a dispensation of the gospel is committed unto me. What is my
reward then? Verily that when I preach the gospel, I may
make the gospel of Christ without charge, that I abuse not
my power in the gospel."

**Reason 2.**     Thirdly, As there is neither precept nor example for this
forced and stinted maintenance in the scripture, so the
apostle, in his solemn farewell to the pastors and elders of
the church of Ephesus, guards them against it, Acts xx.
33, 34, 35. But if the thing had been either lawful or
practised, he would rather have exhorted them to be content with their stinted hire, and not to covet more; whereas
he showeth them, first, by his own example, that they were
Paul covet- not to covet or expect any man's silver or gold; secondly,
ed no bo-  that they ought to work with their hands for an honest
dy's silver
or gold.   livelihood, as he had done; and lastly, he exhorts them so
to do from the words of Christ, "because it is a more
blessed thing to give than to receive;" showing that it is
so far from a thing that a true minister ought to aim at, or
expect, that it is rather a burden to a true minister, and
cross to him, to be reduced to the necessity of wanting it.

**Reason 4.**     § XXX. Fourthly, If a forced and stinted maintenance
were to be supposed, it would make the ministers of Christ
No hireling just one with those hirelings whom the prophets cried out
fitting the
gospel of  against. For certainly if a man make a bargain to preach
Christ.    to people for so much a year, so as to refuse to preach
unless he have it, and seek to force the people to give it
by violence, it cannot be denied that such a one preacheth
Mich. iii. 5. for hire, and so "looks for his gain from his quarter," yea
and "prepares war against such as put not into his mouth;"
but this is the particular special mark of a false prophet
and an hireling, and therefore can no ways belong to a
true minister of Christ.

Next, that a superfluous maintenance, that is, more than
in reason is needful, ought not to be received by Christian
ministers, will not need much proof, seeing the more
moderate and sober, both among Papists and Protestants,
readily confess it, who with one voice exclaim against the
excessive revenues of the clergy; and that it may not
want a proof from scripture, what can be more plain than
that of the apostle to Timothy? 1 Tim. vi. 7, 8, 9, 10, 11,
where he both shows wherewith we ought to be content,
and also the hazard of such as look after more; and
indeed, since that very obligation of giving maintenance
to a minister is founded upon their need, and such as have
opportunity to work are commended rather in not receiving than in receiving, it can no ways be supposed lawful
for them to receive more than is sufficient. And indeed,
were they truly pious and right, though necessitous, they
would rather incline to take too little, than be gaping after
too much.

§ XXXI. Now that there is great excess and abuse
hereof among Christians, the vast revenues which the
bishops and priests have, both Papists and Protestants, do
declare; since I judge it may be said without any hyper-
bole, that some particular persons have more paid them
yearly than Christ and his apostles made use of in their
whole lifetime, who yet wanted not what was needful as to
the outward man, and no doubt deserved it far better than
those that enjoy that fulness. But it is manifest these
bishops and priests love their fat benefices, and the pleasure and honour that attends them, so well, that they purpose neither to follow Christ nor his apostles' example or
advice in this matter.

But it is usually objected, That Christians are become
so hard-hearted, and generally so little heed spiritual things,
that if ministers had not a settled and stinted maintenance
secured them by law, they and their families might starve
for want of bread.

I answer, This objection might have some weight as to
a carnal ministry, made up of natural men, who have no

Moderate Protestants and Papists exclaim against the excess of the clergy's revenues.

II. The excess of the priests and bishops' revenues.

OBJECT.

ANSW.

life, power, nor virtue with them, and so may insinuate some need of such a maintenance for such a ministry; but it saith nothing as to such as are called and sent of God, **They wanted nothing whom God sent; they laboured with their hands.** who sends no man a wayfaring upon his own charges; and so go forth in the authority and power of God, to turn people from darkness to light; for such can trust to him that sendeth them, and do believe that he will provide for them, knowing that he requireth nothing of any but what he giveth power to perform; and so when they return, if he inquire, can say they wanted nothing. And such also when they stay in a place, being immediately furnished by God, and not needing to borrow and steal what they preach from books, and take up their time that way, fall a working at their lawful employments and labour with their hands, as Paul did when he gathered the church at Corinth. And indeed if this objection had any weight, the apostles and primitive pastors should never have gone forth to convert the nations, for fear of want. Doth not the doctrine of Christ teach us to venture all, and part with all, to serve God? Can they then be accounted ministers of Christ who are afraid to preach him lest they get not money for it, or will not do it until they be sure of their payment? What serves the ministry for but to perfect the saints, and so to convert them from that hard-heartedness?

**OBJECT.**   But thou wilt say, I have laboured and preached to them, and they are hard-hearted still, and will not give me any thing:

**ANSW.**   Then surely thou hast either not been sent to them of God, and so thy ministry and preaching hath not been among them in the power, virtue, and life of Christ, and so thou deservest nothing; or else they have rejected thy testimony, and so are not worthy, and from such thou **Mat. x. 14. If they reject thy testimony, shake the dust from off thy feet** oughtest not to expect, yea nor yet receive any thing, if they would give thee, but thou oughtest to "shake off the dust from thy feet," and leave them. And how frivolous this objection is, appears, in that in the darkest and most superstitious times the priests' revenues increased most, and they were most richly rewarded, though they deserved least. So that he that is truly sent of God, as he needs not, so neither will he be afraid of want, so long as he serves so good a master; neither will he ever forbear to do his work for that cause. And indeed such as make this objection show truly that they serve not the Lord Christ, but their own belly, and that makes them so anxious for want of food to it.

§ XXXII. But lastly, As to the abuses of this kind of maintenance, indeed he that would go through them all, though he did it passingly, might make of it alone a huge volume, they are so great and numerous. For this abuse, as others, crept in with the apostasy, there being nothing of this in the primitive times: then the ministers claimed no tithes, neither sought they a stinted or forced maintenance; but such as wanted had their necessity supplied by the church, and others wrought with their hands. But the persecutions being over, and the emperors and princes coming under the name of Christians, the zeal of those great men was quickly abused by the covetousness of the clergy, who soon learned to change their cottages with the palaces of princes, and rested not until by degrees some of them came to be princes themselves, nothing inferior to them in splendour, luxury, and magnificence; a method of living that honest Peter and John the fishermen, and Paul the tent-maker, never coveted; and perhaps as little imagined that men pretending to be their successors should have arrived to these things. And so soon as the bishops were thus seated and constituted, forgetting the life and work of a Christian, they went usually by the ears together about the precedency and revenues, each coveting the chiefest and fattest benefice. It is also to be regretted to think how soon this mischief crept in among Protestants, who had scarce well appeared when the clergy among them began to speak at the old rate, and show that though they had forsaken the bishop of Rome, they were not resolved to part with their old benefices; and therefore so soon as any princes or states shook off the pope's authority, and

*(marginal notes:)* The many abuses priests' maintenance brings.

The Protestants having forsaken the pope, yet would not forsake the rich popish revenues.

so demolished the abbeys, nunneries, and other monuments of superstition, the reformed clergy began presently to cry out to the magistrates to beware of meddling with the church's patrimony, severely exclaiming against making a lawful use of those vast revenues that had been superstitiously bestowed upon the church, so called, to the good and benefit of the commonwealth, as no less than sacrilege.

1. The clergy's covetousness.

But by keeping up of this kind of maintenance for the ministry and clergymen, so called, there is first a bait laid for covetousness, which is idolatry, and of all things most hurtful; so that for covetousness' sake, many, being led by the desire of filthy lucre, do apply themselves to be ministers, that they may get a livelihood by it. If a man have several children, he will allot one of them to be a minister; which if he can get him to be, he reckons it as good as a patrimony: so that a fat benefice hath always many expectants; and then what bribing, what courting, what industry, and shameful actions are used to acquire these things, is too openly known, and needs not to be proved.

The scandal that by these means is raised among Christians is so manifest, that it is become a proverb, that the

The greedy kirk a proverb.

kirk is always greedy. Whereby the gift and grace of God being neglected, they have for the most part no other motive or rule in applying themselves to one church more than another but the greater benefice. For though they hypocritically pretend, at their accepting of and entering into their church, that they have nothing before them but the glory of God and the salvation of souls; yet if a richer benefice offer itself, they presently find it more for God's glory to remove from the first, and go thither. And thus they make no difficulty often to change, while notwithstanding they accuse us that we allow ministers to go from place to place, and not to be tied to one place; but we allow this not for the gaining of money, but as moved of God. For if a minister be called to minister in a particular place, he ought not to leave it, except God call him from it, and then he ought to obey: for we make the will of

God inwardly revealed, and not the love of money and more gain, the ground of removing.

Secondly, From this abuse hath proceeded that luxury and idleness that most of the clergy live in, even among Protestants as well as Papists, to the great scandal of Christianity. For not having lawful trades to work with their hands, and being so superfluously and sumptuously provided for, they live in idleness and luxury; and there doth more pride, vanity, and worldly glory appear in their wives and children than in most others, which is open and evident to all. *2. The clergy's luxury*

Thirdly, They become hereby so glued to the love of money, that there is none like them in malice, rage, and cruelty. If they be denied their hire, they rage like drunken men, fret, fume, and as it were go mad. A man may sooner satisfy the severest creditor than them; the general voice of the poor doth confirm this. For indeed they are far more exact in taking up the tithes of sheep, geese, swine, and eggs, &c., and look more narrowly to it than to the members of their flock: they will not miss the least mite; and the poorest widow cannot escape their avaricious hands. Twenty lies they will hear unreproved; and as many oaths a man may swear in their hearing without offending them; and greater evils than all this they can overlook. But if thou owest them aught, and refusest to pay it, then nothing but war will they thunder against thee, and they will stigmatize thee with the horrible title of sacrilege, and send thee to hell without mercy, as if thou hadst committed the sin against the Holy Ghost. Of all people we can best bear witness to this; for God having shown us this corrupt and antichristian ministry, and called us out from it, and gathered us unto his own power and life, to be a separate people, so that we dare not join with, nor hear these anti-christian hirelings, neither yet put into their mouths or feed them; oh! what malice, envy, and fury hath this raised in their hearts against us! That though we get none of their wares, neither will buy them, as knowing them to be naught, yet will they force us to

*3. The clergy's cruelty.*

*Poor widow's mite cannot escape the priests' greedy hands.*

*The work of Antichrist is fury, envy, malice.*

27 *

give them money: and because we cannot for conscience
sake do it, our sufferings have upon that account been unutterable. Yea, to give account of their cruelty, and
several sorts of inhumanity used against us, would make
no small history. These avaricious hirelings have come to
that degree of malice and rage, that several poor labouring
men have been carried hundreds of miles from their own
dwellings, and shut up in prison, some two, some three,
yea, some seven years together, for the value of one pound

A widow
for the tithe
of geese
about four
years in
prison.

sterling, and less. I know myself a poor widow, that for
the tithes of her geese, which amounted not to five shillings,
was about four years kept in prison, thirty miles from her
house. Yea, they by violence for this cause have plun-
dered of men's goods the hundred-fold, and prejudiced
much more ; yea, hundreds have hereby spilt their innocent blood, by dying in the filthy noisome holes and pri-

Some lost
their lives
in nasty
holes, some
wounded by
the priests,
&c.

sons. And some of the priests have been so enraged, that
goods thus ravished could not satisfy them, but they must
also satisfy their fury by beating, knocking, and wounding
with their hands innocent men and women, for refusing,
for conscience' sake, to put into their mouths.

The only way then soundly to reform and remove all
these abuses, and take away the ground and occasion of
them, is, to take away all stinted and forced maintenance
and stipends. And seeing those things were anciently
given by the people, that they return again into the public
treasure ; and thereby the people may be greatly benefited
by them, for that they may supply for those public taxa-
tions and impositions, that are put upon them, and may

Whoso
heap teach-
ers to them-
selves, let
them pro
vide their
stipend.

ease themselves of them. And whoever call or appoint
teachers to themselves, let them accordingly entertain
them : and for such as are called and moved to the ministry by the Spirit of God, those that receive them, and taste
of the good of their ministry, will no doubt provide things
needful for them, and there will be no need of a law to
force a hire for them : for he that sends them, will take
care for them ; and they also, having food and raiment,
will therewith be content.

§ XXXIII. The sum then of what is said is, That the ministry that we have pleaded for, and which also the Lord hath raised up among us is, in all its parts, like the true ministry of the apostles and primitive church. Whereas the ministry our adversaries seek to uphold and plead for, as it doth in all its parts differ from them, so, on the other hand, it is very like the false prophets and teachers testified against and condemned in the scripture, as may be thus briefly illustrated: *The differ-ence be-tween the ministry of the Qua-kers and their adver-saries.*

I. The ministry and ministers we plead for, are such as are immediately called and sent forth by Christ and his Spirit unto the work of the ministry: so were the holy apostles and prophets, as appears by these places, Mat. x. 1, 5; Eph. iv. 11; Heb. v. 4. *The true ministers' call.*

1. But the ministry and ministers our opposers plead for, are such as have no immediate call from Christ, to whom the leading and motion of the Spirit is not reckoned necessary; out who are called, sent forth, and ordained by wicked and ungodly men: such were of old the false prophets and teachers, as appears by these places, Jer. xiv. 14, 15; *item*, chap. xxiii. 21, and xxvii. 15.

II. The ministers we plead for, are such as are actuated and led by God's Spirit, and by the power and operation of his grace in their hearts, are in some measure converted and regenerate, and so are good, holy, and gracious men: such were the holy prophets and apostles, as appears from 1 Tim. iii. 2, 3, 4, 5, 6; Tit. i. 7, 8, 9. *True min-isters' guide.*

2. But the ministers our adversaries plead for, are such to whom the grace of God is no needful qualification; and so may be true ministers, according to them, though they be ungodly, unholy, and profligate men: such were the false prophets and apostles, as appears from Mic. iii. 5, 11; 1 Tim. vi. 5, 6, 7, 8, &c.; 2 Tim. iii. 2; 2 Pet. ii. 1, 2, 3.

III. The ministers we plead for, are such as act, move, and labour in the work of the ministry, not from their own mere natural strength and ability, but as they are actuated, moved, supported, assisted and influenced by the Spirit of *True min-isters' work.*

God, and minister according to the gift received, as good stewards of the manifold grace of God: such were the holy prophets and apostles, 1 Pet. iv. 10, 11; 1 Cor. i. 17, ii. 3, 4, 5, 13; Acts ii. 4; Mat. x. 20; Mark xiii. 11; Luke xii. 12; 1 Cor. xiii. 2.

3. But the ministers our adversaries plead for, are such as wait not for, nor expect, nor need the Spirit of God to actuate and move them in the work of the ministry; but what they do they do from their own mere natural strength and ability, and what they have gathered and stolen from the letter of the scripture, and other books, and so speak it forth in the strength of their own wisdom and eloquence, and not in the evidence and demonstration of the Spirit and power: such were the false prophets and apostles, as appears, Jer. xxiii. 30, 31, 32, 34, &c.; 1 Cor. iv. 18; Jude 16.

True ministers' humility.

IV. The ministers we plead for, are such as, being holy and humble, contend not for precedency and priority, but rather strive to prefer one another, and serve one another in love; neither desire to be distinguished from the rest by their garments and large phylacteries, nor seek the greetings in the market-places, nor uppermost rooms at feasts, nor the chief seats in the synagogues; nor yet to be called of men master, &c., such were the holy prophets and apostles, as appears from Mat. xxiii. 8, 9, 10, and xx. 25, 26, 27.

4. But the ministers our adversaries plead for, are such as strive and contend for superiority, and claim precedency over one another; affecting and ambitiously seeking after the forementioned things: such were the false prophets and apostles in time past, Mat. xxiii. 5, 6, 7.

True ministers' free gift.

V. The ministers we plead for, are such as having freely received, freely give; who covet no man's silver, gold, or garments; who seek no man's goods, but seek them, and the salvation of their souls: whose hands supply their own necessities, working honestly for bread to themselves and their families. And if at any time they be called of God, so as the work of the Lord hinder them from the use of their trades, take what is freely given them by such to whom they have communicated spirituals; and having food and raiment, are therewith content: such were the holy prophets and apostles, as appears from Mat. x. 8; Acts xx. 33, 34, 35; 1 Tim. vi. 8.

5. But the ministers our adversaries plead for, are such as not having freely received, will not freely give; but are covetous, doing that which they ought not, for filthy lucre's sake; as to preach for hire, and divine for money, and look for their gain from their quarter, and prepare war against such as put not into their mouths, &c. Greedy dogs, which can never have enough. Shepherds who feed themselves, and not the flock; eating the fat, and clothing themselves with the wool; making merchandize of souls; and following the way of Balaam, that loved the wages of unrighteousness: such were the false prophets and apostles, Isai. lvi. 11; Ezek. xxxiv. 2, 3, 8; Mic. iii. 5, 11; Tit. i. 10, 11; 2 Pet. ii. 1, 2, 3, 14, 15.

And in a word, We are for a holy, spiritual, pure and living ministry, where the ministers are both called, qualified and ordered, actuated and influenced in all the steps of their ministry by the Spirit of God; which being wanting, we judge they cease to be the ministers of Christ.

*True ministers' l fs and qua ification.*

But they, judging this life, grace, and Spirit no essential part of their ministry, are therefore for the upholding of a human, carnal, dry, barren, fruitless and dead ministry; of which, alas! we have seen the fruits in the most part of their churches: of whom that saying of the Lord is certainly verified, Jer. xxiii. 32—"I sent them not, nor commanded them, therefore they shall not profit this people at all, saith the LORD."

---

## PROPOSITION XI.

### *Concerning Worship.*

All true and acceptable worship to God is offered in the inward and immediate moving and drawing of his own

What the
true wor-
ship is, tha
is accepta-
ble to God.
How to be
performed.

Spirit, which is neither limited to places, times, nor persons. For though we are to worship him always, and continually to fear before him; yet as to the outward signification thereof, in prayers, praises or preachings, we ought not to do it in our own will, where and when we will; but where and when we are moved thereunto by the stirring and secret inspiration of the Spirit of God in our hearts; which God heareth and accepteth of, and is never wanting to move us thereunto, when need is; of which he himself is the alone proper judge. All other worship then, both praises, prayers or preachings, which man sets about in his own will, and at his own appointment, which he can both begin and end at his pleasure, do or leave undone as himself seeth meet, whether they be a prescribed form, as a liturgy, &c., or prayers conceived extempore by the natural strength and faculty of the mind, they are all but superstition, will-worship, and abominable idolatry in the sight of God, which are now to be denied and rejected, and separated from, in this day of his spiritual arising: however it might have pleased him (who winked at the times of ignorance, with a respect to the simplicity and integrity of some, and of his own innocent seed, which lay as it were buried in the hearts of men under that mass of superstition) to blow upon the dead and dry bones, and to raise some breathings of his own, and answer them; and that until the day should more clearly dawn and break forth.

§ I. THE duty of man towards God lieth chiefly in these two generals: 1. In an holy conformity to the pure law and light of God, so as both to forsake the evil, and be found in the practice of those perpetual and moral precepts of righteousness and equity. And, 2. In rendering that reverence, honour and adoration to God, that he requires and demands of us; which is comprehended under worship. Of the former we have already spoken, as also of the different relations of Christians, as they are distinguished by the several measures of grace received, and given to

...... ; and in that respect have their several offices in the body of Christ, which is the church. Now I come to speak of worship, or of those acts, whether private or public, general or particular, whereby man renders to God that part of his duty which relates immediately to him : and as obedience is better than sacrifice, so neither is any sacrifice acceptable, but that which is done according to the will of him to whom it is offered. But men, finding it easier to sacrifice in their own wills, than obey God's will, have heaped up sacrifices without obedience; and thinking to deceive God, as they do one another, give him a show of reverence, honour and worship, while they are both inwardly estranged and alienated from his holy and righteous life, and wholly strangers to the pure breathings of his Spirit, in which the acceptable sacrifice and worship is only offered up. Hence it is, that there is not anything relating to man's duty towards God, which among all sorts of people hath been more vitiated, and in which the devil hath more prevailed, than in abusing man's mind concerning this thing : and as among many others, so among those called Christians, nothing hath been more out of order, and more corrupted, as some Papists, and all Protestants, do acknowledge. As I freely approve whatsoever the Protestants have reformed from Papists in this respect; so I meddle not at this time with their controversies about it : only it suffices me with them to deny, as no part of the true worship of God, that abominable superstition and idolatry the Popish mass, the adoration of saints and angels, the veneration of relics, the visitation of sepulchres, and all those other superstitious ceremonies, confraternities, and endless pilgrimages of the Romish synagogue. Which all may suffice to evince to Protestants, that Antichrist hath wrought more in this than in any other part of the Christian religion; and so it concerns them narrowly to consider, whether herein they have made a clear and perfect reformation; as to which stands the controversy betwixt them and us. For we find many of the branches lopped off by them, but the root yet remaining; to wit, a worship acted in and from man's

*True worship and duty to God-ward corrupted.*

*The Popish mass (idolatry) denied, with all their trumpery.*

*If Protestants have made a perfect reformation?*

will and spirit, and not by and from the Spirit of God : for the true Christian and spiritual worship of God hath been so early lost, and man's wisdom and will hath so quickly and thoroughly mixed itself herein, that both the apostasy in this respect hath been greatest, and the reformation here from, as to the evil root, most difficult. Therefore let not the reader suddenly stumble at the account of our propo- sition in this matter, but patiently hear us explain ourselves in this respect, and I hope (by the assistance of God) to make it appear, that though our manner of speaking and doctrine seem most singular and different from all other sorts of Christians; yet it is most according to the purest Christian religion, and indeed most needful to be observed and followed. And that there be no ground of mistake, (for that I was necessitated to speak in few words, and therefore more obscurely and dubiously in the proposition itself) it is fit in the first place to declare and explain our sense, and clear the state of the controversy.

1.

What wor- ship here is spoken of.

§ II. And first, let it be considered, that what is here affirmed, is spoken of the worship of God in these gospel- times, and not of the worship that was under or before the law : for the particular commands of God to men then, are not sufficient to authorize us now to do the same things ; else we might be supposed at present acceptably to offer sacrifice as they did, which all acknowledge to be ceased. So that what might have been both commendable and ac- ceptable under the law, may justly now be charged with superstition, yea, and idolatry. So that impertinently, in this respect, doth Arnoldus rage against this proposition, [Exercit. Theolog. sect. 44,] saying ; That I deny all public worship, and that according to me, such as in Enoch's time publicly began to call upon the name of the Lord ; and such as at the command of God went thrice up to Jerusalem to worship ; and that Anna, Simeon, Mary, &c., were idolaters, because they used the public worship of those times ; such a consequence is most impertinent, and no less foolish and absurd, than if I should infer from Paul's expostulating with the Galatians for their returning to the

Jewish ceremonies, that he therefore condemned Moses and all the prophets as foolish and ignorant, because they used those things: the forward man, not heeding the different dispensations of times, ran into this impertinency. Though a spiritual worship might have been, and no doubt was practised by many under the law in great simplicity; yet will it not follow, that it were no superstition to use all those ceremonies that they used, which were by God dispensed to the Jews, not as being essential to true worship, or necessary as of themselves for transmitting and entertaining a holy fellowship betwixt him and his people; but in condescension to them, who were inclinable to idolatry. Albeit then in this, as in most other things, the substance was enjoyed under the law by such as were spiritual indeed; yet was it veiled and surrounded with many rites and ceremonies, which it is no ways lawful for us to use now under the gospel.

*Ceremonies under the law were not essential to true worship.*

§ III. Secondly; Albeit I say, that this worship is neither limited to times, places, nor persons; yet I would not be understood, as if I intended the putting away of all set times and places to worship: God forbid I should think of such an opinion. Nay, we are none of those that forsake the assembling of ourselves together; but have even certain times and places, in which we carefully meet together, nor can we be driven therefrom by the threats and persecutions of men, to wait upon God, and worship him. To meet together we think necessary for the people of God; because, so long as we are clothed with this outward tabernacle, there is a necessity to the entertaining of a joint and visible fellowship, and bearing of an outw rd testimony for God, and seeing of the faces of one another, that we concur with our persons as well as spirits: to be accompanied with that inward love and unity of spirit, doth greatly tend to encourage and refresh the saints.

*II. True worship is not limited to place or person.*

*Necessity of meetings.*

But the limitation we condemn, is, that whereas the Spirit of God should be the immediate actor, mover, persuader and influencer of man in the particular acts of wor-

*1. Will-worship doth limit the Spirit of God.*

28

ship, when the saints are met together, this Spirit is limited
in its operations, by setting up a particular man or men to
preach and pray in man's will; and all the rest are excluded from so much as believing that they are to wait for
God's Spirit to move them in such things; and so they
neglecting that in themselves which should quicken them,
and not waiting to feel the pure breathings of God's Spirit,
so as to obey them, are led merely to depend upon the
preacher, and hear what he will say.

**2. True
teaching of
the word of
God.**     Secondly; In that these peculiar men come not thither
to meet with the Lord, and to wait for the inward motions
and operations of his Spirit; and so to pray as they feel
the Spirit to breathe through them, and in them; and to
preach, as they find themselves actuated and moved by
God's Spirit, and as he gives utterance, so as to speak a
word in season to refresh weary souls, and as the present
condition and state of the people's hearts require; suffering God by his Spirit both to prepare people's hearts, and
also give the preacher to speak what may be fit and seasonable for them; but he [viz., the preacher] hath ham-
mered together in his closet, according to his own will, by
his human wisdom and literature, and by stealing the words
of truth from the letter of the scriptures, and patching
together other men's writings and observations, so much
as will hold him speaking an hour, while the glass runs;

**Priests
preach by
hap-hazard
their studi-
ed sermons**   and without waiting or feeling the inward influence of the
Spirit of God, he declaims that by hap-hazard, whether it
be fit or seasonable for the people's condition, or not; and
when he has ended his sermon, he saith his prayer also in
his own will; and so there is an end of the business.
Which customary worship, as it is no ways acceptable to
God, so how unfruitful it is, and unprofitable to those that
are found in it, the present condition of the nations doth
sufficiently declare. It appears then, that we are not against
set times for worship, as Arnoldus against this proposition,
Sect. 45, no less impertinently allegeth; offering need-
lessly to prove that which is not denied: only these times
being appointed for outward conveniency, we may not

therefore think with the Papists, that these days are holy, and lead people into a superstitious observation of them; being persuaded that all days are alike holy in the sight of God. And although it be not my present purpose to make a long digression concerning the debates among Protestants about the first day of the week, commonly called the Lord's day, yet forasmuch as it comes fitly in here, I shall briefly signify our sense thereof.

*Whether days are holy.*

§ IV. We, not seeing any ground in scripture for it, cannot be so superstitious as to believe, that either the Jewish sabbath now continues, or that the first day of the week is the anti-type thereof, or the true Christian sabbath; which with Calvin we believe to have a more spiritual sense: and therefore we know no moral obligation by the fourth command, or elsewhere, to keep the first day of the week more than any other, or any holiness inherent in it. But first, forasmuch as it is necessary that there be some time set apart for the saints to meet together to wait upon God; and that secondly, it is fit at some times they be freed from their other outward affairs; and that thirdly, reason and equity doth allow that servants and beasts have some time allowed them to be eased from their continual labour; and that fourthly, it appears that the apostles and primitive Christians did use the first day of the week for these purposes; we find ourselves sufficiently moved for these causes to do so also, without superstitiously straining the scriptures for another reason: which, that it is not to be there found, many Protestants, yea, Calvin himself, upon the fourth command, hath abundantly evinced. And though we therefore meet, and abstain from working upon this day, yet doth not that hinder us from having meetings also for worship at other times.

*Of the first day of the week, commonly called the Lord's day*

§ V. Thirdly; Though according to the knowledge of God, revealed unto us by the Spirit, through that more full dispensation of light which we believe the Lord hath brought about in this day, we judge it our duty to hold forth that pure and spiritual worship which is acceptable to God, and answerable to the testimony of Christ and his apostles, and likewise to testify against and deny not only manifest superstition and idolatry, but also all formal will worship, which stands not in the power of God; yet, I say, we do not deny the whole worship of all those that have borne the name of Christians even in the apostasy, as if God had never heard their prayers, nor accepted any of them: God forbid we should be so void of charity! The latter part of the proposition showeth the contrary. And as we would not be so absurd on the one hand to conclude, because of the errors and darkness that many were covered and surrounded with in Babylon, that none of their prayers were heard or accepted of God, so will we not be so unwary on the other, as to conclude, that because God heard and pitied them, so we ought to continue in these errors and darkness, and not come out of Babylon, when it is by God discovered unto us. The Popish mass and vespers I do believe to be, as to the matter of them, abominable idolatry and superstition, and so also believe the Protestants; yet will neither I or they affirm, that in the darkness of Popery no upright-hearted men, though zealous in these abominations, have been heard of God, or accepted of him. Who can deny, but that both Bernard and Bonaventure, Taulerus, Thomas à Kempis, and divers others have both known and tasted of the love of God, and felt the power and virtue of God's Spirit working with them for their salvation? And yet ought we not to forsake and deny those superstitions which they were found in? The Calvinistical Presbyterians do much upbraid, and I say not without reason, the formality and deadness of the Episcopalian and Lutheran liturgies; and yet, as they will not deny but there have been some good men among them, so neither dare they refuse, but that when that good step was brought in by them, of turning the public prayers into the vulgar tongues, though continued in a liturgy, it was acceptable to God, and sometimes accompanied with his power and presence: yet will not the Presbyterians have it from thence concluded, that the common prayers should still continue; so likewise, though we should confess, that

The worship in the apostasy.

The Popish mass and vespers.

Bernard and Bonaventure, Taulerus, Thomas à Kempis, have tasted of the love of God.

The bishops' liturgy.

through the mercy and wonderful condescension of God, there have been upright in heart both among Papists and Protestants, yet can we not therefore approve of their way in the general, or not go on to the upholding of that spiritual worship, which the Lord is calling all to, and so to the testifying against whatsoever stands in the way of it.

§ VI. Fourthly; To come then to the state of the con- *Assemblies of worship in public described.* troversy, as to the public worship, we judge it the duty of all to be diligent in the assembling of themselves toge- ther, and what we have been, and are, in this matter, our enemies in Great Britain, who have used all means to hinder our assembling together to worship God, may bear witness; and when assembled, the great work of one and all ought to be to wait upon God; and returning out of their own thoughts and imaginations, to feel the Lord's presence, and know a gathering into his name indeed, where he is in the midst, according to his promise. And as every one is thus gathered, and so met together in- wardly in their spirits, as well as outwardly in their persons, there the secret power and virtue of life is known to re- fresh the soul, and the pure motions and breathings of God's Spirit are felt to arise; from which, as words of declaration, prayers or praises arise, the acceptable worship is known, which edifies the church, and is well-pleasing to God. And no man here limits the Spirit of God, nor bringeth forth his own conned and gathered stuff; but every one puts that forth which the Lord puts into their hearts: and it is uttered forth not in man's will and wis- *The glori- ous dispen- sation of the Spirit.* dom; but in the evidence and demonstration of the Spirit, and of power. Yea, though there be not a word spoken, yet is the true spiritual worship performed, and the body of Christ edified; yea, it may, and hath often fallen out among us, that divers meetings have past without one word; and yet our souls have been greatly edified and refreshed, and our hearts wonderfully overcome with the secret sense of God's power and Spirit, which without words hath been ministered from one vessel to another. This is indeed strange and incredible to the mere natural and carnally-minded man, who will be apt to judge all time lost where there is not something spoken that is obvious to the outward senses ; and therefore I shall insist a little upon this subject, as one that can speak from a certain experience, and not by mere hearsay, of this wonderful and glorious dispensation ; which hath so much the more of the wisdom and glory of God in it, as it is contrary to the nature of man's spirit, will, and wisdom.

The silent waiting upon God obtained. § VII. As there can be nothing more opposite to the natural will and wisdom of man than this silent waiting upon God, so neither can it be obtained, nor rightly comprehended by man, but as he layeth down his own wisdom and will, so as to be content to be thoroughly subject to God. And therefore it was not preached, nor can be so practised, but by such as find no outward ceremony, no observations, no words, yea, not the best and purest words, even the words of scripture, able to satisfy their weary and afflicted souls : because where all these may be, the life, power, and virtue, which make such things effectual, may be wanting. Such, I say, were necessitated to cease from all externals, and to be silent before the Lord; and being directed to that inward principle of life and light in themselves, as the most excellent teacher, which " can never be removed into a corner," came thereby to be taught to wait upon God in the measure of life and grace received from him, and to cease from their own forward words and actings, in the natural willing and comprehension, and feel after this inward seed of life ; that, as it moveth, they may move with it, and be actuated by its power, and influenced, whether to pray, preach or sing. And so from this principle of man's being silent, and not acting in the things of God of himself, until thus actuated by God's light and grace in the heart, did naturally spring that manner of sitting silent together, and waiting together upon the Lord. For many thus principled, meeting together in the pure fear of the Lord, did not apply themselves presently to speak, pray, or sing, &c., being afraid to be found acting

[Isa. xxx. 20.]

forwardly in their own wills; but each made it their work to retire inwardly to the measure of grace in themselves, not being only silent as to words, but even abstaining from all their own thoughts, imaginations and desires; so watching in a holy dependence upon the Lord, and meeting together not only outwardly in one place, but thus inwardly in one Spirit, and in one name of Jesus, which is his power and virtue, they come thereby to enjoy and feel the arisings of this life, which, as it prevails in each particular, becomes as a flood of refreshment, and overspreads the whole meeting: for man, and man's part and wisdom, being denied and chained down in every individual, and God exalted, and his grace in dominion in the heart, thus his name comes to be one in all, and his glory breaks forth, and covers all; and there is such a holy awe and reverence upon every soul, that if the natural part should arise in any, or the wise part, or what is not one with the life, it would presently be chained down, and judged out. And when any are, through the breaking forth of this power, constrained to utter a sentence of exhortation or praise, or to breathe to the Lord in prayer, then all are sensible of it; for the same life in them answers to it, "as in water face answereth to face." This is that divine and spiritual worship, which the world neither knoweth nor understandeth, which the vulture's eye seeth not into. Yet many and great are the advantages, which my soul, with many others, hath tasted of hereby, and which would be found of all such as would seriously apply themselves hereunto: for, when people are gathered thus together, not merely to hear men, nor depend upon them, but all are inwardly taught to stay their minds upon the Lord, and wait for his appearance in their hearts; thereby the forward working of the spirit of man is stayed and hindered from mixing itself with the worship of God; and the form of this worship is so naked and void of all outward and worldly splendor, that all occasion for man's wisdom to be exercised in that superstition and idolatry hath no lodging here; and so there being also an inward quietness and

*What it is to meet in the name of Jesus.*

*Prov. xxvii 19.*

*Advantages of silent meetings.*

*Isa. x. 20, & xxvi 3*

retiredness of mind, the witness of God ariseth in the heart, and the light of Christ shineth, whereby the soul cometh to see its own condition. And there being many joined together in this same work, there is an inward travail and wrestling; and also, as the measure of grace is abode in, an overcoming of the power and spirit of darkness; and thus we are often greatly strengthened and renewed in the spirits of our minds without a word, and we enjoy and Eph. iv. 23. possess the holy fellowship and communion of the body and blood of Christ, by which our inward man is nourished and fed; which makes us not to dote upon outward water, and bread and wine, in our spiritual things. Now as many thus gathered together grow up in the strength, power, and virtue of truth, and as truth comes thus to have victory and dominion in their souls, then they receive an utterance, Speaking to and speak steadily to the edification of their brethren, and edification. the pure life hath a free passage through them, and what is thus spoken edifieth the body indeed. Such is the evident certainty of that divine strength that is communicated by thus meeting together, and waiting in silence upon God, that sometimes when one hath come in that hath been unwatchful and wandering in his mind, or suddenly out of the hurry of outward business, and so not inwardly gathered with the rest, so soon as he retires himself inwardly, this power being in a good measure raised in the whole meeting, will suddenly lay hold upon his spirit, and wonderfully help to raise up the good in him, and beget him into the sense of the same power, to the melting and warming of his heart; even as the warmth would take hold upon a man that is cold coming in to a stove, or as a flame will lay hold upon some little combustible matter being near unto it. Yea, if it fall out that several met together be straying in their minds, though outwardly silent, and so wandering from the measure of grace in themselves, which through the working of the enemy, and negligence of some, may fall out, if either one come in, or may be in, who is watchful, and in whom the life is raised in a great measure, as that one keeps his place, he will feel a secret travail for the rest in a sympathy with the seed which is oppressed in the other, and kept from arising by their thoughts and wanderings; and as such a faithful one waits in the light, and keeps in this divine work, God often-times answers the secret travail and breathings of his own seed through such a one, so that the rest will find them-selves secretly smitten without words, and that one will be as a midwife through the secret travail of his soul to bring forth the life in them, just as a little water thrown into a pump brings up the rest, whereby life will come to be raised in all, and the vain imaginations brought down; and such a one is felt by the rest to minister life unto them without words. Yea, sometimes, when there is not a word in the meeting, but all are silently waiting, if one come in that is rude and wicked, and in whom the power of darkness prevaileth much, perhaps with an intention to mock or do mischief, if the whole meeting be gathered into the life, and it be raised in a good measure, it will strike terror into such a one, and he will feel himself unable to resist; but by the secret strength and virtue thereof, the power of darkness in him will be chained down: and if the day of his visitation be not expired, it will reach to the measure of grace in him, and raise it up to the redeeming of his soul. And this we often bear witness of, so that we have had frequent occasion in this respect, since God hath gathered us to be a people, to renew this old saying of many, "Is Saul also among the prophets?" For not a few have come to be convinced of the truth after this manner, of which I myself, in part, am a true witness, who not by strength of arguments, or by a particular disquisition of each doctrine, and convincement of my understanding thereby, came to receive and bear witness of the truth, but by being secretly reached by this life; for when I came into the silent assemblies of God's people, I felt a secret power among them, which touched my heart, and as I gave way unto it, I found the evil weakening in me, and the good raised up, and so I became thus knit and united unto them, hungering more and more after the increase of

*A secret travail one for another in silent meetings.*

*The mocker struck with terror when no word is spoken.*

*1 Sam. x. 12.*

*The true convincement.*

this power and life, whereby I might feel myself p rfectly redeemed. And indeed this is the surest way to become a Christian, to whom afterwards the knowledge and understanding of principles will not be wanting, but will grow up so much as is needful, as the natural fruit of this good root, and such a knowledge will not be barren nor unfruitful. After this manner we desire therefore all that come among us to be proselyted, knowing that though thousands should be convinced in their understandings of all the truths we maintain, yet if they were not sensible of this inward life, and their souls not changed from unrighteousness to righteousness, they could add nothing to us. For 1 Cor vi.17. this is that cement whereby we are joined "as to the Lord," so to one another, and without this none can worship with us. Yea, if such should come among us, and from that understanding and convincement they have of the truth, speak ever so true things, and utter them forth with ever so much excellency of speech, if this life were wanting, it would not edify us at all, but be as "sounding brass, or a tinkling cymbal," 1 Cor. xiii. 1.

*1 Cor vi.17. The ife of righteousness doth join us to the Lord.*

§ VIII. Our work then and worship is, when we meet together, for every one to watch and wait upon God in themselves, and to be gathered from all visibles thereunto. And as every one is thus stated, they come to find the good arise over the evil, and the pure over the impure, in which God reveals himself, and draweth near to every individual, and so he is in the midst in the general, whereby each not only partakes of the particular refreshment and strength which comes from the good in himself, but is a sharer in the whole body, as being a living member of the body, having a joint fellowship and communion with all. And as this worship is steadfastly preached and kept to, it becomes easy, though it be very hard at first to the natural man, whose roving imaginations and running worldly desires are not so easily brought to silence. And therefore the Lord often-times, when any turn towards him, and have true desires thus to wait upon him, and find great difficulty through the unstayedness of their

*Our work and worship in our meetings.*

minds, doth in condescension and compassion cause his power to break forth in a more strong and powerful manner. And when the mind sinks down, and waits for the appearance of life, and that the power of darkness in the soul wrestles and works against it, then the good seed, as it ariseth, will be found to work as physic in the soul, especially if such a weak one be in the assembly of divers others in whom the life is arisen in greater dominion, and through the contrary workings of the power of darkness there will be found an inward striving in the soul as really in the mystery as ever Esau and Jacob strove in Rebecca's womb. And from this inward travail, while the darkness seeks to obscure the light, and the light breaks through the darkness, which it always will do, if the soul gives not its strength to the darkness, there will be such a painful travail found in the soul, that will even work upon the outward man, so that often-times, through the working thereof, the body will be greatly shaken, and many groans, and sighs, and tears, even as the pangs of a woman in travail, will lay hold upon it; yea, and this not only as to one, but when the enemy, who, when the children of God assemble together, is not wanting to be present, to see if he can let their comfort, hath prevailed in any measure in a whole meeting, and strongly worketh against it by spreading and propagating his dark power, and by drawing out the minds of such as are met from the life in them, as they come to be sensible of this power of his that works against them, and to wrestle with it by the armour of light, sometimes the power of God will break forth into a whole meeting, and there will be such an inward travail, while each is seeking to overcome the evil in themselves, that by the strong contrary workings of these opposite powers, like the going of two contrary tides, every individual will be strongly exercised as in a day of battle, and thereby trembling and a motion of body will be upon most, if not upon all, which, as the power of truth prevails, will from pangs and groans end with a sweet sound of thanksgiving and praise. And from this the name of Quakers, i. e., Tremblers, was

*Esau and Jacob strove in Rebecca's womb.*

*The travail crowned with a victorious song.*

first reproachfully cast upon us; which though it be none of our choosing, yet in this respect we are not ashamed of it, but have rather reason to rejoice therefore, even that we are sensible of this power that hath oftentimes laid hold of our adversaries, and made them yield unto us, and join with us, and confess to the truth, before they had any distinct or discursive knowledge of our doctrines, so that sometimes many at one meeting have been thus convinced: and this power would sometimes also reach to and wonderfully work even in little children, to the admiration and astonishment of many.

§ IX. Many are the blessed experiences which I could relate of this silence and manner of worship; yet I do not so much commend and speak of silence as if we had bound ourselves by any law to exclude praying or preaching, or tied ourselves thereunto; not at all: for as our worship consisteth not in words, so neither in silence, as silence; but in a holy dependence of the mind upon God: from which dependence silence necessarily follows in the first place, until words can be brought forth, which are from God's Spirit. And God is not wanting to move in his children to bring forth words of exhortation or prayer, when it is needful; so that of the many gatherings and meetings of such as are convinced of the truth, there is scarce any in whom God raiseth not up some or other to minister to his brethren; and there are few meetings that are altogether silent. For when many are met together in this one life and name, it doth most naturally and frequently excite them to pray to and praise God, and stir up one another by mutual exhortation and instructions; yet we judge it needful there be in the first place some time of silence, during which every one may be gathered inward to the word and gift of grace, from which he that ministereth may receive strength to bring forth what he ministereth; and that they that hear may have a sense to discern betwixt the precious and the vile, and not to hurry into the exercise of these things so soon as the bell rings, as other Christians do. Yea, and we doubt not, but assuredly know hat the meeting may be good and refreshful, though from he sitting down to the rising up thereof there hath not been a word as outwardly spoken, and yet life may have been known to abound in each particular, and an inward growing up therein and thereby, yea, so as words might have been spoken acceptably, and from the life: yet there being no absolute necessity laid upon any so to do, all might have chosen rather quietly and silently to possess and enjoy the Lord in themselves, which is very sweet and comfortable to the soul that hath thus learned to be gathered out of all its own thoughts and workings, to feel the Lord to bring forth both the will and the deed, which many can declare by a blessed experience: though indeed it cannot but be hard for the natural man to receive or believe this doctrine, and therefore it must be rather by a sensible experience, and by coming to make proof of it, than by arguments, that such can be convinced of this thing, seeing it is not enough to believe it, if they come not also to enjoy and possess it; yet in condescension to, and for the sake of, such as may be the more willing to apply themselves to the practice and experience hereof, if they found their understandings convinced of it, and that it is founded upon scripture and reason, I find a freedom of mind to add some few considerations of this kind, for the confirmation hereof, besides what is before mentioned of our experience.

§ X. That to wait upon God, and to watch before him, is a duty incumbent upon all, I suppose none will deny; and that this also is a part of worship will not be called in question, since there is scarce any other so frequently commanded in the holy scriptures, as may appear from Psalm xvii. 14, and xxxvii. 7, 34; Prov. xx. 22; Isai. xxx. 18; Hosea xii. 6; Zeph. iii. 8; Mat. xxiv. 42, and xxv. 13, and xxvi. 41; Mark xiii. 33, 35, 37; Luke xxi. 36; Acts . 4, and xx. 31; 1 Cor. xvi. 13; Col. iv. 2; 1 Thess. v. ; 2 Tim. iv. 5; 1 Pet. iv. 7. Also this duty is often recommended with very great and precious promises, as 'salm xxv. 3, and xxxvii. 9, and lxix. 6; Isai. xlii. 23;

*Marginal notes:*
No absolute necessity for words, though from the life at times

To wait and watch commanded in the scripture.

**Lam.** iii. 25, 26. They that wait upon the Lord shal
renew their strength, &c., Isa. xl. 31. Now how is thi.
waiting upon God, or watching before him, but by thi.
silence of which we have spoken? Which as it is in it
self a great and principal duty, so it necessarily in orde
both of nature and time precedeth all other. But that i
may be the better and more perfectly understood, as it i
not only an outward silence of the body, but an inwar
silence of the mind from all its own imaginations and self
cogitations, let it be considered according to truth, and t
the principles and doctrines heretofore affirmed and proved
that man is to be considered in a twofold respect, to wit
in his natural, unregenerate, and fallen state, and in hi
spiritual and renewed condition; from whence ariseth tha
distinction of the natural and spiritual man so much use
by the apostle, and heretofore spoken of. Also these tw
births of the mind proceed from the two seeds in man re
spectively, to wit, the good seed and the evil; and from
the evil seed doth not only proceed all manner of gross an
abominable wickedness and profanity, but also hypocrisy

Whence
wicked-
nesses arise
that are
spiritual.
and those wickednesses which the scripture calls spiritual
because it is the serpent working in and by the natural ma
in things that are spiritual, which having a show and appear
ance of good, are so much the more hurtful and dangerous.
as it is Satan transformed and transforming himself into a
angel of light; and therefore doth the scripture so pressing'y
and frequently, as we have heretofore had occasion to observe, shut out and exclude the natural man from med
dling with the things of God, denying his endeavour
therein, though acted and performed by the most eminen
of his parts, as of wisdom and utterance.

Also this spiritual wickedness is of two sorts, thoug
both one in kind, as proceeding from one root, yet differ
ing in their degrees, and in the subjects also sometimes
The one is, when as the natural man, meddling with an
working in the things of religion, doth from his own con
ceptions and divinations affirm or propose wrong an
erroneous notions and opinions of God and things spiritual

and invent superstitions, ceremonies, observations, and rites in worship, from whence have sprung all the heresies and superstitions that are among Christians. The other 's, when as the natural man, from a mere conviction of his understanding, doth in the forwardness of his own will, and by his own natural strength, without the influence and leading of God's Spirit, go about either in his understanding to imagine, conceive, or think of the things of God, or actually to perform them by preaching or praying. The first is a missing both in matter and form; the second is a retaining of the form without the life and substance of Christianity; because Christian religion consisteth not in a mere belief of true doctrines, or a mere performance of acts good in themselves, or else the bare letter of the scripture, though spoken by a drunkard, or a devil, might be said to be spirit and life, which I judge none will be so absurd as to affirm; and also it would follow, that where the form of godliness is, there the power is also, which is contrary to the express words of the apostle. For the form of godliness cannot be said to be, where either the notions and opinions believed are erroneous and ungodly, or the acts performed evil and wicked; for then it would be the form of ungodliness, and not of godliness: but of this more hereafter, when we shall speak particularly of preaching and praying. Now though this last be not so bad as the former, yet it hath made way for it; for men having first departed from the life and substance of true religion and worship, to wit, from the inward power and virtue of the Spirit, so as therein to act, and thereby to have all their actions enlivened, have only retained the form and show, to wit, the true words and appearance; and so acting in their own natural and unrenewed wills in this form, the form could not but quickly decay, and be vitiated. For the working and active spirit of man could not contain itself within the simplicity and plainness of truth, but giving way to his own numerous inventions and imaginations, began to vary in the form, and adapt it to his own inventions, until by degrees the form of godliness for the most part came to be lost, as well as the power.

For this kind of idolatry, whereby man loveth, idolizeth and embraceth his own conceptions, inventions, and product of his own brain, is so incident unto him, and seated in his fallen nature, that so long as his natural spirit is the first author and actor of him, and is that by which he only is guided and moved in his worship towards God, so as not first to wait for another guide to direct him, he can never perform the pure spiritual worship, nor bring forth anything but the fruit of the first, fallen, natural, and corrupt root. Wherefore the time appointed of God being come, wherein by Jesus Christ he hath been pleased to restore the true spiritual worship, and the outward form of worship, which was appointed by God to the Jews, and whereof the manner and time of its performance was particularly determined by God himself, being come to an end,

we find that Jesus Christ, the author of the Christian religion, prescribes no set form of worship to his children under the more pure administration of the new covenant,* save that he only tells them, that the worship now to be performed is spiritual, and in the Spirit. And it is especially to be observed, that in the whole New Testament there is no order nor command given in this thing, but to follow the revelation of the Spirit, save only that general one of

---

* If any object here, That the Lord's Prayer is a prescribed form of prayer, and therefore of worship given by Christ to his children:

I answer, First, This cannot be objected by any sort of Christian that I know, because there are none who use not other prayers, or that limit their worship to this. Secondly, This was commanded to the disciples, while yet weak, before they had received the dispensation of the gospel; not that they should only use it in praying, but that he might show them by one example how that their prayers ought to be short, and not like the long prayers of the Pharisees. And that this was the use of it, appears by all their prayers, which divers saints afterwards made use of, whereof the scripture makes mention; for none made use of this, neither repeated it, but used other words, according as the thing required, and as the Spirit gave utterance. Thirdly, That this ought to be so understood, appears from Rom. viii. 26, of which afterwards mention shall be made at greater length, where the apostle saith, " We know not what we should pray for as we ought, but the Spirit itself maketh intercession for us," &c. But if this prayer had been such a prescribed form of prayer to the church, that had not been true, neither had they been ignorant what to pray for, nor should they have needed the help of the Spirit to teach them.

meeting together; a thing dearly owned and diligently practised by us, as shall hereafter more appear. True it is, mention is made of the duties of praying, preaching, and singing; but what order or method should be kept in so doing, or that presently they should be set about so soon as the saints are gathered, there is not one word to be found: yea, these duties, as shall afterwards be made appear, are always annexed to the assistance, leadings, and motions of God's Spirit. Since then man in his natural state is thus excluded from acting or moving in things spiritual, how or what way shall he exercise this first and previous duty of waiting upon God but by silence, and by bringing that natural part to silence? Which is no other ways but by abstaining from his own thoughts and imaginations, and from all the self-workings and motions of his own mind, as well in things materially good as evil; that he being silent, God may speak in him, and the good seed may arise. This, though hard to the natural man, is so answerable to reason, and even natural experience in other things, that it cannot be denied. He that cometh to learn of a master, if he expect to hear his master and be instructed by him, must not continually be speaking of the matter to be taught, and never be quiet, otherwise how shall his master have time to instruct him? Yea, though the scholar were never so earnest to learn the science, yet would the master have reason to reprove him, as untoward and indocile, if he would always be meddling of himself, and still speaking, and not wait in silence patiently to hear his master instructing and teaching him, who ought not to open his mouth until by his master he were commanded and allowed so to do. So also if one were about to attend a great prince, he would be thought an impertinent and imprudent servant, who, while he ought patiently and readily to wait, that he might answer the king when he speaks, and have his eye upon him to observe the least motions and inclinations of his will, and to do accordingly, would be still deafening him with discourse, though it were in praises of him; and running to and fro, without any particular and

*Marginal notes:*

I pray, preach, and sing in Spirit.

To wait on God, by what it is performed.

A simile of a master and his scholar.

Of a prince and his servant.

29 *

immediate order, to do things that perhaps might be good
in themselves, or might have been commanded at other
times to others; would the kings of the earth accept of
such servants or service? Since then we are commanded

**To wait in silence.** to wait upon God diligently, and in so doing it is promised
that our strength shall be renewed, this waiting cannot be
performed but by a silence or cessation of the natural part
on our side, since God manifests himself not to the outward man or senses, so much as to the inward, to wit, to
the soul and spirit. If the soul be still thinking and working in her own will, and busily exercised in her own ima-

**The thinking busy soul excludes the voice of God.** ginations, though the matters as in themselves may be good
concerning God, yet thereby she incapacitates herself from
discerning the still, small voice of the Spirit, and so hurts
herself greatly, in that she neglects her chief business of
waiting upon the Lord: nothing less than if I should busy
myself, crying out and speaking of a business, while in the
mean time I neglect to hear one who is quietly whispering
into my ear, and informing me in those things which are
most needful for me to hear and know concerning that
business. And since it is the chief work of a Christian to
know the natural will in its own proper motions crucified,
that God may both move in the act and in the will, the
Lord chiefly regards this profound subjection and self-denial. For some men please themselves as much, and gratify
their own sensual wills and humours in high and curious

**Religious speculations.** speculations of religion, affecting a name and reputation
that way, or because those things by custom or otherways
are become pleasant and habitual to them, though not a
whit more regenerated or inwardly sanctified in their spirits,

**Sensual recreations.** as others gratify their lusts in acts of sensuality, and therefore both are alike hurtful to men, and sinful in the sight
of God, it being nothing but the mere fruit and effect of
man's natural and unrenewed will and spirit. Yea, should
one, as many no doubt do, from a sense of sin, and fear of
punishment, seek to terrify themselves from sin, by multiplying thoughts of death, hell, and judgment, and by presenting to their imaginations the happiness and joys of

Leaven, and also by multiplying prayers and other religious performances, as these things could never deliver him from one iniquity, without the secret and inward power of God's Spirit and grace, so would they signify no more than the fig-leaves wherewith Adam thought to cover his nakedness. And seeing it is only the product of man's own natural will, proceeding from a self-love, and seeking to save himself, and not arising purely from that divine seed of righteousness which is given of God to all for grace and salvation, it is rejected of God, and no ways acceptable unto him ; since the natural man, as natural, while he stands in that state, is, with all his arts, parts, and actings, reprobated by him. This great duty then of waiting upon God, must needs be exercised in man's denying self, both in- wardly and outwardly, in a still and mere dependence upon God, in abstracting from all the workings, imaginations, and speculations of his own mind, that being emptied as it were of himself, and so thoroughly crucified to the natural products thereof, he may be fit to receive the Lord, who will have no co-partner nor co-rival of his glory and power. And man being thus stated, the little seed of righteousness which God hath planted in his soul, and Christ hath purchased for him, even the measure of grace and life, which is burdened and crucified by man's natural thoughts and imaginations, receives a place to arise, and becometh a holy birth and geniture in man ; and is that divine air in and by which man's soul and spirit comes to be leavened ; and by waiting therein he comes to be accepted in the sight of God, to stand in his presence, hear his voice, and observe the motions of his holy Spirit. And so man's place is to wait in this ; and as hereby there are any objects presented to his mind concerning God, or things relating to religion, his soul may be exercised in them without hurt, and to the great profit both of himself and others ; because those things have their rise not from his own will, but from God's Spirit : and therefore as in the arisings and movings of this his mind is still to be exercised in thinking and meditating, so also in the more obvious acts of preaching

No Qua-
kers are
against a
meditating
mind.
From na-
ture's
thoughts
all errors
rise.

and praying. And so it may hence appear we are not against meditation, as some have sought falsely to infer from our doctrine; but we are against the thoughts and imaginations of the natural man in his own will, from which all errors and heresies concerning the Christian religion in the whole world have proceeded. But if it please God at any time, when one or more are waiting upon him, not to present such objects as give them occasion to exercise their minds in thoughts and imaginations, but purely to keep them in this holy dependence, and as they persist therein, to cause his secret refreshment and the pure incomes of his holy life to flow in upon them, then they have good reason to be content, because by this, as we know by good and blessed experience, the soul is more strengthened, renew-

The soul renewed, by what? The holy life of God.

ed, and confirmed in the love of God, and armed against the power of sin, than any way else; this being a foretaste of that real and sensible enjoyment of God, which the saints in heaven daily possess, which God frequently affords to his children here for their comfort and encouragement, especially when they are assembled together to wait upon him.

Whatever man does act without the power of God is not accept-ed.

§ XI. For there are two contrary powers or spirits, to wit, the power and spirit of this world, in which the prince of darkness bears rule, and over as many as are acted by it, and work from it; and the power or Spirit of God, in which God worketh and beareth rule, and over as many as act in and from it. So whatever be the things that a man thinketh of, or acteth in, however spiritual or religious as to the notion or form of them, so long as he acteth and moveth in the natural and corrupt spirit and will, and not from, in, and by the power of God, he sinneth in all, and

Prov. xxi. 4.

is not accepted of God. For hence both the "ploughing and praying of the wicked is sin;" as also whatever a man acts in and from the Spirit and power of God, having his understanding and will influenced and moved by it, whether it be actions religious, civil, or even natural, he is accepted in so doing in the sight of God, and is

Ja. i. 25.

"blessed in them." From what is said, it doth appear

now frivolous and impertinent their objection is, that say they wait upon God in praying and preaching, since waiting doth of itself imply a passive dependence, rather than an acting. And since it is, and shall yet be more shown, that preaching and praying without the Spirit is an offending of God, not a waiting upon him, and that praying and preaching by the Spirit pre-supposes necessarily a silent waiting to feel the motions and influence of the Spirit to lead thereunto; and lastly, that in several of these places where praying is commanded, as Mat. xxvi. 41; Mark xiii. 33; Luke xxi. 36; 1 Peter iv. 7, watching is specially prefixed as a previous preparation thereunto; we do well and certainly conclude, that since waiting and watching are so particularly commanded and recommended, and cannot be truly performed but in this inward silence of the mind from men's own thoughts and imaginations, this silence is and must necessarily be a special and principal part of God's worship.

To pray and preach without the Spirit is offence to God.

§ XII. But secondly, The excellency of this silent waiting upon God doth appear, in that it is impossible for the enemy, viz., the devil, to counterfeit it, so as for any soul to be deceived or deluded by him in the exercise thereof. Now in all other matters he may mix himself with the natural mind of man, and so by transforming himself he may deceive the soul, by busying it about things perhaps innocent in themselves, while yet he keeps them from beholding the pure light of Christ, and so from knowing distinctly their duty, and doing of it. For that envious spirit of man's eternal happiness knoweth well how to accommodate himself, and fit his snares for all the several dispositions and inclinations of men; if he find one not fit to be engaged with gross sins, or worldly lusts, but rather averse from them, and religiously inclined, he can fit himself to beguile such a one, by suffering his thoughts and imaginations to run upon spiritual matters, and so hurry him to work, act, and meditate in his own will. For he well knoweth that so long as self bears rule, and the Spirit of God is not the principal and chief actor, man is not put

II. This silent waiting the devil cannot counterfeit.

Altar,pray-
ers, pulpit,
study, can-
not shut the
devil out.

out of his reach; so therefore he can accompany the priest
to the altar, the preacher to the pulpit, the zealot to his
prayers, yea, the doctor and professor of divinity to his
study, and there he can cheerfully suffer him to labour and
work among his books, yea, and help him to find out and
invent subtile distinctions and quiddities, by which both
his mind and others through him, may be kept from heeding God's Light in the conscience, and waiting upon him.
There is not any exercise whatsoever, wherein he cannot
enter and have a chief place, so as the soul many times
cannot discern it, except in this alone: for he can only
work in and by the natural man, and his faculties, by
secretly acting upon his imaginations and desires, &c., and
therefore, when he, to wit, the natural man, is silent, there
he must also stand. And therefore when the soul comes
to this silence, and as it were is brought to nothingness, as
to her own workings, then the devil is shut out; for the
pure presence of God and shining of his Light he cannot
abide, because so long as a man is thinking and meditating
as of himself, he cannot be sure but the devil is influencing
him therein; but when he comes wholly to be silent, as
the pure Light of God shines in upon him, then he is sure
that the devil is shut out; for beyond the imaginations he
cannot go, which we often find by sensible experience.
For he that of old is said to have come to the gathering
together of the children of God, is not wanting to come to
our assemblies. And indeed he can well enter and work
in a meeting, that is silent only as to words, either by keeping the minds in various thoughts and imaginations, or by
stupefying them, so as to overwhelm them with a spirit of
heaviness and slothfulness: but when we retire out of all,
and are turned in, both by being diligent and watchful
upon the one hand, and also silent and retired out of all
our thoughts upon the other, as we abide in this sure place,
we feel ourselves out of his reach. Yea, oftentimes the
power and glory of God will break forth and appear, just
as the bright sun through many clouds and mists, to the
dispelling of that power of darkness; which will also be

sensibly felt, seeking to cloud and darken the mind, and wholly to keep it from purely waiting upon God.

§ XIII. Thirdly, the excellency of this worship doth appear, in that it can neither be stopped nor interrupted by the malice of men or devils, as all others can. Now interruptions and stoppings of worship may be understood in a twofold respect, either as we are hindered from meeting, as being outwardly by violence separated one from another; or when permitted to meet together, as we are interrupted by the tumult, noise, and confusion which such as are malicious may use to molest or distract us. Now in both these respects, this worship doth greatly overpass all others: for how far soever people be separate or hindered from coming together, yet as every one is inwardly gathered to the measure of life in himself, there is a secret unity and fellowship enjoyed, which the devil and all his instruments can never break or hinder. But, secondly, It doth as well appear, as to those molestations which occur, when we are met together, what advantage this true and spiritual worship gives us beyond all others; seeing in despite of a thousand interruptions and abuses, one of which were sufficient to have stopped all other sorts of Christians, we have been able, through the nature of this worship, to keep it uninterrupted as to God, and also at the same time to show forth an example of our Christian patience towards all, even oftentimes to the reaching and convincing of our opposers. For there is no sort of worship used by others which can subsist, though they be permitted to meet, unless they be either authorized and protected by the magistrate, or defend themselves with the arm of flesh: but we at the same time exercise worship towards God, and also patiently bear the reproaches and ignominies which Christ prophesied should be so incident and frequent to Christians. For how can the Papists say their mass, if there be any there to disturb and interrupt them? Do but take away the mass-book, the chalice, the host, or the priest's garments, yea, do but spill the water, or the wine, or blow out the candles, a thing quickly done,

III. The worship of the Quakers not stopped or interrupted by men or devils.

The worship of the Papists soon interrupted.

and the whole business is marred, and no sacrifice can be
offered. Take from the Lutherans or Episcopalians their
Liturgy or Common-Prayer-Book, and no service can be
said. Remove from the Calvinists, Arminians, Socinians,
Independents, or Anabaptists, the pulpit, the bible, and
the hour-glass, or make but such a noise as the voice of
the preacher cannot be heard, or disturb him but so before
he come, or strip him of his bible or his books, and he
must be dumb: for they all think it an heresy to wait to
speak as the Spirit of God giveth utterance; and thus
easily their whole worship may be marred. But when
people meet together, and their worship consisteth not in
such outward acts, and they depend not upon any one's
speaking, but merely sit down to wait upon God, and to
be gathered out of all visibles, and to feel the Lord in
Spirit, none of these things can hinder them, of which we
may say of a truth, we are sensible witnesses. For when
the magistrates, stirred up by the malice and envy of our
opposers, have used all means possible, and yet in vain, to
deter us from meeting together, and that openly and publicly in our own hired houses for that purpose, both death,
banishments, imprisonments, finings, beatings, whippings,
and other such devilish inventions, have proved ineffectual
to terrify us from our holy assemblies. And we having, I
say, thus oftentimes purchased our liberty to meet, by deep
sufferings, our opposers have then taken another way, by
turning in upon us the worst and wickedest people, yea,
the very off-scourings of men, who by all manner of inhu
man, beastly and brutish behaviour, have sought to pro
voke us, weary us, and molest us, but in vain. It would
be almost incredible to declare, and indeed a shame, that
among men pretending to be Christians, it should be mentioned, what things of this kind men's eyes have seen, and
I myself, with others, have shared of in suffering! There
they have often beaten us, and cast water and dirt upon
us; there they have danced, leaped, sung, and spoken all
manner of profane and ungodly words; offered violence
and shameful behaviour to grave women and virgins;

*Side notes:* The Protestants the like, and Anabaptists.

The sufferings of the Quakers for their religious meetings.

jeered, mocked and scoffed, asking us, if the Spirit was not yet come? And much more, which were tedious here to relate: and all this while we have been seriously and silently sitting together, and waiting upon the Lord. So that by these things our inward and spiritual fellowship with God, and one with another, in the pure life of righteousness, hath not been hindered. But on the contrary, the Lord knowing our sufferings and reproaches for his testimony's sake, hath caused his power and glory more to abound among us, and hath mightily refreshed us by the sense of his love, which hath filled our souls; and so much the rather, as we found ourselves gathered into the "name of the Lord," which is the strong tower of the righteous; whereby we felt ourselves sheltered from receiving any inward hurt through their malice: and also that he had delivered us from that vain name and profession of Christianity, under which our opposers were not ashamed to bring forth those bitter and cursed fruits. Yea, sometimes in the midst of this tumult and opposition, God would powerfully move some or other of us by his Spirit, both to testify of that joy, which notwithstanding their malice we enjoyed, and powerfully to declare, in the evidence and demonstration of the Spirit, against their folly and wickedness; so as the power of truth hath brought them to some measure of quietness and stillness, and stopped the impetuous streams of their fury and madness: that even as of old Moses by his rod divided the waves of the Red Sea, that the Israelites might pass; so God hath thus by his Spirit made a way for us in the midst of this raging wickedness, peaceably to enjoy and possess him, and accomplish our worship to him: so that sometimes upon such occasions several of our opposers and interrupters have hereby been convinced of the truth, and gathered from being persecutors to be sufferers with us. And let it not be forgotten, but let it be inscribed and abide for a constant remembrance of the thing, that in these beastly and brutish pranks, used to molest us in our spiritual meetings, none have been more busy than the

*Prov. xviii. 10.*

*The rod of Moses divided the sea: the Spirit maketh way through the raging waves.*

30

What bru-
tish pranks
did not that
young fry
of the cler-
gy commit? young students of the universities, who were learning philosophy and divinity, so called, and many of them prepar-
ing themselves for the ministry. Should we commit to
writing all the abominations committed in this respect by
the young fry of the clergy, it would make no small
volume; as the churches of Christ, gathered into his pure
worship in Oxford and Cambridge in England, and Edinburgh and Aberdeen in Scotland, where the universities
are, can well bear witness.

How the
old cove-
nant-wor-
ship doth
differ from
the new. § XIV. Moreover, in this we know, that we are partakers of the new covenant's dispensation, and disciples
of Christ indeed, sharing with him in that spiritual worship, which is performed in the Spirit and in truth; because
as he was, so are we in this world. For the old covenant-
worship had an outward glory, temple and ceremonies, and
was full of outward splendour and majesty, having an outward tabernacle and altar, beautified with gold, silver, and
precious stones; and their sacrifices were confined to a particular place, even the outward Mount Sion; and those
that prayed, were to pray with their faces towards that outward temple; and therefore all this was to be protected by
an outward arm. Nor could the Jews peaceably have
enjoyed it, but when they were secured from the violence
of their outward enemies; and therefore when at any time
their enemies prevailed over them, their glory was darkened,
and their sacrifices stopped, and the face of their worship
marred: hence they complain, lament, and bewail the de-
The new
covenant-
worship is
inward.
J hn xviii.
36 stroying of the temple, as a loss irreparable. But Jesus
Christ, the author and institutor of the new covenant-wor-
ship, testifies, that God is neither to be worshipped in this
nor that place, but in the Spirit and in Truth; and forasmuch as his kingdom is not of this world, neither doth his
worship consist in it, or need either the wisdom, glory,
riches or splendour of this world to beautify or adorn it:
nor yet the outward power or arm of flesh to maintain, uphold, or protect it: but it is and may be performed by
those that are spiritually minded, notwithstanding all the
opposition, violence, and malice of men; because it being

purely spiritual, it is out of the reach of natural men to interrupt or obstruct it. Even as Jesus Christ, the author thereof, did enjoy and possess his spiritual kingdom, while oppressed, persecuted, and rejected of men; and as, in despite of the malice and rage of the devil, " he spoiled Col. ii. 15. principalities and powers, triumphing over them, and through death destroyed him that had the power of death, Heb. ii. 14. that is, the devil;" so also all his followers both can and do worship him, not only without the arm of flesh to protect them, but even when oppressed. For their worship being spiritual, is by the power of the Spirit defended and maintained; but such worships as are carnal, and consist Carnal worships canin carnal and outward ceremonies and observations, need not stand a carnal and outward arm to protect and defend them, else without the arm of they cannot stand and subsist. And therefore it appears, flesh. that the several worships of our opposers, both Papists and Protestants, are of this kind, and not the true spiritual and new covenant worship of Christ; because, as hath been observed, they cannot stand without the protection or countenance of the outward magistrate, neither can be performed, if there be the least opposition: for they are not in the patience of Jesus, to serve and worship him with sufferings, ignominies, calumnies, and reproaches. And from hence have sprung all those wars, fightings, and bloodshed among Christians, while each by the arm of flesh endeavoured to defend and protect their own way and worship; and from this also sprung up that monstrous opinion of persecution; of which we shall speak more at length hereafter.

§ XV. But fourthly; The nature of this worship, which IV. True woris performed by the operation of the Spirit, the natural ship in man being silent, doth appear from these words of Christ, Spirit established John iv. 23, 24: " But the hour cometh, and now is, when by Christ the true worshippers shall worship the Father in Spirit and in Truth: for the Father seeketh such to worship him. God is a Spirit, and they that worship him, must worship him in Spirit and in Truth." This testimony is the more specially to be observed, for that it is both the first, chiefest, and most ample testimony, which Christ gives us of his Christian worship, as different and contra-distinguished from that under the law. For first, he showeth that the season is now come, wherein the worship must be in Spirit and in Truth : for the Father seeketh such to worship him. so then it is no more a worship consisting in outward observations, to be performed by man at set times or opportunities, which he can do in his own will, and by his own natural strength : for else it would not differ in matter, but **The reason Christ gives for a worship in Spirit.** only in some circumstances from that under the law. Next, as for a reason of this worship, we need not give any other, and indeed none can give a better than that which Christ giveth, which I think should be sufficient to satisfy every Christian, to wit, " GOD IS A SPIRIT, and they that worship him, must worship him in Spirit and in Truth." As this ought to be received, because it is the words of Christ, so also it is founded upon so clear a demonstration of reason, as sufficiently evidenceth its verity. For Christ excellently argues from the analogy that ought to be betwixt the object, and the worship directed thereunto :

**Arg.**   God is a Spirit ;

Therefore he must be worshipped in Spirit.

This is so certain, that it can suffer no contradiction ; yea, and this analogy is so necessary to be minded, that under the law, when God instituted and appointed that ceremonial worship to the Jews, because that worship was outward, that there might be an analogy, he saw it necessary to condescend to them as in a special manner, to dwell betwixt the cherubims within the tabernacle, and afterwards to make the temple of Jerusalem in a sort his habitation, and cause something of an outward glory and majesty to appear, by causing fire from heaven to consume **The glory of the outward temple.** the sacrifices, and filling the temple with a cloud : through and by which mediums, visible to the outward eye, he manifested himself proportionably to that outward worship which he had commanded them to perform. So now under the new covenant, he seeing meet in his heavenly wisdom to lead his children in a path more heavenly and spiritual, and in a way more easy and familiar, and also purposing to disappoint carnal and outward observations, that his may have an eye more to an inward glory and kingdom than to an outward, he hath given us for an example hereof the appearance of his beloved Son, the Lord Jesus Christ, who (as Moses delivered the Israelites out of their outward bondage, and by outwardly destroying their enemies) hath delivered and doth deliver us by suffering, and dying by the hands of his enemies; thereby triumphing over the devil, and his and our inward enemies, and delivering us therefrom. He hath also instituted an inward and spiritual worship: so that God now tieth not his people to the temple of Jerusalem, nor yet unto outward ceremonies and observations; but taketh the heart of every Christian for a temple to dwell in; and there immediately appeareth, and giveth him directions how to serve him in any outward acts. Since, as Christ argueth, God is a Spirit, he will now be worshipped in the Spirit, where he reveals himself, and dwelleth with the contrite in heart. Now, since it is the heart of man that now is become the temple of God, in which he will be worshipped, and no more in particular outward temples, since, as blessed Stephen said, out of the prophet, to the professing Jews of old, "The most High dwelleth not in temples made with hands," as before the glory of the Lord descended to fill the outward temple, it behoved to be purified and cleansed, and all polluted stuff removed out of it; yea, and the place for the tabernacle was overlaid with gold, the most precious and cleanest of metals; so also before God be worshipped in the inward temple of the heart, it must also be purged of its own filth, and all its own thoughts and imaginations, that so it may be fit to receive the Spirit of God, and to be actuated by it. And doth not this directly lead us to that inward silence, of which we have spoken, and exactly pointed out? And further, This worship must be in truth; intimating, that this spiritual worship, thus acted, is only and properly

*As Moses did from outward, so Christ delivers his from inward slavery.*

30 *  2 u

a true worship; as being that which, for the reasons above observed, cannot be counterfeited by the enemy, nor yet performed by the hypocrite.

§ XVI. And though this worship be indeed very different from the divers established invented worships among Christians, and therefore may seem strange to many, yet hath it been testified of, commended and practised, by the most pious of all sorts, in all ages, as by many evident testimonies might be proved. So that from the professing and practising thereof the name of Mystics hath arisen, as of a certain sect, greatly commended by all, whose writings are full both of the explanation and of the commendation of this sort of worship; where they plentifully assert this inward introversion and abstraction of the mind, as they call it, from all images and thoughts, and the prayer of the will: yea, they look upon this as the height of Christian perfection; so that some of them, though professed Papists, do not doubt to affirm, "That such as have attained this method of worship, or are aiming at it, as in a book, called Sancta Sophia, put out by the English Benedictines, printed at Doway, Anno, 1657, Tract I., sect. ii., cap. 5, need not, nor ought to trouble or busy themselves with frequent and unnecessary confessions, with exercising corporal labours and austerities, the using of vocal voluntary prayers, the hearing of a number of masses, or set devotions, or exercises to saints, or prayers for the dead, or having solicitous and distracting cares to gain indulgences, by going to such and such churches, or adjoining one's self to confraternities, or entangling one's self with vows and promises; because such kind of things hinder the soul from observing the operations of the Divine Spirit in it, and from having liberty to follow the Spirit whither it would draw her." And yet who knows not that in such kind of observations the very substance of the Popish religion consisteth? Yet nevertheless, it appears by this, and many other passages, which out of their Mystic writers might be mentioned, how they look upon this worship as excelling all other; and that such as arrived here

*A certain sect of Mystics, among the Papists, their inward exercise. See Sancta Sophia, printed An. Dom. 1657.*

*The English Benedictines' testimony for the spiritual worship, against their masses and set devotions.*

unto, hal no absolute need of the others: yea, see the Life of Balthazar Alvares, in the same Sancta Sophia, Tract III., sect. i., cap. 7, such as tasted of this, quickly confessed, that the other forms and ceremonies of worship were useless as to them; neither did they perform them as things necessary, but merely for order or example's sake. And therefore, though some of them were so over-clouded with the common darkness of their profession, yet could they affirm that this spiritual worship was still to be retained and sought for, even though it should become necessary to omit their outward ceremonies. Hence Bernard, as in many other places, so in his Epistle to William, abbot of the same order, saith, " Take heed to the rule of God; the kingdom of God is within you :" and afterwards, saying, That their outward orders and rules should be observed, he adds: " But otherwise, when it shall happen that one of these two must be omitted, in such a case these are much rather to be omitted than those former : for by how much the Spirit is more excellent and noble than the body, by so much are spiritual exercises more profitable than corporal." Is not that then the best of worships, which the best of men in all ages, and of all sects, have commended, and which is most suitable to the doctrine of Christ? I say, Is not that worship to be followed and performed? And so much the rather, as God hath raised a people to testify for it, and preach it, to their great refreshment and strengthening, in the very face of the world, and notwithstanding much opposition; who do not, as these Mystics, make of it a mystery, only to be attained by a few men or women in a cloister ; or, as their mistake was, after wearying themselves with many outward ceremonies and observations, as if it were the consequence of such a labour; but who in the free love of God, who respects not persons, and was near to hear and reveal himself, as well to Cornelius, a centurion and a Roman, as to Simeon and Anna; and who discovered his glory to Mary, a poor handmaid, and to the poor shepherds, rather than to the high priests and devout proselytes among the

*Be nard preferring the Spirit above Popish orders*

*Those Mystics did confine that mystery to a cloister*

Jews, in and according to his free love, finding that God is revealing and establishing this worship, and making many poor tradesmen, yea, young boys and girls, witnesses of it, do entreat and beseech all to lay aside their own will-worships, and voluntary acts, performed in their own wills, and by their own mere natural strength and power, without retiring out of their vain imaginations and thoughts, or feeling the pure Spirit of God to move and stir in them; that they may come to practise this acceptable worship, which is in Spirit and in Truth. But against this worship they object.

OBJ. 1

§ XVII. First, it seem to be an unprofitable exercise for a man to be doing or thinking nothing; and that one might be much better employed, either in meditating upon some good subject, or otherwise praying to or praising God.

ANSW.

I answer; That is not unprofitable, which is of absolute necessity before any other duty can be acceptably performed, as we have shown this waiting to be. Moreover, those have but a carnal and gross apprehension of God, and of the things of his kingdom, who imagine that men please him by their own workings and actings: whereas, as hath been shown, the first step for a man to fear God, is to cease from his own thoughts and imaginations, and suffer God's Spirit to work in him. For we must "cease to do evil," ere we "learn to do well;" and this meddling in things spiritual by man's own natural understanding, is one of the greatest and most dangerous evils that man is incident to; being that which occasioned our first parents' fall, to wit, a forwardness to desire to know things, and a meddling with them, both without and contrary to the Lord's command.

Isa. i. 16, 17.
We must cease to do ill, ere we learn to do well.

OBJ. 2.

Secondly, Some object, If your worship merely consist in inwardly retiring to the Lord, and feeling of his Spirit arise in you, and then to do outward acts as ye are led by it, what need ye have public meetings at set times and places, since every one may enjoy this at home? Or should not every one stay at home, until they be particularly moved to go to such a place at such a time; since to

Set times and places for meetings.

meet at set times and places seems to be an outward observation and ceremony, contrary to what ye at other times
assert?

I answer, first; To meet at set times and places is not A *sw.*
any religious act, or part of worship in itself; but only an Public
outward conveniency, necessary for our seeing one another, meetings,
their use
so long as we are clothed with this outward tabernacle: and reason
asserted.
and therefore our meeting at set times and places is not a
part of our worship, but a preparatory accommodation of
our outward man, in order to a public visible worship;
since we set not about the visible acts of worship when we
meet together, until we be led thereunto by the Spirit of
God. Secondly, God hath seen meet, so long as his children are in this world, to make use of the outward senses,
not only as a means to convey spiritual life, as by speaking,
praying, praising, &c., which cannot be done to mutual
edification, but when we hear and see one another; but
also to entertain an outward, visible testimony for his name
in the world: he causeth the inward life (which is also
many times not conveyed by the outward senses) the more
to abound, when his children assemble themselves diligently
together to wait upon him; so that "as iron sharpeneth Prov xxvii
iron," the seeing of the faces one of another, when both 17.
are inwardly gathered unto the life, giveth occasion for the
life secretly to rise, and pass from vessel to vessel. And
as many candles lighted, and put in one place, do greatly
augment the light, and make it more to shine forth, so
when many are gathered together into the same life, there
is more of the glory of God, and his power appears, to the
refreshment of each individual; for that he partakes not
only of the light and life raised in himself, but in all the
rest. And therefore Christ hath particularly promised a
blessing to such as assemble together in his name, seeing
he will be "in the midst of them," Matth. xviii. 20. And
the author to the Hebrews doth precisely prohibit the neglect of this duty, as being of very dangerous and dreadful
consequence, in these words: Heb. x. 24, "And let us
consider one another, to provoke unto love, and to good

works; not forsaking the assembling of ourselves together, as the manner of some is; — For if we sin wilfully, after that we have received the knowledge of the truth, there remaineth no more sacrifice for sins." And therefore the Lord hath shown that he hath a particular respect to such as thus assemble themselves together, because that thereby a public testimony for him is upheld in the earth, and his name is thereby glorified; and therefore such as are right in their spirits, are naturally drawn to keep the meetings of God's people, and never want a spiritual influence to lead them thereunto: and if any do it in a mere customary way, they will no doubt suffer condemnation for it. Yet cannot the appointing of places and times be accounted a ceremony and observation, done in man's will, in the worship of God, seeing none can say that it is an act of worship, but only a mere presenting of our persons in order to it, as is abovesaid. Which that it was practised by the primitive church and saints, all our adversaries do acknowledge.

Lastly, Some object, That this manner of worship in silence is not to be found in all the scripture:

I answer; We make not silence to be the sole matter of our worship; since, as I have said above, there are many meetings, which are seldom altogether silent; some or other are still moved either to preach, pray, or praise: and so in this our meetings cannot be but like the meetings of the primitive churches recorded in scripture, since our adversaries confess that they did preach and pray by the Spirit. And then what absurdity is it to suppose, that at some times the Spirit did not move them to these outward acts, and that then they were silent? Since we may well conclude they did not speak until they were moved; and so no doubt had sometimes silence. Acts ii. 1, before the Spirit came upon them, it is said, — " They were all with one accord in one place;" and then it is said, The Spirit suddenly came upon them; but no mention is made of any one speaking at that time; and I would willingly know what absurdity our adversaries can infer, should we conclude they were a while silent?

But if it be urged, That a whole silent meeting cannot Inst.
be found in scripture;

I answer; Supposing such a thing were not recorded, it Answ.
will not therefore follow that it is not lawful; since it naturally followeth from other scripture precepts, as we have Silent
proved this doth. For seeing the scripture commands to meetings
are proved
meet together, and when met, the scripture prohibits prayers from scrip
or preachings, but as the Spirit moveth thereunto; if people reason.
meet together, and the Spirit move not to such acts, it will
necessarily follow that they must be silent. But further,
there might have been many such things among the saints
of old though not recorded in scripture; and yet we have
enough in scripture, signifying that such things were. For
Job sat silent seven days with his friends together; here
was a long silent meeting: see also Ezra ix. 4, and Ezekiel
xiv. 1, and xx. 1. Thus having shown the excellency of
this worship, proving it from scripture and reason, and answered the objections which are commonly made against
it, which, though it may suffice to the explanation and
proof of our proposition, yet I shall add something more
particularly of preaching, praying, and singing, and so proceed to the following proposition.

§ XVIII. Preaching, as it is used both among Papists
and Protestants, is for one man to take some place or verse I.
of scripture, and thereon speak for an hour or two, what he What
preaching
hath studied and premeditated in his closet, and gathered is with the
Protestants
together from his own inventions, or from the writings and and Papists.
observations of others; and then having got it by heart, as A studied
talk an
a school-boy doth his lesson, he brings it forth, and repeats hour or
it before the people: and how much the more fertile and two.
strong a man's invention is, and the more industrious and
laborious he is in collecting such observations, and can
utter them with the excellency of speech and human eloquence, so much the more is he accounted an able and
excellent preacher.

To this we oppose, that when the saints are met toge
ther, and every one gathered to the gift and grace of God
in themselves, he that ministereth, being actuated thereunto
by the arising of the grace in himself, ought to speak forth
what the Spirit of God furnisheth him with; not minding
the eloquence and wisdom of words, but the demonstration
of the Spirit and of power: and that either in the interpreting some part of scripture, in case the Spirit, which is the
good remembrancer, lead him so to do, or otherwise words
of exhortation, advice, reproof, and instruction, or the sense
of some spiritual experiences: all which will still be agreeable to the scripture, though perhaps not relative to, nor
founded upon any particular chapter or verse, as a text.
Now let us examine and consider which of these two sorts
of preaching is most agreeable to the precepts and practice
of Christ and his apostles, and the primitive church, recorded
in scripture? For, first, as to their preaching upon a text, if
it were not merely customary or premeditated, but done by
the immediate motion of the Spirit, we should not blame
it; but to do it as they do, there is neither precept nor
practice, that ever I could observe, in the New Testament,
as a part of the instituted worship thereof.

But they allege, That Christ took the book of Isaiah, and
read out of it, and spake therefrom; and that Peter preached from a sentence of the prophet Joel.

ANSW.
1. Christ's
and Peter's
speaking
was not by
premedita-
ion.

I answer, That Christ and Peter did it not but as immediately actuated and moved thereunto by the Spirit of
God, and that without premeditation, which I suppose our
adversaries will not deny; in which case we willingly approve of it. But what is this to their customary conned
way, without either waiting for or expecting the movings
or leadings of the Spirit? Moreover, that neither Christ
nor Peter did it as a settled custom or form, to be constantly practised by all the ministers of the church, appears,
in that most of all the sermons recorded of Christ and his
apostles in scripture were without this, as appears from
Christ's sermon upon the mount, Mat. v. 1, &c.; Mark iv.
1, &c., and Paul's preaching to the Athenians, and to the

Jews, &c. As then it appears that this method of preaching is not grounded upon any scripture precept, so the nature of it is contrary to the preaching of Christ under the new covenant, as expressed and recommended in scripture; for Christ, in sending forth his disciples, expressly mentioneth, that they are not to speak of or from themselves, or to forecast beforehand, but that which the Spirit in the same hour shall teach them, as is particularly mentioned in the three evangelists, Mat. x. 20; Mark xiii. 11; Luke xii. 12. Now if Christ gave this order to his disciples before he departed from them, as that which they were to practise during his abode outwardly with them, much more were they to do it after his departure, since then they were more especially to receive the Spirit, "to lead them in all things," and to "bring all things to their remembrance," John xiv. 26. And if they were to do so when they appeared before the magistrates and princes of the earth, much more in the worship of God, when they stand specially before him; seeing, as is above shown, his worship is to be performed in Spirit; and therefore after their receiving of the Holy Ghost it is said, Acts ii. 4, "They spake as the Spirit gave them utterance," not what they had studied and gathered from books in their closets in a premeditated way.

Franciscus Lambertus, before cited, speaketh well and showeth their hypocrisy, Tract. v., of Prophecy, chap. 3, saying, "Where are they now that glory in their inventions, who say, a fine invention! a fine invention! This they call invention, which themselves have made up; but what have the faithful to do with such kind of inventions? It is not figments, nor yet inventions, that we will have, but things that are solid, invincible, eternal, and heavenly; not which men have invented, but which God hath revealed: for if we believe the scriptures, our invention profiteth nothing, but to provoke God to our ruin." And afterwards, "Beware," saith he, "that thou determine not precisely to speak what before thou hast meditated, whatsoever it be; for though it be lawful to determine the text

Franciscus Lambertus's testimony against the priests' studied inventions and figments.

which thou art to expound, yet not at all the interpretation; lest if thou so dost, thou take from the Holy Spirit that which is his, to wit, to direct thy speech, that thou mayest prophesy in the name of the Lord, void of all learning, meditation, and experience, and as if thou hadst studied nothing at all, committing thy heart, thy tongue, and thyself wholly unto his Spirit, and trusting nothing to thy former studying or meditation; but saying with thyself, in great confidence of the divine promise, 'The Lord will give a word with much power unto those that preach the gospel.' But above all things be careful thou follow not the manner of hypocrites, who have written almost word for word what they are to say, as if they were to repeat some verses upon a theatre, having learned all their preaching as they do that act tragedies. And afterwards, when they are in the place of prophesying, pray the Lord to direct their tongue; but in the mean time, shutting up the way of the Holy Spirit, they determine to say nothing but what they have written. O unhappy kind of prophets, yea and truly cursed, which depend not upon God's Spirit, but upon their own writings or meditation! Why prayest thou to the Lord, thou false prophet, to give thee his holy Spirit, by which thou mayest speak things profitable, and yet thou repellest the Spirit? Why preferrest thou thy meditation or study to the Spirit of God? Otherwise why committest thou not thyself to the Spirit?"

2. The words man's wisdom brings beget not faith.

§ XIX. Secondly, This manner of preaching as used by them, considering that they also affirm that it may be and often is performed by men who are wicked, or void of true grace, cannot only not edify the church, beget or nourish true faith, but is destructive to it, being directly contrary to the nature of the Christian and apostolic ministry mentioned in the scriptures: for the apostle preached the gospel " not in the wisdom of words, lest the cross of Christ should be of none effect," 1 Cor. i. 17. But this preaching not being done by the actings and movings of God's Spirit, but by man's invention and eloquence, in his own will, and through his natural and acquired parts and learning, is in the wisdom of words, and therefore the cross of Christ is thereby made of none effect. The apostle's speech and preaching was not "with enticing words of man's wisdom, but in demonstration of the Spirit and of power," that the faith of their hearers "should not stand in the wisdom of men, but in the power of God," 1 Cor. ii. 3, 4, 5. But this preaching having nothing of the Spirit and power in it, both the preachers and hearers confessing they wait for no such thing, nor yet are sometimes sensible of it, must needs stand in the enticing words of man's wisdom, since it is by the mere wisdom of man it is sought after, and the mere strength of man's eloquence and enticing words it is uttered ; and therefore no wonder if the faith of such as hear and depend upon such preachers and preachings stand in the wisdom of men, and not in the power of God. The apostles declared, That they "spake not in the words which man's wisdom teacheth, but which the Holy Ghost teacheth," 1 Cor. ii. 13. But these preachers confess that they are strangers to the Holy Ghost, his motions and operations, neither do they wait to feel them, and therefore they speak in the words which their own natural wisdom and learning teach them, mixing them in, and adding them to, such words as they steal out of the scripture and other books, and therefore speak not what the Holy Ghost teacheth.

Thirdly, This is contrary to the method and order of the primitive church mentioned by the apostle, 1 Cor. xiv. 30, &c., where in preaching every one is to wait for his revelation, and to give place one unto another, according as things are revealed; but here there is no waiting for a revelation, but the preacher must speak, and not that which is revealed unto him, but what he hath prepared and premeditated before hand. *3. True church's method was to speak by revelation.*

Lastly, By this kind of preaching the Spirit of God, which should be the chief instructer and teacher of God's people, and whose influence is that only which makes all preaching effectual and beneficial for the edifying of souls, is shut out, and man's natural wisdom, learning, and parts *4. The Spirit is shut out by priests from being the teacher.*

set up and exalted; which no doubt is a great and chief reason why the preaching among the generality of Christians is so unfruitful and unsuccessful. Yea, according to this doctrine, the devil may preach, and ought to be heard also, seeing he both knoweth the truth, and hath as much eloquence as any. But what avails excellency of speech, if the demonstration and power of the Spirit be wanting, which toucheth the conscience? We see that when the devil confessed to the truth, yet Christ would have none of his testimony. And as these pregnant testimonies of the scripture do prove this part of preaching to be contrary to the doctrine of Christ, so do they also prove that of ours before affirmed to be comformable thereunto.

*Object.*

§ XX. But if any object after this manner, Have not many been benefited, yea, and both converted and edified by the ministry of such as have premeditated their preaching? Yea, and hath not the Spirit often concurred by its divine influence with preachings thus premeditated, so as they have been powerfully borne in upon the souls of the hearers to their advantage?

*Answ.*

I answer, Though that be granted, which I shall not deny, it will not infer that the thing was good in itself,

*Paul persecuting was converted, is therefore persecuting good?*

more than because Paul was met with by Christ to the converting of his soul riding to Damascus to persecute the saints, that he did well in so doing. Neither particular actions, nor yet whole congregations, as we above observed, are to be measured by the acts of God's condescension in times of ignorance. But besides, it hath oftentimes fallen out, that God, having a regard to the simplicity and integrity either of the preacher or hearers, hath fallen in upon the heart of a preacher by his power and holy influence, and thereby hath led him to speak things that were not in his premeditated discourse, and which perhaps he never thought on before; and those passing ejaculations and unpremeditated but living exhortations, have proved more beneficial and refreshing both to preacher and hearers than all their premeditated sermons. But all that will not allow them to continue in these things which in themselves are not approved, but contrary to the practice of the apostles, when God is raising up a people to serve him, according to the primitive purity and spirituality; yea, such acts of God's condescension, in times of darkness and ignorance, should engage all more and more to follow him, according as he reveals his most perfect and spiritual way.

§ XXI. Having hitherto spoken of preaching, now it is fit to speak of praying, concerning which the like controversy ariseth. Our adversaries, whose religion is all for the most part outside, and such whose acts are the mere product of man's natural will and abilities, as they can preach, so can they pray when they please, and therefore have their set particular prayers. I meddle not with the controversies among themselves concerning this, some of them being for set prayers, as a liturgy, others for such as are conceived extempore: it suffices me that all of them agree in this, That the motions and influence of the Spirit of God are not necessary to be previous thereunto; and therefore they have set times in their public worship, as before and after preaching, and in their private devotion, as morning and evening, and before and after meat, and other such occasions, at which they precisely set about the performing of their prayers, by speaking words to God, whether they feel any motion or influence of the Spirit or not; so that some of the chiefest have confessed that they have thus prayed without the motions or assistance of the Spirit, acknowledging that they sinned in so doing; yet they said they looked upon it as their duty to do so, though to pray without the Spirit be sin. We freely confess that prayer is both very profitable, and a necessary duty commanded, and fit to be practised frequently by all Christians; but as we can do nothing without Christ, so neither can we pray without the concurrence and assistance of his Spirit. But that the state of the controversy may be the better understood, let it be considered, first, that prayer is two-fold, inward and outward. Inward prayer is that secret turning of the mind towards God, whereby,

*Marginal notes:*
II. Of prayer, how the outward is distinguished from the inward.

The priests set times to preach and pray, deny the Spirit.

What inward prayer is.

31 *

being secretly touched and awakened by the light of Christ in the conscience, and so bowed down under the sense of its iniquities, unworthiness, and misery, it looks up to God, and joining with the secret shinings of the seed of God, it breathes towards him, and is constantly breathing forth some secret desires and aspirations towards him. It is in this sense that we are so frequently in scripture commanded to pray continually, Luke xviii. 1; 1 Thess. v. 17; Eph. vi. 18; Luke xxi. 36, which cannot be understood of outward prayer, because it were impossible that men should be always upon their knees, expressing words of prayer; and this would hinder them from the exercise of those duties no less positively commanded. Outward prayer is, when as the Spirit being thus in the exercise of inward retirement, and feeling the breathing of the Spirit of God to arise powerfully in the soul, receives strength and liberty by a superadded motion and influence of the spirit to bring forth either audible sighs, groans or words, and that either in public assemblies, or in private, or at meat, &c.

*What outward prayer is.*

As then inward prayer is necessary at all times, so, so long as the day of every man's visitation lasteth, he never wants some influence less or more, for the practice of it; because he no sooner retires his mind, and considers himself in God's presence, but he finds himself in the practice of it.

*Inward prayer necessary at all times.*

The outward exercise of prayer, as needing a greater and superadded influence and motion of the Spirit, as it cannot be continually practised, so neither can it be so readily, so as to be effectually performed, until his mind be some time acquainted with the inward; therefore such as are diligent and watchful in their minds, and much retired in the exercise of this inward prayer, are more capable to be frequent in the use of the outward, because that this holy influence doth more constantly attend them, and they being better acquainted with, and accustomed to, the motions of God's Spirit, can easily perceive and discern them. And indeed, as such who are most diligent

*Outward prayer doth require a superadded influence.*

nave a near access to God, and he taketh most delight to draw them by his Spirit to approach and call upon him, so when many are gathered together in this watchful mind, God doth frequently pour forth the Spirit of prayer among them and stir them thereunto, to the edifying and building up of one another in love. But because this outward prayer depends upon the inward, as that which must follow *We cannot fix set times to speak and pray.* it, and cannot be acceptably performed but as attended with a superadded influence and motion of the Spirit, therefore cannot we prefix set times to pray outwardly, so as to lay a necessity to speak words at such and such times, whether we feel this heavenly influence and assistance or no ; for that we judge were a tempting of God, and a coming before him without due preparation. We think it fit for us to present ourselves before him by this inward retirement of the mind, and so to proceed further, as his Spirit shall help us and draw us thereunto ; and we find that the Lord accepts of this, yea, and seeth meet sometimes to exercise us in this silent place for the trial of our patience, without allowing us to speak further, that he may teach us not to rely upon outward performances, or satisfy ourselves, as too many do, with the saying of our prayers ; and that our dependence upon him may be the more firm and constant, to wait for the holding out of his sceptre, and for his allowance to draw near unto him, with greater freedom and enlargement of Spirit upon our hearts towards him. Yet nevertheless we do not deny but sometimes God, upon particular occasions, very suddenly, yea, upon the very first turning in of the mind, may give power and liberty to bring forth words or acts of outward prayer, so as the soul can scarce discern any previous motion, but the influence and bringing forth thereof may be as it were *simul & semel :* nevertheless that saying of Bernard is true, that all prayer is lukewarm, which hath not an inspiration preceding it. Though we affirm that none ought to go about prayer without this motion, yet we do not deny but such sin as neglect prayer ; but their sin is in that they *Such sin as are neglecting prayer.* come not to that place where they may feel that which would lead them thereunto. And therefore we question not but many, through neglect of this inward watchfulness and retiredness of mind, miss many precious opportunities to pray, and thereby are guilty in the sight of God; yet would they sin if they should set about the act until they first felt the influence. For as he grossly offends his master that lieth in his bed and sleeps, and neglects to do his master's business; yet if such a one should suddenly get up, without putting on his clothes, or taking along with him those necessary tools and instruments, without which he could not possibly work, and should forwardly fall a doing to no purpose, he would be so far thereby from repairing his former fault, that he would justly incur a new censure: and as one that is careless and otherways busied may miss to hear one speaking unto him, or even not hear the bell of a clock, though striking hard by him, so may many, through negligence, miss to hear God oftentimes calling upon them, and giving them access to pray unto him; yet will not that allow them, without his liberty, in their own wills to fall to work.

*A forward and a careless servant answers not his duty.*

And lastly, Though this be the only true and proper method of prayer, as that which is alone acceptable to God, yet shall we not deny but he oftentimes answered the prayers and concurred with the desires of some, especially in times of darkness, who have greatly erred herein; so that some that have sat down in formal prayer, though far wrong in the matter as well as manner, without the assistance or influence of God's Spirit, yet have found him to take occasion there-through to break in upon their souls, and wonderfully tender and refresh them; yet as in preaching and elsewhere hath afore been observed, that will not prove any such practices, or be a just let to hinder any from coming to practise that pure, spiritual, and acceptable prayer, which God is again restoring and leading his people into, out of all superstitions and mere empty formalities. The state of the controversy, and our sense thereof, being thus clearly stated, will both obviate many objections, and make the answer to others more brief and easy. I shall

*In times of darkness God did often hear their prayers.*

first prove this spiritual prayer by some short considerations from scripture, and then answer the objections of our opposers, which will also serve to refute their method and manner thereof.

First, spiritual prayer proved from scripture.

§ XXII. And first, That there is a necessity of this inward retirement of the mind as previous to prayer, that the Spirit may be felt to draw thereunto, appears, for that in most of those places where prayer is commanded, watching is prefixed thereunto, as necessary to go before, as Matt. xxiv. 42; Mark xiii. 33, and xiv. 38; Luke xxi. 36, from which it is evident that this watching was to go before prayer. Now to what end is this watching, or what is it, but a waiting to feel God's Spirit to draw unto prayer, that so it may be done acceptably? For since we are to pray always in the Spirit, and cannot pray of ourselves without it acceptably, this watching must be for this end recommended to us, as preceding prayer, that we may watch and wait for the seasonable time to pray, which is when the Spirit moves thereunto.

I. God's Spirit must be felt to move the mind to prayer.

Eph. vi. 18

Secondly, This necessity of the Spirit's moving and concurrence appears abundantly from that of the apostle Paul, Rom. viii. 26, 27: "Likewise the Spirit also helpeth our infirmities: for we know not what we should pray for as we ought; but the Spirit itself maketh intercession for us with groanings which cannot be uttered. And he that searcheth the hearts knoweth what is the mind of the Spirit, because he maketh intercession for the saints according to the will of God." Which first holds forth the incapacity of men as of themselves to pray or call upon God in their own wills, even such as have received the faith of Christ, and are in measure sanctified by it, as was the church of Rome, to whom the apostle then wrote. Secondly, It holds forth that which can only help and assist men to pray, to wit, the Spirit, as that without which they cannot do it acceptably to God, nor beneficially to their own souls. Thirdly, The manner and way of the Spirit's intercession, with sighs and groans which are unutterable. And fourthly, That God receiveth graciously the prayers of such as are

II. We know not how to pray but as the Spirit helps.

presented and offered unto himself by the Spirit, knowing
it to be according to his will.   Now it cannot be conceived
but this order of prayer thus asserted by the apostle is most
consistent with those other testimonies of scripture, commending and recommending to us the use of prayer.   From
which I thus argue,

**ARG.**

If any man know not how to pray, neither can do it
without the help of the Spirit, then it is to no purpose for
him, but altogether unprofitable, to pray without it.

But the first is true, therefore also the last.

**III.**
**Pray al-**
**ways in the**
**Spirit, and**
**watching**
**thereunto.**

Thirdly, This necessity of the Spirit to true prayer appears from Eph. vi. 18, and Jude 20, where the apostle
commands " to pray always in the Spirit, and watching
thereunto ;" which is as much as if he had said, that we
were never to pray without the Spirit, or watching thereunto.   And Jude showeth that such prayers as are in the
Holy Ghost only, tend to the building up of ourselves in
our most holy faith.

**IV.**
**Man can-**
**not call**
**Christ Lord**
**but by the**
**Holy**
**Ghost.**

Fourthly, The apostle Paul saith expressly, 1 Cor. xii.
3 : " That no man can say that Jesus is the Lord but by
the Holy Ghost :" if then Jesus cannot be thus rightly
named but by the Holy Ghost, far less can he be acceptably called upon.   Hence the same apostle declares, 1 Cor.
xiv. 15, that he " will pray with the Spirit," &c.   A clear
evidence that it was none of his method to pray without it.

**V.**
**God will**
**not hear the**
**prayers of**
**the wicked**

But fifthly, All prayer without the Spirit is abomination,
such as are the prayers of the wicked,   Prov. xxviii. 9.
And the confidence that the saints have that God will hear
them, is, if they " ask any thing according to his will,"
1 John v. 14.   So if the prayer be not according to his
will, there is no ground of confidence that he will hear.
Now our adversaries will acknowledge that prayers without
the Spirit are not according to the will of God, and therefore such as pray without it have no ground to expect an
answer : for indeed to bid a man pray without the Spirit is
all one as to bid one see without eyes, work without hands,
or go without feet.   And to desire a man to fall to prayer

ere the Spirit in some measure less or more move him thereunto, is to desire a man to see before he opens his eyes, or to walk before he rises up, or to work with his hands before he moves them.

§ XXIII. But lastly, From this false opinion of praying without the Spirit, and not judging it necessary to be waited for, as that which may be felt to move us thereunto, hath proceeded all the superstition and idolatry that is among those called Christians, and those many abominations wherewith the Lord is provoked, and his Spirit grieved; so that many deceive themselves now, as the Jews did of old, thinking it sufficient if they pay their daily sacrifices, and offer their customary oblations; from thence thinking all is well, and creating a false peace to themselves, as the whore in the Proverbs, because they have offered up their sacrifices of morning and evening prayers. And therefore it is manifest that their constant use of these things doth not a whit influence their lives and conversations, but they remain for the most part as bad as ever. Yea, it is frequent both among Papists and Protestants, for them to leap as it were out of their vain, light, and profane conversations at their set hours and seasons, and fall to their customary devotion; and then, when it is scarce finished, and the words to God scarce out, the former profane talk comes after it; so that the same wicked profane spirit of this world actuates them in both. If there be any such thing as vain oblations, or prayers that are abomination, which God heareth not, (as is certain there are, and the scripture testifies, Isa. lxvi. 3; Jer. xiv. 12,) certainly such prayers as are acted in man's will, and by his own strength, without God's Spirit, must be of that number.

*VI. All sacrifice is sin, not offered by the Spirit.*

§ XXIV. Let this suffice for proof. I shall now proceed to answer their objections, when I have said something concerning joining in prayer with others. Those that pray together with one accord use not only to concur in their spirits, but also in the gesture of their body, which we also willingly approve of. It becometh those who approach

*Concerning joining in prayer with others.*

before God to pray, that they do it with bowed knees, and with their heads uncovered, which is our practice.

**OBJ. 1.** But here ariseth a controversy, Whether it be lawful to join with others by those external signs of reverence, albeit not in heart, who pray formally, not waiting for the motion of the Spirit, nor judging it necessary.

**ANSW.**
**The reason why we cannot join in prayer.**
We answer, Not at all; and for our testimony in this thing we have suffered not a little. For when it hath fallen out, that either accidentally, or to witness against their worship, we have been present during the same, and have not found it lawful for us to bow with them thereunto, they have often persecuted us, not only with reproaches, but also with strokes and cruel beatings. For this cause they used to accuse us of pride, profanity, and madness, as if we had no respect or reverence to the worship of God, and as if we judged none could pray, or were heard of God, but ourselves. Unto all which, and many more reproaches of this kind, we answer briefly and modestly, That it sufficeth us that we are found so doing, neither through pride, nor madness, nor profanity, but merely lest we should hurt our consciences; the reason of which is plain and evident: for since our principle and doctrine oblige us to believe that the prayers of those who themselves confess they are not actuated by the Spirit, are abominations, how can we with a safe conscience join with them?

**OB. 2** If they urge, That this is the height of uncharitableness and arrogancy, as if we judged ourselves always to pray by the Spirit's motion, but they never; as if we were never deceived by praying without the motions of the Spirit, and that they were never actuated by it, seeing albeit they judge not the motion of the Spirit always necessary, they confess nevertheless, that it is very profitable and comfortable, and they feel it often influencing them; which that it sometimes falls out we cannot deny;

**ANSW.** To all which I answer distinctly, If it were their known and avowed doctrine not to pray without the motion of the Spirit, and that, seriously holding thereunto, they did not bind themselves to pray at certain prescribed times pre

cisely, at which times they determine to pray, though without the Spirit, then indeed we might be accused of uncharitableness and pride, if we never joined with them;
and if they so taught and practised, I doubt not but it
would be lawful for us so to do, unless there should appear
some manifest and evident hypocrisy and delusion. But
seeing they confess that they pray without the Spirit, and
seeing God hath persuaded us that such prayers are abominable, how can we with a safe conscience join with an
abomination? That God sometimes condescends to them,
we do not deny; although now, when the spiritual worship
is openly proclaimed, and all are invited unto it, the case
is otherwise than in those old times of apostasy and darkness; and therefore, albeit any should begin to pray in our
presence, not expecting the motion of the Spirit; yet if it
manifestly appear that God in condescension did concur
with such a one, then according to God's will we should
not refuse to join also; but this is rare, lest thence they
should be confirmed in their false principle. And although
this seems hard in our profession, nevertheless it is so confirmed by the authority both of scripture and right reason,
that many convinced thereof have embraced this part before other truths, which were easier, and, as they seemed
to some, clearer. Among whom is memorable of late years
Alexander Skein, a magistrate of the city of Aberdeen, a
man very modest, and very averse from giving offence to
others, who nevertheless being overcome by the power of
truth in this matter, behoved for this cause to separate
himself from the public assemblies and prayers, and join
himself unto us; who also gave the reason of his change,
and likewise succinctly, but yet substantially, comprehended this controversy concerning worship in some short questions, which he offered to the public preachers of the city,
and which I think meet to insert in this place.

1. Whether or not should any act of God's worship be
gone about without the motions, leadings, and actings of
the Holy Spirit?

2 If the motions of the Spirit be necessary to every par-

32

*Shall we confirm the hypocrites when pray-ing?*

*Some ques-tions of A. Skein pro-posed to t: preachers in Aber-deen.*

ticular duty, whether should he be waited upon, that all
our acts and words may be according as he gives utterance
and assistance?

3. Whether every one that bears the name of a Christian, or professes to be a Protestant, hath such an uninterrupted measure thereof, that he may, without waiting, go
immediately about the duty?

4. If there be an indisposition and unfitness at some times
for such exercises, at least as to the spiritual and lively
performance thereof, whether ought they to be performed
in that case, and at that time?

5. If any duty be gone about, under pretence that it is
in obedience to the external command, without the spiritual
life and motion necessary, whether such a duty thus performed can in faith be expected to be accepted of God,
Lev. xvi. 1. and not rather reckoned as a bringing of strange fire before
the Lord, seeing it is performed at best by the strength of
natural and acquired parts, and not by the strength and
assistance of the Holy Ghost, which was typified by the
fire that came down from heaven, which alone behoved to
consume the sacrifice and no other?

6. Whether duties gone about in the mere strength of
natural and acquired parts, whether in public or private,
be not as really, upon the matter, an image of man's invention as the popish worship, though not so gross in the
outward appearance? And therefore whether it be not as
real superstition to countenance any worship of that nature,
as it is to countenance popish worship, though there be a
difference in the degree?

7. Whether it be a ground of offence or just scandal to
countenance the worship of those whose professed principle
it is neither to speak for edification, nor to pray, but as the
Holy Ghost shall be pleased to assist them in some measure
less or more; without which they rather choose to be silent,
than to speak without this influence?

Unto these they answered but very coldly and faintly.
whose answers likewise long ago he refuted.

Seeing then God hath called us to his spiritual worship, and to testify against the human and voluntary worships of the apostasy, if we did not this way stand immovable to the truth revealed, but should join with them, both our testimony for God would be weakened and lost, and it would be impossible steadily to propagate this worship in the world, whose progress we dare neither retard nor hinder by any act of ours; though therefore we shall lose not only worldly honour, but even our lives. And truly many Protestants, through their unsteadiness in this thing, for politic ends complying with the Popish abominations, have greatly scandalized their profession, and hurt the reformation; as appeared in the example of the Elector of Saxony; who, in the convention at Augsburg, in the year 1530, being commanded by the Emperor Charles the Fifth to be present at the mass, that he might carry the sword before him, according to his place; which when he justly scrupled to perform, his preachers taking more care for their prince's honour than for his conscience, persuaded him that it was lawful to do it against his conscience. Which was both a very bad example, and great scandal to the reformation, and displeased many; as the author of the History of the Council of Trent, in his first book, well observes. But now I hasten to the objections of our adversaries against this method of praying.

*We must not lose our witnessing for God.*

*Elector of Saxony's scandal given to Protestants.*

*Secondly, Objections against spiritual prayer answered.*

§ XXV. First; They object, That if such particular influences were needful to outward acts of worship, then they should also be needful to inward acts, as to wait, desire, and love God. But this is absurd; therefore also that from whence it follows.

*Obj. 1.*

I answer; That which was said in the state of the controversy cleareth this; because, as to those general duties, there never wants an influence, so long as the day of a man's visitation lasteth; during which time God is always near to him, and wrestling with him by his Spirit, to turn him to himself; so that if he do but stand still, and cease from his evil thoughts, the Lord is near to help him, &c.

*Answ*

But as to the outward acts of prayer, they need a more special motion and influence, as hath been proved.

Obj. 2.   Secondly; They object, That it might be also alleged, that men ought not to do moral duties, as children to honour their parents, men to do right to their neighbours, except the Spirit move them to it.

Answ.   I answer; There is a great difference betwixt these general duties betwixt man and man, and the particular express acts of worship towards God: the one is merely spiritual, and commanded by God to be performed by his Spirit; the other answer their end, as to them whom they are immediately directed to and concern, though done from a mere natural principle of self-love; even as beasts have natural affections one to another, and therefore may be thus performed. Though I shall not deny, but that they are not works accepted of God, or beneficial to the soul, but as they are done in the fear of God, and in his blessing, in which his children do all things, and therefore are accepted and blessed in whatsoever they do.

Obj. 3.   Thirdly; They object, That if a wicked man ought not to pray without a motion of the Spirit, because his prayer would be sinful; neither ought he to plough by the same Prov xxi.4. reason, because the ploughing of the wicked, as well as his praying, is sin.

Answ.   This objection is of the same nature with the former, and therefore may be answered the same way; seeing How acts of there is a great difference betwixt natural acts, such as nature differ from eating, drinking, sleeping, and seeking sustenance for the the Spirit's. body, which things man hath common with beasts, and spiritual acts. And it doth not follow, because man ought not to go about spiritual acts without the Spirit, that therefore he may not go about natural acts without it. The analogy holds better thus, and that for the proof of our affirmation, That as man for the going about natural acts needs his natural spirit; so to perform spiritual acts he needs the Spirit of God. That the natural acts of the wicked and unregenerate are sinful, is not denied; though no* as in themselves, but in so far as man in that state is in all things reprobated in the sight of God.

Fourthly; They object, That wicked men may, according to this doctrine, forbear to pray for years together, alleging, they want a motion to it. Obj. 4.

I answer; The false pretences of wicked men do nothing Answ. invalidate the truth of this doctrine; for at that rate there is no doctrine of Christ, which men might not set aside. That they ought not to pray without the Spirit, is granted; but then they ought to come to that place of watching, That wick- where they may be capable to feel the Spirit's motion. ed men neglect the They sin indeed in not praying; but the cause of this sin motions of the Spirit is their not watching: so their neglect proceeds not from to pray. this doctrine, but from their disobedience to it; seeing if they did pray without this, it would be a double sin, and no fulfilling of the command to pray: nor yet would their prayer, without this Spirit, be useful unto them. And this our adversaries are forced to acknowledge in another case: for they say, It is a duty incumbent on Christians to frequent the sacrament of the Lord's supper, as they call it; yet they say, No man ought to take it unworthily: yea, they plead, that such as find themselves unprepared, must abstain; and therefore do usually excommunicate them from the table. Now, though according to them it be necessary to partake of this sacrament; yet it is also necessary that those that do it, do first examine themselves, lest they eat and drink their own condemnation; and though they reckon it sinful for them to forbear, yet they account it more sinful for them to do it without this examination.

Fifthly; They object Acts viii. 22, where Peter com- Obj. 5. manded Simon Magus, that wicked sorcerer, to pray; from thence inferring, That wicked men may and ought to pray.

I answer; That in the citing of this place, as I have Answ. often observed, they omit the first and chiefest part of the verse, which is thus, Acts viii. vers. 22, " Repent there- The sorcerer may fore of this thy wickedness, and pray God, if perhaps the pray, but not without thought of thine heart may be forgiven thee:" so here he repentance bids him first " Repent." Now the least measure of true repentance cannot be without somewhat of that inward retirement of the mind which we speak of: and indeed where true repentance goeth first, we do not doubt but the Spirit of God will be near to concur with, and influence such to pray to and call upon God.

**OBJ 6**   And lastly; They object, That many prayers begun without the Spirit have proved effectual; and that the prayers of wicked men have been heard, and found acceptable, as Ahab's.

**ANSW.**   This objection was before solved. For the acts of God's compassion and indulgence at some times, and to some persons, upon singular extraordinary occasions, are not to be a rule of our actions. For if we should make that the measure of our obedience, great inconveniences would follow; as is evident, and will be acknowledged by all. Next, We do not deny, but wicked men are sensible of the motions and operations of God's Spirit oftentimes, before their day be expired; from which they may at times pray acceptably; not as remaining altogether wicked, but as entering into piety, from whence they afterwards fall away.

**III.**
**Of singing psalms.**   § XXVI. As to the singing of psalms, there will not be need of any long discourse; for that the case is just the same as in the two former of preaching and prayer. We confess this to be a part of God's worship, and very sweet and refreshing, when it proceeds from a true sense of God's love in the heart, and arises from the divine influence of the Spirit, which leads souls to breathe forth **A sweet harmonious** either a sweet harmony, or words suitable to the present **ound.** condition; whether they be words formerly used by the saints, and recorded in scripture, such as the Psalms of David, or other words; as were the hymns and songs of **But formal** Zacharias, Simeon, and the blessed Virgin Mary. But as **singing has** for the formal customary way of singing, it hath no foun- **no ground** **inscripture.** dation in scripture, nor any ground in true Christianity; yea, besides all the abuses incident to prayer and preaching, it hath this more peculiar, that oftentimes great and

horrid lies are said in the sight of God: for all manner of wicked profane people take upon them to personate the experiences and conditions of blessed David; which are not only false, as to them, but also as to some of more sobriety, who utter them forth: as where they will sing sometimes, Psalm xxii. 14, — "My heart is like wax, it is melted in the midst of my bowels:" and verse 15, "My strength is dried up like a potsherd, and my tongue cleaveth to my jaws; and thou hast brought me into the dust of death:" and Psalm vi. 6, "I am weary with my groaning, all the night make I my bed to swim: I water my couch with my tears:" and many more, which those that speak know to be false, as to them.  And sometimes will confess just after, in their prayers, that they are guilty of the vices opposite to those virtues, which but just before they have asserted themselves endued with.  Who can suppose that God accepts of such juggling?  And indeed such singing doth more please the carnal ears of men, than the pure ears of the Lord, who abhors all lying and hypocrisy.

That singing then that pleaseth him must proceed from that which is PURE in the heart, even from the Word of Life therein, in and by which, richly dwelling in us, spiritual songs and hymns are returned to the Lord, according to that of the apostle, Col. iii. 16.

But as to their artificial music, either by organs, or other instruments, or voice, we have neither example nor precept for it in the New Testament.

§ XXVII. But lastly ; The great advantage of this true worship of God, which we profess and practice, is, that it consisteth not in man's wisdom, arts or industry; neither needeth the glory, pomp, riches, nor splendour of this world to beautify it, as being of a spiritual and heavenly nature; and therefore too simple and contemptible to the natural mind and will of man, that hath no delight to abide in it, because he finds no room there for his imaginations and inventions, and hath not the opportunity to gratify his outward and carnal senses: so that this form being observed, is not likely to be long kept pure without the power; for it is of itself so naked without it, that it hath nothing in it to invite and tempt men to dote upon it, further than it is accompanied with the power. Whereas the worship of our adversaries, being performed in their own wills, is self-pleasing, as in which they can largely exercise their natural parts and invention: and so, as to most of them, having somewhat of an outward and worldly splendour, delectable to the carnal and worldly senses, they can pleasantly continue it, and satisfy themselves, though without the Spirit and power; which they make no ways essential to the performance of their worship, and therefore neither wait for, nor expect it.

*The carnal worship pleases self.*

§ XXVIII. So that to conclude, The worship, preaching, praying and singing, which we plead for, is such as proceedeth from the Spirit of God, and is always accompanied with its influence, being begun by its motion, and carried on by the power and strength thereof; and so is a worship purely spiritual: such as the scripture holds forth, John iv. 23, 24; 1 Cor. xiv. 15; Eph. vi. 18, &c.

*The worship of the Quakers.*

But the worship, preaching, praying and singing, which our adversaries plead for, and which we oppose, is a worship which is both begun, carried on, and concluded in man's own natural will and strength, without the motion or influence of God's Spirit, which they judge they need not wait for; and therefore may be truly performed, both as to the matter and manner, by the wickedest of men. Such was the worship and vain oblations which God always rejected, as appears from Isa. lxvi. 3; Jer. xiv. 12, &c.; Isa. i. 13; Prov. xv. 29; John ix. 31.

*Our adversaries' worship.*

---

# PROPOSITION XII.

## *Concerning Baptism.*

As there is one Lord, and one faith, so there is one baptism; which is not the putting away the filth of the flesh, but the answer of a good conscience before God, by the

*Eph. iv. 5.*
*1 Pet. iii. 21.*
*Rom. vi. 4.*

resurrection of Jesus Christ. And this baptism is a
pure and spiritual thing, to wit, the baptism of the Spirit
and fire, by which we are buried with him, that being
washed and purged from our sins, we may walk in newness of life: of which the baptism of John was a figure,
which was commanded for a time, and not to continue
for ever. As to the baptism of infants, it is a mere
human tradition, for which neither precept nor practice
is to be found in all the scripture.

Gal. iii. 27.
Col. ii. 12.
John iii. 30
1 Cor. i.
17.

§ I. I DID sufficiently demonstrate, in the explanation
and proof of the former proposition, how greatly the professors of Christianity, as well Protestants as Papists, were
degenerated in the matter of worship, and how much
strangers to, and averse from that true and acceptable worship that is performed in the Spirit of Truth, because of
man's natural propensity in his fallen state to exalt his own
inventions, and to intermix his own work and product in
the service of God: and from this root sprung all the idle
worships, idolatries, and numerous superstitious inventions
among the heathen. For when God, in condescension to
his chosen people the Jews, did prescribe to them by his
servant Moses many ceremonies and observations, as types
and shadows of the substance, which in due time was to
be revealed; which consisted for the most part in washings,
outward purifications and cleansings, which were to continue until the time of reformation, until the spiritual worship should be set up; and that God, by the more plentiful
pouring forth of his Spirit, and guiding of that anointing,
should lead his children into all truth, and teach them to
worship him in a way more spiritual and acceptable to
him, though less agreeable to the carnal and outward
senses; yet notwithstanding God's condescension to the
Jews in such things, we see that that part in man, which
delights to follow its own inventions, could not be re-
strained, nor yet satisfied with all these observations, but
that oftentimes they would be either declining to the other
superstitions of the Gentiles, or adding some new obser-

From
whence ido
latries and
heathen su
perstitions
did spring.

vations and ceremonies of their own; to which they were so devoted, that they were still apt to prefer them before the commands of God, and that under the notion of zeal and piety. This we see abundantly in the example of the Pharisees, the chiefest sect among the Jews, whom Christ so frequently reproves for making void the commandments of God by their traditions. Mat. xv. 6, 9, &c. This complaint may at this day be no less justly made as to many bearing the name of Christians, who have introduced many things of this kind, partly borrowed from the Jews, which they more tenaciously stick to, and more earnestly contend for, than for the weightier points of Christianity; because that self, yet alive, and ruling in them, loves their own inventions better than God's commands. But if they can by any means stretch any scripture practice, or conditional precept or permission, fitted to the weakness or capacity of some, or appropriate to some particular dispensation, to give some colour for any of these their inventions; they do then so tenaciously stick to them, and so obstinately and obstreperously plead for them, that they will not patiently hear the most solid Christian reasons against them. Which zeal, if they would but seriously examine it, they would find to be but the prejudice of education, and the love of self, more than that of God, or his pure worship. This is verified concerning those things which are called sacraments, about which they are very ignorant in religious controversies, who understand not how much debate, contention, jangling, and quarrelling there has been among those called Christians: so that I may safely say the controversy about them, to wit, about their number, nature, virtue, efficacy, administration, and other things, hath been more than about any other doctrine of Christ, whether as betwixt Papists and Protestants, or among Protestants betwixt themselves. And how great prejudice these controversies have brought to Christians is very obvious; whereas the things contended for among them are for the most part but empty shadows, and mere

*(marginal notes:)*

The Pharisees the chiefest among the Jews.

Many things in Christendom are borrowed from the Jews and Gentiles.

Of sacraments so many controversies.

outside things: as I hope hereafter to make appear to the patient and unprejudicate reader.

§ II. That which comes first under observation, is the name *sacrament*, which it is strange that Christians should stick to and contend so much for, since it is not to be found in all the scripture; but was borrowed from the military oaths among the heathen, from whom the Christians, when they began to apostatize, did borrow many superstitious terms and observations, that they might thereby ingratiate themselves, and the more easily gain the heathen to their religion; which practice, though perhaps intended by them for good, yet, as being the fruit of human policy, and not according to God's wisdom, has had very pernicious consequences. I see not how any, whether Papists or Protestants, especially the latter, can in reason quarrel with us for denying this term, which it seems the Spirit of God saw not meet to inspire the penmen of the scriptures to leave unto us. *The name of sacrament (not found in scripture) is borrowed from the heathen.*

But if it be said, That it is not the name, but the thing they contend for; *Obj. 1.*

I answer; Let the name then, as not being scriptural, be laid aside, and we shall see at first entrance how much benefit will redound by laying aside this traditional term, and betaking us to plainness of scripture language. For presently the great contest about the number of them will vanish; seeing there is no term used in scripture that can be made use of, whether we call them institutions, ordinances, precepts, commandments, appointments, or laws, &c., that would afford ground for such a debate; since neither will Papists affirm, that there are only seven, or Protestants only two, of any of these afore-mentioned. *Answ.*

If it be said, That this controversy arises from the definition of the thing, as well as from the name; *Obj. 2.*

It will be found otherwise: for whatever way we take their definition of a sacrament, whether as an outward visible sign, whereby inward grace is conferred, or only signified, this definition will agree to many things, which neither Papists nor Protestants will acknowledge to be *Answ. The definition of sacrament agrees to many other things.*

sacraments. If they be expressed under the name of seal-ing ordinances, as by some they are, I could never see, either by reason or scripture, how this title could be ap-propriate to them more than to any other Christian, re-ligious performance: for that must needs properly be a sealing ordinance, which makes the persons receiving it infallibly certain of the promise or thing sealed to them.

What seal-ing ordi-nance doth mean.

Obj. 3.

If it be said, It is so to them that are faithful;

Answ.

I answer; So is praying and preaching, and doing of every good work. Seeing the partaking or performing of the one gives not to any a more certain title to heaven, yea, in some respect, not so much, there is no reason to call them so, more than the other.

Besides, we find not any thing called the seal and pledge of our inheritance, but the Spirit of God. It is by that we are said to be sealed, Eph. i. 14, and iv. 30, which is also termed the "earnest of our inheritance," 2 Cor. i. 22, and not by outward water, or eating and drinking; which as the wickedest of men may partake of, so many that do, do, notwithstanding it, go to perdition. For it is not out-ward washing with water that maketh the heart clean, by which men are fitted for heaven; and as that which goeth into the mouth doth not defile a man, because it is put forth again, and so goeth to the dunghill; neither doth any thing which man eateth purify him, or fit him for heaven. What is said here in general may serve for an introduction, not only to this proposition, but also to the other concern-ing the supper. Of these sacraments (so called) baptism is always first numbered, which is the subject of the pre-sent proposition; in whose explanation I shall first demon-strate and prove our judgment, and then answer the objec-tions, and refute the sentiments of our opposers. As to the first part, these things following, which are briefly com-prehended in the proposition, come to be proposed and proved.

That out-ward wash-ing doth not cleanse the heart.

Part I.

Prop. 1.

§ III. First: There is but one baptism, as well as but one Lord, one faith, &c.

Prop. II

Secondly, That this one baptism, which is the baptism

of Christ, is not a washing with, or dipping in water, but a being baptized by the Spirit.

Thirdly, That the baptism of John was but a figure of this; and therefore, as the figure, to give place to the substance; which though it be to continue, yet the other ceaseth. **Prop. III**

As for the first, viz., That there is but one baptism, there needs no other proof than the words of the text, Eph. iv. 5: "One Lord, one faith, one baptism:" where the apostle positively and plainly affirms, that as there is but one body, one Spirit, one faith, one God, &c., so there is but "one baptism." **Prop. 1. One baptism proved.**

As to what is commonly alleged by way of explanation upon the text, That the baptism of water and of the Spirit make up this one baptism, by virtue of the sacramental union; **Obj. 1.**

I answer; This exposition hath taken place, not because grounded upon the testimony of the scripture, but because it wrests the scripture to make it suit to their principle of water baptism; and so there needs no other reply, but to deny it, as being repugnant to the plain words of the text; which saith not, that there are two baptisms, to wit, one of water, the other of the Spirit, which do make up one baptism; but plainly, that there is one baptism, as there is one faith, and one God. Now as there go not two faiths, nor two Gods, nor two Spirits, nor two bodies, whereof the one is outward and elementary, and the other spiritual and pure, to the making up the one faith, the one God, the one body, and the one Spirit; so neither ought there to go two baptisms to make up the one baptism. **Answ. Whether two baptisms make up the one.**

But secondly, if it be said, The baptism is but one, whereof water is the one part, to wit, the sign; and the Spirit, the thing signified, the other; **Obj. 2.**

I answer; This yet more confirmeth our doctrine: for if water be only the sign, it is not the matter of the one baptism (as shall further hereafter by its definition in scripture appear), and we are to take the one baptism for the matter of it, not for the sign, or figure and type that went before. **Answ. If water be the type, the substance must remain.**

Ever as where Christ is called the one offering in scripture, though he was typified by many sacrifices and offerings under the law, we understand only by the one offering, his offering himself upon the cross; whereof though those many offerings were signs and types, yet we say not that they go together with that offering of Christ, to make up the one offering: so neither, though water baptism was a sign of Christ's baptism, will it follow, that it goeth now to make up the baptism of Christ. If any should be so absurd as to affirm, That this one baptism here was the baptism of water, and not of the Spirit; that were foolishly to contradict the positive testimony of the scripture, which saith the contrary; as by what followeth will more amply appear.

PROP. II.     Secondly, That this one baptism, which is the baptism of Christ, is not a washing with water, appears, first, from PROOF I. the testimony of John, the proper and peculiar administra-
The differ- tor of water baptism, Mat. iii. 11, "I indeed baptize you
ence be- with water unto repentance; but he that cometh after me
tween
John's bap- is mightier than I, whose shoes I am not worthy to bear;
tism and he shall baptize you with the Holy Ghost, and with fire."
Christ's. Here John mentions two manners of baptizing, and two different baptisms; the one with water, and the other with the Spirit; the one whereof he was the minister of; the other whereof Christ was the minister of: and such as were baptized with the first, were not therefore baptized with the second: I indeed baptize you, but he shall baptize you. Though in the present time they were baptized with the baptism of water; yet they were not as yet, but were to be, baptized with the baptism of Christ. From all which I thus argue:

ARG. 1.     If those that were baptized with the baptism of water, were not therefore baptized with the baptism of Christ; then the baptism of water is not the baptism of Christ:

But the first is true;

Therefore also the last.

And again,

ARG. 2.     If he, that truly and really administered the baptism of water, did notwithstanding declare, that he neither could, nor did, baptize with the baptism of Christ; then the baptism of water is not the baptism of Christ:

But the first is true;

Therefore, &c.

And indeed to understand it otherwise, would make John's words void of good sense: for if their baptisms had been all one, why should he have so precisely contra-distinguished them? Why should he have said, that those whom he had already baptized, should yet be baptized with another baptism?

If it be urged, That baptism with water was the one part, and that with the Spirit the other part, or effect only of the former; *Object.*

I answer; This exposition contradicts the plain words of the text. For he saith not, I baptize you with water, and he that cometh after me shall produce the effects of this my baptism in you by the Spirit, &c., or he shall accomplish this baptism in you; but, He shall baptize you. So then, if we understand the words truly and properly, when he saith, I baptize you, as consenting that thereby is really signified that he did baptize with the baptism of water; we must needs, unless we offer violence to the text, understand the other part of the sentence the same way; viz., where he adds presently, "But he shall baptize you," &c., that he understood it of their being truly to be baptized with another baptism, than what he did baptize with: else it had been nonsense for him thus to have contra-distinguished them. *Answ. One baptism is no part nor effect of the other*

Secondly, This is further confirmed by the saying of Christ himself, Acts i. 4, 5, "But wait for the promise of the Father, which, saith he, ye have heard of me: for John truly baptized with water, but ye shall be baptized with the Holy Ghost not many days hence." There can scarce two places of scripture run more parallel than this doth with the former, a little before mentioned; and therefore concludeth the same way as did the other. For Christ here grants fully that John completed his baptism, as to the matter and *Proof II. Who were baptized by John were still to wait for Christ's baptism with the Spirit.*

substance of it: "John," saith he, "truly baptized with water;" which is as much as if he had said, John did truly and fully administer the baptism of water; "But ye shall be baptized with," &c. This showeth that they were to be baptized with some other baptism than the baptism of water; and that although they were formerly baptized with the baptism of water, yet not with that of Christ, which they were to be baptized with.

**PROOF III.**

**The baptism with the Holy Ghost and that with water differ.**

Thirdly, Peter observes the same distinction, Acts xi 16, "Then remembered I the word of the Lord, how that he said, John indeed baptized with water; but ye shall be baptized with the Holy Ghost." The apostle makes this application upon the Holy Ghost's falling upon them; whence he infers, that they were then baptized with the baptism of the Spirit. As to what is urged from his calling afterwards for water, it shall be spoken to hereafter. From all which three sentences, relative one to another, first of John, secondly of Christ, and thirdly of Peter, it doth evidently follow, that such as were truly and really baptized with the baptism of water, were notwithstanding not baptized with the baptism of the Spirit, which is that of Christ; and such as truly and really did administer the baptism of water, did, in so doing, not administer the baptism of Christ. So that if there be now but one baptism, as we have already proved, we may safely conclude that it is that of the Spirit, and not of water; else it would follow, that the one baptism, which now continues, were the baptism of water, i. e., John's baptism, and not the baptism of the Spirit, i. e., Christ's; which were most absurd.

**OBJECT.**

If it be said further, That though the baptism of John, before Christ's was administered, was different from it, as being the figure only; yet now, that both it as the figure, and that of the Spirit as the substance, is necessary to make up the one baptism;

I answer; This urgeth nothing, unless it be granted also that both of them belong to the essence of baptism; so that baptism is not to be accounted as truly administered, where both are not; which none of our adversaries will acknow

.edge: but on the contrary, account not only all those truly baptized with the baptism of Christ, who are baptized with water, though they be uncertain whether they be baptized with the Spirit, or not; but they even account such truly baptized with the baptism of Christ, because sprinkled, or baptized with water, though it be manifest and most certain that they are not baptized with the Spirit, as being enemies thereunto in their hearts by wicked works. So here, by their own confession, baptism with water is without the Spirit. Wherefore we may far safer conclude, that the baptism of the Spirit, which is that of Christ, is and may be without that of water; as appears in that of Acts xi. 15, where Peter testifies of these men, that they were baptized with the Spirit, though then not baptized with water. And indeed the controversy in this, as in most other things, stands betwixt us and our opposers, in that they oftentimes prefer the form and shadow to the power and substance; by denominating persons as inheritors and possessors, of the thing, from their having the form and shadow, though really wanting the power and substance; and not admitting those to be so denominated, who have the power and substance, if they want the form and shadow. This appears evidently, in that they account those truly baptized with the one baptism of Christ, who are not baptized with the Spirit, which in scripture is particularly called the baptism of Christ, if they be only baptized with water, which themselves yet confess to be but the shadow or figure. And moreover, in that they account not those who are surely baptized with the baptism of the Spirit baptized, neither will they have them so denominated, unless they be also sprinkled with, or dipped in water: but we, on the contrary, do always prefer the power to the form, the substance to the shadow; and where the substance and power is, we doubt not to denominate the person accordingly, though the form be wanting. And therefore we always seek first, and plead for the substance and power, as knowing that to be indispensably necessary, though the form sometimes may be dispensed with, and the figure or type may cease, when

*Water baptism is not the true baptism of Christ.*

*The baptism of the Spirit needeth no sprinkling or dipping in water.*

33 *

the substance and anti-type come to be enjoyed, as it doth
in this case, which shall hereafter be made appear.

PROOF IV.

* Or, as it
should be
translated,
' Whose
model bap-
tism does
also now
save us.'
The plain-
est defini-
tion of the
baptism of
Christ in all
the bible.

§ IV. Fourthly, That the one baptism of Christ is not a
washing with water, appears from 1 Pet. iii. 21: "The
like figure* whereunto, even baptism, doth also now save
us (not the putting away of the filth of the flesh, but the
answer of a good conscience towards God) by the resurrection of Jesus Christ." So plain a definition of baptism
is not in all the bible; and therefore, seeing it is so plain,
it may well be preferred to all the coined definitions of the
school-men. The apostle tells us first negatively what it is
not, viz., "Not a putting away of the filth of the flesh:"
then surely it is not a washing with water, since that is so.
Secondly, he tells us affirmatively what it is, viz., "The
answer of a good conscience towards God, by the resurrection of Jesus Christ;" where he affirmatively defines it
to be the "answer (or confession, as the Syriac version
hath it) of a good conscience." Now this answer cannot
be but where the Spirit of God hath purified the soul, and
the fire of his judgment hath burned up the unrighteous
nature; and those in whom this work is wrought may be
truly said to be baptized with the baptism of Christ, i. e.
of the Spirit and of fire. Whatever way then we take this
definition of the apostle of Christ's baptism, it confirmeth
our sentence: for if we take the first or negative part, viz.,
That it is not a putting away of the filth of the flesh, then

Water
baptism
shut out
from bap-
tism of
Christ.

it will follow that water baptism is not it, because that is a
putting away the filth of the flesh. If we take the second
and affirmative definition, to wit, That it is the answer or
confession of a good conscience, &c., then water baptism
is not it; since, as our adversaries will not deny, water
baptism doth not always imply it, neither is it any necessary consequence thereof. Moreover, the apostle in this
place doth seem especially to guard against those that
might esteem water baptism the true baptism of Christ;
because, lest by the comparison induced by him in the
preceding verse, betwixt the souls that were saved in
Noah's ark, and us that are now saved by baptism; lest, I

say, any should have thence hastily concluded, that because the former were saved by water, this place must needs be taken to speak of water baptism, to prevent such a mistake, he plainly affirms, that it is not that, but another thing. He saith not that it is the water, or the putting away of the filth of the flesh, as accompanied with the answer of a good conscience, whereof the one, viz., water, is the sacramental element, administered by the minister; and the other, the grace or thing signified conferred by Christ; but plainly, That it is not the putting away, &c., than which there can be nothing more manifest to men unprejudicate and judicious. Moreover, Peter calls this here which saves ἀντίτυπον, the anti-type or the ' thing figured ;' whereas it is usually translated, ' as if the like figure did now save us ;' thereby insinuating that as they were saved by water in the ark, so are we now by water baptism. But this interpretation crosseth his sense, he presently after declaring the contrary, as hath above been observed; and likewise it would contradict the opinion of all our opposers. For Protestants deny it to be absolutely necessary to salvation; and though Papists say, none are saved without it, yet in this they admit an exception, as of martyrs, &c., and they will not say that all that have it are saved by water baptism; which they ought to say, if they will understand by baptism, by which the apostle saith we are saved, water baptism. For seeing we are saved by this baptism, as all those that were in the ark were saved by water, it would then follow, that all those that have this baptism are saved by it. Now this consequence would be false, if it were understood of water baptism; because many, by the confession of all, are baptized with water that are not saved; but this consequence holds most true, if it be understood as we do, of the baptism of the Spirit; since none can have this answer of a good conscience, and, abiding in it, not be saved by it.

*The Protestants denying water baptism its absolute necessity to men's salvation; although the Papists say none can be saved with out it, yet grant exceptions.*

Fifthly, That the one baptism of Christ is not a washing with water, as it hath been proved by the definition of the one baptism, so it is also manifest from the necessary fruits *Proof V.*

The effects and fruits of the baptism of Christ. and effects of it, which are three times particularly ex pressed by the apostle Paul; as first, Rom. vi. 3, 4, where he saith, " That so many of them as were baptized into Jesus Christ, were baptized into his death. buried with him by baptism into death, that they should walk in new- ness of life." Secondly, to the Galatians, iii. 27, he saith positively, " For as many of you as have been baptized into Christ, have put on Christ." And thirdly, to the Colossians, ii. 12, he saith, That they were " buried with him in baptism," and risen " with him through the faith of the operation of God." It is to be observed here, that the apostle speaks generally, without any exclusive term, but comprehensive of all. He saith not, Some of you that were baptized into Christ, have put on Christ, but " as many of you;" which is as much as if he had said, Every one of you that hath been baptized into Christ, hath put on Christ. Whereby it is evident that this is not meant of

Which ef- fects water baptism wants. water baptism, but of the baptism of the Spirit; because else it would follow, that whosoever had been baptized with water baptism had put on Christ, and were risen with him, which all acknowledge to be most absurd. Now supposing all the visible members of the churches of Rome, Galatia, and Colosse had been outwardly baptized with water, (I do not say they were, but our adversaries will not only readily grant it, but also contend for it,) suppose, I say, the case so, they will not say they had all put on Christ, since divers expressions in these epistles to them show the contrary. So that the apostle cannot mean bap- tism with water; and yet that he meaneth the baptism of Christ, i. e., of the Spirit, cannot be denied; or that the baptism wherewith these were baptized, of whom the apostle here testifies that they had put on Christ, was the one baptism, I think none will call in question. Now admit, as our adversaries contend, that many in these churches who had been baptized with water had not put on Christ, it will follow, that notwithstanding that water baptism, they were not baptized into Christ, or with the baptism of Christ, seeing as many of them as were bap-

tized into Christ had put on Christ, &c. From all which
I thus argue :

If the baptism with water were the one baptism, i. e., Arg. 1.
the baptism of Christ, as many as were baptized with wa-
er would have put on Christ :

But the last is false,

Therefore also the first.

And again :

Since as many as are baptized into Christ, i. e., with the Arg. 2.
one baptism, which is the baptism of Christ, have put on
Christ, then water baptism is not the one baptism, viz., the
baptism of Christ.

But the first is true,

Therefore also the last.

§ V. Thirdly, Since John's baptism was a figure, and Pro. III.
seeing the figure gives way to the substance, although the Proved.
thing figured remain, to wit, the one baptism of Christ, yet
the other ceaseth, which was the baptism of John.

That John's baptism was a figure of Christ's baptism, I I.
judge will not readily be denied ; but in case it should, John's bap
it can easily be proved from the nature of it. John's bap- tism was a
tism was a being baptized with water, but Christ's is a figure of Christ's
baptizing with the Spirit ; therefore John's baptism must
have been a figure of Christ's. But further, that water
baptism was John's baptism, will not be denied : that
water baptism is not Christ's baptism, is already proved.
From which doth arise the confirmation of our proposition
thus :

There is no baptism to continue now, but the one baptism of Christ.

Therefore water baptism is not to continue now, because
t is not the one baptism of Christ.

That John's baptism is ceased, many of our adversaries II.
confess ; but if any should allege it is otherwise, it may be John's bap
easily proved by the express words of John, not only as tism is
being insinuated there, where he contra-distinguisheth his ceased our
baptism from that of Christ, but particularly where he confess.
saith, John iii. 30, "He [Christ] must increase, but I

[John] must decrease." From whence it clearly follows, that the increasing or taking place of Christ's baptism is the decreasing or abolishing of John's baptism; so that if water baptism was a particular part of John's ministry, and is no part of Christ's baptism, as we have already proved. it will necessarily follow that it is not to continue.

**Arg.** Secondly, If water baptism had been to continue a perpetual ordinance of Christ in his church, he would either have practised it himself, or commanded his apostles so to do.

But that he practised it not, the scripture plainly affirms, John iv. 2. And that he commanded his disciples to baptize with water, I could never yet read. As for what is alleged, that, Mat. xxviii. 19, &c., where he bids them baptize, is to be understood of water baptism, that is but to beg the question, and the grounds for that shall be hereafter examined.

Therefore, to baptize with water is no perpetual ordinance of Christ to his church.

This hath had the more weight with me, because I find not any standing ordinance or appointment of Christ necessary to Christians, for which we have not either Christ's own practice or command, as to obey all the commandments which comprehend both our duty towards God and man, &c., and where the gospel requires more than the law, which is abundantly signified in the 5th and 6th chapters of Matthew, and elsewhere. Besides, as to the duties of worship, he exhorts us to meet, promising his presence; commands to pray, preach, watch, &c., and gives precepts concerning some temporary things, as the washing of one another's feet, the breaking of bread, hereafter to be discussed; only for this one thing of baptizing with water, though so earnestly contended for, we find not any precept of Christ.

III.
The gospel puts an end to carnal ordinances.

§ VI. But to make water baptism a necessary institution of the Christian religion, which is pure and spiritual, and not carnal and ceremonial, is to derogate from the new covenant dispensation, and set up the legal rites and ceremonies, of which this of baptism, or washing with water, was one, as appears from Heb. ix. 10. where the apostle speaking thereof saith, that " it stood only in meats and drinks, and divers washings, and carnal ordinances, imposed until the time of reformation." If then the time of reformation, or the dispensation of the gospel, which puts an end to the shadows, be come, then such baptisms and carnal ordinances are no more to be imposed. For how baptism with water comes now to be a spiritual ordinance, more than before in the time of the law, doth not appear, seeing it is but water still, and a washing of the outward man, and a putting away of the filth of the flesh still: and as before, those that were so washed, were not thereby made perfect, as pertaining to the conscience, neither are they at this day, as our adversaries must needs acknowledge, and experience abundantly showeth. So that the matter of it, which is a washing with water, and the effect of it, which is only an outward cleansing, being still the same, how comes water baptism to be less a carnal ordinance now than before ?

If it be said, That God confers inward grace upon some Obj. 1. that are now baptized ;

So no doubt he did also upon some that used those baptisms among the Jews. Answ

Or if it be said, Because it is commanded by Christ Obj. 2 now, under the new covenant ;

I answer, First, That is to beg the question ; of which Answ. hereafter.

But Secondly, We find that where the matter of ordinances is the same, and the end the same, they are never accounted more or less spiritual, because of their different times. Now was not God the author of the purifications and baptisms under the law? Was not water the matter of them, which is so now? Was not the end of them to signify an inward purifying by an outward washing? And is not that alleged to be the end still? And are the necessary effects or consequences of it any better now than before, since men are now by the virtue of water baptism,

Men are no more now than before by water baptism inwardly cleansed.

as a necessary consequence of it, no more than before made inwardly clean? And if some by God's grace that are baptized with water are inwardly purified, so were some also under the law; so that this is not any necessary consequence or effect, neither of this nor that baptism. It is then plainly repugnant to right reason, as well as to the scripture testimony, to affirm that to be a spiritual ordinance now, which was a carnal ordinance before, if it be still the same, both as to its author, matter, and end, however made to vary in some small circumstances. The spirituality of the new covenant, and of its worship established by Christ, consisted not in such superficial alterations of circumstances, but after another manner. Therefore let our adversaries show us, if they can, without begging the question, and building upon some one or other of their own principles denied by us, where ever Christ appointed or ordained any institution or observation under the new covenant, as belonging to the nature of it, or such a necessary part of its worship as is perpetually to continue; which being one in substance and effects, (I speak of necessary, not accidental effects,) yet, because of some small difference in form or circumstance, was before carnal, notwithstanding it was commanded by God under the law, but now is become spiritual, because commanded by Christ under the gospel? And if they cannot do this, then if water baptism was once a carnal ordinance, as the apostle positively affirms it to have been, it remains a carnal ordinance still; and if a carnal ordinance, then no necessary part of the gospel or new covenant dispensation; and if no necessary part of it, then not needful to continue, nor to be practised by such as live and walk under this dispensation. But in this, as in most other things, according as we have often observed, our adversaries judaize, and renouncing the glorious and spiritual privileges of the new covenant, are sticking in and cleaving to the rudiments of the old, both in doctrine and worship, as being more suited and agreeable to their carnal apprehensions and natural senses. But we, on the contrary, travail above all to lay hold upon and cleave unto the Light of the glorious gospel revealed unto us. And the harmony of the truth we profess in this may appear, by briefly observing how in all things we follow the spiritual gospel of Christ, as contra-distinguished from the carnality of the legal dispensation; while our adversaries, through rejecting this gospel, are still labouring under the burden of the law, which neither they nor their fathers were able to bear. The law distinguished from the gospel.

For the law and rule of the old covenant and Jews was outward, written in tables of stone and parchment; so also is that of our adversaries. But the law of the new covenant is inward and perpetual, written in the heart; so is ours. The outward baptism, worship, law, distinguished from the outward

The worship of the Jews was outward and carnal, limited to set times, places, and persons, and performed according to set prescribed forms and observations; so is that of our adversaries. But the worship of the new covenant is neither limited to time, place, nor person, but is performed in the Spirit and in truth; and it is not acted according to set forms and prescriptions, but as the Spirit of God immediately actuates, moves, and leads, whether it be to preach, pray, or sing; and such is also our worship.

So likewise the baptism among the Jews under the law was an outward washing with outward water, only to typify an inward purification of the soul, which did not necessarily follow upon those that were thus baptized; but the baptism of Christ under the gospel is the baptism of the Spirit and of fire; not the putting away of the filth of the flesh, but the answer of a good conscience towards God; and such is the baptism that we labour to be baptized withal, and contend for.

§ VII. But again, If water baptism had been an ordinance of the gospel, then the apostle Paul would have been sent to administer it; but he declares positively, 1 Cor. i. 17: "That Christ sent him not to baptize, but to preach the gospel." The reason of that consequence is undeniable, because the apostle Paul's commission was as Arg

**IV.**
**That wa-**
**ter baptism**
**is no badge**
**of Chris-**
**tians, like**
**circumci-**
**sion of the**
**Jews.**

large as that of any of them; and consequently he being in special manner the apostle of Christ to the Gentiles, if water baptism, as our adversaries contend, be to be accounted the badge of Christianity, he had more need than any of the rest to be sent to baptize with water, that he might mark the Gentiles converted by him with that Christian sign. But indeed the reason holds better thus, that since Paul was the apostle of the Gentiles, and that in his ministry he doth through all, as by his epistles appears, labour to wean them from the former Jewish ceremonies and observations, though in so doing he was sometimes undeservedly judged by others of his brethren, who were unwilling to lay aside those ceremonies, therefore his commission, though as full as to the preaching of the gospel and new covenant dispensation as that of the other apostles, did not require of him that he should lead those converts into such Jewish observations and baptisms: however that practice was indulged in and practised by the other apostles among their Jewish proselytes, for which

**1 Cor. i. 14.**

**Paul was**
**not sent to**
**baptize.**

cause he thanks God that he had baptized so few: intimating that what he did therein he did not by virtue of his apostolic commission, but rather in condescension to their weakness, even as at another time he circumcised Timothy.

**OBJ. 1.**

Our adversaries, to evade the truth of this testimony, usually allege, That by this is only to be understood that he was not sent principally to baptize, not that he was not sent at all.

**ANSW.**

But this exposition, since it contradicts the positive words of the text, and has no better foundation than the affirmation of its assertors, is justly rejected as spurious, until they bring some better proof for it. He saith not, I was not sent principally to baptize, but, " I was not sent to baptize."

**CONFIR.**

**Mat. ix. 13.**
**Hos. vi. 6.**

As for what they urge, by way of confirmation, from other places of scripture, where *not* is to be so taken, as where it is said, " I will have mercy, and *not* sacrifice," which is to be understood that God requires principally mercy, not excluding sacrifice:

I say this place is abundantly explained by the follow- **Refut.** ing words, " And the knowledge of God more than burnt-offerings ;" by which it clearly appears that burnt-offerings, which are one with sacrifices, are not excluded; but there is no such word added in that of Paul, and therefore the parity is not demonstrated to be alike, and consequently the instance not sufficient, unless they can prove that it ought so to be admitted here; else we might interpret by the same rule all other places of scripture the same way, as where the apostle saith, 1 Cor. ii. 5 : " That your faith might not stand in the wisdom of men, but in the power of God," it might be understood, it shall not stand principally so. How might the gospel, by this liberty of interpretation be perverted ?

If it be said, That the abuse of this baptism among the **Obj. 2.** Corinthians, in dividing themselves according to the persons by whom they were baptized, made the apostle speak so ; but that the abuse of a thing doth not abolish it ;

I answer, It is true, it doth not, provided the thing be **Answ.** lawful and necessary ; and that no doubt the abuse abovesaid gave the apostle occasion so to write. But let it from this be considered how the apostle excludes baptizing, not preaching, though the abuse (mark) proceeded from that, no less than from the other. For these Corinthians did denominate themselves from those different persons by whose preaching, as well as from those by whom they were baptized, they were converted, as by the 4th, 5th, 6th, 7th, and 8th verses of chap. iii. may appear : and yet *That* to remove that abuse the apostle doth not say he was not *preaching* sent to preach, nor yet doth he rejoice that he had only *ing ordi-* preached to a few ; because preaching, being a standing *nance, and* ordinance in the church, is not, because of any abuse that *forborne* the devil may tempt any to make of it, to be forborne by such as are called to perform it by the Spirit of God : wherefore the apostle accordingly, chap. iii. 8, 9, informs them, as to that, how to remove that abuse. But as to water baptism, for that it was no standing ordinance of Christ, but only practised as in condescension to the Jews, and by some apostles to some Gentiles also, therefore, so soon as the apostle perceived the abuse of it, he let the Corinthians understand how little stress was to be laid upon it, by showing them that he was glad that he had administered this ceremony to so few of them ; and by telling them plainly that it was no part of his commission, neither that which he was sent to administer.

QUERY.

Some ask us, How we know that baptizing here is meant of water, and not of the Spirit; which if it be, then it will exclude baptism of the Spirit, as well as of water.

ANSW.

That which converts to Christ is the baptism of the Spirit.

I answer, Such as ask the question, I suppose, speak it not as doubting that this was said of water baptism, which is more than manifest. For since the apostle Paul's message was, to turn people from darkness to light, and convert them to God; and that as many as are thus turned and converted, so as to have the answer of a good conscience towards God, and to have put on Christ, and be risen with him in newness of life, are baptized with the baptism of the Spirit. But who will say that only those few mentioned there to be baptized by Paul were come to this ? Or that to turn or bring them to this condition was not, even admitting our adversaries' interpretation, as principal a part of Paul's ministry as any other ? Since then our adversaries do take this place for water baptism, as indeed it is, we may lawfully, taking it so also, urge it upon them. Why the word *baptism* and *baptizing* is used by the apostle, where that of water and not of the Spirit is only understood, shall hereafter be spoken to. I come

PART II.

now to consider the reasons alleged by such as plead for water baptism, which are also the objections used against the discontinuance of it.

OBJ. 1.

John iii. 34.

§ VIII. First, Some object, That Christ, who had the Spirit above measure, was notwithstanding baptized with water. As Nic. Arnoldus against this Thesis, Sect. xlvi of his Theological Exercitation.

I answer, So was he also circumcised: it will not follow Answ.
from thence that circumcision is to continue: for it behoved Christ to fulfil all righteousness, not only the minis- WhyChrist
try of John, but the law also; therefore did he observe the was bap-
Jewish feasts and rites, and keep the passover.   It will not John.
thence follow that Christians ought to do so now; and
therefore Christ, Matt. iii. 15, gives John this reason of his
being baptized, desiring him to " suffer it to be so now :"
whereby he sufficiently intimates that he intended not
thereby to perpetuate it as an ordinance to his disciples.

Secondly, They object, Matt. xxviii. 19 : " Go ye there- Obj. 2.
fore and teach all nations, baptizing them in the name of
the Father, and of the Son, and of the Holy Ghost."

This is the great objection, and upon which they build Answ.
the whole superstructure; whereunto the first general and
sound answer is, by granting the whole; but putting them
to prove that water is here meant, since the text is silent What bap-
of it.   And though in reason it be sufficient upon our part tism Christ
that we concede the whole expressed in the place, but in Matt.
deny that it is by water, which is an addition to the text, xxviii.
yet I shall premise some reasons why we do so, and then
consider the reasons alleged by those that will have water
to be here understood.

The first is a maxim yielded to by all, That we ought Arg. 1.
not to go from the literal signification of the text, except
some urgent necessity force us thereunto.

But no urgent necessity in this place forceth us thereunto :

Therefore we ought not to go from it.

Secondly, That baptism which Christ commanded his Arg. 2.
apostles was the one baptism, id est, his own baptism;

But the one baptism, which is Christ's baptism, is not
with water, as we have already proved :

Therefore the baptism commanded by Christ to his apostles was not water baptism.

Thirdly, That baptism which Christ commanded his Arg. 3.
apostles was such, that as many as were therewith baptized
did put on Christ;

But this is not true of water baptism:

Therefore, &c.

ARG. 4.   Fourthly, The baptism commanded by Christ to his apostles was not John's baptism;

But baptism with water was John's baptism:

Therefore, &c.

ALLE. I.   But first, They allege, That Christ's baptism, though a baptism with water, did differ from John's, because John only baptized with water unto repentance, but Christ commands his disciples to baptize in the name of the Father, Son, and Holy Ghost; reckoning that in this form there lieth a great difference betwixt the baptism of John and that of Christ.

I answer, In that John's baptism was unto repentance, the difference lieth not there, because so is Christ's also; yea, our adversaries will not deny but that adult persons that are to be baptized ought, ere they are admitted to water baptisu, to repent, and confess their sins; and that infants also, with a respect to and consideration of their baptism, ought to repent and confess; so that the difference lieth not here, since this of repentance and confession agrees as well to Christ's as to John's baptism. But in this our adversaries are divided: for Calvin will have Christ's and John's to be all one, Inst. lib. iv., cap. 15, sect. 7, 8, yet they do differ, and the difference is, in that the one is by water, the other not, &c.

Secondly, As to what Christ saith, in commanding them to "baptize in the name of the Father, Son, and Spirit," I confess that states the difference, and it is great; but that lies not only in admitting water baptism in this different form, by a bare expressing of these words: for as the text says no such thing, neither do I see how it can be inferred from it. For the Greek is εἰς τὸ ὄνομα, that is, *into the* name; now the name of the Lord is often taken in scripture for something else than a bare sound of words, or literal expression, even for his virtue and power, as may appear from Psal. liv. 1; Cant. i. 3; Prov. xviii. 10, and in many more. Now that the apostles were by their minis

Of the name of the Lord, how taken in scripture

try to baptize the nations into this name, virtue and power, The baptism into the name, what it is. and that they did so, is evident by these testimonies of Paul above mentioned, where he saith, "That as many of them as were baptized into Christ, have put on Christ;" this must have been a baptizing into the name, i. e., power and virtue, and not a mere formal expression of words adjoined with water baptism ; because, as hath been above observed, it doth not follow as a natural or necessary consequence of it. I would have those who desire to have their faith built upon no other foundation than the testimony of God's Spirit and scriptures of truth, thoroughly to consider whether there can be any thing further alleged for this interpretation than what the prejudice of education and influence of tradition hath imposed. Perhaps it may stumble the unwary and inconsiderate reader, as if the very character of Christianity were abolished, to tell him plainly that this scripture is not to be understood of baptizing with water, and that this form of " baptizing in the name of the Father, Son, and Spirit," hath no warrant from Matt. xxviii., &c.

For which, besides the reason taken from the significa- Whether Christ did prescribe a form of baptism in Matt. xxviii. tion of "the name" as being the virtue and power above expressed, let it be considered, that if it had been a form prescribed by Christ to his apostles, then surely they would have made use of that form in the administering of water baptism to such as they baptized with water; but though particular mention be made in divers places of the Acts who were baptized, and how ; and though it be particularly expressed that they baptized such and such, as Acts ii. 41, and viii. 12, 13, 38, and ix. 18, and x. 48, and xvi. 15, and xviii. 8, yet there is not a word of this form. And in two places, Acts viii. 16, and xix. 5, it is said of some that they were " baptized in the name of the Lord Jesus ;" by which it yet more appears, that either the author of this history hath been very defective, who having so often occasion to mention this, yet omitteth so substantial a part of baptism (which were to accuse the Holy Ghost, by whose guidance Luke wrote it), or else that the apostles did no ways understand that Christ by his commiss. on, Matt. xxviii., did enjoin them such a form of water baptism, seeing they did not use it. And therefore it is safer to conclude, that what they did in administering water baptism, they did not by virtue of that commission, else they would have so used it: for our adversaries I suppose would judge it a great heresy to administer water baptism without that, or only in the name of Jesus, without mention of Father or Spirit, as it is expressly said they did, in the two places above cited.

**ALLE. II.**   Secondly, They say, If this were not understood of water baptism, it would be a tautology, and all one with teaching.

**ANSW.**   I say, Nay: Baptizing with the Spirit is somewhat further than teaching, or informing the understanding; for it

*How teaching and baptizing differ.*   imports a reaching to, and melting the heart, whereby it is turned, as well as the understanding informed. Besides, we find often in the scripture, that *teaching* and *instructing* are put together, without any absurdity, or needless tautology; and yet these two have a greater affinity than *teaching* and *baptizing* with the Spirit.

**ALLE. III.**   Thirdly, They say, Baptism in this place must be understood with water, because it is the action of the apostles; and so cannot be the baptism of the Spirit, which is the work of Christ, and his grace; not of man, &c.

**ANSW.**
*The baptism with the Spirit ascribed to godly men as instruments.*   I answer; Baptism with the Spirit, though not wrought without Christ and his grace, is instrumentally done by men fitted of God for that purpose; and therefore no absurdity follows, that baptism with the Spirit should be expressed as the action of the apostles. For though it be Christ by his grace that gives spiritual gifts, yet the apostle, Rom. i. 11, speaks of his imparting to them spiritual gifts; and he tells the Corinthians, that he had " begotten them through the gospel," 1 Cor. iv. 15. And yet to beget people to the faith, is the work of Christ and his grace, not of men. To convert the heart, is properly the work of Christ; and yet the scripture oftentimes ascribes it to men, as being the instruments: and since Paul's commission

was, To turn people from darkness to light, though that be not done without Christ co-operating by his grace, so may also baptizing with the Spirit be expressed, as performable by man as the instrument, though the work of Christ's grace be needful to concur thereunto. So that it is no absurdity to say, that the apostles did administer the baptism of the Spirit.

Lastly, They say, That since Christ saith here, that he ALLE. IV will be with his disciples to the end of the world, therefore water baptism must continue so long.

If he had been speaking here of water baptism, then that ANSW. might have been urged; but seeing that is denied, and proved to be false, nothing from thence can be gathered: he speaking of the baptism of the Spirit, which we freely confess doth remain to the end of the world; yea, so long as Christ's presence abideth with his children.

§ IX. Thirdly, They object the constant practice of the OBJ. 3. apostles in the primitive church, who, they say, did always administer water baptism to such as they converted to the faith of Christ; and hence also they further urge that of Mat. xxviii. to have been meant of water; or else the apostles did not understand it, because in baptizing they used water; or that in so doing they walked without a commission.

I answer; That it was the constant practice of the apos- ANSW. tles, is denied; for we have shown, in the example of Paul, that it was not so; since it were most absurd to judge that he converted only those few, even of the church of Corinth, whom he saith he baptized; nor were it less absurd to think that that was a constant apostolic practice, which he, who was not inferior to the chiefest of the apostles, and who declares he laboured as much as they all, rejoiceth he was so little in. But further; the conclusion inferred from the How the apost'es' practice of baptizing with water, to evince that apostles baptized they understood Mat. xxviii. of water baptism, doth not hold: for though they baptized with water, it will not follow that either they did it by virtue of that commission, or that they mistook that place; nor can there be any me lium

brought, that will infer such a conclusion. As to the other
insinuated absurdity, That they did it without a commission ; it is none at all : for they might have done it by a
permission, as being in use before Christ's death ; and because the people, nursed up with outward ceremonies,
could not be weaned wholly from them. And thus they
used other things, as circumcision and legal purifications,
which yet they had no commission from Christ to do : to
which we shall speak more at length in the following proposition concerning the supper.

Ob.

But if from the sameness of the word, because Christ
bids them baptize, and they afterwards in the use of water
are said to baptize, it be judged probable that they did understand that commission, Mat. xxviii., to authorize them
to baptize with water, and accordingly practised it ;

Answ.

Although it should be granted, that for a season they did
so far mistake it, as to judge that water belonged to that
baptism, which however I find no necessity of granting, yet
I see not any great absurdity would thence follow. For it
is plain they did mistake that commission, as to a main part
of it, for a season ; as where he bids them " Go, teach all
nations ;" since some time after they judged it unlawful to
teach the Gentiles ; yea, Peter himself scrupled it, until by
a vision constrained thereunto ; for which, after he had done
it, he was for a season, until they were better informed,
judged by the rest of his brethren. Now, if the education
of the apostles as Jews, and their propensity to adhere and
stick to the Jewish religion, did so far influence them, that
even after Christ's resurrection, and the pouring forth of
the Spirit, they could not receive nor admit of the teaching
of the Gentiles, though Christ, in his commission to them,
commanded them to preach to them ; what further absurdity
were it to suppose, that, through the like mistake, the
chiefest of them having been the disciples of John, and his
baptism being so much prized there among the Jews, they
also took Christ's baptism, intended by him of the Spirit,
to be that of water, which was John's, and accordingly
practised it for a season ? It suffices us, that if they were

The apos-
tles did
scruple the
teaching
the Gen-
tiles.

ѕυ mistaken, though I say not that they were so, they did not always remain under that mistake: else Peter would not have said of the baptism which now saves, " that it is not a putting away of the filth of the flesh," which certainly water baptism is.

But further, They urge much Peter's baptizing Cornelius; in which they press two things, First, That water baptism is used, even to those that had received the Spirit. Secondly, That it is said positively, "he commanded them to be baptized," Acts x. 47, 48.

But neither of these doth necessarily infer water baptism to belong to the new covenant dispensation, nor yet to be a perpetual standing ordinance in the church. For first, all that this will amount to, was, that Peter at that time baptised these men; but that he did it by virtue of that commission, Mat. xxviii., remains yet to be proved. And how doth the baptizing with water, after the receiving of the Holy Ghost, prove the case, more than the use of circumcision, and other legal rites, acknowledged to have been performed by him afterwards? Also, it is no wonder if Peter, who thought it so strange, notwithstanding all that had been professed before, and spoken by Christ, that the Gentiles should be made partakers of the gospel, and with great difficulty, not without an extraordinary impulse thereunto, was brought to come to them, and eat with them, was apt to put this ceremony upon them; which being, as it were, the particular dispensation of John, the forerunner of Christ, seemed to have greater affinity with the gospel, than the other Jewish ceremonies then used by the church; but that will no ways infer our adversaries' conclusion. Secondly, As to these words, "And he commanded them to be baptized;" it declareth matter of fact, not of right, and amounteth to no more, than that Peter did at that time, *pro hic & nunc*, command those persons to be baptized with water, which is not denied: but it saith nothing that Peter commanded water baptism to be a standing and perpetual ordinance to the church; neither can any man of sound reason say, if he heed what he says, that a command in

Whether Peter's baptizing some with water makes it a standing ordinance to the church.

matter of fact to particular persons, doth infer the thing commanded to be of general obligation to all, if it be not otherwise bottomed upon some positive precept. Why doth Peter's commanding Cornelius and his household to be baptized at that time infer water baptism to continue, more than his constraining, which is more than commanding, the Gentiles in general to be circumcised, and observe the law? We find at that time, when Peter baptized Cornelius, it was not yet determined whether the Gentiles should not be circumcised; but on the contrary, it was the most general sense of the church that they should: and therefore no wonder if they thought it needful at that time that they should be baptized; which had more affinity with the gospel, and was a burthen less grievous.

Obj. 4.

§ X. Fourthly; They object from the signification of the word *baptize*, which is as much as to dip and wash with water; alleging thence, that the very word imports a being baptized with water.

Answ.

This objection is very weak. For since baptizing with water was a rite among the Jews, as Paulus Riccius showeth, even before the coming of John; and that the ceremony received that name from the nature of the practice, as used both by the Jews and by John; yet we find that Christ and his apostles frequently make use of these terms to a more spiritual signification. Circumcision was only used and understood among the Jews to be that of the flesh; but the apostle tells us of the circumcision of the heart and spirit made without hands. So that though baptism was used among the Jews only to signify a washing with water, yet both John, Christ, and his apostles, speak of a being "baptized with the Spirit, and with fire;" which they make the peculiar baptism of Christ, as contradistinguished from that of water, which was John's, as is above shown. So that though baptism among the Jews was only understood of water, yet among Christians it is very well understood of the Spirit without water: as we see Christ and his apostles spiritually to understand things, under the terms of what had been shadows before. Thus

Baptizing signifies dipping or washing with water.

Christ, speaking of his body, though the Jews mistook him, said, "Destroy this temple, and in three days I will raise it up;" and many more that might be instanced. But if the etymology of the word should be tenaciously adhered to, it would militate against most of our adversaries, as well as against us; for the Greek Βαπτίζω signifies *immergo*, that is, to *plunge* and *dip in;* and that was the proper use of water baptism among the Jews, and also by John, and the primitive Christians, who used it; whereas our adversaries, for the most part, only sprinkle a little water upon the forehead, which doth not at all answer to the word *baptism.* Yea, those of old among Christians that used water baptism, thought this dipping or plunging so needful, that they thus dipped children: and forasmuch as it was judged that it might prove hurtful to some weak constitutions, sprinkling, to prevent that hurt, was introduced; yet then it was likewise appointed, that such as were only sprinkled, and not dipped, should not be admitted to have any office in the church, as not being sufficiently baptized. So that if our adversaries will stick to the word, they must alter their method of sprinkling.

*Βαπτίζω, immergo, intingo, to plunge and dip in.*

Those that of old used water baptism were dipped and plunged, and those that were only sprinkled, were not admitted to any office in the church, and why.

Fifthly, They object John iii. 5, "Except a man be born of water, and of the Spirit," &c., hence inferring the necessity of water baptism, as well as of the Spirit.

Obj. 5.

But if this prove any thing, it will prove water baptism to be of absolute necessity; and therefore Protestants rightly affirm, when this is urged upon them by Papists, to evince the absolute necessity of water baptism, that *water* is not here understood of outward water; but mystically, of an inward cleansing and washing. Even as where Christ speaks of being baptized with fire, it is not to be understood of outward material fire, but only of purifying, by a metonymy; because to purify is a proper effect of fire, as to wash and make clean is of water; therefore the scripture alludes to water, where it can as little be so understood, as where we are said to be saved by the washing of regeneration, Tit. iii. 5. Yea, Peter saith expressly, in the place often cited, as * Calvin well observes, "That the baptism which saves, is

Answ.

The water that regenerates, is mystical and inward.

*In the 4th book of his Instit., c.15

not the putting away of the filth of the flesh." So that since *water* cannot be understood of outward water, this can serve nothing to prove water baptism.

OBJECT.

If it be said, that *water* imports here *necessitatem præcepti*, though not *medii;*

ANSW.

I answer; That is first to take it for granted that outward water is here understood; the contrary whereof we have already proved. Next, *water* and the *Spirit* are

*Necessitas præcepti and medii urged.*

placed here together, "Except a man be born of *water* and the *Spirit*," where the necessity of the one is urged as much as of the other. Now if the Spirit be absolutely necessary, so will also water; and then we must either say, that to be born of the Spirit is not absolutely necessary, which all acknowledge to be false; or else, that water is absolutely necessary; which, as Protestants, we affirm, and have proved, is false: else, we must confess, that water is not here understood of outward water. For to say that when water and the Spirit are placed here just together, and in the same manner, though there be not any difference or ground for it visible in the text, or deducible from it, That the necessity of water is here *præcepti*, but not *medii*, but the necessity of the Spirit is both *medii* and *præcepti*, is indeed confidently to affirm, but not to prove.

OBJ. 6.

Sixthly and lastly; They object, That the baptism of water is a visible sign or badge to distinguish Christians from Infidels, even as circumcision did the Jews.

ANSW.

I answer; This saith nothing at all, unless it be proved to be a necessary precept, or part of the new covenant dispensation; it not being lawful for us to impose outward ceremonies and rights, and say, they will distinguish us

*Circumcision a seal of the first covenant.*

from infidels. Circumcision was positively commanded, and said to be a seal of the first covenant; but as we have already proved that there is no such command for

*Water baptism falsely called a badge of Christianity.*

baptism, so there is not any word in all the New Testament, calling it a badge of Christianity, or seal of the new covenant: and therefore to conclude it is so, because circumcision was so, unless some better proof be alleged for it, is miserably to beg the question   The professing of faith in Christ, and a holy life answering thereunto, is a far better badge of Christianity than any outward washing; which yet answers not to that of circumcision, since that affixed a character in the flesh, which this doth not: so that a Christian is not known to be a Christian by his being baptized, especially when he was a child, unless he tell them so much: and may not the professing of faith in Christ signify that as well? I know there are divers of those called the Fathers, that speak much of water baptism, calling it *Characterem Christianitatis:* but so did they also of the sign of the cross, and other such things, justly rejected by Protestants. For the mystery of iniquity, which began to work in the apostles' days, soon spoiled the simplicity and purity of the Christian worship; insomuch that not only many Jewish rites were retained, but many heathenish customs and ceremonies introduced into the Christian worship; as particularly that word *sacrament.* So that it is a great folly, especially for Protestants, to plead any thing of this from tradition or antiquity; for we find that neither Papists nor Protestants use those rites exactly as the ancients did; who in such things, not walking by the most certain rule of God's Spirit, but doting too much upon externals, were very uncertain. For most of them all, in the primitive times, did wholly plunge and dip those they baptized, which neither Papists, nor most Protestants, do: yea, several of the Fathers accused some as heretics in their days, for holding some principles common with Protestants concerning it; as particularly Augustine doth the Pelagians, for saying that infants dying unbaptized may be saved. And the Manichees were condemned, for denying that grace is universally given by baptism; and Julian the Pelagian by Augustine, for denying exorcism and insufflation in the use of baptism: all which things Protestants deny also. So that Protestants do but foolishly to upbraid us, as if we could not show any among the ancients that denied water baptism; seeing they cannot show any, whom they acknowledge not to have been heretical in several things, that used it; nor yet,

*Marginal notes:*

Which is the badge of Christianity.

What the Fathers say of water baptism, and of the sign of the cross.

Heathenish ceremonies introduced into the Christian worship.

Exorcism or adjuration.

The sign of
the cross.

Many in
former ages
testified
against wa-
ter bap-
tism.

Ten canon-
ics burnt
at Orleans,
and why?

who using it, did not also use the sign of the cross, and
other things with it, which they deny.  There were some
nevertheless in the darkest times of Popery, who testified
against water baptism.  For one Alanus, pag. 103, 104,
107, speaks of some in his time that were burnt for the
denying of it: for they said, That baptism had no efficacy,
either in children or adult persons ; and therefore men
were not obliged to take baptism : particularly ten canonics, so called, were burnt for that crime, by the order
of king Robert of France.  And P. Pithæus mentions it in
his fragments of the history of Guienne, which is also confirmed by one Johannes Floracensis, a monk, who was
famous at that time, in his epistle to Oliva, abbot of the
Ausonian church : " I will," saith he, " give you to understand concerning the heresy that was in the city of Orleans
on Childermas-day ; for it was true, if ye have heard any
thing, that king Robert caused to be burnt alive near four-
teen of that city, of the chief of their clergy, and the more
noble of their laics, who were hateful to God, and abominable to heaven and earth ; for they did stiffly deny the
grace of holy baptism, and also the consecration of the
Lord's body and blood."  The time of this deed is noted
in these words by Papir. Masson, in his Annals of France,
lib. iii. ; in Hugh and Robert, *Actum Aureliæ publice anno
Incarnucionis Domini* 1022 ; *Regni Roberti Regis* 28 ; *In-
dictione* 5, *quando Stephanus Hæresiarcha & Complices ejus
damnati sunt & exusti Aureliæ.*

Now for their calling them Heretics and Manichees, we
have nothing but the testimony of their accusers, which
will no more invalidate their testimony for this truth against
the use of water baptism, or give more ground to charge
us, as being one with the Manichees, than because some,
called by them Manichees, do agree with Protestants in
some things, that therefore Protestants are Manichees or
Heretics, which Protestants can no ways shun.  For the
question is, Whether, in what they did, they walked according to the truth testified of by the Spirit in the holy
scriptures ?  So that the controversy is brought back again

to the scriptures, according to which, I suppose, I have
already discussed it.

As for the latter part of the thesis, denying the use of The bap-
infant baptism, it necessarily follows from what is above tism of in-<br>fants a
said.  For if water baptism be ceased, then surely baptiz- human tra
ing of infants is not warrantable.  But those that take dition.
upon them to oppose us in this matter, will have more to
do as to this latter part: for after they have done what
they can to prove water baptism, it remains for them to
prove that infants ought to be baptized.  For he that
proves water baptism ceased, proves that infant baptism is
vain: but he that should prove that water baptism con
tinues, has not thence proved that infant baptism is necessary; that needs something further.  And therefore it was
a pitiful subterfuge of Nic. Arnoldus against this, to say,
That the denying of infant baptism belonged to the gan-
grene of the Anabaptists, without adding any further
proof.

---

## PROPOSITION XIII.

*Concerning the Communion, or Participation of the Body
and Blood of Christ.*

The communion of the body and blood of Christ is inward 1 Cor. x.
and spiritual, which is the participation of his flesh and 16, 17.<br>John vi. 32
blood, by which the inward man is daily nourished in 33, 35.
the hearts of those in whom Christ dwells.  Of which 1 Cor. v. 8
things the breaking of bread by Christ with his disciples
was a figure, which even they who had received the substance used in the church for a time, for the sake of the
weak; even as abstaining from things strangled, and from Acts xv. 20
blood, the washing one another's feet, and the anointing John xiii<br>14.
of the sick with oil: all which are commanded with no James v.
less authority and solemnity than the former; yet seeing 14.
they are but shadows of better things, they cease in
such as have obtained the substance.

35 *

§ I. The communion of the body and blood of Christ is a mystery hid from all natural men, in their first fallen and degenerate state, which they cannot understand, reach to, nor comprehend, as they there abide; neither, as they there are, can they be partakers of it, nor yet are they able to discern the Lord's body. And forasmuch as the Christian world, so called, for the most part hath been still labouring, working, conceiving and imagining, in their own natural and unrenewed understandings, about the things of God and religion; therefore hath this mystery been much hid and sealed up from them, while they have been contending, quarrelling and fighting one with another about the mere shadow, outside and form, but strangers to the substance, life and virtue.

§ II. The body then of Christ, which believers partake of, is spiritual, and not carnal; and his blood, which they drink of, is pure and heavenly, and not human or elementary, as Augustine also affirms of the body of Christ, which is eaten, in his Tractat., Psal. xcviii., "Except a man eat my flesh, he hath not in him life eternal:" and he saith, "The words which I speak unto you are Spirit and life; understand spiritually what I have spoken. Ye shall not eat of this body which ye see, and drink this blood which they shall spill, which crucify me—I am the living bread, who have descended from heaven. He calls himself the bread, who descended from heaven, exhorting that we might believe in him," &c.

*The body and blood of Christ is spiritual.*

Object. If it be asked then, What that body, what that flesh and blood is?

Answ. I answer; It is that heavenly seed, that divine, spiritual, celestial substance, of which we spake before in the fifth and sixth propositions. This is that spiritual body of Christ, whereby and through which he communicateth life to men, and salvation to as many as believe in him, and receive him; and whereby also man comes to have fellowship and communion with God. This is proved from the 6th of John, from verse 32, to the end, where Christ speaks more at large of this matter, than in any other place: and

*What the heavenly seed is, whereby formerly, and also now, life and salvation was and is communicated.*

indeed this evangelist and beloved disciple, who lay in the bosom of our Lord, gives us a more full account of the spiritual sayings and doctrine of Christ than any other : and 'tis observable, that though he speaks nothing of the ceremony used by Christ of breaking bread with his disciples, neither in his evangelical account of Christ's life and sufferings, nor in his epistles ; yet he is more large in this account of the participation of the body, flesh and blood of Christ, than any of them all.   For Christ, in this chapter, perceiving that the Jews did follow him for love of the loaves, desires them, verse 27, to " labour not for the meat which perisheth, but for that meat which endureth for ever :" but forasmuch as they, being carnal in their apprehensions, and not understanding the spiritual language and doctrine of Christ, did judge the manna, which Moses gave their fathers, to be the most excellent bread, as coming from heaven ; Christ, to rectify that mistake, and better inform them, affirmeth, First, That it is not Moses, but his Father, that giveth the true bread from heaven, vers. 32 and 48.   Secondly, This bread he calls himself, vers. 35, " I am the bread of life :" and vers. 51, " I am the living bread, which came down from heaven."   Thirdly, He declares that this bread is his flesh, vers. 51, " The bread that I will give, is my flesh ;" and vers. 55, " For my flesh is meat indeed, and my blood is drink indeed." Fourthly, The necessity of partaking thereof, vers. 53, " Except ye eat the flesh of the Son of man, and drink his blood, ye have no life in you."   And lastly, The blessed fruits and necessary effects of this communion of the body and blood of Christ, vers. 33, " This bread giveth life to the world."   Vers. 50, He that eateth thereof, dieth not.   Vers. 58, "He that eateth of this bread shall live for ever."   Vers. 54, Whoso eateth this flesh, and drinketh this blood, shall live for ever.   Vers. 56, And he dwelleth in Christ, and Christ in him.   Vers. 57, And shall live by Christ.   From this large description of the origin, nature, and effects of this body, flesh and blood of Christ, it is apparent that it is spiritual, and to be under-

*The origin nature and effects of the body flesh and blood of Christ.*

stood of a spiritual body, and not of that body, or temple of Jesus Christ, which was born of the Virgin Mary, and in which he walked, lived, and suffered in the land of Judea; because it is said, that it came down from heaven, yea, that it is he that came down from heaven. Now all Christians at present generally acknowledge, that the outward body of Christ came not down from heaven; neither was it that part of Christ which came down from heaven. And to put the matter out of doubt, when the carnal Jews would have been so understanding it, he tells them plainly, ver. 63, "It is the Spirit that quickeneth, but the flesh profiteth nothing." This is also founded upon most sound and solid reason; because it is the soul, not the body, that is to be nourished by this flesh and blood. Now outward flesh cannot nourish nor feed the soul; there is no proportion nor analogy betwixt them; neither is the communion of the saints with God by a conjunction and mutual participation of flesh, but of the Spirit: "He that is joined to the Lord is one Spirit," not one flesh. For the flesh (I mean outward flesh, even such as was that wherein Christ lived and walked when upon earth; and not flesh, when transformed by a metaphor, to be understood spiritually) can only partake of flesh, as spirit of spirit: as the body cannot feed upon spirit, neither can the spirit feed upon flesh. And that the flesh here spoken of is spiritually to be understood, appears further, inasmuch as that which feedeth upon it shall never die; but the bodies of all men once die; yea, it was necessary that the body of Christ himself should die. That this body, and spiritual flesh and blood of Christ, is to be understood of that divine and heavenly seed, before spoken of by us, appears both by the nature and fruits of it. First, it is said, it is that which cometh down from heaven, and giveth life unto the world: now this answers to that light and seed, which is testified of, John i., to be the light of the world, and the life of men. For that spiritual light and seed, as it receives place in men's hearts, and room to spring up there, is as bread to the hungry and fainting soul, that is, as it were,

Solid reasons that it is his spiritual body Christ speaks of.

1 Cor. vi. 17.

This spiritual light and seed is as bread to the hungry soul.

buried and dead in the lusts of the world; which receives life again, and revives, as it tasteth and partaketh of this heavenly bread: and they that partake of it are said to come to Christ; neither can any have it, but by coming to him, and believing in the appearance of his light in their hearts; by receiving which, and believing in it, the participation of this body and bread is known. And that Christ understands the same thing here by his body, flesh and blood, which is understood, John i., by the "light enlightening every man," and the life, &c., appears; for the light and life, spoken of John i., is said to be Christ; "He is the true light:" and the bread and flesh, &c., spoken of in John vi., is called Christ; "I am the bread of life," saith he. Again, They that received that light and life, John i. 12, obtained power to become the sons of God, by believing in his name: so also here, John vi. 35, he that cometh unto this bread of life shall not hunger; and he that believes in him, who is this bread, shall never thirst. So then, as there was the outward visible body and temple of Jesus Christ, which took its origin from the Virgin Mary; there is also the spiritual body of Christ, by and through which He that was the "Word in the beginning with God," and was and is GOD, did reveal himself to the sons of men in all ages, and whereby men in all ages come to be made partakers of eternal life, and to have communion and fellowship with God and Christ. Of which body of Christ, and flesh and blood, if both Adam, and Seth, and Enoch, and Noah, and Abraham, and Moses, and David, and all the prophets and holy men of God, had not eaten, they had not had life in them; nor could their inward man have been nourished. Now as the outward body and temple was called Christ, so was also his spiritual body, no less properly, and that long before that outward body was in being. Hence the apostle saith, 1 Cor. x. 3, 4, that the "Fathers did all eat the same spiritual meat, and did all drink the same spiritual drink: for they drank of that spiritual rock that followed them, and that rock was Christ." This cannot be understood otherwise than of this spiritual body

*Christ's outward and spiritual body distinguished.*

*The patriarchs did eat of the body of Christ.*

3 c

of Christ; which spiritual body of Christ, though it was the saving food of the righteous both before the law and under the law; yet under the law it was veiled and shadowed, and covered under divers types, ceremonies, and observations; yea, and not only so, but it was veiled and hid, in some respect, under the outward temple and body of Christ, or during the continuance of it; so that the Jews could not understand Christ's preaching about it while on earth; and not the Jews only, but many of his disciples, judging it a hard saying, murmured at it; and many from that time went back from him, and walked no more with him. I doubt not but that there are many also at this day, professing to be the disciples of Christ, that do as little understand this matter as those did, and are as apt to be offended, and stumble at it, while they are gazing and following after the outward body, and look not to that by which the saints are daily fed and nourished. For as Jesus Christ, in obedience to the will of the Father, did by the eternal Spirit offer up that body for a propitiation for the remission of sins, and finished his testimony upon earth thereby, in a most perfect example of patience, resignation and holiness, that all might be made partakers of the fruit of that sacrifice; so hath he likewise poured forth into the hearts of all men a measure of that divine light and seed wherewith he is clothed; that thereby, reaching unto the consciences of all, he may raise them up out of death and darkness by his life and light, and thereby may be made partakers of his body, and therethrough come to have fellowship with the Father and with the Son.

§ III. If it be asked, How and after what manner man comes to partake of it, and to be fed by it?

I answer in the plain and express words of Christ, "I am the bread of life," saith he; "he that cometh to me shall never hunger; he that believeth in me shall never thirst." And again, "For my flesh is meat indeed, and my blood is drink indeed." So whosoever thou art that askest this question, or readest these lines, whether thou accountest thyself a believer, or really feelest, by a certain

*Marginal notes:*
John vi. 60, 66.

The divine light of Christ doth make the saints partakers of his body.

Quest.

Answ.
John vi 35 and 55

and sad experience, that thou art yet in the unbelief, and findest that the outward body and flesh of Christ is so far from thee, that thou canst not reach it, nor feed upon it; yea, though thou hast often swallowed down and taken in that which the Papists have persuaded thee to be the real flesh and blood of Christ, and hast believed it to be so, though all thy senses told thee the contrary; or, being a Lutheran, hast taken that bread, in and with and under which the Lutherans have assured thee that the flesh and blood of Christ is; or, being a Calvinist, hast partaken of that which the Calvinists say, though a figure only of the body, gives them who take it a real participation of the body, flesh, and blood of Christ, though they never knew how nor what way; I say, if for all this thou findest thy soul yet barren, yea, hungry, and ready to starve, for want of something thou longest for; know that that light that discovers thy iniquity to thee, that shows thee thy barrenness, thy nakedness, thy emptiness, is that body which thou must partake of, and feed upon: but that till by forsaking iniquity thou turnest to it, comest unto it, receivest it, though thou mayest hunger after it, thou canst not be satisfied with it; for it hath no communion with darkness, nor canst thou drink of the cup of the Lord, and the cup of devils: and be partaker of the Lord's table, and the table of devils," 1 Cor. x. 21. But as thou sufferest that small seed of righteousness to arise in thee, and to be formed into a birth; that new substantial birth, that is brought forth in the soul, naturally feeds upon and is nourished by this spiritual body; yea, as this outward birth lives not but as it draws in breath by the outward elementary air, so this new birth lives not in the soul, but as it draws in and breathes by that spiritual air or vehicle. And as the outward birth cannot subsist without some outward body to feed upon, some outward flesh, and some outward drink, so neither can this inward birth, unless it be fed by this inward flesh and blood of Christ, which answers to it after the same manner, by way of analogy. And this is most agreeable to the doctrine of Christ concerning this

*The Lutherans and Calvinists' opinions of the flesh and blood of Christ in the supper, so called.*

*2 Cor. vi. 14*

*How the inward man is nourished.*

matter. For as without outward food the natural body
John vi. 53. hath not life, so also saith Christ, "Except ye eat the flesh
of the Son of man, and drink his blood, ye have no life in
you." And as the outward body, eating outward food,
John vi. 57. lives thereby, so Christ saith, that he that eateth him shall
live by him. So it is this inward participation of this inward man, of this inward and spiritual body, by which man
is united to God, and has fellowship and communion with
him. "He that eateth my flesh, and drinketh my blood,"
John vi. 56. saith Christ, "dwelleth in me, and I in him." This cannot
be understood of outward eating of outward bread; and
as by this the soul must have fellowship with God, so also,
so far as all the saints are partakers of this one body and
one blood, they come also to have a joint communion.
Hence the apostle, 1 Cor. x. 17, in this respect saith, that
they "being many, are one bread, and one body;" and to
Verse 16. the wise among the Corinthians he saith, "The bread which
we break is it not the communion of the body of Christ?"
The true
spiritual
supper of
the Lord.
This is the true and spiritual supper of the Lord, which
men come to partake of, by hearing the voice of Christ,
and opening the door of their hearts, and so letting him in
in the manner abovesaid, according to the plain words of
the scripture, Rev. iii. 20, "Behold I stand at the door
and knock; if any man hear my voice, and open the door,
I will come in to him, and will sup with him, and he with
me." So that the supper of the Lord, and the supping with
the Lord, and partaking of his flesh and blood, is no ways
limited to the ceremony of breaking bread and drinking
wine at particular times, but is truly and really enjoyed, as
often as the soul retires into the light of the Lord, and feels
and partakes of that heavenly life by which the inward man
is nourished; which may be and is often witnessed by the
faithful at all times, though more particularly when they are
assembled together to wait upon the Lord.

§ IV. But what confusion the professors of Christianity
have run into concerning this matter, is more than obvious;
who, as in most other things they have done, for want of
a true spiritual understanding, have sought to tie this sup-

per of the Lord to that ceremony used by Christ before his death, of breaking bread and drinking wine with his disci-ples. And though they for the most part agree generally in this, yet how do they contend and debate one against another! How strangely are they pinched, pained, and straitened to make the spiritual mystery agree to that cere-mony! And what monstrous and wild opinions and con-ceptions have they invented, to inclose or affix the body of Christ to their bread and wine? From which opinion not only the greatest, and fiercest, and most hurtful con-tests, both among the professors of Christianity in general, and among Protestants in particular, have arisen; but also such absurdities, irrational and blasphemous consequences have ensued, as make the Christian religion odious and hateful to Jews, Turks, and heathen. The professors of Christianity do chiefly divide in this matter into three opinions.

*Man is not tied to the ceremony of breaking bread and drinking wine which Christ did use with his disciples; this only was a shadow.*

*What makes the Christian religion hateful to Jews, Turks, and heathen.*

The first is of those that say, The substance of the bread is transubstantiated into the very substance of that same body, flesh, and blood of Christ, which was born of the Virgin Mary, and crucified by the Jews; so that after the words of consecration, as they call them, it is no more bread, but the body of Christ.

*The Papists' faith of Christ's flesh.*

The second is of such who say, The substance of the bread remains, but that also that body is in, and with, and under the bread; so that both the substance of bread, and of the body, flesh, and blood of Christ, is there also.

*The Lutherans' faith.*

The third is of those, that, denying both these do affirm, That the body of Christ is not there corporally or substan-tially, but yet that it is really and sacramentally received by the faithful in the use of bread and wine; but how or what way it is there, they know not, nor can they tell; only we must believe it is there, yet so that it is only properly in heaven.

*The Calvinists' faith.*

It is not my design to enter into a refutation of these several opinions; for each of their authors and assertors have sufficiently refuted one another, and are all of them no less strong both from scripture and reason in refuting

36

each their contrary parties' opinion, than they are weak in establishing their own. For I often have seriously observed. in reading their respective writings, and so it may be have others, that all of them do notably, in so far as they refute the contrary opinions; but that they are mightily pained, when they come to confirm and plead for their own. Hence I necessarily must conclude, that none of them had attained to the truth and substance of this mystery. Let us see if Calvin,* after he had refuted the two former opinions, be more successful in what he affirms and asserts for the truth of his opinion, who, after he hath much laboured in over-turning and refuting the two former opinions, plainly con-fesseth, that he knows not what to affirm instead of them. For after he has spoken much, and at last concluded "that the body of Christ is there, and that the saints must needs partake thereof," at last he lands in these words, sect. 32, "But if it be asked me how it is? I shall not be ashamed to confess, that it is a secret too high for me to comprehend in my spirit, or explain in words." Here he deals very ingenuously; and yet who would have thought that such a man would have been brought to this strait in the confirming of his opinion? considering that a little before, in the same chapter, sect. 15, he accuseth the school-men among the Papists, and I confess truly, in that they neither understand nor explain to others how Christ is in the eucharist, which shortly after he confesseth himself he cannot do. If then the school-men among the Papists do neither understand nor yet explain to others their doc-trine in this matter, nor Calvin can comprehend it in his spirit, which I judge is as much as not to understand it, nor express it in words, and then surely he cannot explain it to others, then no certainty is to be had from either of them. There have been great endeavours used for recon-cilement in this matter, both betwixt Papists and Lutherans, Lutherans and Calvinists, yea, and Calvinists and Papists, but all to no purpose; and many forms and manners of expressions drawn up, to which all might yield; which in the end proved in vain, seeing every one understood them

*Inst. lib. iv. cap. 17.

J. Calvin's faith of Christ's flesh and blood un-certain.

The like the Papists

and interpreted them in their own way; and so they did thereby but equivocate and deceive one another. The reason of all this contention is, because they had not a clear understanding of the mystery, and were doting about shadows and externals. For both the ground and matter of their contest lies in things extrinsic from, and unnecessary to, the main matter. And this hath been often the policy of Satan, to busy people, and amuse them with outward signs, shadows, and forms, making them contend about that, while in the mean time the substance is neglected; yea, and in contending for these shadows he stirs them up to the practice of malice, heat, revenge, and other vices, by which he establisheth his kingdom of darkness among them, and ruins the life of Christianity. For there have been more animosities and heats about this one particular, and more bloodshed and contention, than about any other. And surely they are little acquainted with the state of Protestant affairs, who know not that their contentions about this have been more hurtful to the reformation than all the opposition they met with from their common adversaries. Now all those uncertain and absurd opinions, and the contentions therefrom arising, have proceeded from their all agreeing in two general errors concerning this thing; which being denied and receded from, as they are by us, there would be an easy way made for reconciliation, and we should all meet in one spiritual and true understanding of this mystery: and as the contentions, so would also the absurdities which follow from all the three forementioned opinions, cease and fall to the ground.

*Satan busies people in outward signs, shadows, and forms, whilst they neglect the substance.*

*What hath been hurtful to the reformation.*

*Two errors the ground of the contention about the supper.*

The first of these errors is, in making the communion or participation of the body, flesh, and blood of Christ to relate to that outward body, vessel, or temple, that was born of the Virgin Mary, and walked and suffered in Judea; whereas it should relate to the spiritual body, flesh, and blood of Christ, even that heavenly and celestial light and life, which was the food and nourishment of the regenerate in all ages, as we have already proved.

The second error is, in tying this participation of the

body and blood of Christ to that ceremony used by him with his disciples in the breaking of bread, &c., as if it had only a relation thereto, or were only enjoyed in the use of that ceremony, which it neither hath nor is. For this is that bread which Christ in his prayer teaches to call for, terming it τὸν ἄρτον τον ἐπιέσιον, i. e., the *super-substantial bread*, as the Greek hath it, and which the soul partakes of, without any relation or necessary respect to this ceremony, as shall be hereafter proved more at length.

These two errors being thus laid aside, and the contentions arising therefrom buried, all are agreed in the main positions, viz. : First, that the body, flesh, and blood of Christ is necessary for the nourishing of the soul. Secondly, that the souls of believers do really and truly partake and feed upon the body, flesh, and blood of Christ. But while men are not content with the spirituality of this mystery, going in their own wills, and according to their own inventions, to strain and wrest the scriptures to tie this spiritual communion of the flesh and blood of Christ to outward bread and wine, and such like carnal ordinances, no wonder if by their carnal apprehensions they run into confusion. But because it hath been generally supposed that the communion of the body and blood of Christ had some special relation to the ceremony of breaking bread, I shall first refute that opinion, and then proceed to consider the nature and use of that ceremony, and whether it be now necessary to continue ; answering the reasons and objections of such as plead its continuance as a necessary and standing ordinance of Jesus Christ.

§ V. First, it must be understood that I speak of a necessary and peculiar relation otherwise than in a general respect : for inasmuch as our communion with Christ is and ought to be our greatest and chiefest work, we ought to do all other things with a respect to God, and our fellowship with him ; but a special and necessary respect or relation is such as where the two things are so tied and united together, either of their own nature, or by the command of God, that the one cannot be enjoyed, or at least is not,

Believers' souls do really feed upon the flesh and blood of Christ.

I.
That the communion of the body and blood of Christ has no special relation to the ceremony of breaking bread, neither by nature nor precept.

except very extraordinarily, without the other.  Thus salvation hath a necessary respect to holiness, because " without holiness no man shall see God ;" and the eating of the flesh and blood of Christ hath a necessary respect to our having life, because if we eat not his flesh, and drink not his blood, we cannot have life ; and our feeling of God's presence hath a necessary respect to our being found meeting in his name by divine precept, because he has promised where two or three are met together in his name, he will be in the midst of them.  In like manner our receiving benefits and blessings from God has a necessary respect to our prayer, because if we ask, he hath promised we shall receive.  Now the communion or participation of the flesh and blood of Christ hath no such necessary relation to the breaking of bread and drinking of wine : for if it had any such necessary relation, it would either be from the nature of the thing, or from some divine precept ; but we shall show it is from neither ; therefore, &c.

First, It is not from the nature of it; because to partake of the flesh and blood of Christ is a spiritual exercise, and all confess that it is by the soul and spirit that we become real partakers of it, as it is the soul, and not the body, that is nourished by it.  But to eat bread and drink wine is a natural act, which in itself adds nothing to the soul, neither has any thing that is spiritual in it ; because the most carnal man that is can as fully, as perfectly, and as wholly eat bread and drink wine as the most spiritual.  Secondly, Their relation is not by nature, else they would infer one another ; but all acknowledge that many eat of the bread and drink of the wine, even that which they say is consecrate and transubstantiate into the very body of Christ, who notwithstanding have not life eternal, have not Christ dwelling in them, nor do live by him, as all do who truly partake of the flesh and blood of Christ without the use of this ceremony, as all the patriarchs and prophets did before this ordinance, as they account it, was instituted. Neither was there any thing under the law that had any direct or necessary relation hereunto ; though to partake

*The patriarchs and prophets, without this ceremony's use, were true partakers of Christ's flesh and blood.*

36 *                          3 D

of the flesh and blood of Christ in all ages was indispen

The paschal lamb its end.
sably necessary to salvation. For as for the paschal lamb, the whole end of it is signified particularly, Exod. xiii. 8, 9, to wit, That the Jews might thereby be kept in remembrance of their deliverance out of Egypt.

Secondly, It hath not relation by divine precept; for if it had, it would be mentioned in that which our adversaries account the institution of it, or else in the practice of it by the saints recorded in scripture; but so it is not. For as to the institution, or rather narration, of Christ's practice in this matter, we have it recorded by the evangelists Matthew, Mark, and Luke. In the first two there

Mat. xxvi. 26. Mark xiv. 22. Luke xxii. 19.
is only an account of the matter of fact, to wit, That Christ brake bread, and gave it his disciples to eat, saying, "This is my body;" and blessing the cup, he gave it them to drink, saying, "This is my blood;" but nothing of

The institution of the supper, or narration of Christ's practice therein.
any desire to them to do it. In the last, after the bread (but before the blessing, or giving them the wine), he bids them do it in remembrance of him. What we are to think of this practice of Christ shall be spoken of hereafter. But what necessary relation hath all this to the believers partaking of the flesh and blood of Christ? The end of this for which they were to do it, if at all, is to remember Christ; which the apostle yet more particularly expresses, 1 Cor. xi. 26, "to show forth the Lord's death;" but to remember the Lord, or declare his death, which are the special and particular ends annexed to the use of this ceremony, is not at all to partake of the flesh and blood of Christ; neither have they any more necessary relation to it than any other two different spiritual duties. For though they that partake of the flesh and blood of Christ cannot but remember him, yet the Lord and his death may be remembered, as none can deny, where his flesh and blood is not truly partaken of. So that since the very particular and express end of this ceremony may be witnessed, to wit, the remembrance of the Lord's death, and yet the flesh and blood of Christ not partaken of, it cannot have had any necessary relation to it, else the partaking thereof

would have been the end of it, and could not have been attained without this participation. But on the contrary, we may well infer hence, that since the positive end of this ceremony is not the partaking of the flesh and blood of Christ, and that whoever partakes of the flesh and blood of Christ cannot but remember him, that therefore such need not this ceremony to put them in remembrance of him.

But if it be said, That Jesus Christ calls the bread here OBJECT. his body, and the wine his blood, therefore he seems to have had a special relation to his disciples partaking of his flesh and blood in the use of this thing;

I answer, His calling the bread his body, and the wine ANSW. his blood, would yet infer no such thing; though it is not denied but that Jesus Christ, in all things he did, yea, and from the use of all natural things, took occasion to raise the minds of his disciples and hearers to spirituals. Hence from the woman of Samaria her drawing water, he took The wo-occasion to tell her of that living water, which "whoso man of Sa-maria, drinketh of shall never thirst;" which indeed is all one John iv. 14. with his blood here spoken of; yet it will not follow that that well or water had any necessary relation to the living The well, water, or the living water to it, &c. So Christ takes occa-the loaves, the bread sion, from the Jews following him for the loaves, to tell and wine, them of this spiritual bread and flesh of his body, which takes occa-was more necessary for them to feed upon; it will not sion from, to show the therefore follow that their following him for the loaves had inward any necessary relation thereunto. So also Christ here, feeding. being at supper with his disciples, takes occasion, from the bread and wine which was before them, to signify unto them, That as that bread which he brake unto them, and that wine which he blessed and gave unto them, did con-tribute to the preserving and nourishing of their bodies, so was he also to give his body and shed his blood for the salvation of their souls. And therefore the very end pro-posed in this ceremony to those that observe it is, to be a memorial of his death.

But if it be said, That the apostle, 1 Cor. x. 16, calls

the bread which he brake the communion of the body of
Christ, and the cup the communion of his blood;

I do most willingly subscribe unto it; but do deny that
this is understood of the outward bread, neither can it be
evinced, but the contrary is manifest from the context:
for the apostle in this chapter speaks not one word of that
ceremony; for having in the beginning of it shown them
how the Jews of old were made partakers of the spiritual
food and water, which was Christ, and how several of
them, through disobedience and idolatry, fell from that
good condition, he exhorts them, by the example of those
Jews whom God destroyed of old, to flee those evils;
showing them that they, to wit, the Corinthians, are likewise partakers of the body and blood of Christ; of which
communion they would rob themselves if they did evil,
because "they could not drink of the cup of the Lord and
the cup of devils, and partake of the Lord's table and the
table of devils," ver. 21, which shows that he understands
not here the using of outward bread and wine; because
those that do drink the cup of devils, and eat of the table

The wick-
edest may
take the
outward
bread and
wine.

of devils, yea, the wickedest of men, may partake of the
outward bread and outward wine. For there the apostle
calls the bread one, ver. 17, and he saith, "We being
many, are one bread, and one body; for we are all partakers of that one bread." Now if the bread be one, it
cannot be the outward, or the inward would be excluded;
whereas it cannot be denied but that it is the partaking of
the inward bread, and not the outward, that makes the
saints truly one body and one bread. And whereas they

The sacra-
mental
union pre-
tended, a
figment.

say, that the one bread here comprehendeth both the outward and inward, by virtue of the sacramental union; that
indeed is to affirm, but not to prove. As for that figment
of a sacramental union, I find not such a thing in all the
scripture, especially in the New Testament; nor is ther
any thing can give a rise for such a thing in this chapter,
where the apostle, as is above observed, is not at all treating of that ceremony, but only, from the excellency of that
privilege which the Corinthians had, as believing Chris-

tians. to partake of the flesh and blood of Christ, dehorts
them from idolatry, and partaking of the sacrifices offered
to idols, so as thereby to offend or hurt their weak brethren.

But that which they most of all cry out for in this mat- Object.
ter, and are always urging, is from 1 Cor. xi., where the
apostle is particularly treating of this matter, and therefore,
from some words here, they have the greatest appearance
of truth for their assertion, as ver. 27, where he calls the
cup the "cup of the Lord;" and saith, "That they who
eat of it and drink it unworthily, are guilty of the body and
blood of the Lord;" and ver. 29, Eat and drink their
own damnation; intimating hence, that this hath an immediate or necessary relation to the body, flesh, and blood
of Christ.

Though this at first view may catch the unwary reader, Answ
yet being well considered, it doth no ways evince the matter in controversy. As for the Corinthians being in the
use of this ceremony, why they were so, and how that
obliges not Christians now to the same, shall be spoken of
hereafter: it suffices at this time to consider that they were
in the use of it. Secondly, That in the use of it they were
guilty of and committed divers abuses. Thirdly, That the
apostle here is giving them directions how they may do it
aright, in showing them the right and proper use and end
of it.

These things being premised, let it be observed, that the
very express and particular use of it, according to the
apostle, is "to show forth the Lord's death," &c. But
to show forth the Lord's death, and partake of the flesh
and blood of Christ, are different things. He saith not,
As often as ye eat this bread, and drink this cup, ye partake of the body and blood of Christ; but, "ye show forth
the Lord's death." So I acknowledge that this ceremony,
by those that practise it, hath an immediate relation to the
outward body and death of Christ upon the cross, as being
properly a memorial of it; but it doth not thence follow
that it hath any inward or immediate relation to believers
communicating or partaking of the spiritual body and blood

of Christ, or that spiritual supper spoken of Rev. iii. 20
For though, in a general way, as every religious action in
some respect hath a common relation to the spiritual communion of the saints with God, so we shall not deny but
this hath a relation as others. Now for his calling the cup
" the cup of the Lord," and saying, They are guilty of
the body and blood of Christ, and eat their own damnation in not discerning the Lord's body, &c., I answer,
That this infers no more necessary relation than any other
religious act, and amounts to no more than this, That since
the Corinthians were in the use of this ceremony, and so
performed it as a religious act, they ought to do it worthily,
or else they should bring condemnation upon themselves.
Now this will not more infer the thing so practised by them
to be a necessary religious act obligatory upon others, than
when the apostle saith, Rom. xiv. 6, " He that regardeth
the day, regardeth it unto the Lord," it can be thence inferred that the days that some esteemed and observed did
lay an obligation upon others to do the same. But yet, as
he that esteemed a day, and placed conscience in keeping
it, was to regard it to the Lord, and so it was to him, in
so far as he dedicated it unto the Lord, the Lord's day, he
was to do it worthily; and if he did it unworthily, he
would be guilty of the Lord's day, and so keep it to his
own damnation; so also such as observe this ceremony of
bread and wine, it is to them the bread of the Lord, and
the cup of the Lord, because they use it as a religious
act; and forasmuch as their end therein is to show forth
the Lord's death, and remember his body that was crucified for them, and his blood that was shed for them, if,
notwithstanding, they believe it is their duty to do it, and
make it a matter of conscience to forbear, if they do it
without that due preparation and examination which every
religious act ought to be performed in, then, instead of
truly remembering the Lord's death, and his body and his
blood, they render themselves guilty of it, as being in one
spirit with those that crucified him, and shed his blood,
though pretending with thanksgiving and joy to remember

**it.** Thus the Scribes and Pharisees of old, though in memory of the prophets they garnished their sepulchres, yet are said by Christ to be guilty of their blood. And that no more can be hence inferred, appears from another saying of the same apostle, Rom. xiv. 23, "He that doubteth is damned if he eat," &c., where he, speaking of those that judged it unlawful to eat flesh, &c., saith, If they eat doubting, they eat their own damnation. Now it is manifest from all this, that either the doing or forbearing of this was to another, that placed no conscience in it, of no moment. So I say, he that eateth that which in his conscience he is persuaded it is not lawful for him to eat, doth eat his own damnation; so he also that placeth conscience in eating bread and wine as a religious act, if he do it unprepared, and without that due respect wherein such acts should be gone about, he eateth and drinketh his own damnation, not discerning the Lord's body, i. e., not minding what he doth, to wit, with a special respect to the Lord, and by way of special commemoration of the death of Christ.

The Pharisees guilty of the blood of the prophets.

§ VI. Having now sufficiently shown what the true communion of the body and blood of Christ is, how it is partaken of, and how it has no necessary relation to that ceremony of bread and wine used by Christ with his disciples: it is fit now to consider the nature and constitution of that ceremony (for as to the proper use of it, we have had occasion to speak before), whether it be a standing ordinance in the church of Christ obligatory upon all, or indeed whether it be any necessary part of the worship of the new covenant dispensation, or hath any better or more binding foundation than several other ceremonies appointed and practised about the same time, which the most of our opposers acknowledge to be ceased, and now no ways binding upon Christians. We find this ceremony only mentioned in scripture in four places, to wit, Matthew, Mark, and Luke, and by Paul to the Corinthians. If any would infer any thing from the frequency of the mentioning of it, that will add nothing: for it being a matter of

II.<br>Whether this ceremony be a necessary part of the new covenant, and obligatory.

fact, is therefore mentioned by the evangelists; and there
are other things less memorable as often, yea, oftener mentioned.    Matthew and Mark give only an account of the
matter of fact, without any precept to do so afterwards;
simply declaring, that Jesus at that time did desire them to
eat of the bread, and ·drink of the cup; to which Luke
adds these words, " This do in remembrance of me."    If
we consider this action of Christ with his apostles, there
will appear nothing singular in it for a foundation to such
a strange superstructure as many in their airy imaginations
have sought to build upon it: for both Matthew and Mark
express it as an act done by him as he was eating.    Matthew saith, " And as they were eating;" and Mark, "And
as they did eat, Jesus took bread," &c.    Now this act was
no singular thing, neither any solemn institution of a gospel
ordinance; because it was a constant custom among the
Jews, as Paulus Riccius observes at length in his Celestial
Agriculture, that when they did eat the passover, the master of the family did take bread, and bless it, and breaking
it, gave of it to the rest; and likewise taking wine, did the
same; so that there can nothing further appear in this, than
that Jesus Christ, who fulfilled all righteousness, and also
observed the Jewish feasts and customs, used this also
among his disciples only, that as in most other things he
laboured to draw their minds to a further thing, so in the
use of this he takes occasion to put them in mind of his
death and sufferings, which were shortly to be; which he
did the oftener inculcate unto them, for that they were
averse from believing it.    And as for that expression of
Luke, " Do this in remembrance of me," it will amount to
no more than this, that being the last time that Christ did
eat with his disciples, he desired them, that in their eating
and drinking they might have regard to him, and by the
remembering of that opportunity, be the more stirred up
to follow him diligently through sufferings and death, &c.
But what man of reason, laying aside the prejudice of
education, and the influence of tradition, will say, that this
account of the matter of fact given by Matthew and Mark,

---

*Side notes (left margin):*

Matt. xxvi. 26.
Mark xiv. 22.
Luke xxii. 19.
1 Cor. xi. 23, &c.

The break-
ing of bread
was no
singular
thing, but a
custom
among the
Jews.
P. Riccius.

What it is
to do this
in remem-
brance of
Christ.

oɪ this expression of Luke, to "do that in remembrance of him," will amount to these consequences, which the generality of Christians have sought to draw from it; as calling it, *Augustissimum Eucharistiæ Sacramentum; venerabile altaris Sacramentum;* the principal seal of the covenant of grace, by which all the benefits of Christ's death are sealed to believers; and such like things? But t̄ give a further evidence, how these consequences have not any bottom from the practice of that ceremony, nor fiom the words following, "do this," &c., let us consider another of the like nature, as it is at length expressed by John, chap. xiii. 4, 5, 8, 12, 14, 15: "Jesus riseth from supper, and laid aside his garments, and took a towel, and girded himself: after that, he poureth water into a bason, and began to wash the disciples' feet; and to wipe them with the towel wherewith he was girded: Peter said unto him, Thou shalt never wash my feet: Jesus answered him, If I wash thee not, thou hast no part with me. So after he had washed their feet, he said, Know ye what I have done to you? If I then your Lord and Master have washed your feet, ye also ought to wash one another's feet: for I have given you an example, that ye should do as I have done to you." As to which, let it be observed, that John relates this passage to have been done at the same time with the other of breaking bread; both being done the night of the passover, after supper. If we regard the narration of this, and the circumstances attending it, it was done with far more solemnity, and prescribed far more punctually and particularly than the former. It is saɪd only, "As he was eating, he took bread;" so that this would seem to be but an occasional business; but here he rose up, he laid by his garments, he girded himself, he poured out the water, he washed their feet, he wiped them with a towel; he did this to all of them; which are circumstances surely far more observable than those noted ɪn the other. The former was a practice common among the Jews, used by all masters of families upon that occasion; but this, as to the manner, and person acting it,

*Christ's washing of feet, and its manner related.*

*Compared with the breaking of bread.*

to wit, for the master to rise up, and wash the feet of his servants and disciples, was more singular and observable. In the breaking of bread, and giving of wine, it is not pleaded by our adversaries, nor yet mentioned in the text, that he particularly put them into the hands of all; but breaking it, and blessing it, gave it the nearest, and so they from hand to hand; but here it is mentioned, that he washed not the feet of one or two, but of many. He saith not in the former, that if they do not eat of that bread, and drink of that wine, they shall be prejudiced by it; but here he saith expressly to Peter, that if he wash him not, he hath no part with him; which being spoken upon Peter's refusing to let him wash his feet, would seem to import no less, than not the continuance only, but even the necessity of this ceremony. In the former he saith, as it were passingly, Do this in remembrance of me; but here he sitteth down again, he desires them to consider what he hath done, tells them positively, that as he hath done to them, so ought they to do to one another; and yet again, he re-doubles that precept, by telling them, he has given them an example, that they should do so likewise. If we respect the nature of the thing, it hath as much in it as either baptism or the breaking of bread; seeing it is an outward element of a cleansing nature, applied to the outward man, by the command and the example of Christ, to signify an inward purifying. I would willingly propose this seriously to men, who will be pleased to make use of that reason and understanding that God hath given them, and not be imposed upon, nor abused by the custom or tradition of others; Whether this ceremony, if we respect either the time that it was appointed in, or the circumstances wherewith it was performed, or the command enjoining the use of it, hath not as much to recommend it for a standing ordinance of the gospel, as either water baptism, or bread and wine, or any other of that kind? I wonder then what reason the Papists can give, why they have not numbered it among their sacraments, except merely *Voluntas Ecclesiæ* and *Traditio Patrum*.

*The washing one another's feet was left as an example.*

But if they say, That it is used among them, in .hat the Obje:t.
Pope, and some other persons among them, use to do it
once a year to some poor people;

I would willingly know what reason they have why this Answ.
should not be extended to all, as well as that of the eucharist, as they term it, or whence it appears from the text,
that " Do this in remembrance of me," should be interpreted that the bread and wine were every day to be taken
by all priests, or the bread every day, or every week, by
the people; and that that other command of Christ, " Ye
ought to do as I have done to you," &c., is only to be
understood of the Pope, or some other persons, to be done
only to a few, and that once a year? Surely there can be
no other reason for this difference assigned from the text.
And as to Protestants, who use not this ceremony at all, The Pro-
if they will but open their eyes, they may see how that by testants use
custom and tradition they are abused in this matter, as washing of
were their fathers in divers Popish traditions. For if we feet.
look into the plain scripture, what can be thence inferred
to urge the one, which may not be likewise pleaded for
the other; or for laying aside the one, which may not be
likewise said against the continuance of the other? If they
say, That the former, of washing the feet, was only a ceremony; what have they, whence they can show, that this
breaking of bread is more? If they say, That the former
was only a sign of humility and purifying; what have they
to prove that this was more? If they say, That one was
only for a time, and was no evangelical ordinance; what
hath this to make it such, that the other wanted? Surely
there is no way of reason to evade this; neither can any
thing be alleged, that the one should cease, and not the
other; or the one continue, and not the other, but the
mere opinion of the affirmers; which by custom, education
and tradition, hath begotten in the hearts of people a
greater reverence for, and esteem of the one than the other;
which if it had fallen out to be as much recommended to
us by tradition, would no doubt have been as tenaciously
pleaded for, as ha ing no less foundation in scripture. But

since the former, to wit, the washing of one another's feet
is justly laid aside, as not binding upon Christians; so
ought also the other for the same reason.

The breaking of bread not used now in the same manner as Christ did.

§ VII. But it is strange that those who are so clamorous for this ceremony, and stick so much to it, take liberty to dispense with the manner or method that Christ did it in; since none that ever I could hear of, except some Baptists, who now do it, use it in the same way that he did: Christ did it at supper, while they were eating; but the generality of Protestants do it in the morning only by itself. What rule walk they by in this change?

OBJECT.

If it be said, These are but circumstances, and not the matter; and if the matter be kept to, the alteration of circumstances is but of small moment;

ANSW.

What if it should be said the whole is but a circumstance, which fell out at that time when Christ eat the passover? For if we have regard to that which alone can be pleaded for an institution, viz., these words, " Do this in remembrance of me ;" it doth as properly relate to the manner as matter. For what may or can they evince in reason, that these words, " Do this," only signify eat bread, and drink wine, but it is no matter when ye eat, nor how ye eat it; and not as ye have seen me eat it at supper with you, who take bread, and break it, and give it you; and take the cup, and bless it, and give it you; so do ye likewise? And seeing Christ makes no distinction in those words, " Do this," it cannot be judged in reason but to relate to the whole; which if it do, all those that at present use this ceremony among Christians, have not yet obeyed this precept, nor fulfilled this institution, for all their clamours concerning it.

OBJECT.

If it be said, That the time and manner of doing it by Christ was but accidentally, as being after the Jewish passover, which was at supper;

ANSW.
The breaking of bread was a Jewish ceremony.

Besides that it may be answered, and easily proved, that the whole was accidental, as being the practice of a Jewish ceremony, as is above observed; may it not the same way be urged, that the drinking of wine was accidental, as being the natural product of that country; and so be pleaded, that in those countries where wine doth not grow, as in our nation of Scotland, we may make use of beer or ale in the use of this ceremony; or bread made of other grain than that which Christ used? And yet would not our adversaries judge this an abuse, and not right performing of this sacrament? Yea, have not scruples of this kind occasioned no little contention among the professors of Christianity? What great contest and strife hath been betwixt the Greek and Latin churches concerning the bread? While the one will have it unleavened, reckoning, because the Jews made use of unleavened bread in the passover, that it was such kind of bread that Christ did break to his disciples; the other leavened: therefore the Lutherans make use of unleavened bread, the Calvinists of leavened. And this contest was so hot, when the reformation was beginning at Geneva, that Calvin and Farellus were forced to fly for it. But do not Protestants, by these uncertainties, open a door to Papists for their excluding the people from the cup? Will not "Do this" infer positively, that they should do it in the same manner, and at the same time, as Christ did it; as well as that they should use the cup, and not the bread only? Or what reason have they to dispense with the one, more than the Papists have to do with the other? Oh! what strange absurdities and inconveniences have Christians brought upon themselves, by superstitiously adhering to this ceremony! Out of which difficulties it is impossible for them to extricate themselves, but by laying it aside, as they have done others of the like nature. For besides what is above mentioned, I would gladly know how from the words they can be certainly resolved that these words "Do this" must be understood to the clergy, Take, bless, and break this bread, and give it to others; but to the laity only, Take and eat, but do not bless, &c.

If it be said, That the clergy were only present;

Then will not that open a door for the Popish argument against the administration of the cup to the people? Or

*Contests between the Greek and Latin churches, concerning the leavened and unleavened bread in the supper.*

*Farellus.*

*The clergy taking bread, do bless and give it: the laity must take and eat, not bless it.*

*Object.*

*Answ.*

37 *

may not another from thence as easily infer, that the
clergy only ought to partake of this ceremony; because
they were the apostles only then present, to whom it was
said, Do this? But if this [Do this] be extended to all,
how comes it all have not liberty to obey it, in both blessing, breaking, and distributing, as well as taking and
eating? Besides all these, even the Calvinist Protestants
of Great Britain could never yet accord among themselves
about the manner of taking it, whether sitting, standing,
or kneeling; whether it should be given to the sick, and
those that are ready to die, or not? Which controversies,
though they may be esteemed of small moment, yet have
greatly contributed, with other things, to be the occasion
not only of much contention, but also of bloodshed and
devastation; so that in this last respect the Prelatic Calvinists have termed the Presbyterians schismatical and pertinacious; and they them again superstitious, idolatrous,
and papistical. Who then, that will open their eyes, but
may see that the devil hath stirred up this contention and
zeal, to busy men about things of small moment, that
greater matters may be neglected, while he keeps them in
such ado about this ceremony; though they lay aside others
of the like nature, as positively commanded, and as punctually practised; and from the observation of which half
so many difficulties will not follow?

§ VIII. How then? Have we not reason, not finding
the nature of this practice to be obligatory upon us, more
than those others which our adversaries have laid aside, to
avoid this confusion; since those that use it can never
agree, neither concerning the nature, efficacy, nor manner
of doing it? And this proceeds, because they take it not
plainly, as it lies in the scripture; but have so much inter-
mixed their own inventions. For would they take it as it
lies, it would import no 'more, than that Jesus Christ at
that time did thereby signify unto them, that his body and
blood was to be offered for them; and desired them, that
whensoever they did eat or drink, they might do it in remembrance of him; or with a regard to him, whose blood

was shed for them. Now that the primitive church, gathered immediately after his ascension, did so understand it, doth appear from their use and practice, if we admit those places of the Acts where breaking of bread is spoken of, to have relation hereto; which as our adversaries do, so we shall willingly agree to: as first, Acts ii. 42, "And they continued steadfastly in the apostles' doctrine and fellowship, and in breaking of bread," &c. This cannot be understood of any other than of their ordinary eating; for as nothing else appears from the text, so the context makes it plain; for they had all things in common: and therefore it is said, vers. 46, "And they continuing daily with one accord in the temple, and breaking bread from house to house, did eat their meat with gladness and singleness of heart." Those who will not wilfully close their eyes, may see here, that the breaking being joined with their eating, shows, that nothing else is here expressed, but that having all things in common, and so continuing together, they also did break their bread, and eat their meat together: in doing whereof, I cannot doubt but they remembered the Lord; to follow whom they had, with so much zeal and resignation, betaken themselves. This is further manifest from Acts vi. 2, for the apostles, having the care and distribution of that money, which the believers, having sold their possessions, gave unto them, and finding themselves overcharged with that burthen, appointed deacons for that business, that they might give themselves continually to prayer, and to the ministry of the word; not leaving that, to serve tables. This cannot be meant of any sacramental eating, or religious act of worship; seeing our adversaries make the distributing of that the proper act of ministers, not of deacons: and yet there can be no reason alleged, that that breaking of bread, which they are said to have continued in, and to have done from house to house, was other than those tables which the apostles served; but here gave over, as finding themselves overcharged with it. Now as the increase of the disciples did incapacitate the apostles any more to manage this; so it would seem their further

By breaking of bread they had all things in common, remembering the Lord.

Deacons appointed for serving tables.

increase, and dispersing in divers places, hindered the continuance of that practice of having things in common: but
notwithstanding, so far at least to remember or continue
that ancient community they did at certain times come together, and break bread together.    Hence it is said, Acts

At Troas
the supper
deferred till
midnight.
xx. 7, on Paul's coming to Troas, that " upon the first day
of the week, when the disciples came together to break
bread, Paul preached unto them, ready to depart on the
morrow, and continued his speech until midnight."    Here
is no mention made of any sacramental eating; but only
that Paul took occasion from their being together to preach
unto them.    And it seems it was a supper they intended,
not a morning bit of bread, and sup of wine, else it is not
very probable that Paul would from the morning have
preached until midnight.    But the 11th verse puts the
matter out of dispute, which is thus: " When he therefore
was come up again, and had broken bread, and eaten, and
talked a long while, even till break of day, so he departed."    This shows, that the breaking of bread was deferred
till that time; for these words [and when he had broken
bread, and eaten] do show, that it had a relation to the
breaking of bread before mentioned, and that that was the
time he did it.    Secondly, These words joined together
[and when he had broken bread, and eaten, and talked]

They only
did eat for
refreshing
the body.
show, it was no religious act of worship, but only an eating
for bodily refreshment, for which the Christians used to
meet together some time; and doing it in God's fear, and
singleness of heart, doth notwithstanding difference it from

By some
called a
love-feast.
the eating or feasting of profane persons.    And this by some
is called a love-feast, or a being together, not merely to
feed their bellies, or for outward ends; but to take thence
occasion to eat and drink together, in the dread and presence of the Lord, as his people; which custom we shall
not condemn.    But let it be observed, that in all the Acts
there is no other nor further mention of this matter.    But
if that ceremony had been some solemn sacrifice, as some
will have it, or such a special sacrament as others plead it
to be; it is strange that that history, which in many less

things gives a particular account of the Christians' behaviour, should have been so silent in the matter: only we find, that they used sometimes to meet together to break bread, and eat. Now as the early Christians began by degrees to depart from that primitive purity and simplicity, so did they also to accumulate superstitious traditions, and vitiate the innocent practices of their predecessors, by the intermixing either of Jewish or heathenish rites; and likewise in the use of this, abuses began very early to creep in among Christians, so that it was needful for the apostle Paul to reform them, and reprove them for it, as he doth at large, 1 Cor. xi., from vers. 17, to the end: which place we shall particularly examine, because our adversaries lay the chief stress of their matter upon it; and we shall see whether it will infer any more than we have above granted. First, Because they were apt to use that practice in a superstitious mind beyond the true use of it, so as to make of it some mystical supper of the Lord, he tells them, vers. 20, That their " coming together into one place, is not to eat the Lord's supper;" he saith not, This is not the right manner to eat; but, " This is NOT to eat the Lord's supper;" because the supper of the Lord is spiritual, and a mystery. Secondly, He blames them, in that they came together for the worse, and not for the better; the reason he gives of this is, vers. 21, " For in eating every one hath taken before his own supper; and one is hungry, and another is drunken." Here it is plain that the apostle condemns them in that, because this custom of supping in general was used among Christians to increase their love, and as a memorial of Christ's supping with the disciples, they had so vitiated it, as to eat it apart, and to come full, who had abundance; and hungry, who had little at home; whereby the very use and end of this practice was lost and perverted: and therefore he blames them, that they did not either eat this in common at home; or reserve their eating till they came all together to the public assembly. This appears plainly by the following vers. 22: " Have ye not houses to eat and drink in? Or despise ye the church of

*The Christians began by degrees to depart from the primitive purity.*

*1 Cor. xi. 17. Concerning the supper of the Lord (so called) explained.*

*Why the custom of supping in common was used among Christians.*

God, and shame them that have not?" Where he blames them for their irregular practice herein, in that they despised to eat orderly, or reserve their eating to the public assembly; and so shaming such as not having houses, nor fulness at home, came to partake of the common table; who, being hungry, thereby were ashamed, when they observed others come thither full and drunken. Those that without prejudice will look to the place, will see this must have been the case among the Corinthians: for supposing the use of this to have been then, as now used either by Papists, Lutherans, or Calvinists, it is hard making sense of the apostle's words, or indeed to conceive what was the abuse the Corinthians committed in this thing. Having thus observed what the apostle said above, because this

The rise of that custom.

custom of eating and drinking together some time, had its rise from Christ's act with the apostles, the night he was betrayed; therefore the apostle proceeds, vers. 23, to give them an account of that: "For I have received of the Lord that which also I delivered unto you, that the Lord Jesus, the same night in which he was betrayed, took bread," &c. Those that understand the difference betwixt a narration of a thing, and a command, cannot but see, if they will, that there is no command in this place, but only an account of matter of fact; he saith not, I received of the Lord, that as he took bread, so I should command it to you to do so likewise; there is nothing like this in the place: yea, on the contrary, vers. 25, where he repeats Christ's imperative words to his apostles, he placeth them so as they import no command; " This do ye, as oft as ye drink it, in remembrance of me:" and then he adds, " For as often as ye eat

That [as often] imports no command of this supper.

this bread, and drink this cup, ye do show the Lord's death till he come:" but these words " as often" import no more a command, than to say, As often as thou goest to Rome, see the Capitol, will infer a command to me to go thither.

Object.

But whereas they urge the last words, " Ye show forth the Lord's death till he come;" insinuating, That this imports a necessary continuance of that ceremony, until Christ come at the end of the world to judgment;

I answer: They take two of the chief parts of the con- <sub>Answ.</sub> troversy here for granted, without proof. First, that "as often" imports a command; the contrary whereof is shown; neither will they ever be able to prove it. Secondly, That Christ's this coming is to be understood of Christ's last outward outward coming, and not of his inward and spiritual, that remains coming. t· be proved: whereas the apostle might well understand it of his inward coming and appearance, which perhaps some of those carnal Corinthians, that used to come drunken together, had not yet known; and others, being weak among them, and inclinable to dote upon outwards, this might have been indulged to them for a season, and even used by those who knew Christ's appearance in Spirit (as other things were, of which we shall speak hereafter), especially by the apostle, who became weak to the weak, and all to all, that he might save some. Now those weak To remem-and carnal Corinthians might be permitted the use of this, ber Christ's death till he to show forth, or remember Christ's death, till he came to come to arise in them; for though such need those outward things heart. to put them in mind of Christ's death, yet those who are dead with Christ, and not only dead with Christ, but buried, and also arisen with him, need not such signs to remember him: and to such therefore the apostle saith, Col. iii. 1, "If ye then be risen with Christ, seek those things which are above, where Christ sitteth on the right hand of God:" but bread and wine are not those things that are above, but are things of the earth. But that this whole matter was a mere act of indulgence and condescension of the apostle Paul to the weak and carnal Corinthians, appears yet more by the Syriac* copy, which, vers. 17, in his entering upon this matter, hath it thus; "In that concerning which I am about to command you (or instruct you) I commend you not, because ye have not gone forward, but are descended unto that which is less, or of less consequence:" clearly importing that the apostle was grieved that such was their condition, that he was forced

---

* And likewise the other Oriental versions, as the Arabic and Æthiopic, have it the same way.

to give them instructions concerning those outward things and doting upon which, they showed they were not gone forward in the life of Christianity, but rather sticking in beggarly elements. And therefore, vers. 20, the same version hath it thus, " When then ye meet together, ye do not do it, as it is just ye should do in the day of the Lord, ye eat and drink it:" therefore showing to them, that to meet together to eat and drink outward bread and wine, was not the labour and work of that day of the Lord. But since our adversaries are so zealous for this ceremony, because used by the church of Corinth, though with how little ground is already shown, how come they to pass over far more positive commands of the apostles, as matters of no moment? As first, Acts xv. 29, where the apostles peremptorily command the Gentiles, as that which was the mind of the Holy Ghost, " To abstain from things strangled, and from blood:" and James v. 14, where it is expressly commanded, That the sick be anointed with oil in the name of the Lord.

*To abstain from things strangled.*

*The anointing with oil.*

OBJECT. If they say, These were only temporary things, but not to continue;

ANSW. What have they more to show for this; there being no express repeal of them?

OBJECT. If they say, The repeal is implied, because the apostle saith, We ought not to be judged in meats and drinks;

ANSW. I admit the answer; but how can it be prevented from militating the same way against the other practice? Surely not at all: nor can there be any thing urged for the one more than for the other, but custom and tradition.

OBJECT As for that of James, they say, There followed a miracle upon it, to wit, the recovery of the sick; but this being ceased, so should the ceremony.

ANSW. Though this might many ways be answered, to wit, That prayer then might as well be forborne, to which also the saving of the sick is there ascribed; yet I shall accept of it, because I judge indeed that ceremony is ceased. only methinks, since our adversaries, and that rightly, think a ceremony ought to cease where the virtue fails,

*A ceremony ought to cease, its virtue failing.*

they ought by the same rule to forbear the laying on of Thus lay ing on of hands. hands, in imitation of the apostles, since the gift of the Holy Ghost doth not follow upon it.

§ IX. But since we find that several testimonies of scripture do sufficiently show, that such external rites are no necessary part of the new covenant dispensation, therefore not needful now to continue, however they were for a season practised of old, I shall instance some few of them, whereby from the nature of the thing, as well as those testimonies, it may appear, that the ceremony of bread and The cere- mony of bread and wine is ceased. wine is ceased, as well as those other things confessed by our adversaries to be so. The first is Rom. xiv. 17, "For the kingdom of God is not meat and drink, but righteousness and peace, and joy in the Holy Ghost:" here the apostle evidently shows, that the kingdom of God, or gospel of Christ, stands not in meats and drinks, and such like things, but in righteousness, &c., as by the context doth appear, where he is speaking of the guilt and hazard of judging one another about meats and drinks. So then, if the kingdom of God stand not in them, nor the gospel, nor work of Christ, then the eating of outward bread and wine can be no necessary part of the gospel worship, nor any perpetual ordinance of it. Another of the same apostle is yet more plain, Col. ii. 16, the apostle throughout this whole second chapter doth clearly plead for us, and against the formality and superstition of our opposers: for in the beginning he holds forth the great privileges which Christians have by Christ, who are indeed come to the life of Christianity; and therefore he desires them, vers. 6, As they have received Christ, so to walk in him; and to beware, lest they be spoiled through philosophy and vain deceit, after the rudiments or elements of the world; because that in Christ, whom they have received, is all fulness: and that they are circumcised with the circumcision made without hands (which he calls the circumcision of Christ), and being buried with him by baptism, are also arisen with him through the faith of the operation of God. Here also they did partake of the true baptism of Christ;

38

and being such as are arisen with him, let us see whether he thinks it needful they should make use of such meat and drink as bread and wine, to put them in remembrance of Christ's death; or whether they ought to be judged, that they did it not; ver. 16, "Let no man therefore judge you in meat or in drink:" Is not bread and wine meat and drink? But why? "Which are a shadow of things to come: but the body is of Christ." Then since our adversaries confess, that their bread and wine is a sign or shadow; therefore, according to the apostle's doctrine, we ought not to be judged in the non-observation of it. But is it not fit for those that are dead with Christ to be subject to such ordinances? See what he saith, vers. 20, "Wherefore, if ye be dead with Christ from the rudiments of the world, why, as though living in the world, are ye subject to ordinances, (Touch not, taste not, handle not: which all are to perish with the using) after the commandments and doctrines of men?" What can be more plain? If this serve not to take away the absolute necessity of the use of bread and wine, what can it serve to take away? Sure I am, the reason here given is applicable to them, "which all do perish with the using;" since bread and wine perish with the using, as much as other things. But further, if the use of water, and bread and wine, were that wherein the very seals of the new covenant stood, and did pertain to the chief sacraments of the gospel and evangelical ordinances (so called), then would not the gospel differ from the law, or be preferable to it. Whereas the apostle shows the difference, Heb. ix. 10, in that such kind of observations of the Jews were as a sign of the gospel, for that they "stood only in meats and drinks, and divers washings." But if the gospel worship and service stand in the same, where is the difference?

If it be said, These under the gospel have a spiritual signification;

So had those under the law; God was the author of those, as well as Christ is pretended to be the author of these. But doth not this contending for the use of water,

**Marginal notes:**

'Tis but a sign and shadow they confess.

And which do perish with the using.

The law was meats and drinks; not so the gospel.

Object

Answ.

bread and wine, as necessary parts of the gospel worship, destroy the nature of it, as if the gospel were a dispensation of shadows, and not of the substance? Whereas the apostle, in that of the Colossians above mentioned, argues against the use of these things, as needful to those that are dead and arisen with Christ, because they are but shadows. And since, through the whole Epistle to the Hebrews, he argues with the Jews, to wean them from their old worship, for this reason, because it was typical and figurative; is it agreeable to right reason to bring them to another of the same nature? What ground from scripture or reason can our adversaries bring us, to evince that one shadow or figure should point to another shadow or figure, and not to the substance? And yet they make the figure of circumcision to point to water baptism, and the paschal lamb to bread and wine. But was it ever known that one figure was the anti-type of the other, especially seeing Protestants make not these their anti-types to have any more virtue and efficacy than the type had? For since, as they say, and that truly, That their sacraments confer not grace, but that it is conferred according to the faith of the receiver, it will not be denied but the faithful among the Jews received also grace in the use of their figurative worship. And though Papists boast that their sacraments confer grace *ex opere operato*, yet experience abundantly proveth the contrary.

*The law has shadows, the gospel brings the substance.*

*Their sacraments confer not grace.*

§ X. But supposing the use of water baptism and bread and wine to have been in the primitive church, as was also that of " abstaining from things strangled, and from blood," the use of legal purification, Acts xxi. 23, 24, 25, and anointing of the sick with oil, for the reasons and grounds before mentioned; yet it remains for our adversaries to show us how they come by power or authority to administer them. It cannot be from the letter of the scripture, else they ought also to do those other things, which the letter declares also they did, and which in the letter have as much foundation. Then their power must be derived from the apostles, either mediately or immediately;

*Opposers claim a power to give their sacraments; from whence do they derive it?*

but we have shown before, in the tenth proposition, that they have no mediate power, because of the interruption made by the apostasy; and for an immediate power or command by the Spirit of God to administer these things, none of our adversaries pretend to it. We know that in this, as in other things, they make a noise of the constant consent of the church, and of Christians in all ages; but *Tradition* as tradition is not a sufficient ground for faith, so in this *no sufficient* matter especially it ought to have but small weight; for that *ground for* in this point of ceremonies and superstitious observations *faith.* the apostacy began very early, as may appear in the epistles of Paul to the Galatians and Colossians; and we have no ground to imitate them in those things, whose entrance the apostle so much withstood, so heavily regretted, and so sharply reproved. But if we look to antiquity, we find, that in such kind of observances and traditions they were very uncertain and changeable; so that neither Protestants *The supper* nor Papists do observe this ceremony as they did, both in *they gave* that they gave it to young boys, and to little children: and *to young* *boys and* for aught can be learned, the use of this and infant bap- *children.* tism are of a like age, though the one be laid aside both by Papists and Protestants, and the other, to wit, baptism of infants, be stuck to. And we have so much the less reason to lay weight upon antiquity, for that if we consider their profession of religion, especially as to worship, and the ceremonial part of it, we shall not find any church now, whether Popish or Protestant, who differ not widely *Dailæus.* from them in many things, as Dallæus, in his treatise concerning the Use of the Fathers, well observeth and demonstrateth. And why they should obtrude this upon us because of the ancients' practice, which they themselves follow not, or why we may not reject this, as well as they do other things no less zealously practised by the ancients, no sufficient reason can be assigned.

Nevertheless I doubt not but many, whose understandings have been clouded with these ceremonies, have notwithstanding, by the mercy of God, had some secret sense of the mystery, which they could not clearly understand.

because it was veiled from them by their sticking to such outward things; and that through that secret sense diving in their comprehensions they ran themselves into these carnal apprehensions, as imagining the substance of the bread was changed, or that if the substance was not changed, yet the body was there, &c. And indeed I am inclinable very favourably to judge of Calvin in this particular, in that he deals so ingenuously to confess he "neither comprehends it, nor can express it in words; but yet by a feeling experience can say, The Lord is spiritually present." Calvin's ingenuous confession commended. Now as I doubt not but Calvin sometimes had a sense of his presence without the use of this ceremony, so as the understanding given him of God made him justly reject the false notions of transubstantiation and consubstantiation, though he knew not what to establish instead of them, if he had fully waited in the light that makes all Eph. v. 13 things manifest, and had not laboured in his own comprehension to settle upon that external ceremony, by affixing the spiritual presence as chiefly or principally, though not only, as he well knew by experience, there, or especially to relate to it, he might have further reached unto the knowledge of this mystery than many that went before him.

§ XI. Lastly, If any now at this day, from a true tenderness of spirit, and with real conscience towards God, did practice this ceremony in the same way, method, and manner as did the primitive Christians recorded in scripture, I should not doubt to affirm but they might be indulged in it, and the Lord might regard them, and for a season appear to them in the use of these things, as many of us have known him to do to us in the time of our ignorance; providing always they did not seek to obtrude them upon others, nor judge such as found themselves delivered from them, or that they do not pertinaciously adhere to them. For we certainly know that the day is dawned, in which God hath arisen, and hath dismissed all those ceremonies and rites, and is only to be worshipped n Spirit, and that he appears to them who wait upon him; and that In tenderness of conscience, God winketh at our ignorance. The day is dawned wherein God is risen and worshipped n Spirit.

to seek God in these things is, with Mary at the sepulchre, to seek the living among the dead: for we know that he is risen, and revealed in Spirit, leading his children out of these rudiments, that they may walk with him in his light: to whom be glory for ever.   Amen.

---

## PROPOSITION XIV.

*Concerning the Power of the Civil Magistrate in Matters purely Religious, and pertaining to the Conscience.*

Since God hath assumed to himself the power and dominion of the conscience, who alone can rightly instruct and govern it, therefore it is not lawful for any, whosoever, by virtue of any authority or principality they bear in the government of this world, to force the consciences of others; and therefore all killing, banishing, fining, imprisoning, and other such things which are inflicted upon men for the alone exercise of their conscience, or difference in worship or opinion, proceedeth from the spirit of Cain the murderer, and is contrary to the truth; providing always, that no man, under the pretence of conscience, prejudice his neighbour in his life or estate, or do any thing destructive to, or inconsistent with, human society; in which case the law is for the transgressor, and justice is to be administered upon all, without respect of persons.

Luke ix.
55, 56.
Mat. vii. 12,
13, 29.
Tit. iii. 10.

§ I. LIBERTY of conscience from the power of the civil magistrate hath been of late years so largely and learnedly handled, that I shall need to be but brief in it; yet it is to be lamented that few have walked answerably to this principle, each pleading it for themselves, but scarce allowing it to others, as hereafter I shall have occasion more at length to observe.

It will be fit in the first place, for clearing of mistakes

to say something of the state of the controversy, that what follows may be the more clearly understood.

By conscience then, as in the explanation of the fifth and sixth propositions I have observed, is to be understood *What conscience is* that persuasion of the mind which arises from the understanding's being possessed with the belief of the truth or falsity of any thing; which though it may be false or evil upon the matter, yet if a man should go against his persuasion or conscience, he would commit a sin; because what a man doth contrary to his faith, though his faith be wrong, is no ways acceptable to God. Hence the apostle saith, "Whatsoever is not of faith, is sin; and he that *Rom. xiv.* doubteth is damned if he eat;" though the thing might *23.* have been lawful to another; and that this doubting to eat some kind of meats (since all the creatures of God are good, and for the use of man, if received with thanksgiving) might be a superstition, or at least a weakness, which were better removed. Hence Ames. de Cas. Cons. saith, "The conscience, although erring, doth evermore bind, so as that he sinneth who doth contrary to his conscience,* be- *i. e. As he supposeth.* cause he doth contrary to the will of God, although not *poseth.* materially and truly, yet formally and interpretatively."

So the question is, First, Whether the civil magistrate hath power to force men in things religious to do contrary to their conscience; and if they will not, to punish them in their goods, liberties, or lives? This we hold in the negative. But Secondly, As we would have the magistrate to avoid this extreme of encroaching upon men's consciences, so on the other hand we are far from joining with or strengthening such libertines as would stretch the liberty of their consciences to the prejudice of their neighbours, or to the ruin of human society. We understand therefore by matters of conscience such as immediately relate betwixt God and man, or men and men, that are under the same persuasion, as to meet together and worship God in that way which they judge is most acceptable unto him, and not to encroach upon, or seek to force their neighbours, otherwise than by reason, or such other means as Christ

and his apostles used, viz. : Preaching and instructing such
as will hear and receive it; but not at all for men, under
the notion of conscience, to do any thing contrary to the
moral and perpetual statutes generally acknowledged by
all Christians; in which case the magistrate may very lawfully use his authority; as on those, who, under a pretence
of conscience, make it a principle to kill and destroy all
the wicked, *id est*, all that differ from them, that they, to
wit, the saints, may rule, and who therefore seek to make
all things common, and would force their neighbours to
share their estates with them, and many such wild notions,
as is reported of the Anabaptists of Munster; which evidently appears to proceed from pride and covetousness,
and not from purity or conscience; and therefore I have
sufficiently guarded against that in the latter part of the
proposition. But the liberty we lay claim to is such as
the primitive church justly sought under the heathen emperors, to wit, for men of sobriety, honesty, and a peaceable conversation, to enjoy the liberty and exercise of their
conscience towards God and among themselves, and to
admit among them such as by their persuasion and influence come to be convinced of the same truth with them,
without being therefore molested by the civil magistrate.
Thirdly, Though we would not have men hurt in their
temporals, nor robbed of their privileges as men and members of the commonwealth, because of their inward persuasion; yet we are far from judging that in the church of
God there should not be censures exercised against such
as fall into error, as well as such as commit open evils;
and therefore we believe it may be very lawful for a Christian church, if she find any of her members fall into any
error, after due admonitions and instructions according to
gospel order, if she find them pertinacious, to cut them off
from her fellowship by the sword of the Spirit, and deprive
them of those privileges which they had as fellow-mem-
bers; but not to cut them off from the world by the temporal sword, or rob them of their common privileges as
men, seeing they enjoy not these as Christians, or under

such a fellowship, but as men, and members of the creation. Hence Chrysostom saith well, (de Anath.) "We must condemn and reprove the evil doctrines that proceed from heretics; but spare the men, and pray for their salvation."

§ II. But that no man, by virtue of any power or principality he hath in the government of this world, hath power over the consciences of men, is apparent, because the conscience of man is the seat and throne of God in him, of which God is the alone proper and infallible judge, who by his power and Spirit can alone rectify the mistakes of conscience, and therefore hath reserved to himself the power of punishing the errors thereof as he seeth meet. Now for the magistrate to assume this, is to take upon him to meddle with things not within the compass of his jurisdiction: for if this were within the compass of his jurisdiction, he should be the proper judge in these things; and also it were needful to him, as an essential qualification of his being a magistrate, to be capable to judge in them. But that the magistrate, as a magistrate, is neither proper judge in these cases, nor yet that the capacity so to be is requisite in him as a magistrate, our adversaries cannot deny; or else they must say, That all the heathen magistrates were either no lawful magistrates, as wanting something essential to magistracy, and this were contrary to the express doctrine of the apostle, Rom. xiii., or else (which is more absurd) that those heathen magistrates were proper judges in matters of conscience among Christians. As for that evasion that the magistrates ought to punish according to the church censure and determination, which is indeed no less than to make the magistrate the church's hangman, we shall have occasion to speak of it hereafter. But if the chief members of the church, though ordained to inform, instruct, and reprove, are not to have dominion over the faith nor consciences of the faithful, as the apostle expressly affirms, 2 Cor. i. 24, then far less ought they to usurp this dominion, or stir up the magistrate to persecute and murder those who cannot yield to them therein.

*Conscience the throne of God.*

Secondly, This pretended power of the magistrate is both contrary unto, and inconsistent with the nature of the gospel, which is a thing altogether extrinsic to the rule and government of political states, as Christ expressly signified, saying, His kingdom was not of this world; and if the propagating of the gospel had had any necessary relation thereunto, then Christ had not said so. But he abundantly hath shown by his example, whom we are chiefly to imitate in matters of that nature, that it is by persuasion and the power of God, not by whips, imprisonments, banishments, and murderings, that the gospel is to be propagated; and that those that are the propagators of it are often to suffer by the wicked, but never to cause the wicked to suffer. When he sends forth his disciples, he tells them, he sends them forth as " lambs among wolves," to be willing to be devoured, not to devour; he tells them of their being whipped, imprisoned, and killed for their conscience; but never that they shall either whip, imprison, or kill; and indeed if Christians must be as lambs, it is not the nature of lambs to destroy or devour any. It serves nothing to allege, that in Christ's and his apostles' times the magistrates were heathen, and therefore Christ and his apostles, nor yet any of the believers, being no magistrates, could not exercise the power; because it cannot be denied but Christ, being the Son of God, had a true right to all kingdoms, and was righteous heir of the earth. Next, as to his power, it cannot be denied but he could, if he had seen meet, have called for legions of angels to defend him, and have forced the princes and potentates of the earth to be subject unto him, Mat. xxvi. 53. So that it was only because it was contrary to the nature of Christ's gospel and ministry to use any force or violence in the gathering of souls to him. This he abundantly expressed in his reproof to the two sons of Zebedee, who would have been calling for fire from heaven to burn those that refused to receive Christ: it is not to be doubted but this was as great a crime as now to be in an error concerning the faith and doctrine of Christ. That there was not power wanting

*Matt. x 16.*

*Matt. xxviii. 18.*

to have punished those refusers of Christ cannot be doubted; for they that could do other miracles, might have done this also. And moreover, they wanted not the precedent of a holy man under the law, to wit, Elias; yet we see what Christ saith to them, "Ye know not what spirit ye are of," Luke ix. 55, "For the Son of Man is not come to destroy men's lives, but to save them." Here Christ shows that such kind of zeal was no ways approved of by him; and such as think to make way for Christ or his gospel by this means, do not understand what spirit they are of. But if it was not lawful to call for fire from heaven to destroy such as refused to receive Christ, it is far less lawful to kindle fire upon earth to destroy those that believe in Christ, because they will not believe, nor can believe, as the magistrates do, for conscience' sake. And if it was not lawful for the apostles, who had so large a measure of the Spirit, and were so little liable to mistake, to force others to their judgment, it can be far less lawful now for men, who as experience declareth, and many of themselves confess, are fallible, and often mistaken, to kill and destroy all such as cannot, because otherwise persuaded in their minds, judge and believe in matters of conscience just as they do. And if it was not according to the wisdom of Christ, who was and is King of kings, by outward force to constrain others to believe him or receive him, as being a thing inconsistent with the nature of his ministry and spiritual government, do not they grossly offend him, who will needs be wiser than he, and think to force men against their persuasion to conform to their doctrine and worship? The word of the Lord said, "Not by power and by might, but by my Spirit saith the Lord," Zech. iv. 6. But these say, Not by the Spirit of the Lord, but by might and carnal power. The apostle saith plainly, "We wrestle not with flesh and blood;" and "the weapons of our warfare are not carnal, but mighty through God," &c.; but these men will needs wrestle with flesh and blood, when they cannot prevail with the Spirit and the understanding; and not having spiritual weapons, go about with carnal weapons to estab-

2 Cor. x. 4

lish Christ's kingdom, which they can never do : and there fore when the matter is well sifted, it is found to be more out of love to self, and from a principle of pride in man to have all others to bow to him, than from the love of God. Christ indeed takes another method ; for he saith, "His people shall be a willing people in the day of his power ;" but these men labour against men's wills and consciences, not by Christ's power, but by the outward sword, to make men the people of Christ, which they never can do, as shall hereafter be shown.

But Thirdly, Christ fully and plainly declareth to us his sense in this matter in the parable of the tares, Mat. xiii. 25, of which we have himself the interpreter, ver. 38, 39, 40, 41, where he expounds them to be the " children of the wicked one," and yet he will not have the servants to meddle with them, lest they pull up the wheat therewith Now it cannot be denied but heretics are here included ; and although these servants saw the tares, and had a certain discerning of them ; yet Christ would not they should meddle, lest they should hurt the wheat : thereby intimating, that that capacity in man to be mistaken, ought to be a bridle upon him, to make him wary in such matters ; and therefore, to prevent this hurt, he gives a positive prohibition, " But he said, Nay," ver. 29. So that they who will notwithstanding be pulling up that which they judge is tares, do openly declare, that they make no scruple to break the commands of Christ. Miserable is that evasion which some of our adversaries use here, in alleging these tares are meant of hypocrites, and not of heretics ! But how to evince that, seeing heretics, as well as hypocrites, are children of the wicked one, they have not any thing but their own bare affirmation, which is therefore justly rejected.

OBJECT. 　　If they say, Because hypocrites cannot be discerned, but so may heretics ;

Answ. 　　This is both false, and a begging of the question. For those that have a spiritual discerning, can discern both hypocrites and heretics ; and those that want it, cannot

*Psal. cx 3.*

certainly discern either.  Seeing the question will arise,
Whether that is a heresy which the magistrate saith is so?
and seeing it is both possible, and confessed by all to have
often fallen out, that some magistrates have judged that
heresy which was not, punishing men accordingly for truth,
instead of error; there can be no argument drawn from the
obviousness or evidence of heresy, unless we should conclude heresy could never be mistaken for truth nor truth
for heresy; whereof experience shows daily the contrary,
even among Christians.  But neither is this shift applicable
to this place; for the servants did discern the tares, and
yet were liable to hurt the wheat, if they had offered to pull
them up.

§ III.  But they object against this liberty of conscience, Object.
Deut. xiii. 5, where false prophets are appointed to be put
to death; and accordingly they give example thereof.

The case no way holds parallel; those particular com- Answ.
mands to the Jews, and practices following upon them, are
not a rule for Christians; else we might by the same rule
say, It were lawful for us to borrow of our neighbours their
goods, and so carry them away, because the Jews did so
by God's command; or that it is lawful for Christians to
invade their neighbours' kingdoms, and cut them all off
without mercy, because the Jews did so to the Canaanites,
by the command of God.

If they urge, That these commands ought to stand, ex- Object.
cept they be repealed in the gospel;

I say, The precepts and practices of Christ and his apos- Answ.
tles mentioned are a sufficient repeal: for if we should
plead, that every command given to the Jews is binding
upon us, except there be a particular repeal; then would
it follow, that because it was lawful for the Jews, if any
man killed one, for the nearest kindred presently to kill the
murderer, without any order of law, it were lawful for us
to do so likewise.  And doth not this command of Deut
xiii. 9, openly order him who is enticed by another to forsake the Lord, though it were his brother, his son, his
daughter, or his wife, presently to kill him or her? " Thou

39                      3 H

shalt surely kill him, thy hand shall be first upon h m to
put him to death." If this command were to be follow d,
there needed neither inquisition nor magistrate to do the
business; and yet there is no reason why they should
shuffle by this part, and not the other; yea, to argue this
way from the practice among the Jews, were to overturn
the very gospel, and to set up again the carnal ordinances
among the Jews, to pull down the spiritual ones of the
gospel.   Indeed we can far better argue from the analogy
betwixt the figurative and carnal state of the Jews, and the
real and spiritual one under the gospel; that as Moses delivered the Jews out of outward Egypt, by an outward
force, and established them in an outward kingdom, by
destroying their outward enemies for them; so Christ, not
by overcoming outwardly, and killing others, but by suffer
ing and being killed, doth deliver his chosen ones, the inward Jews, out of mystical Egypt, destroying their spiritual
enemies before them, and establishing among them his
spiritual kingdom, which is not of this world.   And as such
as departed from the fellowship of outward Israel were to
be cut off by the outward sword, so those that depart from
the inward Israel are to be cut off by the sword of the
Spirit: for it answers very well, that as the Jews were to
cut off their enemies outwardly, in order to establish their
kingdom and outward worship, so they were to uphold it
the same way: but as the kingdom and gospel of Christ
was not to be established or propagated by cutting off or
destroying the Gentiles, but by persuading them, so neither
is it to be upheld otherwise.

OBJECT.        But Secondly, they urge, Rom. xiii., where the magistrate is said not to bear the sword in vain, because he is
the minister of God, to execute wrath upon such as do
evil.   But heresy, say they, is evil.   Ergo.

ANSW.        But so is hypocrisy also; yet they confess he ought not
to punish that.   Therefore this must be understood of moral
evils, relative to affairs betwixt man and man, not of matters of judgment or worship; or else what great absurdities
would follow, considering that Paul wrote here to the

church of Rome, which was under the government of Nero, an impious heathen and persecutor of the church? Now if a power to punish in point of heresy be here included, it will necessarily follow, that Nero had this power; yea, and that he had it of God; for because the power was of God, therefore the apostle urges their obedience. But can there be any thing more absurd, than to say that Nero had power to judge in such cases? Surely if Christian magistrates be not to punish for hypocrisy, because they cannot outwardly discern it; far less could Nero punish anybody for heresy, which he was incapable to discern. And if Nero had not power to judge or punish in point of heresy, then nothing can be urged from this place; since all that is said here, is spoken as applicable to Nero, with a particular relation to whom it was written. And if Nero had such a power, surely he was to exercise it according to his judgment and conscience, and in doing thereof he was not to be blamed; which is enough to justify him in his persecuting of the apostles, and murdering the Christians.

Thirdly, They object that saying of the apostle to the Galatians, v. 12, " I would they were even cut off which trouble you." *Object*

But how this imports any more than a cutting off from *Answ.* the church, is not, nor can be shown. Beza upon the place saith, " We cannot understand that otherwise than of excommunication, such as was that of the incestuous Corinthian. And indeed it is madness to suppose it otherwise; for Paul would not have these cut off otherwise than he did Hymenæus and Philetus, who were blasphemers; which was by giving them over to Satan, not by cutting off their heads."

The same way may be answered that other argument, drawn from Rev. ii. 20, where the church of Thyatira is reproved for suffering the woman Jezebel: which can be no otherways understood, than that they did not excommunicate her, or cut her off by a church censure. For as to corporal punishment, it is known that at that time the

Christians had not power to punish neretics so. it the y had had a mind to it.

OBJECT.    Fourthly, They allege, that heresies are numbe. ed among the works of the flesh, Gal. v. 20. Ergo, &c.

ANSW.    That magistrates have power to punish all the works of the flesh is denied, and not yet proved. Every evil is a work of the flesh, but every evil comes not under the magistrate's cognizance. Is not hypocrisy a work of the flesh, which our adversaries confess the magistrats ough not to punish? Yea, are not hatred and envy there mentioned as works of the flesh? And yet the magistrate cannot punish them, as they are in themselves, until they exert themselves in other acts which come under his power. But so long as heresy doth not exert itself in any act destructive to human society, or such like things, but is kept within the sphere of those duties of doctrine or worship which stand betwixt a man and God, they no ways come under the magistrate's power.

§ IV. But Secondly; This forcing of men's consciences is contrary to sound reason, and the very law of nature. For man's understanding cannot be forced by all the bodily sufferings another man can inflict upon him, especially in matters spiritual and supernatural: 'T is argument, and evident demonstration of reason, together with the power of God reaching the heart, that can change a man's mind from one opinion to another, and not knocks and blows, and such like things, which may well destroy the body, but never can inform the soul, which is a free agent, and must either accept or reject matters of opinion as they are borne in upon it by something proportioned to its own nature. To seek to force minds in any other manner, is to deal with men as if they were brutes, void of understanding; and at last is but to lose one's labour, and as the proverb is, "To seek to wash the black-moor white." By that course indeed men may be made hypocrites, but can never be made Christians; and surely the products of such compulsion, even where the end is obtained, to wit, an outward assent or conformity, whether in doctrine or worship, can be no ways acceptable to God, who desireth not any sacrifice, except that which cometh thoroughly from the heart, and will have no constrained ones : so that men, by constraining force, are so far from being members of the church, that they are made ten times more the servants of Satan than before ; in that to their error is added hypocrisy, the worst of evils in matters of religion, and that which above all things the Lord's soul most abhors.

But if it be said, Their error notwithstanding is thereby Object suppressed, and the scandal removed ;

I answer ; Besides that this is a method no ways allowed Answ. by Christ, as is above proved, surely the church can be no ways bettered by the accession of hypocrites, but greatly corrupted and endangered ; for open heresies men may be aware of, and shun such as profess them, when they are separated from the church by her censures ; but secret hypocrites may putrefy the body, and leaven it, ere men be aware. And if the dissenters prove resolute, and suffer boldly for the opinions they esteem right, experience showeth that such sufferings often tend to the commendation of the sufferers, but never of the persecutors. For such suffering ordinarily breeds compassion, and begets a curiosity in others to enquire the more diligently into the things for which they see men suffer such great losses so boldly ; and is also able to beget an opinion, that it is for some good they do so suffer : it being no ways probable that men will venture all merely to acquire fame ; which may as well be urged to detract from the reputation of all the martyrs, unless some better arguments be brought against it than a halter or a faggot. But supposing this principle, That the magistrate hath power to force the consciences of his subjects, and to punish them if they will not comply, very great inconveniences and absurdities will follow, and even such as are inconsistent with the nature of the Christian religion.

For First, It will naturally follow that the magistrate ought to do it, and sinneth by omission of his duty, if he do it not. Will it not then hence be inferred that Christ

39 *

was defective to his church, who having power to force men, and to call for legions of angels so to do, did notwithstanding not exert that power, but left his church to the mercy of the wicked, without so necessary a bulwark?

Secondly, Seeing every magistrate is to exercise his power according to the best understanding he hath, being obliged so to do, for the promoting of what he in conscience is persuaded to be truth, will not this justify all the heathen emperors in their persecutions against Christians? Will not this justify the Spanish inquisition, which yet is odious not only to Protestants, but to many moderate Papists? How can Protestants in reason condemn the Papists for persecuting them, seeing they do but exercise a lawful power according to their conscience and best understanding, and do no more to them than the sufferers profess they would do to them, if they were in the like capacity? Which takes away all ground of commiseration from the sufferers: whereas that was the ground which of old gained reputation to the Christians, that they being innocent, suffered, who neither had, nor by principle could, hurt any. But there is little reason to pity one that is but dealt by according as he would deal with others. For to say, They have no reason to persecute us, because they are in the wrong, and we in the right, is but miserably to beg the question. Doth not this doctrine strengthen the hands of the persecutors every where, and that rationally, from a principle of self-preservation; For who can blame me for destroying him that I know waits but for an occasion to destroy me, if he could? Yea, this makes all suffering for religion, which of old was the glory of Christians, to be but of pure necessity; whereby they are not led as lambs to the slaughter, as was the captain of their salvation; but rather as wolves catched in the snare, who only bite not again because they are not able; but could they get force, would be as ready to lead those the same way that led them. Where is the faith and patience of the saints? For indeed it is but a small glory to make a virtue of necessity, and suffer because I cannot help it

Every thief and murderer would be a martyr at that rate: experience hath abundantly proved this in these last centuries; for however each party talk of passively obeying the magistrate in such cases, and that the power resides in him, yet it is apparent, that from this principle it naturally follows, that any party, supposing themselves right, should, so soon as they are able, endeavour at any rate to get uppermost, that they might bring under those of another opinion, and force the magistrate to uphold their way, to the ruin of all others. What engine the pope of Rome used to make of his pretended power in this thing, upon any pretence of dislike to any prince or state, even for very small heresies in their own account, to depose princes, and set up their subjects against them, and give their dominions to other princes to serve his interest, they cannot be ignorant who have read the life of Hildebrand; and how Protestants have vindicated the liberty of their consciences after this same manner is apparent. They suffered much in France, to the great increase and advantage of their party; but as soon as they found themselves considerable, and had gotten some princes upon their side, they began to let the king know, that they must either have the liberty of their consciences, or else they would purchase it; not by suffering, but by fighting. And the experience of other Protestant states shows, that if Henry the Fourth, to please the Papists, had not quitted his religion, to get the crown the more peaceably, and so the Protestants had prevailed with the sword, they would as well have taught the Papists with the faggot, and led them to the stake: so that this principle of persecution on all hands is the ground of all those miseries and contentions. For so long as any party is persuaded that it is both lawful for them, and their duty, if in power, to destroy those that differ from them, it naturally follows they ought to use all means possible to get that power, whereby they may secure themselves in the ruin of their adversaries. And that Papists judge it not unlawful to compel the magistrate, if they be strong enough to do it, to effect this, experience shows it to be a known

popish principle, That the Pope may depose an heretic
prince, and absolve the people from the oath of fidelity:
And the Pope, as is above said. hath done so to divers
princes; and this doctrine is defended by Bellarmine
against Barclay. The French refused Henry the Fourth
till he quitted his religion. And as for Protestants, many
of them scruple not to affirm, That wicked kings and magis
trates may be deposed, and killed: yea, our Scotch Presbyterians are as positive in it as any Jesuits, who would
not admit king Charles the Second, though otherwise a
Protestant prince, unless he would swear to renounce episcopacy; a matter of no great difference, though contrary
to his conscience. Now how little proportion these things
bear with the primitive Christians, and the religion propagated by Christ and his apostles, needs no great demonstration; and it is observable, that notwithstanding many
other superstitions crept into the church very early, yet this
of persecution was so inconsistent with the nature of the
gospel, and liberty of conscience, as we have asserted it,
such an innate and natural part of the Christian religion,
that almost all the Christian writers, for the first three hundred years, earnestly contended for it, condemning the
contrary opinion.

Athan. in
epist. ad
solit. vit.
ag. ibid.

§ V. Thus Athanasius; "It is the property of piety not
to force, but to persuade, in imitation of our Lord, who
forced nobody, but left it to the will of every one to follow
him, &c. But the devil, because he hath nothing of truth,
uses knocks and axes, to break up the doors of such
as receive him. But our Saviour is meek, teaching the
truth; whosoever will come after me, and whosoever will
be my disciple, &c., but constraining none; coming to us,
and knocking rather, and saying, My sister, my spouse
open to me, &c. And entereth when he is opened to, and
retires if they delay, and will not open unto him; because
it is not with swords, nor darts, nor soldiers, nor armour,
that truth is to be declared, but with persuasion and counsel." And it is observable, that they were the impious
Arians who first of all brought in this doctrine, to perse-

**cute** others among Christians, whose successors both Papists and Protestants are in this matter, whom Athanasius thus reproveth further: " Where," saith he, " have they learned to persecute? Certainly they cannot say they have learned it from the saints; but this hath been given them, and taught them of the devil. The Lord commanded indeed sometimes to flee, and the saints sometimes fled; but to persecute is the invention and argument of the devil, which he seeks against all." And after, he saith, " In so far as the Arians banish those that will not subscribe their decrees, they show that they are contrary to Christians, and friends of the devil." Athan. apol. 1, de fuga sua, tom. 1.

" But now, O lamentable!" saith Hilarius, " they are the suffrages of the earth that recommend the religion of God, and Christ is found naked of his virtue, while ambition must give credit to his name. The church reproves and fights by banishment and prisons, and forceth herself to be believed, which once was believed because of the imprisonments and banishments herself suffered. She that once was consecrated by the terrors of her persecutors, depends now upon the dignity of those that are in her communion. She that once was propagated by her banished priests, now banisheth the priests. And she boasts now, that she is loved of the world, who would not have been Christ's if she had not been hated of the world." Hil. contra Aux.

" The church," saith Hierom, " was founded by shedding of blood, and by suffering, and not in doing of hurt. The church increased by persecutions, and was crowned by martyrdom." Hierom, epist. 62, ad The.

Ambrose, speaking of Auxentius, saith thus, " Whom he (viz., Auxentius) could not deceive by discourse, he thinks ought to be killed with the sword, making bloody laws with his mouth, writing them with his own hands, and imagining that an edict can command faith." Amb., epist. 32, tom. 3

And the same Ambrose saith, That going into France, he would not communicate with those bishops that required that heretics should be put to death. Amb., epist. 27

The emperor Martianus, who assembled the council of

Mart.,
epist. ad
Archi-
mand, &c.
Mon. Eg.
in acta
concil.
Chalced.,
tom. 2,
conc. gen.
a Hosii,
epist. ad—
Constit.
apud Ath.
in Eph. ad
solit. vit.
tom. 1.
b Hil. l. 1,
ad Const.

Chalcedon, protests, That he would not force nor constrain any one to subscribe the council of Chalcedon
against his will.

a Hosius, bishop of Corduba, testifies, That the emperor
Constans would not constrain any to be orthodox.

b Hilarius saith further, That God teacheth, rather than
exacteth, the knowledge of himself, and authorizing his
commandments by the miracles of his heavenly works; he
wills not that any should confess him with a forced will,
&c. He is the God of the whole universe, he needs not
a forced obedience, nor requires a constrained confession.

c Ambr.
comm. in
Luc. l. 7.

c "Christ," saith Ambrose, "sent his apostles to sow
faith; not to constrain, but to teach; not to exercise coer-
cive power, but to extol the doctrine of humility."

d Cypr.,
epist. 62.

Hence Cyprian,d comparing the old covenant with the
new, saith, "Then were they put to death with the outward sword; but now the proud and contumacious are cut
off with the spiritual sword, by being cast out of the
church." And this answers very well that objection before observed, taken from the practice of the Jews under
the law.

e Tertul.,
Apol. c. 24.

e "See," saith Tertullian to the heathen, "if it be not
to contribute to the renown of irreligion, to seek to take
away the liberty of religion, and to hinder men their choice
of God, that I may not be admitted to adore whom I will,
but must be constrained to serve him whom I will not.
There is none, nay, not a man, that desires to be adored
by any against their will. And again, It is a thing that
easily appears to be unjust, to constrain and force men to
sacrifice against their wills; seeing to do the service of
God there is required a willing heart." And again, "It
is a human right and natural power that every one worship
what he esteems; and one man's religion doth not profit
nor hurt another. Neither is it any piece of religion to
enforce religion; which must be undertaken by consent,
and not by violence, seeing that the sacrifices themselves
are not required, but from a willing mind."

Id. Apol.
c. 28.

Idem ad
Scapul. c.
2.

Now how either Papists or Protestants, that boast of antiquity, can get by these plain testimonies, let any rational man judge. And indeed I much question if in any one point owned by them, and denied by us, they can find all the old fathers and writers so exactly unanimous. Which shows how contrary all of them judged this to be to the nature of Christianity, and that in the point of persecution lay no small part of the apostasy; which, from little to more, came to that, that the pope, upon every small discontent, would excommunicate princes, absolve their subjects from obeying them, and turn them in and out at his pleasure. Now if Protestants do justly abhor these things among Papists, is it not sad that they should do the like themselves? A thing that at their first appearance, when they were in their primitive innocency, they did not think on, as appears by that saying of Luther; "Neither pope nor bishop, nor any other man, hath power to oblige a Christian to one syllable, except it be by his own consent." And again, "I call boldly to all Christians, that neither man nor angel can impose any law upon them, but so far as they will: for we are free of all." And when he appeared at the diet of Spiers, before the emperor, in a particular conference he had before the archbishop of Triers and Joachim, elector of Brandenburgh, when there seemed no possibility of agreeing with his opposers, they asking him, What remedy seemed to him most fit? He answered, "The counsel that Gamaliel proposed to the Jews, to wit, That if this design was of God, it would stand; if not, it would vanish; which he said ought to content the pope:" he did not say, Because he was in the right he ought to be spared. For this counsel supposeth, that those that are tolerated may be wrong; and yet how soon did the same Luther, ere he was well secure himself, press the elector of Saxony to banish poor Carolostadius, because he could not in all things submit to his judgment? And certainly it is not without ground reported, that it smote Luther to the heart; so that he needed to be comforted, when he was informed, that Carolostadius, in his letter to his con-

Luth. lib. de captivitate Babylon.

History of the council of Trent

gregation, styled himself "A man banished for conscience. by the procurement of Martin Luther." And since, both the Lutherans and Calvinists not admitting one another to worship in those respective dominions, showeth how little better they are than either Papists or Arians in this par-

Calv. inst.
. 3, c. 19
sect. 14.

ticular. And yet Calvin saith, That "the conscience is free from the power of all men:" if so, why then did he cause Castellio to be banished, because he could not, for conscience' sake, believe as he did, That God had ordained men to be damned? And Servetus to be burned for denying the divinity of Christ, if Calvin's report of him be to be credited? Which opinion, though indeed it was to be abominated, yet no less was Calvin's practice in causing him to be burned, and afterwards defending that it was lawful to burn heretics; by which he encouraged the Papists to lead his followers the more confidently to the stake, as having for their warrant the doctrine of their own sect-master; which they omitted not frequently to twit them with, and indeed it was to them unanswerable. Hence, upon this occasion, the judicious author of the History of the Council of Trent, in his fifth book, where giving an account of several Protestants that were burned for their religion, well and wisely observeth it, as a matter of astonishment, that those of the new reformation did offer to punish in the case of religion. And afterwards, taking notice that Calvin justifies the punishing of heretics; he adds, "But since the name of heresy may be more or less restricted, yea, or diversely taken, this doctrine may be likewise taken in divers senses, and may at one time hurt those, whom at another time it may have benefited."

*Protestant persecution strengthens the popish inquisition.*

So that this doctrine of persecution cannot be maintained by Protestants without strengthening the hands of popish inquisitors; and indeed in the end lands in direct popery; seeing, if I may not profess and preach that religion, which I am persuaded in my own conscience is true, it is to no purpose to search the scriptures, or to seek to choose my own faith by convictions thence derived; since whatever I there observe, or am persuaded of, I must either subject to the judgment of the magistrate and church of that place I am in, or else resolve to remove or die. Yea, doth not this heretical and antichristian doctrine, both of Papists and Protestants, at last resolve into that cursed policy of Mahomet, who prohibited all reason or discourse about religion, as occasioning factions and divisions? And indeed those that press persecution, and deny liberty of conscience, do thereby show themselves more the disciples of Mahomet than of Christ; and that they are no ways followers of the apostle's doctrine, who desired the Thessalonians " to prove all things, and hold fast that which is good," 1 Thess. v. 21. And also saith, " Unto such as are otherwise minded, God shall reveal it," Phil. iii. 15, not that by beatings and banishments it must be knocked into them.

§ VI. Now the ground of persecution, as hath been above shown, is an unwillingness to suffer; for no man, that will persecute another for his conscience, would suffer for his own, if he could avoid it, seeing his principle obliges him, if he had power, by force to establish that which he judges is the truth, and so to force others to it. Therefore I judge it meet, for the information of the nations, briefly to add something in this place concerning the nature of true Christian sufferings, whereunto a very faithful testimony hath been borne by God's witnesses, which he hath raised up in this age, beyond what hath been generally known or practised for these many generations, yea, since the apostasy took place. Yet it is not my design here in any wise to derogate from the sufferings of the Protestant martyrs, whom I believe to have walked in faithfulness towards God, according to the dispensation of light in that day appearing, and of which many were utter enemies to persecution, as by their testimonies against it might be made appear.

*The ground of persecution.*

But the true, faithful and Christian suffering is for men to profess what they are persuaded is right, and so practise and perform then worship towards God, as being their true right so to do; and neither to do more in that, because of

*What true suffering is.*

outward encouragement from men; nor any whit less, because of the fear of their laws and acts against it. Thus for a Christian man to vindicate his just liberty with so much boldness, and yet innocency, will in due time, though through blood, purchase peace, as this age hath in some measure experienced, and many are witnesses of it; which yet shall be more apparent to the world, as truth takes place in the earth. But they greatly sin against this excellent rule, that in time of persecution do not profess their own way so much as they would if it were otherwise; and yet, when they can get the magistrate upon their side, not only stretch their own liberty to the utmost, but seek to establish the same by denying it to others.

**The innocent sufferings of the people called Quakers.**

But of this excellent patience and sufferings, the witnesses of God, in scorn called Quakers, have given a manifest proof: for so soon as God revealed his truth among them, without regard to any opposition whatsoever, or what they might meet with, they went up and down, as they were moved of the Lord, preaching and propagating the truth in market-places, highways, streets, and public temples, though daily beaten, whipped, bruised, haled, and imprisoned therefore. And when there was any where a church or assembly gathered, they taught them to keep their meetings openly, and not to shut the door, nor do it by stealth, that all might know it, and those who would might enter. And as hereby all just occasion of fear of plotting against the government was fully removed, so this their courage and faithfulness in not giving over their meeting together (but more especially the presence and glory of God manifested in the meeting being terrible to the consciences of the persecutors), did so weary out the malice of their adversaries, that oftentimes they were forced to leave their work undone. For when they came to break up a meeting, they were obliged to take every individual out by force, they not being free to give up their liberty by dissolving at their command: and when they were haled out, unless they were kept forth by violence, they presently returned peaceably to their place. Yea, when sometimes the magistrates have pulled down their meeting-houses, they have met the next day openly upon the rubbish, and so by innocency kept their possession and ground, being properly their own, and their right to meet and worship God being not forfeited to any. So that when armed men have come to dissolve them, it was impossible for them to do it, unless they had killed every one; for they stood so close together, that no force could move any one to stir, until violently pulled thence: so that when the malice of their opposers stirred them to take shovels, and throw the rubbish upon them, there they stood unmoved, being willing, if the Lord should so permit, to have been there buried alive, witnessing for him. As this patient but yet courageous way of suffering made the persecutors' work very heavy and wearisome unto them, so the courage and patience of the sufferers, using no resistance, nor bringing any weapons to defend themselves, nor seeking any ways revenge upon such occasions, did secretly smite the hearts of the persecutors, and made their chariot wheels go on heavily. Thus after much and many kind of sufferings thus patiently borne, which to rehearse would make a volume of itself, which may in due time be published to the nations (for we have them upon record) a kind of negative liberty has been obtained; so that at present for the most part we meet together without disturbance from the magistrate. But on the contrary, most Protestants, when they have not the allowance and toleration of the magistrate, meet only in secret, and hide their testimony; and if they be discovered, if there be any probability of making their escape by force (or suppose it were by cutting off those that seek them out) they will do it; whereby they lose the glory of their sufferings, by not appearing as the innocent followers of Christ, nor having a testimony of their harmlessness in the hearts of their pursuers, their fury, by such resistance, is the more kindled against them. As to this last part, of resisting such as persecute them, they can lay claim to no precept from Christ, nor any example of him or his apostles approved.

OBJECT.    But as to the first part, for fleeing and meeting secretly
and not openly testifying for the truth, they usually object
that saying of Christ, Mat. x. 23, " When they persecute
you in this city, flee ye into another." And John xx. 19,
That the disciples met secretly for fear of the Jews.
And Acts ix. 25, That Paul was let out of Damascus in a
basket down by the wall.

ANSW    To all which I answer, First, As to that saying of Christ,
it is a question if it had any further relation than to that
particular message with which he sent them to the Jews;
yea, the latter end of the words seem expressly to hold
forth so much; " For ye shall not have gone over the cities
of Israel till the Son of man be come." Now a particular
practice or command for a particular time will not serve
for a precedent to any at this day to shun the cross of
Christ. But supposing this precept to reach farther, it
must be so understood to be made use of only according
as the Spirit giveth liberty, else no man that could flee
Fleeing in    might suffer persecution. How then did not the apostles
time of per-  John and Peter flee, when they were the first time perse-
secution      cuted at Jerusalem? But, on the contrary, went the next
not allow-
ed.           day, after they were discharged by the council, and
preached boldly to the people. But indeed many are but
too capable to stretch such sayings as these for self-per--
servation, and therefore have great ground to fear, when
they interpret them, that they shun to witness for Christ,
for fear of hurt to themselves, lest they mistake them. As
for that private meeting of the disciples, we have only an
account of the matter of fact, but that suffices not to make
of it a precedent for us; and men's aptness to imitate them
in that (which, for aught we know, might have been an act
of weakness) and not in other things of a contrary nature,
shows that it is not a true zeal to be like those disciples,
but indeed a desire to preserve themselves, which moves
them so to do. Lastly, As to that of Paul's being conveyed out of Damascus, the case was singular; and is not
to be doubted but it was done by a special allowance from
God, who having designed him to be a principal minister

of his gospel, saw meet in his wisdom to disappoint the wicked counsel of the Jews. But our adversaries have no such pretext for fleeing, whose fleeing proceeds from self-preservation, not from immediate revelation. And that Paul made not this the method of his procedure, appears, in that at another time, notwithstanding the persuasion of his friends, and certain prophecies of his sufferings to come, he would not be dissuaded from going up to Jerusalem, which according to the forementioned rule he should have done.

But Lastly, To conclude this matter, glory to God, and our Lord Jesus Christ, that now these twenty-five years, since we were known to be a distinct and separate people, hath given us faithfully to suffer for his name, without shrinking or fleeing the cross; and what liberty we now enjoy, it is by his mercy, and not by any outward working or procuring of our own, but it is He has wrought upon the hearts of our opposers. Nor was it any outward interest hath procured it unto us, but the testimony of our harmlessness in the hearts of our superiors: for God hath preserved us hitherto in the patient suffering of Jesus, that we have not given away our cause by persecuting any, which few if any Christians that I know can say. Now against our unparalleled yet innocent and Christian cause our malicious enemies have nothing to say, but that if we had power, we would do so likewise. This is a piece of mere unreasonable malice, and a privilege they take to judge of things to come, which they have not by immediate revelation; and surely it is the greatest height of harsh judgment to say men would do contrary to their professed principle if they could, who have from their practice hitherto given no ground for it, and wherein they only judge others by themselves: such conjectures cannot militate against us, so long as we are innocent. And if ever we prove guilty of persecution, by forcing other men by corporal punishment to our way, then let us be judged the greatest of hypocrites, and let not any spare to persecute us. Amen, saith my soul.

## PROPOSITION XV.

*Concerning Salutations and Recreations, &c.*

Ephes. v.
11.
1 Pet. i. 14.
John v. 44.
Jer. x. 3.
Acts x. 26.
Mat. xv. 13
Col. ii. 8.

Seeing the chief end of all religion is to redeem men from the spirit and vain conversation of this world, and to lead into inward communion with God, before whom if we fear always we are accounted happy; therefore all the vain customs and habits thereof, both in word and deed, are to be rejected and forsaken by those who come to this fear; such as taking off the hat to a man, the bowings and cringings of the body, and such other salutations of that kind, with all the foolish and superstitious formalities attending them; all which man hath invented in his degenerate state, to feed his pride in the vain pomp and glory of this world: as also the unprofitable plays, frivolous recreations, sportings, and gamings, which are invented to pass away the precious time, and divert the mind from the witness of God in the heart, and from the living sense of his fear, and from that evangelical spirit wherewith Christians ought to be leavened, and which leads into sobriety, gravity, and godly fear; in which as we abide, the blessing of the Lord is felt to attend us in those actions in which we are necessarily engaged, in order to the taking care for the sustenance of the outward man.

§ I. HAVING hitherto treated of the principles of religion, both relating to doctrine and worship, I am now to speak of some practices which have been the product of this principle, in those witnesses whom God hath raised up in this day to testify for his truth. It will not a little commend them, I suppose, in the judgment of sober and judicious men, that taking them generally, even by the confession of their adversaries, they are found to be free of those abominations which abound among other professors, such as are swearing, drunkenness, whoredom, riotousness, &c.; and that generally the very coming among this people doth naturally work such a change, so that many vicious and profane persons have been known, by coming to this truth, to become sober and virtuous; and many light, vain, and wanton ones to become grave and serious, as our adversaries dare not deny:* yet that they may not want something to detract us for, cease not to accuse us for those things which, when found among themselves, they highly commend; thus our gravity they call sullenness, our seriousness melancholy, our silence sottishness. Such as have been vicious and profane among them, but by coming to us have left off those evils, lest they should commend the truth of our profession, they say, that whereas they were profane before, they are become worse, in being hypocritical and spiritually proud. If any before dissolute and profane among them, by coming to the truth with us, become frugal and diligent, then they will charge them with covetousness: and if any eminent among them for seriousness, piety, and discoveries of God, come unto us, then they will say, they were always subject to melancholy and to enthusiasm; though before, when among them, it was esteemed neither melancholy nor enthusiasm in an evil sense, but Christian gravity and divine revelation. Our boldness and Christian suffering they call obstinacy and pertinacity; though half as much, if among themselves, they would account Christian courage and nobility. And though thus by their envy they strive to read all relating to us backwards, counting those things vices in us, which in themselves they would extol as virtues, yet hath the strength of truth extorted this confession often from them, That we are generally a pure and clean people, as to the outward conversation.

But this, they say, is but in policy to commend our heresy.

---

* After this manner the Papists used to disapprove the sobriety of the Waldenses, of whom Reinerus, a Popish author, so writeth: "But this sect of the Leonists hath a great show of truth; for that they live righteously before men, and believe all things well of God, and all the articles which are contained in the creed; only they blaspheme and hate the church of Rome."

But such policy it is, say I, as Christ and his apostles made use of, and all good Christians ought to do; yea, so far hath truth prevailed by the purity of its followers, that if one that is called a Quaker do but that which is common among them, as to laugh and be wanton, speak at large, and keep not his word punctually, or be overtaken with hastiness or anger, they presently say, O this is against your profession! As if indeed so to do were very consistent with theirs; wherein though they speak the truth, yet they give away their cause. But if they can find any under our name in any of those evils common among themselves (as who can imagine but among so many thousands there will be some chaff, since of twelve apostles one was found to be a devil), O how will they insult, and make more noise of the escape of one Quaker, than of an hundred among themselves!

§ II. But there are some singular things, which most of all our adversaries plead for the lawfulness of, and allow themselves in, as no ways inconsistent with the Christian religion, which we have found to be no ways lawful unto us, and have been commanded of the Lord to lay them aside; though the doing thereof hath occasioned no small sufferings and buffetings, and hath procured us much hatred and malice from the world. And because the nature of these things is such, that they do upon the very sight distinguish us, and make us known, so that we cannot hide ourselves from any, without proving unfaithful to our testimony; our trials and exercises have here-through proved the more numerous and difficult, as will after appear. These I have laboured briefly to comprehend in this proposition; but they may more largely be exhibited in these six following propositions:

Flattering titles.

I. That it is not lawful to give to men such flattering titles, as Your Holiness, Your Majesty, Your Eminency, Your Excellency, Your Grace, Your Lordship, Your Honour, &c., nor use those flattering words, commonly called COMPLIMENTS.

II. That it is not lawful for Christians to kneel, or pros

trate themselves to any man, or to bow the body, or to un- Hat and knee.
cover the head to them.

III. That it is not lawful for a Christian to use super- Apparel.
fluities in apparel, as are of no use, save for ornament and
vanity.

IV. That it is not lawful to use games, sports, plays, Gaming.
nor among other things comedies among Christians, under
the notion of recreations, which do not agree with Christian silence, gravity, and sobriety ; for laughing, sporting,
gaming, mocking, jesting, vain talking, &c., is not Christian liberty, nor harmless mirth.

V. That it is not lawful for Christians to swear at all Swearing.
under the gospel, not only not vainly, and in their common
discourse, which was also forbidden under the Mosaical
law, but even not in judgment before the magistrate.

VI. That it is not lawful for Christians to resist evil, or Fighting
to war or fight in any case.

Before I enter upon a particular disquisition of these Degrees of
things, I shall first premise some general considerations, to precedency
prevent all mistakes ; and next add some general consider- allowed.
ations, which equally respect all of them.   I would not
have any judge, that hereby we intend to destroy the
mutual relation that either is betwixt prince and people,
master and servants, parents and children ; nay, not at all :
we shall evidence, that our principle in these things hath
no such tendency, and that these natural relations are
rather better established, than any ways hurt by it.   Next,
Let not any judge, that from our opinion in these things,
any necessity of levelling will follow, or that all men must
have things in common.   Our principle leaves every man
to enjoy that peaceably, which either his own industry, or
his parents, have purchased to him ; only he is thereby instructed to use it aright, both for his own good, and that
of his brethren ; and all to the glory of God : in which
also his acts are to be voluntary, and no ways constrained.
And further, we say not hereby, that no man may use the
creation more or less than another : for we know, that as
it hath pleased God to dispense it diversly, giving to some

**Education differs accordingly.**

more, and some less, so they may use it accordingly. The several conditions, under which men are diversly stated, together with their educations answering thereunto, do sufficiently show this : the servant is not the same way educated as the master ; nor the tenant as the landlord ; nor the rich as the poor ; nor the prince as the peasant. Now, though it be not lawful for any, however great abundance they may have, or whatever their education may be, to use that which is merely superfluous; yet seeing their education has accustomed them thereunto, and their capacity enables them so to do, without being profuse or extravagant, they may use things better in their kind, than such whose education hath neither accustomed them to such things, nor their capacity will reach to compass them. For it is beyond question, that whatever thing the creation affords is for the use of man, and the moderate use of them is lawful ; yet, *per accidens*, they may be unlawful to some, and not to others. As for instance, he that by reason of his estate and education hath been used to eat flesh and drink wine, and to be clothed with the finest wool, if his estate will bear it, and he use it neither in superfluity, nor immoderately, he may do it ; and perhaps, if he should apply himself to feed, or be clothed as are the peasants, it might prejudice the health of his body, and nothing advance his soul. But if a man, whose estate and education had accustomed him to both coarser food and raiment, should stretch himself beyond what he had, or were used to, to the manifest prejudice of his family and children, no doubt it would be unlawful to him, even so to eat or be clothed as another, in whom it is lawful ; for that the other may be as much mortified, and have denied himself as much in coming down to that, which this aspires to, as he, in willing to be like him, aspires beyond what he either is able, or hath accustomed to do. The safe place then is, for such as have fulness, to watch over themselves, that they use it moderately, and rescind all superfluities; being willing, as far as they can, to help the need of those to whom Providence hath allotted a smaller allowance. Let

**The lawful or unlawful use of the creation.**

**The rich to help the poor.**

the brother of high degree rejoice, in that he is abased; and such as God calls in a low degree, be content with their condition, not envying those brethren who have greater abundance, knowing they have received abundance, as to the inward man; which is chiefly to be regarded. And therefore beware of such a temptation, as to use their calling as an engine to be richer, knowing, they have this advantage beyond the rich and noble that are called, that the truth doth not any ways abase them, nay, not in the esteem of the world, as it doth the other; but that they are rather exalted thereby, in that as to the inward and spiritual fellowship of the saints, they become the brethren and companions of the greatest and richest; and in this respect, Let him of low degree rejoice that he is exalted.

These things premised, I would seriously propose unto all such, as choose to be Christians indeed, and that in nature, and not in name only, whether it were not desirable, and would not greatly contribute to the commendation of Christianity, and to the increase of the life and virtue of Christ, if all superfluous titles of honour, profuseness and prodigality in meat and apparel, gaming, sporting and playing, were laid aside and forborne? And whether such as lay them aside, in so doing, walk not more like the disciples of Christ and his apostles, and are therein nearer their example, than such as use them? Whether the laying them aside would hinder any from being good Christians? Or if Christians might not be better without them, than with them? Certainly the sober and serious among all sorts will say, Yea. Then surely such as lay them aside, as reckoning them unsuitable for Christians, are not to be blamed, but rather commended for so doing: because that in principle and practice they effectually advance that, which others acknowledge were desirable, but can never make effectual, so long as they allow the use of them as lawful. And God hath made it manifest in this age, that by discovering the evil of such things, and leading his witnesses out of them, and to testify against them, he hath produced effectually in many that mortification and abstraction from the love and cares of this world, who daily are conversing in the world, but inwardly redeemed out of it, both in wedlock, and in their lawful employments, which was judged could only be obtained by such as were shut up in cloisters and monasteries. Thus much in general.

§ III. As to the first we affirm positively, That it is not lawful for Christians either to give or receive these titles of honour, as, Your Holiness, Your Majesty, Your Excellency, Your Eminency, &c.

**Titles.**

First, Because these titles are no part of that obedience which is due to magistrates or superiors; neither doth the giving them add to or diminish from that subjection we owe to them, which consists in obeying their just and lawful commands, not in titles and designations.

**Under the law and gospel.**

Secondly, We find not that in the scripture any such titles are used, either under the law or the gospel: but that in the speaking to kings, princes, or nobles, they used only a simple compellation, as O King! and that without any further designation, save perhaps the name of the person, as, O King Agrippa, &c.

**Lying titles.**

Thirdly, It lays a necessity upon Christians most frequently to lie; because the persons obtaining these titles, either by election or hereditarily, may frequently be found to have nothing really in them deserving them, or answering to them: as some, to whom it is said, Your Excellency, having nothing of excellency in them; and he who is called, Your Grace, appears to be an enemy to grace; and he who is called, Your Honour, is known to be base and

**Patents do not oblige to a lie.**

ignoble. I wonder what law of man, or what patent ought to oblige me to make a lie, in calling good, evil; and evil, good? I wonder what law of man can secure me, in so doing, from the just judgment of God, that will make me account for every idle word? And to lie is something more. Surely Christians should be ashamed that such laws, manifestly crossing the law of God, should be among them.

**Object.**

If it be said, We ought in charity to suppose that they

have these virtues, because the king has bestowed those titles upon them, or that they are descended of such as deserved them;

I answer, Charity destroys not knowledge: I am not ANS·. obliged by charity, either to believe or speak a lie. Now it is apparent, and cannot be denied by any, but that those virtues are not in many of the persons expressed by the titles they bear; neither will they allow to speak so to such, in whom these virtues are, unless they be so dignified by outward princes. So that such as are truly virtuous, must not be styled by their virtues, because not privileged by the princes of this world; and such as have them not, must be so called, because they have obtained a patent so to be: and all this is done by those, who pretend to be his followers, that commanded his disciples, Not to be called of men, Master; and told them, such could not believe, as received honour one from another, and sought not the honour which cometh from God only. This is so plain, to such as will indeed be Christians, that it needs no consequence.

Fourthly, As to those titles of Holiness, Eminency and Your Holi-Excellency, used among the Papists to the Pope and Car- ness, Your dinals, &c., and Grace, Lordship, and Worship, used to Grace &c. the clergy among the Protestants, it is a most blasphemous usurpation. For if they use Holiness and Grace, because these things ought to be in a Pope or in a Bishop, how come they to usurp that peculiarly to themselves? Ought not holiness and grace to be in every Christian? And so every Christian should say, Your Holiness, and Your Grace, one to another. Next, how can they in reason claim any more titles, than were practised and received by the apostles and primitive Christians, whose successors they pretend they are, and as whose successors (and no otherwise) themselves, I judge, will confess any honour they seek, is due to them? Now if they neither sought, received, nor admitted such honour nor titles, how came these by them? If they say they did, let them prove it if they can: we find no such thing in the scripture. The

Christians speak to the apostles without any such denomination, neither saying, If it please Your Grace, Your
Holiness, Your Lordship, nor Your Worship; they are
neither called, My Lord Peter, nor My Lord Paul; nor
yet Master Peter, nor Master Paul; nor Doctor Peter, nor
Doctor Paul; but singly Peter and Paul; and that not
only in the scripture, but for some hundreds of years after:
so that this appears to be a manifest fruit of the apostasy.
For if these titles arise either from the office or worth of
the persons, it will not be denied, but the apostles deserved
them better than any now that call for them. But the case
is plain, the apostles had the holiness, the excellency, the
grace; and because they were holy, excellent, and gracious, they neither used, nor admitted of such titles: but
Hypocrites these having neither holiness, excellency, nor grace, will
want titles. needs be so called, to satisfy their ambitious and ostentatious minds, which is a manifest token of their hypocrisy.

Fifthly, As to that title of Majesty, usually ascribed to
princes, we do not find it given to any such in the holy
scripture; but that it is specially and peculiarly ascribed
unto God, as 1 Chron. xxix. 11; Job xxxvii. 22; Psal.
xxi. 5, and xxix. 4, and xlv. 3, and xciii. 1, and xcvi. 6;
Isa. ii. 10, and xxiv. 14, and xxvi. 10; Heb. i. 3; 2 Pet.
i. 16, and many more places. Hence saith Jude, ver. 25,
"To the only wise God our Saviour, be glory and majesty," &c., not to men. We find in scripture the proud
king Nebuchadnezzar assuming this title to himself, Dan.
iv. 30, who at that time received a sufficient reproof, by a
sudden judgment which came upon him. Therefore in all
the compellations used to princes in the Old Testament, it
is not to be found, nor yet in the New. Paul was very
civil to Agrippa, yet he gives him no such title: neither
was this title used among Christians in the primitive times.
Hence the Ecclesiastical History of the Reformation of
France, relating the speech of the Lord Rochefort, at the
assembly of the estates of France, held under Charles the
Ninth, in the year 1560, saith, That this harangue was
well remarked, in that he used not the word Majesty, in-

vented by flatterers of late years. And yet this author minded not how his master Calvin used this flattering title to Francis the First, King of France; and not only so, but calls him Most Christian King, in the epistle to his Institutions; though by his daily persecuting of the reformers, it was apparent, he was far from being such, even in Calvin's own esteem. Surely the complying with such vain titles, imposed and introduced by anti-christ, greatly tended to stain the reformation, and to render it defective in many things.

Eccles. Hist. l. 4. p. 445. Your Majesty not used; how taken notice of in 1560.

Lastly, All these titles and styles of honour are to be rejected by Christians, because they are to seek the honour that comes from above, and not the honour that is from below: but these honours are not that honour that comes from above, but are from below. For we know well enough what industry, and what pains men are at to get these things, and what part it is that seeks after them, to wit, the proud, insolent, haughty, aspiring mind. For judge, Is it the meek and innocent Spirit of Christ that covets that honour? Is it that Spirit that must be of no reputation in this world, that has its conversation in heaven, that comes to have fellowship with the sons of God? Is it that Spirit, I say, that loves that honour, that seeks after that honour, that pleads for the upholding of that honour, that frets, and rages, and fumes, when it is denied that honour? Or is it not rather the lordly insulting spirit of Lucifer, the prince of this world, he that of old affected and sought after this honour, and loved not to abide in the submissive low place? And so all his children are possessed with the same ambitious proud mind, seeking and coveting titles of honour, which indeed belong not to them. For let us examine, * Who they are that are honourable indeed? Is it not the righteous man? Is it not the holy man? Is it

The proud mind loves titles.

Phil. iii. 20.

Lucifer's spirit.

1 Sam. ii. 30

---

* Hierom, in his epistle to Celant, admonisheth her, That she was to be preferred to none for her nobility, for the Christian religion admits not of respect of persons; neither are men to be esteemed because of their outward condition, but according to the disposition of the mind to be esteemed either noble or base; he that obeyeth not sin, is free who is strong in virtue, is noble. Let the Epistle of James be read.

not the humble-hearted man, the meek-spirited man? And are not such those that ought to be honoured among Christians? Now of these, may there not be poor men, labourers, silly fishermen? And if so, how comes it that the titles of honour are not bestowed upon such? But who are they that generally receive and look for this honour? Are they not the rich ones, such as have abundance of the earth, as be like the rich glutton, such as are proud and ambitious, such as are oppressors of the poor, such as swell with lust and vanity, and all superfluity of naughtiness, who are the very abomination and plague of the nations? Are not these they that are accounted honourable, that require and receive the titles of honour, proud Hamans? Now whether is this the honour that comes from God, or the honour from below? Doth God honour such as daily dishonour him, and disobey him? And if this be not the honour that comes from God, but the honour of this world, which the children of this world give and receive one from another; how can the children of God, such as are Christians indeed, give or receive that honour among themselves, without coming under the reproof of Christ, who saith, that such as do cannot believe? But further, if we respect the cause that most frequently procures to men these titles of honour, there is not one of a thousand that shall be found to be, because of any Christian virtue; but rather for things to be discommended among Christians: as by the favour of princes, procured by flattering, and often by worse means. Yea, the most frequent, and accounted among men most honourable, is fighting, or some great martial exploit, which can add nothing to a Christian's worth: since, sure it is, it were desirable there were no fightings among Christians at all; and in so far as there are, it shows they are not right Christians. And James tells us, that fighting proceeds from the lusts. So that it were fitter for Christians, by the sword of God's Spirit, to fight against their lusts, than by the prevalency of their lusts to destroy one another. Whatever honour any might have attained of old under the

**Law** this way, we find under the Gospel Christians commended for suffering, not for fighting; neither did any of Christ's disciples, save one, offer outward violence by the sword, in cutting off Malchus's ear; for which he received no title of honour, but a just reproof. Finally, if we look either to the nature of this honour, the cause of it, the ways it is conveyed, the terms in which it is delivered, it cannot be used by such as desire to be Christians in good earnest.

§ IV. Now besides these general titles of honour, what gross abuses are crept in among such as are called Christians in the use of compliments, wherein not servants to masters, or others, with respect to any such kind of relations, but others who have no such relation, do say and write to one another, at every turn, Your humble servant, Your most obedient servant, &c. Such wicked customs have, to the great prejudice of souls, accustomed Christians to lie ; and to use lying is now come to be accounted civility. O horrid apostasy ! for it is notoriously known, that the use of these compliments imports not any design of service, neither are any such fools as to think so : for if we should put them to it that say so, they would not doubt to think we abused them ; and would let us us know they gave us words in course, and no more. It is strange, that such as pretend to scripture as their rule should not be ashamed to use such things ; since Elihu, who had not the scriptures, could by the Light within him (which these men think insufficient), say, Job xxxii. 21, 22 : "Let me not accept any man's person, neither let me give flattering titles unto man. For I know not to give flattering titles ; in so doing my Maker would soon take me away." A certain ancient devout man, in the primitive time, subscribed himself to a bishop, Your humble servant ; wherein I doubt not but he was more real than our usual complimenters ; and yet he was sharply reproved for it.*

---

* This history is reported by Casaubonus, in his book of Manners and Customs, p. 160. In this last age he is esteemed an uncivil man, who will not either to his inferior or equal subscribe himself Servant. But Sulpitius Severus was heretofore sharply reproved by Paulinus,

But they usually object, to defend themselves, That Luke saith, Most Excellent Theophilus; and Paul, Most Noble Festus.

I answer; Since Luke wrote that by the dictates of the infallible Spirit of God, I think it will not be doubted but Theophilus did deserve it, as being really endued with that virtue: in which case we shall not condemn those that do it by the same rule. But it is not proved that Luke gave Theophilus this title, as that which was inherent to him, either by his father, or by any patent Theophilus had obtained from any of the princes of the earth; or that he would have given it him, in case he had not been truly excellent; and without this be proved (which never can), there can nothing hence be deduced against us. The like

*Concerning the title Paul gave to Festus.* may be said of that of Paul to Festus, whom he would not have called such, if he had not been truly noble; as indeed he was, in that he suffered him to be heard in his own cause, and would not give way to the fury of the Jews against him: it was not because of any outward title bestowed upon Festus, that he so called him, else he would have given the same appellation to his predecessor, Felix, who had the same office; but being a covetous man, we find he gives him no such style.

*The singular number to one person used in the Latin.* § V. It will not be unfit in this place to say something concerning the using of the singular number to one person; of this there is no controversy in the Latin. For when we speak to one, we always use the pronoun *tu*, and he that would do otherwise, would break the rules of grammar. For what boy, learning his rudiments, is ignorant, that it is incongruous to say *vos amas, vos legis*, that is, *you lovest, you readest*, speaking to one? But the pride of man, that hath corrupted many things, refuses also to use this simplicity of speaking in the vulgar languages. For being puffed up with a vain opinion of themselves, as if the singu-

bishop of Nola, because in his epistle he had subscribed himself his Servant, saying, "Beware thou subscribe not thyself his Servant, who is thy Brother: for flattery is sinful, not a testimony of humility to give those honours to men, which are only due to the One Lord, Master and GOD."

lar number were not sufficient for them, they will have others to speak to them in the plural. Hence Luther, in his plays, reproves and mocks this manner of speaking, saying, *Magister, vos es iratus:* which corruption Erasmus sufficiently refutes in his book of writing epistles: concerning which likewise James Howel, in his epistle to the nobility of England, before the French and English Dictionary, takes notice, " That both in France, and in other nations, the word *thou* was used in speaking to one; but by succession of time, when the Roman commonwealth grew into an empire, the courtiers began to magnify the emperor (as being furnished with power to confer dignities and offices), using the word *you*, yea, and deifying him with more remarkable titles; concerning which matter, we read in the epistles of Symmachus to the emperors Theodosius and Valentinianus, where he useth these forms of speaking, Vestra Æternitas, Your Eternity; Vestrum Numen, Your Godhead; Vestra Serenitas, Your Serenity; Vestra Clementia, Your Clemency. So that the word *you* in the plural number, together with the other titles and compellations of honour, seem to have taken their rise from monarchical government; which afterwards, by degrees, came to be derived to private persons."

*How the word* you *came to be used to a single person.*

The same is witnessed by John Maresius, of the French academy, in the preface of his Clovis: " Let none wonder," saith he, " that the word *thou* is used in this work to Princes and Princesses; for we use the same to God: and of old the same was used to Alexanders, Cæsars, Queens and Empresses. The use of the word *you*, when one person is spoken to, was only introduced by these base flatterers of men of latter ages, to whom it seemed good to use the plural number to one person, that he may imagine himself alone to be equal to many others in dignity and worth; from whence at last it came to persons of lower quality."

To the same purpose speaketh also M. Godeau, in his preface to the New Testament translation: " I had rather," saith he, " faithfully keep to the express words of Paul,

than exactly follow the polished style of our tongue; therefore I always use that form of calling God in the singular
number, not in the plural; and therefore I say rather *thou*
than *you*. I confess indeed, that the civility and custom
of this world requires him to be honoured after that manner; but it is likewise on the contrary true, that the original tongue of the New Testament hath nothing common
with such manners and civility; so that not one of these
many old versions we have doth observe it. Let not men
believe, that we give not respect enough to God, in that
we call him by the word *thou*, which is nevertheless far
otherwise; for I seem to myself (may be by the effect of
custom) more to honour his Divine Majesty, in calling
him after this manner, than if I should call him after the
manner of men, who are so delicate in their forms of
speech."

The word
*thou*, a
greater
horour to
one than
*you*.

See how clearly and evidently these men witness, that
this form of speaking, and these profane titles, derive their
origin from the base flattery of these last ages, and from
the delicate haughtiness of worldly men, who have invented these novelties, that thereby they might honour
one another, under I know not what pretence of civility
and respect. From whence many of the present Christians (so accounted) are become so perverse, in commending most wicked men, and wicked customs, that the simplicity of the Gospel is wholly lost; so that the giving of
men and things their own names is not only worn out of
custom, but the doing thereof is accounted absurd and
rude by such kind of delicate parasites, who desire to
ascribe to this flattery and abuse, the name of civility.
Moreover, that this way of speaking proceeds from a high
and proud mind, hence appears; because that men commonly use the singular number to beggars, and to their
servants; yea, and in their prayers to God. Thus the
superior will speak to his inferior, who yet will not bear
that the inferior so speak to him, as judging it a kind of
reproach unto him. So hath the pride of men placed God
and the beggar in the same category. I think I need not

use arguments to prove to such as know congruous language, that we ought to use the singular number speaking
to one; which is the common dialect of the whole scripture, as also the most interpreters do translate it. Seeing
therefore it is manifest to us, that this form of speaking to
men in the plural number doth proceed from pride, as
well as that it is in itself a lie, we found a necessity upon
us to testify against this corruption, by using the singular
equally unto all. And although no reason can be given
why we should be persecuted upon this account, especially
by Christians, who profess to follow the rule of scripture, *Scripture dialect the plain language.*
whose dialect this is; yet it would perhaps seem incredible
if I should relate how much we have suffered for this
thing, and how these proud ones have fumed, fretted, and
gnashed their teeth, frequently beating and striking us,
when we have spoken to them thus in the singular number:
whereby we are the more confirmed in our judgment, as
seeing that this testimony of truth, which God hath given
us to bear in all things, doth so vex the serpentine nature
in the children of darkness.

§ VI. Secondly, Next unto this of titles, the other part *Bowing to men, &c.*
of honour used among Christians is the kneeling, bowing,
and uncovering of the head to one another. I know
nothing our adversaries have to plead for them in this
matter, save some few instances of the Old Testament, and
the custom of the country.

The first are, such as Abraham's bowing himself to the
children of Heth, and Lot, to the two angels, &c.

But the practice of these patriarchs, related as matter
of fact, is not to be a rule to Christians now; neither are
we to imitate them in every practice, which has not a particular reproof added to it: for we find not Abraham reproved for taking Hagar, &c. And indeed to say all
things were lawful for us which they practised, would pro-
duce great inconveniences obvious enough to all. And *The custom of the nations no rule to Christians.*
as to the customs of the nations, it is a very ill argument
for a Christian's practice: we should have a better rule to
walk by than the custom of the Gentiles; the apostle

desires us not to be " conformed to this world," &c.   We
see how little they have to say for themselves in this matter
Let it be observed then, whether our reasons for laying
aside these things be not considerable and weighty enough
to uphold us in so doing.

First, We say, That God, who is the creator of man,
and he to whom he oweth the dedication both of soul and
body, is over all to be worshipped and adored, and that
not only by the spirit, but also with the prostration of body.

**Bowing is
adoring,
and is only
due to God.** Now kneeling, bowing, and uncovering of the head, is
the alone outward signification of our adoration towards
God and therefore it is not lawful to give it unto man.   He
that kneeleth, or prostrates himself to man, what doth he
more to God ?   He that boweth, and uncovereth his head
to the creature, what hath he reserved to the Creator?
Now the apostle shows us, that the uncovering of the head
is that which God requires of us in our worshipping of
him, 1 Cor. xi. 4.   But if we make our address to men in
the same manner, where lieth the difference ?   Not in the
outward signification, but merely in the intention ; which
opens a door for the popish veneration of images, which
hereby is necessarily excluded.

Secondly, Men being alike by creation, though their
being stated under their several relations requires from
them mutual services according to those respective relations, owe not worship one to another, but all equally are
to return it to God: because it is to him, and his name
alone, that every knee must bow, and before whose throne
the four and twenty elders prostrate themselves.   Therefore for men to take this one from another, is to rob God
of his glory : since all the duties of relations may be performed one to another without these kind of bowings,
which therefore are no essential part of our duty to man,
but to God.   All men, by an inward instinct, in all nations
have been led to prostrate and bow themselves to God.
And it is plain that this bowing to men took place from a
slavish fear possessing some, which led them to set up
others as gods : when also an ambitious proud spirit got

up in those others, to usurp the place of God over their brethren.

Thirdly, We see that Peter refused it from Cornelius, saying, He was a man. Are then the popes more, or more excellent than Peter, who suffer men daily to fall down at their feet, and kiss them? This reproof of Peter to Cornelius doth abundantly show, that such manners were not to be admitted among Christians. Yea, we see, that the angel twice refused this kind of bowing from John, Rev. xix. 10, and xxii. 9, for this reason, "Because I am thy fellow-servant, and of thy brethren;" abundantly intimating that it is not lawful for fellow-servants thus to prostrate themselves one to another: and in this respect all men are fellow-servants.

*Peter and the angel refused bowing.*

If it be said, John intended here a religious worship, and not a civil:

*Object.*

I answer; This is to say, not to prove: neither can we suppose John, at that time of the day, so ill-instructed as not to know it was unlawful to worship angels; only it should seem, because of those great and mysterious things revealed to him by that angel, he was willing to signify some more than ordinary testimony of respect, for which he was reproved. These things being thus considered, it is remitted to the judgment of such as are desirous to be found Christians indeed, whether we are worthy of blame for waving it to men. Let those then that will blame us consider whether they might not as well accuse Mordecai of incivility, who was no less singular than we in this matter. And forasmuch as they accuse us herein of rudeness and pride, though the testimony of our consciences in the sight of God be a sufficient guard against such calumnies, yet there are of us known to be men of such education, as forbear not these things for want of that they call good breeding; and we should be very void of reason, to purchase that pride at so dear a rate, as many have done the exercise of their conscience in this matter; many of us having been sorely beaten and buffeted, yea, and several months imprisoned, for no other reason but because we

*Answ.*

*To forbear bowing to man is no incivility, nor pride, nor rudeness*

could not so satisfy the proud unreasonable humours of proud men, as to uncover our heads, and bow our bodies. Nor doth our innocent practice, in standing still, though upright, not putting off our hats, any more than our shoes, the one being the covering of our heads, as well as the other of our feet, show so much rudeness, as their beating and knocking us, &c., because we cannot bow to them contrary to our consciences: which certainly shows less meekness and humility upon their part, than it doth of rudeness or pride upon ours. Now suppose it were our weakness, and we really under a mistake in this thing, since it is not alleged to be the breach of any Christian precept, are we not to be indulged, as the apostle commanded should be done to such as scrupled to eat flesh? And do not persecuting and reviling us upon this account show them to be more like unto proud Haman, than the disciples or followers of the meek, self-denying Jesus? And this I can say boldly, in the sight of God, from my own experience, and that of many thousands more, that however small or foolish this may seem, yet we behoved to choose death rather than do it, and that for conscience' sake: and that in its being so contrary to our natural spirits, there are many of us, to whom the forsaking of these bowings and ceremonies was as death itself; which we could never have left, if we could have enjoyed our peace with God in the use of them. Though it be far from us to judge all those to whom God hath not shown the evil of them under the like hazard; yet nevertheless we doubt not but to such as would prove faithful witnesses to Christ's divine light in their consciences, God will also show the evil of these things.

§ VII. The third thing to be treated of, is the vanity and superfluity of apparel. In which, first, two things are to be considered, the condition of the person, and the country he lives in. We shall not say that all persons are to be clothed alike, because it will perhaps neither suit their bodies nor their estates. And if a man be clothed soberly, and without superfluity, though they may be finer

*Apparel in its vanity and superfluity disallowed.*

than that which his servant is clothed with, we shall not blame him for it: the abstaining from superfluities, which his condition and education have accustomed him to, may be in him a greater act of mortification than the abstaining from finer clothes in the servant, who never was accustomed to them. As to the country, what it naturally produces may be no vanity to the inhabitants to use, or what is commonly imparted to them by way of exchange, seeing it is without doubt that the creation is for the use of man. So where silk abounds, it may be worn as well as wool; and were we in those countries, or near unto them, where gold or silver were as common as iron or brass, the one might be used as well as the other. The iniquity lies then here, First, When from a lust of vanity, and a desire to adorn themselves, men and women, not content with what their condition can bear, or their country easily affords, do stretch to have things, that from their rarity, and the price that is put upon them, seem to be precious, and so feed their lust the more; and this all sober men of all sorts will readily grant to be evil.

Secondly, When men are not content to make a true use of the creation, whether the things be fine or coarse, and do not satisfy themselves with what need and conveniency call for, but add thereunto things merely superfluous, such as is the use of ribbands and lace, and much more of that kind of stuff, as painting the face, and plaiting the hair, which are the fruits of the fallen, lustful, and corrupt nature, and not of the new creation, as all will acknowledge. And though sober men among all sorts will say, that it were better these things were not, yet will they not reckon them unlawful, and therefore do admit the use of them among their church members: but we do account them altogether unlawful, and unsuitable to Christians, and that for these reasons:

First, The use of clothes came originally from the fall. If man had not fallen, it appears he would not have needed them; but this miserable state made them necessary in two respects: 1. To cover his nakedness; 2. To keep him from

The proper use of clothes.

42

the cold; which are both the proper and principal use of them. Now for man to delight himself in that which is the fruit of his iniquity, and the consequence of his sin, can be no ways lawful for him: so to extend things beyond their real use, or to superadd things wholly superfluous, is a manifest abuse of the creation, and therefore not lawful to Christians.

Secondly, Those that will needs so adorn themselves in the use of their clothes, as to beset them with things having no real use or necessity, but merely for ornament sake, do openly declare, that the end of it is either to please their lust, for which end these things are chiefly invented and contrived, or otherwise to gratify a vain, proud, and ostentatious mind; and it is obvious these are their general ends in so doing. Yea, we see how easily men are puffed up with their garments, and how proud and vain they are, when adorned to their mind. Now how far these things are below a true Christian, and how unsuitable, needs very little proof. Hereby those who love to be gaudy and superfluous in their clothes, show they concern themselves little with mortification and self-denial, and that they study to beautify their bodies more than their souls; which prove they think little upon mortality, and so certainly are more nominal than real Christians.

*Not to please their lusts.*

*Contrary to scripture.*

Thirdly, The scripture severely reproves such practices, both commending and commanding the contrary; as Isa. iii., how severely doth the prophet reprove the daughters of Israel for their tinkling ornaments, their cauls, and their round tires, their chains and bracelets, &c., and yet is it not strange to see Christians allow themselves in these things, from whom a more strict and exemplary conversation is required? Christ desires us not to be anxious about our clothing, Mat. vi. 25, and to show the vanity of such as glory in the splendour of their clothing, tells them, That even Solomon, in all his glory, was not to be compared to the lily of the field, which to-day is, and to-morrow is cast into the oven. But surely they make small reckoning of Christ's words and doctrine that are so curious in their clothing, and so industrious to deck themselves, and so earnest to justify it, and so enraged when they are reproved for it. The apostle Paul is very positive in this respect, 1 Tim. ii. 9, 10, "I will therefore in like manner also that women adorn themselves in modest apparel, with shame-facedness and sobriety, and not with broidered hair, or gold, or pearls, or costly array, but (which becometh women professing godliness) with good works." To the same purpose saith Peter, 1 Pet. iii. 3, 4, "Whose adorn-ing let it not be that outward adorning of plaiting the hair, and wearing of gold, or of putting on of apparel; but let it be the hidden man of the heart, in that which is not cor-ruptible, even the ornament of a meek and quiet spirit," &c. Here both the apostles do very positively and ex-pressly assert two things. First, That the adorning of Christian women (of whom it is particularly spoken, I judge, because this sex is most naturally inclined to that vanity, and that it seems that Christian men in those days deserved not in this respect so much to be reproved) ought not to be outward, nor consist in the apparel. Se-condly, That they ought not to use the plaiting of the hair, or ornaments, &c., which was at that time the custom of the nations. But is it not strange, that such as make the scripture their rule, and pretend they are guided by it, should not only be so generally in the use of these things, which the scripture so plainly condemns, but also should attempt to justify themselves in so doing? For the apostles not only commend the forbearance of these things, as an attainment commendable in Christians, but condemn the use of them as unlawful; and yet may it not seem more strange, that in contradiction to the apostles' doctrine, as if they had resolved to slight their testimony, they should condemn those that out of conscience apply themselves seriously to follow it, as if in so doing they were singular, proud, or superstitious? This certainly betokens a sad apostasy in those that will be accounted Christians, that they are so offended with those who love to follow Christ and his apostles, in denying of, and departing from, the

*Plaiting the hair, &c.*

lying vanities of this perishing world; and so doth much evidence their affinity with those who hate to be reproved, and neither will enter themselves, nor suffer those that would.

**Sports, &c., inconsistent with the gospel.** § VIII. Fourthly, Let us consider the use of games, sports, comedies, and other such things, commonly and indifferently used by all the several sorts of Christians, under the notion of divertisement and recreation, and see whether these things can consist with the seriousness, gravity, and Godly fear, which the gospel calls for. Let us but view and look over the notions of them that call themselves Christians, whether Papists or Protestants, and see if generally there be any difference, save in mere name and profession, from the heathen? Doth not the same folly, the same vanity, the same abuse of precious and irrevocable time abound? The same gaming, sporting, playing, and from thence quarrelling, fighting, swearing, ranting, revelling? Now how can these things be remedied, so long as the preachers and professors, and those who are the leaders of the people, do allow these things, and account them not inconsistent with the profession of Christianity? And it is strange to see that these things are tolerated every where; the inquisition lays no hold on them, neither at Rome, nor in Spain, where in their masquerades all manner of obscenity, folly, yea, and Atheism is generally practised in the face of the world, to the great scandal of the Christian name; but if any man reprove them in these things, and forsake their superstitions, and come seriously to serve God, and worship him in the Spirit, he becomes their prey, and is immediately exposed to cruel sufferings. Doth this bear any relation to Christianity? Do these things look any thing like the churches of the primitive Christians? Surely not at all. I shall first cite some few scripture testimonies, being very positive precepts to Christians, and then see whether such as obey them can admit of these forementioned things. The apostle commands us, That " whether we eat or drink, or whatever we do, we do it all to the glory of God." But

I judge none will be so impudent as to affirm, That in the use of these sports and games God is glorified: if any should so say, they would declare they neither knew God nor his glory. And experience abundantly proves, that in the practice of these things men mind nothing less than the glory of God, and nothing more than the satisfaction of their own carnal lusts, wills, and appetites. The apostle desires us, 1 Cor. vii. 29, 31 : Because the time is short, that they that buy should be as though they possessed not ; and they that use this world, as not abusing it, &c. But how can they be found in the obedience of this precept that plead for the use of these games and sports, who, it seems, think the time so long, that they cannot find occasion enough to employ it, neither in taking care for their souls, nor yet in the necessary care for their bodies; but invent these games and sports to pass it away, as if they wanted other work to serve God in, or be useful to the creation? The apostle Peter desires us, "To pass the time of our sojourning here in fear," 1 Pet. i. 17. But will any say, That such as use dancing and comedies, carding and dicing, do so much as mind this precept in the use of these things? Where there is nothing to be seen but lightness and vanity, wantonness and obscenity, contrived to draw men from the fear of God, and therefore no doubt calculated for the **service of the** devil. There is no duty more frequently commanded, nor more incumbent upon Christians, than the fear of the Lord, to stand in awe before him, to walk as in his presence ; but if such as use these games and sports will speak from their consciences, they can, I doubt not, experimentally declare, that this fear is forgotten in their gaming; and if God by his light secretly touch them, or mind them of the vanity of their way, they strive to shut it out, and use their gaming as an engine to put away from them that troublesome guest, and thus make merry over the Just One, whom they have slain and crucified in themselves. But further, if Christ's reasoning be to be heeded, who saith, Matt. xii. 35, 36 : That "the good man, out of the good treasure of the **heart,** bringeth forth good things ; and an evil man, out of the evil treasure, bringeth forth evil things," and that " of every idle word we shall give an account in the day of judgment," it may be easily gathered from what treasure these inventions come ; and it may be easily proved, that it is from the evil, and not the good. How many idle words do they necessarily produce ? Yea, what are come-

Comedies a studied complex of idle lying words.

dies but a studied complex of idle and lying words ? Let men that believe their souls are immortal, and that there will be a day of judgment, in which these words of Christ will be accomplished, answer me, how all these will make account in that great and terrible day, of all these idle words that are necessarily made use of about dancing, gaming, carding, and comedies acting? And yet how is it that by Christians not condemning these things, but allowing of them, many that are accounted Christians take up their whole time in them, yea, make it their trade and employment? Such as the dancing-masters and come-dians, &c., whose hellish conversations do sufficiently de-clare what master they serve, and to what end these things contribute. And it cannot be denied, as being obviously manifest by experience, that such as are masters of these occupations, and are most delighted in them, if they be not open Atheists and profligates, are such at best as make religion or the care of their souls their least business. Now if these things were discountenanced by Christians, as in-consistent with their profession, it would remove these things : for these wretches would be necessitated then to betake themselves to some honest livelihood, if they were not fed and upholden by these. And as hereby a great scandal and stumbling-block would be removed from off the Christian name, so also would that in part be taken out of the way which provokes the Lord to withhold his blessing, and by occasion of which things the minds of many remain chained in darkness, and drowned in lust, sensuality, and worldly pleasures, without any sense of God's fear, or their own souls' salvation. Many of those called fathers of the church, and other serious persons, have signified their regret for these things, and their desires they might be remedied; of whom many citations might be alleged, which for brevity's sake I have omitte l.

§ IX. But they object, That men's spirits could not Object. subsist, if they were always intent upon serious and spiritual matters, and that therefore there is need of some divertisement to recreate the mind a little, whereby it being refreshed, is able with greater vigour to apply itself to these things.

I answer; Though all this were granted, it would no Answ. ways militate against us, neither plead the use of these things, which we would have wholly laid aside. For that men should be always in the same intentiveness of mind, we do not plead, knowing how impossible it is, so long as we are clothed with this tabernacle of clay. But this will not allow us at any time so to recede from the remembrance of God, and of our souls' chief concern, as not still to retain a certain sense of his fear; which cannot be so The fear of much as rationally supposed to be in the use of these things God the which we condemn. Now the necessary occasions in tion in the which all are involved, in order to the care and sustenta- world. tion of the outward man, are a relaxation of the mind from the more serious duties; and those are performed in the blessing, as the mind is so leavened with the love of God, and the sense of his presence, that even in doing these things the soul carrieth with it that divine influence and spiritual habit, whereby, though these acts, as of eating, drinking, sleeping, working, be upon the matter one with what the wicked do, yet they are done in another spirit; and in doing of them we please the Lord, serve him, and answer our end in the creation, and so feel and are sensible of his blessing: whereas the wicked and profane, being not come to this place, are in whatsoever they do, cursed, and their ploughing as well as praying is sin. Now if any will plead, that for relaxation of mind, there may be a liberty allowed beyond these things, which are of absolute need to the sustenance of the outward man, I shall not much conter.d against it; provided these things

be not such as are wholly superfluous, or in their propes
nature and tendency lead the mind into lust, vanity, and
wantonness, as being chiefly contrived and framed for that
end, or generally experienced to produce these effects, or
being the common engines of such as are so minded to
feed one another therein, and to propagate their wickedness, to the impoisoning of others; seeing there are o<sup>+</sup>her

**Lawful di-
vertise-
ments.**

innocent divertisements which may sufficiently serve for
relaxation of the mind, such as for friends to visit one another; to hear or read history; to speak soberly of the
present or past transactions; to follow after gardening; to
use geometrical and mathematical experiments, and such
other things of this nature. In all which things we are
not so to forget God, in whom we both live and are moved,
Acts xvii. 28, as not to have always some secret reserve
to him, and sense of his fear and presence; which also
frequently exerts itself in the midst of these things by
some short aspiration and breathings. And that this may
neither seem strange nor troublesome, I shall clear it by
one manifest instance, answerable to the experience of all
men. It will not be denied but that men ought to be more
in the love of God than of any other thing; for we ought
to love God above all things. Now it is plain, that men
that are taken with love, whether it be of a woman, or of
any other thing, if it hath taken a deep place in the heart,
and possess the mind, it will be hard for the man so in love
to drive out of his mind the person or thing so loved;
yea, in his eating, drinking, and sleeping, his mind will
always have a tendency that way; and in business or recreations, however intent he be in it, there will but a very
short time be permitted to pass, but the mind will let some

**The love
towards its
beloved
shuns its
offence.**

ejaculation forth towards its beloved. And albeit such a
one must be conversant in those things that the care of this
body and such like things call for; yet will he avoid as
death itself to do those things that may offend the party so
beloved, or cross his design in obtaining the thing so earnestly desired: though there may be some small use in
them, the great design, which is chiefly in his eye, will so

balance him, that he will easily look over and dispense with such petty necessities, rather than endanger the loss of the greater by them. Now that men ought to be thus in love with God, and the life to come, none will deny; and the thing is apparent from these scriptures, Mat. vi. 20, "But lay up for yourselves treasures in heaven." Col. iii. 2, "Set your affection on things above," &c. And that this hath been the experience and attainment of some, the scripture also declares, Psalm lxiii. 1, 8; 2 Cor. v. 4

And again, That these games, sports, plays, dancing, comedies, &c., do naturally tend to draw men from God's fear, to make them forget heaven, death, and judgment, to foster lust, vanity, and wantonness, and therefore are most loved, as well as used, by such kind of persons, experience abundantly shows, and the most serious and conscientious among all will scarcely deny; which if it be so, the application is easy.

*Sports and plays draw men from the fear of God.*

§ X. Fifthly, The use of swearing is to be considered, which is so frequently practised almost among all Christians; not only profane oaths among the profane, in their common discourses, whereby the most HOLY NAME of GOD is in a horrible manner daily blasphemed; but also solemn oaths, with those that have some show of piety, whereof the most part do defend swearing before the magistrate with so great zeal, that not only they are ready themselves to do it upon every occasion, but also have stirred up the magistrates to persecute those, who, out of obedience to Christ, their Lord and master, judge it unlawful to swear; upon which account not a few have suffered imprisonment, and the spoiling of their goods.

But considering these clear words of our Saviour, Mat. v. 33, 34, "Again, ye have heard that it hath been said by them of old time, Thou shalt not forswear thyself, but shalt perform unto the Lord thine oaths. But I say unto you, SWEAR NOT AT ALL, neither by heaven," &c. "But let your communication be yea, yea; nay, nay; for whatsoever is more than these cometh of evil." As also the

*All swearing is forbidden—*

words of the apostle James, v. 12, " But above all things,
my brethren, swear not, neither by heaven, neither by the
earth, neither by any other oath ; but let your yea be yea,
and your nay, nay, lest ye fall into condemnation." I
say, considering these clear words, it is admirable how any
one that professeth the name of Christ can pronounce any
oath with a quiet conscience, far less to persecute other
Christians, that dare not swear, because of their master
Christ's authority. For did any one purpose seriously,
and in the most rigid manner, to forbid any thing comprehended under any general, can they use a more full and
general prohibition, and that without any exception? I
think not. For Christ, First, proposeth it to us negatively, Swear not all, neither by heaven, nor by the
earth, nor by Jerusalem, nor by thy head, &c. And
again, " Swear not by heaven, nor by earth, nor by any
other oath." Secondly, he presseth it affirmatively, " But
let your communication be yea, yea, and nay, nay ; for
whatsoever is more than these, cometh of evil." And saith
James, " Lest ye fall into condemnation."

Without
exception.
Which words both all and every one of them do make
such a full prohibition, and so free of all exception, that it
is strange how men that boast the scripture is the rule of
their faith and life, can counterfeit any exception ! Certainly reason ought to teach every one, that it is not lawful to make void a general prohibition coming from God
by such opposition, unless the exception be as clearly and
evidently expressed as the prohibition : neither is it enough
to endeavour to confirm it by consequences and proba-
bilities, which are obscure and uncertain, and not sufficient
to bring quiet to the conscience. For if they say, that
there is therefore an exception and limitation in the words,
because there are found exceptions in the other general
prohibition of the fifth chapter, as in the forbidding of
divorcement, where Christ saith, " It hath been said, Whosoever shall put away his wife, let him give her a writing
of divorcement : but I say unto you, That whosoever shall
put away his wife, saving for the cause of fornication, caus

eth her to commit adultery;" if, I say, they plead this, they not only labour in vain, but also fight against themselves, because they can produce no exception of this general command of not swearing, expressed by God to any under the new covenant, after Christ gave this prohibition so clear as that which is made in the prohibition itself. More- Also oaths before a magistrate. over, if Christ would have excepted oaths made before magistrates, certainly he had then expressed, adding, Except in judgment, before the magistrate, or the like ; as he did in that of divorcement by these words, " saving for the cause of fornication :" which being so, it is not lawful for us to except or distinguish, or, which is all one, make void this general prohibition of Christ; it would be far less agreeable to Christian holiness to bring upon our heads the crimes of so many oaths, which by reason of this corruption and exception are so frequent among Christians.

Neither is it to be omitted that without doubt the most The concurrence of the ancient fathers therein. learned doctors of each sect know, that these fore-mentioned words were understood by the ancient fathers of the first three hundred years after Christ to be a prohibition of all sorts of oaths. It is not then without reason that we wonder that the Popish doctors and priests bind themselves by an oath to interpret the holy scriptures according to the universal exposition of the holy fathers; who nevertheless understood those controverted texts quite contrary to what these modern doctors do. And from thence also do clearly appear the vanity and foolish certainty (so to speak) of Popish traditions; for if by the writings of the fathers, so called, the faith of the church of those ages may be demonstrated, it is clear they have departed from the faith of the church of the first three ages in the point of swearing. Moreover, because not only Papists, but also Lutherans and Calvinists, and some others, do restrict the words of Christ and James, I think it needful to make manifest the vain foundation upon which their presumption in this matter is built.

§ XI. First, They object, That Christ only forbids these Object oaths that are made by creatures, and things created ; and they prove it thence, because he numbers some of these things.

Secondly, All rash and vain oaths in familiar discourses; because he saith, " Let your communication be yea, yea, and nay, nay."

**Ans. 1.**

To which I answer, First, That the law did forbid all oaths made by the creatures, as also all vain and rash oaths in our common discourses, commanding, That men should only swear by the name of God, and that neither falsely nor rashly ; for that is to take his name in vain.

**Ans. 2.**

*To swear by God himself forbidden by Christ.*

Secondly, It is most evident that Christ forbids somewhat that was permitted under the law, to wit, to swear by the name of God, because it was not lawful for any man to swear but by God himself. And because he saith, " Neither by heaven, because it is the throne of God ;' therefore he excludes all other oaths, even those which are made by God; for he saith, chap. xxiii. 22, " He that shall swear by heaven, sweareth by the throne of God, and by him that sitteth thereon :" which is also to be understood of the rest.

**Ans. 3.**

Lastly, That he might put the matter beyond all controversy, he adds, " Neither by any other oath :" therefore seeing to swear before the magistrate by God is an oath, it is here without doubt forbidden.

**Object.**

Secondly, They object, That by these words oaths by God's name cannot be forbidden, because the Heavenly Father hath commanded them ; for the Father and the Son are one, which could not be, if the Son had forbid that which the Father commanded.

**Answ.**

*Oaths under the old covenant.*

I answer, They are indeed one, and cannot contradict one another : nevertheless the Father gave many things to the Jews for a time, because of their infirmity under the old covenant, which had only a shadow of good things to come, not the very substance of things, until Christ should come, who was the substance, and by whose coming all these things vanished, to wit, sabbaths, circumcision, the paschal lamb : men used then sacrifices, who lived in controversies with God, and one with another, which all are abrogated in the coming of the Son, who is the Substance, Eternal Word, and Essential Oath and Amen, in whom the promises of God are Yea and Amen: who came that men might be redeemed out of strife, and might make an end of controversy.

Thirdly, They object, But all oaths are not ceremonies, Object. nor any part of the ceremonial law.

I answer, Except it be shown to be an eternal, im- Answ. mutable, and moral precept, it withstands not; neither are they of so old an origin as tithes, and the offering of the Tithes, &c first fruits of the ground, which by Abel and Cain were $\begin{smallmatrix} \text{unlawful} \\ \text{now.} \end{smallmatrix}$ offered long before the ceremonial law, or the use of oaths; which, whatever may be alleged against it, were no doubt ceremonies, and therefore no doubt unlawful now to be practised.

Fourthly, They object, That to swear by the name of Object. God is a moral precept of continual duration, because it is marked with his essential and moral worship, Deut. vi. 13, and x. 20, " Thou shalt fear the Lord thy God, and serve him alone: thou shalt cleave to him, and swear by his name."

I answer, This proves not that it is a moral and eternal Answ. precept; for Moses adds that to all the precepts and cere- monies in several places; as Deut. x. 12, 13, saying, "And now, Israel, what doth the Lord thy God require of thee, but to fear the Lord thy God, to walk in all his ways, and to love him, and to serve the Lord thy God with all thy heart, and with all thy soul; to keep the commandments of the Lord, and his statutes, which I command thee this day?" And chap. xiv. 23, the fear of the Lord is men- tioned together with the tithes. And so also Levit. xix. 2, 3, 6, the sabbaths and regard to parents are mentioned with swearing.

Fifthly, They object, That solemn oaths, which God Object commanded, cannot be here forbidden by Christ; for he saith, that they come from evil: but these did not come from evil; for God never commanded any thing that was evil, or came from evil.

Answ.    I answer, There are things which are good because commanded, and evil because forbidden; other things are commanded because good, and forbidden because evil.

Oaths are evil, because forbidden    As circumcision and oaths, which were good, when and because they were commanded, and in no other respect; and again, when and because prohibited under the gospel, they are evil.

And in all these Jewish constitutions, however ceremonial, there was something of good, to wit, in their season, as prefiguring some good: as by circumcision, the purifications, and other things, the holiness of God was typified, and that the Israelites ought to be holy, as their God was holy. In the like manner, oaths, under the shadows and ceremonies, signified the verity of God, his faithfulness and certainty; and therefore that we ought in Truth was before all oaths. all things to speak and witness the truth. But the witness of truth was before all oaths, and remains when all oaths are abolished; and this is the morality of all oaths; and so long as men abide therein, there is no necessity nor place for oaths, as Polybius witnessed, who said, "The use of oaths in judgment was rare among the ancients; but by the growing of perfidiousness, so grew also the use of oaths." To which agreeth Grotius, saying, "An oath is only to be used as a medicine, in case of necessity: a Oaths supply presupposed defects of men's inconstancy. solemn oath is not used but to supply defect. The lightness of men, and their inconstancy, begot diffidence; for which swearing was sought out as a remedy." Basil the Great saith, That "swearing is the effect of sin." And Ambrose, That "oaths are only a condescendency for defect." Chrysostom saith, That "an oath entered when evil grew, when men exercised their frauds, when all foundations were overturned: that oaths took their beginning from the want of truth." These and the like are witnessed by many others with the fore-mentioned authors. But what need of testimonies, where the evidence of things speaks itself? For who will force another to swear, of whom he is certainly persuaded that he abhors to lie in his words? And again, as Chrysostom and others say,

For what end wilt thou force him to swear, whom thou believest not that he will speak the truth?

§ XII. That then which was not from the beginning, which was of no use in the beginning, which had not its beginning first from the will of God, but from the work of the devil, occasioned from evil, to wit, from unfaithfulness, lying, deceit; and which was at first only invented by man, as a mutual remedy of this evil, in which they called upon the names of their idols; yea, that which, as Hierom, Chrysostom, and others testify, was given to the Israelites by God, as unto children, that they might abstain from the idolatrous oaths of the heathen, Jer. xii. 16, whatsoever is so, is far from being a moral and eternal precept. And lastly, whatsoever by its profanation and abuse is polluted with sin, such as are abundantly the oaths of these times, by so often swearing and forswearing, far differs from any necessary and perpetual duty of a Christian: but oaths are so; therefore, &c.

Sixthly, They object, That God swore, therefore to swear is good.

I answer with Athanasius; "Seeing it is certain it is proper in swearing to swear by another, thence it appears, that God, to speak properly, did never swear but only improperly: whence, speaking to men, he is said to swear, because those things which he speaks, because of the certainty and immutability of his will, are to be esteemed for oaths. Compare Psalm cx. 4, where it is said, The Lord did swear, and it did not repent him, &c. 'And I swore,' saith he, 'by myself:' and this is not an oath; for he did not swear by another, which is the property of an oath, but by himself. Therefore God swears not according to the manner of men, neither can we be induced from thence to swear. But let us so do and say, and show ourselves such by speaking and acting, that we need not an oath with those who hear us; and let our words of themselves have the testimony of truth: for so we shall plainly imitate God."

Answ. Athan. in pass. & cruc. Dom.

God swears not by another, but by himself.

**OBJECT.** Seventhly, They object, Christ did swear, and we ought to imitate him.

**ANSW.** I answer, That Christ did not swear; and albeit he had sworn, being yet under the law, this would no ways oblige us under the gospel; as neither circumcision, or the cele-

Hier. lib.
Ep. part. 3.
tract. 1.
Ep. 2.

bration of the paschal lamb. Concerning which Hierom saith, "All things agree not unto us, who are servants, that agreed unto our Lord," &c. "The Lord swore as Lord, whom no man did forbid to swear; but unto us, that are servants, it is not lawful to swear, because we are forbidden by the law of our Lord. Yet, lest we should suffer scandal by his example, he hath not sworn, since he commanded us not to swear."

**OBJECT.** Eighthly, They object, That Paul swore, and that often, Rom. i. 9; Phil. i. 8, saying, "For God is my record." 2 Cor. xi. 10, "As the truth of Christ is in me." 2 Cor. i. 23, "I call God for a record upon my soul." Rom. ix. 1, "I speak the truth in Christ, I lie not." Gal. i. 20, "Behold, before God I lie not," and also requires oaths of others. 1 Tim. v. 21, "I charge thee before God and our Lord Jesus Christ." 1 Thess. v. 27, "I charge you by the Lord, that this epistle be read to all the brethren." But Paul would not have done so, if all manner of oaths had been forbidden by Christ, whose apostle he was.

**ANSW.** To all which I answer, First, That the using of such forms of speaking is neither swearing, nor so esteemed by our adversaries. For when upon occasion, in matters of great moment, we have said, "We speak the truth in the fear of God, and before him, who is our witness, and the searcher of our hearts," adding such kind of serious attestations, which we never refused in matters of conse-

The ceremonies of an oath.

quence; nevertheless an oath hath moreover been required of us, with the ceremony of putting our hands upon the book, the kissing of it, the lifting up of the hand or fingers, together with this common form of imprecation, "So help me God;" or, "So truly let the Lord God Almighty help me." Secondly, This contradicts the opinion of our adversaries, because that Paul was neither before a magistrate that was requiring an oath of him, nor did he himself administer the office of a magistrate, as offering an oath to any other. Thirdly, The question is not what Paul or Peter did, but what their and our Master taught to be done; and if Paul did swear (which we believe not) he had sinned against the command of Christ, even according to their own opinion, because he swore not before a magistrate, but in an epistle to his brethren.

Ninthly, They object, Isa. lxv. 16, where, speaking of OBJECT. the evangelical times, he saith, "That he who blesseth himself in the earth, shall bless himself in the God of truth; and he that sweareth in the earth, shall swear by the God of truth; because the former troubles are forgotten, and because they are hid from mine eyes. For behold I create new heavens, and a new earth." Therefore in these times we ought to swear by the name of the Lord.

I answer, It is ordinary for the prophets to express the ANSW. greatest duties of evangelical times in mosaical terms, as appears among others from Jer. xxxi. 38, 39, 40; Ezek. xxxvi. 25, and 30; and Isa. xlv. 23: "I have sworn by myself, that unto me every knee shall bow, every tongue shall swear." Where the righteousness of the new Jerusalem, the purity of the gospel, with its spiritual worship, and the profession of the name of Christ, are expressed under forms of speaking used to the old Jerusalem, under the washings of the law, under the names of ceremonies, the temple, services, sacrifices, oaths, &c. Yea, that which the prophet speaks here of swearing, the apostle Paul in- *Swearing is* terprets expressly of confessing, saying, Rom. xiv. 11: *expressed* *by confess-* "For it is written, As I live, saith the Lord, every knee *ing under* shall bow to me, and every tongue shall confess to God:" *the gospel.* which being rightly considered, none can be ignorant but these words which the prophet writes under the law, when the ceremonial oaths were in use, to wit, "Every tongue shall swear," were by the apostle, being under the gospel, when those oaths became abolished, expressed by "Every tongue shall confess."

Tenthly, They object, But the apostle Paul approves OBJECT.

43 *

oaths used among men, when he writes, Heb. vi. 16: "For men verily swear by the greater, and an oath for confirmation is to them an end of all strife." But there are as many contests, fallacies, and diffidences, at this time, as there ever were; therefore the necessity of oaths doth yet remain.

I answer; The apostle tells indeed in this place what men at that time did, who lived in controversies and incredulity; not what they ought to have done, nor what the saints did, who were redeemed from strife and incredulity, and had come to Christ, the Truth and Amen of God. Moreover, he only alludes to a certain custom usual among men, that he might express the firmness of the divine promise, in order to excite in the saints so much the more confidence in God promising to them; not that he might instigate them to swear against the law of God, or confirm them in that; no, not at all: for neither doth 1 Cor. ix. 24 teach Christians the vain races, whereby men oftentimes, even to the destruction of their bodies, are wearied to obtain a corruptible prize; so neither doth Christ, who is the Prince of Peace, teach his disciples to fight, albeit he takes notice, Luke xiv. 31, what it behoveth such kings to do who are accustomed to fight, as prudent warriors therein. Secondly, as to what pertains to contests, perfidies, and diffidences among men, which our adversaries affirm to have grown to such a height, that swearing is at present as necessary as ever, that we deny not at all: for we see, and daily experience teacheth us, that all manner of deceit and malice doth increase among worldly men and false Christians; but not among true Christians. But because men cannot trust one another, and therefore require oaths one of another, it will not therefore follow that true Christians ought to do so, whom Christ has brought to faithfulness and honesty, as well towards God as one towards another, and therefore has delivered them from contests, perfidies, and consequently from oaths.

Eleventhly, They object, We grant, that among true Christians there is not need of oaths; but by what means shall we infallibly know them? It will follow then that oaths are at present needful, and that it is lawful for Christians to swear, to wit, that such may be satisfied who wih not acknowledge this and the other man to be a Christian.

I answer, It is no ways lawful for a Christian to swear, Answ. whom Christ has called to his essential truth, which was before all oaths, forbidding him to swear; and on the con- Truth was trary, commanding him to speak the truth in all things, before oaths. to the honour of Christ who called him; that it may appear that the words of his disciples may be as truly believed as the oaths of all the worldly men. Neither is it lawful for them to be unfaithful in this, that they may please others, or that they may avoid their hurt: for thus the primitive Christians for some ages remained faithful, who being required to swear, did unanimously answer, I am a Christian, I do not swear. What shall I say of the heathen, some of whom arrived to that degree? For Heathen Diodorus Siculus relates, lib. xvi., That "the giving of testimonies against the right hand was among the Persians, a sign of speaking oaths. the truth." And the Scythians, as Qu. Curtius relates, said, in their conferences with Alexander the Great, "Think not that the Scythians confirm their friendship by swearing; they swear by keeping their promises." Stobæus, Serm. 3, relates, That Solon said, "A good man ought to be in that estimation that he need not an oath; because it is to be reputed a lessening of his honour if he be forced to swear." Pythagoras, in his oration, among other things hath this maxim, as that which concerns the administration of the commonwealth: "Let no man call God to witness by an oath, no not in judgment; but let every man so accustom himself to speak, that he may become worthy to be trusted even without an oath." Basil the Great commends Clinias an heathen, "That he had rather pay three talents, which are about three thousand pounds, than swear." Socrates, as Stobæus relates, Serm. 14, had this sentence, "The duty of good men requires that they show to the world that their manners and actions are more

firm thar. oaths." The same was the judgment of Iso-
crates. Plato also stood against oaths in his judgment
de Leg. 12. Quintilianus takes notice, " That it was of
old a kind of infamy, if any was desired to swear ; but to
require an oath of a nobleman, was like an examining him
by the hangman." The Emperor Marcus Aurelius Anto-
ninus saith, in his description of a good man, " Such is
his integrity, that he needs not an oath." So also some
Jews did witness, as Grotius relates out of Maimonides,
" It is best for a man to abstain from all oaths." The
Essenes, as Philo Judæus relates, " did esteem their words
more firm than oaths ; and oaths were esteemed among
them as needless things." And Philo himself, speaking
of the third commandment, explains his mind thus, viz. :
" It were better altogether not to swear, but to be accustomed always to speak the truth, that naked words might
have the strength of an oath." And elsewhere he saith,
" It is more agreeable to natural reason altogether to
abstain from swearing ; persuading, That whatsoever a
good man saith may be equivalent with an oath."

Oaths ab-
rogated by
Christ.

Who then needs further to doubt, but that since Christ
would have his disciples attain the highest pitch of per
fection, he abrogated oaths, as a rudiment of infirmity,
and in place thereof established the use of truth ? Who
can now any more think that the holy martyrs and ancient
fathers of the first three hundred years, and many others
since that time, have so opposed themselves to oaths, that
they might only rebuke vain and rash oaths by the creatures, or heathen idols, which were also prohibited under
the mosaical law ; and not also swearing by the true God,
in truth and righteousness, which was there commanded ?
as Polycarpus, Justin Martyr, Apolog. 2, and many mar-

The testi-
monies of
the fathers
against
oaths and
swearing.

tyrs, as Eusebius relates. Tertullian, in his Apol., cap.
32 ; ad Scap., cap. 1 ; of Idolatry, cap. 11. Clem. Alexandrinus, Strom., lib. 7. Origen, in Mat., Tract. 25.
Cyprianus, lib. 3. Athanasius, in pass. & cruc., Domini
Christi. Hilarius in Mat. v. 34. Basilius Magn. in Psalm
xiv. Greg. Nyssenus, in Cant. Orat. 13. Greg. Nazian-

zenus in dialog. contra juramenta. Epiphanius adversus
heres., lib. 1. Ambros. de Virg., lib. 3; Idem in Mat. v
Chrysostom in Genes. homil. 15; Idem homil., in Ac⁺
Apost., cap. 3. Hieronimus Epistol., lib. part 3, Ep. 2.
Idem in Zech., lib. 2, cap. 8. Idem in Mat., lib. 1, cap. 5.
Augustinus de serm. Dom. serm. 28. Cyrillus in Jer. iv.
Theodoretus in Deut. vi. Isidorus Pelusiota, Ep. lib. 1,
Epist. 155. Chromatius in Mat. v. Johannes Damas-
cenus, lib. 3, cap. 16. Cassiodorus in Psalm xciv. Isidorus Hispalensis, cap. 31. Antiochus in Pandect. script.
hom. 62. Beda in Jac. v. Haimo in Apoc. Ambrosius
Ansbertus in Apoc. Theophylactus in Mat. v. Pascha-
sius Radbertus in Mat. v. Otho Brunsfelsius in Mat. v.
Druthmarus in Mat. v. Euthymius Eugubinus Bibliotheca
vet. patr. in Mat. v. Œcumenius in Jac., cap. v., ver. 12.
Anselmus in Mat. v.; the Waldenses, Wickliffe, Erasmus,
in Mat. v., and in Jac. v. Who can read these places and
doubt of their sense in this matter? And who, believing
that they were against all oaths, can bring so great an indignity to the name of Christ, as to seek to subject again
his followers to so great an indignity? Is it not rather
time that all good men should labour to remove this abuse
and infamy from Christians?

Lastly, They object, This will bring in fraud and con- Objec1
fusion; for impostors will counterfeit probity, and under
the benefit of this dispensation will lie without fear of
punishment.

I answer, There are two things which oblige a man to Answ.
speak the truth : First, either the fear of God in his heart,
and love of truth ; for where this is, there is no need of
oaths to speak the truth ; or Secondly, The fear of punishment from the judge. Therefore let there be the same, The
or rather greater punishment appointed to those who pre- punishment
o' liars.
tend so great truth in words, and so great simplicity in
heart that they cannot lie, and so great reverence towards
the law of Christ, that for conscience' sake they deny to
swear in any wise, if they fail; and so there shall be the
same good order, yea, greater security against deceivers,

as if oaths were continued; and also, by that more severe punishment, to which these false dissemblers shall be liable. Hence wicked men shall be more terrified, and good men delivered from all oppression, both in their liberty and goods: for which respect to tender consciences, God hath often a regard to magistrates and their state, as a thing most acceptable to him. But if any can further doubt of this thing, to wit, if without confusion it can be practised in the commonwealth, let him consider the state The United of the United Netherlands, and he shall see the good effect Nether-lands in-stanced. of it: for there, because of the great number of merchants more than in any other place, there is most frequent occasion for this thing; and though the number of those that are of this mind be considerable, to whom the States these hundred years have condescended, and yet daily condescend, yet nevertheless there has nothing of prejudice followed thereupon to the commonwealth, government, or good order; but rather great advantage to trade, and so to the commonwealth.

§ XIII. Sixthly, The last thing to be considered, is revenge and war, an evil as opposite and contrary to the Spirit and doctrine of Christ as light to darkness. For, as is manifest by what is said, through contempt of Christ's Reverge law the whole world is filled with various oaths, cursings, and war contrary to blasphemous profanations, and horrid perjuries; so likeChrist. wise, through contempt of the same law, the world is filled with violence, oppression, murders, ravishing of women and virgins, spoilings, depredations, burnings, devastations, and all manner of lasciviousness and cruelty: so that it is strange that men, made after the image of God, should have so much degenerated, that they rather bear the image and nature of roaring lions, tearing tigers, devouring wolves, and raging boars, than of rational creatures endued with reason. And is it not yet much more admirable, that this horrid monster should find place, and be fomented, among those men that profess themselves disciples of our peaceable Lord and master Jesus Christ, who by excellency is called the Prince of Peace, and hath expressly prohibited his children all violence; and on the contrary, commanded them, that, according to his example, they should follow patience, charity, forbearance, and other virtues worthy of a Christian?

Hear then what this great prophet saith, whom every soul is commanded to hear, under the pain of being cut off, Matt. v., from verse 38, to the end of the chapter. For thus he saith: "Ye have heard that it hath been said, An eye for an eye, and a tooth for a tooth: But I say unto you, That ye resist not evil; but whosoever shall smite thee on thy right cheek, turn to him the other also. And if any man will sue thee at the law, and take away thy coat, let him have thy cloak also. And whosoever shall compel thee to go a mile, go with him twain. Give to him that asketh thee; and from him that would borrow of thee, turn not thou away. Ye have heard that it has been said, Thou shalt love thy neighbour, and hate thine enemy; but I say unto you, Love your enemies, bless them that curse you, do good to them that hate you, and pray for them which despitefully use you, and persecute you, that ye may be the children of your Father which is in heaven. For he maketh his sun to rise on the evil and on the good, and sendeth rain on the just and on the unjust. For if ye love them which love you, what reward have ye? Do not even the publicans the same? And if ye salute your brethren only, what do you more than others? Do not even the publicans so? Be ye therefore perfect, even as your Father which is in heaven is perfect." *Revenge forbidden by Christ.*

These words, with respect to revenge, as the former in the case of swearing, do forbid some things, which in time past were lawful to the Jews, considering their condition and dispensation; and command unto such as will be the disciples of Christ, a more perfect, eminent, and full signification of charity, as also patience and suffering, than was required of them in that time, state, and dispensation of the law of Moses. This is not only the judgment of most, if not all, the ancient fathers, so called, of the first three hundred years after Christ, but also of many others, *The law of Christ more perfect than that of Moses.*

and in general of all those who have rightly understood and propagated the law of Christ concerning swearing, as appears from Justin Martyr in Dialog. cum Tryph. ejusdemque Apolog. 2. Item ad Zenam. Tertul. de Corona Militis. It. Apolog., cap. 21, and 37. It. lib. de Idolol., cap. 17, 18, 19. It. ad Scapulam., cap. 1. It. adversus Jud., cap. 7, and 9. It. adv. Gnost., cap. 13. It. ad. Marc., cap. 4. It. lib. de Patientia, c. 6, 10. Orig. cont. Celsum, lib. 3, 5, 8. It. in Josuam hom. 12, cap. 9. It. in Matt., cap. 26. Tract. 35. Cyp. Epist. 56. It. ad. Cornel. Lactan. de just., lib. 5, c. 18; lib. 6, c. 20. Ambr. in Luc. xxii. Chrysost. in Matt. v., hom. 18. It. in Matt. xxvi., hom. 85. It. lib. 2, de Sacerdotio. It. in 1 Cor. xiii. Chromat. in Matt. v. Hierom. ad. Ocean. It. lib. Epist., p. 3; Tom. 1, Ep. 2. Athan. de Inc. Verb. Dei. Cyrill. Alex., lib. 11, in Johan., cap. xxv. 26. Yea, Augustine, although he vary much in this matter, notwithstanding in these places he did condemn fighting, Epist. 158, 159, 160. It. ad. Judices, Epist. 203. It. ad. Darium, and lib. 21. It. ad. Faustum., cap. 76, lib. 22, de Civit. ad. Marc., cap. 6, as Sylburgius relates. Euthym. in Matt. xxvi, and many others of this age. Erasmus in Luc., cap. 3, and 22. Ludov. Vives in Introduc. ad. Sap. J. Ferus, lib. 4; Comment. in Matt. vii., and Luc. xxii.

From hence it appears, that there is so great a connection betwixt these two precepts of Christ, that as they were uttered and commanded by him at one and the same time, so the same way they were received by men of all ages, not only in the first promulgation by the little number of the disciples, but also after the Christians increased in the first three hundred years. Even so in the apostasy, the one was not left and rejected without the other; and now again in the restitution, and renewed preaching of the eternal gospel, they are acknowledged as eternal and unchangeable laws, properly belonging to the evangelical state and perfection thereof; from which if any withdraw, he falls short of the perfection of a Christian man.

And truly the words are so clear in themselves, that, 'n

*Testimonies of the fathers against fighting.*

*The laws of Christ in the New Testament are irreconcilable to persecution, wars, and fighting*

my judgment, they need no illustration to explain their
sense : for it is as easy to reconcile the greatest contradictions, as these laws of our Lord Jesus Christ with the
wicked practices of wars : for they are plainly inconsistent.
Whoever can reconcile this, " Resist not evil," with, Resist violence by force : again, " Give also thy other cheek,"
with, Strike again ; also " Love thine enemies," with, Spoil
them, make a prey of them, pursue them with fire and
sword ; or, " Pray for those that persecute you, and those
that calumniate you," with, Persecute them by fines, imprisonments, and death itself ; and not only such as do not
persecute you, but who heartily seek and desire your eternal
and temporal welfare : whoever, I say, can find a means to
reconcile these things, may be supposed also to have found
a way to reconcile God with the devil, Christ with Antichrist, light with darkness, and good with evil. But if
this be impossible, as indeed it is, so will also the other be
impossible ; and men do but deceive themselves and others,
while they boldly adventure to establish such absurd and
impossible things.

§ XIV. Nevertheless, because some, perhaps through
inadvertency, and by the force of custom and tradition, do
transgress this command of Christ, I shall briefly show
how much war doth contradict this precept, and how much
they are inconsistent with one another ; and consequently,
that war is no ways lawful to such as will be the disciples
of Christ. For,

First, Christ commands, That " we should love our ene- Matt. v. 44
mies ;" but war, on the contrary, teacheth us to hate and
destroy them.

Secondly, The apostle saith, That " we war not after Eph. vi. 12
the flesh," and that " we fight not with flesh and blood ;"
but outward war is according to the flesh, and against flesh
and blood : for the shedding of the one, and destroying
of the other.

Thirdly, The apostle saith, That " the weapons of our 2 Cor. x. 4
warfare are not carnal, but mighty through God ;" but the
weapons of outward warfare are carnal, such as cannon,

muskets, spears, swords, &c., of which there is no mention in the armour described by Paul.

*James iv. 1.*
*Gal. v. 24.*
Fourthly, Because James testifies, That wars and strifes come from the lusts, which war in the members of carnal men; but Christians, that is, those that are truly saints, "have crucified the flesh, with its affections and lusts;" therefore they cannot indulge them by waging war.

*Isa. ii. 4.*
*Mic. iv. 3.*
Fifthly, Because the prophets Isaiah and Micah have expressly prophesied, That in the mountain of the house of the Lord, Christ shall judge the nations, and then "they shall beat their swords into ploughshares," &c.

*Primitive Christians most averse from war.*
And the ancient fathers of the first three hundred years after Christ did affirm these prophecies to be fulfilled in the Christians of their times, who were most averse from war; concerning which Justin Martyr, Tertullian, and others may be seen: which need not seem strange to any, since Philo Judæus abundantly testifies of the Essenes, That "there was none found among them that would make instruments of war." But how much more did Jesus come, that he might keep his followers from fighting, and might bring them to patience and charity?

*Isa. lxv. 25.*
Sixthly, Because the prophet foretold, That there should none hurt nor kill in all the holy mountain of the Lord; but outward war is appointed for killing and destroying.

*John xviii. 36.*
Seventhly, Because Christ said, That "his kingdom is not of this world," and therefore that his servants shall not fight; therefore those that fight are not his disciples nor servants.

*Mat. xxvi. 52.*
Eighthly, Because he reproved Peter for the use of the sword, saying, "Put up again thy sword into his place: for all they that take the sword, shall perish with the sword." Concerning which Tertullian speaks well, lib. de Idol., "How shall he fight in peace without a sword, which the Lord did take away? For although soldiers came to John, and received a form of observation; if also the centurion believed afterwards, he disarmed every soldier in disarming of Peter." Idem. de Coron. Mil. asketh, "Shall it

oe lawful to use the sword, the Lord saying, That he that useth the sword, shall perish by the sword."

Ninthly, Because the apostle admonisheth Christians, That they defend not themselves, neither revenge by rendering evil for evil; but give place unto wrath, because vengeance is the Lord's. Be not overcome of evil, but overcome evil with good. If thine enemy hunger, feed him; if he thirst, give him drink. But war throughout teacheth and enjoineth the quite contrary. *Rom. xii 17 to 21.*

Tenthly, Because Christ calls his children to bear his cross, not to crucify or kill others; to patience, not to revenge; to truth and simplicity, not to fraudulent stratagems of war, or to play the sycophant, which John himself forbids; to flee the glory of this world, not to acquire it by warlike endeavours; therefore war is altogether contrary unto the law and Spirit of Christ. *Mark viii. 34.*

§ XV. But they object, That it is lawful to war, because Abraham did war before the giving of the law, and the Israelites after the giving of the law. *Object.*

I answer as before, 1. That Abraham offered sacrifices at that time, and circumcised the males; which nevertheless are not lawful for us under the gospel. *Answ.*

2. That neither defensive nor offensive war was lawful to the Israelites of their own will, or by their own counsel or conduct; but they were obliged at all times, if they would be successful, first to inquire of the oracle of God. *Israelites going to war inquired of the oracle of God.*

3. That their wars against the wicked nations were a figure of the inward war of the true Christians against their spiritual enemies, in which we overcome the devil, the world, and the flesh.

4. Something is expressly forbidden by Christ, Mat. v. 38, &c., which was granted to the Jews in their time, because of their hardness; and on the contrary, we are commanded that singular patience and exercise of love which Moses commanded not to his disciples. From whence Tertullian saith well against Marc., "Christ truly teacheth a new patience, even forbidding the revenge of an injury, which was permitted by the Creator." And lib. de patien., *Some things permitted in the Old Testament because of hardness of heart.*

"The law finds more than it lost, by Christ's saying, Love your enemies." And in the time of Clem. Alex. Christians were so far from wars, that he testified that they had no marks or signs of violence among them, saying, "Neither are the faces of idols to be painted, to which so much as to regard is forbidden: neither sword nor bow to them that follow peace; nor cups to them who are moderate and temperate," as Sylvius Disc. de Rev. Belg.

OBJECT.    Secondly, They object, That defence is of natural right, and that religion destroys not nature.

ANSW.    I answer, Be it so; but to obey God, and commend ourselves to him in faith and patience, is not to destroy nature, but to exalt and perfect it; to wit, to elevate it from the natural to the supernatural life, by Christ living therein, and comforting it, that it may do all things, and be rendered more than conqueror.

OBJECT.    Thirdly, They object, That John did not abrogate or condemn war, when the soldiers came unto him.

ANSW.    I answer, What then? The question is not concerning John's doctrine, but Christ's, whose disciples we are, not John's: for Christ, and not John, is that prophet whom
Luke vii. 28. we ought all to hear. And although Christ said, "That a greater than John the Baptist was not among men born of women," yet he adds, "That the least in the kingdom of God is greater than he." But what was John's answer, that we may see if it can justify the soldiers of this time? For if it be narrowly observed, it will appear, that what he proposeth to soldiers doth manifestly forbid them that
Luke iii. 14. employment; for he commands them "not to do violence to any man, nor to accuse any falsely;" but to "be content with their wages." Consider then what he dischargeth to soldiers, viz.: Not to use violence or deceit against any; which being removed, let any tell how soldiers can war? For are not craft, violence, and injustice three properties of war, and the natural consequences of battles?

OBJECT.    Fourthly, They object, That Cornelius, and that centurion of whom there is mention made, Mat. viii. 5, were soldiers, and there is no mention that they laid down their military employments.

I answer, Neither read we that they continued in them. Answ. But it is most probable that if they continued in the doctrine of Christ (and we read not any where of their falling from the faith) that they did not continue in them ; especially if we consider, that two or three ages afterwards Christians altogether rejected war, or at least a long while after that time, if the emperor Marc. Aurel. Anton. be to be credited, who writes thus: — "I prayed to my country gods; but when I was neglected by them, and observed myself pressed by the enemy, considering the fewness of my forces, I called to one, and entreated those who with Christians us are called Christians, and I found a great number of instanced<br>that did not them ; and I forced them with threats, which ought not to war. have been, because afterwards I knew their strength and force:" therefore they betook themselves neither to the use of darts nor trumpets, "for they use not so to do, for the cause and name of their God, which they bear in their consciences:" and this was done about an hundred and sixty years after Christ. To this add those words, which in Justin Martyr the Christians answer, ἐ πολεμῦμεν τοῖς ἐχθροῖς, that is, ' We fight not with our enemies.' And moreover the answer of Martin to Julian the apostate, related by Sulpitius Severus, "I am a soldier of Christ, therefore I cannot fight;" which was three hundred years after Christ. It is not therefore probable that they continued in warlike employments. How then are Vincentius Lyrinensis and the Papists consistent with their maxim, "That which always, every where, and by all was received," &c. And what becomes of the priests, with their oath, That they neither ought nor will interpret the scripture but according to the universal consent of the fathers, so called? For it is as easy to obscure the sun at mid-day, as to deny that the primitive Christians renounced all revenge and war.

And although this thing be so much known, yet it is as well known that almost all the modern sects live in the neglect and contempt of this law of Christ, and likewise

Persecu-
tion for not
bearing
arms, and
not fasting
and praying
for victory.

oppress others, who in this agree not with them for conscience' sake towards God: even as we have suffered much
in our country, because we neither could ourselves bea.
arms, nor send others in our place, nor give our money
for the buying of drums, standards, and other military
attire.   And lastly, Because we could not hold our doors,
windows, and shops close, for conscience' sake, upon such
days as fasts and prayers were appointed, to desire a blessing upon, and success for, the arms of the kingdom or
commonwealth under which we live; neither give thanks
for the victories acquired by the effusion of much blood.
By which forcing of the conscience, they would have constrained our brethren, living in divers kingdoms at war
together, to have implored our God for contrary and contradictory things, and consequently impossible: for it is
impossible that two parties fighting together, should both
obtain the victory.   And because we cannot concur with
them in this confusion, therefore we are subject to persecution.   Yea, and others, who with us do witness that
the use of arms is unlawful to Christians, do look asquint
upon us; but which of us two do most faithfully observe
this testimony against arms?   Either they, who at certain
times, at the magistrate's order, do close up their shops
and houses, and meet in their assembly, praying for the
prosperity of their arms, or giving thanks for some victory
or other, whereby they make themselves like to those that
approve wars and fighting; or we, who cannot do these
things for the same cause of conscience, lest we should
destroy, by our works, what we establish in words, we
shall leave to the judgment of all prudent men.

Fifthly, They object, That Christ, Luke xxii. 36, speaking to his disciples, commands them, That he that then had
not a sword, should sell his coat, and buy a sword; therefore, say they, arms are lawful.

I answer, Some indeed understand this of the outward
sword, nevertheless regarding only that occasion; otherwise judging, that Christians are prohibited wars under the
gospel.   Among which is Ambrose, who upon this place

speaks thus: "O Lord! why commandest thou me to buy
a sword, who forbiddest me to smite with it? Why commandest thou me to have it, whom thou prohibitest to draw
it? Unless perhaps a defence be prepared, not a necessary revenge; and that I may seem to have been able to
revenge, but that I would not. For the law forbids me to
smite again; and therefore perhaps he said to Peter, offering two swords, 'It is enough,' as if it had been lawful
until the gospel times, that in the law there might be a
learning of equity, but in the gospel a perfection of goodness." Others judge Christ to have spoken here mystically, and not according to the letter; as Origen upon
Matt. xix., saying, "If any looking to the letter, and not
understanding the will of the words, shall sell his bodily
garment, and buy a sword, taking the words of Christ contrary to his will, he shall perish; but concerning which
sword he speaks, is not proper here to mention." And
truly when we consider the answer of the disciples, "Master, behold here are two swords;" understanding it of outward swords; and again Christ's answer, "It is enough:"
it seems that Christ would not that the rest, who had not
swords (for they had only two swords), should sell their
coats, and buy an outward sword. Who can think that,
matters standing thus, he should have said, Two was
enough? But however, it is sufficient that the use of arms
is unlawful under the gospel.

Sixthly, They object, That the scriptures and old fathers,
so called, did only prohibit private revenge, not the use of
arms for the defence of our country, body, wives, children,
and goods, when the magistrate commands it, seeing the
magistrate ought to be obeyed; therefore although it be
not lawful for private men to do it of themselves, nevertheless they are bound to do it by the command of the
magistrate.

I answer, If the magistrate be truly a Christian, or desires to be so, he ought himself, in the first place, to obey
the command of his master, saying, "Love your enemies,"
&c., and then he could not command us to kill them: but

*Peter offer-
ed two
swords.*

*Object*

*Answ*

Christian
magistrates
ought to
obey the
command
of their
master,
Christic.
if he be not a true Christian, then ought we to obey our Lord and King, Jesus Christ, whom he ought also to obey: for in the kingdom of Christ all ought to submit to his laws, from the highest to the lowest, that is, from the king to the beggar, and from Cæsar to the clown. But alas! where shall we find such an obedience? O deplorable fall!

Lud. Vives
against
arms.
concerning which Ludov. Viv. writes well, lib. de con. vit. Christ. sub. Turc., by relation of Fredericus Sylvius, Disc. de Revol. Belg., p. 85: "The prince entered into the church, not as a true and plain Christian, which had indeed been most happy and desirable; but he brought in with him his nobility, his honours, his ARMS, his ensigns, his triumphs, his haughtiness, his pride, his superciliousness, that is, he came into the house of Christ, accompanied with the devil; and which could no ways be done; he would have joined two houses and two cities together, God's and the devil's, which could not more be done than Rome and Constantinople, which are distant by so long a tract both of sea and land. What communion, saith Paul, is there betwixt Christ and Belial? Their zeal cooled by degrees, their faith decreased, their whole piety degenerated; instead whereof we make now use of shadows and images, and, as he saith, I would we could but retain these." Thus far Vives. But lastly, as to what relates to this thing, since nothing seems more contrary to man's nature, and seeing of all things the defence of one's self seems most tolerable, as it is most hard to men, so it is the most perfect part of the Christian religion, as that wherein the denial of self and entire confidence in God doth most appear; and therefore Christ and his apostles left us hereof

Concerning
the present
magistrates
of the
Christian
world.
a most perfect example. As to what relates to the present magistrates of the Christian world, albeit we deny them not altogether the name of Christians, because of the public profession they make of Christ's name, yet we may boldly affirm, that they are far from the perfection of the Christian religion; because in the state in which they are (as in many places before I have largely observed), they have not come to the pure dispensation of the gospel. And there-

fore, while they are in that condition, we shall not say, That war, undertaken upon a just occasion, is altogether unlawful to them. For even as circumcision and the other ceremonies were for a season permitted to the Jews, not because they were either necessary of themselves, or lawful at that time, after the resurrection of Christ, but because that Spirit was not yet raised up in them, whereby they could be delivered from such rudiments; so the present confessors of the Christian name, who are yet in the mixture, and not in the patient suffering spirit, are not yet fitted for this form of Christianity, and therefore cannot be undefending themselves until they attain that perfection. But for such whom Christ has brought hither, it is not lawful to defend themselves by arms, but they ought over all to trust to the Lord.

§ XVI. But Lastly, to conclude, If to give and receive flattering titles, which are not used because of the virtues inherent in the persons, but are for the most part bestowed by wicked men upon such as themselves; if to bow, scrape, and cringe to one another; if at every time to call themselves each others' humble servants, and that most frequently without any design of real service; if this be the honour that comes from God, and not the honour that is from below, then indeed our adversaries may be said to be believers, and we condemned as proud and stubborn, in denying all these things. *The conclusion*

But if with Mordecai, to refuse to bow to proud Haman, and with Elihu not to give flattering titles to men, lest we should be reproved of our Maker; and if, according to Peter's example and the angel's advice, to bow only to God, and not to our fellow-servants; and if to call no man lord nor master, except under particular relations, according to Christ's command; I say, if these things are not to be reproved, then are we not blameworthy in so doing. *Esther iii 5. Job xxxii 21, 22.*

If to be vain and gaudy in apparel; if to paint the face and plait the hair; if to be clothed with gold and silver, and precious stones; and if to be filled with ribands and lace be to be clothed in modest apparel; and if these be the ornaments of Christians; and if that be to be humble, meek, and mortified, then are our adversaries good Christians indeed, and we proud, singular, and conceited, in contenting ourselves with what need and conveniency calls for, and condemning what is more as superfluous: but not otherwise.

If to use games, sports, plays; if to card, dice, and dance; if to sing, fiddle, and pipe; if to use stage-plays and comedies, and to lie, counterfeit, and dissemble, be to fear always; and if that be to do all things to the glory of God; and if that be to pass our sojourning here in fear; and if that be to use this world as if we did not use it; and if that be not to fashion ourselves according to our former lusts; to be not conformable to the spirit and vain conversation of this world; then are our adversaries, notwithstanding they use these things, and plead for them, very good, sober, mortified, and self-denying Christians, and we justly to be blamed for judging them: but not otherwise.

If the profanation of the holy name of God; if to exact oaths one from another upon every light occasion; if to call God to witness in things of such a nature, in which no earthly king would think himself lawfully and honourably to be a witness, be the duties of a Christian man, I shall confess that our adversaries are excellent good Christians, and we wanting in our duty: but if the contrary be true, of necessity our obedience to God in this thing must be acceptable.

If to revenge ourselves, or to render injury, evil for evil, wound for wound, to take eye for eye, tooth for tooth; if to fight for outward and perishing things, to go a warring one against another, whom we never saw, with whom we never had any contest, nor any thing to do; being moreover altogether ignorant of the cause of the war, but only that the magistrates of the nations foment quarrels one against another, the causes whereof are for the most part unknown to the soldiers that fight, as well as upon whose side the right or wrong is; and yet to be so furious, and rage one against another, to destroy and spoil all, that this or the other worship may be received or abolished; if to do this, and much more of this kind, be to fulfil the law of Christ, then are our adversaries indeed true Christians, and we miserable heretics, that suffer ourselves to be spoiled, taken, imprisoned, banished, beaten, and evilly entreated, without any resistance, placing our trust only in GOD, that he may defend us, and lead us by the way of the cross unto his kingdom. But if it be other-ways, we shall certainly receive the reward which the Lord hath promised to those that cleave to him, and, in denying themselves, confide in him.

And to sum up all, if to use all these things, and many more that might be instanced, be to walk in the strait way that leads to life, be to take up the cross of Christ, be to die with him to the lusts and perishing vanities of this world, and to arise with him in newness of life, and sit down with him in the heavenly places, then our adversaries may be accounted such, and they need not fear they are in the broad way that leads to destruction, and we are greatly mistaken, that have laid aside all these things for Christ's sake, to the crucifying of our own lusts, and to the pro-curing to ourselves shame, reproach, hatred, and ill-will from the men of this world: not as if by so doing we judged to merit heaven, but as knowing they are contrary to the will of Him who redeems his children from the love of this world, and its lusts, and leads them in the ways of truth and holiness, in which they take delight to walk.

# THE

# CONCLUSION.

~~~~~~~~~~~

IF in God's fear, candid reader, thou appliest thyself to consider this system of religion here delivered, with its consistency and harmony, as well in itself as with the scriptures of truth, I doubt not but thou wilt say with me and many more, that this is the spiritual day of Christ's appearance, wherein he is again revealing the ancient paths of truth and righteousness. For thou mayest observe here the Christian religion in all its parts truly established and vindicated, as it is a living, inward, spiritual, pure, and substantial thing, and not a mere form, show, shadow, notion, and opinion, as too many have hitherto held it, whose fruits declare they wanted that which they bear the name of: and yet many of those are so in love with their empty forms and shadows, that they cease not to calumniate us for commending and calling them to the substance, as if we therefore denied or neglected the true form and outward part of Christianity, which indeed is, as God the searcher of hearts knows, a very great slander. Thus, because we have desired people earnestly to feel after God near and in themselves, telling them that their notions of God, as he is beyond the clouds, will little avail them, if they do not feel him near; hence they have sought maliciously to infer that we deny any God except that which is within us. Because we tell people, that it is the light and law within, and not the letter without, that can truly tell them their condition, and lead them out of all evil; hence they say, we vilify the scriptures, and set up our own imaginations above them. Because we tell them, that it is not their talking or believing of Christ's outward

life, sufferings, death, and resurrection, no more than the
Jews crying, "the temple of the Lord, the temple of the
Lord," that will serve their turn, or justify them in the
sight of God; but that they must know Christ in them,
whom they have crucified, to be raised, and to justify
them, and redeem them from their iniquities: hence they
say, we deny the life, death, and sufferings of Christ, justification by his blood, and remission of sins through him.
Because we tell them, while they are talking and determin-
ing about the resurrection, that they have more need to
know the Just One, whom they have slain, raised in themselves, and to be sure they are partakers of the first resurrection; and that if this be, they will be the more capable
to judge of the second: hence they say, that we deny the
resurrection of the body. Because when we hear them
talk foolishly of heaven and hell, and the last judgment,
we exhort them to come out of that hellish condition they
are in, and come down to the judgment of Christ in their
own hearts, and believe in the light, and follow it, that so
they may come to sit in the heavenly places that are in
Christ Jesus: hence they maliciously say, that we deny
any heaven or hell but that which is within us, and that
we deny any general judgment; which slanders the Lord
knows are foully cast upon us, whom God hath raised for
this end, and gathered us, that by us he might confound
the wisdom of the wise, and bring to nought the understanding of the prudent; and might, in and by his own
Spirit and power in a despised people (that no flesh might
glory in his presence), pull down that dead, dark, corrupt
image, and mere shadow and shell of Christianity wherewith Antichrist hath deceived the nations: for which end
he hath called us to be a first-fruits of those that serve him,
and worship him no more in the oldness of the letter, but
in the newness of the Spirit. And though we be few in
number, in respect of others, and weak as to outward
strength, which we also altogether reject, and foolish if
compared with the wise ones of this world; yet as God
hath prospered us, notwithstanding much opposition, so

will he yet do, that neither the art, wisdom, nor violence of men or devils shall be able to quench that little spark that hath appeared; but it shall grow to the consuming of whatsoever shall stand up to oppose it. The mouth of the Lord hath spoken it! yea, he that hath arisen in a small remnant shall arise and go on by the same arm of power in his spiritual manifestation, until he hath conquered all his enemies, until all the kingdoms of the earth become the kingdom of Christ Jesus.

Unto Him that hath begun this work, not among the rich or great ones, but among the poor and small, and hath revealed it not to the wise and learned, but unto the poor, unto babes and sucklings; even to him, the Only-wise and Omnipotent GOD, be Honour, Glory, Thanks-giving, and renown, from henceforth and for ever. Amen.    Hallelu-JAH.

# A

# TABLE OF THE AUTHORS CITED IN THIS BOOK.

~~~~~~~~~~~~

## A.

*Abraham's* Faith, 43.

*Adam*; see *Man, Sin, Redemption.* What happiness he lost by the fall, 99. What death he died, *ibid.* He retained in his nature no will or light capable of itself to manifest spiritual things, *ibid.* Whether there be any relics of the heavenly image left in him, 103, 141.

*Alexander Skein's* queries proposed to the preachers, 373, 374.

*Anabaptists of Great Britain,* 63, 348.

*Anabaptists of Munster,* how their mischievous actings nothing touch the Quakers, 61 to 65.

*Anicetus,* 62.

*Anointing,* the anointing teacheth all things; it is and abideth for ever a common privilege, and sure rule to all saints, 59, 60.

*Antichrist* is exalted when the seed of God is pressed, 142. His work, 299, 300, 305, 306.

*Antinomians,* their opinion concerning justification, 200.

*Apostasy,* 249, 296.

*Apostle,* who he is, their number was not limited, and whether any may be now-a-days so called, 301, 302, 303, 304.

*Appearances;* see *Faith.*

*Arians,* they first brought in the doctrine of persecution upon the account of religion, 465.

*Arius,* by what he fell into error, 295, 296.

*Arminians;* see *Remonstrants.*

*Assemblings* are needful, and what

**45 ***

sort, 325, 326, &c., see *Worship,* they are not to be forsaken, 341.

*Astronomer,* 69.

*Aurelia,* there ten canonics were burnt, and why, 412.

## B.

*Baptism* is one, its definition, 380, 383 to 390. It is the baptism of Christ, and of the Spirit, not of water, 390 to 393. The baptism of water, which was John's baptism, was a figure of this baptism, and is not to be continued, 393 to 413.

*Baptism* with water doth not cleanse the heart, 384, 395. Nor is it a badge of Christianity, as was circumcision to the Jews, 398, 410. That Paul was not sent to baptize is explained, 398 to 400. Concerning what baptism Christ speaks, Mat xxviii. 19, it is explained, 401. How the apostles baptized with water is explained, 404 to 408. To *baptize* signifies to *plunge,* and how sprinkling was brought in, 408, 409. Those of old that used water baptism were plunged, and they that were only sprinkled were not admitted to an ecclesiastical function, and why, 409. Against the use of water baptism many heretofore have testified, 412.

*Infant Baptism* is a mere human tradition, 381, 413.

*Bible,* the last translations always find fault with the first, 84.

*Birth,* the spiritual birth, 71. Holy birth, 343; see *Justification.*

*Bishop of Rome,* concerning his

*God*, how he hath always manifested himself, 28. Unless he speak within, the preacher makes a rustling to no purpose, 32, 33. None can know him aright, unless he receive it of the Holy Ghost, *ibid.* God is to be sought within, 33. He is known by sensation, and not by mere speculation and syllogistic demonstrations, 33. He is the fountain, root, and beginning of all good works, and he hath made all things by his eternal word, 36. God speaking is the object of faith, 42. Among all, he hath his own chosen ones, 30. He delights not in the death of the wicked; see *Redemption.* He hath manifested his love in sending his son, 194, 215, 216; see *Justification.* He rewards the good works of his children, 226, 227. Whether it be possible to keep his commandments, 230, 231. He is the Lord, and the only judge of the conscience, 450, 453. He will have a free exercise, 460.

*Gospel;* see *Redemption.*—The truths of it are as lies in the mouths of profane and carnal men, 39, 40, The nature of it is explained, 56, 57. It is distinguished from the law, and is more excellent than it, 57, 77, 78; see *Covenant, Law.* Whether any ought to preach it in this or that place, is not found in scripture, 280. Its works are distinguished from the works of the law, 220. How it is to be propagated, and of its propagation, 454. The worship of it is inward, 397. It is an inward power, 163.

*Grace*, the grace of God can be lost through disobedience, 249, &c. Saving grace (see *Redemption*) which is required in the calling and qualifying of a minister; see *Minister.* In some it worketh in a special and prevalent manner, that they necessarily obtain salvation, 148, 149

*Your Grace*; see *Titles.*

## H.

*Hai Eben Yokdan*, 186.

*Hands*, laying on of hands, 281, 445.

*Head*, of uncovering the head in salutations, 474, 477, 489 to 492, 525.

*Heart*, the heart is deceitful and wicked, 82, 100, 101.

*Heathen*, albeit they were ignorant of the history, yet they were sensible of the loss by the fall, 184. Some heathen would not swear, 511. Heathenish ceremonies were brought into the Christian religion, 411.

*Henry IV.*, king of France, 463, 464.

*Heresies*, whence they proceeded, 339.

*Heretics*, 456.

*High ;* see *Priest.*

*History* of Christ; see *Quakers, Redemption.*

*Holy of Holies*, the high priest entered into it once a year, 41, 58. But now all of us at all times have access unto God, 58.

*Holiness*, Your Holiness; see *Titles.*

*Honour ;* see *Titles.*

*Hypocrite*, 456, 460, 461.

## I.

*Jacob*, 335.

*James* the Apostle, there were of old divers opinions concerning his epistle, 75.

*Idolatry*, 323, 324, 340. Whence it proceeded, 381.

*Jesting ;* see *Plays, Games.*

*Jesuits ;* see *Sect, Ignatian.*

*Jesus :* see *Christ.*—What it is to be saved, and to be assembled in his name, 178, 193, 331.

*Jews*, among them there may be

3 s

members of the church, 259. Their error concerning the outward succession from Abraham, 269. Their worship is outward, 397.

*Illiterate;* see *Mechanics.*

*Indulgences,* 191.

*Infants;* see *Sin.*

*Iniquities,* spiritual iniquities, or wickedness, 338.

*Inquisition,* 462.

*Inspiration,* where that doth not teach, words without do make a noise to no purpose, 31, 32.

*John* the Apostle, concerning his second and third epistles, and the revelation, there were sometime divers opinions, 75.

*John* the Baptist did not miracles, 279.

*John Hus* is said to have prophesied, 96.

*John Knox,* in what respect he was called the apostle of Scotland, 304.

*Judas* fell from his apostleship, 271. Who was his vicar, 286. His ministry was not purely evangelical, 288. He was called immediately of Christ, and who are inferior to him, and plead for him, as a pattern of their ministry, 289.

*Justification,* the doctrine thereof is and hath been greatly vitiated among the Papists, 189, 190, 191, and wherein we place it, 215, 216. Luther and the Protestants with good reason opposed the Popish doctrine, though many of them ran soon into another extreme; and wherein they place it; and that they agree in one, 192, 193, 198. It comes from the love of God, 194, 215. To *justify,* signifies to *make really just,* not to *repute just,* which many Protestants are forced to acknowledge, 206, 207, 209 to 213. The revelation of Christ formed in the heart is the formal cause of justification, not

works (to speak properly), which are only an effect, and so also many Protestants have said, 188, 189, 191 to 194, 205 to 226. We are justified in works, and how, 188, 189 197, 198, 199, 218 to 226. This is so far from being a Popish doctrine, that Bellarmine and others opposed it, 197, 225, 226, 227.

K.

*Kingdom* of God, 355, 445, 454.

*Knowledge,* the height of man's happiness is placed in the true knowledge of God, 13. Error in the entrance of this knowledge is dangerous, 25. Superstition, idolatry, and thence atheism, have proceeded from the false and feigned opinions concerning God, and the knowledge of him, 27. The uncertain knowledge of God is divers ways attained, but the true and certain only by the inward and immediate revelation of the Holy Spirit, 30. It hath been brought out of use, and by what devices, 34, 35. There is no knowledge of the Father but by the Son, nor of the Son but by the Spirit, 27 36 to 41. The knowledge of Christ, which is not by the revelation of his Spirit in the heart, is no more the knowledge of Christ, than the prattling of a parrot, which hath been taught a few words, may be said to be the voice of a man, 40.

L.

*Laics,* 301, 302.

*Laity,* 305, 306, 307.

*Lake of Bethesda,* 145.

*Law,* the law is distinguished from the gospel, 57, 58, 397. The difference thereof, 57, 239, 240. See *Gospel.*—Under the law the people were not in any doubt who should be priests and ministers, 266. See *Minister of the Law, Worship.*

he will procure to himself tenderness of heart, 144. Whatsoever he doth, while he doth it not by, in, and through the power of God, he is not approved of God, 344. How the inward man is nourished, 416 to 420. How his understanding cannot be forced by sufferings, and how his understanding is changed, 460, 461.

*Merchandise,* what it is to make merchandise with the Scriptures, 296.

*Mass,* 323, 328, 347, 375.

*Mathematician,* 69.

*Mechanics,* 306, 307. They contributed much to the reformation *ibid.*

*Merit* ; see *Justification.*

*Metaphysics,* 294.

*Minister of the Gospel,* it is not found in scripture if any be called, 79, 80, 280, 281. Teachers are not to go before the teaching of the Spirit, 88. The Popish and Protestant errors concerning the grace of a minister are rejected, 97, 305, 306. They are given for the perfecting of the saints, &c., 237. Concerning their call, and wherein it is placed, 256, 257, 264 to 280. Qualities, 257, 281 to 298. Orders and distinction of laity and clergy, 300 to 305. Of separating men for the ministry, *ibid.* Concerning the sustentation and maintenance of ministers, and their abuse ; of the idleness, riot, and cruelty of ministers, 306 to 318. What kind of ministry and ministers the Quakers are for, and what sort their adversaries are for, 319 to 321.

*Minister of the Law,* there was no doubtfulness concerning them under the law, 266. Their ministry was not purely spiritual, and while they performed it, they behoved to be purified from their

outward pollutions, as now those under the gospel from their inward 265, 266, 288.

*Miracles,* whether they be needful to those who place their faith in objective revelation, 44, 279.

*Moses,* 183, 349, 353, 381, 415.

*Munster* ; see *Anabaptists,* their mischievous actings, 60.

*Music,* 379, 380.

*Mystery* of iniquity, 300.

*Mystics,* 354, 355.

## N.

*Name of the Lord,* 402, 403. To anoint in the name of the Lord. 444.

*Nero,* 459.

*Noah's* faith had neither the scripture nor the prophecy of those going before him, 43. It is said of him, that he was a perfect man, 242.

*Number,* of using the singular number to one person, 486, 487.

## O.

*Oath,* that it is not lawful to swear, 477, 501 to 514.

*Obedience* is better than sacrifice, 80.

*Object* of faith ; see *Faith.*

*Oil,* to anoint with oil, 413, 444, 447.

*Ordinance,* sealing ordinance, 384.

## P.

*Papists,* the rule of their faith 62. They are forced ultimately to recur unto the immediate and inward revelations of the Holy Spirit, 70. What difference there is betwixt the cursed deeds of those of Munster and theirs, 64 to 67. They have taken away the second commandment in their catechism. 84. They make philosophy the handmaid of divinity, 89. They exalt

selves they extol as notable virtues, and make more noise about the escape of one Quaker, than of an hundred among themselves, 476. They destroy not the mutual relation that is betwixt prince and people, master and servant, father and son, nor do they introduce community of goods, 477. Nor say that one man may not use the creation more or less than another, 478.

## R.

*Ranters*, the blasphemy of the Ranters or Libertines, saying, that there is no difference betwixt good and evil, 239.

*Reason*, what need we set up corrupt reason, 54. Concerning reason, 63, 64, 142, 143.

*Rebecca*, 335.

*Reconciliation*, how reconciliation with God is made, 199 to 206.

*Recreations;* see *Plays*.

*Redemption* is considered in a twofold respect; first, performed by Christ without us; and secondly, wrought in us, 195, 196, 197. It is universal: God gave his only begotten Son Jesus Christ for a light, that whosoever believeth in him may be saved, 109, 110, 156, 157. The benefit of his death is no less universal than the seed of sin, 110, 111. There is scarce found any article of the Christian religion that is so expressly confirmed in the holy scriptures, 118 to 125. This doctrine was preached by the fathers (so called) of the first six hundred years, and is proved by the sayings of some, 125, 126, 127. Those that since the time of the reformation have affirmed it, have not given a clear testimony how that benefit is communicated to all, nor have sufficiently taught the truth, because they have added the absolute ne-

cessity of the outward knowledge of the history of Christ; yea, they have thereby given the contrary party a stronger argument to defend their precise decree of reprobation, among whom were the Remonstrants of Holland, 112, 127, 128, 129. God hath now raised up a few illiterate men to be dispensers of this truth, 130, 131, 174, 175. This doctrine showeth forth the mercy and justice of God, 132, 148, 149. It is the foundation of salvation, 132. It answers to the whole tenor of the gospel promises and threats, *ibid.* It magnifies and commends the merits and death of Christ, *ibid.* It exalts above all the grace of God, *ibid.* It overturns the false doctrine of the Pelagians, Semi-Pelagians, and others, who exalt the light of nature, and the freedom of man's will, *ibid.* It makes the salvation of man solely to depend upon God, and his condemnation wholly and in every respect to be of himself, 132, 133. It takes away all ground of despair, and feeds none in security, 133. It commends the Christian religion among infidels, *ibid.* It showeth the wisdom of God, *ibid.* And it is established, though not in words, yet by deeds, even by those ministers that oppose this doctrine, 133, 134. It derogates not from the atonement and sacrifice of Jesus Christ, but doth magnify and exalt it, 139. There is given to every one (none excepted) a certain day and time of visitation, in which it is possible for them to be saved, 131, 149 to 156. The testimony of Cyrillus concerning this thing, 155. It is explained what is understood and not understood by *this day*, 135. To some it may be longer, to others shorter, *ibid.* Many may outlive their day of visitation, after which

there is no possibility of salvation
to them, *ibid*. Some examples are
alleged, *ibid*. The objections, and
those places of scripture which others
abuse, to prove that God incites men
necessarily to sin, are easily solved,
if they be applied to these men, after
the time of their visitation is past,
135, 149. There is given to every
one a measure of the light, seed,
grace, and word of God, whereby
they can be saved, 131, 132, 149,
150, 161 to 169. Which is also
confirmed by the testimonies of Cyrillus and others, 159 to 168. What
that light is; see *Light*.— Many,
though ignorant of the outward history, yet have been sensible of the
loss that came by Adam, which is
confirmed by the testimonies of
Plato and others, 184, 185. Many
have known Christ within, as a remedy to redeem them, though not
under that denomination, witness
Seneca, Cicero, and others, 184, 185,
186. Yet all are obliged to believe
the outward history of Christ to
whom God bringeth the knowledge
of it, 139, 140.

*Reformation*, wherein it is not
placed, 267. Mechanic men have
contributed much to it, 307. What
hath been pernicious to it, 423.

*Relation ;* see *Quakers.*

*Religion*, the Christian religion;
see *Christianity.*— How it is made
odious to Jews, Turks, and Heathen,
421.

*Remonstrants of Holland ;* see
*Arminians, Redemption.*—They deny absolute reprobation, 63. How
we differ from them, 145, 146. They
exalt too much the natural power
and free will of man, and what they
think of the saving light, 171, 172.
Their worship can easily be stopped,
348.

*Reprobation ;* see also *Redemp-*

*tion*.—What absolute reprobation is,
is described, 112. Its doctrine is
horrible, impious, and blasphemous
112 to 117. It is also so called by
Lucas Osiander, 128. It is a new
doctrine, and Augustine laid the first
foundation thereof, which Dominicus, Calvin, and the Synod of Dor'
maintained, 113, 127, 128. Also
Luther, whom notwithstanding Lutherans afterwards deserted, *ibid*. it
is injurious to God, and makes him
the author of sin; proved by the
sayings of Calvin, Beza, Zanchius,
Paræus, Martyr, Zuinglius, and Piscator, 114. It makes the preaching
of the gospel a mere mock and illusion, 116. It makes the coming of
Christ and his propitiatory sacrifice
to have been a testimony of God's
wrath, *ibid*. It is injurious to mankind, and makes his condition worse
than the condition of devils, beasts,
Jews under Pharaoh, and the same
which the poets applied to Tantalus,
117.

*Revelation*, God always manifested himself by the revelations of the
Spirit, 13, 38, 39, 68. They are
made several ways, 13. They have
been always the formal object of
faith, and so remain, 13, 41 to 56.
And that not only subjectively, but
also objectively, 56, 57. They are
simply necessary unto true faith, 11.
28, 61, 70. They are not uncertain.
59, 60, 61. Yea, it is horrible sacrilege to accuse them of uncertainty, 52, 53. The examples of the
Anabaptists of Munster do not a whit
weaken this doctrine, 60, 61, 64, 65,
67. They can never contradict the
holy scripture, nor sound reason, 14,
68, 89, 90. They are evident and
clear of themselves, nor need they
another's testimony, 13, 68, 69.
They are the only, sure, certain,
and unmovable foundation of all

THE END.